Let ...... your dream home

Ultimate
BOOK OF Home Plans

CREATIVE HOMEOWNER®, Mahwah, New Jersey

COPYRIGHT © 2012

CREATIVE
HOMEOWNER®

A Division of Federal Marketing Corp.
Mahwah, NJ

Home Plans Editor: Kenneth D. Stuts, CPBD

Design and Layout: Kroha Direct (David Kroha, Cindy DiPierdomenico, Judith Kroha)

Cover Design: David Geer

Vice President and Publisher: Timothy O. Bakke

Current Printing (last digit)
10 9 8 7 6 5 4 3 2 1

Manufactured in the United States of America

The Ultimate Book of Home Plans
Library of Congress Control Number: 2012931476
ISBN-10: 1-58011-561-6
ISBN-13: 978-1-58011-561-2

CREATIVE HOMEOWNER®
A Division of Federal Marketing Corp.
One International Blvd.
Suite #400
Mahwah, NJ 07458
www.creativehomeowner.com

Note: The homes as shown in the photographs and renderings in this book may differ from the actual blueprints. When studying the house of your choice, please check the floor plans carefully.

Front cover: *top plan 161024, page 229; main plan 211011,* page 133; bottom, *left to right: plan 101022, page 181; plan 291015, page 291;* **page 1:** *plan 121023, page 149* **page 3:** *top to bottom: plan 391040, page 579; plan 391055, page 569; plan 391069, page 538* **page 4:** *plan 391053, page 576* **page 5:** *plan 391056, page 252* **page 6:** *top to bottom: plan 271024, page 529; plan 271007, page 553* **page 7:** *plan 391052, page 321* **page 110-117:** *all illustrations* Steve Buchanan **page 196:** Harpur Garden Images **page 197:** *top* John Glover; *bottom* David Cavagnaro **page 198:** *all* Carolyn L. Bates **page 199:** *top* Jerry Pavia; *bottom* David Cavagnaro **pages 200–201:** *all* Red Cover **page 202:** David Cavagnaro **page 203:** *top* Red Cover; *bottom* David Cavagnaro **pages 282–283:** *both* George Ross/CH **page 284:** *all* Christine Elasigue/CH **page 285:** *top right* George Ross/CH; *bottom all* Christine Elasigue/CH **page 286:** *left* George Ross/CH; *right all* Christine Elasigue/CH **pages 287–289:** *all* Christine Elasigue/CH **334–341:** illustrations by Warren Cutler, Tony Davis (site plans), Elizabeth Eaton, Biruta Hansen, Paul Mirocha, Gordon Morrison, Michael Rothman, Michael Wanke **pages 456:** courtesy of Central Fireplaces **pages 457–459:** courtesy of Aladdin Steel Products **page 461:** George Ross/CH **page 462:** Randall Perry **page 463:** courtesy of Heatilator **page 597:** *plan 161016, page 154* **page 601:** *top to bottom plan 211011, page 133; plan 211007, page 529; plan 121153, page 261* **page 608:** *plan 391066, page 547; plan 271001, page 495; plan 211071, page 528* **back cover:** *top plan 481035, page 431;* bottom *left to right: plan 121023, page 149; plan 351003, page 390; plan 291015, page 435*

Contents

Getting Started

Maybe you can't wait to bang the first nail. Or you may be just as happy leaving town until the windows are cleaned. The extent of your involvement with the construction phase is up to you. Your time, interests, and abilities can help you decide how to get the project from lines on paper to reality. But building a house requires more than putting pieces together. Whoever is in charge of the process must competently manage people as well as supplies, materials, and construction. He or she will have to

- Make a project schedule to plan the orderly progress of the work. This can be a bar chart that shows the time period of activity by each trade.
- Establish a budget for each category of work, such as foundation, framing, and finish carpentry.
- Arrange for a source of construction financing.
- Get a building permit and post it conspicuously at the construction site.
- Line up supply sources and order materials.
- Find subcontractors and negotiate their contracts.
- Coordinate the work so that it progresses smoothly with the fewest conflicts.
- Notify inspectors at the appropriate milestones.
- Make payments to suppliers and subcontractors.

You as the Builder

You'll have to take care of every logistical detail yourself if you decide to act as your own builder or general contractor. But along with the responsibilities of managing the project, you gain the flexibility to do as much of your own work as you want and subcontract out the rest. Before taking this path, however, be sure you have the time and capabilities. Do you also have

the time and ability to schedule the work, hire and coordinate subs, order materials, and keep ahead of the accounting required to manage the project successfully? If you do, you stand to save the amount that a general contractor would charge to take on these responsibilities, normally 15 to 30 percent of the construction cost. If you take this responsibility on but mismanage the project, the potential savings will erode and may even cost you more than if you had hired a builder in the first place. A subcontractor might charge extra for hav-

Acting as the builder, above, requires the ability to hire and manage subcontractors.

Building a home, opposite, includes the need to schedule building inspections at the appropriate milestones.

ing to return to the site to complete work that was originally scheduled for an earlier date. Or perhaps because you didn't order the windows at the beginning, you now have to pay for a recent cost increase. (If you had hired a builder in the first place he or she would absorb the increase.)

Hiring a Builder to Handle Construction

A builder or general contractor will manage every aspect of the construction process. Your role after signing the construction contract will be to make regular progress payments and ensure that the work for which you are paying has been completed. You will also consult with the builder and agree to any changes that may have to be made along the way.

Leads for finding builders might come from friends or neighbors who have had contractors build, remodel, or add to their homes. Real-estate agents and bankers may have some names handy but are more likely familiar with the builder's ability to complete projects on time and budget than the quality of the work itself.

The next step is to narrow your list of candidates to three or four who you think can do a quality job and work harmoniously with you. Phone each builder to see whether he or she is interested in being considered for your project. If so, invite the builder to an interview at your home. The meeting will serve two purposes. You'll be able to ask the candidate about his or her experience, and you'll be able to see whether or not your personalities are compatible. Go over the plans with the builder to make certain that he or she understands the scope of the project. Ask if they have constructed similar houses. Get references, and check the builder's standing with the Better Business Bureau. Develop a short list of builders, say three, and ask them to submit bids for the project.

Contracts

Lump-Sum Contracts

A lump-sum, or fixed-fee, contract lets you know from the beginning just what the project will cost, barring any changes made because of your requests or unforeseen conditions. This form works well for projects that promise few surprises and are well defined from the outset by a complete set of contract documents. You can enter into a fixed-price contract by negotiating with a single builder on your short list or by obtaining bids from three or four builders. If you go the latter route, give each bidder a set of documents and allow at least two weeks for them to submit their bids. When you get the bids, decide who you want and call the others to thank them for their efforts. You don't have to accept the lowest bid, but it probably makes sense to do so since you have already honed the list to builders you trust. Inform this builder of your intentions to finalize a contract.

Cost-Plus-Fee Contracts

Under a cost-plus-fee contract, you agree to pay the builder for the costs of labor and materials, as verified by receipts, plus a fee that represents the builder's overhead and profit. This arrangement is sometimes referred to as "time and materials." The fee can range between 15 and 30 percent of the incurred costs. Because you ultimately pick up the tab—whatever the costs—the contractor is never at risk, as he is with a lump-sum contract. You won't know the final total cost of a cost-plus-fee contract until the project is built and paid for. If you can live with that uncertainty, there are offsetting advantages. First, this form allows you to accommodate unknown conditions much more easily than does a lump-sum contract. And rather than being tied down by the project documents, you will be free to make changes at any point along the way. This can be a trap, though. Watching the project take shape will spark the desire to add something or do something differently. Each change costs more, and the accumulation can easily exceed your budget. Because of the uncertainty of the final tab and the built-in advantage to the contractor, you should think twice before entering into this form of contract.

Contract Content

The conditions of your agreement should be spelled out thoroughly in writing and signed by both parties, whatever contractual arrangement you make with your builder. Your contract should include provisions for the following:

- The names and addresses of the owner and builder.
- A description of the work to be included ("As described in the plans and specifications dated . . .").
- The date that the work will be completed if time is of the essence.
- The contract price for lump-sum contracts and the builder's allowed profit and overhead costs for changes.
- The builder's fee for cost-plus-fee contracts and the method of accounting and requesting payment.
- The criteria for progress payments (monthly, by project milestones) and the conditions of final payment.
- A list of each drawing and specification section that is to be included as part of the contract.
- Requirements for guarantees. (One year is the standard period for which contractors guarantee the entire project, but you may require specific guarantees on

When submitting bids, all of the builders should base their estimates on the same specifications. Once the work begins, communicate with your builder to keep the work proceeding smoothly.

Inspect your newly built home, if possible, before the builder closes it up and finishes it.

certain parts of the project, such as a 20-year guarantee on the roofing.)

■ Provisions for insurance.

■ A description of how changes in the work orders will be handled.

The builder may have a standard contract that you can tailor to the specifics of your project. These contain complete specific conditions with blanks that you can fill in to fit your project and a set of "general conditions" that cover a host of issues from insurance to termination provisions. It's always a good idea to have an attorney review the draft of your completed contract before signing it.

Working with Your Builder

The construction phase officially begins when you have a signed copy of the contract and copies of any insurance required from the builder. It's not unheard of for a builder to request an initial payment of 10 to 20 percent of the total cost to cover mobilization costs, those costs associated with obtaining permits and getting set up to begin the actual construction. If you agree to this, keep a careful eye on the progress of the work to ensure that the total paid out at any one time doesn't get too far out of sync with the actual work completed.

What about changes? From here on, it's up to you and your builder to proceed in good faith and to keep the channels of communication open. Even so, changes of one sort or another beset every project, and they usually add to its cost.

Light at the End of the Tunnel.

The builder's request for a final inspection marks the end of the construction phase—almost. At the final inspection meeting, you and the builder will inspect the work, noting any defects or incomplete items on a "punch list." When the builder tidies up the punch list items, you should reinspect. Sometimes, builders go on to another job and take forever to clean up the last few details, so only after all items on the list have been completed satisfactorily should you release the final payment, which often accounts for the builder's profit.

Some Final Words

Having a positive attitude is important when undertaking a project as large as building a home. A positive attitude can help you ride out the rigors and stress of the construction process.

Stay Flexible. Expect problems, because they certainly will occur. Weather can upset the schedule you have established for subcontractors. A supplier may get behind on deliveries, which also affects the schedule. An unexpected pipe may surprise you during excavation. Just as certain, every problem that comes along has a solution if you are open to it.

Be Patient. The extra days it may take to resolve a construction problem will be forgotten once the project is completed.

Express Yourself. If what you see isn't exactly what you thought you were getting, don't be afraid to look into changing it. Or you may spot an unforeseen opportunity for an improvement. Changes usually cost more money, though, so don't make frivolous decisions.

Finally, watching your home go up is exciting, so stay upbeat. Get away from your project from time to time. Dine out. Take time to relax. A positive attitude will make for smoother relations with your builder. An optimistic outlook will yield better-quality work if you are doing your own construction. And though the project might seem endless while it is under way, keep in mind that all the planning and construction will fade to a faint memory at some time in the future, and you will be getting a lifetime of pleasure from a home that is just right for you.

Plan #131033

Dimensions: 84'10" W x 48' D
Levels: 1.5
Square Footage: 2,813
Main Level Sq. Ft.: 1,890
Upper Level Sq. Ft.: 923
Bedrooms: 5
Bathrooms: 3½
Foundation: Crawl space or slab; basement for fee
Materials List Available: Yes
Price Category: G

Contemporary styling, luxurious amenities, and the classics that make a house a home are all available here.

Features:

- Family Room: A sloped ceiling with skylight and a railed overlook to make this large space totally up to date.

- Living Room: Sunken for comfort and with a cathedral ceiling for style, this room features a fireplace flanked by windows and sliding glass doors.

- Master Suite: Unwind in this room, with its cathedral ceiling, with a skylight, walk-in closet, and private access to the den.

- Upper Level: A bridge overlooks the living room and foyer and leads through the family room to three bedrooms and a bath.

- Optional Guest Suite: 500 sq. ft. above the master suite and den provides total comfort.

Images provided by designer/architect.

Main Level Floor Plan

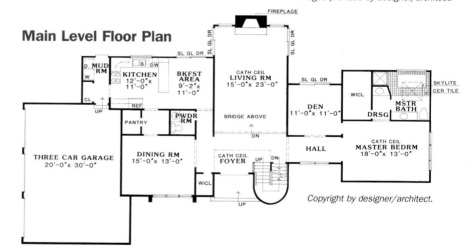

Copyright by designer/architect.

Upper Level Floor Plan

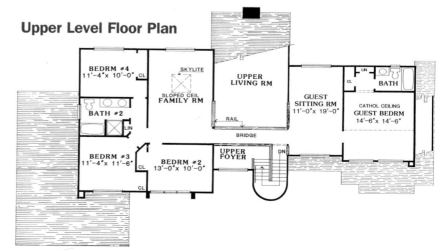

Entry

Living Room / Foyer

Living Room

Rear View

Plan #271016

Dimensions: 45'4" W x 49'6" D
Levels: 2
Square Footage: 2,170
Main Level Sq. Ft.: 1,169
Upper Level Sq. Ft.: 1,001
Bedrooms: 3
Bathrooms: 2½
Foundation: Basement
Materials List Available: Yes
Price Category: D

Images provided by designer/architect.

With plenty of living space, this attractive design is just right for a growing family.

Features:

• **Entry:** This two-story reception area welcomes guests with sincerity and style. A coat closet stands ready to take winter wraps.

• **Great Room:** This sunken and vaulted space hosts gatherings and formal meals of any size, and a handsome fireplace adds warmth and ambiance.

• **Kitchen:** A U-shaped counter keeps the family cook organized. A bayed breakfast nook overlooks a backyard deck.

• **Family Room:** The home's second fireplace adds a cozy touch to this casual area. Relax here with the family after playing in the snow!

• **Master Suite:** A vaulted ceiling presides over the master bedroom. The private bath hosts a separate tub and shower, a dual-sink vanity, and two walk-in closets.

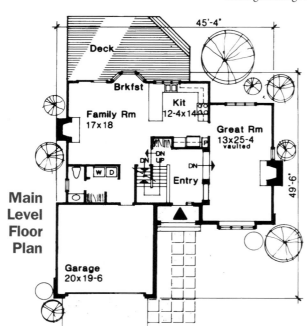

Main Level Floor Plan

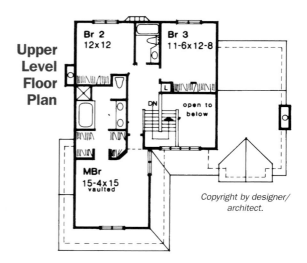

Upper Level Floor Plan

Copyright by designer/architect.

Plan #441029

Dimensions: 70' W x 71' D

Levels: 2

Square Footage: 3,217

Main Level Sq. Ft.: 2,292

Upper Level Sq. Ft.: 925

Bedrooms: 3

Bathrooms: 3½

Foundation: Crawl space; slab or basement available for fee

Material List Available: Yes

Price Category: I

Images provided by designer/architect.

Influenced by the Modernist movement, this California contemporary design is grand in façade and comfortable to live in.

Features:

- Entry: The two-story foyer opens to the formal dining room (also two-story) and the great room. Decorative columns help define these spaces. The curved wall of glass overlooking the rear patio brightens the great room.

- Master Suite: This suite, which has a salon with curved window wall, features a private bath with spa tub and walk-in closet.

- Bedrooms: The two family bedrooms share the upper level with the library, which has built-ins. Each upper-level bedroom has its own bathroom and walk-in closet.

- Home Office: The left wing of the main level contains this space, which features a curved window wall.

Upper Level Floor Plan

Copyright by designer/architect.

Main Level Floor Plan

◀ 70' ▶

71'

Rear View

Plan #161031

Dimensions: 99'8" W x 68'8" D

Levels: 2

Square Footage: 3,793

Opt. Lower Level Sq. Ft.: 1,588

Bedrooms: 3

Bathrooms: 2½

Foundation: Walkout

Materials List Available: Yes

Price Category: F

This home, as shown in the photograph, may differ from the actual blueprints. For more detailed information, please check the floor plans carefully.

Images provided by designer/architect.

If you're looking for a compatible mixture of formal and informal areas in a home, look no further!

Features:

• Great Room: Columns at the entry to this room and the formal dining room set a gracious tone that is easy around which to decorate.

• Library: Set up an office or just a cozy reading area in this quiet room.

• Hearth Room: Spacious and inviting, this hearth room is positioned so that friends and family can flow from here to the breakfast area and kitchen.

• Master Suite: The luxury of this area is capped by the access it gives to the rear yard.

• Lower Level: Enjoy the 9-ft.-tall ceilings as you walk out to the rear yard from this area.

Entry

Rear View

Main Level Floor Plan

Copyright by designer/architect.

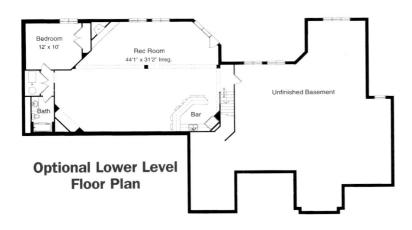

**Optional Lower Level
Floor Plan**

Rear Elevation

Left Elevation

Dining Room

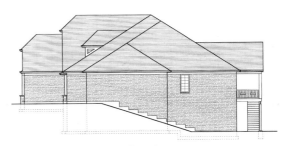

Right Elevation

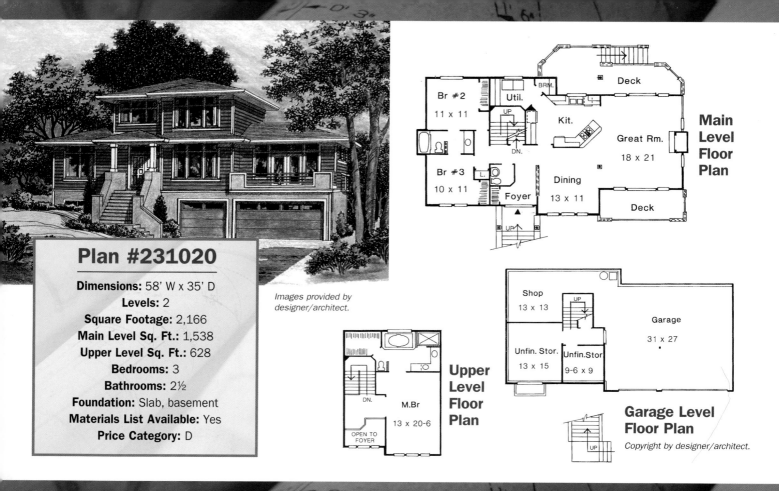

Plan #231020

Dimensions: 58' W x 35' D
Levels: 2
Square Footage: 2,166
Main Level Sq. Ft.: 1,538
Upper Level Sq. Ft.: 628
Bedrooms: 3
Bathrooms: 2½
Foundation: Slab, basement
Materials List Available: Yes
Price Category: D

Images provided by designer/architect.

Main Level Floor Plan

Br #2 11 x 11
Util.
BRM.
Deck
Kit.
Great Rm. 18 x 21
UP
DN.
Br #3 10 x 11
Foyer
Dining 13 x 11
Deck
UP

Upper Level Floor Plan

DN.
M.Br 13 x 20-6
OPEN TO FOYER

Garage Level Floor Plan

Shop 13 x 13
UP
Garage 31 x 27
Unfin. Stor. 13 x 15
Unfin.Stor. 9-6 x 9
UP

Copyright by designer/architect.

Plan #321036

Dimensions: 78'4" W x 68'6" D
Levels: 1
Square Footage: 2,900
Bedrooms: 4
Bathrooms: 2½
Foundation: Basement
Materials List Available: Yes
Price Category: F

Images provided by designer/architect.

CAD FILE AVAILABLE

78'-4"
68'-6"

Patio
Morning Rm 19-0x12-0
Great Rm 24-0x21-2 vaulted
MBr 16-0x17-5 coffered clg.
Kitchen 16-7x16-6
Dining 14-8x13-6 coffered clg.
Dn
Br 2 11-0x12-0
Entry
Br 4 12-10x14-9
Br 3 14-4x12-0
Porch
Garage 22-4x32-2

Optional Basement Level Floor Plan

Wet Bar
Family 19-8x31-1
storage
Up
Br 5 14-4x12-0

Copyright by designer/architect.

Main Level Floor Plan

Upper Level Floor Plan

Copyright by designer/architect.

Plan #181061

Dimensions: 56' W x 53'2" D

Levels: 2

Square Footage: 2,111

Main Level Sq. Ft.: 1,545

Upper Level Sq. Ft.: 566

Bedrooms: 2

Bathrooms: 2½

Foundation: Crawl space, basement

Materials List Available: Yes

Price Category: F

Images provided by designer/architect.

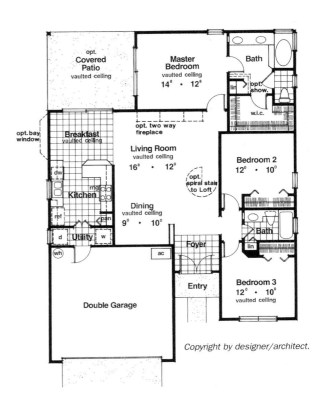

Plan #661033

Dimensions: 40' W x 55' D

Levels: 1

Square Footage: 2,036

Bedrooms: 3

Bathrooms: 2

Foundation: Slab

Materials List Available: Yes

Price Category: D

Images provided by designer/architect.

Copyright by designer/architect.

Plan #161027

Dimensions: 59'10" W x 37'4" D

Levels: 2

Square Footage: 2,388

Main Level Sq. Ft.: 1,207

Upper Level Sq. Ft.: 1,181

Bedrooms: 4

Bathrooms: 2½

Foundation: Basement

Materials List Available: Yes

Price Category: E

Double gables, wood trim, an arched window, and sidelights at the entry give elegance to this family-friendly home.

Features:

- Foyer: Friends and family will see the angled stairs, formal dining room, living room, and library from this foyer.

- Family Room: A fireplace makes this room cozy in the evenings on those chilly days, and multiple windows let natural light stream into it.

- Kitchen: You'll love the island and the ample counter space here as well as the butler's pantry. A breakfast nook makes a comfortable place to snack or just curl up and talk to the cook.

- Master Suite: Tucked away on the upper level, this master suite provides both privacy and luxury.

- Additional Bedrooms: These three additional bedrooms make this home ideal for any family.

Images provided by designer/architect.

Main Level Floor Plan

Deck

Breakfast 16'11" x 15'10"

Family Room 20'0" x 13'6"

Kitchen

Two-car Garage 21' x 22'2"

pantry

butler's pantry

Laun.

Bath

Living Room /Library 11'6" x 15'4"

stairs dn.

Dining Room 13'2" x 12'0"

Foyer

Porch

37'4"

59'10"

Upper Level Floor Plan

Bedroom 16'8" x 10'8"

walk-in closet

Dress.

Bedroom 12'11" x 10'

Bath

Bedroom 12'11" x 11'

stairs dn.

Master Bedroom 12' x 17'6"

Balcony

Copyright by designer/architect.

Plan #151495

Dimensions: 67'2" W x 64'8" D
Levels: 1
Square Footage: 2,121
Bedrooms: 3
Bathrooms: 2
Foundation: Slab; basement for fee
CompleteCost List Available: Yes
Price Category: D

Images provided by designer/architect.

Treasure the countless amenities that make this home ideal for family and welcoming guests.

Features:

- **Great Room:** This large gathering area, which is open to the kitchen, boasts a 10-ft.-high ceiling. The sliding glass doors allow natural light into the room and provide access to the rear lanai.

- **Master Suite:** A convenient private office with French door entry and built-ins is part of this extravagant master suite. The master bath pampers you with its whirlpool tub and separate toilet area.

- **Secondary Bedrooms:** Two additional bedrooms share the second bathroom. Bedroom 3 features a vaulted ceiling.

- **Garage:** This two-car front-loading garage includes a storage area and easy access to the kitchen through the laundry room.

Copyright by designer/architect.

Plan #211009

Dimensions: 72' W x 60' D
Levels: 1
Square Footage: 2,396
Bedrooms: 4
Bathrooms: 2
Foundation: Slab
Materials List Available: Yes
Price Category: E

Images provided by designer/architect.

Beautiful arched windows lend a luxurious feeling to the exterior of this one-story home.

Features:

- Ceiling Height: 9 ft. unless otherwise noted.

- Entry: Guests will be greeted by a dramatic 12-ft. ceiling in this elegant foyer.

- Living Room: The 12-ft. ceiling continues through the foyer into this inviting living room. Everyone will feel welcomed by the crackling fire in the handsome fireplace.

- Covered Porch: When the weather is warm, invite guests to step out of the living room directly into this covered porch.

- Kitchen: This bright and cheery kitchen is designed for the way we live today. It includes a pantry and an angled eating bar that will see plenty of impromptu family meals.

- Energy-Efficient Walls: All the outside walls are framed with 2x6 lumber instead of 2x4. The extra thickness makes room for more insulation to lower your heating and cooling bills.

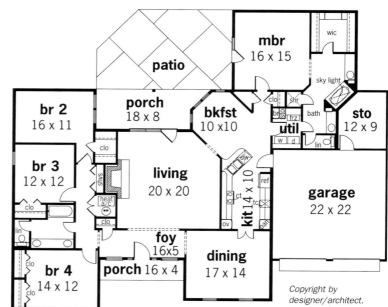

Copyright by designer/architect.

SMARTtip

Ornaments in a Garden

Placement is everything with ornaments in a garden. Some elements are best sitting by themselves. Others are better when they are part of a cohesive whole, perhaps placed in the greenery at a corner or flanking a structure.

Plan #271025

Dimensions: 61'4" W x 56'4" D
Levels: 2
Square Footage: 2,223
Main Level Sq. Ft.: 1,689
Upper Level Sq. Ft.: 534
Bedrooms: 3
Bathrooms: 2½
Foundation: Basement
Materials List Available: Yes
Price Category: E

This traditional home's unique design combines a dynamic, exciting exterior with a fantastic floor plan.

Features:

- Living Room: To the left of the column-lined, barrel-vaulted entry, this inviting space features a curved wall and corner windows.

- Dining Room: A tray ceiling enhances this formal meal room.

- Kitchen: This island-equipped kitchen includes a corner pantry and a built-in desk. Nearby, the sunny breakfast room opens onto a backyard deck via sliding glass doors.

- Family Room: A corner bank of windows provides a glassy backdrop for this room's handsome fireplace. Munchies may be served on the snack bar from the breakfast nook.

- Master Suite: This main-floor retreat is simply stunning, and includes a vaulted ceiling, access to a private courtyard, and of course, a sumptuous bath with every creature comfort.

Main Level Floor Plan

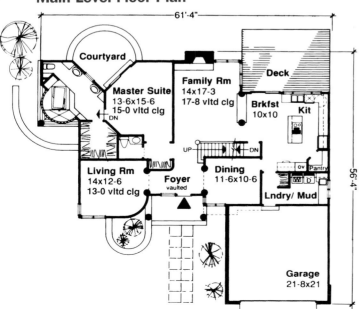

Upper Level Floor Plan

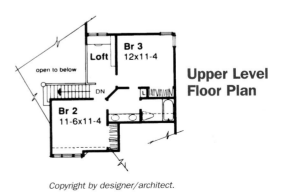

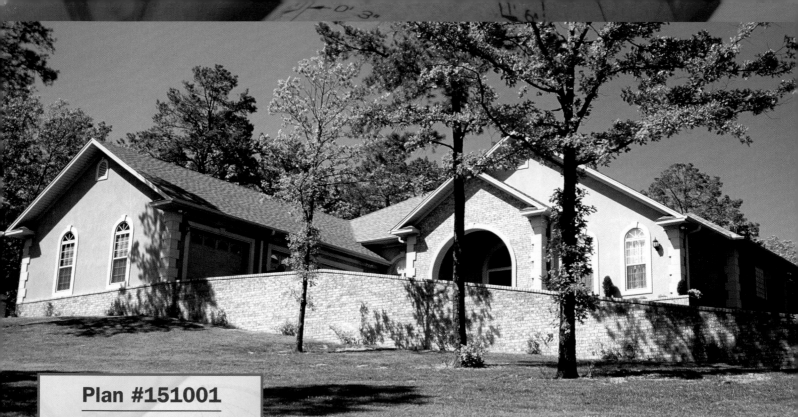

Plan #151001

Dimensions: 70' W x 88'2" D

Levels: 1

Square Footage: 3,124

Bedrooms: 4

Bathrooms: 3½

Foundation: Crawl space, slab

CompleteCost List Available: Yes

Price Category: G

This home, as shown in the photograph, may differ from the actual blue-prints. For more detailed information, please check floor plans carefully.

Images provided by designer/architect.

From the double front doors to sleek arches, columns, and a gallery with arched openings to the bedrooms, you'll love this elegant home.

Features:

- **Grand Room:** With a 13-ft. pan ceiling and column entry, this room opens to the rear covered porch as well as through French doors to the bay-windowed morning room that, in turn, leads to the gathering room.

- **Gathering Room:** A majestic fireplace, built-in entertainment center, and book shelves give comfort and ease.

- **Kitchen:** A double oven, built-in desk, and a work island add up to a design for efficiency.

- **Master Suite:** Enjoy the practicality of walk-in closets, the comfort of a private sitting area, and the convenience of an adjacent study or nursery. The bath features a step-up whirlpool tub and separate shower.

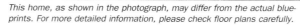

Copyright by designer/architect.

Plan #121009

Dimensions: 50' W x 58' D
Levels: 1
Square Footage: 1,422
Bedrooms: 3
Bathrooms: 2
Foundation: Basement
Materials List Available: Yes
Price Category: B

Images provided by designer/architect.

This amenity-filled home is perfect for the growing family or as a retirement retreat.

Features:

- Ceiling Height: 8 ft. unless otherwise noted.
- Great Room: This inviting space is the perfect place for gatherings of all sizes. It shares 12-ft. ceilings with the dining room and kitchen.

- Dining Room: In addition to the 12-ft. ceiling, arched openings, and built-in book cases make this an elegant place to dine.
- Private Porch: After dinner, step through a door in the dining room to enjoy a summer breeze in this inviting porch.
- Master Suite: The boxed ceiling lends drama to this suite and a walk-in closet adds convenience. Luxury comes from the whirlpool bath.
- Garage: You won't be short of parking and storage space in this two-bay garage. As a bonus there is space for a workbench.

SMARTtip
Window Cornices

You can transform plain rooms by making jogs in cornice molding that will hold shades, blinds, and other window treatments. You can create individual pockets over each window or continue the molding past narrow wall sections between windows to form a more expansive detail. Housings below the cornice can be painted or papered.

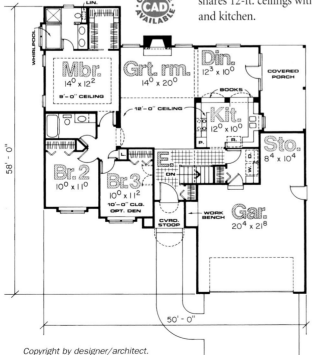

Copyright by designer/architect.

Plan #131045

Dimensions: 81'4" W x 68'3" D
Levels: 1
Square Footage: 2,347
Bedrooms: 4
Bathrooms: 2½
Foundation: Crawl space or slab; basement for fee
Materials List Available: Yes
Price Category: F

You'll love the character and flexibility in sitting that the angled design gives to this contemporary ranch-style home.

Features:

• Porch: A wraparound rear porch adds distinction to this lovely home.

• Great Room: Facing the rear of the house, this great room has a high, stepped ceiling, fireplace, and ample place for built-ins.

• Kitchen: This large room sits at an angle to the great room and is adjacent to both a laundry room and extra powder room.

• Office: Use the 4th bedroom as a home office, study, or living room, depending on your needs.

• Master Suite: This area is separated from the other bedrooms in the house to give it privacy. The beautiful bay window at the rear, two large walk-in closets, and luxurious bath make it an ideal retreat after a hectic day.

Images provided by designer/architect.

Great Room

Main Level Floor Plan

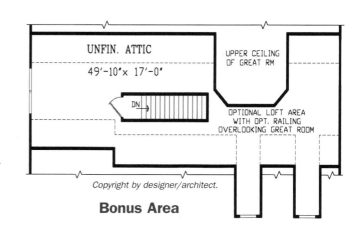

Copyright by designer/architect.

Bonus Area

Plan #391013

Dimensions: 52' W x 41'4" D
Levels: 2
Square Footage: 1,894
Main Level Sq. Ft.: 1,108
Upper Level Sq. Ft.: 786
Bedrooms: 3
Bathrooms: 2½
Foundation: Crawl space, slab, or basement
Materials List Available: Yes
Price Category: D

Images provided by designer/architect.

This home hints at Tudor lineage, with its rising half-timber-effects and peaked roofline. Inside, it's a different, more contemporary story.

Features:

- Living Room. The foyer opens to this room, which basks in the light of a two-story arched window. Even the open dining room enjoys the brightness.

- Family Room: This room warms up with a fireplace, plus a built-in desk, wet bar, and entry to an outdoor deck.

Rear View

- Kitchen: The angular plan of this room, with a convenient pass-through to the dining area, features a picture window with built-in seat for taking time to meditate. Excellent shelving, storage, half-bath, and hall coat closet offer behind-the-scenes support.

- Bedrooms: Bedroom 2 looks over the front yard and shares a bath with bedroom 3, which oversees the backyard.

Main Level Floor Plan

- Master Bedroom: The second level master bedroom overlooks the living room from a beautiful balcony. Double windows along one wall fill the area with natural light, and a windowed corner illuminates the master bath.

Copyright by designer/architect.

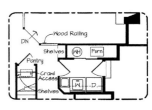

Second Floor Plan

Upper Level Floor Plan

Optional Crawl Space/Slab Floor Plan

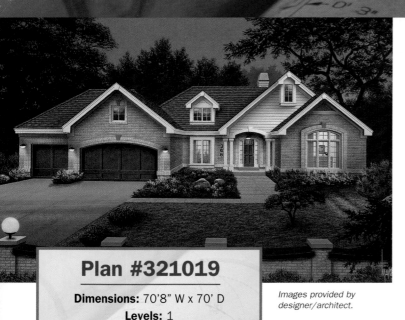

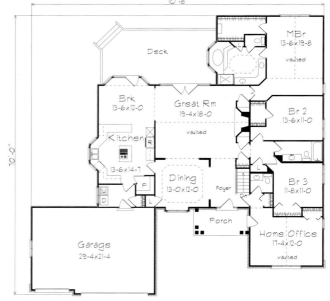

Plan #321019

Dimensions: 70'8" W x 70' D

Levels: 1

Square Footage: 2,452

Bedrooms: 4

Bathrooms: 2½

Foundation: Basement

Materials List Available: Yes

Price Category: E

Images provided by designer/architect.

Copyright by   designer/ architect.

Plan #401001

Dimensions: 56' W x 43'4" D

Levels: 2

Square Footage: 2,071

Main Level Sq. Ft.: 1,204

Upper Level Sq. Ft.: 867

Bedrooms: 3

Bathrooms: 2½

Foundation: Basement

Materials List Available: Yes

Price Category: D

Images provided by designer/architect.

Main Level Floor Plan

Upper Level Floor Plan

Copyright by designer/architect.

Plan #741005

Dimensions: 62'5" W x 62' D

Levels: 1

Square Footage: 2,231

Bedrooms: 3

Bathrooms: 2

Foundation: Slab

Materials List Available: Yes

Price Category: D

Images provided by designer/architect.

Copyright by designer/architect.

Rear Elevation

Plan #441214

Dimensions: 77' W x 65' D

Levels: 1

Square Footage: 4,600

Main Level Sq. Ft.: 2,624

Lower Level Sq. Ft.: 1,976

Bedrooms: 4

Bathrooms: 3½

Foundation: Walkout

Material List Available: Yes

Price Category: I

Images provided by designer/architect.
Copyright by designer/architect

Main Level Floor Plan

Rear Elevation

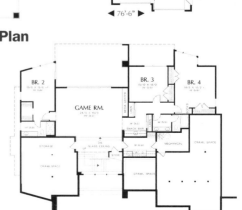

Lower Level Floor Plan

Plan #271086

Dimensions: 56'6" W x 67'6" D
Levels: 2
Square Footage: 1,910
Main Level Sq. Ft.: 1,324
Upper Level Sq. Ft.: 586
Bedrooms: 3
Bathrooms: 2
Foundation: Crawl space, daylight basement
Materials List Available: Yes
Price Category: D

Images provided by designer/architect.

A passive-solar sunroom is the highlight of this popular home and helps to minimize heating costs.

Features:

- Living/Dining Area: This expansive space is brightened by numerous windows and offers panoramic views of the outdoor scenery. A handsome woodstove gives the area a delightful ambiance, especially when the weather outside is frightful. Your dining table goes in the corner by the sun room.

- Kitchen: This room's efficient design keeps all of the chef's supplies at the ready. A snack bar could be used to help serve guests during parties.

- Bedrooms: With three bedrooms to choose from, all of your family members will be able to find secluded spots of their very own.

- Lower Level: This optional space includes a recreation room with a second woodstove. Let the kids gather here and make as much noise as they want.

Optional Basement Level Floor Plan

Copyright by designer/architect.

Main Level Floor Plan

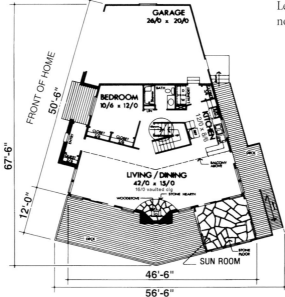

Upper Level Floor Plan

Plan #121017

Dimensions: 54' W x 50' D

Levels: 2

Square Footage: 2,353

Main Level Sq. Ft.: 1,653

Upper Level Sq. Ft.: 700

Bedrooms: 4

Bathrooms: 2½

Foundation: Basement; slab for fee

Materials List Available: Yes

Price Category: E

The dramatic two-story entry with bent staircase is the first sign that this is a gracious home.

Features:

• Ceiling Height: 8 ft. except as noted.

• Great Room: A row of transom-topped windows and a tall, beamed ceiling add a sense of spaciousness to this family gathering area.

• Formal Dining Room: The bayed window helps make this an inviting place to entertain.

• See-through Fireplace: This feature spreads warmth and coziness throughout the informal areas of the home.

• Breakfast Area: This sunny area shares a see-through fireplace with the great room. It's the perfect place to start the day.

• Master Suite: Here are all the features you expect to find in large luxury homes. Wake up to tall, sloped ceilings, and enjoy the corner whirlpool, separate shower, and vanity. A large walk-in closet provides plenty of wardrobe storage.

Main Level Floor Plan

Upper Level Floor Plan

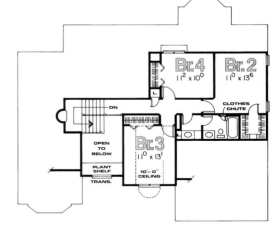

Copyright by designer/architect.

Plan #121025

Dimensions: 60' W x 59'4" D

Levels: 2

Square Footage: 2,562

Main Level Sq. Ft.: 1,875

Upper Level Square Footage: 687

Bedrooms: 4

Bathrooms: 2½

Foundation: Basement; crawl space or slab for fee

Materials List Available: Yes

Price Category: E

Images provided by designer/architect.

Dramatic arches are the reoccurring architectural theme in this distinctive home.

Features:

- Ceiling Height: 8 ft. unless otherwise noted.

- Foyer: This is a grand two-story entrance. Plants will thrive on the plant shelf thanks to light streaming through the arched window.

- Great Room: The foyer flows into the great room through dramatic 15-ft.-high arched openings.

- Kitchen: An island is the centerpiece of this highly functional kitchen that includes a separate breakfast area.

- Office: French doors open into this versatile office that features a 10-ft. ceiling and transom-topped windows.

- Master Suite: The master suite features a volume ceiling, built-in dresser, and two closets. You'll unwind in the beautiful corner whirlpool bath with its elegant window treatment.

CAD FILE AVAILABLE — **CAD**

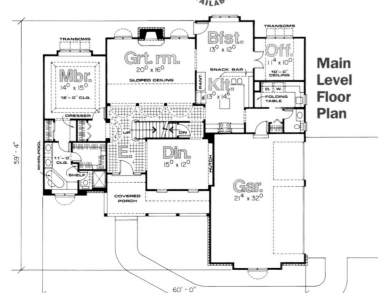

Main Level Floor Plan

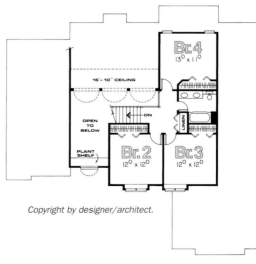

Upper Level Floor Plan

Copyright by designer/architect.

Plan #121029

Dimensions: 58'8" W x 54' D
Levels: 2
Square Footage: 2,576
Main Level Sq. Ft.: 1,735
Upper Level Sq. Ft.: 841
Bedrooms: 4
Bathrooms: 2½
Foundation: Basement
Materials List Available: Yes
Price Category: E

Images provided by designer/architect.

This gracious home is designed with the contemporary lifestyle in mind.

Features:

- **Ceiling Height:** 8 ft. unless otherwise noted.
- **Great Room:** This room features a fireplace and entertainment center. It's equally suited for family gatherings and formal entertaining.
- **Breakfast Area:** The fireplace is two-sided so it shares its warmth with this breakfast area — the perfect spot for informal family meals.
- **Master Suite:** Halfway up the staircase you'll find double-doors into this truly distinctive suite featuring a barrel-vault ceiling, built-in bookcases, and his and her walk-in closets. Unwind at the end of the day by stretching out in the oval whirlpool tub.
- **Computer Loft:** This loft overlooks the great room. It is designed as a home office with a built-in desk for your computer.
- **Garage:** Two bays provide plenty of storage in addition to parking space.

CAD FILE AVAILABLE

Main Level Floor Plan

Upper Level Floor Plan

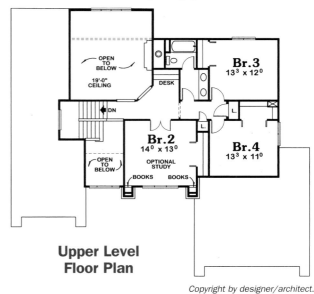

Copyright by designer/architect.

Plan #121031

Dimensions: 52' W x 51'4" D

Levels: 2

Square Footage: 1,772

Main Level Sq. Ft.: 1,314

Upper Level Sq. Ft.: 458

Bedrooms: 3

Bathrooms: 2½

Foundation: Basement; crawl space or slab for fee

Materials List Available: Yes

Price Category: C

This home features architectural details reminiscence of earlier fine homes.

Features:

- Ceiling Height: 8 ft. unless otherwise noted.

- Foyer: This grand entry soars two-stories high. The U-shaped staircase with window leads to a second-story balcony.

- Great Room: You'll be drawn to the impressive views through the triple-arch windows at the front and rear of this room.

- Kitchen: Designed for maximum efficiency, this kitchen is a pleasure to be in. It features a center island, a full pantry, and a desk for added convenience.

- Breakfast Area: This area adjoins the kitchen. Both rooms are flooded with sunlight streaming from a shared bay window.

- Master Suite: The stylish bedroom includes a walk-in closet. Luxuriate in the whirlpool tub at the end of a long day .

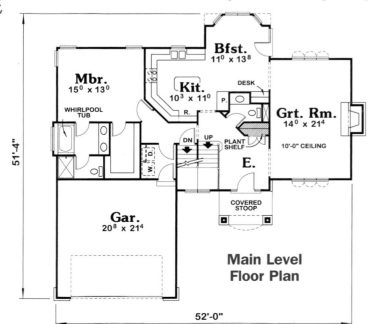

Main Level Floor Plan

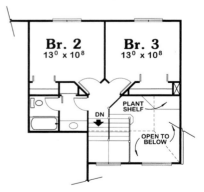

Copyright by designer/architect.

Upper Level Floor Plan

Plan #401029

Dimensions: 37'6" W x 48'4" D
Levels: 2
Square Footage: 2,163
Main Level Sq. Ft.: 832
Upper Level Sq. Ft.: 1,331
Bedrooms: 3
Bathrooms: 2½
Foundation: Basement
Materials List Available: Yes
Price Category: D

This two-level plan has a bonus--a roof deck with hot tub! A variety of additional outdoor spaces make this one wonderful plan.

Features:

• First Level: Family bedrooms, a full bath room, and a cozy den are on the first level, along with a two-car garage.

• Living Area: The living spaces are on the second floor and nclude a living/dining room combination with a deck and a fireplace. The dining room has buffet space.

• Family Room: Featuring a fireplace and a built-in entertainment center, the gathering area is open to the breakfast room and sky lighted kitchen.

• Master Bedroom: This room features a private bath with a whirlpool tub and two-person shower, a walk-in closet, and access to still another deck.

CAD FILE AVAILABLE

Master Bathroom

Rear Elevation

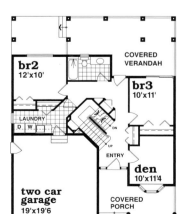

Main Level Floor Plan

Upper Level Floor Plan

Copyright by designer/architect.

Plan #121015

Dimensions: 52' W x 47'4" D

Levels: 2

Square Footage: 1,999

Main Level Sq. Ft.: 1,421

Upper Level Sq. Ft.: 578

Bedrooms: 4

Bathrooms: 2½

Foundation: Basement

Materials List Available: Yes

Price Category: D

CAD FILE AVAILABLE

This home, as shown in the photograph, may differ from the actual blueprints. For more detailed information, please check the floor plans carefully.

Images provided by designer/architect.

Hipped roofs and a trio of gables bring distinction to this plan.

Features:

- Ceiling Height: 8 ft.

- Open Floor Plan: The rooms flow into each other and are flanked by an abundance of windows. The result is a light and airy space that seems much larger than it really is.

- Formal Dining Room: Here is the perfect room for elegant entertaining.

- Breakfast Nook: This bright, bayed nook is the perfect place to start the day. It's also great for intimate get-togethers.

- Great Room: The family will enjoy gathering in this spacious area.

- Bedrooms: This large master bedroom, along with three secondary bedrooms and an extra room, provides plenty of room for a growing family.

- Attached Garage: The garage provides two bays of parking plus plenty of storage space.

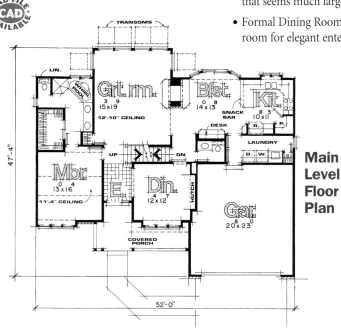

Main Level Floor Plan

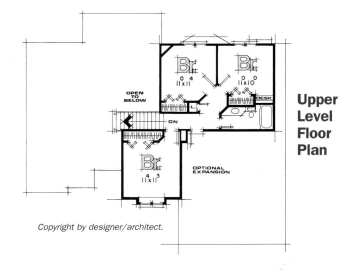

Upper Level Floor Plan

Copyright by designer/architect.

Plan #401048

Dimensions: 57'8" W x 103'6" D
Levels: 2
Square Footage: 5,159
Main Level Sq. Ft.: 2,473
Upper Level Sq. Ft.: 2,686
Bedrooms: 4
Bathrooms: 4½
Foundation: Basement
Materials List Available: Yes
Price Category: I

Images provided by designer/architect.

This unusual stucco-and-siding design opens with a grand portico to a foyer that extends to the living room with a fireplace.

Features:

• Dining Room: Step up a fw steps to this dining room, withi ts coffered ceiling and butler's pantry, which connects to the gourmet kitchen.

• Hearth Room: Attached to the kitchen, this hearth room has the requisite fireplace and three sets of french doors that lead to the covered porch.

• Family Room: This room features a coffered ceiling and a fireplace flanked by French doors.

• Master Suite: This area includes a tray ceiling, covered deck, and lavish bath.

• Bedrooms: All bedrooms are located on the second floor. Two full bathrooms serve the family bedrooms and a bonus room that might be used as an additional bedroom or hobby space.

Great Room

Rear Elevation

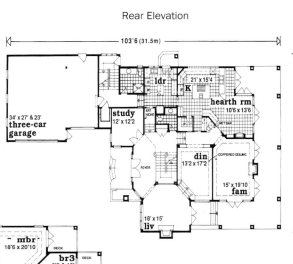

Upper Level Floor Plan

Copyright by designer/architect.

Main Level Floor Plan

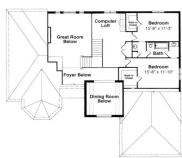

Main Level Floor Plan

Copyright by designer/architect.

Plan #161097

Dimensions: 70' W x 56'10" D
Levels: 2
Square Footage: 3,144
Main Level Sq. Ft.: 2,237
Upper Level Sq. Ft.: 900
Optional Basement Level Sq. Ft.: 1,450
Bedrooms: 3
Bathrooms: 2½
Foundation: Walkout; basement for fee
Material List Available: Yes
Price Category: G

Images provided by designer/architect.

Upper Level Floor Plan

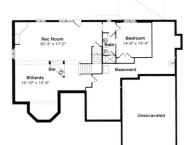

Optional Lower Level Floor Plan

Main Level Floor Plan

Plan #391462

Dimensions: 32' W x 34' D
Levels: 2
Square Footage: 1,487
Main Level Sq. Ft.: 911
Upper Level Sq. Ft.: 576
Bedrooms: 3
Bathrooms: 1½
Foundation: Basement
Material List Available: yes
Price Category: B

Images provided by designer/architect.

Upper Level Floor Plan

Copyright by designer/architect.

Main Level Floor Plan

Images provided by architect.

designer/

Plan #661057

Dimensions: 50' W x 40' D

Levels: 2

Square Footage: 1,887

Main Level Sq. Ft.: 1,371

Upper Level Sq. Ft.: 516

Bedrooms: 3

Bathrooms: 2½

Foundation: Slab

Materials List Available: Yes

Price Category: D

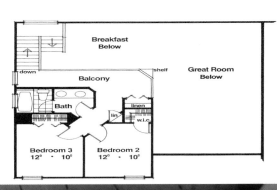

Upper Level Floor Plan

Copyright by designer/architect.

Main Level Floor Plan

Copyright by designer/architect.

Plan #181162

Dimensions: 38' W x 38' D

Levels: 2

Square Footage: 1,867

Main Level Sq. Ft.: 911

Upper Level Sq. Ft.: 956

Bedrooms: 3

Bathrooms: 2½

Foundation: Basement

Materials List Available: Yes

Price Category: F

Images provided by designer/architect.

CAD FILE AVAILABLE

Upper Level Floor Plan

Plan #151021

Dimensions: 75'2" W x 89'6" D
Levels: 2
Square Footage: 3,385
Main Level Sq. Ft.: 2,633
Upper Level Sq. Ft.: 752
Bedrooms: 4
Bathrooms: 4
Foundation: Crawl space, or slab
CompleteCost List Available: Yes
Price Category: F

From the fireplace in the master suite to the well-equipped game room, the amenities in this home will surprise and delight you.

Features:

- **Great Room:** A bank of windows on the far wall lets sunlight stream into this large room. The fireplace is located across the room and is flanked by the built-in media center and built-in bookshelves. Gracious brick arches create an entry into the breakfast area and kitchen.

- **Breakfast Room:** Move easily between this room with 10-foot ceiling either into the kitchen or onto the rear covered porch.

- **Game Room:** An icemaker and refrigerator make entertaining a snap in this room.

- **Master Suite:** A 10-ft. boxed ceiling, fireplace, and access to the rear porch give romance, while the built-ins in the closet, whirlpool tub with glass blocks, and glass shower give practicality.

Main Level Floor Plan

Upper Level Floor Plan

Plan #161113

Dimensions: 120'2" W x 60'4" D
Levels: 2
Square Footage: 4,365
Main Level Sq. Ft.: 3,298
Upper Level Sq. Ft.: 1,067
Optional Lower Level Sq. Ft.: 1,761
Bedrooms: 3
Bathrooms: 2½
Foundation: Basement, or walkout
Materials List Available: Yes
Price Category: I

Images provided by designer/architect.

A covered porch welcomes friends and family to this elegant home.

Features:

• Library: Just off the foyer is this library, which can be used as a home office. Notice the connecting door to the master bathroom.

• Kitchen: Release the chef inside of you into this gourmet kitchen, complete with seating at the island and open to the breakfast area. Step through the triple sliding door, and arrive on the rear porch.

• Master Suite: This luxurious master suite features a stepped ceiling in the sleeping area and private access to the rear patio. The master bath boasts an oversized stall shower, a whirlpool bath, dual vanities, and an enormous walk-in closet.

• Lower Level: For family fun times, this lower level is finished to provide a wet bar, billiard room, and media room. The area also includes two additional bedrooms and an exercise room.

• Garage: You'll have storage galore in this four-car garage, complete with an additional set of stairs to the unfinished part of the basement.

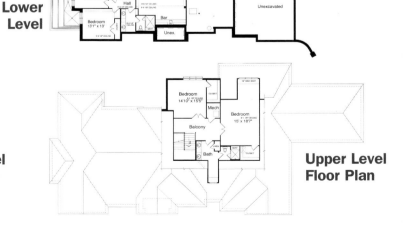

Optional Lower Level

Copyright by designer/architect.

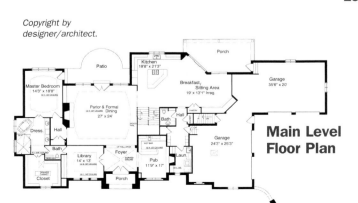

Main Level Floor Plan

Upper Level Floor Plan

Plan #271061

Dimensions: 68' W x 52' D
Levels: 1
Square Footage: 1,750
Bedrooms: 1
Bathrooms: 1½
Foundation: Walkout basement
Material List Available: Yes
Price Category: C

Stucco and a contemporary design give this home a simplistically elegant look.

Images provided by designer/architect.

Features:

- Entry: A small porch area welcomes guests out of the weather and into the warmth. Inside, this entryway provides an inviting introduction to the rest of the home.

- Kitchen: Opening to both the full dining room and a bayed dinette, this kitchen is both beautifully and efficiently designed. The space includes a walk-in pantry and plenty of work-space for the budding gourmet.

- Master Suite: This space is fit for the king (or queen) of the castle. Separated from the rest

of the house by a small entry, the suite includes its own full bath with dual sinks, bathtub, shower stall, and water closet.

- Basement: This area can be finished to include two bedrooms with wide closets, a full bathroom, a family room, and storage space.

- Garage: Whether you actually have three cars you need kept from the climate, you are a collector of things, or you prefer a hobby area, this three-bay garage has plenty of space to fit your needs.

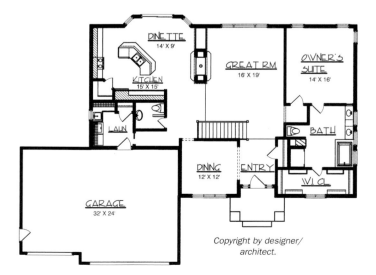

Copyright by designer/architect.

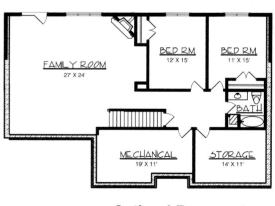

Optional Basement Level Floor Plan

Plan #271034

Dimensions: 45' W x 43' D

Levels: 2

Square Footage: 1,531

Main Level Sq. Ft.: 1,062

Upper Level Sq. Ft.: 469

Bedrooms: 4

Bathrooms: 2

Foundation: Basement

Materials List Available: Yes

Price Category: C

Images provided by designer/architect.

This versatile home design adapts to today's constantly changing and nontraditional families.

Features:

• Great Room: Both old and young are sure to enjoy this great room's warm and charming fireplace. The vaulted ceiling and high fixed windows add volume and light to the room.

• Family/Kitchen: This joined space is perfect for weekend get-togethers. On warm evenings, step through the sliding glass doors to the backyard deck.

• Den/Bedroom: The flexible den can serve as a nursery or as a guestroom for visiting family members of any age.

• Master Bedroom: When the golden years near, you'll appreciate its main-floor locale.

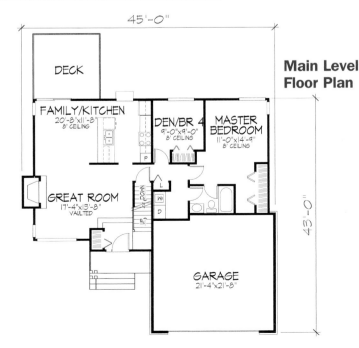

Main Level Floor Plan

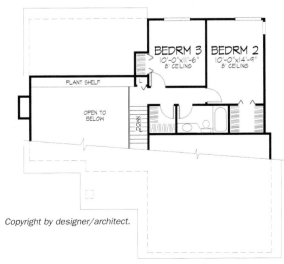

Upper Level Floor Plan

Copyright by designer/architect.

Plan #451237

Dimensions: 66' W x 69'6" D
Levels: 1
Square Footage: 1,898
Bedrooms: 3
Bathrooms: 2½
Foundation: Slab
Material List Available: Yes
Price Category: D

Images provided by designer/architect.

Copyright by designer/architect.

Side Elevation

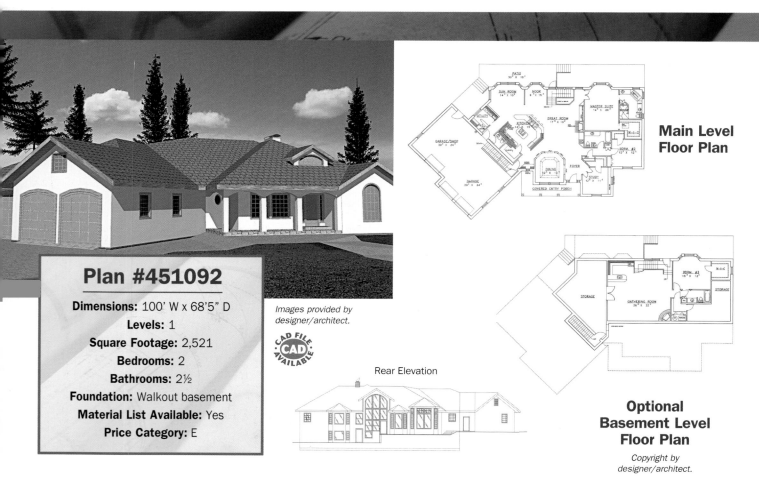

Plan #451092

Dimensions: 100' W x 68'5" D
Levels: 1
Square Footage: 2,521
Bedrooms: 2
Bathrooms: 2½
Foundation: Walkout basement
Material List Available: Yes
Price Category: E

Images provided by designer/architect.

Main Level Floor Plan

Optional Basement Level Floor Plan

Copyright by designer/architect.

Rear Elevation

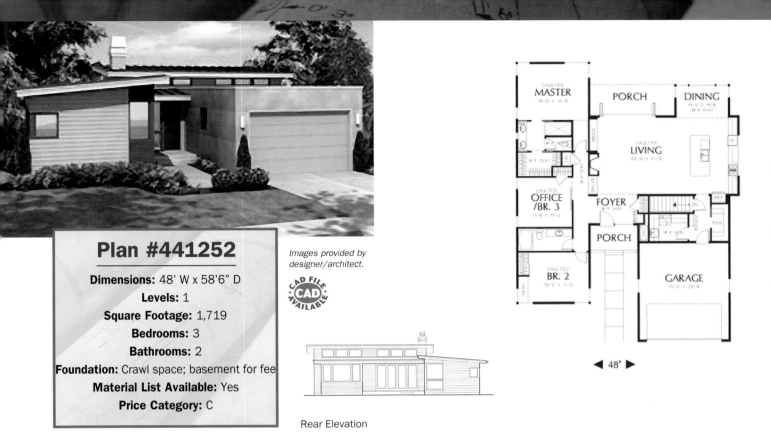

Plan #441252

Dimensions: 48' W x 58'6" D

Levels: 1

Square Footage: 1,719

Bedrooms: 3

Bathrooms: 2

Foundation: Crawl space; basement for fee

Material List Available: Yes

Price Category: C

Images provided by designer/architect.

Rear Elevation

Copyright by designer/architect.

Plan #641008

Dimensions: 66' W x 32' D

Levels: 1.5

Square Footage: 2,767

Bedrooms: 4

Bathrooms: 2½

Foundation: Basement or crawl space; slab or walkout for fee

Materials List Available: Yes

Price Category: F

Images provided by designer/architect.

Upper Level Floor Plan

Main Level Floor Plan

Copyright by designer/architect.

Plan #271036

Dimensions: 43'4" W x 50' D
Levels: 2
Square Footage: 1,602
Main Level Sq. Ft.: 1,112
Upper Level Sq. Ft.: 490
Bedrooms: 3
Bathrooms: 2½
Foundation: Basement
Materials List Available: Yes
Price Category: C

A country-styled home, like this one, is a perfect fit for any neighborhood.

Features:

- **Living Room:** Just off the entry you will find this large gathering area with a cozy fireplace. The front wall of windows will allow the area to be flooded with natural light.

- **Kitchen:** The chef in the family will love the layout of this efficiently designed kitchen. On nice days step out the glass doors onto the rear patio, and dine in the sunshine.

- **Master Bedroom:** This main-level retreat features an elegant double-door entry. The master bath offers efficiency in a compact design.

- **Secondary Bedrooms:** Located on the upper level, these two bedrooms offer adequate space for furniture and toys. The second full bathroom is located close by.

Upper Level Floor Plan

Br 2 10-6x13-8
Br 3 10x10
DN
open to below
unfinished storage
Plant Shelf

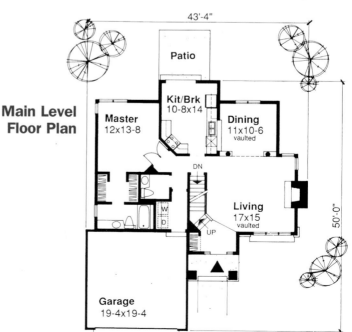

Main Level Floor Plan

43'-4"
Patio
Kit/Brk 10-8x14
Master 12x13-8
Dining 11x10-6 vaulted
DN
Living 17x15 vaulted
UP
W D
50'-0"
Garage 19-4x19-4

Plan #321058

Dimensions: 39' W x 42'8" D
Levels: 2
Square Footage: 1,700
Main Level Sq. Ft.: 896
Upper Level Sq. Ft.: 804
Bedrooms: 4
Bathrooms: 2½
Foundation: Basement
Materials List Available: Yes
Price Category: C

Images provided by designer/architect.

Graceful architectural details, including unique window designs, create an exterior that mirrors the beauty and efficiency of the interior.

Features:

- Entry: This two-story entry is illuminated by a decorative oval window.

- Family Room: This large family room will be bathed in warm light no matter the time of day thanks to plenty of windows and a built-in fireplace.

- Kitchen: A built-in pantry and ample counter space make a great work area for the family cook and the aspiring chef alike. An open transition to the breakfast area simplifies

morning chaos, while a defined separation formalizes the dining room.

- Bedrooms: Having the bedrooms separated from the other living areas means a restful space for sleep and a quiet place for study or work. The master suite is spacious and features a walk-in closet and full bath. The three secondary bedrooms are all near a full bathroom, and all have generous closet storage. If three bedrooms are one too many, use one as an office, study, or entertainment space.

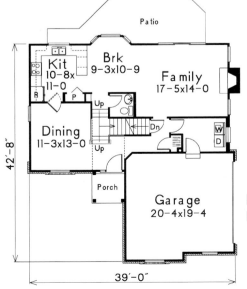

Main Level Floor Plan

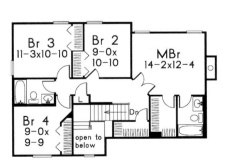

Upper Level Floor Plan

Copyright by designer/architect.

Plan #301001

Dimensions: 99'10" W x 46'2" D
Levels: 1
Square Footage: 2,720
Bedrooms: 3
Bathrooms: 2
Foundation: Crawl space or basement
Materials List Available: Yes
Price Category: F

Images provided by designer/architect.

Copyright by designer/architect.

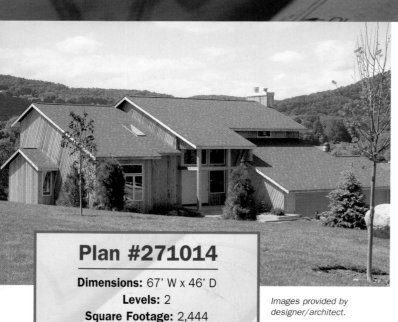

Plan #271014

Dimensions: 67' W x 46' D
Levels: 2
Square Footage: 2,444
Main Level Sq. Ft.: 1,364
Upper Level Sq. Ft.: 1,080
Bedrooms: 3
Bathrooms: 3
Foundation: Basement
Material List Available: Yes
Price Category: E

Images provided by designer/architect.

Main Level Floor Plan

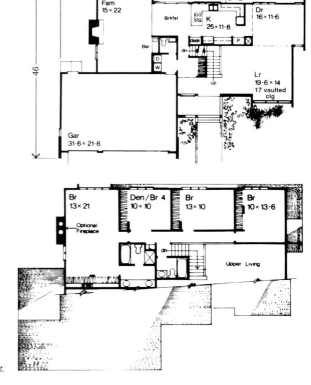

Upper Level Floor Plan

Copyright by designer/architect.

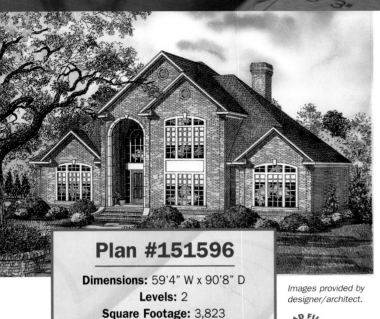

Main Level Floor Plan

Copyright by designer/ architect.

Upper Level Floor Plan

Images provided by designer/architect.

Plan #151596

Dimensions: 59'4" W x 90'8" D

Levels: 2

Square Footage: 3,823

Main Level Sq. Ft.: 2,654

Upper Level Sq. Ft.: 1,169

Bedrooms: 3

Bathrooms: 3½

Foundation: Crawl space, slab

CompleteCost List Available: Yes

Price Category: H

CAD FILE AVAILABLE

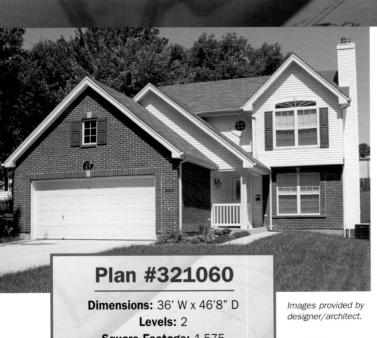

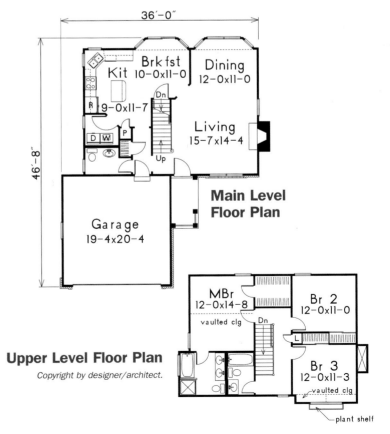

Plan #321060

Dimensions: 36' W x 46'8" D

Levels: 2

Square Footage: 1,575

Main Level Sq. Ft.: 802

Upper Level Sq. Ft.: 773

Bedrooms: 3

Bathrooms: 2½

Foundation: Basement

Materials List Available: Yes

Price Category: C

Images provided by designer/architect.

CAD FILE AVAILABLE

Main Level Floor Plan

Upper Level Floor Plan

Copyright by designer/ architect.

Plan #151384

Dimensions: 76'8" W x 77'7" D
Levels: 1.5
Square Footage: 2,742
Bedrooms: 3
Bathrooms: 2½
Foundation: Crawl space or slab
CompleteCost List Available: Yes
Price Category: F

With its fine detailing, this is a home created for the ages.

CAD FILE AVAILABLE

Features:

- **Great Room:** A fireplace nicely settled between built-ins punctuates this enormous room.

This home, as shown in the photograph, may differ from the actual blueprints. For more detailed information, please check the floor plans carefully. *Images provided by designer/architect.*

- **Hobby Room:** This oversized room offers space galore for those do-it-yourself home projects.

- **Master Suite:** This elaborate suite presents an entire wall of built-ins, along with an angled private entrance to the porch.

- **Bedrooms:** The two secondary bedrooms are located on the opposite side of the home from the master suite and share the full bathroom adjacent to Bedroom 2.

Copyright by designer/architect.

Bonus Area Floor Plan

Front View

Plan #121059

Dimensions: 52' W x 59'4" D
Levels: 1
Square Footage: 1,782
Bedrooms: 3
Bathrooms: 2
Foundation: Basement
Materials List Available: Yes
Price Category: C

This home is ideal for families looking for luxury and style mixed with convenience.

Features:

• Great Room: This large room is enhanced by the three-sided fireplace it shares with adjacent living areas.

• Hearth Room: Enjoy the fireplace here, too, and decorate to emphasize the bayed windows.

• Kitchen: This kitchen was designed for efficiency and is flooded with natural light.

• Breakfast Area: Picture-awing windows are the highlight in this area.

• Master Suite: A boxed ceiling and walk-in closet as well as a bath with a double-vanity, whirlpool tub, shower, and window with a plant ledge make this suite a true retreat.

• Bedrooms: These lovely bedrooms are served by a luxurious full bath.

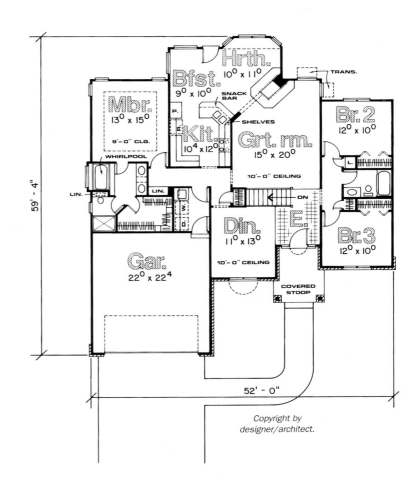

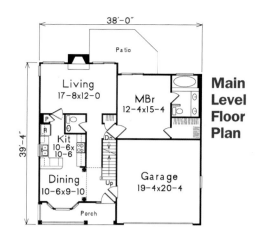

Main Level Floor Plan

38'-0"

39'-4"

Patio

Living 17-8x12-0

MBr 12-4x15-4

Kit 10-6x 10-6

Dn

Up

Dining 10-6x9-10

Garage 19-4x20-4

Porch

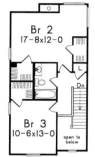

Images provided by designer/architect.

CAD FILE AVAILABLE

Plan #321057

Dimensions: 38' W x 39'4" D

Levels: 2

Square Footage: 1,524

Main Level Sq. Ft.: 951

Upper Level Sq. Ft.: 573

Bedrooms: 3

Bathrooms: 2½

Foundation: Basement

Materials List Available: Yes

Price Category: C

Upper Level Floor Plan

Br 2 17-8x12-0

Dn

Br 3 10-6x13-0

open to below

Copyright by designer/ architect.

Upper Level Floor Plan

WHIRLPOOL

BALCONY

BEDROOM 11⁸ x 13⁸

BATH

SEAT

MASTER BEDROOM 17⁸ x 15⁴

DRESS. RM

WALK-IN CLOSET

SHELVES

CL

CL

LINEN

BATH

RAILING

DN

UPPER FOYER

BEDROOM 12⁸ x 11⁰

WALK-IN CLOSET

Plan #741007

Dimensions: 40' W x 58' D

Levels: 2

Square Footage: 3,315

Main Level Sq. Ft.: 1,096

Upper Level Sq. Ft.: 1,115

Lower Level Sq. Ft.: 1,104

Bedrooms: 4

Bathrooms: 3½

Foundation: Walkout

Material List Available: Yes

Price Category: G

Images provided by designer/architect.

Copyright by designer/architect.

Main Level Floor Plan

DECK

DINING RM. 13⁰ x 11⁸

DECK

BALCONY ABOVE

GATHERING RM 17⁸ x 15⁴

BRKFST RM 10⁸ x 14⁸

KITCHEN 10⁸ x 11⁴

DESK

OPEN ABOVE

MUD RM

WASH RM

FOYER

P

CL

RAILING

COVERED PORCH

GARAGE 21⁴ x 21⁸

Lower Level Floor Plan

TERRACE

HOBBIES 13⁰ x 11⁸

TERRACE

GUEST BEDROOM 11⁸ x 18⁸

FURN.

MECH. RM

ACTIVITIES RM 17⁰ x 15⁴

BATH

LINEX

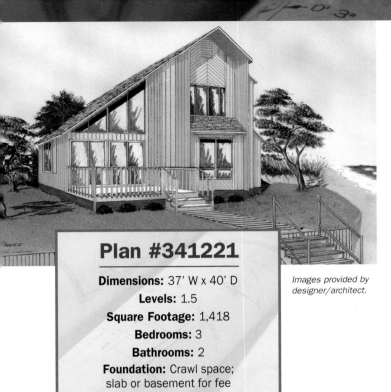

**Main Level
Floor Plan**

37'-0"

PORCH

BEDROOM
11'-8" x 11'-5"

LIVING ROOM
13'-7" x 19'-2"

CLOSET

BATH

40'-0"

CLOS

LIN

VAULTED
CEILING

KITCHEN / DINING
15'-2" x 13'-3"

PANTRY

STOOP

DECK

Lower Level

*Images provided by
designer/architect.*

Plan #341221

Dimensions: 37' W x 40' D

Levels: 1.5

Square Footage: 1,418

Bedrooms: 3

Bathrooms: 2

Foundation: Crawl space;
slab or basement for fee

Material List Available: Yes

Price Category: B

open to below

MBr
15-4 x 12-8

Dn

open to
below

Upper Level Floor Plan

Br 2
12-11 x 11-8

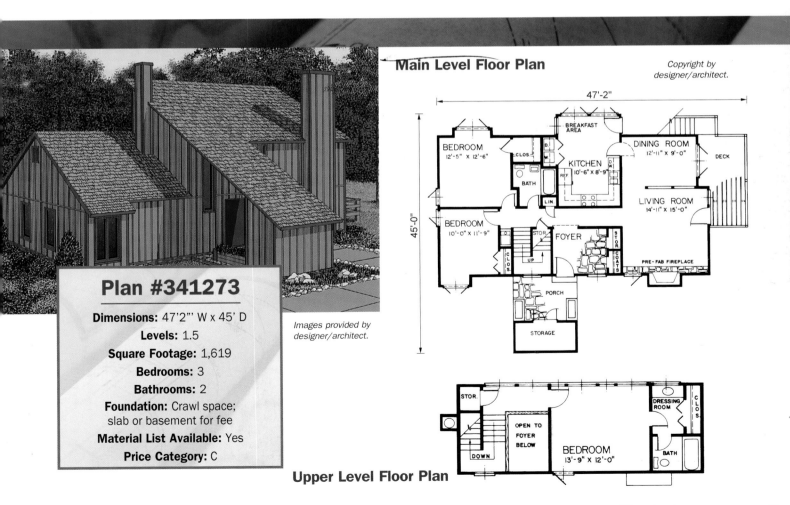

Main Level Floor Plan

47'-2"

BEDROOM
12'-5" x 12'-6"

CLOS

BREAKFAST
AREA

KITCHEN
10'-6" x 8'-9"

DINING ROOM
12'-11" x 9'-0"

DECK

BATH

REF

45'-0"

LIN

LIVING ROOM
14'-11" x 15'-0"

BEDROOM
10'-0" x 11'-9"

STOR

CLOS

FOYER

STOR

COATS

UP

PRE-FAB FIREPLACE

PORCH

STORAGE

*Images provided by
designer/architect.*

Plan #341273

Dimensions: 47'2"' W x 45' D

Levels: 1.5

Square Footage: 1,619

Bedrooms: 3

Bathrooms: 2

Foundation: Crawl space;
slab or basement for fee

Material List Available: Yes

Price Category: C

STOR.

OPEN TO
FOYER
BELOW

DRESSING
ROOM

CLOS

DOWN

BEDROOM
13'-9" x 12'-0"

BATH

Upper Level Floor Plan

Plan #161096

Dimensions: 67'6" W x 75'6" D
Levels: 2
Square Footage: 3,435
Main Level Sq. Ft.: 2,479
Upper Level Sq. Ft.: 956
Bedrooms: 4
Bathrooms: 3½
Foundation: Walkout basement;
basement for fee
Material List Available: Yes----
Price Category: G

A stone-and-brick exterior is excellently coordinated to create a warm and charming showplace.

Features:

- **Great Room:** The spacious foyer leads directly into this room, which visually opens to the rear yard, providing natural light and outdoor charm.

- **Kitchen:** This fully equipped kitchen is located to provide the utmost convenience in serving the formal dining room and the breakfast area, which is surrounded by windows and has a double-soffit ceiling treatment. The combination of breakfast room, hearth room, and kitchen creatively forms a comfortable family gathering place.

- **Master Suite:** A tray ceiling tops this suite and its luxurious dressing area, which will pamper you after a hard day.

- **Balcony:** Wood rails decorate the stairs leading to this balcony, which offers a dramatic view of the great room and foyer below.

- **Bedrooms:** A secondary private bedroom suite with personal bath, plus two bedrooms that share a Jack-and-Jill bathroom, complete the exciting home.

Great Room

Main Level Floor Plan

Deck

Hearth Room
15'11" X 17'3"
Irregular

Breakfast
12'5" X 12'10"
Irregular

Kitchen
13'6" X 16'11"
Irregular

Laun.

Dressing

WALK-IN CLOSET

Great Room
18'6" X 22'3"

Master Bedroom
13'8" X 17'0"
Tray Ceiling

Foyer

Hall

Bath

Dining Room
12'4" X 13'10"
Double Soffit Ceiling

Porch

Library
12'4" X 12'3"
Irregular

Garage
21'2" X 33'10"
Irregular

Main Level Floor Plan

Copyright by designer/architect.

Upper Level Floor Plan

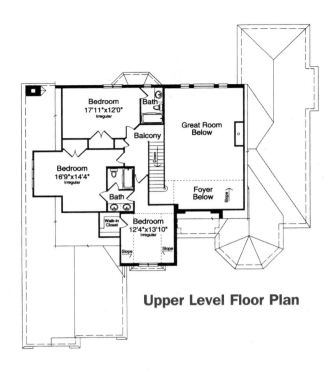

Bedroom
17'11"x12'0"
Irregular

Bath

Balcony

Great Room Below

Bedroom
16'9"x14'4"
Irregular

Bath

Foyer Below

Slope

Walk-in Closet

Bedroom
12'4"x13'10"
Irregular

Slope   Slope

Upper Level Floor Plan

Hearth Room

Front View

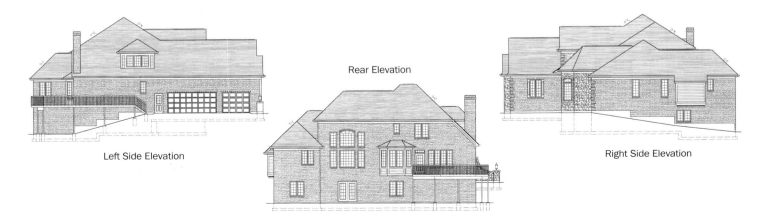

Left Side Elevation

Rear Elevation

Right Side Elevation

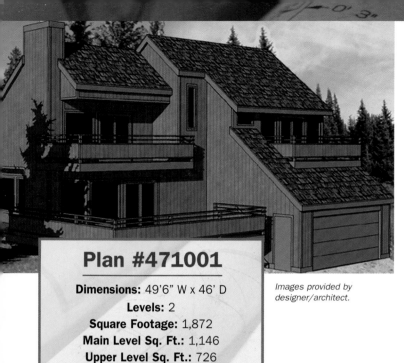

Plan #471001

Dimensions: 49'6" W x 46' D
Levels: 2
Square Footage: 1,872
Main Level Sq. Ft.: 1,146
Upper Level Sq. Ft.: 726
Bedrooms: 3
Bathrooms: 2
Foundation: Crawl space
Material List Available: Yes
Price Category: D

Images provided by designer/architect.

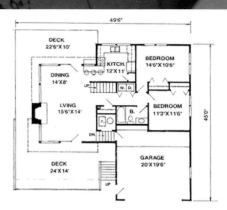

Main Level Floor Plan

Upper Level Floor Plan

Copyright by designer/architect.

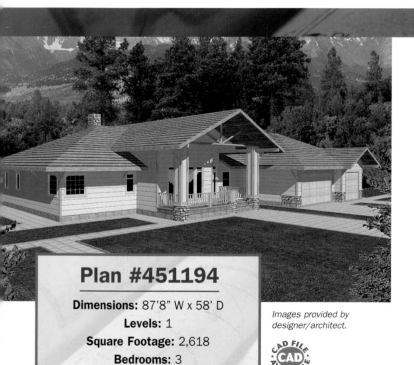

Plan #451194

Dimensions: 87'8" W x 58' D
Levels: 1
Square Footage: 2,618
Bedrooms: 3
Bathrooms: 2½
Foundation: Crawl space
Materials List Available: Yes
Price Category: F

Images provided by designer/architect.

CAD FILE AVAILABLE

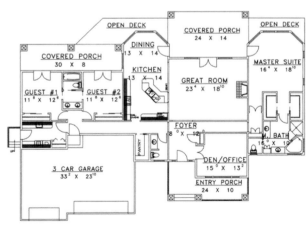

Copyright by designer/architect.

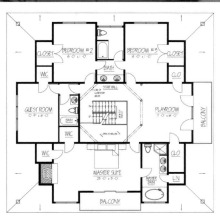

Plan #641007

Dimensions: 50' W x 50' D
Levels: 2
Square Footage: 3,650
Main Level Sq. Ft.: 1,686
Upper Level Sq. Ft.: 1,964
Bedrooms: 4
Bathrooms: 3½
Foundation: Crawl space; slab,
basement or walkout for fee
Material List Available: Yes
Price Category: H

Images provided by designer/architect.

CAD FILE AVAILABLE

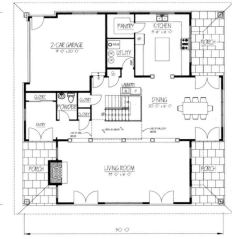

Main Level
Floor Plan

Copyright by designer/architect.

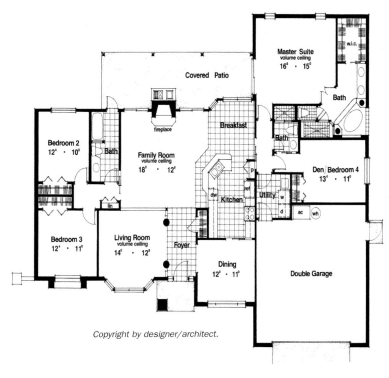

Plan #661109

Dimensions: 70' W x 58'8" D
Levels: 1
Square Footage: 2,321
Bedrooms: 4
Bathrooms: 3
Foundation: Slab
Material List Available: Yes
Price Category: E

Images provided by designer/architect.

Copyright by designer/architect.

Plan #151383

Dimensions: 70'4" W x 57'2" D

Levels: 1

Square Footage: 2,534

Bedrooms: 3

Bathrooms: 2

Foundation: Crawl space or slab

CompleteCost List Available: Yes

Price Category: G

The arched entry of the covered porch welcomes you to this magnificent home.

Features:

- **Foyer:** Welcome your guests in this warm foyer before leading them into the impressive dining room with magnificent columns framing the entry.

- **Great Room:** After dinner, your guests will enjoy conversation in this spacious room, complete with fireplace and built-ins.

- **Study:** Beautiful French doors open into this quiet space, where you'll be able to concentrate on that work away from the office.

- **Rear Porch:** This relaxing spot may be reached from the breakfast room or your secluded master suite.

This home, as shown in the photograph, may differ from the actual blueprints. *Images provided by designer/architect.* For more detailed information, please check the floor plans carefully.

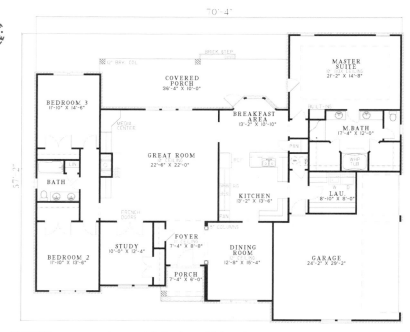

Copyright by designer/architect.

Front View

Plan #121111

Dimensions: 52' W x 45'4" D
Levels: 1.5
Square Footage: 1,685
Main Level Sq. Ft.: 1,297
Upper Level Sq. Ft.: 388
Bedrooms: 3
Bathrooms: 2½
Foundation: Basement;
crawl space for fee
Materials List Available: Yes
Price Category: C

This home, as shown in the photograph, may differ from the actual blueprints. For more detailed information, please check the floor plans carefully.

Images provided by designer/architect.

Beauty meets practicality in this charming home. Lovely architectural details and an interior designed with daily living in mind create an ideal environment for the growing family.

Features:

• Great Room: When the day is done and its time to relax, this is the place where the family will gather. The fireplace is a great start to creating an atmosphere tailored to your family's lifestyle.

• Kitchen: Great for the busy family, the kitchen has all the workspace and storage that the family chef needs, as well as a snack bar that acts as a transition to the large breakfast room.

• Dining Room: A triplet of windows projecting onto the covered front porch creates a warm atmosphere for formal dining.

• Master Bedroom: A romantic space, this master bedroom features a window seat facing the front elevation and a compartmentalized full master bath that includes his and her sinks, a walk-in closet, and a whirlpool tub with a skylight.

• Second Floor: In a quiet space of their own, the two secondary bedrooms both include ample closet space and access to the second full bathroom.

Main Level Floor Plan

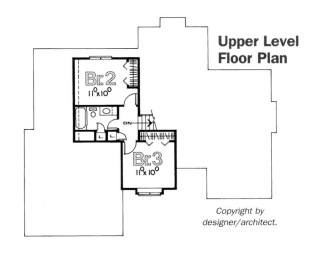

Upper Level Floor Plan

Copyright by designer/architect.

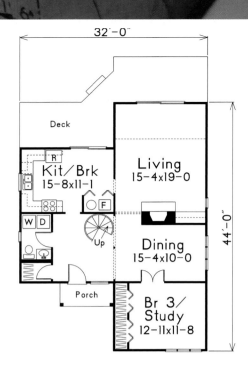

Main Level Floor Plan

Deck

R

Kit/Brk
15-8x11-1

Living
15-4x19-0

W D

F

Up

Dining
15-4x10-0

Porch

Br 3/
Study
12-11x11-8

32'-0"

44'-0"

Plan #321339

Dimensions: 32' W x 44' D

Levels: 2

Square Footage: 1,836

Main Level Sq. Ft.: 1,088

Upper Level Sq. Ft.: 748

Bedrooms: 3

Bathrooms: 2½

Foundation: Crawl space or slab

Materials List Available: Yes

Price Category: D

Images provided by designer/architect.

CAD FILE AVAILABLE

open to below

MBr
15-4x12-8

Dn

open to below

Br 2
12-11x11-8

Upper Level Floor Plan

Copyright by designer/architect.

Plan #741002

Dimensions: 66'6" W x 38' D

Levels: 1

Bedrooms: 3

Bathrooms: 2

Foundation: Slab

Materials List Available: Yes

Price Category: B

Images provided by designer/architect.

BED RM.
12 x 15

PORCH

MASTER BED RM.
15 x 15

BATH

PDR. RM.

ENTRY

KIT.

BATH

PDR. RM.

BED RM.
9 x 7

PANTRY

REF'S.

STOR.

AIR COND.

LIVING
31 x 13

DINING

TERRACE

Copyright by designer/architect.

Rear View

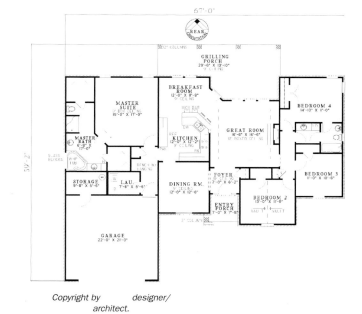

Images provided by designer/architect.

Copyright by   designer/architect.

Plan #151240

Dimensions: 67' W x 59'2" D

Levels: 1

Square Footage: 2,007

Bedrooms: 4

Bathrooms: 2

Foundation: Crawl space or slab

CompleteCost List Available: Yes

Price Category: E

Main Level Floor Plan

Copyright by designer/architect.

Images provided by designer/architect.

Upper Level Floor Plan

Plan #321291

Dimensions: 34' W x 54' D

Levels: 2

Square Footage: 1,873

Main Level Sq. Ft.: 896

Upper Level Sq. Ft.: 977

Bedrooms: 3

Bathrooms: 2½

Foundation: Crawl space, slab or basement

Materials List Available: Yes

Price Category: D

Plan #271019

Dimensions: 40'4" W x 41'8" D

Levels: 2

Square Footage: 1,556

Main Level Sq. Ft.: 834

Upper Level Sq. Ft.: 722

Bedrooms: 3

Bathrooms: 2½

Foundation: Basement

Materials List Available: Yes

Price Category: C

This traditional home features a combination of stone and wood, lending it a distinctive old-world flavor.

Features:

- Kitchen: The centerpiece of the home, this country kitchen features ample work surfaces, a nice-sized eating area with built-in bookshelves, and access to a large backyard deck.

- Dining Room: This formal eating space is highlighted by a dramatic three-sided fireplace that is shared with the adjoining living room.

- Living Room: Enhanced by a dramatic vaulted ceiling, this living room also boasts corner windows that flood the area with natural light.

- Master Suite: Residing on the upper floor along with two other bedrooms, the master bedroom features a vaulted ceiling and a plant shelf that tops the entry to a private bath and walk-in closet.

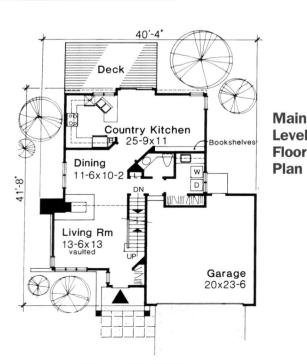

Main Level Floor Plan

40'-4"

Deck

Country Kitchen
25-9x11

Bookshelves

Dining
11-6x10-2

Living Rm
13-6x13
vaulted

Garage
20x23-6

41'-8"

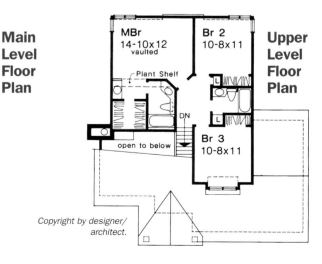

Upper Level Floor Plan

MBr
14-10x12
vaulted

Br 2
10-8x11

Plant Shelf

open to below

Br 3
10-8x11

Plan #151711

Dimensions: 64' W x 60'2" D
Levels: 1
Square Footage: 2,554
Bedrooms: 4
Bathrooms: 2½
Foundation: Crawl space or slab
CompleteCost List Available: Yes
Price Category: E

An alluring arched entry welcomes guests into your home, giving them a taste of the lavishness they'll find once inside.

CAD FILE AVAILABLE

Features:

- **Kitchen:** Counter space on all sides and a center island provide ample space for the budding chef. This kitchen is located across the hall from the dining room and opens into the hearth room, providing easy transitions between preparing and serving. A snack bar acts as a shift between the kitchen and hearth room.

- **Hearth Room:** This spacious area is lined with windows on one side, shares a gas fire place with the great room, and opens onto the grilling porch, which makes it ideal for gatherings of all kinds and sizes.

- **Master Suite:** Larger than any space in the house, this room will truly make you feel like the master. The bedroom is a blank canvas waiting for your personal touch and has a door opening to the backyard. The compartmentalized master bath includes his and her walk-in closets and sinks, a glass shower stall, and a whirlpool bathtub.

- **Secondary Bedrooms:** If three bedrooms is one too many, the second bedroom can easily be used as a study with optional French doors opening from the foyer. Every additional bedroom has a large closet and access to the central full bathroom.

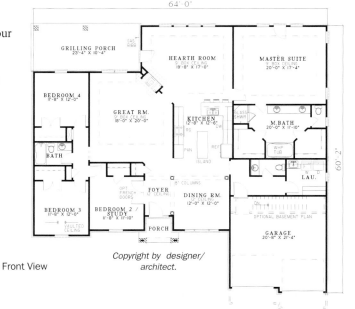

Copyright by designer/architect.

Front View

This home, as shown in the photograph, may differ from the actual blueprints. For more detailed information, please check the floor plans carefully.

Plan #391036

Dimensions: 28' W x 32' D
Levels: 2
Square Footage: 1,710
Main Level Sq. Ft.: 728
Upper Level Sq. Ft.: 573
Lower Level Sq. Ft.: 409
Bedrooms: 3
Bathrooms: 2
Foundation: Basement
Materials List Available: Yes
Price Category: C

This home is a vacation haven, with views from every room, whether it is situated on a lake or a mountaintop.

Features:

- Main Floor: A fireplace splits the living and dining rooms in this area.

- Kitchen: This kitchen flows into the dining room and is gracefullly separated by a bar.

- Master Suite: A large walk-in closet, full bathroom, and deck make this private area special.

- Bedroom or Loft: The second floor has this bedroom or library loft, with clerestory windows, which opens above the living room.

- Lower Level: This lower floor has a large recreation room with a whirlpool tub, bar, laundry room, and garage.

Images provided by designer/architect.

Main Level Floor Plan

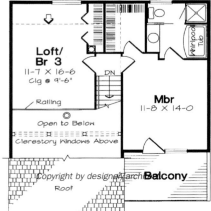

Upper Level Floor Plan

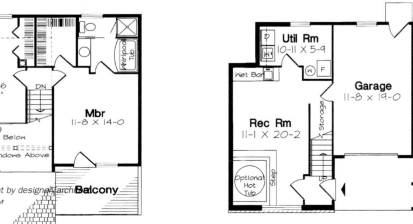

Lower Level Floor Plan

Plan #271015

Dimensions: 48' W x 28' D
Levels: 2
Square Footage: 1,359
Main Level Sq. Ft.: 668
Upper Level Sq. Ft.: 691
Bedrooms: 3
Bathrooms: 2½
Foundation: Basement
Materials List Available: Yes
Price Category: B

Images provided by designer/architect.

Strong vertical lines and pairs of narrow windows give this compact home an airy feel. Its clever floor plan makes good use of every square foot of space.

Features:

- **Living Room:** Beyond the sidelighted front door, the living room enjoys a vaulted ceiling and a flood of light from a striking corner window arrangement.

- **Kitchen/Dining:** A central fireplace separates the living room from this kitchen/dining room, where a French door opens to a rear deck.

- **Master Suite:** Sacrifice no luxuries in this sweet, upper-floor retreat, where a boxed-out window catches morning rays or evening stars. Next to the roomy walk-in closet, the private split bath enjoys a window of its own.

- **Secondary Bedrooms:** A balcony overlooks the living room and leads to one bedroom and the flexible loft.

Main Level Floor Plan

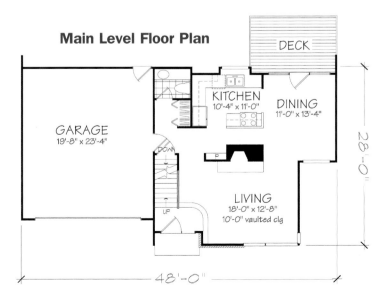

Upper Level Floor Plan

Copyright by designer/architect.

Copyright by designer/architect.

Plan #151203

Dimensions: 46' W x 38'10" D

Levels: 1

Square Footage: 1,214

Bedrooms: 3

Bathrooms: 2

Foundation: Crawl space, slab; basement or walkout basement option for fee

CompleteCost List Available: Yes

Price Category: B

Images provided by designer/architect.

CAD FILE AVAILABLE

Plan #321272

Dimensions: 48' W x 40' D

Levels: 2

Square Footage: 2,087

Bedrooms: 4

Bathrooms: 2½

Foundation: Crawl space, slab or basement

Material List Available: Yes

Price Category: D

Images provided by designer/architect.

CAD FILE AVAILABLE

Main Level Floor Plan

Copyright by designer/architect.

Upper Level Floor Plan

Copyright by designer/architect.

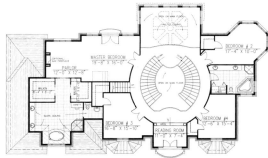

Main Level Floor Plan

Copyright by designer/architect.

Images provided by designer/architect.

Plan #571036

Dimensions: 87'6" W x 51'3" D
Levels: 2
Square Footage: 6,175
Main Level Sq. Ft.: 2,628
Upper Level Sq. Ft.: 3,024
Bonus Area Sq. Ft.: 523
Bedrooms: 4
Bathrooms: 2½
Foundation: Basement
Material List Available: Yes
Price Category: K

Bonus Area Floor Plan

Upper Level Floor Plan

Plan #391168

Dimensions: 93'6" W x 48' D
Levels: 1
Square Footage: 2,352
Main Level Sq. Ft.: 2,352
Bedrooms: 3
Bathrooms: 2½
Foundation: Basement
Material List Available: Yes
Price Category: E

Images provided by designer/architect.

Plan #661191

Dimensions: 58'8" W x 68' D
Levels: 2
Square Footage: 2,998
Main Level Sq. Ft.: 2,227
Upper Level Sq. Ft.: 771
Bedrooms: 4
Bathrooms: 4
Foundation: Slab
Material List Available: Yes
Price Category: F

A soaring, two-story ceiling and dramatic staircase help create the "wow factor" in the grand entryway of this home.

This home, as shown in the photograph, may differ from the actual blueprints. For more detailed information, please check the floor plans carefully.

Images provided by designer/architect.

Features:

- Family Room: This open, airy space is wonderful for entertaining guests or enjoying a movie with the family. Close proximity to the kitchen makes getting a quick snack even easier.

- Kitchen: This gourmet kitchen offers easy access to everything the family cook requires. A large pantry and plentiful counter space are just two of the special amenities.

- Rear Patio: This versatile covered patio at the back of the house is great for entertaining guests or watching the kids play in the backyard. It is conveniently accessed through the family room and kitchen, creating a wonderful flow during large get-togethers.

- Master Suite: You'll love to escape to this luxurious master suite, made complete with his and her sinks, walk-in closet, and large tub.

Main Level Floor Plan

Copyright by designer/architect.

Upper Level Floor Plan

Plan #131054

Dimensions: 107'4" W x 75'3" D
Levels: 1
Square Footage: 2,753
Bedrooms: 3
Full Bathrooms: 2 1/2
Foundation: Crawl space, slab, basement or walk-out
Materials List Available: Yes
Price Category: G

Images provided by designer/architect.

This beautifully designed interior area combined with plenty of outdoor living space create a striking and efficient home.

Features:

• Outdoor Living: Sit on the front porch and watch the world go by, enjoy a peaceful moment on the screened-in porch, or entertain on the wooden deck. If you enjoy the outdoors, this home is for you.

• Great Room: A vaulted ceiling, built-in fireplace, and flanking windows create a bright and comfortable space for entertaining or simply hanging out with the family.

• Kitchen: With plenty of workspace and storage, this kitchen suits all cooking styles. An exit onto the back deck and screened-in porch provide outdoor meal options for any kind of weather.

• Master Suite: Down a hallway of its own, this oasis inspires total relaxation. It features two walk-in closets, a desk, his and her vanities, extra large tub, and separate stall shower.

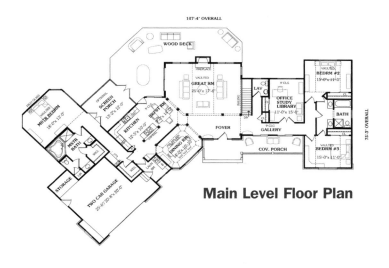

Main Level Floor Plan

Optional Basement Level Floor Plan

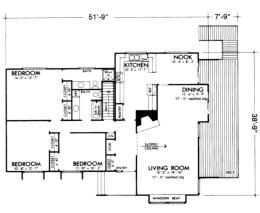

Copyright by designer/architect.

Plan #271084

Dimensions: 51'9" W x 38'9" D

Levels: 1

Square Footage: 1,602

Bedrooms: 3

Bathrooms: 1½

Foundation: Daylight

Materials List Available: Yes

Price Category: C

Images provided by designer/architect.

Optional Basement Level Floor Plan

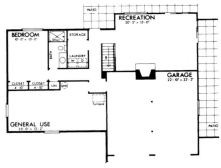

Plan #391022

Dimensions: 39' W x 48' D

Levels: 2

Square Footage: 1,908

Main Level Sq. Ft.: 1,316

Upper Level Sq. Ft.: 592

Bedrooms: 3

Bathrooms: 2

Foundation: Crawl space, slab or basement

Material List Available: Yes

Price Category: D

Images provided by designer/architect.

CAD FILE AVAILABLE

Rear View

Upper Level Floor Plan

Mstr. Suite 17-8 x 16-4

Balcony

Second Floor

Main Level Floor Plan

Copyright by designer/architect.

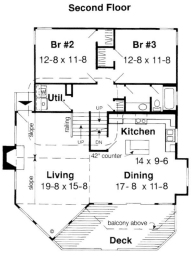

Br #2 12-8 x 11-8

Br #3 12-8 x 11-8

Util.

Kitchen 14 x 9-6

Living 19-8 x 15-8

Dining 17-8 x 11-8

Deck

balcony above

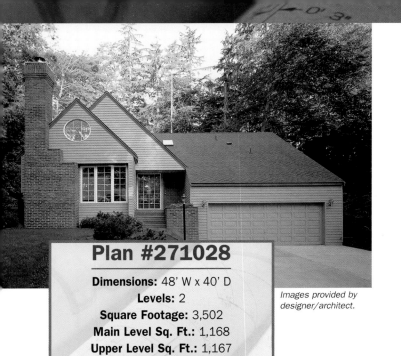

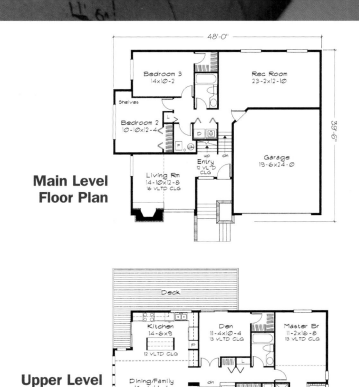

Main Level Floor Plan

Bedroom 3
14x10-2

Shelves

Bedroom 2
10-10x12-4

Living Rm
14-10x12-8
16 VLTD CLG

Entry
12 VLTD CLG

Rec Room
23-2x12-10

Garage
19-6x24-0

48'-0"

39'-6"

Images provided by designer/architect.

Upper Level Floor Plan

Deck

Kitchen
14-6x9
12 VLTD CLG

Den
11-4x10-4
13 VLTD CLG

Master Br
11-2x16-8
13 VLTD CLG

Dining/Family
16-4x14-4
13 VLTD CLG

living rm below

Copyright by designer/architect.

Plan #271028

Dimensions: 48' W x 40' D

Levels: 2

Square Footage: 3,502

Main Level Sq. Ft.: 1,168

Upper Level Sq. Ft.: 1,167

Lower Level Sq. Ft.: 1,167

Bedrooms: 3

Bathrooms: 3

Foundation: Basement, crawl space

Materials List Available: Yes

Price Category: E

Upper Level Floor Plan

BEDROOM 3
11'-4" X 11'-6"

LIVING ROOM BELOW

BEDROOM 2
11'-0" X 11'-4"

DRESSING AREA

SEAT

SLOPE   SLOPE

M. BEDROOM
14'-8" X 11'-4"

Copyright by designer/architect.

Main Level Floor Plan

DECK

LIVING RM.
13'-4" X 19'-8"

SLOPE   SLOPE

KITCHEN
9'-6" X 12'-0"

BRKFST.
9'-6" X 11'-0"

DINING
11'-0" X 11'-4"

FOYER

GARAGE
21'-4" X 21'-8"

Images provided by designer/architect.

CAD FILE AVAILABLE

Plan #391212

Dimensions: 34' W x 58''4" D

Levels: 2

Square Footage: 1,701

Upper Level Sq. Ft. 928

Lower Level Sq. Ft.: 773

Bedrooms: 3

Bathrooms: 2 1/2

Foundation: Basement

Materials List Available: Yes

Price Category: B

Plan #271011

Dimensions: 36' W x 40'8" D
Levels: 2
Square Footage: 1,296
Main Level Sq. Ft.: 891
Upper Level Sq. Ft.: 405
Bedrooms: 3
Bathrooms: 2
Foundation: Basement
Materials List Available: Yes
Price Category: B

Images provided by designer/architect.

Perfectly sized for a narrow lot, this charming modern cottage boasts space efficiency and affordability.

Features:

- Living Room: The inviting raised foyer steps down into this vaulted living room, with its bright windows and eye-catching fireplace.
- Dining Room: This vaulted formal eating space includes sliding-glass-door access to a backyard deck.

- Kitchen: Everything is here: U-shaped efficiency, handy pantry—even bright windows.
- Master Suite: Main-floor location ensures accessibility in later years, plus there's a walk-in closet and full bathroom.
- Secondary Bedrooms: On the upper floor, a bedroom and a loft reside near a full bath. The loft can be converted easily to a third bedroom, or use it as a study or play space.

Main Level Floor Plan

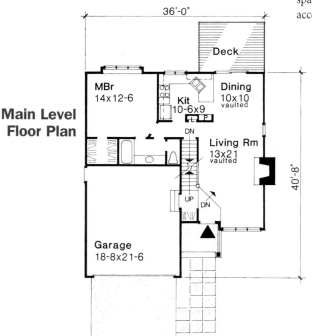

Upper Level Floor Plan

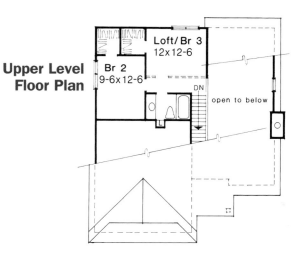

Plan #131067

Dimensions: 60'8" W x 29'4" D

Levels: 2

Square Footage: 1,909

Main Level Sq. Ft.: 1,159

Upper Level Sq. Ft.: 750

Bedrooms: 3

Bathrooms: 2½

Foundation: Crawl Space, Slab, or basement

Materials List Available: Yes

Price Category: E

This dramatic contemporary home features large dormers and windows.

Features:

• Foyer: This cathedral-ceiling entry welcomes you into this home. The open and airy feeling of the space makes you feel comfortable.

• Family Room: This sunken room is the comfortable space in which you and your family can relax after a busy day. The sliding glass doors lead out to the rear patio.

• Kitchen: This U-shaped kitchen is open to the adjacent breakfast area and only a few steps to the washer and dryer.

• Master Suite: Located on the upper level with two secondary bedrooms, this retreat offers two large closets. The master bath is an added plus.

Images provided by designer/architect.

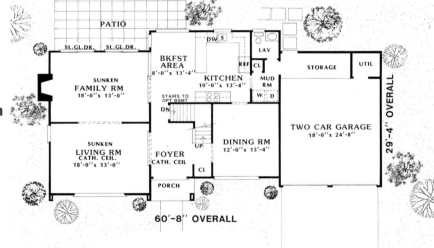

Main Level Floor Plan

PATIO
SL.GL.DR. SL.GL.DR.
BKFST AREA 8'-0" x 13'-4"
DW S
LAV
SUNKEN FAMILY RM 18'-0" x 13'-0"
KITCHEN 10'-0" x 13'-4"
REF CL
STORAGE
UTIL
MUD RM
STAIRS TO OPT BSMT
W D
TWO CAR GARAGE 18'-0" x 24'-8"
DN
UP
SUNKEN LIVING RM CATH. CEIL. 18'-0" x 13'-0"
FOYER CATH. CEIL
DINING RM 12'-0" x 13'-4"
CL
PORCH
29'-4" OVERALL
60'-8" OVERALL

Upper Level Floor Plan

MAST BATH
CL
BEDRM #1 11'-0" x 10'-4"
CL
MASTER BEDRM 15'-8" x 13'-0"
LIN
LIN
BATH #2
DN
CL
DN
OPT. RM OVER GARAGE 18'-0" x 11'-8"
DN
BEDRM #2 12'-0" x 10'-0"
CL

Copyright by designer/architect.

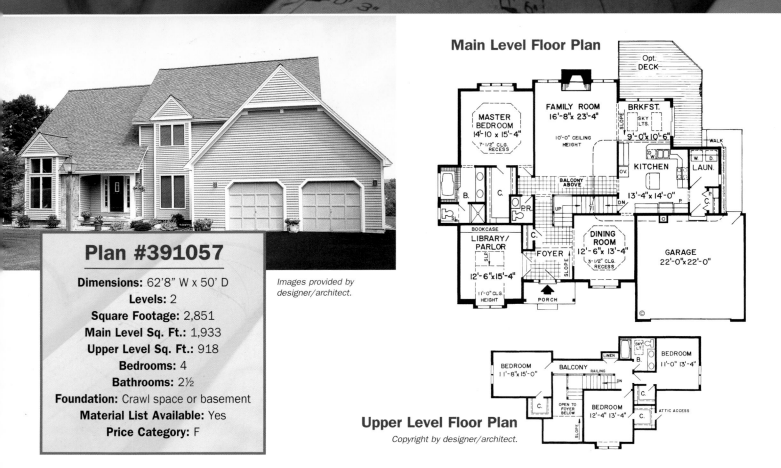

Main Level Floor Plan

MASTER BEDROOM 14'-10 x 15'-4" 7-1/2" CLG. RECESS

FAMILY ROOM 16'-8" x 23'-4" 10'-0" CEILING HEIGHT

Opt. DECK

BRKFST. 9'-0"x10'-6" SKY LTS.

WALK

KITCHEN 13'-4"x 14'-0"

LAUN.

W. D.

BALCONY ABOVE

B.

C.

PR.

UP

DN

DINING ROOM 12'-6"x 13'-4" 3-1/2" CLG. RECESS

GARAGE 22'-0"x 22'-0"

BOOKCASE

C.

LIBRARY/ PARLOR 12'-6"x15'-4" 11'-0" CLG. HEIGHT

FOYER

PORCH

Plan #391057

Dimensions: 62'8" W x 50' D
Levels: 2
Square Footage: 2,851
Main Level Sq. Ft.: 1,933
Upper Level Sq. Ft.: 918
Bedrooms: 4
Bathrooms: 2½
Foundation: Crawl space or basement
Material List Available: Yes
Price Category: F

Images provided by designer/architect.

BEDROOM 11'-8"x15'-0"

BALCONY RAILING

LINEN

SKY LT

B.

BEDROOM 11'-0" 13'-4"

C.

OPEN TO FOYER BELOW

DN

BEDROOM 12'-4" 13'-4"

C.

C.

ATTIC ACCESS

SLOPE

Upper Level Floor Plan

Copyright by designer/architect.

Plan #271078

Dimensions: 83' W x 52' D
Levels: 1
Square Footage: 3,620
Main Level Sq. Ft.: 1,855
Lower Level Sq. Ft.: 1,765
Bedrooms: 2
Bathrooms: 2½
Foundation: Walk-out
Materials List Available: Yes
Price Category: H

Images provided by designer/architect.

CAD FILE AVAILABLE

OWNER'S SUITE 14 X 16

SCREEN PORCH 15 X 14

BATH

GREAT RM 21 X 19

DINING 14 X 12

GARAGE 30 X 28

ENTRY

KITCHEN 14 X 13

STUDY 14 X 9

PORCH

LAUN

Main Level Floor Plan

BED RM 14 X 16

BA

EXERCISE ROOM 9' X 11'

LIVING ROOM 21' X 19'

SHOP 13' X 21'

MECHANICAL 18' X 9'

STORAGE 13' X 8'

STORAGE 13' X 13'

Lower Level Floor Plan

Copyright by designer/architect.

Main Level Floor Plan

CAD FILE AVAILABLE CAD

Third Floor Bedroom Floor Plan

Copyright by designer/ architect.

Images provided by designer/architect.

This home, as shown in the photograph, may differ from the actual blueprints. For more detailed information, please check the floor plans carefully.

Upper Level Floor Plan

Plan #121049

Dimensions: 82' W x 60'8" D

Levels: 2

Square Footage: 3,335

Main Level Sq. Ft.: 2,054

Upper Level Sq. Ft.: 1,281

Bedrooms: 4

Bathrooms: 3½

Foundation: Slab; basement for fee

Materials List Available: Yes

Price Category: G

Plan #151121

Dimensions: 66'8" W x 60'4" D

Levels: 2

Square Footage: 3,108

Main Level Sq. Ft.: 2,107

Upper Level Sq. Ft.: 1,001

Bedrooms: 3

Bathrooms: 2½

Foundation: Crawl space, slab; basement option for fee

CompleteCost List Available: Yes

Price Category: G

Images provided by designer/architect.

CAD FILE AVAILABLE CAD

This home, as shown in the photograph, may differ from the actual blueprints. For more detailed information, please check the floor plans carefully.

Upper Level Floor Plan

Main Level Floor Plan

Copyright by designer/architect.

Plan #151020

Dimensions: 96'10" W x 75'10" D
Levels: 2
Square Footage: 4,532
Main Level Sq. Ft.: 3,732
Upper Level Sq. Ft.: 800
Bedrooms: 3
Bathrooms: 3½
Foundation: Crawl space or slab; basement available for fee
CompleteCost List Available: Yes
Price Category: I

From the arched entry to the lanai and exercise and game rooms, this elegant home is a delight.

CAD FILE AVAILABLE

Images provided by designer/architect.

Features:

- Foyer: This spacious foyer with 12-ft. ceilings sets an open-air feeling for this home.
- Hearth Room: This cozy hearth room shares a 3-sided fireplace with the breakfast room. French doors open to the rear lanai.
- Dining Room: Entertain in this majestic dining room, with its arched entry and 12-ft. ceilings.
- Master Suite: This stunning suite includes a sitting room and access to the lanai. The bath features two walk-in closets, a step-up whirlpool tub with 8-in. columns, and glass-block shower.
- Upper Level: You'll find an exercise room, a game room, and attic storage space upstairs.

Rear View

Main Level Floor Plan

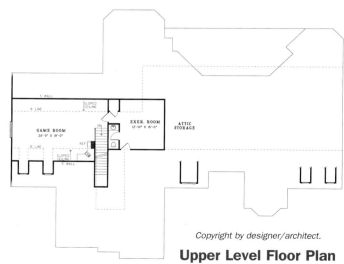

Copyright by designer/architect.

Upper Level Floor Plan

Plan #271002

Dimensions: 44'8" W x 50'8" D
Levels: 1
Square Footage: 1,252
Bedrooms: 3
Bathrooms: 2
Foundation: Basement
Materials List Available: Yes
Price Category: B

This traditional home combines a modest square footage with stylish extras.

Features:

• Living Room: Spacious and inviting, this gathering spot is brightened by a Palladian window arrangement, warmed by a fireplace, and topped by a vaulted ceiling.

• Dining Room: The vaulted ceiling also crowns this room, which shares the living room's fireplace. Sliding doors lead to a backyard deck.

• Kitchen: Smart design ensures a place for everything.

• Master Suite: The master bedroom boasts a vaulted ceiling, cheery windows, and a private bath.

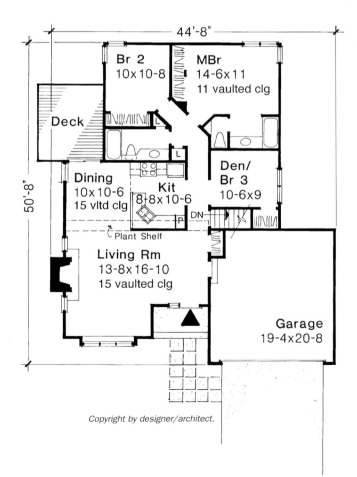

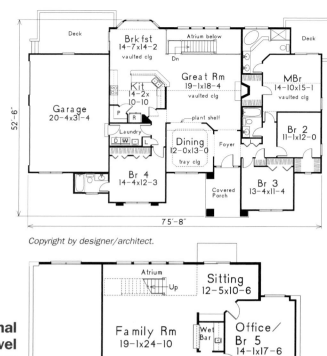

Copyright by designer/architect.

Plan #321034

Dimensions: 75'8" W x 52'6" D
Levels: 1
Square Footage: 3,508
Bedrooms: 4
Bathrooms: 3
Foundation: Basement, walkout
Material List Available: Yes
Price Category: H

Images provided by designer/architect.

Optional Basement Level Floor Plan

Plan #661203

Dimensions: 74' W x 67'2" D
Levels: 2
Square Footage: 3,182
Main Level Sq. Ft.: 2,136
Upper Level Sq. Ft.: 1,046
Bedrooms: 3
Bathrooms: 2
Foundation: Slab
Materials List Available: Yes
Price Category: G

Images provided by designer/architect.

Main Level Floor Plan

Upper Level Floor Plan

Copyright by designer/architect.

Plan #661102

Dimensions: 58' W x 71'8" D

Levels: 1

Square Footage: 2,278

Bedrooms: 3

Bathrooms: 2

Foundation: Slab

Materials List Available: Yes

Price Category: E

Images provided by designer/architect.

Copyright by designer/architect.

Plan #271042

Dimensions: 69'8" W x 71'4" D

Levels: 2

Square Footage: 3,469

Main Level Sq. Ft.: 2,132

Upper Level Sq. Ft.: 1,337

Bedrooms: 5

Bathrooms: 3½

Foundation: Basement

Materials List Available: Yes

Price Category: G

Images provided by designer/architect.

Upper Level Floor Plan

Main Level Floor Plan

Copyright by designer/architect.

Plan #121117

Dimensions: 76' W x 46' D
Levels: 1
Square Footage: 2,172
Bedrooms: 4
Bathrooms: 3
Foundation: Basement;
Crawl space for fee
Materials List Available: Yes
Price Category: D

Tall ceilings and an efficient design complement this home's stately exterior.

Features:

• Great Room: Whether welcoming guests in
for an elegant evening or just spending time
with the family, this great room provides plenty
of space and is warmed by a built-in fireplace.

• Kitchen: This unique design includes a walk-
in pantry, desk, and large square island, the
kitchen drinks in the sunlight from the adjacent
breakfast room, which provides a simple transition from meal preparation to dining.

• Master Suite: With windows flanking one
wall of the bedroom and a skylight in the bathroom, natural light romanticizes this space,
Other features include a large walk-in closet, a
whirlpool tub with a view, and a separate stall
shower.

• Secondary Bedrooms: Two equally sized
bedrooms each have access to their own semi-
private full bathrooms. A living area by the

entry can serve as a third bedroom for a growing
family or a guest bedroom for the occasional
visitor.

Images provided by designer/architect.

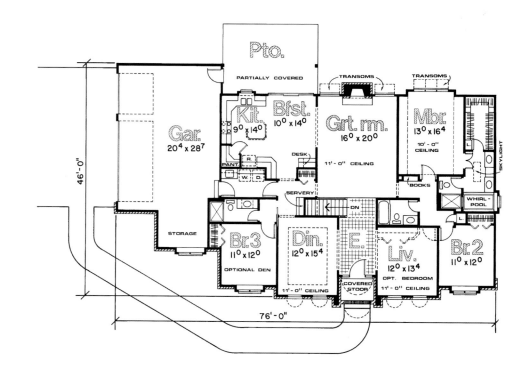

Plan #391030

Dimensions: 60' W x 82'6" D
Levels: 1
Square Footage: 3,903
Main Level Sq. Ft.: 2,376
Lower Level Sq. Ft.: 1,241
Bedrooms: 4
Bathrooms: 3
Foundation: Basement
Materials List Available: Yes
Price Category: H

This home as shown in the photograph, may differ from the actual blueprints. For more detailed infloration, please check the floor plans carefully.

Images provided by designer/architect.

All decked out with rich wood decking that sweeps around the family room to the dining and kitchen areas as well as to the main-floor family room, this home has the feel of living in harmony with nature.

Features:

• Dining Room: A greenhouse window adds exotic flair to this formal dining room.

• Master Suite: This master suite is lavish with amenities--skylight over the tub, double vanitysinks, separate shower, two walk-in closets, and a dressing room.

• Bedroom: Teenagers an appreciate the seond bedroom with built-in cabinet and private bath. Plus, its ideally situated near the kitchen for late night snacking, close to the laundry room for quick wardrobe freshening, and its only a quick jog to the garage.

• Dramatic Features: The house is outfitted with a massive family-room fireplace, built-in shelves, and a soaring loft with study.

Main Level Floor Plan

Lower Level Floor Plan

Copyright by designer/architect.

Plan #181063

Dimensions: 55' W x 41' D
Levels: 2
Square Footage: 2,037
Main Level Sq. Ft.: 1,347
Upper Level Sq. Ft.: 690
Bedrooms: 4
Bathrooms: 2
Foundation: Full basement
Materials List Available: Yes
Price Category: F

Quaint brick and stone, plus deeply pitched rooflines, create the storybook aura folks fall for when they see this home, but it's the serenely versatile interior layout that captures their hearts.

Features:

- Family Room: The floor plan is configured to bring a panoramic view to nearly every room, beginning with this room, with its fireplace and towering cathedral ceiling.

- Kitchen: This kitchen, with its crowd-pleasing island, has an eye on the outdoors. It also has all the counter and storage space a cook would want, plus a lunch counter with comfy seats and multiple windows to bring in the breeze.

- Bedrooms: Downstairs, you'll find the master bedroom, with its adjoining master bath. Upstairs, three uniquely shaped bedrooms, styled with clever nooks and windows to dream by, easily share a large bathroom.

- Mezzanine: This sweeping mezzanine overlooks the open living and dining rooms.

Images provided by designer/architect.

This home, as shown in the photograph, may differ from the actual blueprints. For more detailed information, please check the floor plans carefully.

Front View

Living Room

Master Bath

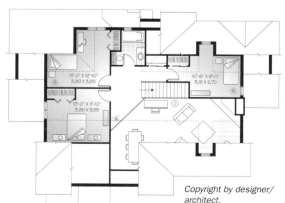

Upper Level Floor Plan

Copyright by designer/architect.

Main Level Floor Plan

Plan #271005

Dimensions: 48'4" W x 48'4" D

Levels: 1

Square Footage: 1,368

Bedrooms: 3

Bathrooms: 2

Foundation: Basement

Materials List Available: Yes

Price Category: B

This traditional home boasts an open floor plan that is further expanded by soaring vaulted ceilings.

Features:

- **Great Room:** Front and center, this large multipurpose room features a gorgeous corner fireplace, an eye-catching boxed out window, and dedicated space for casual dining—all beneath a vaulted ceiling.

- **Kitchen:** A vaulted ceiling crowns this galley kitchen and its adjoining breakfast nook.

- **Master Suite:** This spacious master bedroom, brightened by a boxed-out window, features a vaulted ceiling in the sleeping chamber and the private bath.

Images provided by designer/architect.

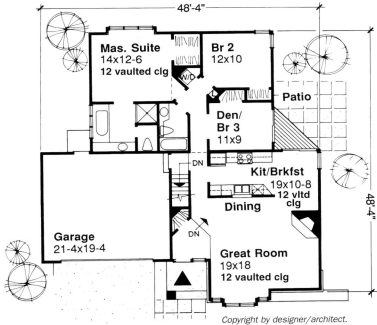

Copyright by designer/architect.

SMARTtip

Design with Computers

Consider using a computer-aided design (CAD) program to plan your deck. Some programs let you see three-dimensional views of your design complete with railings, stairs, planters, hot tubs, and the surrounding landscaping.

Plan #281030

Dimensions: 50' W x 48'6" D
Levels: 2
Square Footage: 2,517
Main Level Sq. Ft.: 1,384
Upper Level Sq. Ft.: 1,133
Bedrooms: 4
Bathrooms: 3
Foundation: Basement
Materials List Available: Yes
Price Category: E

A tall covered entry welcomes you home.

Images provided by designer/architect.

Features:

- Entry: This spacious entry, accented by a regal curved stairway and a full two-story-high ceiling, sets the theme for this unique home.

- Living Room: This formal gathering area is just off of the foyer and is open into the formal dining room. The gas fireplace will add an elegant feel.

- Family Room: This large casual gathering area is open to the kitchen and the breakfast nook.

French doors open to the rear covered patio.

- Master Suite: Located on the upper level, this retreat features a private sitting area. The master bath boasts dual vanities, a whirlpool tub, and a stand-up shower.

- Garage: This side-loading two-car garage gives the front of the home a nice, clean look.

Main Level Floor Plan

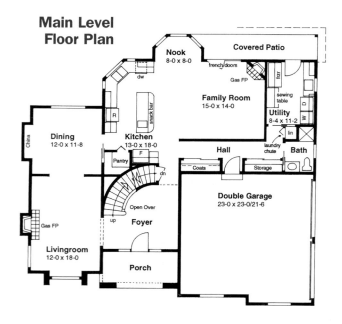

Upper Level Floor Plan

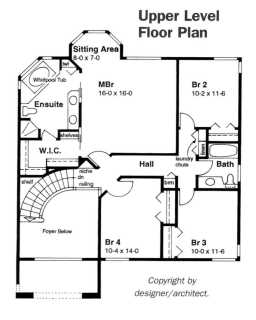

Copyright by designer/architect.

Plan #181329

Dimensions: 30' W x 45' D
Levels: 1
Square Footage: 1,116
Bedrooms: 2
Bathrooms: 1
Foundation: Basement
Materials List Available: Yes
Price Category: C

Round-top window and a large front porch make this home bright and airy.

Features:

- **Foyer:** This sunken entry, complete with a coat closet, introduces you to the wonderful home. Up two steps, and you are in the dining room.

- **Living Room:** Open to the dining room and the kitchen, this gathering area has plenty of room for friends and family. The large triple window will flood the area with natural light.

- **Kitchen:** A large open kitchen, complete with an island, is just what the family chef ordered. Sliding glass doors open to the front porch.

- **Bedrooms:** Two bedrooms share a the full bathroom and complete this floor plan. The larger bedroom has two closets.

Images provided by designer/architect.

Rear Elevation

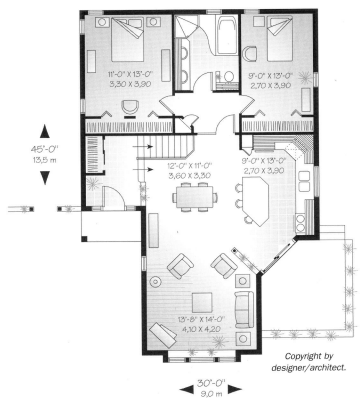

Copyright by designer/architect.

Plan #211125

Dimensions: 94' W x 92' D

Levels: 2

Square Footage: 4,440

Main Level Sq. Ft.: 3,465

Upper Level Sq. Ft.: 975

Bedrooms: 4

Bathrooms: 5½

Foundation: Crawl space

Materials List Available: Yes

Price Category: I

Images provided by designer/architect.

Main Level Floor Plan

porch 40 x 10

family 23 x 20

kit & den 35 x 17

util

mbr 20 x 16

books / books / books

fireplace / wet bar / fireplace / fireplace

built in entertainment center and library / built in entertainment center and library

clo

gallery

bar

sto

phone niche

dining 18 x 12

study 18 x 12

br 2 13 x 12

clo / clo / lin / shr

foy

golf cart & sto 18 x 17

garage 22 x 22

work bench

Upper Level Floor Plan

open to lower level

DOWN

clo / library / clo

ttic / to

br 3 18 x 12 / br 4 18 x 12

open to lower level

books / desk / desk / books

Bonus Area Floor Plan

future space 36 x 12

Copyright by designer/architect.

Plan #271456

Dimensions: 54' W x 48'6" D

Levels: 2

Square Footage: 2,167

Main Level Sq. Ft.: 1,323

Upper Level Sq. Ft.: 844

Bedrooms: 3

Bathrooms: 2

Foundation: Crawl space or basement

Material List Available: Yes

Price Category: D

Images provided by designer/architect.

Upper Level Floor Plan

SKYLIGHTS

BEDROOM 14'-6" x 11'-0" / BEDROOM 12'-0" x 13'-0"

OPEN TO LIVING RM.

STORAGE

BALCONY RAILING

BATH

HEAT

OPEN TO ENTRY

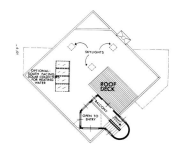

Roof Deck Floor Plan

SKYLIGHTS

OPTIONAL SOUTH FACING SOLAR COLLECTORS FOR HEATING WATER

ROOF DECK

BALCONY

OPEN TO ENTRY

Main Level Floor Plan

DECK

LIVING ROOM 20'-0" x 20'-0" 18' ceiling

DINING 14'-0" x 11'-0"

BEDROOM 12'-0" x 16'-0"

KITCHEN 11'-6"

BATH

ENTRY 27' clg

CARPORT 21'-6" x 24'-0"

Copyright by designer/architect.

Upper Level Floor Plan

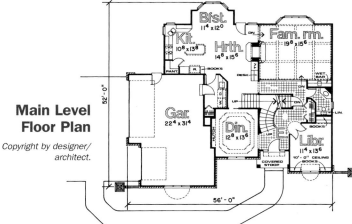

Main Level Floor Plan

Copyright by designer/ architect.

Plan #121061

Dimensions: 56' W x 52' D

Levels: 2

Square Footage: 3,025

Main Level Sq. Ft.: 1,583

Upper Level Sq. Ft.: 1,442

Bedrooms: 4

Bathrooms: 3½

Foundation: Basement

Materials List Available: Yes

Price Category: G

Images provided by designer/architect.

CAD FILE AVAILABLE CAD

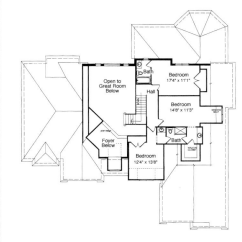

Upper Level Floor Plan

Copyright by designer/architect.

Main Level Floor Plan

Plan #161035

Dimensions: 75' W x 64'11" D

Levels: 2

Square Footage: 3,688

Main Level Sq. Ft.: 2,702

Upper Level Sq. Ft.: 986

Bedrooms: 4

Bathrooms: 3½

Foundation: Basement

Materials List Available: Yes

Price Category: H

Images provided by designer/architect.

Plan #181228

Dimensions: 68' W x 36' D
Levels: 2
Square Footage: 2,393
Main Level Sq. Ft.: 1,279
Upper Level Sq. Ft.: 1,114
Bedrooms: 4
Bathrooms: 2
Foundation: Slab
Materials List Available: Yes
Price Category: G

Come home to this fine home, and relax on the front or rear porch.

Features:

- **Living Room:** This large, open entertaining area has a cozy fireplace and is flooded with natural light.

- **Kitchen:** This fully equipped kitchen has an abundance of cabinets and counter space. Access the rear porch is through a glass door.

- **Laundry Room:** Located on the main level, this laundry area also has space for storage.

- **Upper Level:** Climb the U-shaped staircase, and you'll find four large bedrooms that share a common bathroom.

Images provided by designer/architect.

Main Level Floor Plan

Copyright by designer/architect.

Upper Level Floor Plan

Rear View

Dining Room

Living Room

Living Room

Kitchen

Master Bath

Plan #441007

Dimensions: 70' W x 64' D
Levels: 1
Square Footage: 2,197
Bedrooms: 4
Bathrooms: 2½
Foundation: Crawl space
Materials List Available: Yes
Price Category: F

Welcome to this roomy ranch, embellished with a brick facade, intriguing roof peaks, and decorative quoins on all the front corners.

Features:

• Great Room: There's a direct sightline from the front door through the trio of windows in this room. The rooms are defined by columns and changes in ceiling height rather than by walls, so light bounces from dining room to breakfast nook to kitchen.

• Kitchen: The primary workstation in this kitchen is a peninsula, which faces the fireplace. The peninsula is equipped with a sink, dishwasher, downdraft cooktop, and snack counter.

• Den/Home Office: Conveniently located off the foyer, this room would work well as a home office.

• Master Suite: The double doors provide an air of seclusion for this suite. The vaulted bedroom features sliding patio doors to the backyard and an arch-top window. The adjoining bath is equipped with a whirlpool tub, shower, double vanity, and walk-in closet.

• Secondary Bedrooms: The two additional bedrooms, each with direct access to the shared bathroom, occupy the left wing of the ranch.

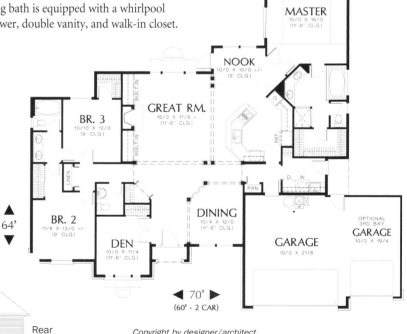

Rear Elevation

Copyright by designer/architect.

Plan #131040

Dimensions: 50' W x 37' D
Levels: 1
Square Footage: 1,630
Bedrooms: 3
Bathrooms: 2
Foundation: Crawl space, slab, or basement
Materials List Available: Yes
Price Category: D

Images provided by designer/architect.

The raised main level of this home makes this plan ideal for any site that has an expansive view, and you can finish the lower level as an office, library, or space for the kids to play.

Features:

- **Living Room:** This sunken living room with a prow-shaped front is sure to be a focal point where both guests and family gather in this lovely ranch home. A see-through fireplace separates this room from the dining room.

- **Dining Room:** A dramatic vaulted ceiling covers both this room and the adjacent living room, creating a spacious feeling.

- **Kitchen:** Designed for efficiency, you'll love the features and location of this convenient kitchen.

- **Master Suite:** Luxuriate in the privacy this suite affords and enjoy the two large closets, sumptuous private bath, and sliding glass doors that can open to the optional rear deck.

Rear Elevation

Main Level Floor Plan

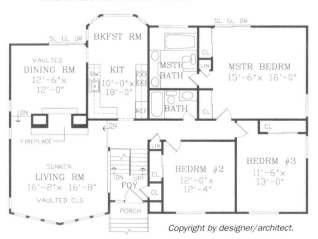

Copyright by designer/architect.

Lower Level Floor Plan

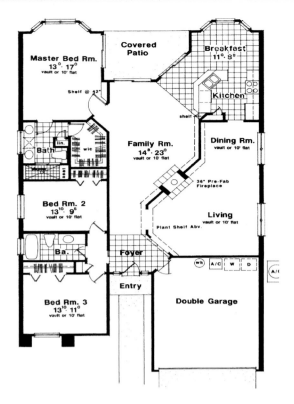

Copyright by designer/architect.

Plan #661055

Dimensions: 40' W x 66'8" D

Levels: 1

Square Footage: 1,872

Bedrooms: 3

Bathrooms: 2

Foundation: Slab

Materials List Available: Yes

Price Category: D

Images provided by designer/architect.

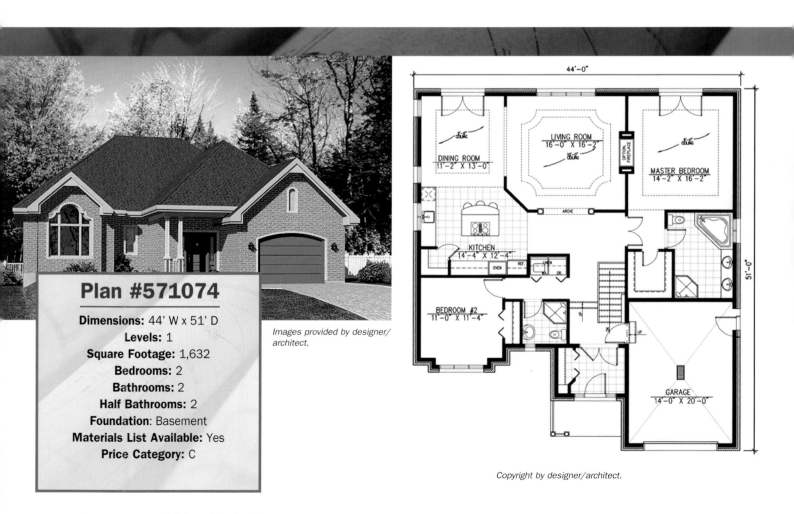

Plan #571074

Dimensions: 44' W x 51' D

Levels: 1

Square Footage: 1,632

Bedrooms: 2

Bathrooms: 2

Half Bathrooms: 2

Foundation: Basement

Materials List Available: Yes

Price Category: C

Images provided by designer/architect.

Copyright by designer/architect.

Main Level Floor Plan

MAIN FLOOR

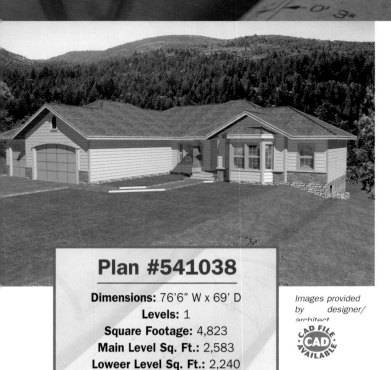

Plan #541038

Dimensions: 76'6" W x 69' D
Levels: 1
Square Footage: 4,823
Main Level Sq. Ft.: 2,583
Loweer Level Sq. Ft.: 2,240
Bedrooms: 7
Bathrooms: 3½
Foundation: Basement
Materials List Available: Yes
Price Category: I

Images provided by designer/architect

CAD FILE AVAILABLE

Lower Level Floor Plan

LOWER LEVEL

Copyright by designer/architect.

Plan #461202

Dimensions: 48' W x 78'4" D
Levels: 1
Square Footage: 2,215
Bedrooms: 3
Bathrooms: 2½
Foundation: Slab
Materials List Available: Yes
Price Category: E

Images provided by designer/architect.

Main Level Floor Plan

FIRST FLOOR PLAN

Upper Level Floor Plan

SECOND FLOOR PLAN

Copyright by designer/architect.

Plan #371092

Dimensions: 71'6" W x 70'8" D
Levels: 2
Square Footage: 3,836
Main Level Sq. Ft.: 2,981
Upper Level Sq. Ft.: 855
Bedrooms: 5
Bathrooms: 4
Foundation: Slab, crawl space
or basement for fee
Materials List Available: Yes
Price Category: H

Images provided by designer/architect.

Front View

This grand home has an arched covered entry and great styling that would make this home a focal point of the neighborhood.

CAD FILE AVAILABLE

Features:

- **Family Room:** This large gathering area boasts a fireplace flanked by a built-in media center. Large windows flood the room with natural light, and there is access to the rear porch.

- **Kitchen:** This large island kitchen has a raised bar and is open to the family room. Its walk-in pantry has plenty of room for supplies.

- **Master Suite:** This retreat features a stepped ceiling and a see-through fireplace to the master bath, which has a large walk-in closet, dual vanities, a glass shower, and a marble tub.

- **Secondary Bedrooms:** Bedrooms 2 and 3 are located on the main level and share a common bathroom. Bedrooms 4 and 5 are located on the upper level and share a Jack-and-Jill bathroom.

Copyright by designer/architect.

Main Level Floor Plan

Upper Level Floor Plan

Plan #101019

Dimensions: 58'4" W x 55'2" D

Levels: 2

Square Footage: 2,954

Main Level Sq. Ft. 2,093

Upper Level Sq. Ft. 861

Bedrooms: 4

Bathrooms: 3½

Foundation: Crawl space, slab, or basement

Materials List Available: Yes

Price Category: F

Images provided by designer/architect.

This luxurious home features a spectacular open floor plan and a brick exterior.

Features:

- Ceiling Height: 9 ft. unless otherwise noted.
- Foyer: This inviting two-story foyer, which vaults to 18 ft., will greet guests with an impressive "welcome."
- Dining Room: To the right of the foyer is this spacious dining room surrounded by decorative columns.

- Family Room: There's plenty of room for all kinds of family activities in this enormous room, with its soaring two-story ceiling.
- Master Suite: This sumptuous retreat boasts a tray ceiling. Optional pocket doors provide direct access to the study. The master bath features his and her vanities and a large walk-in closet.
- Breakfast Area: Perfect for informal family meals, this bayed breakfast area has real flair.
- Secondary Bedrooms: Upstairs are three large bedrooms with 8-ft. ceilings. One has a private bath.

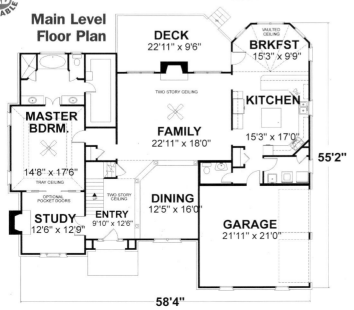

Main Level Floor Plan

DECK 22'11" x 9'6"

BRKFST 15'3" x 9'9" — VAULTED CEILING

KITCHEN 15'3" x 17'0"

TWO STORY CEILING

MASTER BDRM. 14'8" x 17'6" — TRAY CEILING

OPTIONAL POCKET DOORS

FAMILY 22'11" x 18'0"

55'2"

STUDY 12'6" x 12'9"

ENTRY 9'10" x 12'6" — TWO STORY CEILING — UP

DINING 12'5" x 16'0"

GARAGE 21'11" x 21'0"

58'4"

Upper Level Floor Plan

OPEN BELOW

BEDRM 4 13'0" x 11'6"

OPEN BELOW — PLANT SHELF

DN

BEDRM 2 12'5" x 12'5"

BEDRM 3 11'3" x 17'1"

Copyright by designer/architect.

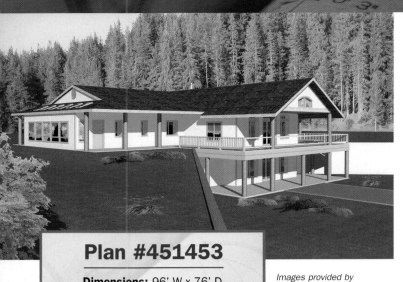

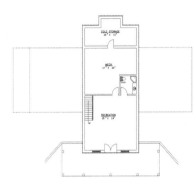

**Main Level
Floor Plan**

*Images provided by
designer/architect.*

Plan #451453

Dimensions: 96' W x 76' D

Levels: 1

Square Footage: 4,868

Main Level Sq. Ft.: 3,296

Lower Level Sq. Ft.: 1,572

Bedrooms: 3

Bathrooms: 3½

Foundation: Basement or Walk-out

Materials List Available: Yes

Price Category: I

**Lower Level

Floor Plan**

Copyright by designer/architect.

**Main Level
Floor Plan**

*Images provided by
designer/architect.*

Plan #571037

Dimensions: 95' W x 84' D

Levels: 2

Square Footage: 6,440

Main Level Sq. Ft.: 4,409

Upper Level Sq. Ft.: 2,031

Bedrooms: 4

Bathrooms: 3½

Foundation: Basement

Material List Available: Yes

Price Category: K

**Upper Level
Floor Plan**

*Copyright by
designer/architect.*

Plan #321051

Dimensions: 69'8" W x 46' D

Levels: 2

Square Footage: 2,624

Main Level Sq. Ft.: 1,774

Upper Level Sq. Ft.: 850

Bedrooms: 4

Bathrooms: 2½

Foundation: Basement

Materials List Available: Yes

Price Category: F

The dramatic exterior design allows natural light to flow into the spacious living area of this home.

Features:

- **Entry:** This two-story area opens into the dining room through a classic colonnade.

- **Dining Room:** A large bay window, stately columns, and doorway to the kitchen make this room both beautiful and convenient.

- **Great Room:** Enjoy light from the fireplace or the three Palladian windows in the 18-ft. ceiling.

- **Kitchen:** The step-saving design features a walk-in pantry as well as good counter space.

- **Breakfast Room:** You'll love the light that flows through the windows flanking the back door.

- **Master Suite:** The vaulted ceiling and bayed areas in both the bed and bath add elegance. You'll love the two walk-in closets and bath with a sunken tub, two vanities, and separate shower.

This home, as shown in the photograph, may differ from the actual blueprints. Images provided by designer/architect. For more detailed information, please check the floor plans carefully.

Main Level Floor Plan

Copyright by designer/architect.

Master Bath

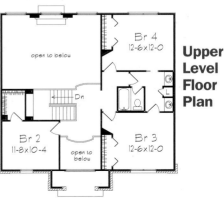

Upper Level Floor Plan

Plan #151055

Dimensions: 82'4" W x 81'6" D
Levels: 1
Square Footage: 3,183
Bedrooms: 4
Bathrooms: 2½
Foundation: Crawl space or slab; basement or walkout available for fee
CompleteCost List Available: Yes
Price Category: E

meals. The family will enjoy lazy weekend mornings in the adjoining breakfast room and intimate hearth room.

- **Master Suite:** This retreat, with its built-in media center and romantic fireplace in the sleeping area, features a boxed ceiling. The

master bath boasts a whirlpool tub, his and her vanities and lavatories, and a glass shower.

- **Bedrooms:** These three family bedrooms are located on the opposite side of the home from the master suite for privacy and share a common bathroom.

This stunning large ranch home has a well-designed floor plan that is perfect for today's family.

CAD FILE AVAILABLE

Features:

- **Living Room:** This large gathering area features a beautiful fireplace and a vaulted ceiling. On nice days, exit through the atrium doors and relax on the grilling porch.

- **Kitchen:** The raised bar in this island kitchen provides additional seating for informal

Copyright by designer/architect.

Front View

Main Level Floor Plan

Plan #271032

Dimensions: 78' W x 40' D

Levels: 2

Square Footage: 3,195

Main Level Sq. Ft.: 1,758

Upper Level Sq. Ft.: 1,437

Bedrooms: 4

Bathrooms: 2½

Foundation: Basement

Materials List Available: Yes

Price Category: E

Images provided by designer/architect.

CAD FILE AVAILABLE

Upper Level Floor Plan

Copyright by designer/architect.

Main Level Floor Plan

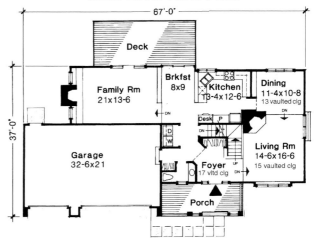

Plan #271018

Dimensions: 67' W x 37' D

Levels: 2

Square Footage: 2,445

Main Level Sq. Ft.: 1,290

Upper Level Sq. Ft.: 1,155

Bedrooms: 4

Bathrooms: 2½

Foundation: Basement; walkout for fee

Materials List Available: Yes

Price Category: E

Images provided by designer/architect.

Upper Level Floor Plan

Copyright by designer/architect.

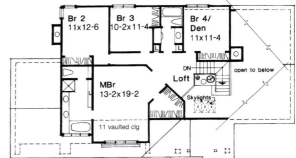

Plan #121026

Dimensions: 66'8" W x 76' D

Levels: 2

Square Footage: 3,926

Main Level Sq. Ft.: 2,351

Upper Level Sq. Ft.: 1,575

Bedrooms: 4

Bathrooms: 3 full, 2 half

Foundation: Basement; slab for fee

Materials List Available: Yes

Price Category: H

Images provided by designer/architect.

Plenty of space and architectural detail make this a comfortable and gracious home.

Features:

• Ceiling Height: 8 ft. unless otherwise noted.

• Great Room: A soaring cathedral ceiling makes this great room seem even more spacious than it is, while the fireplace framed by windows lends warmth and comfort.

• Eating Area: There's a dining room for more formal entertaining, but this informal eating area to the left of the great room will get plenty of daily use. It features a built-in desk for compiling shopping lists and recipes and access to the backyard.

• Kitchen: Next door to the eating area, this kitchen is designed to make food preparation a pleasure. It features a center cooktop, a recycling area, and a corner pantry.

CAD FILE AVAILABLE

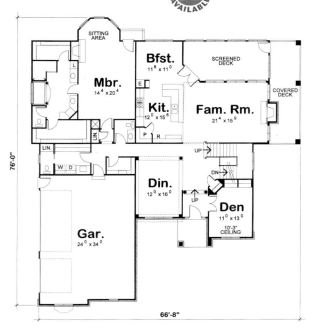

Main Level Floor Plan

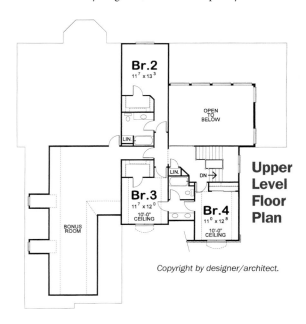

Upper Level Floor Plan

Copyright by designer/architect.

Plan #391009

Dimensions: 73'4" W x 60'4" D

Levels: 2

Square Footage: 3,440

Main Level Sq. Ft.: 2,486

Upper Level Sq. Ft.: 954

Bedrooms: 4

Bathrooms: 3½

Foundation: Basement, Crawl Space, Slab

Materials List Available: Yes

Price Category: G

This home, as shown in the photograph, may differ from the actual blueprints. For more detailed information, please check the floor plans carefully.   *Images provided by designer/architect.*

This home offers classic Victorian detils combined with modern amenities.

Features:

• Ceiling Height: 9 ft. unless otherwise noted

• Porch: Enjoy summer breezes on this large wraparound porch, with its classic turret corner.

• Family Room: This room has a fireplace and two sets of French doors. One set of doors leads to the porch; the other leads to a rear sun deck.

• Living Room: This large room at the front of the house is designed for entertaining.

• Kitchen: This convenient kitchen features an island and a writing desk.

• Master Bedroom: Enjoy the cozy sitting area in the turret corner. The bedroom offers access to a second story balcony.

• Laundry: The second-floor laundry means that you won't have to haul clothing up and down stairs.

Main Level Floor Plan

Upper Level Floor Plan

Plan #271052

Dimensions: 57' W x 67' D

Levels: 2

Square Footage: 1,779

Main Level Sq. Ft.: 1,309

Upper Level Sq. Ft.: 470

Bedrooms: 3

Bathrooms: 2

Foundation: Crawl space, daylight basement

Materials List Available: Yes

Price Category: C

Images provided by designer/architect.

Main Level Floor Plan

Copyright by designer/architect.

Optional Basement Level Floor Plan

Upper Level Floor Plan

Plan #181100

Dimensions: 74'6" W x 44' D

Levels: 2

Square Footage: 4,200

Main Level Sq. Ft.: 2,207

Upper Level Sq. Ft.: 1,993

Bedrooms: 4

Bathrooms: 3½

Foundation: Basement

Material List Available: Yes

Price Category: K

Images provided by designer/architect.

Main Level Floor Plan

Upper Level Floor Plan

Copyright by designer/architect.

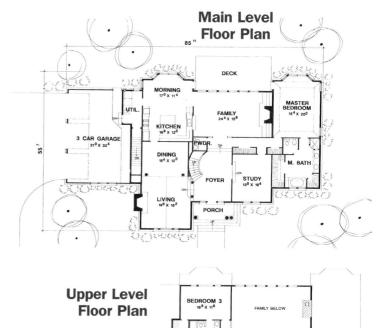

Main Level Floor Plan

Plan #331005

Dimensions: 85'11" W x 55'7" D
Levels: 2
Square Footage: 3,585
Main Level Sq. Ft.: 2,691
Upper Level Sq. Ft.: 894
Bedrooms: 4
Bathrooms: 3½
Foundation: Crawl space, slab, or basement
Materials List Available: Yes
Price Category: H

Upper Level Floor Plan

Rear View

Main Level Floor Plan

Plan #451448

Dimensions: 90' W x 39' D
Levels: 2
Square Footage: 2,717
Main Level Sq. Ft.: 2,064
Upper Level Sq. Ft.: 653
Bedrooms: 2
Bathrooms: 2
Foundation: Walk-out
Materials List Available: Yes
Price Category: F

Upper Level Floor Plan

Lower Level Floor Plan

Plan #271031

Dimensions: 87'4" W x 66' D
Levels: 2
Square Footage: 3,062
Main Level Sq. Ft.: 2,389
Upper Level Sq. Ft.: 673
Bedrooms: 4
Bathrooms: 3½
Foundation: Basement
Materials List Available: Yes
Price Category: G

Images provided by designer/architect.

The distinctive look of this elegant, trendsetting estate reflects a refined sense of style and taste.

Features:

• Parlor/Dining: Off the vaulted foyer, this cozy sunken parlor boasts a vaulted ceiling and a warm fireplace. Opposite the parlor, this formal dining room is serviced by a stylish wet bar.

• Kitchen: This open room features an angled snack bar and serves a skylighted breakfast room.

• Family Room: Defined by columns, this skylighted, vaulted family room offers a handsome fireplace with a built-in log bin. Sliding glass doors open to a backyard deck.

• Master Suite: This deluxe getaway boasts a vaulted ceiling and unfolds to a skylighted sitting area and a private deck. The garden tub in the master bath basks under its own skylight.

• Library/Guest Room: This versatile room enjoys a high ceiling and a walk-in closet.

• Secondary Bedrooms: Two reside on the upper floor.

Main Level Floor Plan

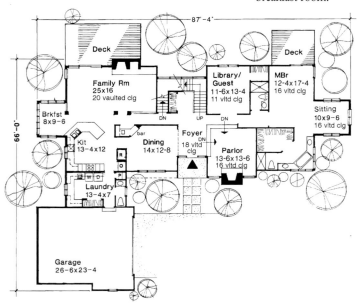

Upper Level Floor Plan

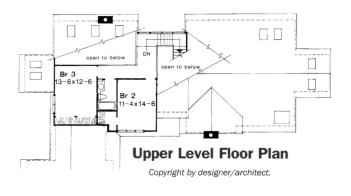

Copyright by designer/architect.

Plan #131031

Dimensions: 69'8" W x 48'4" D
Levels: 2
Square Footage: 4,027
Main Level Sq. Ft.: 2,198
Upper Level Sq. Ft.: 1,829
Bedrooms: 5
Bathrooms: 4½
Foundation: Slab; basement for fee
Materials List Available: Yes
Price Category: I

If you love dramatic lines and contemporary design, you'll be thrilled by this lovely home.

Features:

• Foyer: A gorgeous vaulted ceiling sets the stage for a curved staircase flanked by a formal living room and dining room.

• Living Room: The foyer ceiling continues in this room, giving it an unusual presence.

• Family Room: This sunken family room features a fireplace and a wall of windows that look out to the backyard. It's open to the living room, making it an ideal spot for entertaining.

• Kitchen: With a large island, this kitchen flows into the breakfast room.

• Master Suite: The luxurious bedroom has a dramatic tray ceiling and includes two-walk-in closets. The dressing room is fitted with a sink, and the spa bath is sumptuous.

Images provided by designer/architect.

Main Level Floor Plan

Copyright by designer/architect.

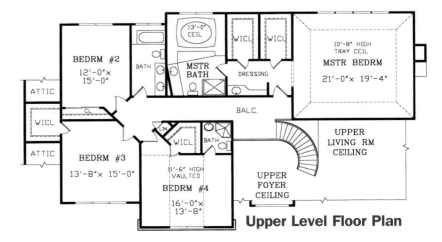

Upper Level Floor Plan

Plan #151030

Dimensions: 59' W x 73' D

Levels: 2

Square Footage: 2,949

Main Level Sq. Ft.: 2,126

Upper Level Sq. Ft.: 823

Bonus Room Sq. Ft.: 442

Bedrooms: 3

Bathrooms: 3½

Foundation: Crawl space or slab; basement or walkout for fee

CompleteCost List Available: Yes

Price Category: F

Images provided by designer/ architect.

Main Level Floor Plan

Upper Level Floor Plan

Copyright by designer/ architect.

Plan #151723

Dimensions: 49'10" W x 64'4" D

Levels: 1

Square Footage: 1,552

Bedrooms: 4

Bathrooms: 2

Foundation: Crawl space or slab; basement or walkout for fee

CompleteCost List Available: Yes

Price Category: C

Images provided by designer/architect.

Copyright by designer/architect.

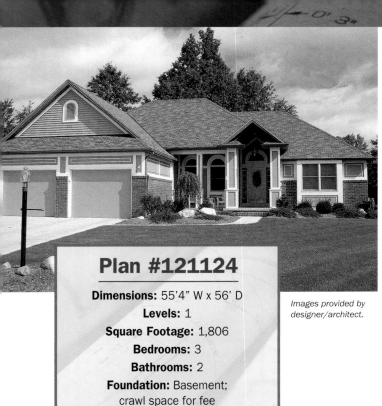

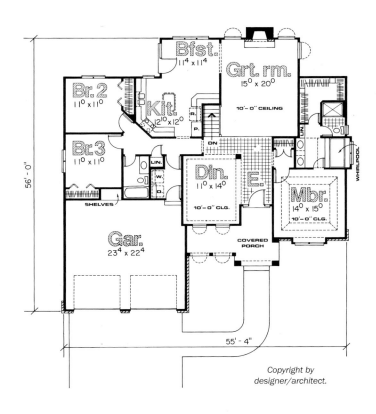

Plan #121124

Dimensions: 55'4" W x 56' D

Levels: 1

Square Footage: 1,806

Bedrooms: 3

Bathrooms: 2

Foundation: Basement;
crawl space for fee

Material List Available: Yes

Price Category: D

Images provided by designer/architect.

Copyright by designer/architect.

Plan #271013

Dimensions: 43' W x 45'8" D

Levels: 2

Square Footage: 1,498

Main Level Sq. Ft.: 1,044

Upper Level Sq. Ft.: 454

Bedrooms: 2

Bathrooms: 2½

Foundation: Basement

Materials List Available: Yes

Price Category: B

Images provided by designer/architect.

Main Level Floor Plan

Upper Level Floor Plan

Copyright by designer/architect.

Plan #391021

Dimensions: 54' W x 48'4" D
Levels: 1
Square Footage: 1,568
Bedrooms: 3
Bathrooms: 2
Foundation: Crawl space, slab, or basement
Materials List Available: Yes
Price Category: C

Images provided by designer/architect.

• Master Suite: This private retreat is situated far from the public areas. A large walk-in closet with a private bath and double vanity add to the suite's intimate appeal.

• Bedrooms: The two additional bedrooms boast large closets and bright windows. The generous hall bathroom is located conveniently nearby.

A peaked porch roof and luminous Palladian window play up the exterior appeal of this ranch home, while other archectectural components dramatize the interior.

Features:

• Living Room: There is a soaring ceiling in this living room, where a corner fireplace and built-in bookshelves provide cozy comfort.

• Dining Room: Open to the living room, this room features sliders to the wood deck, which makes it conductive to both casual and formal entertaining.

• Kitchen: This well-planned kitchen seems to have it all--a built-in pantry, a double sink, and a breakfast bar that feeds into the dining room. The bar provides additional serving space when needed.

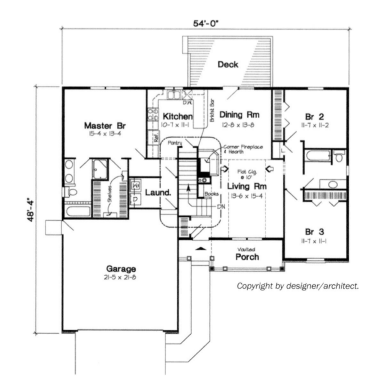

Copyright by designer/architect.

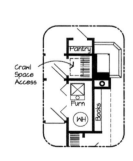

Plan #401023

Dimensions: 76' W x 63'4" D
Levels: 1
Square Footage: 2,806
Bedrooms: 3
Bathrooms: 2½
Foundation: Basement, walkout
Materials List Available: Yes
Price Category: F

Images provided by designer/architect.

The lower level of this magnificent home includes unfinished space that could have a future as a den and a family room with a fireplace. This level could also house extra bedrooms or an in-law suite.

Features:

- Foyer: On the main level, this foyer spills into a tray ceiling living room with a fireplace and an arched, floor-to-ceiling window wall.

- Family Room: Up from the foyer, a hall introduces this vaulted room with built-in media center and French doors that open to an expansive railed deck.

- Kitchen: Featured in this gourmet kitchen are a food-preparation island with a salad sink, double-door pantry, corner-window sink, and breakfast bay.

- Master Bedroom: The vaulted master bedroom opens to the deck, and the deluxe bath offers a raised whirlpool spa and a double-bowl vanity under a skylight.

- Bedroom: Two family bedrooms share a compartmented bathroom.

Rear Elevation

Copyright by designer/architect.

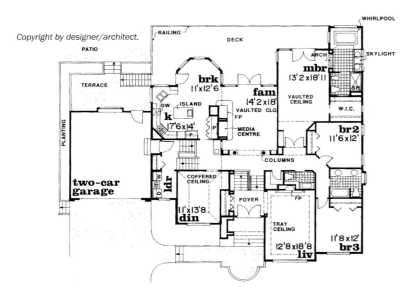

Optional Floor Plan

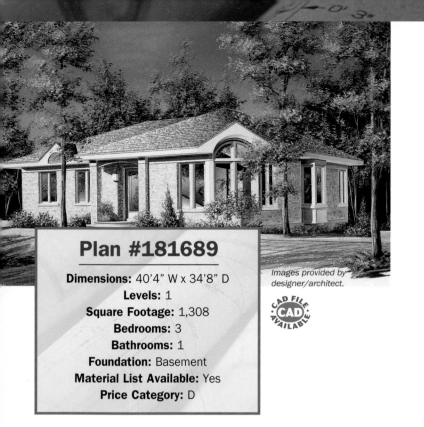

Plan #181689

Dimensions: 40'4" W x 34'8" D
Levels: 1
Square Footage: 1,308
Bedrooms: 3
Bathrooms: 1
Foundation: Basement
Material List Available: Yes
Price Category: D

Images provided by designer/architect.

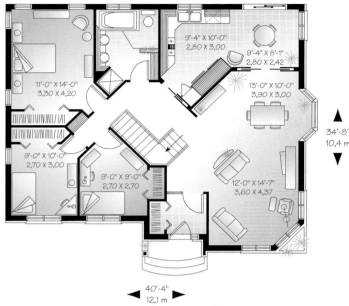

34'-8"
10,4 m

40'-4"
12,1 m

Plan #451138

Dimensions: 64'4" W x 73' D
Levels: 1
Square Footage: 4,484
Main Level Sq. Ft.: 2,242
Basement Level Sq. Ft.: 2,242
Bedrooms: 4
Bathrooms: 3
Foundation: Basement – insulated concrete form
Material List Available: Yes
Price Category: I

Images provided by designer/architect.

Basement Level Floor Plan

Copyright by designer/architect.

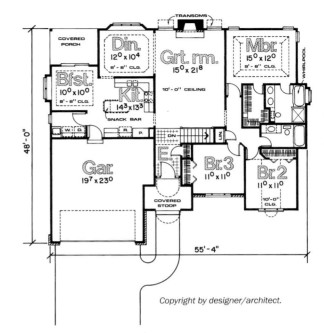

Images provided by designer/architect.

Plan #121004

Dimensions: 55'4" W x 48' D

Levels: 1

Square Footage: 1,666

Bedrooms: 3

Bathrooms: 2

Foundation: Basement

Materials List Available: Yes

Price Category: C

Copyright by designer/architect.

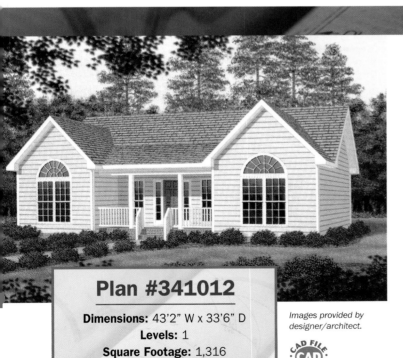

Copyright by designer/architect.

Plan #341012

Dimensions: 43'2" W x 33'6" D

Levels: 1

Square Footage: 1,316

Bedrooms: 3

Bathrooms: 2

Foundation: Crawl space, slab, or basement

Materials List Available: Yes

Price Category: B

Images provided by designer/architect.

Plan #271037

Dimensions: 66' W x 65' D

Levels: 2

Square Footage: 4,220

Main Level Sq. Ft.: 2,768

Upper Level Sq. Ft.: 1,452

Bedrooms: 3

Bathrooms: 4½

Foundation: Basement

Materials List Available: Yes

Price Category: I

This design allows family members to carry out their work and leisure activities inside the home. The options for leisure and study are almost countless!

Features:

- "Us" Room: The home's sunken "Us" room is the center of attention, with its vaulted ceiling and two-story fireplace. The room is surrounded by the family living areas.

- Master Suite: Relax in this oasis, which offers twin walk-in closets and a lovely bath.

- Upper Floor: Study areas, an office, and an exercise space are just the beginning!

Dining Room / "Us" Room

Copyright by designer/architect.

CAD FILE AVAILABLE

Main Level Floor Plan

66—0

Patio

Activity Area
18—4x13—8
13 vaulted clg

glass block

Master Suite
17x18—4
13 vaulted clg

Lndry tub

Lndry
6x16

desk

shower tub

Garden

Kit

bar

Frzr

Dining
11—4x12
10 clg

'US' Room
27—4x19—8
23—6 clg

10—6 clg

Garden

halfwall

65—0

DN

cabinet

Entry
10 clg

Garage
22—4x21

stor

Mud

Porch

sink

Multi-Purpose
17—4x19
13 vaulted clg

Upper Level Floor Plan

glass block

Exercise
11—8x9—4
9—6 clg

DN

cabinet

desk

Kid's Study
11—6 clg

open to below

desk

Office
11—6
sloped clg

skylight above

glass block

Stor.

Br 2
11—4x13
9—6 vltd clg

Br 3
11—4x13
9—6 vltd clg

Plan #271033

Dimensions: 40' W x 41'4" D

Levels: 2

Square Footage: 1,516

Main Level Sq. Ft.: 817

Upper Level Sq. Ft.: 699

Bedrooms: 3

Bathrooms: 2½

Foundation: Basement

Materials List Available: Yes

Price Category: C

Images provided by designer/architect.

A pronounced roofline and a pleasing mix of brick and lap siding give a sunny disposition to this charming home.

Features:

- Great Room: Introduced by the sidelighted entry, this large space offers tall corner windows for natural light and a cheery corner fireplace for warmth.

- Dining Room: Joined to the great room only by air, this formal dining room basks in the glow from a broad window.

- Kitchen: Plenty of open space allows this kitchen to include ample counter space and incorporate an eating area into it. From here, a door leads to the backyard.

- Family Room: Flowing directly from the kitchen, this large family room allows passage to a backyard deck via sliding glass doors.

- Master Suite: Secluded to the upper floor, the master bedroom offers a private bath with a walk-in closet beyond.

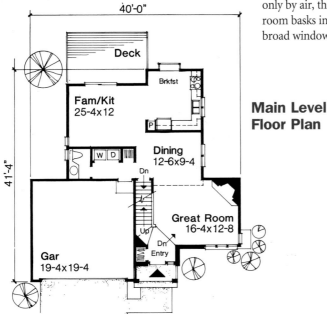

Main Level Floor Plan

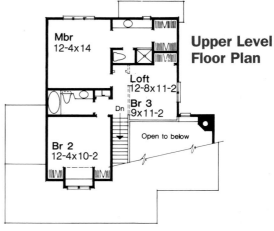

Upper Level Floor Plan

Copyright by designer/architect.

Plans and Ideas for Your Landscape

Landscapes change over the years. As plants grow, the overall look evolves from sparse to lush. Trees cast cool shade where the sun used to shine. Shrubs and hedges grow tall and dense enough to provide privacy. Perennials and ground covers spread to form colorful patches of foliage and flowers. Meanwhile, paths, arbors, fences, and other structures gain the patina of age.

Constant change over the years—sometimes rapid and dramatic, sometimes slow and subtle—is one of the joys of landscaping. It is also one of the challenges. Anticipating how fast plants will grow and how big they will eventually get is difficult, even for professional designers, and was a major concern in formulating the designs for this book.

To illustrate the kinds of changes to expect in a planting, these pages show a landscape design at three different "ages." Even though a new planting may look sparse at first, it will soon fill in. And because of careful spacing, the planting will look as good in 10 to 15 years as it does after 3 to 5. It will, of course, look different, but that's part of the fun.

At Planting

Crape myrtle

Carolina jasmine or clematis

Spirea

Bluebeard

Barberry

Annuals

Mondo grass

Three to Five Years

Carolina jasmine or clematis

Crape myrtle

Spirea

Barberry

Mondo grass

At Planting—Here's how a corner planting might appear in spring immediately after planting. The fence and mulch look conspicuously fresh, new, and unweathered. The crape myrtle is only 4 to 5 ft. tall, with trunks no thicker than broomsticks. It hasn't leafed out yet. The spirea and barberries are 12 to 18 in. tall and wide, and the Carolina jasmine (or clematis) just reaches the bottom rail of the fence. Evenly spaced tufts of mondo grass edge the sidewalk. The bluebeards are stubby now but will grow 2 to 3 ft. tall by late summer, when they bloom. Annuals such as vinca and ageratum start flowering right away and soon form solid patches of color. The first year after planting, be sure to water during dry spells, and to pull or spray any weeds that pop through the mulch.

Three to Five Years—Shown in summer now, the planting has begun to mature. The mondo grass has spread to make a continuous, weed-proof patch. The Carolina jasmine (or clematis) reaches partway along the fence. The spirea and barberries have grown into bushy, rounded specimens. From now on, they'll get wider but not much taller. The crape myrtle will keep growing about 1 ft. taller every year, and its crown will broaden. As you continue replacing the annuals twice a year, keep adding compost or organic matter to the soil and spreading fresh mulch on top.

Ten to Fifteen Years—As shown here in late summer, the crape myrtle is now a fine specimen, about 15 ft. tall, with a handsome silhouette, beautiful flowers, and colorful bark on its trunks. The bluebeards recover from an annual spring pruning to form bushy mounds covered with blooms. The Carolina jasmine, (or clematis) spirea, and barberry have reached their mature size. Keep them neat and healthy by pruning out old, weak, or dead stems every spring. If you get tired of replanting annuals, substitute low-growing perennials or shrubs in those positions.

Ten to Fifteen Years

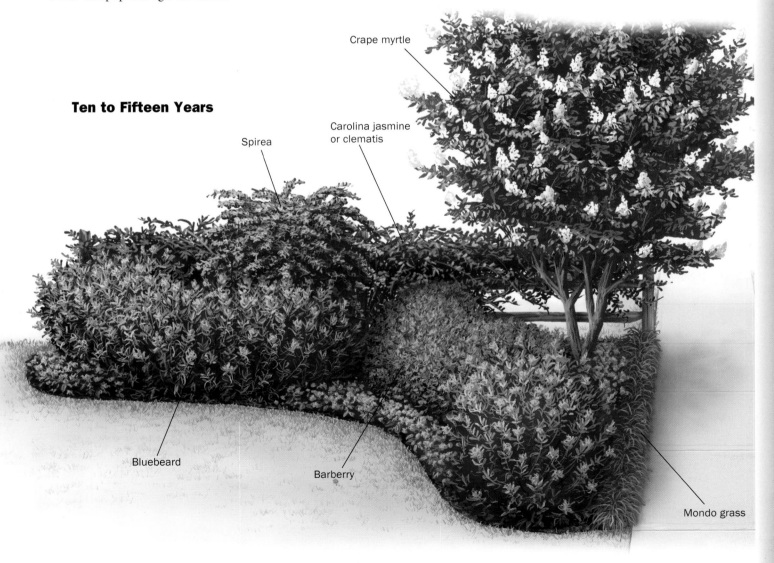

Crape myrtle

Carolina jasmine or clematis

Spirea

Bluebeard

Barberry

Mondo grass

"Around Back"

Dress Up the Area between the House and a Detached Garage

When people think of landscaping the entrance to their home, the public entry at the front of the house comes immediately to mind. It's easy to forget that the back door often gets more use. If you make the journey between back door and driveway or garage many times each day, why not make it as pleasant a trip as possible? For many properties, a simple planting can trans-form the space bounded by the house, garage, and driveway, making it at once more inviting and more functional.

In a high-traffic area frequented by ball-bouncing, bicycle-riding children as well as busy adults, delicate, fussy plants have no place. The design shown here employs a few types of tough low-care plants, all of which look good year-round. The low yew hedge links the house and the garage and separates the more private backyard from the busy driveway. The star magnolia is just the right size for its spot. Its early-spring flowers will be a delight whether viewed coming up the driveway or from a window overlooking the back-yard. The wide walk makes passage to and from the car easy—even with your arms full of groceries.

Note: All plants are appropriate for USDA Hardiness Zones 5, 6, and 7.

A Star magnolia

See site plan for **F**

Site: Sunny
Season: Summer
Concept: A planting to raise spirits when weighed down by shopping bags and to separate activities in the backyard from the driveway.

C 'Steeds' Japanese holly

B 'Hicksii' hybrid yew

D 'Hidcote' hypericum

E 'Big Blue' lilyturf

Walkway **G**

'Big Blue' lilyturf **E**

Plants & Projects

The watchword in this planting is evergreen. Except for the magnolia, all the plants here are fully evergreen or are nearly so. Spring and summer see lovely flowers from the magnolia and hypericum, and the carpet of lilyturf turns a handsome blue in August. For a bigger splash in spring, underplant the lilyturf with daffodils. Choose a single variety for uniform color, or select several varieties for a mix of colors and bloom times. Other than shearing the hedge, the only maintenance required is cutting back the lilyturf and hypericum in late winter.

A **Star magnolia** *Magnolia stellata* (use 1 plant)
Lovely white flowers cover this small deciduous tree before the leaves appear. Starlike blooms, slightly fragrant and sometimes tinged with pink, appear in early spring and last up to two weeks. In summer, the dense leafy crown of dark green leaves helps provide privacy in the backyard. A multitrunked specimen will fill the space better and display more of the interesting winter bark.

B **'Hicksii' hybrid yew** *Taxus x media* (use 9)
A fast-growing evergreen shrub is ideal for this 3-ft.-tall, neatly sheared hedge. Needles are glossy dark green and soft, not prickly. Eight plants form the L-shaped portion, while a single sheared plant extends the hedge on the other side of the walk connecting it to the house. (If the hedge needs to play a part in confining a family pet, you could easily set posts either side of the walk and add a gate.)

C **'Steeds' Japanese holly** *Ilex crenata* (use 3 or more)
Several of these dense, upright evergreen shrubs can be grouped at the corner as specimen plants or to tie into an existing foundation planting. You could also extend them along the house to create a foundation planting, as shown here. The small dark green leaves are thick and leathery and have tiny spines. Plants attain a pleasing form when left to their own devices. Resist the urge to shear them; just prune to control size if necessary.

R **'Hidcote' hypericum** *Hypericum* (use 1)
All summer long, clusters of large golden flowers cover the arching stems of this tidy semievergreen shrub, brightening the entrance to the backyard.

E **'Big Blue' lilyturf** *Liriope muscari* (use 40 or more)
Grasslike evergreen clumps of this perennial ground cover grow together to carpet the ground flanking the driveway and walk. (Extend the planting as far down the drive as you like.) Slim spires of tiny blue flowers rise above the dark green leaves in June. Lilyturf doesn't stand up to repeated tromping. If the drive is also a basket ball court, substitute periwinkle (*Vinca minor*) a tough ground cover with late-spring lilac flowers.

F **Stinking hellebor**
Helleborus foetidus (use 5 or more) This clump-forming perennial is ideal for filling the space between the walk and house on the backyard side of the hedge. (You might also consider extending the planting along the L-shaped side of the hedge.) Its pale green flowers are among the first to bloom in the spring and continue for many weeks; dark green leaves are attractive year-round.

G **Walkway**
Precast concrete pavers, 2 ft. by 2 ft., replace an existing walk or form a new one.

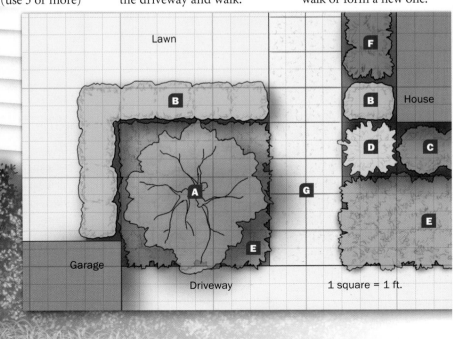

1 square = 1 ft.

Beautify Your Garden Shed

Just as you enhance your living room by hanging paintings on the walls, you can decorate blank walls in your outdoor "living rooms." The design shown here transforms a nondescript shed wall into a living fresco, showcasing lovely plants in a framework of roses and flowering vines. Instead of a view of peeling paint, imagine gazing at this scene from a nearby patio, deck, or kitchen window.

This symmetrical composition frames two crape myrtles between arched lattice-work trellises. Handsome multitrunked shrubs, the crape myrtles perform year-round, providing sumptuous pink flowers in summer, orange-red foliage in fall, and attractive bark in winter. On either side of the crape myrtles, roses and clematis scramble over the trellis in a profusion of yellow and purple flowers.

A tidy low boxwood hedge sets off a shallow border of shrubs and perennials at the bottom of the "frame." Cheerful long-blooming daylilies and asters, airy Russian sage, and elegant daphne make sure that the ground-level attractions hold their own with the aerial performers covering the wall above. The flowers hew to a color scheme of yellows, pinks, blues, and purples.

Wider or narrower walls can be accommodated by expanding the design to include additional "panels," or by reducing it to one central panel. To set off the plants, consider painting or staining the wall and trellises in an off-white, an earth tone, or a light gray color.

Jackman clematis **D**

'Golden Showers' rose **B**

'Carol Mackie' daphne **F** 'Happy Returns' daylily **H** 'Green Beauty' littleleaf boxwood **E**

Plants and Projects

These plants will all do well in the hot, dry conditions often found near a wall with a sunny exposure. Other than training and pruning the vines, roses, and hedge, maintenance involves little more than fall and spring cleanup. The trellises, supported by 4x4 posts and attached to the garage, are well within the reach of average do-it-yourselfers.

A **'Hopi' crape myrtle** *Lagerstroemia indica* (use 2 plants)
Large multitrunked deciduous shrubs produce papery pink flowers for weeks in summer. They also contribute colorful fall foliage and attractive flaky bark for winter interest.

B **'Golden Showers' rose** *Rosa* (use 3)
Tied to each trellis, the long canes of these climbers display large, fragrant, double yellow flowers in abundance all summer long.

C **Golden clematis** *Clematis tangutica* (use 1)
Twining up through the rose canes, this deciduous vine adds masses of small yellow flowers to the larger, more elaborate roses all summer. Feathery silver seed heads in fall.

D **Jackman clematis** *Clematis x jackmanii* (use 2)
These deciduous vines clamber among the rose canes at the corners of the wall. The combination of their large but simple purple flowers and the double yellow roses is spectacular.

E **'Green Beauty' littleleaf boxwood** *Buxus microphylla* (use 15)
Small evergreen leaves make this an ideal shrub for this neat hedge. The leaves stay bright green all winter. Trim it about 12 to 18 in. high so it won't obscure the plants behind.

F **Carol Mackie' daphne** *Daphne x burkwoodii* (use 2)
This small rounded shrub marks the far end of the bed with year-round green-and-cream variegated foliage. In spring, pale pink flowers fill the yard with their perfume.

G **Russian sage** *Perovskia atriplicifolia* (use 7)
Silver-green foliage and tiers of tiny blue flowers create a light airy effect in the center of the design from midsummer until fall. Cut stems back partway in early summer to control the size and spread of this tall perennial.

H **'Happy Returns' daylily** *Hemerocallis* (use 6)
These compact grassy-leaved perennials provide yellow trumpet-shaped flowers from early June to frost. A striking combination of color and texture with the Russian sage behind.

I **'Monch' aster** *Aster x frikartii* (use 4)
Pale purple daisylike flowers bloom gaily from June until frost on these knee-high perennials. Cut stems partway back in midsummer if they start to flop over the hedge.

J **Trellis**
Simple panels of wooden lattice frame the crape myrtles while supporting the roses and clematis.

K **Steppingstones**
Rectangular flagstone slabs provide a place to stand while pruning and tying nearby shrubs and vines.

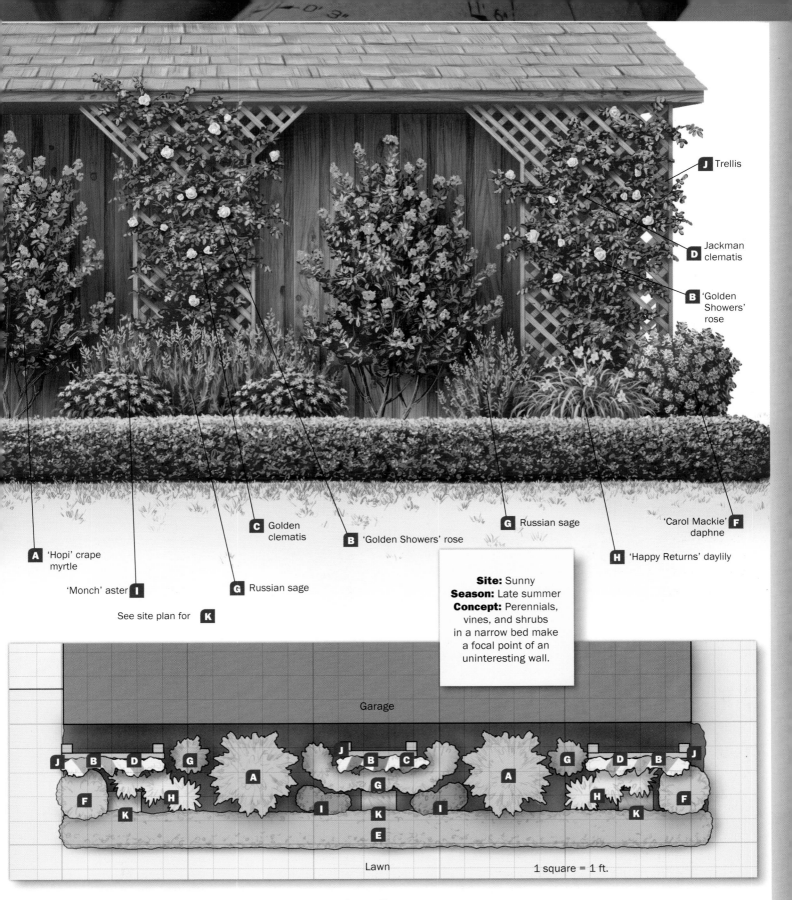

J Trellis

D Jackman clematis

B 'Golden Showers' rose

C Golden clematis

B 'Golden Showers' rose

A 'Hopi' crape myrtle

'Monch' aster **I**

G Russian sage

See site plan for **K**

G Russian sage

G Russian sage

'Carol Mackie' daphne **F**

H 'Happy Returns' daylily

Site: Sunny
Season: Late summer
Concept: Perennials, vines, and shrubs in a narrow bed make a focal point of an uninteresting wall.

Garage

J **B** **D** **G** **A** **J** **B** **C** **A** **G** **D** **B** **J**

F **H** **G** **F**

K **I** **K** **I** **H** **K**

E

Lawn

1 square = 1 ft.

Note: All plants are appropriate for USDA Hardiness Zones 5, 6, and 7.

Pleasing Passage to a Garden Landscape

Entrances are an important part of any landscape. They can welcome visitors onto your property; highlight a special feature, such as a rose garden; or mark passage between two areas with different character or function. The design shown here can serve in any of these situations. A picket fence and perennial plantings create a friendly, attractive barrier, just enough to signal the confines of the front

yard or contain the family dog. The vine-covered arbor provides welcoming access.

The design combines uncomplicated elements imaginatively, creating interesting details to catch the eye and a slightly formal but comfortable overall effect. Picketed enclosures and compact evergreen shrubs

broaden the arbor, giving it greater presence. The wide flagstone apron, flanked by neat deciduous shrubs, reinforces this effect and frames the entrance. Massed perennial plantings lend substance to the fence, which serves as a backdrop to their handsome foliage and colorful flowers.

J Arbor

A White clematis

White clematis A

B 'Green Beauty' littleleaf boxwood

C Pale yellow daylily

C Pale yellow daylily

'Green Beauty' littleleaf boxwood B

G Evergreen candytuft

I White bugleweed

L Walkway

G Evergreen candytuft

See site plan for H

F 'Autumn Joy' sedum

D 'Longwood Blue' bluebeard

Note: All plants are appropriate for USDA Hardiness Zones 5, 6, and 7.

order direct: 1-800-523-6789

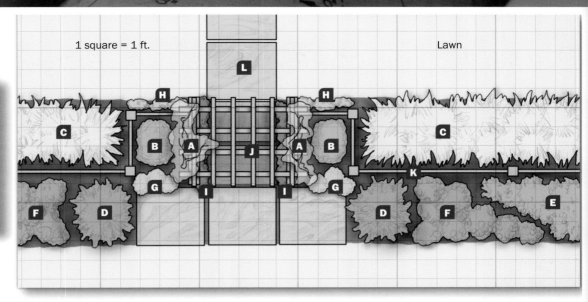

1 square = 1 ft.

Lawn

Plants and Projects

For many people, a picket fence and vine-covered arbor represent old-fashioned "Cottage" style. The plantings here further encourage this feeling.

Pretty white flowers cover the arbor for much of the summer. Massed plantings of daylilies, geraniums, and sedums along the fence produce wide swaths of flowers and attractive foliage from early summer to fall. Plant drifts of snowdrops in these beds; their late-winter flowers are a welcome sign that spring will soon come.

The structures and plantings are easy to build, install, and care for. You can extend the fence and plantings as needed. To use an existing concrete walk, just pour pads either side to create the wide apron in front of the arbor.

A **White clematis** *Clematis* (use 4 plants)
Four of these deciduous climbing vines, one at each post, will cover the arbor in a few years. For large white flowers, try the cultivar 'Henryi', which blooms in early and late summer.

B **'Green Beauty' littleleaf boxwood** *Buxus microphylla* (use 2)
This evergreen shrub forms a neat ball of small bright green leaves without shearing. It is colorful in winter when the rest of the plants are dormant.

C **Pale yellow daylily** *Hemerocallis* (use 24)
A durable perennial whose cheerful trumpet-shaped flowers nod above clumps of arching foliage. Choose from the many yellow-flowered cultivars (some fragrant); mix several to extend the season of bloom.

D **'Longwood Blue' bluebeard** *Caryopteris x clandonensis* (use 2)
A pair of these small deciduous shrubs with soft gray foliage frame the entry. Sky blue late-summer flowers cover the plants for weeks.

E **'Wargrave Pink' geranium** *Geranium endressii* (use 9)
This perennial produces a mass of bright green leaves and a profusion of pink flowers in early summer. Cut it back in July and it will bloom intermittently until frost.

F **'Autumn Joy' sedum** *Sedum* (use 13)
This perennial forms a clump of upright stems with distinctive fleshy foliage. Pale flower buds that appear during summer are followed by pink flowers during fall and rusty seed heads that stand up in winter.

G **Evergreen candytuft** *Iberis sempervirens* (use 12)
A perennial ground cover that spreads to form a small welcome mat at the foot of the boxwoods. White flowers stand out against glossy evergreen leaves in spring.

H **Lamb's ears** *Stachys byzantina* (use 6)
Favorites of children, the long woolly gray leaves of this perennial form a soft carpet. In early summer, thick stalks carry scattered purple flowers.

I **White bugleweed** *Ajuga reptans 'Alba'* (use 20)
Edging the walk under the arbor, this perennial ground cover has pretty green leaves and, in late spring, short spikes of white flowers.

J **Arbor** Thick posts give this simple structure a sturdy visual presence. Paint or stain it, or make it of cedar and let it weather as shown here.

K **Picket fence** Low picket fence adds character to the planting; materials and finish should match the arbor.

L **Walkway** Flagstone walk can be large pavers, as shown here, or made up of smaller rectangular flags.

K Picket fence

E 'Wargrave Pink' geranium

F 'Autumn Joy' sedum

D 'Longwood Blue' bluebeard

Plan #111031

Dimensions: 56' W x 53' D
Levels: 1.5
Square Footage: 2,869
Main Level Sq. Ft.: 2,152
Upper Level Sq. Ft.: 717
Bedrooms: 4
Bathrooms: 3
Foundation: Crawl space, slab
Materials List Available: Yes
Price Category: G

Images provided by designer/architect.

This home is ideal for any family, thanks to its spaciousness, beauty, and versatility.

Features:

- Ceiling Height: 9 ft.
- Front Porch: The middle of the three French doors with circle tops here opens to the foyer.
- Living Room: Archways from the foyer open to both this room and the equally large dining room.
- Family Room: Also open to the foyer, this room features a two-story sloped ceiling and a balcony from the upper level. You'll love the fireplace, with its raised brick hearth and the

two French doors with circle tops, which open to the rear porch.

- Kitchen: A center island, range with microwave, built-in desk, and dining bar that's open to the breakfast room add up to comfort and efficiency.
- Master Suite: A Palladian window and linen closet grace this suite's bedroom, and the bath has an oversized garden tub, standing shower, two walk-in closets, and double vanity.

Copyright by designer/architect.

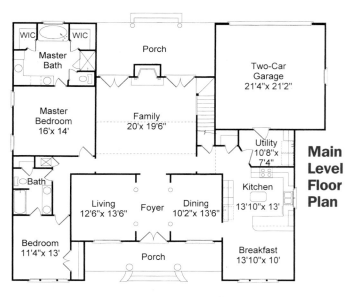

Main Level Floor Plan

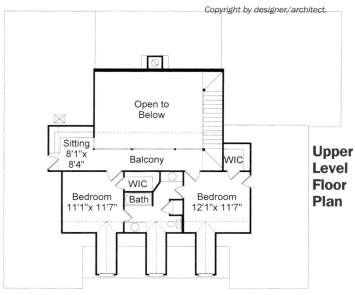

Upper Level Floor Plan

Entry

Kitchen

Living Room

Living Room

SMARTtip

Preparing to Use a Clay Chiminea

Before getting started, there are a couple of general rules about using a clay chiminea. Make sure the chiminea is completely dry before lighting a fire, or else it will crack. Also, line the bottom of the pot with about 4 inches of sand. Finally, always build the fire slowly, and never use kerosene or charcoal lighter fluid.

To cure a new clay chiminea, follow these simple steps:

- Build a small paper fire inside the pot. For kindling, use strips of newspaper rolled into a few balls. Place one newspaper ball on the sand inside the chiminea. Ignite it with a match. Then add another ball, and another, one at a time, until the outside walls of the chiminea are slightly warm. Allow the fire to burn out; then let the pot cool completely before the next step.

- Once the chiminea feels cool, light another small fire, this time using wood. Again, let the fire burn out naturally, and then allow the unit to completely cool.

- Repeat the process of lighting a wood fire three more times, adding more kindling and building a larger fire with each consecutive attempt. Remember to let the chiminea cool completely between fires.

After the fifth fire, the chiminea should be cured and ready to use anytime you want a cozy fire.

Images provided by designer/architect.

Plan #101010

Dimensions: 70' W x 47' D

Levels: 1

Square Footage: 2,187

Bedrooms: 4

Bathrooms: 2½

Foundation: Crawl space, slab, or basement

Materials List Available: Yes

Price Category: D

This stately ranch features a brick-and-stucco exterior, layered trim, and copper roofing returns.

Features:

- Ceiling Height: 11 ft. unless otherwise noted.

- Special Ceilings: Vaulted and raised ceilings adorn the living room, family room, dining room, foyer, kitchen, breakfast room, and master suite.

- Kitchen: This roomy kitchen is brightened by an abundance of windows.

- Breakfast Room: Located off the kitchen, this breakfast room is the perfect spot for informal family meals.

- Master Suite: This truly exceptional master suite features a bath, and a spacious walk in closet.

- Morning Porch: Step out of the master bedroom, and greet the day on this lovely porch.

- Additional Bedrooms: The three additional bedrooms each measure approximately 11 ft. x 12 ft. Two of them have walk-in closets.

Copyright by designer/architect.

SMARTtip

Using Slipcovers in Your Dining Area

Change the look of your dining room by slipcovering chairs. Short-skirted slipcovers give a more informal appearance; fabrics in graphic patterns, such as checks or floral prints, complement this style of slipcover best. Long-skirted covers are elegant additions to a formal dining room, particularly in solid color or tone-on-tone fabrics. Ties, buttons, or trim can add personality.

Plan #351001

Dimensions: 72'8" W x 51' D
Levels: 1
Square Footage: 1,855
Bedrooms: 3
Bathrooms: 2½
Foundation: Crawl space, slab, or basement
Materials List Available: Yes
Price Category: D

From the lovely arched windows on the front to the front and back covered porches, this home is as comfortable as it is beautiful.

Features:

- **Great Room:** Come into this room with 12-ft. ceilings, and you're sure to admire the corner gas fireplace and three windows overlooking the porch.

- **Dining Room:** Set off from the open design, this room is designed to be used formally or not.

- **Kitchen:** You'll love the practical walk-in pantry, broom closet, and angled snack bar here.

- **Breakfast Room:** Brightly lit and leading to the covered porch, this room will be a favorite spot.

- **Bonus Room:** Develop a playroom or study in this area.

- **Master Suite:** The large bedroom is complemented by the private bath with garden tub, separate shower, double vanity, and spacious walk-in closet.

Images provided by designer/architect.

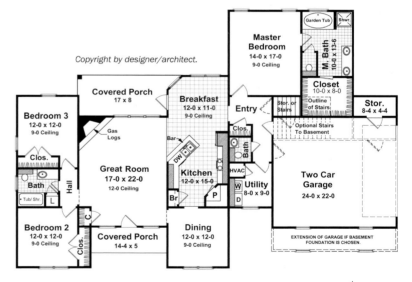

Copyright by designer/architect.

Kitchen

Bonus Area Floor Plan

Plan #151043

Dimensions: 53' W x 59'10" D

Levels: 1

Square Footage: 1,636

Bedrooms: 3

Bathrooms: 2

Foundation: Crawl space, slab; basement option for fee

CompleteCost List Available: Yes

Price Category: E

Images provided by designer/architect.

Copyright by designer/architect.

Plan #211039

Dimensions: 62' W x 64' D

Levels: 1

Square Footage: 1,868

Bedrooms: 3

Bathrooms: 2

Foundation: Slab

Materials List Available: Yes

Price Category: D

Images provided by designer/architect.

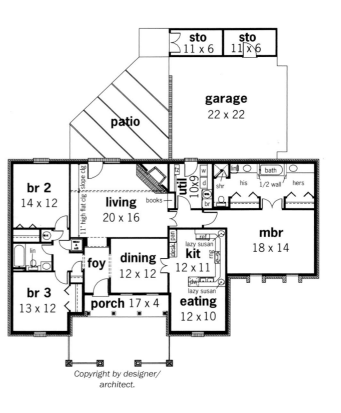

Copyright by designer/architect.

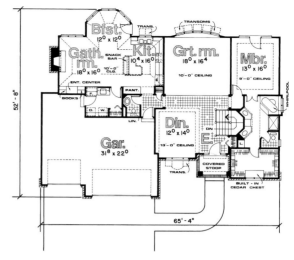

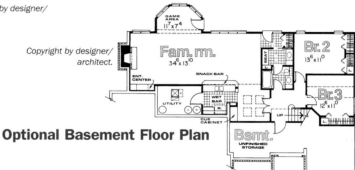

Images provided by designer/
architect.

Copyright by designer/
architect.

Optional Basement Floor Plan

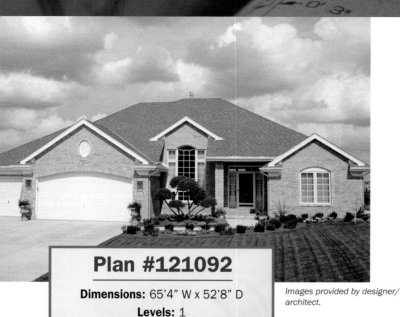

Plan #121092

Dimensions: 65'4" W x 52'8" D

Levels: 1

Square Footage: 1,887

Bedrooms: 3

Bathrooms: 2½

Foundation: Basement

Materials List Available: Yes

Price Category: D

Plan #151054

Dimensions: 67' W x 54'10" D

Levels: 1

Square Footage: 1,746

Bedrooms: 3

Bathrooms: 2

Foundation: Crawl space or slab;
basement option for fee

CompleteCost List Available: Yes

Price Category: C

Images provided by designer/
architect.

CAD FILE AVAILABLE

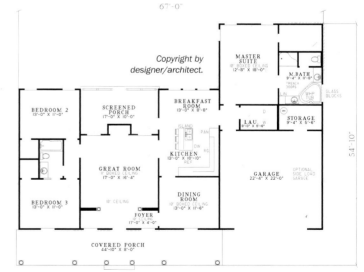

Copyright by
designer/architect.

SMARTtip

Mixing and Matching Windows

Windows, both fixed and operable, are made in various styles and shapes. While mixing styles should be carefully avoided, a variety of interesting window sizes and shapes may nevertheless be combined to achieve symmetry, harmony, and rhythm on the exterior of a home.

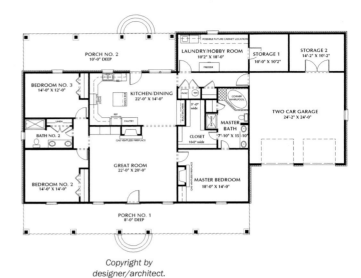

Plan #191032

Dimensions: 80'4" W x 52' D

Levels: 1

Square Footage: 2,091

Bedrooms: 3

Bathrooms: 2

Foundation: Slab

Materials List Available: Yes

Price Category: D

Images provided by designer/architect.

Copyright by designer/architect.

Plan #151003

Dimensions: 51'6" W x 52'4" D

Levels: 1

Square Footage: 1,680

Bedrooms: 3

Bathrooms: 2

Foundation: Crawl space, slab, or basement

CompleteCost List Available: Yes

Price Category: C

Images provided by designer/architect.

This home, as shown in the photograph, may differ from the actual blueprints. For more detailed information, please check the floor plans carefully.

Copyright by designer/architect.

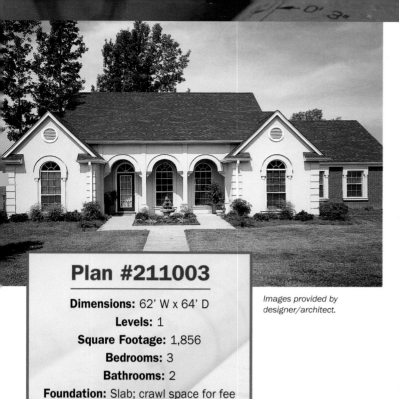

Images provided by designer/architect.

Copyright by designer/architect.

Plan #211003

Dimensions: 62' W x 64' D

Levels: 1

Square Footage: 1,856

Bedrooms: 3

Bathrooms: 2

Foundation: Slab; crawl space for fee

Materials List Available: Yes

Price Category: D

Copyright by designer/architect.

Images provided by designer/architect.

Plan #211058

Dimensions: 74'6" W x 68' D

Levels: 1

Square Footage: 2,564

Bedrooms: 4

Bathrooms: 4

Foundation: Slab

Materials List Available: Yes

Price Category: E

Plan #121003

Dimensions: 76' W x 55'4" D

Levels: 1

Square Footage: 2,498

Bedrooms: 4

Bathrooms: 2½

Foundation: Basement

Materials List Available: Yes

Price Category: E

Repeated arches bring style and distinction to the interior and exterior of this spacious home.

Features:

• Ceiling Height: 8 ft. except as noted.

• Den: A decorative volume ceiling helps make this spacious retreat the perfect place to relax after a long day.

• Formal Living Room: The decorative volume ceiling carries through to the living room that invites large formal gatherings.

• Formal Dining Room: There's plenty of room for all the guests to move into this gracious formal space that also features a decorative volume ceiling.

• Master Suite: Retire to this suite with its glamorous bayed whirlpool, his and her vanities, and a walk-in closet.

• Optional Sitting Room: With the addition of French doors, one of the bedrooms can be converted into a sitting room for the master suite.

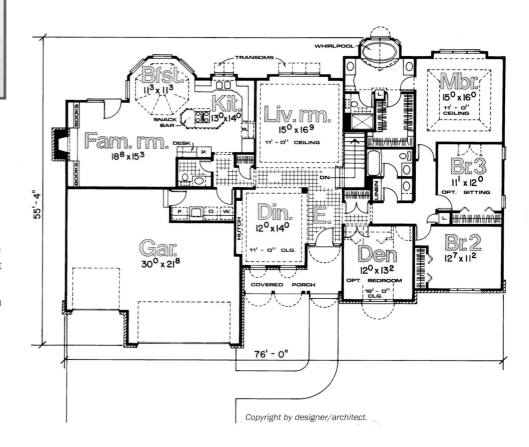

Plan #151002

Dimensions: 67' W x 66' D

Levels: 1

Square Footage: 2,444

Bedrooms: 3

Bathrooms: 2½

Foundation: Crawl space, slab, basement or walkout

CompleteCost List Available: Yes

Price Category: F

This home, as shown in the photograph, may differ from the actual blueprints. For more detailed information, please check the floor plans carefully.

Images provided by designer/architect.

This gracious, traditional home is designed for practicality and convenience.

Features:

- Ceiling Height: 9 ft. except as noted below.

- Great Room: This room is ideal for entertaining, thanks to its lovely fireplace and French doors that open to the covered rear porch. Built-in cabinets give convenient storage space.

- Family Room: With access to the kitchen as well as the rear porch, this room will become your family's "headquarters."

- Study: Enjoy the quiet in this room with its 12-ft. ceiling and doorway to a private patio on the side of the house.

- Dining Room: Take advantage of the 8-in. wood columns and 12-ft. ceilings to create a formal dining area.

- Kitchen: An eat-in bar is a great place to snack, and the handy computer nook allows the kids to do their homework while you cook.

- Breakfast Room: Opening from the kitchen, this area gives added space for the family to gather any time.

- Master Suite: Featuring a 10-ft. boxed ceiling, the master bedroom also has a doorway that opens onto the covered rear porch. The master bathroom has a step-up whirlpool tub, separate shower, and twin vanities with a makeup area.

CAD FILE AVAILABLE · CAD

Copyright by designer/architect.

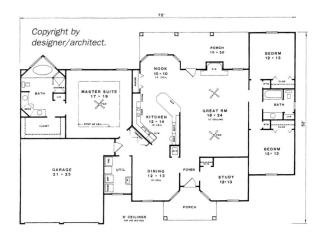

Images provided by designer/architect.

Copyright by designer/architect.

Plan #171004

Dimensions: 72' W x 52' D
Levels: 1
Square Footage: 2,256
Bedrooms: 3
Bathrooms: 2
Foundation: Crawl space, slab
Materials List Available: Yes
Price Category: E

SMARTtip

Windows – Privacy

You can easily stencil a work of art onto a windowpane, perhaps only as a border around the edge. Choose or create a design that gives you as little or as much privacy and light control as you need. Use a ready-made stencil or a piece of openwork fabric such as lace, or mask a design onto the glass using tape and a razor knife. Then apply glass paint or frosted glass spray, referring to the instructions and guidelines that come with the product.

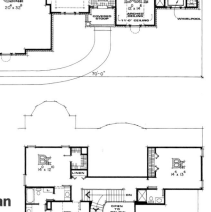

Main Level Floor Plan

Images provided by designer/architect.

Plan #121062

Dimensions: 70' W x 62' D
Levels: 2
Square Footage: 3,448
Main Level Sq. Ft.: 2,375
Upper Level Sq. Ft.: 1,073
Bedrooms: 4
Bathrooms: 3½
Foundation: Basement
Materials List Available: Yes
Price Category: G

Upper Level Floor Plan

Copyright by designer/architect.

Main Level Floor Plan

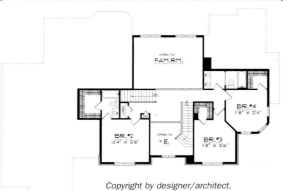

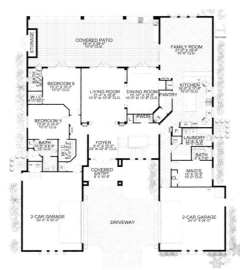

Upper Level Floor Plan

Images provided by designer/architect.

CAD FILE AVAILABLE

Plan #221022

Dimensions: 79' W x 55' D
Levels: 2
Square Footage: 3,382
Main Level Sq. Ft.: 2,376
Upper Level Sq. Ft.: 1,006
Bedrooms: 4
Bathrooms: 3½
Foundation: Basement
Materials List Available: Yes
Price Category: G

Main Level Floor Plan

Plan #611087

Dimensions: 76'8" W x 93' D
Levels: 2
Square Footage: 6,175
Main Level Sq. Ft.: 3,251
Upper Level Sq. Ft.: 2,924
Bedrooms: 6
Bathrooms: 6½
Foundation: Slab
Materials List Available: Yes
Price Category: K

Images provided by designer/architect.

CAD FILE AVAILABLE

Upper Level Floor Plan

Plan #121067

Dimensions: 56' W x 59'4" D

Levels: 2

Square Footage: 2,708

Main Level Sq. Ft.: 1,860

Upper Level Sq. Ft.: 848

Bedrooms: 4

Bathrooms: 3½

Foundation: Basement

Materials List Available: Yes

Price Category: F

Images provided by designer/architect.

You'll love this home because it is such a perfect setting for a family and still has room for guests.

Features:

- **Family Room:** Expect everyone to gather in this room, near the built-in entertainment centers that flank the lovely fireplace.

- **Living Room:** The other side of the see-through fireplace looks out into this living room, making it an equally welcoming spot in chilly weather.

- **Kitchen:** This room has a large center island, a corner pantry, and a built-in desk. It also features a breakfast area where friends and family will congregate all day long.

- **Master Suite:** Enjoy the oversized walk-in closet and bath with a bayed whirlpool tub, double vanity, and separate shower.

Main Level Floor Plan

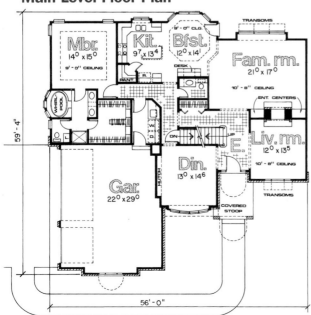

Upper Level Floor Plan

Copyright by designer/architect.

Plan #151004

Dimensions: 64'8" W x 62'1" D

Levels: 1

Square Footage: 2,107

Bedrooms: 4

Bathrooms: 2½

Foundation: Crawl space or slab; basement for fee

CompleteCost List Available: Yes

Price Category: E

This home, as shown in the photograph, may differ from the actual blueprints. For more detailed information, please check the floor plans carefully.

Images provided by designer/architect.

You'll love the spacious feeling in this comfortable home designed for a family.

Features:

- **Foyer:** A 10-ft. ceiling greets you in this home.

- **Great Room:** A 10-ft. ceiling complements this large room, with its fireplace, built-in cabinets, and easy access to the rear covered porch.

- **Dining Room:** The 9-ft. boxed ceiling in this large room helps to create a beautiful formal feeling.

- **Kitchen:** The island in this kitchen is open to the breakfast room for true convenience.

- **Breakfast Room:** Morning light will stream through the bay window here.

- **Master Suite:** A 9-ft. pan ceiling adds a distinctive note to this room with access to the rear porch. In the bath, you'll find a whirlpool tub, separate shower, double vanities, and two walk-in closets.

Copyright by designer/architect.

Plan #161001

Dimensions: 67'2" W x 47' D

Levels: 1

Square Footage: 1,782

Bedrooms: 3

Bathrooms: 2

Foundation: Basement

Materials List Available: Yes

Price Category: C

Images provided by designer/architect.

An all-brick exterior displays the solid strength that characterizes this gracious home.

Features:

- Great Room: A feeling of spaciousness permeates the gathering area created by the foyer, great room, and dining room. Multiple windows provide natural light that dances along a sloped ceiling, spilling onto decorative columns and a fireplace.

- Breakfast Area: A continuation of the sloped ceiling leads to the breakfast area where French doors open to a screened porch.

- Kitchen: An abundance of cabinets and counter space are the hallmarks of this large kitchen with its easy access to a spacious laundry room and storage area.

- Master Suite: A tray ceiling and spacious walk-in closet in the master bedroom, along with a whirlpool tub and double-bowl vanity in the bathroom, enable you to pamper yourself.

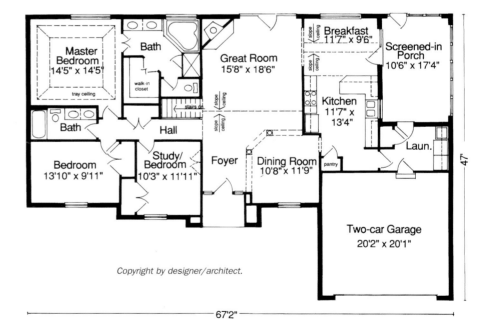

Copyright by designer/architect.

Great Room/Foyer

Rear Elevation

Plan #211011

Dimensions: 84' W x 54' D
Levels: 1
Square Footage: 2,791
Bedrooms: 3 or 4
Bathrooms: 2
Foundation: Slab or crawl space
Materials List Available: Yes
Price Category: F

SMARTtip

Types of Decks

Ground-level decks resemble a low platform and are best for flat locations. They can be the most economical type to build because they don't require stairs.

Raised decks can rise just a few steps up or meet the second story of a house. Lifted high on post supports, they adapt well to uneven or sloped locations.

Multilevel decks feature two or more stories and are connected by stairways or ramps. They can follow the contours of a sloped lot, unifying the deck with the outdoors.

Images provided by designer/architect.

Plenty of room plus an open, flexible floor plan make this a home that will adapt to your needs.

Features:

• Ceiling Height: 8 ft. unless otherwise noted.

• Living Room: This distinctive room features a 12-ft. ceiling and is designed so that it can also serve as a master suite with a sitting room.

• Family Room: The whole family will want to gather in this large, inviting family room.

• Morning Room: The family room blends into this sunny spot, which is perfect for informal family meals.

• Kitchen: This spacious kitchen offers a smart layout. It is also contiguous to the family room.

• Master Suite: You'll look forward to the end of the day when you can enjoy this master suite. It includes a huge, luxurious master bath with two large walk-in closets and two vanity sinks.

• Optional Bedroom: This optional fourth bedroom is located so that it can easily serve as a library, den, office, or music room.

Copyright by designer/architect.

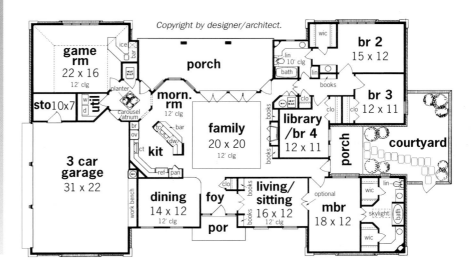

Plan #121050

Dimensions: 64' W x 50' D

Levels: 1

Square Footage: 1,996

Bedrooms: 2

Bathrooms: 2

Foundation: Basement

Materials List Available: Yes

Price Category: D

Images provided by designer/architect.

This compact design includes features usually reserved for larger homes and has styling that is typical of more-exclusive home designs.

Features:

• **Entry:** As you enter this home, you'll see the formal living and dining rooms—both with special ceiling detailing—on either side.

• **Great Room:** Located in the rear of the home for convenience, this great room is likely to be your favorite spot. The fireplace is framed by transom-topped windows, so you'll love curling up here, no matter what the weather or time of day.

• **Kitchen:** Ample counter and cabinet space make this kitchen a dream in which to work.

• **Master Suite:** A tray ceiling and lovely corner windows create an elegant feeling in the bedroom, and two walk-in closets make it easy to keep this space tidy and organized. The private bath has a skylight, corner whirlpool tub, and two separate vanities.

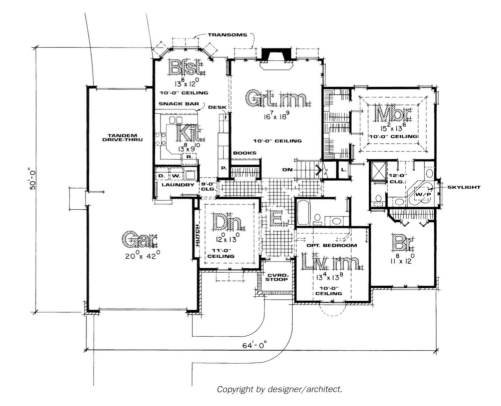

Copyright by designer/architect.

Plan #161028

Dimensions: 84'6" W x 69'4" D
Levels: 1
Square Footage: 3,570
Optional Finished Basement Sq. Ft.: 2,367
Bedrooms: 3
Bathrooms: 3½
Foundation: Basement
Materials List Available: Yes
Price Category: H

From the gabled stone-and-brick exterior to the wide-open view from the foyer, this home will meet your greatest expectations.

Images provided by designer/architect.

Features:

- **Great Room/Dining Room:** Columns and 13-ft. ceilings add exquisite detailing to the dining room and great room.

- **Kitchen:** The gourmet-equipped kitchen with an island and a snack bar merges with the cozy breakfast and hearth rooms.

- **Master Suite:** The luxurious master bed room pampers with a separate sitting room with a fireplace and a dressing room boasting a tub and two vanities.

- **Additional:** Two bedrooms include a private bath and walk-in closet. The optional finished basement solves all your recreational needs: bar, media room, billiards room, exercise room, game room, as well as an office and fourth bedroom.

Rear Elevation

Main Level Floor Plan

Dressing
Sitting 11'2" x 7'9" Irregular
Breakfast 13'6" x 13'11" Irregular
Hearth Room 22'11" x 17'1" Irregular
WALK-IN CLOSET
Master Bedroom 17'8" x 17'4" Irregular
Great Room 19'5" x 17'8"
Kitchen 16'10" x 17'11" Irregular
Bath
WALK-IN CLOSET
Hall
Bedroom 13'4" x 14'0"
WALK-IN CLOSET
Bath
Foyer
DOWN 17 RISERS
Dining Room 14'4" x 15'7" Irregular
Hall
Laun.
Garage 21'4" x 40'11"
Bedroom 13'4" x 12'3"
Porch
84'-6"

Basement Level Floor Plan

Office 12'10" x 11'8" Irregular
Bedroom 12'6" x 14'11" Irregular
WALK-IN CLOSET
Raised Bar
Media Area 20'0" x 13'6" Irregular
Billiards Room 19'8" x 15'11" Irregular
Hall
Bath
Game Room 14'11" x 9'6"
Unexcavated
Basement
UP 17 RISERS
Exercise Area 13'8" x 12'5"
Unexc.

Copyright by designer/architect.

Plan #131036

Dimensions: 72' W x 69'10" D
Levels: 1
Square Footage: 2,585
Bedrooms: 4
Bathrooms: 3
Foundation: Crawl space or slab; basement for fee
Materials List Available: Yes
Price Category: F

Images provided by designer/architect.

This sprawling brick home features living spaces for everyone in the family and makes a lovely setting for any sort of entertaining.

Features:

- **Foyer:** Pass through this foyer, which leads into either the living room or dining room.
- **Living Room:** An elegant 11-ft. stepped ceiling here and in the dining room helps to create the formality their lines suggest.

- **Great Room:** This room, with its 10-ft.-7-in.-high stepped ceiling, fireplace, and many built-ins, leads to the rear covered porch.
- **Kitchen:** This kitchen features an island, a pantry closet, and a wraparound snack bar that serves the breakfast room and gives a panoramic view of the great room.
- **Master Suite:** Enjoy a bayed sitting area, walk-in closet, and private bath with garden tub.
- **Office:** A private entrance and access to a full bath give versatility to this room.

Rear View

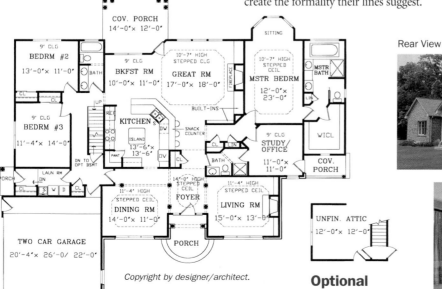

Copyright by designer/architect.

Optional Upper Level Floor Plan

Great Room

Plan #121007

Dimensions: 74' W x 67'8" D

Levels: 1

Square Footage: 2,512

Bedrooms: 3

Bathrooms: 2½

Foundation: Basement

Materials List Available: Yes

Price Category: E

Images provided by designer/architect.

A series of arches brings grace to this home's interior and exterior.

Features:

- Ceiling Height: 8 ft.

- Formal Dining Room: Tapered columns give this dining room a classical look that lends elegance to any dinner party.

- Great Room: Just beyond the dining room is this light-filled room, with its wall of arched windows and see-through fireplace.

- Hearth Room: On the other side of the fire place you will find this cozy area, with its corner entertainment center.

- Dinette: A gazebo-shaped dinette is the architectural surprise of the house layout.

- Kitchen: This well-conceived working kitchen features a generous center island.

- Garage: With three garage bays you'll never be short of parking space or storage.

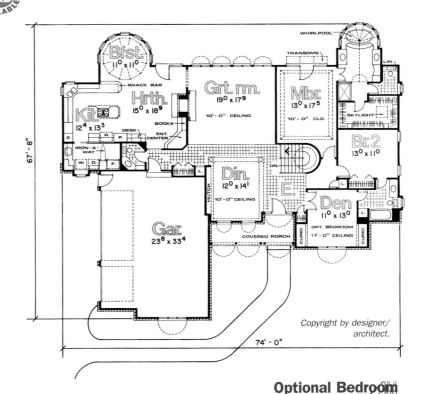

Copyright by designer/architect.

Optional Bedroom

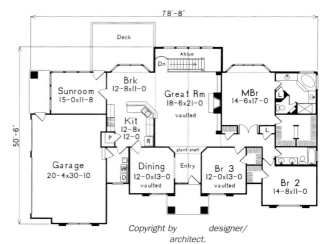

Plan #321037

Dimensions: 78'8" W x 50'6" D

Levels: 1

Square Footage: 2,397

Bedrooms: 3

Bathrooms: 2

Foundation: Basement or walkout

Materials List Available: Yes

Price Category: F

**Optional
Basement Level
Floor Plan**

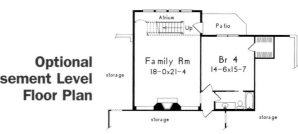

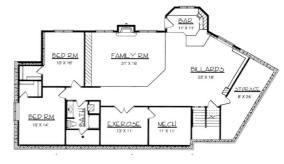

Optional Basement Level Floor Plan

Plan #271079

Dimensions: 104' W x 55' D

Levels: 1

Square Footage: 2,228

Bedrooms: 1-3

Bathrooms: 1½

Foundation: Daylight basement

Materials List Available: Yes

Price Category: E

Plan #211010

Dimensions: 81' W x 84' D

Levels: 1

Square Footage: 2,503

Bedrooms: 3

Bathrooms: 2½

Foundation: Slab

Materials List Available: Yes

Price Category: E

Images provided by designer/architect.

Copyright by designer/architect.

Plan #661179

Dimensions: 74'8" W x 82'8" D

Levels: 1

Square Footage: 2,799

Bedrooms: 5

Bathrooms: 3

Foundation: Slab

Material List Available: Yes

Price Category: F

Images provided by designer/architect.

Copyright by designer/architect.

Plan #121019

Dimensions: 70' W x 60' D
Levels: 2
Square Footage: 3,775
Main Level Sq. Ft.: 1,923
Upper Level Sq. Ft.: 1,852
Bedrooms: 4
Bathrooms: 3
Foundation: Basement
Materials List Available: Yes
Price Category: H

CAD FILE AVAILABLE

Images provided by designer/architect.

The grand exterior presence is carried inside, beginning with the dramatic curved staircase.

Features:

• Den: French doors lead to this sophisticated den, with its bayed windows and wall of bookcases.

• Living Room: A curved wall and a series of arched windows highlight this large space.

• Formal Dining Room: This room shares the curved wall and arched windows found in the living room.

• Screened Porch: This huge space features skylights and is accessible by another French door from the dining room.

• Family Room: Family and guests alike will be drawn to this room, with its trio of arched windows and fireplace flanked by bookcases.

• Kitchen: An island adds convenience and distinction to this large, functional kitchen.

• Garage: This spacious three-bay garage provides plenty of space for cars and storage.

Main Level Floor Plan

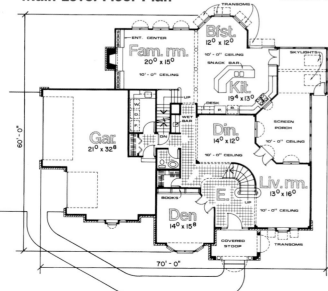

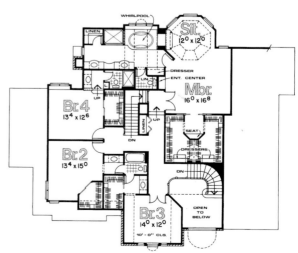

Upper Level Floor Plan

Copyright by designer/architect.

Plan #151007

Dimensions: 54'2" W x 56'2" D
Levels: 1
Square Footage: 1,787
Bedrooms: 3
Bathrooms: 2
Foundation: Crawl space or slab; basement or walkout for fee
CompleteCost List Available: Yes
Price Category: C

This home, as shown in the photograph, may differ from the actual blueprints. For more detailed information, please check the floor plans carefully.

Images provided by designer/architect.

This compact, well-designed home is graced with amenities usually reserved for larger houses.

Features:

- **Foyer:** A 10-ft. ceiling creates unity between the foyer and the dining room just beyond it.

- **Dining Room:** 8-in. boxed columns welcome you to this dining room, with its 10-ft. ceilings.

- **Great Room:** The 9-ft. boxed ceiling suits the spacious design. Enjoy the fireplace in the winter and the rear-grilling porch in the summer.

- **Breakfast Room:** This bright room is a lovely spot for any time of day.

- **Master Suite:** Double vanities and a large walk-in closet add practicality to this quiet room with a 9-ft. pan ceiling. The master bath includes whirlpool tub with glass block and a separate shower.

- **Bedrooms:** Bedroom 2 features a bay window, and both rooms are convenient to the bathroom.

Copyright by designer/architect.

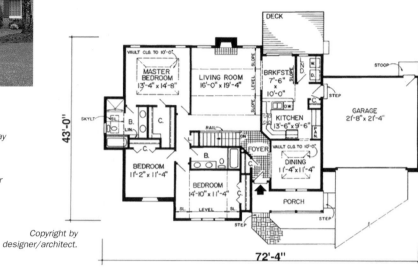

Plan #391034

Dimensions: 72'4" W x 43' D

Levels: 1

Square Footage: 1,737

Bedrooms: 3

Bathrooms: 2

Foundation: Crawl space, slab, or basement

Material List Available: Yes

Price Category: C

Images provided by designer/architect.

This home, as shown in the photograph, may differ from the actual blueprints. For more detailed information, please check the floor plans carefully.

Copyright by designer/architect.

Main Level Floor Plan

Upper Level Floor Plan

Plan #151033

Dimensions: 81'6" W x 93'2" D

Levels: 2

Square Footage: 5,548

Main Level Sq. Ft.: 3,276

Upper Level Sq. Ft.: 2,272

Bedrooms: 5

Bathrooms: 4½

Foundation: Crawl space or slab; basement option for fee

CompleteCost List Available: Yes

Price Category: I

Images provided by designer/architect.

Copyright by designer/architect.

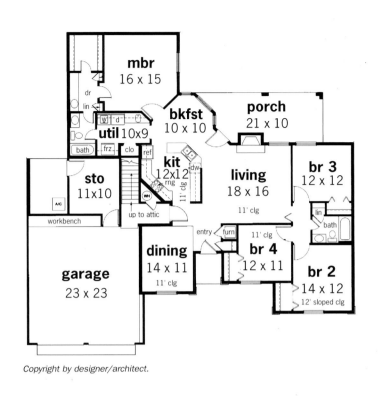

Images provided by designer/architect.

Plan #211004

Dimensions: 64' W x 62' D

Levels: 1

Square Footage: 1,828

Bedrooms: 4

Bathrooms: 2

Foundation: Crawl space, slab, or basement

Materials List Available: Yes

Price Category: D

Copyright by designer/architect.

Images provided by designer/architect.

CAD FILE AVAILABLE

Plan #151057

Dimensions: 73'6" W x 80'6" D

Levels: 1

Square Footage: 2,951

Bedrooms: 4

Bathrooms: 3

Foundation: Crawl space or slab; basement for fee

CompleteCost List Available: Yes

Price Category: G

Plan #121065

Dimensions: 62' W x 55'4" D

Levels: 2

Square Footage: 3,407

Main Level Sq. Ft.: 1,719

Upper Level Sq. Ft.: 1,688

Bedrooms: 4

Bathrooms: 2½

Foundation: Basement

Materials List Available: Yes

Price Category: G

Images provided by designer/architect.

If you love contemporary design, the unusual shapes of the rooms in this home will delight you.

Features:

- Entry: You'll see a balcony from the upper level that overlooks this entryway, as well as the lovely curved staircase to this floor.

- Great Room: This room is sunken to set it apart. A fireplace, wet bar, spider-beamed ceiling, and row of arched windows give it character.

- Dining Room: Columns define this lovely octagon room, where you'll love to entertain guests or create lavish family dinners.

- Master Suite: A multi-tiered ceiling adds a note of grace, while the fireplace and private library create a real retreat. The gracious bath features a gazebo ceiling and a skylight.

Main Level Floor Plan

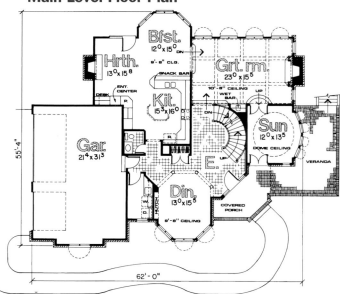

Upper Level Floor Plan

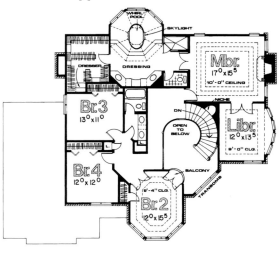

Copyright by designer/architect.

Plan #121073

Dimensions: 70' W x 52' D
Levels: 2
Square Footage: 2,579
Main Level Sq. Ft.: 1,933
Upper Level Sq. Ft.: 646
Bedrooms: 4
Bathrooms: 2½
Foundation: Basement
Materials List Available: Yes
Price Category: E

Luxury will surround you in this home with contemporary styling and up-to-date amenities at every turn.

Features:

• Great Room: This large room shares both a see-through fireplace and a wet bar with the adjacent hearth room. Transom-topped windows add both light and architectural interest to this room.

• Den: Transom-topped windows add visual interest to this private area.

• Kitchen: A center island and corner pantry add convenience to this well-planned kitchen, and a lovely ceiling treatment adds beauty to the bayed breakfast area.

• Master Suite: A built-in bookcase adds to the ambiance of this luxury-filled area, where you're sure to find a retreat at the end of the day.

Main Level Floor Plan

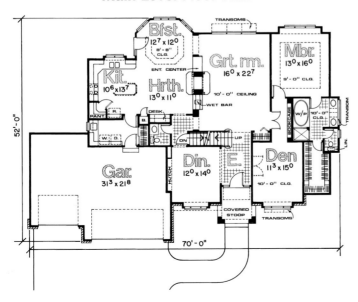

Upper Level Floor Plan

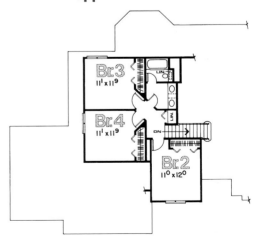

Copyright by designer/architect.

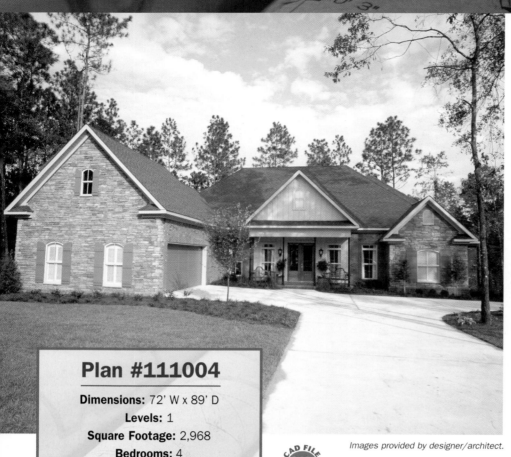

Images provided by designer/architect. Living Room

Plan #111004

Dimensions: 72' W x 89' D

Levels: 1

Square Footage: 2,968

Bedrooms: 4

Full Bathrooms: 3½

Foundation: Crawl space or slab

Materials List Available: Yes

Price Category: G

CAD FILE AVAILABLE — CAD

Copyright by designer/ architect.

If you've been looking for a home that includes a special master suite, this one could be the answer to your dreams.

Features:

- **Living Room:** Make a sitting area around the fireplace here so that the whole family can enjoy the warmth on chilly days and winter evenings. A door from this room leads to the rear covered porch, making this room the heart of your home.

- **Kitchen:** An island with a cooktop makes cooking a pleasure in this well-designed kitchen, and the breakfast bar invites visitors at all times of day.

- **Utility Room:** A sink and a built-in ironing board make this room totally practical.

- **Master Suite:** A private fireplace in the corner sets a romantic tone for this bedroom, and the door to the covered porch allows you to sit outside on warm summer nights. The bath has two vanities, a divided walk-in closet, a standing shower, and a deluxe corner bathtub.

Bonus Area

Gameroom 13'5"x17'

Wood Deck

Covered Porch

Breakfast 14'x12'1"

Living 24'8"x19'3"

Master Bedroom 16'9"x21'5"

Master Bath

WIC

Bedroom 12'4"x12'1"

Kitchen 18'4"x14'10"

Dining 13'1"x14'7"

Foyer

Bedroom 13'x12'

Bedroom 12'1"x13'

Utility

Porch

Garage 21'2"x27'2"

Front Elevation

Kitchen

Dining Room

Master Bath

Master Bath

SMARTtip

How to Quit Smoking — Lighting Your Fireplace

Before attempting to light a wood fire, make certain that the damper is open all the way. This allows a good draft (flow of air up the chimney) to prevent smoke from blowing back into the room. To ensure a good draft— particularly if your home is well insulated —open a window a bit when lighting a fire.

The opposite of draft is downdraft, which occurs when cold air flows down the chimney and into the room. If the fireplace is properly designed and maintained, the smoke shelf will prevent backpuffing from downdraft most of the time by redirecting cold air currents back up the chimney. The open damper also helps prevent backpuffing.

Also, build a fire slowly to let the chimney liner heat up, which will create a good draft and minimize the chances of downdraft.

Don't wait until fall to inspect the chimney. Do this job, or call a chimney sweep, when the weather is mild. Because some repairs take a while to make, it's best to have them done when the fireplace is not normally in use. If you do the inspection yourself, wear old clothes, eye goggles, and a mask.

Plan #151010

Dimensions: 38'4" W x 68'6" D
Levels: 1
Square Footage: 1,379
Bedrooms: 3
Bathrooms: 2
Foundation: Crawl space, slab
CompleteCost List Available: Yes
Price Category: C

This French Country home has a spacious great room for friends and family to gather, but you can sneak away to the covered rear porch or patio off the master suite for cozy tête-à-têtes.

Features:

- Entry: Take advantage of the marvelous 10-ft. ceilings to hang groups of potted flowering plants.

- Great Room: This spacious room, with an optional 10-ft. boxed ceiling, is the place to curl up by the gas fireplace on a cold winter night.

- Kitchen: The kitchen includes a bar for casual meals, and is open to the breakfast room.

- Rear Porch: Enjoy leisurely meals on the covered rear porch that you can access from both the master suite and the breakfast room.

- Master Suite: The 10-ft. boxed ceiling in the bedroom and the master bath with a whirlpool tub and separate shower make this suite a luxurious place to end a long day.

Images provided by designer/architect.

Copyright by designer/architect.

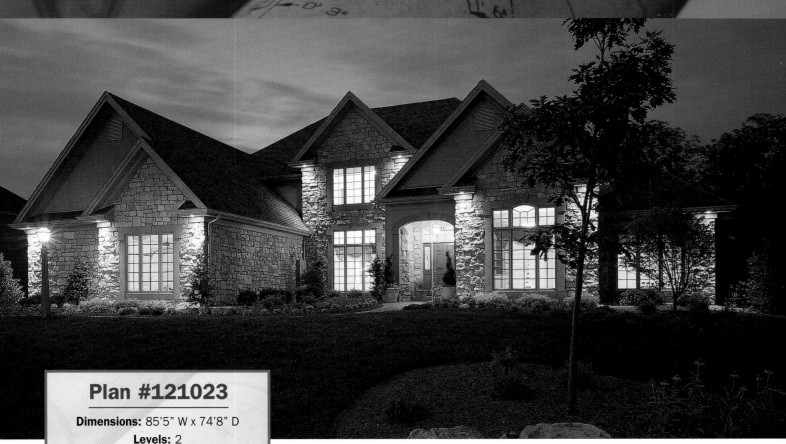

Plan #121023

Dimensions: 85'5" W x 74'8" D

Levels: 2

Square Footage: 3,904

Main Level Sq. Ft.: 2,813

Upper Level Sq. Ft.: 1,091

Bedrooms: 4

Bathrooms: 3½

Foundation: Basement; crawl space, slab, basement or walkout for fee

Materials List Available: Yes

Price Category: H

Images provided by designer/architect.

Spacious and gracious, here are all the amenities you expect in a fine home.

Features:

• Ceiling Height: 8 ft. except as noted.

• Foyer: This magnificent entry features a graceful curved staircase with balcony above.

• Sunken Living Room: This sunken room is filled with light from a row of bowed windows. It's the perfect place for social gatherings both large and small.

• Den: French doors open into this truly distinctive den with its 11-ft. ceiling and built-in bookcases.

• Formal Dining Room: Entertain guests with style and grace in this dining room with corner column.

• Master Suite: Another set of French doors leads to this suite that features two walk-in closets, a tub flanked by vanities, and a private sitting room with built-in bookcases.

Main Level Floor Plan

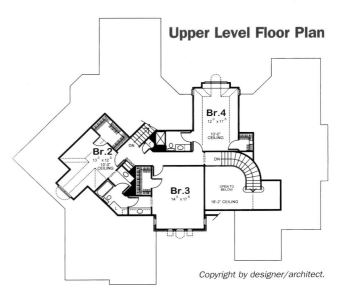

Upper Level Floor Plan

Copyright by designer/architect.

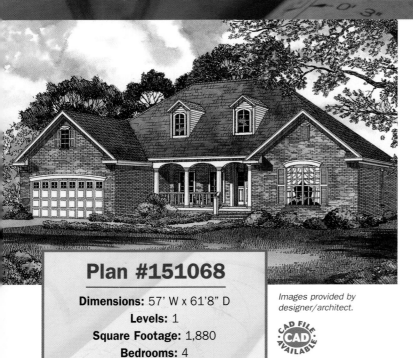

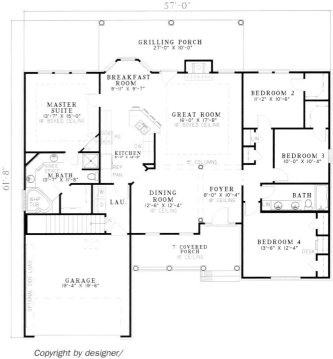

Images provided by
designer/architect.

Plan #151068

Dimensions: 57' W x 61'8" D

Levels: 1

Square Footage: 1,880

Bedrooms: 4

Bathrooms: 2

Foundation: Crawl space, slab, basement or walkout

CompleteCost List Available: Yes

Price Category: D

*Copyright by designer/
architect.*

Plan #221005

Dimensions: 72' W x 42' D

Levels: 1

Square Footage: 1,851

Bedrooms: 3

Bathrooms: 2

Foundation: Basement

Materials List Available: Yes

Price Category: D

Images provided by
designer/architect.

Rear

Copyright by designer/architect.

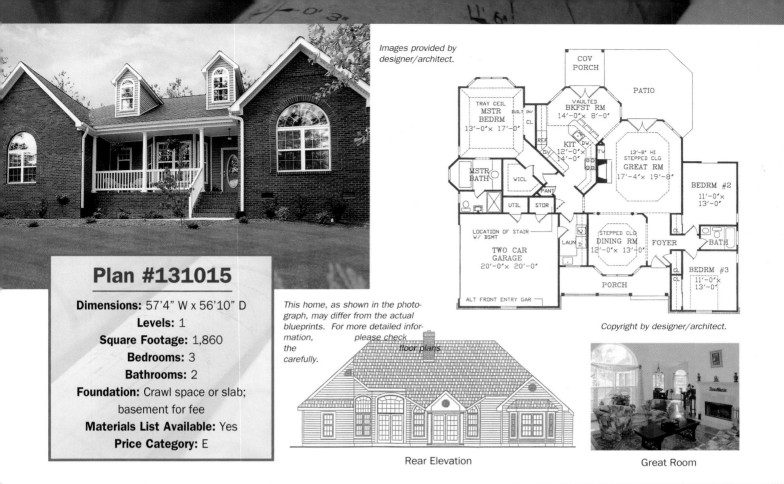

Plan #131015

Dimensions: 57'4" W x 56'10" D
Levels: 1
Square Footage: 1,860
Bedrooms: 3
Bathrooms: 2
Foundation: Crawl space or slab; basement for fee
Materials List Available: Yes
Price Category: E

This home, as shown in the photograph, may differ from the actual blueprints. For more detailed information, please check the floor plans carefully.

Rear Elevation

Great Room

COV PORCH

PATIO

TRAY CEIL MSTR BEDRM 13'-0"x 17'-0"

BUILT IN/CL

VAULTED BKFST RM 14'-0"x 8'-0"

KIT 12'-0"x 14'-0"

REF
OV
DW
TV

13'-8" HI STEPPED CLG GREAT RM 17'-4"x 19'-8"

BEDRM #2 11'-0"x 13'-0"

MSTR BATH

WICL

PANT

UTIL

STOR

LOCATION OF STAIR W/ BSMT

TWO CAR GARAGE 20'-0"x 20'-0"

LAUN

STEPPED CLG DINING RM 12'-0"x 13'-0"

FOYER

BATH

BEDRM #3 11'-0"x 13'-0"

PORCH

ALT FRONT ENTRY GAR

Plan #211006

Dimensions: 61' W x 77' D
Levels: 1
Square Footage: 2,177
Bedrooms: 3
Bathrooms: 2
Foundation: Crawl space or slab
Materials List Available: Yes
Price Category: D

SMARTtip

Deck Furniture Style

Mix-and-match tabletops, frames, and legs are stylish. Combine materials such as glass, metal, wood, and mosaic tiles.

mbr 18 x 12

sitting 11 x 10

porch 29 x 6

eating 11 x 10

living 21 x 17

br 3 12 x 12

kit 13 x 12

bar

sto 10x7

util

sto

dining 15 x 12

foy

por 11x5

br 2 15 x 12

garage 22 x 22

Plan #151011

Dimensions: 59'6" W x 74'4" D
Levels: 2
Square Footage: 3,437
Main Level Sq. Ft.: 2,184
Upper Level Sq. Ft.: 1,253
Bedrooms: 5
Bathrooms: 4
Foundation: Crawl space or slab; basement or daylight basement for fee
CompleteCost List Available: Yes
Price Category: F

Beauty, comfort, and convenience are yours in this luxurious, split-level home.

Features:

- Ceiling Height: 10 ft. unless otherwise noted.

- Master Suite: The 11-ft. pan ceiling sets the tone for this secluded area, with a lovely bay window that opens onto a rear porch, a pass-through fireplace to the great room, and a sitting room.

- Great Room: The pass-through fireplace makes this spacious room a cozy spot, while the French doors leading to a rear porch make it a perfect spot for entertaining.

- Dining Room: Gracious 8-in. columns set off the entrance to this room.

- Kitchen: An island bar provides an efficient work area that's fitted with a sink.

- Breakfast Room: Open to the kitchen, this room is defined by a bay window and a spiral staircase to the second floor.

- Laundry Room: Large enough to accommodate a folding table, this room can also be fitted with a swinging pet door.

- Play Room: French doors in the children's playroom open onto a balcony where they can continue their games.

- Bedrooms: The 9-ft. ceilings on the second story make the rooms feel bright and airy.

**Main Level
Floor Plan**

**Upper Level
Floor Plan**

Plan #321061

Dimensions: 55' W x 49'4" D
Levels: 2
Square Footage: 3,169
Main Level Sq. Ft.: 1,679
Upper Level Sq. Ft.: 1,490
Bedrooms: 4
Bathrooms: 2½
Foundation: Basement
Materials List Available: Yes
Price Category: G

Images provided by designer/architect.

This spacious home combines a truly elegant appearance with family-oriented, comfortable design elements.

Features:

• Entryway: This large area features a hand crafted stairway to the upper floor, French doors leading to the living room, and an adjacent powder room.

• Living Room: This lovely room is ideal for quiet times or lively entertaining.

• Family Room: You'll enjoy all the amenities in this large room, with its lovely bay window, handsome fireplace, and walk-in wet bar.

• Dining Area: This area is open to the living room but is visually set apart by a gracious tray ceiling.

• Study: Adjacent to the front bedroom on the main floor, this study provides a place for quiet times.

• Master Suite: Located on the second floor for privacy, this area is luxurious in every respect.

Main Level Floor Plan

Upper Level Floor Plan

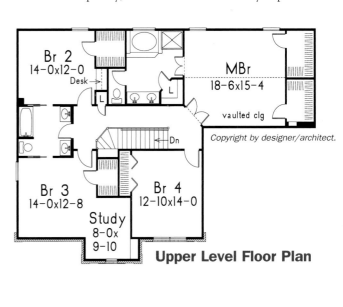

Copyright by designer/architect.

Plan #161016

Dimensions: 59'4" W x 58'8" D

Levels: 1.5

Square Footage: 2,101

Main Level Sq. Ft.: 1,626

Upper Level Sq. Ft.: 475

Bedrooms: 3

Bathrooms: 2½

Foundation: Basement; crawl space option available for fee

Materials List Available: Yes

Price Category: D

Note: Home in photo reflects a modified garage entrance.

Images provided by designer/architect.

Features:

- Great Room: Made for relaxing and entertaining, the great room is sunken to set it off from the rest of the house. A balcony from the second floor looks down into this spacious area, making it easy to keep track of the kids while they are playing.

- Kitchen: Convenience marks this well laid-out kitchen where you'll love to cook for guests and for family.

- Master Suite: A vaulted ceiling complements the unusual octagonal shape

of the master suite. Located on the first floor, this room allows some privacy from the second floor bedrooms. It is also ideal for anyone who no longer wishes to climb stairs to reach a bedroom.

Rear Elevation

You'll love the exciting roofline that sets this elegant home apart from its neighbors as well as the embellished, solid look that declares how well-designed it is—from the inside to the exterior.

CAD FILE AVAILABLE

Main Level Floor Plan

Deck

Sunken Great Room 16-10 x 21

Breakfast 9-2 x 16

Kitchen 8 x 13-4

Bath

Walk-in closet

Dining Room 16 x 11-8

Foyer

Master Bedroom 14 x 17-4

Slope ceiling

Bath

Hall

Laundry

Two-car Garage 21 x 20-8

58'-8"

59'-4"

Copyright by designer/architect.

Upper Level Floor Plan

Bedroom 15x 10-8

Great Room Below

Bath

Bedroom 14x 10-6

Foyer Below

Plan #121008

Dimensions: 62' W x 56' D
Levels: 1
Square Footage: 1,651
Bedrooms: 2
Bathrooms: 2
Foundation: Basement
Materials List Available: Yes
Price Category: C

This elegant home is packed with amenities that belie its compact size.

Features:

- Ceiling Height: 8 ft.

- Dining Room: The foyer opens into a view of the dining room, with its distinctive boxed ceiling.

- Great Room: The whole family will want to gather around the fireplace and enjoy the views and sunlight streaming through the transom-topped window.

- Breakfast Area: Next to the great room and sharing the transom-topped windows, this cozy area invites you to linger over morning coffee.

- Covered Porch: When the weather is nice, take your coffee through the door in the breakfast area and enjoy this large covered porch.

- Master Suite: French doors lead to this comfortable suite featuring a walk-in closet. Enjoy long, luxurious soaks in the corner whirlpool accented with boxed windows.

Images provided by designer/architect.

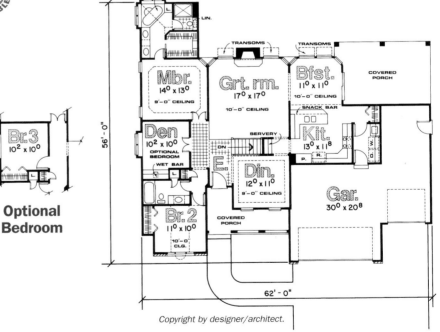

Optional Bedroom

Copyright by designer/architect.

SMARTtip

Finishing Your Fireplace with Tile

An excellent finishing material for a fireplace is tile. Luckily, there are reproductions of art tiles today. Most showrooms carry examples of Arts and Crafts, Art Nouveau, California, Delft, and other European tiles. Granite, limestone, and marble tiles are affordable alternatives to custom stone slabs.

Plan #271096

Dimensions: 66' W x 90' D
Levels: 2
Square footage: 3,190
Main Level Sq. Ft.: 2,152
Upper Level Sq. Ft.: 1,038
Bedrooms: 4
Bathrooms: 3½
Foundation: Crawl space
Materials List Available: Yes
Price Category: G

This traditional home contains quite possibly everything you're dreaming of, and even more!

Features:

- Formal Rooms: These living and dining rooms flank the entry foyer, making a large space for special occasions.

- Family Room: A fireplace is the highlight of this spacious area, where the kids will play with their friends and watch TV.

- Kitchen: A central island makes cooking a breeze. The adjoining dinette is a sunny spot for casual meals.

- Master Suite: A large sleeping area is followed by a deluxe private bath with a whirlpool tub and a walk-in closet. Step through a French door to the backyard, which is big enough to host a deck with an inviting hot tub!

- Guest Suite: One bedroom upstairs has its own private bath, making it perfect for guests.

- A future room above the garage awaits your decision on how to use it.

Main Level Floor Plan

Upper Level Floor Plan

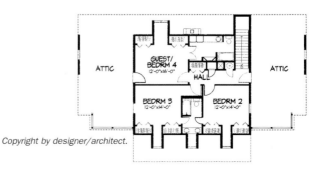

Copyright by designer/architect.

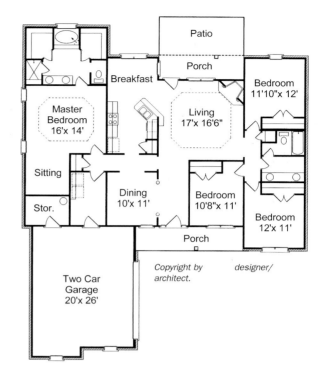

Plan #111015

Dimensions: 64' W x 58' D
Levels: 1
Square Footage: 2,208
Bedrooms: 4
Bathrooms: 2
Foundation: Slab
Materials List Available: Yes
Price Category: F

Images provided by designer/architect.

Copyright by designer/architect.

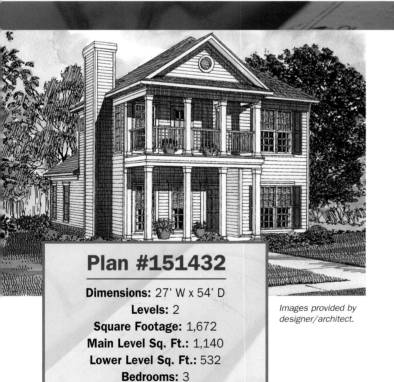

Plan #151432

Dimensions: 27' W x 54' D
Levels: 2
Square Footage: 1,672
Main Level Sq. Ft.: 1,140
Lower Level Sq. Ft.: 532
Bedrooms: 3
Bathrooms: 2½
Foundation: Crawl space or slab; basement or walkout for fee
CompleteCost List Available: Yes
Price Category: C

Images provided by designer/architect.

Main Level Floor Plan

Upper Level Floor Plan

Copyright by designer/architect.

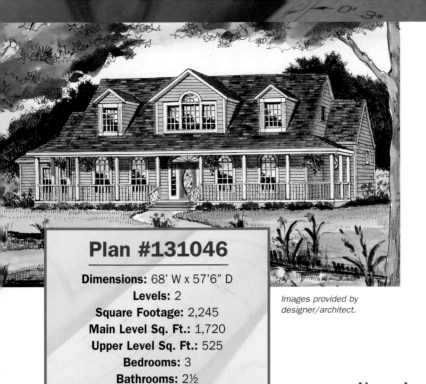

Plan #131046

Dimensions: 68' W x 57'6" D

Levels: 2

Square Footage: 2,245

Main Level Sq. Ft.: 1,720

Upper Level Sq. Ft.: 525

Bedrooms: 3

Bathrooms: 2½

Foundation: Crawl space or slab; basement for fee

Materials List Available: Yes

Price Category: F

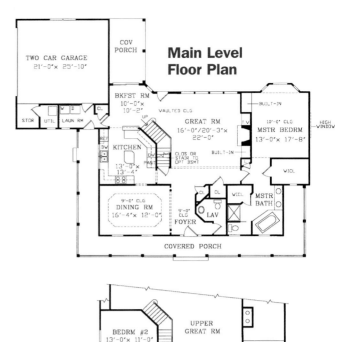

Main Level Floor Plan

Images provided by designer/architect.

Upper Level Floor Plan

Copyright by designer/architect.

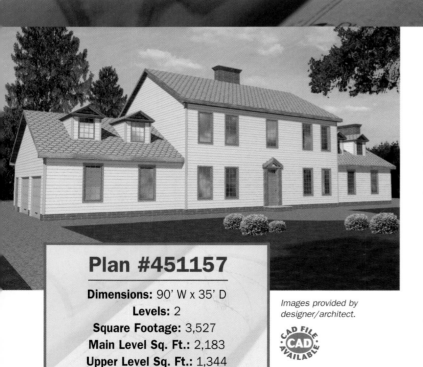

Plan #451157

Dimensions: 90' W x 35' D

Levels: 2

Square Footage: 3,527

Main Level Sq. Ft.: 2,183

Upper Level Sq. Ft.: 1,344

Bedrooms: 4

Bathrooms: 3

Foundation: Crawl space

Material List Available: Yes

Price Category: H

Images provided by designer/architect.

CAD FILE AVAILABLE

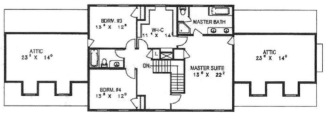

Upper Level Floor Plan

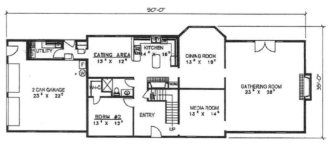

Main Level Floor Plan

Copyright by designer/architect.

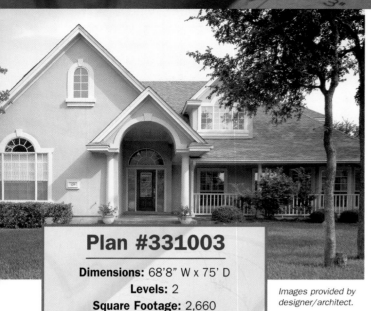

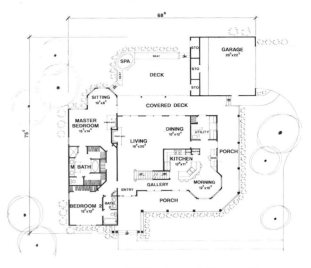

Main Level Floor Plan

Plan #331003

Dimensions: 68'8" W x 75' D

Levels: 2

Square Footage: 2,660

Main Level Sq. Ft.: 2,000

Upper Level Sq. Ft.: 660

Bedrooms: 4

Bathrooms: 3

Foundation: Crawl space, slab or basement

Materials List Available: Yes

Price Category: F

Images provided by designer/architect.

Upper Level Floor Plan

Copyright by designer/architect.

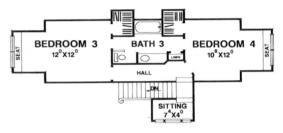

Upper Level Floor Plan

Copyright by designer/architect.

Plan #371065

Dimensions: 92'10" W x 70' D

Levels: 2

Square Footage: 3,266

Main Level Sq. Ft.: 2,313

Upper Level Sq. Ft.: 953

Bedrooms: 4

Bathrooms: 3½

Foundation: Slab

Material List Available: Yes

Price Category: G

Images provided by designer/architect.

Main Level Floor Plan

Plan #111024

Dimensions: 46'10" W x 68'5" D
Levels: 2
Square Footage: 2,356
Main Level Sq. Ft.: 1,516
Upper Level Sq. Ft.: 840
Bedrooms: 4
Bathrooms: 2½
Foundation: Slab
Materials List Available: Yes
Price Category: F

Images provided by designer/architect.

A Southern-style home with a front porch and round-top windows, this is a great place to raise a family.

Features:

- **Living Room:** This gathering area features a ceiling that is two stories tall. The cozy fireplace will add warmth to a cool night.

- **Kitchen:** This U-shape kitchen with an abundance of cabinets and counter space would be a welcome addition to any home. The raised bar, which is open to the breakfast room, adds seating space to the area.

- **Master Suite:** Located on the main level for privacy, this oasis boasts a large walk-in closet. The master bath features his and her vanities, a stall shower, and a whirlpool tub.

- **Upper Level:** Three additional bedrooms and a full bathroom occupy this level. The balcony overlooks the living room.

Main Level Floor Plan

Upper Level Floor Plan

Copyright by designer/architect.

Plan #151101

Dimensions: 87'10" W x 54'6" D
Levels: 1
Square Footage: 2,804
Bedrooms: 4
Bathrooms: 2½
Foundation: Slab; basement for fee
CompleteCost List Available: Yes
Price Category: F

Images provided by designer/architect.

This one-story home has everything you would find in a two-story house more. This home plan is keeping up with the times.

Features:

- Porches: The long covered front porch is perfect for sitting out on warm evenings and greeting passersby. The back grilling porch, which opens through French doors from the great room, is great for entertaining guests with summer barbecues.

- Utility: Accessible from outside as well as the three-car garage, this small utility room is a multipurpose space. Through the breakfast area is the unique hobby/laundry area, a room made large enough for both the wash and the family artist.

- Cooking and Eating Areas: In one straight shot, this kitchen flows into both the sunlit breakfast room and the formal dining room,

for simple transitions no matter the meal. The kitchen features tons of work and storage space, as well as a stovetop island with a seated snack bar and a second eating bar between the kitchen and breakfast room.

- Study: For bringing work home with you or simply paying the bills, this quiet study sits off the foyer through French doors.

- Master Suite: A triplet of windows allows the

morning sun to shine in on this spacious, relaxing area. The full master bath features two separate vanities, a glass shower, a whirlpool tub, and a large walk-in closet.

- Secondary Bedrooms: Two of the three bedrooms include computer centers, keeping pace with the technological times, and all three-share access to the second full bathroom, with its dual sinks and whirlpool tub.

Copyright by designer/architect.

Plan #451109

Dimensions: 90'6" W x 76' D
Levels: 1
Square Footage: 4,475
Main Level Sq. Ft.: 3,235
Basement Level Sq. Ft.: 1,240
Bedrooms: 2
Bathrooms: 2½
Foundation: Crawl space – insulated concrete form
Material List Available: Yes
Price Category: I

Images provided by designer/architect.

CAD FILE AVAILABLE

Basement Level Floor Plan

Copyright by designer/architect.

Plan #271095

Dimensions: 71' W x 75' D
Levels: 2
Square Footage: 3,220
Main Level Sq. Ft.: 2,040
Upper Level Sq. Ft.: 1,180
Bedrooms: 3
Bathrooms: 4
Foundation: Crawl space, slab
Material List Available: Yes
Price Category: G

Images provided by designer/architect.

Main Level Floor Plan

Upper Level Floor Plan

Copyright by designer/architect.

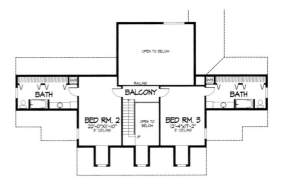

Main Level Floor Plan

GARAGE 23'-6" X 20'-0"

STORAGE

STORAGE

UTIL.

B. 2

NOOK 10'-0" X 12'-0"

PANT

RAISED BAR

FAMILY RM. 16'-0" X 18'-0"

PORCH

GLASS SHR.

10'-0" HIGH CLG.

DINING RM. 12'-0" X 13'-0"

10'-0" HIGH CLG.

KITCH. 11'-0" X 14'-0"

10'-0" HIGH CLG. BATH 1

LIN.

LIN.

STOR.

LIVING RM. 18'-0" X 13'-0"

10'-0" HIGH CLG.

ENTRY

10'-0" HIGH CLG. MASTER SUITE 18'-0" X 13'-0"

PORCH

Images provided by designer/architect.

Upper Level Floor Plan

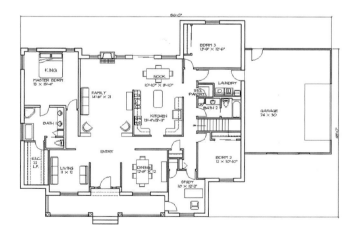

BED RM. 4 12'-6" X 13'-0"

B. 4

LIN.

OPEN ABOVE FAMILY RM.

WOOD RAIL

SHR.

B. 3

LIN.

LOFT

RETURN AIR

STAIR DOWN

BED RM. 3 18'-0" X 13'-0"

WOOD RAIL

OPEN ABOVE ENTRY

BED RM. 2 18'-6" X 13'-0"

Plan #371064

Dimensions: 63' W x 69'4" D

Levels: 2

Square Footage: 3,140

Main Level Sq. Ft.: 1,965

Upper Level Sq. Ft.: 1,175

Bedrooms: 4

Bathrooms: 3½

Foundation: Slab

Materials List Available: Yes

Price Category: G

Plan #451098

Dimensions: 86' W x 48' D

Levels: 1

Square Footage: 2,428

Bedrooms: 3

Bathrooms: 2

Foundation: Walkout – insulated concrete form

Material List Available: Yes

Price Category: E

Images provided by designer/architect.

CAD FILE AVAILABLE CAD

MASTER BDRM 15 X 19'-4"

KING

BDRM 3 13'-6" X 12'-6"

FAMILY 14'-6" X 21

NOOK 10'-10" X 9'-10"

LAUNDRY

STG. PANTRY

BATH 2

GARAGE 24 X 30

BATH

KITCHEN 15'-4" X 12'-1"

W.I.C. 7'-7" L.F.

ENTRY

LIVING 11 X 12

DINING

STUDY 10 X 12'-2"

BDRM 2 12 X 10'-10"

KING

Plan #431001

Dimensions: 58'8" W x 62' D

Levels: 1

Square Footage: 1,792

Bedrooms: 3

Bathrooms: 2½

Foundation: Crawl space or basement

Material List Available: Yes

Price Category: C-

Your neighbors will envy this Southern-style home.

Features:

- Great Room: The entry overlooks this room, where a fireplace warms gatherings on chilly evenings. A large window and French doors allow a view of the yard.

- Kitchen: The primary workstation in this kitchen is a peninsula, which faces the fireplace in the great room. The peninsula is equipped with a sink and snack counter.

- Master Suite: This private space is located on the other side of the home from the other bedrooms. It contains expansive his and her walk-in closets, a spa tub, and a double vanity area in the salon.

- Bedrooms: Two additional bedrooms are separated from the master suite. Both bedrooms have large closets and share a hall bathroom.

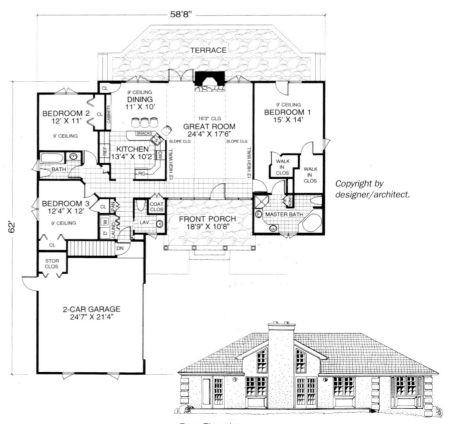

Rear Elevation

Plan #101005

Dimensions: 63' W x 57'2" D

Levels: 1

Square Footage: 1,992

Bedrooms: 3

Bathrooms: 2½

Foundation: Crawl space, slab, or basement

Materials List Available: Yes

Price Category: D

CAD FILE AVAILABLE

Images provided by designer/architect.

Rear View

This midsized ranch is accented with Palladian windows and inviting front porch.

Features:

- Ceiling Height: 9 ft. unless otherwise noted.

- Special Ceilings: Tray or vaulted ceilings adorn the living room, family room, dining room, and master suite.

- Kitchen: This bright and airy kitchen is designed to be a pleasure in which to work. It shares a big bay window with the contiguous breakfast room.

- Breakfast Room: The light streaming in from the bay window makes this the perfect place to linger with coffee and the Sunday paper.

- Master Suite: This lovely suite is exceptional, with its sitting area and direct access to the deck, as well as a full-featured bath, and spacious walk-in closet.

- Secondary Bedrooms: The other bedrooms each measure about 13 ft. x 11 ft. They have walk-in closets and share a "Jack-and-Jill" bath.

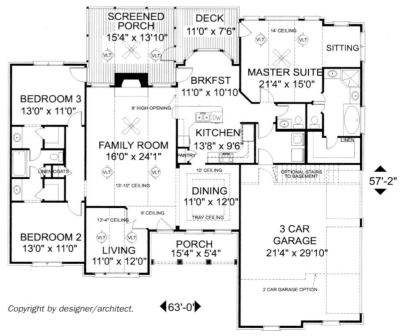

Copyright by designer/architect.

◀63'-0'▶

Plan #181652

Dimensions: 29' W x 44' D
Levels: 2
Square Footage: 1,579
Main Level Sq. Ft.: 709
Upper Level Sq. Ft.: 870
Bedrooms: 3
Bathrooms: 1½
Foundation: Basement
Material List Available: Yes
Price Category: E

This is an attractive home with an appealing Mediterranean look.

Images provided by designer/architect.

Features:

- Entry: This covered entry welcomes you home. The sidelights on the front door flood the interior with light. A coat closet and a half bath add convenience.

- Family Room: Open to the kitchen for an airy feel, this gathering area will be the place to unwind after a long day.

- Kitchen: The family chef will love this kitchen. The room contains extra seating at the island and a convenient breakfast nook. A three-panel sliding-glass door brings plenty of natural light to the area.

- Upper Level: Three bedrooms, a full bathroom, and the laundry area are located on this level.

Copyright by designer/architect.

Main Level Floor Plan

Upper Level Floor Plan

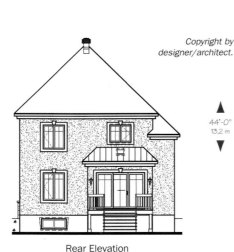

Rear Elevation

Plan #121063

Dimensions: 84' W x 52' D
Levels: 2
Square Footage: 3,473
Main Level Sq. Ft.: 2,500
Upper Level Sq. Ft.: 973
Bedrooms: 4
Bathrooms: 3½
Foundation: Basement; crawl space for fee
Materials List Available: Yes
Price Category: G

Enjoy the many amenities in this well-designed and gracious home.

Features:

- **Entry:** A large sparkling window and a tapering split staircase distinguish this lovely entryway.

- **Great Room:** This spacious great room will be the heart of your new home. It has a 14-ft. spider-beamed ceiling that serves to highlight its built-in bookcase, built-in entertainment center, raised hearth fireplace, wet bar, and lovely arched windows topped with transoms.

- **Kitchen:** Anyone who walks into this kitchen will realize that it's designed for both convenience and efficiency.

- **Master Suite:** The tiered ceiling in the bedroom gives an elegant touch, and the bay window adds to it. The two large walk-in closets and the spacious bath, with columns setting off the whirlpool tub and two vanities, complete this dream of a suite.

Main Level Floor Plan

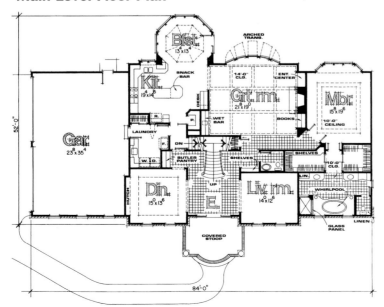

Upper Level Floor Plan

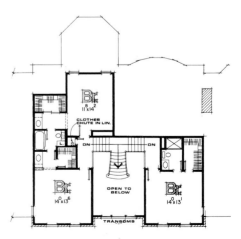

Copyright by designer/architect.

Plan #121070

Dimensions: 50' W x 58' D
Levels: 2
Square Footage: 2,139
Main Level Sq. Ft.: 1,506
Upper Level Sq. Ft.: 633
Bedrooms: 4
Bathrooms: 2½
Foundation: Basement
Materials List Available: Yes
Price Category: D

Images provided by designer/architect.

You'll love this design if you're looking for a bright, airy home where you can easily entertain.

Features:

- Entry: A volume ceiling sets the tone for this home when you first walk in.
- Great Room: With a volume ceiling extending from the entry, this great room has an open feeling. Transom-topped windows contribute natural light during the day.
- Dining Room: Because it is joined to the great room through a cased opening, this dining room can serve as an extension of the great room.
- Kitchen: An island with a snack bar, desk, and pantry make this kitchen a treat, and a door from the breakfast area leads to a private covered patio where dining will be a pleasure.

Main Level Floor Plan

Upper Level Floor Plan

Copyright by designer/architect.

Plan #311003

Dimensions: 70'10" W x 65'4" D

Levels: 2

Square Footage: 2,428

Main Level Sq. Ft.: 2,348

Upper Level Sq. Ft.: 80

Bedrooms: 3

Bathrooms: 2½

Foundation: Crawl space, slab

Materials List Available: Yes

Price Category: F

If you admire the gracious colonnaded porch, curved brick steps, and stunning front windows, you'll fall in love with the interior of this home.

Features:

- **Great Room:** Enjoy the vaulted ceiling, balcony from the upper level, and fireplace with flanking windows that let you look out to the patio.

- **Dining Room:** Columns define this formal room, which is adjacent to the breakfast room.

- **Kitchen:** A bayed sink area and extensive curved bar provide visual interest in this well-designed kitchen, which every cook will love.

- **Breakfast Room:** Huge windows let the sun shine into this room, which is open to the kitchen.

- **Master Suite:** The sitting area is open to the rear porch for a special touch in this gorgeous suite. Two walk-in closets and a vaulted ceiling and double vanity in the bath will make you feel completely pampered.

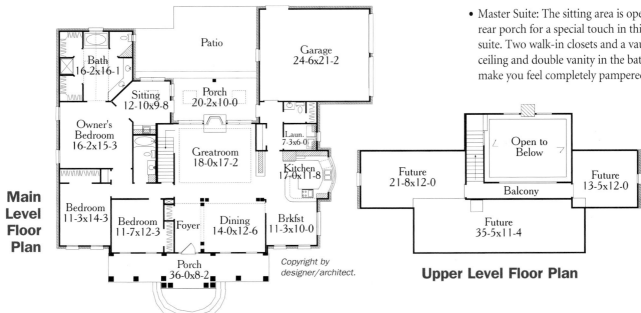

Main Level Floor Plan

Bath 16-2x16-1

Patio

Garage 24-6x21-2

Sitting 12-10x9-8

Porch 20-2x10-0

Owner's Bedroom 16-2x15-3

Greatroom 18-0x17-2

Laun. 7-3x6-0

Kitchen 17-0x11-8

Bedroom 11-3x14-3

Bedroom 11-7x12-3

Foyer

Dining 14-0x12-6

Brkfst 11-3x10-0

Porch 36-0x8-2

Copyright by designer/architect.

Upper Level Floor Plan

Future 21-8x12-0

Open to Below

Future 13-5x12-0

Balcony

Future 35-5x11-4

Plan #311058

Dimensions: 55' W x 76'4" D

Levels: 1

Square Footage: 1,702

Bedrooms: 3

Bathrooms: 2

Foundation: Crawl space, slab, or basement

Material List Available: Yes

Price Category: D

Images provided by designer/architect.

Basement Stair Location

Copyright by designer/architect.

Plan #661213

Dimensions: 77'8" W x 67' D

Levels: 2

Square Footage: 3,393

Main Level Sq. Ft.: 2,422

Upper Level Sq. Ft.: 971

Bedrooms: 5

Bathrooms: 3½

Foundation: Slab

Material List Available: Yes

Price Category: G

Images provided by designer/architect.

CAD FILE CAD AVAILABLE

Upper Level Floor Plan

Copyright by designer/architect.

Main Level Floor Plan

Plan #151850

Dimensions: 66' W x 52' D

Levels: 1

Square Footage: 2,075

Bedrooms: 4

Bathrooms: 3

Foundation: Crawl space or slab; basement or walkout for fee

CompleteCost List Available: Yes

Price Category: D

CAD FILE AVAILABLE

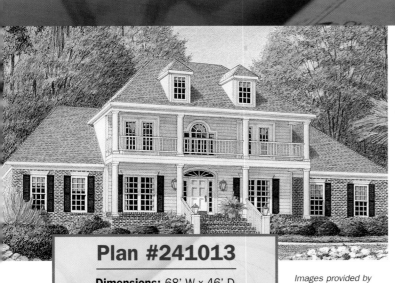

Main Level Floor Plan

Upper Level Floor Plan

Plan #241013

Dimensions: 68' W x 46' D

Levels: 2

Square Footage: 3,033

Main Level Sq. Ft.: 1,918

Upper Level Sq. Ft.: 1,115

Bedrooms: 4

Bathrooms: 3½

Foundation: Crawl space, slab, or walkout

Materials List Available: Yes

Price Category: G

Plan #271100

Dimensions: 69'10" W x 66'5" D
Levels: 2
Square Footage: 3,263
Main Level Sq. Ft.: 2,017
Upper Level Sq. Ft.: 1,246
Bedrooms: 4
Bathrooms: 2½
Foundation: Basement
Material List Available: Yes
Price Category: G

Images provided by designer/architect.

A main level master suite is just the home you have been looking for.

Features:

- **Family Room:** The cathedral ceiling and cozy fireplace strike a balance that creates the perfect gathering place for family and friends. An abundance of space allows you to tailor this room to your needs.

- **Kitchen:** Great for the busy family, this kitchen has all the workspace and storage that the family chef needs, as well as a snack bar that acts as a transition to the large dinette area.

- **Master Bedroom:** Away from the busy areas of the home, this master suite is ideal for shedding your daily cares and relaxing in a romantic atmosphere. It includes a full master bath with his and her sinks, a stall shower, and a whirlpool tub.

- **Second Floor:** Three bedrooms share the second full bathroom. The game room is also located on this level, making it the perfect entertainment area.

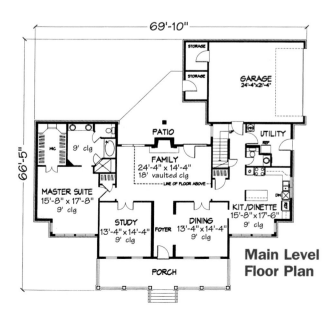

Main Level Floor Plan

Upper Level Floor Plan

Copyright by designer/architect.

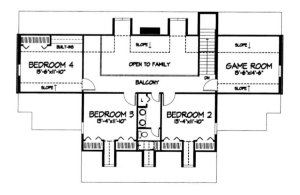

Plan #121047

Dimensions: 67'8" W x 57' D

Levels: 2

Square Footage: 3,072

Main Level Sq. Ft.: 2,116

Upper Level Sq. Ft.: 956

Bedrooms: 4

Bathrooms: 3½

Foundation: Slab; crawl space or basement for fee

Materials List Available: Yes

Price Category: G

Images provided by designer/architect.

A long porch and a trio of roof dormers give this gracious home a sophisticated country look.

Features:

- Ceiling Height: 8 ft. unless otherwise noted.
- Balcony: This balcony overlooks the entry and the staircase hall.
- Dining Room: Columns and a cased opening lend elegance, making this the perfect venue for stylish dinner parties.

- Family Room: A cathedral ceiling gives this room a light and airy feel. The handsome fireplace framed by windows is sure to become a favorite family gathering place.
- Master Suite: This architecturally distinctive suite features a bayed sitting area and a tray ceiling.
- Bedrooms: One of the bedrooms enjoys a private bath, making it a perfect guest room. Other bedrooms feature walk-in closets.

Main Level Floor Plan

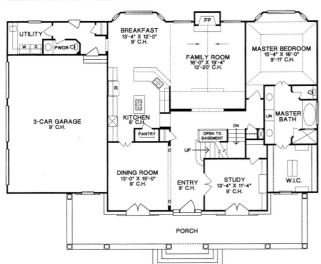

Upper Level Floor Plan

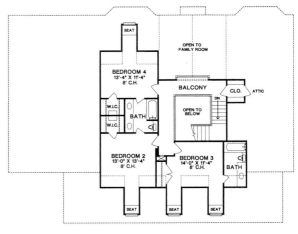

Copyright by designer/architect.

Plan #101006

Dimensions: 63' W x 58' D
Levels: 1
Square Footage: 1,982
Bedrooms: 3
Bathrooms: 2½
Foundation: Crawl space, slab basement, or walkout
Materials List Available: Yes
Price Category: D

SMARTtip

Art in Pools

The tiled walls and floor of a pool make great canvases for art, so incorporate a serious or whimsical design. Also, make the stairs wide and shallow to form a wading area for kids.

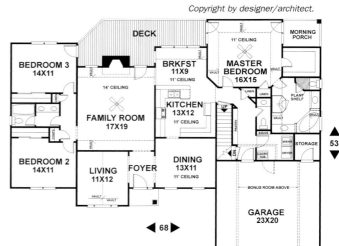

Plan #101008

Dimensions: 68' W x 53' D
Levels: 1
Square Footage: 2,088
Bedrooms: 3
Bathrooms: 2½
Foundation: Crawl space, slab, or basement
Materials List Available: Yes
Price Category: E

SMARTtip

Accentuating Your Bathroom with Details

No matter how big or small the room, details will pull the style together. Some of the best details that you can include are the smallest—drawer pulls from an antique store or shells in a glass jar or just left on the countertop. Add period flavor with crown molding, or dress up contemporary fixtures with polished stone fittings.

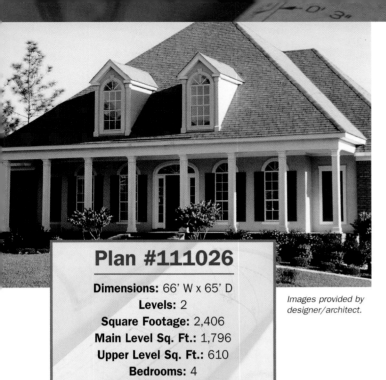

Plan #111026

Dimensions: 66' W x 65' D
Levels: 2
Square Footage: 2,406
Main Level Sq. Ft.: 1,796
Upper Level Sq. Ft.: 610
Bedrooms: 4
Bathrooms: 3½
Foundation: Crawlspace
Materials List Available: Yes
Price Category: F

Images provided by designer/architect.

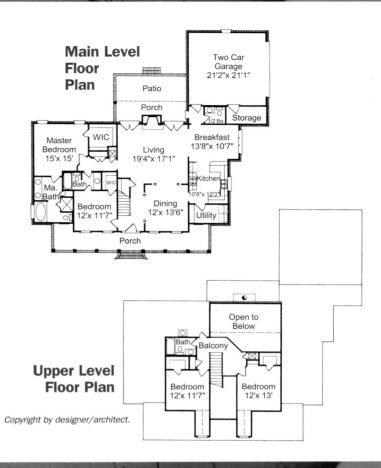

Main Level Floor Plan

Two Car Garage 21'2"x 21'1"

Patio
Porch
½ Ba
Storage

Master Bedroom 15'x 15'
WIC
Living 19'4"x 17'1"
Breakfast 13'8"x 10'7"

Bath
WIC
Kitchen 10'8"x 12'3"

Ma. Bath
Bedroom 12'x 11'7"
Dining 12'x 13'6"

Utility

Porch

Upper Level Floor Plan

Open to Below
Bath
Balcony
Bedroom 12'x 11'7"
Bedroom 12'x 13'

Copyright by designer/architect.

Plan #351104

Dimensions: 84' W x 67'10" D
Levels: 1
Square Footage: 2,755
Bedrooms: 4
Bathrooms: 3½
Foundation: Crawl space or slab
Material List Available: Yes
Price Category: G

Images provided by designer/architect.

CAD FILE AVAILABLE

Bonus Area Floor Plan

STOR.
ATTIC ACCESS
UNFINISHED BONUS ROOM 18'-8" X 18'-0" (CLEAR) 8'-0" C.H.
SLOPED CLG.

Copyright by designer/architect.

Main Level Floor Plan

MASTER BEDROOM 14-6 X 17-6
MASTER BATH 17-4 9-2
JET TUB
LIN.
CLOS. 6-8 X 8
CLOS. 10-4 X 8
OPEN STORAGE

BEDROOM 4 14-0 X 11-6 9-0 C.H.
DESK
CLOSET
COVERED PORCH 20-8 X 10-10
HALL
BREAKFAST 13-8 X 15-2 9-0 C.H.
HALF BATH
ENTRY 8-2 X 6-4
DESK
THREE CAR GARAGE 23-8 X 35-0

BATH 9-10 X 5-6
C
HALL
TV SPACE
VAULT
GREAT ROOM 20-0 X 17-6 (CLEAR)
VAULT
KITCHEN 16-0 X 13-2 9-0 C.H.
DW
MUD ROOM
MASTER BEDROOM

BATH 12-2 X 5-8
GAS LOGS
RANGE/ELEV.
REF.
PAN.
OVEN
STORAGE 5-10 X 9-2

CLOSET
BEDROOM 3 12-2 X 11-6 9-0 C.H.
BEDROOM 2 11-6 X 12-0 9-0 C.H.
FOYER 6-0 X 12-0
DINING OR STUDY 11-6 X 12-0 9-0 C.H.
LAUN. 14-4 X 8-0
BR

COVERED PORCH 35-0 X 6-0

Images provided by designer/architect.

Copyright by designer/architect.

Plan #151841

Dimensions: 53'8" W x 64'8" D

Levels: 1

Square Footage: 1,747

Bedrooms: 3

Bathrooms: 2

Foundation: Crawl space or slab; basement or walkout for fee

CompleteCost List Available: Yes

Price Category: C

Images provided by designer/architect.

Copyright by designer/architect.

Plan #101009

Dimensions: 70'2" W x 59' D

Levels: 1

Square Footage: 2,097

Bedrooms: 3

Bathrooms: 3

Foundation: Crawl space, slab, or basement

Materials List Available: Yes

Price Category: E

SMARTtip

Single-Level Decks

A single-level deck can use a strong vertical element, such as a pergola or a gazebo, to make it interesting. A simple and less-expensive option is a potted conical shrub or a clematis growing on a trellis.

Plan #131001

Dimensions: 72'4" W x 32'4" D
Levels: 1
Square Footage: 1,615
Bedrooms: 3
Bathrooms: 2
Foundation: Crawl space or slab;
basement or walkout for fee
Materials List Available: Yes
Price Category: D

Images provided by designer/architect.

Copyright by designer/architect.

Plan #151014

Dimensions: 70'2" W x 51'4" D
Levels: 1.5
Square Footage: 2,698
Main Level Sq. Ft.: 1,813
Upper Level Sq. Ft.: 885
Bedrooms: 5
Bathrooms: 3
Foundation: Crawl space or slab;
basement or walkout for fee
CompleteCost List Available: Yes
Price Category: F

Images provided by designer/architect.

Main Level Floor Plan

Upper Level Floor Plan

Copyright by designer/architect.

Plan #211076

Dimensions: 95' W x 90' D
Levels: 2
Square Footage: 4,242
Main Level Sq. Ft.: 3,439
Upper Level Sq. Ft.: 803
Bedrooms: 4
Bathrooms: 4 full, 3 half
Foundation: Raised slab
Materials List Available: Yes
Price Category: I

Images provided by designer/architect.

Build this country manor home on a large lot with a breathtaking view to complement its beauty.

Features:

- Foyer: You'll love the two-story ceiling here.
- Living Room: A sunken floor, two-story ceiling, large fireplace, and generous balcony above combine to create an unusually beautiful room.
- Kitchen: Use the breakfast bar at any time of the day. The layout guarantees ample working space, and the pantry gives room for extra storage.

- Master Suite: A sunken floor, wood-burning fireplace, and 200-sq.-ft. sitting area work in concert to create a restful space.
- Bedrooms: The guest room is on the main floor, and bedrooms 2 and 3, both with built-in desks in special study areas, are on the upper level.
- Outdoor Grilling Area: Fitted with a bar, this area makes it a pleasure to host a large group.

Kitchen

Kitchen

Main Level Floor Plan

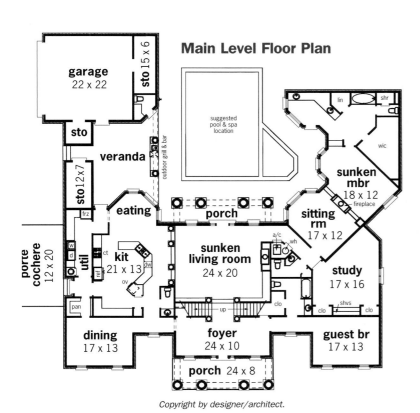

- garage 22 x 22
- sto 15 x 6
- sto
- sto 12 x 7
- veranda
- outdoor grill & bar
- suggested pool & spa location
- eating
- porch
- lin
- shr
- wic
- sunken mbr 18 x 12
- fireplace
- sitting rm 17 x 12
- porte cochere 12 x 20
- util
- kit 21 x 13
- frz
- ct
- ref
- ov
- dw
- pan
- a/c
- wh
- sunken living room 24 x 20
- study 17 x 16
- shvs
- clo
- up
- clo
- clo
- dining 17 x 13
- foyer 24 x 10
- guest br 17 x 13
- porch 24 x 8

Copyright by designer/architect.

Master Bathroom

Upper Level Floor Plan

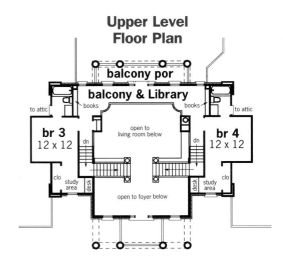

- balcony por
- balcony & Library
- to attic
- books
- books
- to attic
- br 3 12 x 12
- open to living room below
- dn
- dn
- br 4 12 x 12
- clo
- study area
- desk
- open to foyer below
- desk
- study area
- clo

Dining Room

Living Room

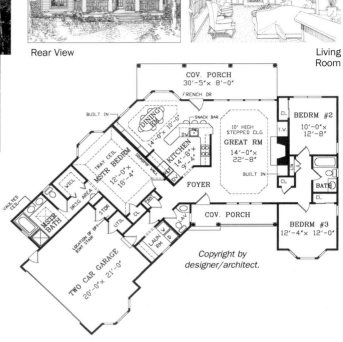

Rear View

Living Room

Plan #131002

Dimensions: 70'1" W x 60'7" D

Levels: 1

Square Footage: 1,709

Bedrooms: 3

Bathrooms: 2½

Foundation: Crawl space or slab; basement or walkout for fee

Materials List Available: Yes

Price Category: D

Images provided by designer/architect.

CAD FILE AVAILABLE

Copyright by designer/architect.

Plan #151015

Dimensions: 72'4" W x 48'4" D

Levels: 2

Square Footage: 2,810

Main Level Sq. Ft.: 2,008

Upper Level Sq. Ft.: 802

Bedrooms: 4

Bathrooms: 3

Foundation: Crawl space or slab; basement or walkout for fee

CompleteCost List Available: Yes

Price Category: G

Images provided by designer/architect.

CAD FILE AVAILABLE

Main Level Floor Plan

Upper Level Floor Plan

Copyright by designer/architect.

Plan #131017

Dimensions: 69'8" W x 39'4" D
Levels: 1
Square Footage: 1,480
Bedrooms: 3
Bathrooms: 2
Foundation: Crawl space or slab; basement for fee
Materials List Available: Yes
Price Category: C

Images provided by designer/architect.

Alternate Floor Plan

Part Plan with Optional Basement

Rear Elevation

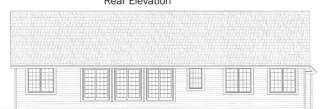

Copyright by designer/architect.

Plan #101022

Dimensions: 66'2" W x 62' D
Levels: 1
Square Footage: 1,992
Bedrooms: 3
Bathrooms: 3
Foundation: Crawl space, slab, or basement
Materials List Available: Yes
Price Category: D

Images provided by designer/architect.

CAD FILE AVAILABLE

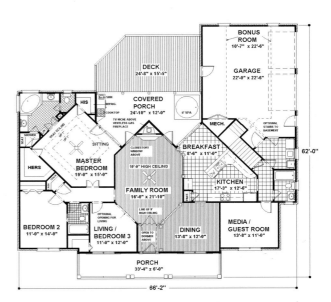

Copyright by designer/architect.

Plan #211127

Dimensions: 94' W x 71' D

Levels: 2

Square Footage: 5,474

Main Level Sq. Ft.: 4,193

Upper Level Sq. Ft.: 1,281

Bedrooms: 4

Bathrooms: 4 full, 2 half

Foundation: Slab; crawl space or walkout for fee

Materials List Available: Yes

Price Category: I

This is a truly grand southern-style home, with stately columns and eye-pleasing symmetry.

Features:

- Ceiling Height: 12 ft.

- Foyer: A grand home warrants a grand entry, and here it is. The graceful curved staircase will impress your guests as they move from this foyer to the fireplace.

- Family Room: Great for entertaining, this family room features a vaulted ceiling. A handsome fireplace adds warmth and ambiance.

- Den: Another fireplace enhances this smaller and cozier den. Here the kids can play, supervised by the family chef working in the adjacent kitchen.

- Verandas: As is fitting for a gracious southern home, you'll find verandas at front and rear.

- Master Suite: A romantic third fireplace is found in this sprawling master bedroom. The master bath provides the utmost in privacy and organization.

Main Level Floor Plan

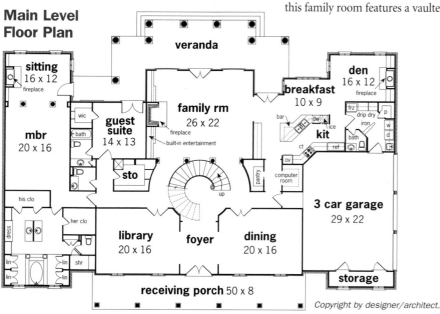

Upper Level Floor Plan

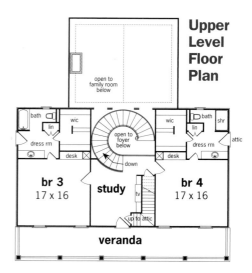

Plan #271030

Dimensions: 55'8" W x 45' D
Levels: 2
Square Footage: 1,926
Main Level Sq. Ft.: 1,490
Upper Level Sq. Ft.: 436
Bedrooms: 3
Bathrooms: 2½
Foundation: Basement or crawl space
Materials List Available: Yes
Price Category: D

Images provided by designer/architect.

This traditional home's main-floor master suite is hard to resist, with its inviting window seat and delightful bath.

Features:

• Master Suite: Just off from the entry foyer, this luxurious oasis is entered through double doors, and offers an airy vaulted ceiling, plus a private bath that includes a separate tub and shower, dual-sink vanity, and walk-in closet.

• Great Room: This space does it all in style, with a breathtaking wall of windows and a charming fireplace.

• Kitchen: A cooktop island makes dinnertime tasks a breeze. You'll also love the roomy pantry. The adjoining breakfast room, with its deck access and built-in desk, is sure to be a popular hangout for the teens.

• Secondary Bedrooms: Two additional bedrooms reside on the upper floor and allow the younger family members a measure of desired—and necessary—privacy.

CAD FILE AVAILABLE

Main Level Floor Plan

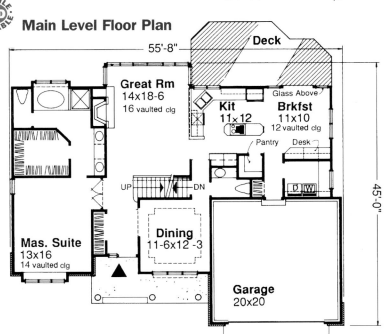

Upper Level Floor Plan

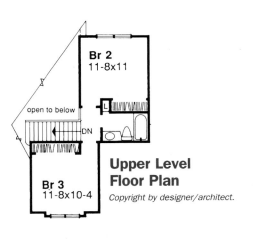

Copyright by designer/architect.

Plan #101004

Dimensions: 55'8" W x 56'6" D

Levels: 1

Square Footage: 1,787

Bedrooms: 3

Bathrooms: 2

Foundation: Crawl space, slab, or basement

Materials List Available: Yes

Price Category: D

This carefully designed ranch provides the feel and features of a much larger home.

Features:

- Ceiling Height: 9 ft. unless otherwise noted.

- Entry: Guests will step up onto the inviting front porch and into this entry, with its impressive 11-ft. ceiling.

- Dining Room: Open to the entry and to its left is this elegant dining room, perfect for entertaining or informal family gatherings.

- Family Room: This family gathering place features an 11-ft. ceiling to enhance its sense of spaciousness.

- Kitchen: This intelligently designed kitchen has an open plan. A breakfast bar and a serving bar are features that add to its convenience.

- Master Suite: This suite is loaded with amenities, including a double-step tray ceiling, direct access to the screened porch, a sitting room, deluxe bath, and his and her walk-in closets.

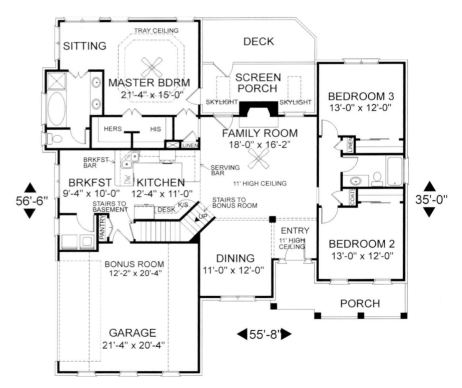

Copyright by designer/architect.

Plan #161101

Dimensions: 136'3" W x 69' D
Levels: 2
Square Footage: 6,209
Main Level Sq. Ft.: 4,011
Upper Level Sq. Ft.: 2,198
Optional Lower Level Sq. Ft.: 2,205
Bedrooms: 4
Bathrooms: 4 full, 2 half
Foundation: Walkout; basement for fee
Material List Available: Yes
Price Category: K

The grandeur of this mansion-style home boasts period stone, two-story columns, an angular turret, a second-floor balcony, and a gated courtyard.

Features:

• Formal Living: Formal areas consist of the charming living room and adjacent music room, which continues to the library, with its sloped ceilings and glass surround. Various ceiling treatments, with 10-ft. ceiling heights, and 8-ft.-tall doors add luxury and artistry to the first floor.

• Hearth Room: This large room, with false wood-beamed ceiling, adds a casual yet rich atmosphere to the family gathering space. Dual French doors on each side of the fireplace create a pleasurable indoor-outdoor relationship.

• Kitchen: This space is an enviable work place for the gourmet cook. Multiple cabinets and expansive counter space create a room that may find you spending a surprisingly enjoyable amount of time on food preparation. The built-in grill on the porch makes outdoor entertaining convenient and fun.

• Master Suite: This suite offers a vaulted ceiling, dual walk-in closets, and his and her vanities. The whirlpool tub is showcased on a platform and surrounded by windows for a relaxing view of the side yard. Private access to the deck is an enchanting surprise.

Rear View

Main Level Floor Plan

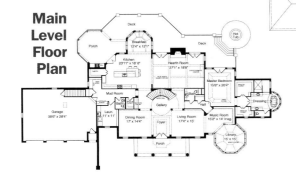

Upper Level Floor Plan

Optional Lower Level Floor Plan

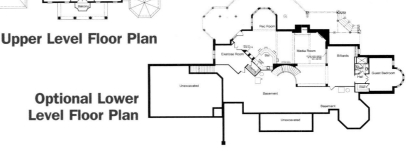

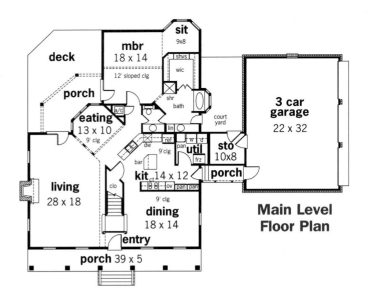

Plan #211071

Dimensions: 72' W x 58' D
Levels: 2
Square Footage: 2,888
Main Level Sq. Ft.: 1,768
Upper Level Sq. Ft.: 1,120
Bedrooms: 4
Bathrooms: 3½
Foundation: Crawl space;slab for fee
Materials List Available: Yes
Price Category: F

Images provided by designer/architect.

Main Level Floor Plan

Upper Level Floor Plan

Copyright by designer/architect.

Plan #151822

Dimensions: 108'10" W x 73'10" D
Levels: 1
Square Footage: 3,602
Bedrooms: 4
Bathrooms: 3½
Foundation: Crawl space or slab; basement or walkout for fee
CompleteCost List Available: Yes
Price Category: G

Images provided by designer/architect.

Copyright by designer/architect.

Plan #281029

Dimensions: 48' W x 59' D

Levels: 1

Square Footage: 1,833

Bedrooms: 3

Bathrooms: 2

Foundation: Basement

Materials List Available: Yes

Price Category: D

Images provided by designer/architect.

Copyright by designer/architect.

Rear Elevation

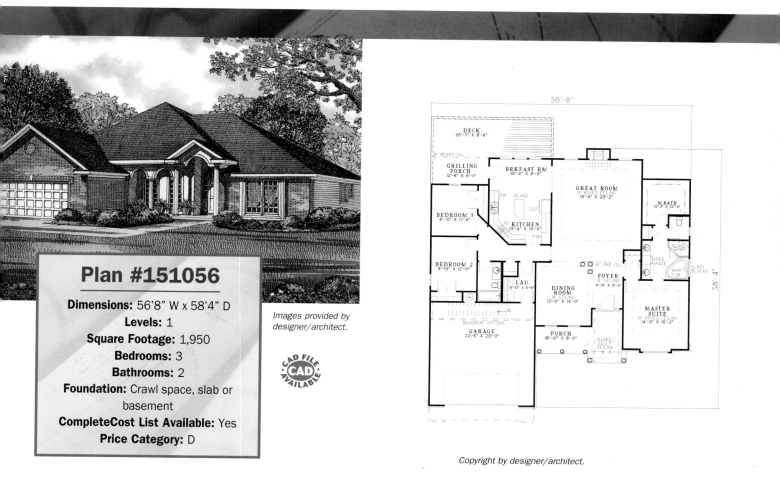

Plan #151056

Dimensions: 56'8" W x 58'4" D

Levels: 1

Square Footage: 1,950

Bedrooms: 3

Bathrooms: 2

Foundation: Crawl space, slab or basement

CompleteCost List Available: Yes

Price Category: D

Images provided by designer/architect.

CAD FILE AVAILABLE

Copyright by designer/architect.

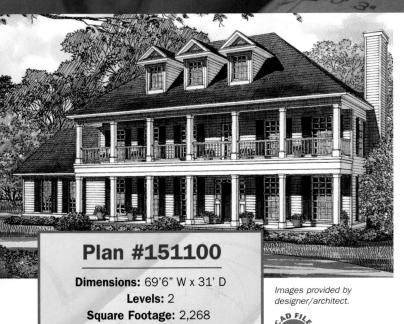

Upper Level Floor Plan

Copyright by designer/architect.

Images provided by designer/architect.

CAD FILE AVAILABLE

Main Level Floor Plan

Plan #151100

Dimensions: 69'6" W x 31' D
Levels: 2
Square Footage: 2,268
Main Level Sq. Ft.: 1,168
Upper Level Sq. Ft.: 1,100
Bedrooms: 3
Bathrooms: 2½
Foundation: Crawl space or slab; basement or walkout for fee
CompleteCost List Available: Yes
Price Category: E

Copyright by designer/architect.

Images provided by designer/architect.

CAD FILE AVAILABLE

Plan #101011

Dimensions: 71'2" W x 58'1" D
Levels: 1
Square Footage: 2,184
Bedrooms: 3
Bathrooms: 3
Foundation: Crawl space, slab, basement, or walkout
Materials List Available: Yes
Price Category: E

Kitchen

Plan #131004

Dimensions: 59'4" W x 35'8" D
Levels: 1
Square Footage: 1,097
Bedrooms: 3
Bathrooms: 2
Foundation: Crawl space or slab; basement or walkout for fee
Materials List Available: Yes
Price Category: B

Images provided by designer/architect.

This home, as shown in the photograph, may differ from the actual blueprints. For more detailed information, please check the floor plans carefully.

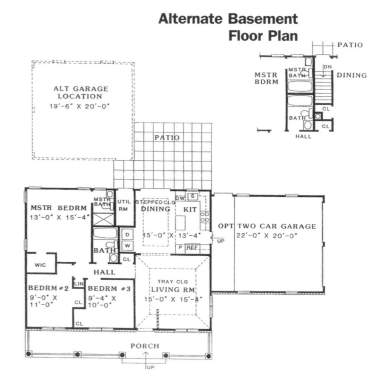

Alternate Basement Floor Plan

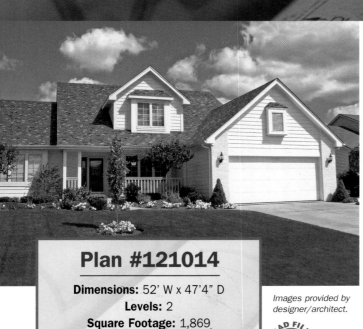

Plan #121014

Dimensions: 52' W x 47'4" D
Levels: 2
Square Footage: 1,869
Main Level Sq. Ft.: 1,421
Upper Level Sq. Ft.: 448
Bedrooms: 3
Bathrooms: 2½
Foundation: Basement, crawl space and slab for fee
Materials List Available: Yes
Price Category: D

Images provided by designer/architect.

CAD FILE AVAILABLE

Upper Level Floor Plan

Main Level Floor Plan

Copyright by designer/architect.

Plan #291016

Dimensions: 69'9" W x 58'3" D
Levels: 2
Square Footage: 2,721
Main Level Sq. Ft.: 1,447
Upper Level Sq. Ft.: 1,274
Bedrooms: 3
Bathrooms: 2½
Foundation: Basement
Materials List Available: Yes
Price Category: F

Images provided by designer/architect.

This fine example of Greek revival architecture begs to be visited!

Features:

- **Entry:** This area is the central hub of the home, with access to the kitchen, dining room, office, and upper level. There are two coat closets here.

- **Living Room:** This gathering area features

a cozy fireplace and has access to the rear sunroom.

- **Kitchen:** Generous in size, this family-oriented kitchen has an informal dining area and a morning room that has access to the rear deck.

- **Upper Level:** Located upstairs are two secondary bedrooms that share the hall bathroom. The master suite, also on this level, features a private bath and a large walk-in closet.

Rear View

Copyright by designer/architect.

Upper Level Floor Plan

Main Level Floor Plan

Plan #121076

Dimensions: 64' W x 60'8" D
Levels: 2
Square Footage: 3,067
Main Level Sq. Ft.: 2,169
Upper Level Sq. Ft.: 898
Bedrooms: 4
Bathrooms: 3½
Foundation: Basement
Materials List Available: Yes
Price Category: G

Images provided by designer/architect.

You'll love the combination of formal features and casual, family-friendly areas in this spacious home with an elegant exterior.

Features:

• Entry: The elegant windows in this two-story area are complemented by the unusual staircase.

• Family Room: This family room features an 11-ft. ceiling, wet bar, fireplace, and trio of windows that look out to the covered porch.

• Living Room: Columns set off both this room and the dining room. Decorate to accentuate their formality, or make them blend into a more casual atmosphere.

• Master Suite: Columns in this suite highlight a bayed sitting room where you'll be happy to relax at the end of the day or on weekend mornings.

• Bedrooms: Bedroom 2 has a private bath, making it an ideal guest room, and you'll find private vanities in bedrooms 3 and 4.

Main Level Floor Plan

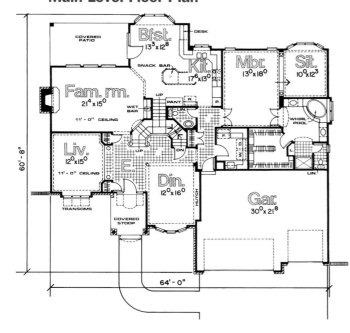

Upper Level Floor Plan

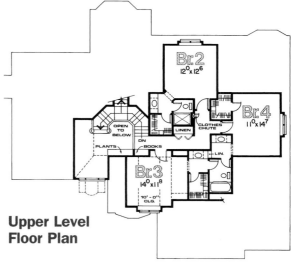

Copyright by designer/architect.

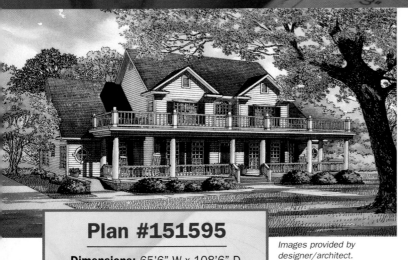

Plan #151595

Dimensions: 65'6" W x 108'6" D
Levels: 2
Square Footage: 3,820
Main Level Sq. Ft.: 2,484
Upper Level Sq. Ft.: 1,336
Bedrooms: 4
Bathrooms: 3½
Foundation: Crawl space, slab
CompleteCost List Available: Yes
Price Category: H

Images provided by designer/architect.

CAD FILE AVAILABLE

Main Level Floor Plan

Upper Level Floor Plan

Copyright by designer/architect.

Plan #101013

Dimensions: 72' W x 66' D
Levels: 1
Square Footage: 2,564
Bedrooms: 3
Bathrooms: 2½
Foundation: Walkout; crawl space, slab or basement for fee
Materials List Available: Yes
Price Category: F

Images provided by designer/architect.

CAD FILE AVAILABLE

Master Bedroom

Copyright by designer/architect.

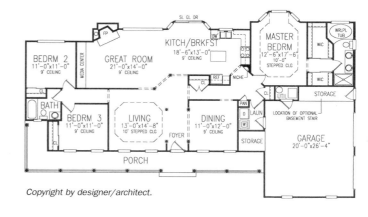

Images provided by designer/architect.

Plan #131016

Dimensions: 75' W x 45' D
Levels: 1
Square Footage: 1,902
Bedrooms: 3
Bathrooms: 2
Foundation: Crawl space or slab; basement for fee
Materials List Available: Yes
Price Category: E

Great Room

Plan #641006

Dimensions: 66' W x 32' D
Levels: 1
Square Footage: 1,232
Bedrooms: 2
Bathrooms: 2
Foundation: Basement; crawl space, slab or walkout for fee
Materials List Available: Yes
Price Category: C

Images provided by designer/architect.

Living Room

Plan #271099

Dimensions: 71' W x 74'2" D
Levels: 2
Square Footage: 2,949
Main Level Sq. Ft.: 2,000
Upper Level Sq. Ft.: 949
Bedrooms: 3
Bathrooms: 2½
Foundation: Crawl space
CompleteCost List Available: Yes
Price Category: F

Gracious symmetry highlights the lovely facade of this traditional two-story home.

Features:

• Foyer: With a high ceiling and a curved staircase, this foyer gives a warm welcome to arriving guests.

• Family Room: At the center of the home, this room will host gatherings of all kinds. A fireplace adds just the right touch.

• Kitchen: An expansive island with a cooktop anchors this space, which easily serves the adjoining nook and the nearby dining room.

• Master Suite: A cozy sitting room with a fireplace is certainly the highlight here. The private bath is also amazing, with its whirlpool tub, separate shower, dual vanities, and walk-in closet.

• Bonus Room: This generous space above the garage could serve as an art studio or as a place for your teenagers to play their electric guitars.

Main Level Floor Plan

Upper Level Floor Plan

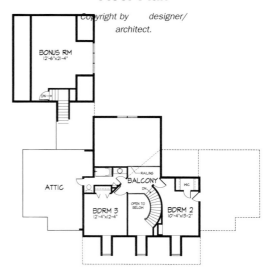

Plan #271047

Dimensions: 68' W x 47' D
Levels: 2
Square Footage: 2,729
Main Level Sq. Ft.: 1,778
Upper Level Sq. Ft.: 951
Bedrooms: 4
Bathrooms: 2½
Foundation: Basement
Materials List Available: Yes
Price Category: F

Constructed with materials chosen with your health in mind, this two-story home promises to pamper your body and soul.

Features:

• Great Room: Not only does this room host a media nook and a two-story ceiling, it also includes a sealed gas fireplace for zero emissions.

• Kitchen: Here, cultured-marble countertops replace traditional pressed-wood and laminate.

• Kitchen: Master Suite: Here's a lovely retreat. A tray ceiling, cavernous walk-in closet, and private bath are just the beginning.

• Air Safety: A radon-detection ystem and exhaust fan in the garage help to eliminate airborne irritants. Tile floors replace carpet in much of the home, too.

CAD FILE AVAILABLE

Main Level Floor Plan

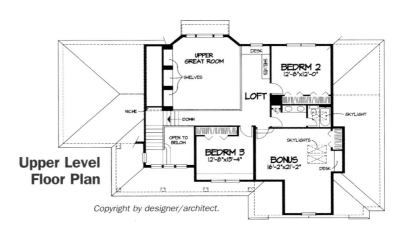

Upper Level Floor Plan

Stone and Water Features

Combining water and stone in landscape design has been popular for millennia. The sight and sound of water imparts feelings of calm, luxury, and rejuvenation no matter how modest or grand your water feature may be. Deciding on the installation that best suits your needs depends upon your local climate, your budget, and your overall landscape design plan. Ultimately, whether you select a simple stone bowl or a formal fountain, a stone and water feature is guaranteed to enhance your outdoor enjoyment.

Water Features

Small water features are relatively inexpensive and easy to install, yet they can have a big impact on the landscape. You can install water bowls and low-flow, gravity-fed fountains and other features virtually anywhere. Water features that rely on pumps also provide an environment for water-loving plants that would otherwise be impossible to maintain.

Circulating pump kits available at home and garden centers make the installation of water features such as streams, ponds, and waterfalls relatively straightforward. Some kits offer the option to combine features, such as a pond with a fountain or a waterfall with a stream.

Carving a Water Bowl

A stone water bowl provides a sculptural feature adaptable to any type of garden. You can use it as a prominent focal point or tuck one in an unexpected place for surprise, texture, or as part of a smaller composition within a larger design. Whether it is polished or rough, geometric or freeform, a bowl of water entices the viewer with a natural show created by the play of light, shadow, depth, and reflection.

Carving a water bowl need not take a lot of time. There is no need to buy expensive specialized equipment—though renting certain professional-grade tools will make the work go along more quickly.

If you want to create a polished surface on the bowl, you will need sophisticated equipment. For this look, consider carving out the bowl yourself and having a stone sculptor polish it.

To create a quick garden accessory, fill an old birdbath with rounded river stones, top.

Use large stones to secure the liner of a man-made pond or to enhance a natural pond or stream, above.

Find Your Stone

Some types of stone are easier to carve than others. A stone with distinct layers is not recommended for carving because it tends to split and break up too easily. Sandstone and limestone are softer and require less muscle to carve than metamorphic rock, such as marble. A more homogeneous stone presents fewer carving challenges in terms of predictability, hence the popularity of marble for carving.

Natural Indentations. Natural or blasted rock that already has an indentation will reduce the amount of time it will take to carve out a basin shape. If you have a circular saw with a masonry blade, a right-angle grinder, and a few good chisels (and your arms are up to the task), you can carve out a 12-inch-diameter by 5-inch-deep basin in an afternoon.

Examine the Stone

Examine your stone for fractures, and note their location in relation to where you will carve out the basin. To check for fractures, thoroughly wet the stone and let it air dry. Fractures will show up as wet lines after the overall surface of the stone has dried. The presence of fractures does mean an increased risk of having the stone break apart while you are working on it. But you can still use it. For best results, carve out small pieces of stone, and calculate the direction and impact as you carve to minimize stress on a fracture line.

Even if your stone has no obvious fractures on the outer surface, it may have some hidden ones. Frequently examine the area where you are working for cracks. An attentive work habit will more likely result in a finished bowl instead of a pile of rubble.

Carving the Bowl

1. Cut pie-shaped wedges using a circular saw with masonry blade, or hammer and chisel.

2. Use the hammer and chisel to remove small sections of stone. Work on small sections to maintain control.

3. You have the option of leaving the surface rough or using a grinder to achieve a smoother surface.

Choosing a Chisel and Hammer

Use a pointed chisel if the stone is soft. For working hard stone, a 1-inch blunt or flat chisel is a good all-purpose size. If your chisel does not have a carbide edge, sharpen it often as you work. If you are unsure about the hardness of your stone and the type of chisel to use, experiment with both. After a little practice, it will become obvious which one is best.

A 2- or 2½-pound sledgehammer is a typical size for this kind of carving. Hammer technology has changed significantly in the last 10 years, so it may make sense to shop for a new one for your carving project. In general, any tool that works for concrete will work well on soft stone.

Rough-out the Bowl

Outline the shape for the top rim of the basin with a nail, graphite, chalk, or a felt tip marker. Holding the chisel at about a 45-degree angle, make a ¼- to ½-inch-deep groove along the outline.

Cut in Sections. Cut pie-shaped sections no more than every 1½ inches using a circular saw with a masonry blade or a chisel and hammer. The smaller you make the pie sections, the easier it is to even out the surface of the basin. Also, the larger the piece you try to remove, the less control you have.

Starting at the rim of the bowl, place your chisel in one of the cuts and hit the opposite end of the chisel with the hammer to remove pieces of stone. Work your way around the rim of the basin; then gradually work toward the center. After you have removed all the stone to the depth of the cuts, again divide the area to be carved into pie-shaped sections and carve out (pitch) the stone you want to remove. Continue in this manner until the bowl is roughly the depth and shape you want.

Finishing the Bowl

After the bowl is roughed out, continue to remove stone in smaller pieces to smooth out the surface. At some point, you will have to decide how smooth you want the surface to be, and what kind of lip or edge you want the bowl to have. The bowl shown in the photos on the opposite page has a crisp edge determined by the original layout. You can round this edge to varying degrees by working it down with your chisel and hammer. You can tool and finish the surface of your bowl in a number of ways, from rough to highly polished. The tools you have available to you and the type of stone with which you're working will determine in part how you finish the bowl.

To achieve a softer, less angular finish, smooth out the surface with a low-grit grinding wheel attachment on a right-angle grinder. (Consider renting a heavy duty professional-grade grinder for large projects.) Soft stone can be worked dry, or wet, which keeps the stone dust to a minimum.

Maintaining the Water Bowl

Because the water in a bowl is stagnant, you will need to change it occasionally. If unwanted moss or lichen grow on the bowl, remove it with a brush. No soap is needed. Use a soft-bristled brush on soft stone.

In climates with below-freezing temperatures, empty water bowls in the fall to reduce the risk of fracturing the stone from freezing water. Tip the bowl upside down; cover it with a tarp; or cover the basin with a piece of plywood to keep out snow and rain.

This carved water bowl serves as a destination in this backyard garden, top.

Carved water bowls are filled with water that can become stagnant after a period of time. Change the water regularly, and clean the stone with a soft-bristle brush, above.

Constructing a Fountain

Fountains are popular additions to sitting areas, and for centuries they have been installed near house entrances in hot, dry climates. Stone fountains come in all sizes, from a dinner-plate-size basin to a prominent garden feature 4 feet or more across. You can install these fountains in a lawn, in a flower bed, or on a terrace or courtyard.

Fountain Types. Because the reservoir is buried, a recirculating water feature that resembles a bubbling spring is a good choice for households with small children. A boulder or pebble fountain is easy to assemble and is adaptable to any landscape aesthetic. They can contribute both moisture and a cooling effect in the area immediately surrounding the fountain. If you have access to electricity, you can install this type of fountain wherever you can excavate a hole large enough for a 5-gallon pail. You can also create the reservoir from a broader, shallower container with a similar volume or form a basin made of flexible pond liner material.

Stone for the Fountain

Stone yards often stock large, predrilled boulders for fountains, or they will custom drill to your specifications. There are many variations of the boulder fountain, including boulders with a basin carved out, a stone bowl, or a basin with a hole drilled in it. An old millstone or an arrangement of stones can also be used with the hardware for a boulder fountain. Smooth, worn stones, sometimes called river stone, are typically used for pebble fountains.

SMARTtip

If you opt to work with an electric grinder on wet stone, plug the tool into a ground-fault circuit-interrupter (GFCI) outlet. All outdoor outlets are required to be equipped with GFCI protection. These types of outlets can cut power to the circuit if there is a grounding fault. You can also use an adapter for a regular electrical outlet.

Create a custom garden fountain by having specimen stones drilled to hold pipes. The pumps are buried in the base, above.

Strive for a natural look when creating a water feature, right. Note how the top piece pushes the water away from the wall.

Assembling a Pump

Vertical gusher spouts or bubblers are usually used with fountain-style water features. They can be adjusted from 3 to 24 inches or higher depending on the size pump you use. If you have questions about matching the size of the pump to the fountain, discuss the project with the fountain supplier. As with any fountain, you need to have easy access to an electrical outlet with GFCI protection.

Installing the Pump

Begin the installation by digging a hole slightly larger than your reservoir. (See illustration at right.) A 5-gallon plastic pail works well as a reservoir. Place the reservoir into the hole, and check to make sure it is plumb. Backfill the hole with soil, and contour the soil at grade level to create a basin that will funnel the water back to the reservoir.

Set the fountain assembly in the reservoir, and drill a hole in the side of the pail near the top for the electrical cord. Place a rectangle of flexible liner material (pond liner or heavy plastic sheeting) over the reservoir, pushing the material down slightly into the pail. The liner material should extend beyond the edge of the reservoir to serve as the catch area to return the water to the reservoir. Use scissors to cut an 8- to 10-inch X-shaped hole in the liner centered over the reservoir.

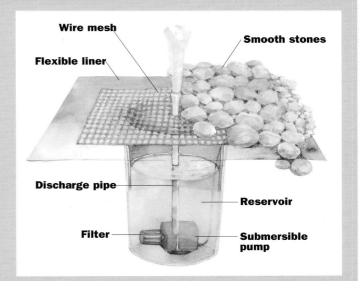

Place a piece of wire mesh (at least 10 inches larger than the diameter of the reservoir) over the liner. Cut a hole in the mesh large enough for the vertical pipe that connects to the fountain pump. For pebble fountains, trim the pipe if needed so that the stones will hide it. Test the assembly by filling the reservoir with water and following the instructions in the fountain kit to adjust the flow rate of the water.

Fountain Maintenance

The amount of water your fountain will lose to evaporation will depend on how often you run the fountain and the ambient temperature. Using a stick, check the level of the reservoir frequently until you can establish a refilling schedule.

Algae. You can remove algae that builds up on the fountain stones by scrubbing them with a soft-bristled brush.

Freezing. Empty the reservoir before freezing temperatures can turn the water to ice. Check the reservoir if you have a midwinter thaw or rain. Remove any water that accumulates from groundwater runoff.

Here's a new slant on a traditional fire pit. Rather than a flame at the center of the seating area, consider a fountain as the focal point.

Dry Streambeds

A dry streambed is a wonderful garden feature that provides visual interest and often serves more than one function. It can create space to display favorite plants, provide a solution to a difficult grade change, disguise a drainage channel, and of course, create the illusion of water where it is impractical to install a water feature.

Design

A dry streambed mimics nature, so let nature be your guide in designing one. Notice how rocks in or adjacent to a stream are dispersed when the water moves at different speeds, and when the terrain is steep or level. Experiment with stones of different sizes and shapes and their placement. Although some trial and error is inevitable, place your stones and plants with both nature and your design goals in mind to achieve the most naturalistic results.

Vary the width and the types of stones used to add interest to your dry streambed.

Installation

Stone in a dry streambed has three uses: it forms the edge or bank of the stream; it takes the place of water; or it makes the streambed itself. Usually, stone for a dry streambed is used 'as is' and is less expensive than wall or patio stone.

Any changes you make after the initial installation can usually be done with hand tools. In fact, you can install many dry streambeds with a shovel, pry bar, and wheelbarrow. Low-tech installation and inexpensive materials make this an ideal project for a homeowner with little do-it-yourself experience.

SMARTtip

Bends in the River

Use bends in a streambed to draw the eye to other garden features, such as a specimen plant or a viewing spot with seating.

CONSTRUCTIONtip

Installation Savvy

- **Use hose or a rope** to lay out the shape of the streambed you desire.
- **Use a plastic barrier** under the streambed for weed control.
- **Set large boulders** and rocks first.
- **Cover any areas** that are not planted at the time of construction with plastic and mulch until you are ready to plant. This will reduce erosion and control weeds.

The Natural Look

The following design guidelines will help you construct a natural-looking dry streambed:

- **Choose a layout** that fits the topography and natural drainage patterns of the site.
- **Change the character** of the streambed if it goes through different parts of the garden. For example, use larger angular stones on a steep grade to indicate a falls.
- **Vary the width** of the bed. Add a beach or dry pond for visual interest.
- **Vary the depth** and steepness of the banks for visual interest and to enhance plantings.
- **Make islands** of vegetation or stone.
- **Place stepping-stones** or a bridge across the streambed.
- **Use shadows** from nearby foliage plants to mimic rippling water.

Dry streambeds can help lead the eye from one landscape feature to another, unifying the design, top right.

Flank a planting bed with a flowing river of stones to separate one area from another, bottom right.

Plan #131027

Dimensions: 62'4" W x 53'6" D
Levels: 1.5
Square Footage: 2,567
Main Level Sq. Ft.: 2,017
Upper Level Sq. Ft.: 550
Bedrooms: 4
Bathrooms: 3
Foundation: Crawl space or slab; basement for fee
Materials List Available: Yes
Price Category: F

This home, as shown in the photograph, may differ from the actual blueprints. For more detailed information, please check the floor plans carefully.

Images provided by designer/architect.

The features of this home are so good that you may have trouble imagining all of them at once.

Features:

- **Great Room:** Imagine a stepped ceiling, corner fireplace, built-media center, and wall of windows with a glass door to the backyard—in one room.

- **Dining Room:** A stepped ceiling and server with a sink add to the elegance of this formal room.

- **Breakfast Room:** Eat at the bar this room shares with the island kitchen, and admire the 12-ft. cathedral ceiling and bayed group of 8- and 9-ft. windows. Or go through the sliding glass door to the covered side porch.

- **Master Suite:** The bedroom has a tray ceiling and cozy sitting area, and a whirlpool tub, shower, and walk-in closet are in the skylighted bath.

- **Optional Study:** The private bath in bedroom 2 makes it ideal for a study or home office.

Breakfast Nook

Rear View

Great Room

Main Level Floor Plan

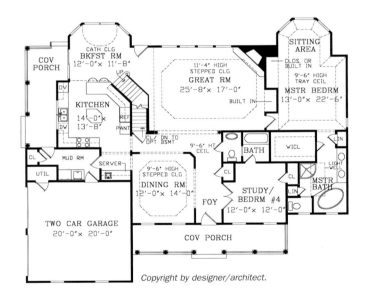

Copyright by designer/architect.

Upper Level Floor Plan

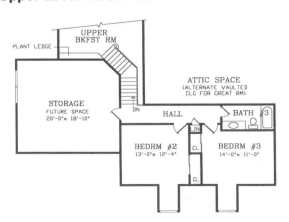

Plan #211074

Dimensions: 64' W x 89' D

Levels: 2

Square Footage: 3,486

Main Level Sq. Ft.: 2,575

Upper Level Sq. Ft.: 911

Bedrooms: 4

Bathrooms: 3

Foundation: Crawl space

Materials List Available: Yes

Price Category: G

Images provided by designer/architect.

This plantation-style home may have an old-fashioned charm, but the energy-efficient design and many amenities inside make it thoroughly contemporary.

Features:

- Ceiling Height: 9 ft.
- Porches: This wraparound front porch is fully 10 ft. wide, so you can group rockers, occasional tables, and even a swing here and save the rear porch for grilling and alfresco dining.

- Entry: A two-story ceiling here sets an elegant tone for the rest of the home.
- Living Room: Somewhat isolated, this room is an ideal spot for quiet entertaining. It has built-in bookshelves and a nearby wet bar.
- Kitchen: You'll love the large counter areas and roomy storage space in this lovely kitchen, where both friends and family are sure to congregate.
- Master Suite: It's easy to pamper yourself in this comfortable bedroom and luxurious bath.

Main Level Floor Plan

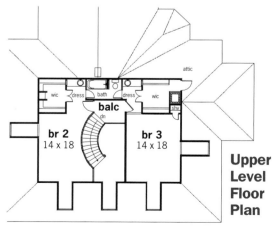

Upper Level Floor Plan

Copyright by designer/architect.

Plan #101020

Dimensions: 55'8" W x 49'2" D

Levels: 2

Square Footage: 2,972

Main Level Sq. Ft.: 1,986

Upper Level Sq. Ft.: 986

Bedrooms: 4

Bathrooms: 3½

Foundation: Crawl space, slab, basement or walkout

Materials List Available: Yes

Price Category: F

Images provided by designer/architect.

This luxurious country home has an open-design main level that maximizes the use of space.

Features:

• Ceiling Height: 9 ft. unless otherwise noted.

• Foyer: Guests will be greeted by this grand two-story entry, with its graceful angled staircase.

• Dining Room: At nearly 12 ft. x 15 ft., this elegant dining room has plenty of room for large parties.

• Family Room: Everyone will be drawn to

this 17-ft. x 19-ft. room, with its dramatic two-story ceiling and its handsome fireplace.

• Kitchen: This spacious kitchen is open to the family room and features a breakfast bar and built-in table in the cooktop island.

• Master Suite: This elegant retreat includes a bayed 18-ft.-5-in. x 14-ft.-9-in. bedroom and a beautiful corner his and her bath/closet arrangement.

• Secondary Bedrooms: Upstairs you'll find three spacious bathrooms, one with a private bath and two with access to a shared bath.

CAD FILE AVAILABLE

Main Level Floor Plan

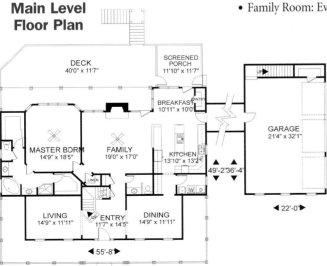

Upper Level Floor Plan

Copyright by designer/architect.

Copyright by designer/architect.

Images provided by
designer/architect.

Rear Elevation

**Bonus Area
Floor Plan**

Plan #351088

Dimensions: 66'8" W x 73'2" D
Levels: 1
Square Footage: 2,500
Bedrooms: 4
Bathrooms: 3
Foundation: Crawl space or slab
Material List Available: Yes
Price Category: G

Plan #211030

Dimensions: 75' W x 37' D
Levels: 1
Square Footage: 1,600
Bedrooms: 3
Bathrooms: 2
Foundation: Slab
Materials List Available: Yes
Price Category: C

Images provided by
designer/architect.

Copyright by designer/architect.

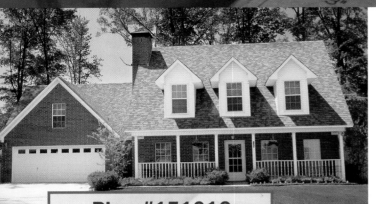

Main Level Floor Plan

Images provided by designer/architect.

Plan #151016

Dimensions: 60'2" W x 39'10" D

Levels: 2

Square Footage: 1,783; 2,107 with bonus

Main Level Sq. Ft.: 1,124

Upper Level Sq. Ft.: 659

Bonus Room Sq. Ft.: 324

Bedrooms: 3

Bathrooms: 2½

Foundation: Crawl space, slab, basement or walkout

CompleteCost List Available: Yes

Price Category: C

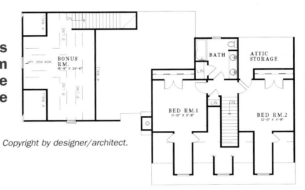

Bonus Room Above Garage

Upper Level Floor Plan

Copyright by designer/architect.

Copyright by designer/architect.

Plan #151089

Dimensions: 84' W x 55'6" D

Levels: 1

Square Footage: 1,921

Bedrooms: 3

Bathrooms: 3

Foundation: Crawl space or slab; basement or walkout for fee

CompleteCost List Available: Yes

Price Category: E

Images provided by designer/architect.

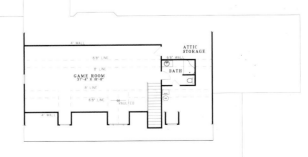

Bonus Area Floor Plan

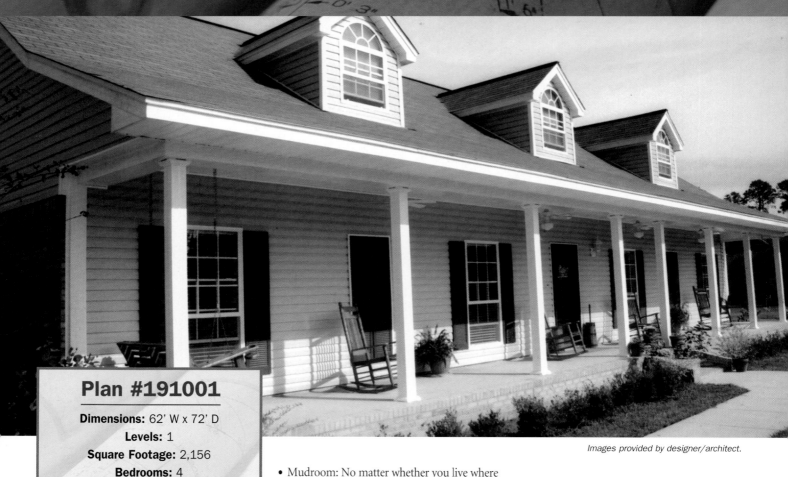

Plan #191001

Dimensions: 62' W x 72' D

Levels: 1

Square Footage: 2,156

Bedrooms: 4

Bathrooms: 3

Foundation: Crawl space, slab, or basement

Materials List Available: Yes

Price Category: D

Images provided by designer/architect.

This lovely home has the best of old and new — a traditional appearance combined with fabulous comforts and conveniences.

Features:

- **Great Room:** A tray ceiling gives stature to this expansive room, and its many windows let natural light stream into it.

- **Kitchen:** When you're standing at the sink in this gorgeous kitchen, you'll have a good view of the patio. But if you turn around, you'll see the island cooktop, wall oven, walk-in pantry, and snack bar, all of which make this kitchen such a pleasure.

- **Master Suite:** Somewhat isolated for privacy, this area is ideal for an evening or weekend retreat. Relax in the gracious bedroom or luxuriate in the spa-style bath, with its corner whirlpool tub, large shower, two sinks, and access to the walk-in closet, which measures a full 8 ft. x 10 ft.

- **Mudroom:** No matter whether you live where mud season is as reliable as spring thaws or where rain is a seasonal event, you'll love having a spot to confine the muddy mess.

Front View

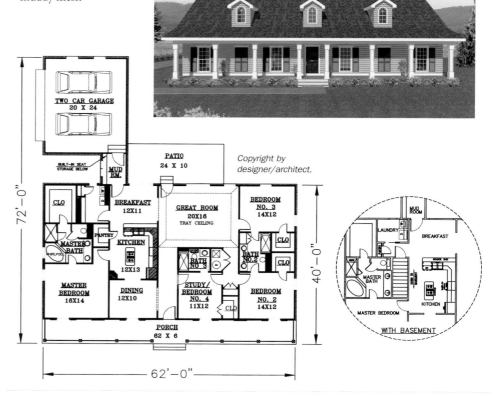

Copyright by designer/architect.

Plan #131022

Dimensions: 54'8" W x 43' D

Levels: 2

Square Footage: 2,092

Main Level Sq. Ft.: 1,152

Upper Level Sq. Ft.: 940

Bedrooms: 4

Bathrooms: 2½

Foundation: Crawl space or slab;
basement for fee

Materials List Available: Yes

Price Category: E

This home, as shown in the photograph, may differ from the actual blueprints. For more detailed information, please check the floor plans carefully.

You'll love the way this charming home reminds you of an old-fashioned farmhouse.

Features:

• Ceiling Height: 8 ft.

• Living Room: This large living room can be used as guest quarters when the need arises.

• Dining Room: This bayed, informal room is large enough for all your dining and entertaining needs. It could also double as an office or den.

• Garage: An expandable loft over the garage offers an ideal playroom or fourth bedroom.

Images provided by designer/architect.

Rear Elevation

Main Level Floor Plan

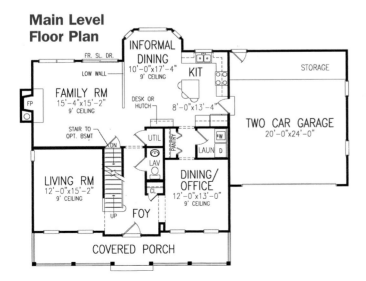

Upper Level Floor Plan

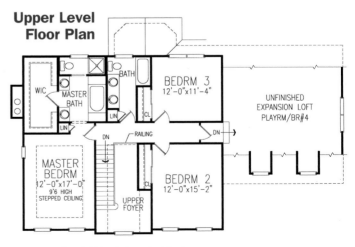

Copyright by designer/architect.

Plan #151113

Dimensions: 62'10" W x 91'4" D

Levels: 1

Square Footage: 2,186

Bedrooms: 4

Bathrooms: 3

Foundation: Crawl space or slab; basement or walkout for fee

CompleteCost List Available: Yes

Price Category: D

Images provided by designer/architect.

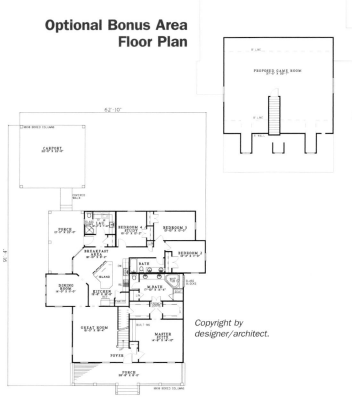

Copyright by designer/architect.

Plan #351008

Dimensions: 64'6" W x 61'4" D

Levels: 1

Square Footage: 2,002

Bedrooms: 3

Bathrooms: 2

Foundation: Crawl space or basement

Materials List Available: Yes

Price Category: E

Images provided by designer/architect.

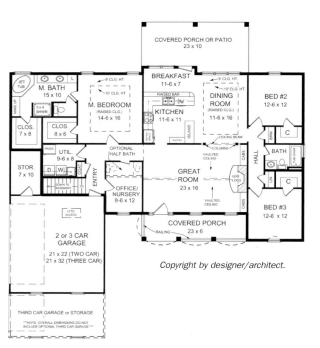

Copyright by designer/architect.

Plan #271074

Dimensions: 68' W x 86' D

Levels: 1

Square Footage: 2,400

Bedrooms: 4

Bathrooms: 3

Foundation: Crawl space, slab or basement

Materials List Available: Yes

Price Category: E

Images provided by designer/architect.

CAD FILE AVAILABLE

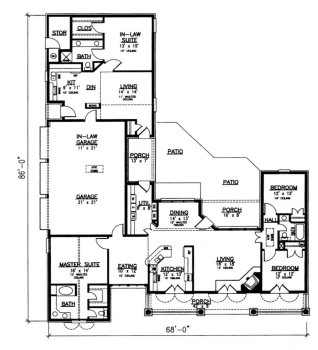

Copyright by designer/architect.

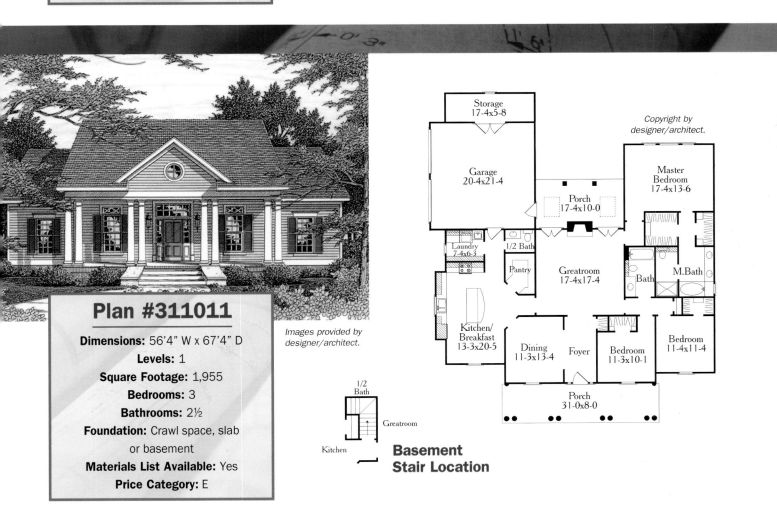

Plan #311011

Dimensions: 56'4" W x 67'4" D

Levels: 1

Square Footage: 1,955

Bedrooms: 3

Bathrooms: 2½

Foundation: Crawl space, slab or basement

Materials List Available: Yes

Price Category: E

Images provided by designer/architect.

Copyright by designer/architect.

Basement Stair Location

Plan #121021

Dimensions: 46' W x 48' D

Levels: 2

Square Footage: 2,270

Main Level Sq. Ft.: 1,150

Upper Level Sq. Ft.: 1,120

Bedrooms: 4

Bathrooms: 2½

Foundation: Basement

Materials List Available: Yes

Price Category: E

This home, as shown in the photograph, may differ from the actual blueprints. For more detailed information, please check the floor plans carefully.

With its wraparound porch, this home evokes the charm of a traditional home.

Features:

• Ceiling Height: 8 ft.

• Foyer: The dramatic two-story entry enjoys views of the formal dining room and great room. A second floor balcony overlooks the entry and a plant shelf.

• Formal Dining Room: This gracious room is perfect for family holiday gatherings and for more formal dinner parties.

• Great Room: All the family will want to gather in this comfortable, informal room which features bay windows, an entertainment center, and a see-through fireplace.

• Breakfast Area: Conveniently located just off the great room, the bayed breakfast area features a built-in desk for household bills and access to the backyard.

• Kitchen: An island is the centerpiece of this kitchen. Its intelligent design makes food preparation a pleasure.

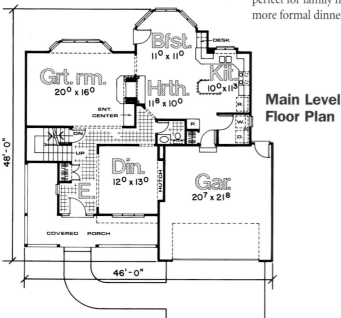

Main Level Floor Plan

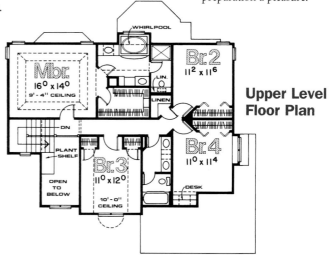

Upper Level Floor Plan

Plan #351020

Dimensions: 54' W x 48' D

Levels: 1

Square Footage: 1,488

Bedrooms: 3

Bathrooms: 2

Foundation: Crawl space, slab, or basement

Materials List Available: Yes

Price Category: C

This is a lot of house for its size and is an excellent example of the popular split bedroom layout.

Features:

- Great Room: This large room is open to the dining room.

- Kitchen: This fully equipped kitchen has a peninsula counter and is open into the dining room.

- Master Suite: This private area, located on the other side of the home from the secondary bedrooms, features large walk-in closets and bath areas.

- Bedrooms: The two secondary bedrooms have large closets and share a hall bathroom.

Images provided by designer/architect.

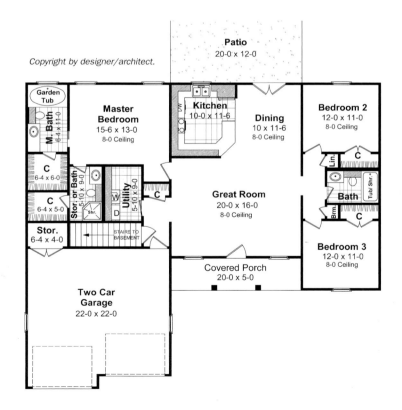

Copyright by designer/architect.

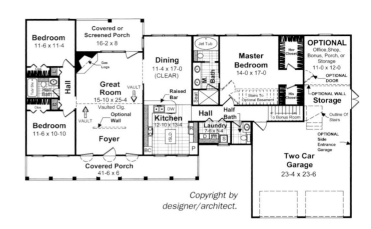

Copyright by designer/architect.

Plan #351004

Dimensions: 78' W x 49'6" D
Levels: 1
Square Footage: 1,852
Bedrooms: 3
Bathrooms: 2½
Foundation: Crawl space, slab, or basement
Materials List Available: Yes
Price Category: D

CAD FILE AVAILABLE CAD

Images provided by designer/architect.

Rear View

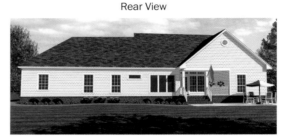

Bonus Room

Plan #131034

Dimensions: 40' W x 32' D
Levels: 2 (upper unfinished)
Square Footage: 1,040
Bedrooms: 5 or 4
Bathrooms: 2½
Foundation: Crawl space or slab; basement for fee
Materials List Available: Yes
Price Category: C

Images provided by designer/architect.

Main Level Floor Plan

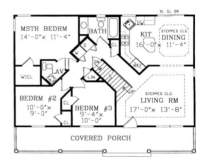

Optional Main Level Floor Plan

Optional Upper Level Floor Plan

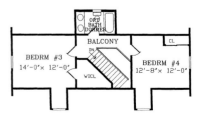

Copyright by designer/architect.

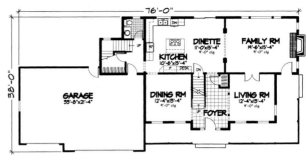

Main Level Floor Plan

Upper Level Floor Plan

Copyright by designer/architect.

Plan #271072

Dimensions: 76' W x 38' D
Levels: 2
Square Footage: 3,081
Main Level Sq. Ft.: 1,358
Upper Level Sq. Ft.: 1,723
Bedrooms: 3
Bathrooms: 2½
Foundation: Crawl space or basement
Materials List Available: Yes
Price Category: G

Images provided by designer/architect.

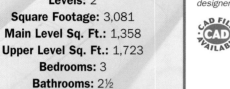

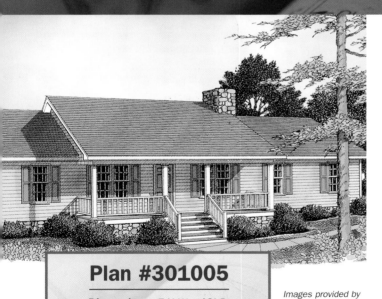

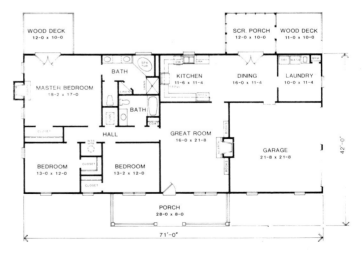

Images provided by designer/architect.

Copyright by designer/architect.

Plan #301005

Dimensions: 71' W x 42' D
Levels: 1
Square Footage: 1,930
Bedrooms: 3
Bathrooms: 2
Foundation: Crawl space, slab
Materials List Available: Yes
Price Category: D

Plan #121083

Dimensions: 72' W x 45'4" D
Levels: 2
Square Footage: 2,695
Main Level Sq. Ft.: 1,881
Upper Level Sq. Ft.: 814
Bedrooms: 4
Bathrooms: 3½
Foundation: Basement
Materials List Available: Yes
Price Category: F

You'll love this home for its soaring entryway ceiling and well-designed layout.

Features:

- **Entry:** A balcony from the upper level looks down into this two-story entry, which features a decorative plant shelf.

- **Great Room:** Comfort is guaranteed in this large room, with its built-in bookcases framing a lovely fireplace and trio of transom-topped windows along one wall.

- **Living Room:** Save both this formal room and the formal dining room, both of which flank the entry, for guests and special occasions.

- **Kitchen:** This convenient work space includes a gazebo-shaped breakfast area where friends and family will gather at any time of day.

Main Level Floor Plan

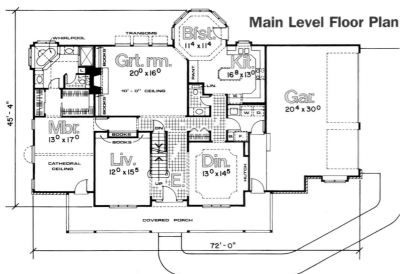

Upper Level Floor Plan

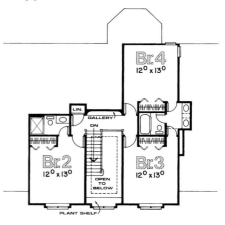

Plan #131047

Dimensions: 69'10" W x 51'8" D
Levels: 1
Square Footage: 1,793
Bedrooms: 3
Bathrooms: 2
Foundation: Crawl space or slab; basement for fee
Materials List Available: Yes
Price Category: D

The country charm of this well-designed home is mixed with the convenience and luxury normally reserved for more contemporary plans.

Images provided by designer/architect.

Features:

- Great Room: The spaciousness of this great room is enhanced by the 11-ft. stepped ceiling. A fireplace makes it cozy on cool evenings or on chilly winter days, and two sets of French sliding glass doors open to the back porch.

- Kitchen: In addition to the convenient layout of this design, you'll also love its bright, airy position. It includes an old-fashioned pantry,

a sink under a window, and a sunny breakfast area that opens to the wraparound porch.

- Master Suite: You'll find 11-ft. ceilings in both the master bedroom and the bayed sitting area that the suite includes. In the bath, the circular spa tub is surrounded by a glass-block wall.

- Bonus Space: A permanent staircase leads to an unfinished bonus space on the upper level.

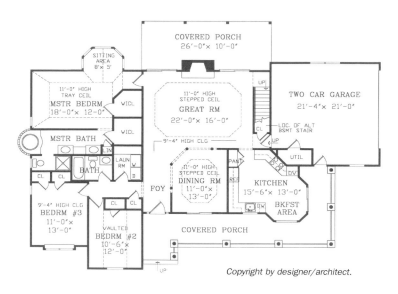

Copyright by designer/architect.

Rear Elevation

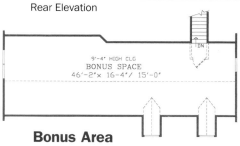

Bonus Area

Plan #131051

Dimensions: 64'4" W x 53'4" D
Levels: 2
Square Footage: 2,431
Main Level Sq. Ft.: 1,293
Upper Level Sq. Ft.: 1,138
Bedrooms: 4
Bathrooms: 2½
Foundation: Crawl space or slab;
basement for fee
Materials List Available: Yes
Price Category: F

Gracious and charming with a wraparound front porch and a backyard terrace, this home also has a ready-to-finish third floor all-purpose room and a full bath.

Features:

- Main Level Ceiling Height: 9 ft.

- Family Room: A comfortable space for the entire family to gather, this delightful room can be warmed by a heat-circulating fireplace.

- Dining Room: A cozy dinette boasts a sliding glass door with access to a gorgeous backyard terrace with an optional calm reflecting pool.

- Kitchen: Adjoining the dining area, the kitchen offers plenty of storage and counter space. The laundry room and half-bath are nearby for convenience.

- Garage: The garage is tucked way back to keep it from intruding into the traditional facade.

Main Level Floor Plan

Images provided by designer/architect.

This home, as shown in the photograph, may differ from the actual blueprints. For more detailed information, please check the floor plans carefully.

Rear Elevation

Upper Level Floor Plan

Optional 3rd Level Floor Plan

Copyright by designer/architect.

Plan #151031

Dimensions: 60'2" W x 60'2" D
Levels: 2
Square Footage: 3,130
Main Level Sq. Ft.: 1,600
Upper Level Sq. Ft.: 1,530
Bedrooms: 3
Bathrooms: 3½
Foundation: Crawl space, slab
CompleteCost List Available: Yes
Price Category: F

If you love traditional Southern plantation homes, you'll want this house with its wraparound porches that are graced with boxed columns.

Features:

- Great Room: Use the gas fireplace for warmth in this comfortable room, which is open to the kitchen.

- Living Room: 8-in. columns add formality as you enter this living and dining room.

- Kitchen: You'll love the island bar with a sink. An elevator here can take you to the other floors.

- Master Suite: A gas fireplace warms this area, and the bath is luxurious.

- Bedrooms: Each has a private bath and built-in bookshelves for easy organizing.

- Optional Features: Choose a 2,559-sq.-ft. basement and add a kitchen to it, or finish the 1,744-sq.-ft. bonus room and add a spiral staircase and a bath.

Images provided by designer/architect.

Main Level Floor Plan

Upper Level Floor Plan

Images provided by designer/architect.

Basement Level Floor Plan

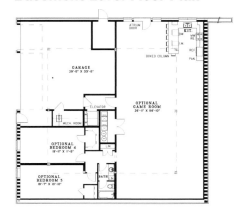

Optional Upper Level Floor Plan

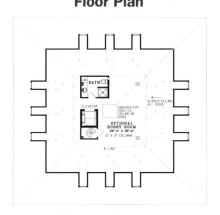

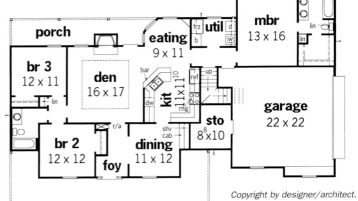

Bonus Room

bonus
10 x 22⁴

Plan #201086

Dimensions: 68'6" W x 46' D

Levels: 1

Square Footage: 1,573

Bedrooms: 3

Bathrooms: 2

Foundation: Crawl space, slab

Materials List Available: Yes

Price Category: C

Images provided by designer/architect.

porch

br 3
12 x 11

den
16 x 17

eating
9 x 11

util

mbr
13 x 16

kit
11x11¹⁰

bar

br 2
12 x 12

foy

dining
11 x 12

sto
8 x 10

garage
22 x 22

Copyright by designer/architect.

Plan #171011

Dimensions: 70' W x 58' D

Levels: 1

Square Footage: 2,069

Bedrooms: 3

Bathrooms: 2½

Foundation: Crawl space, slab

Materials List Available: Yes

Price Category: D

Images provided by designer/architect.

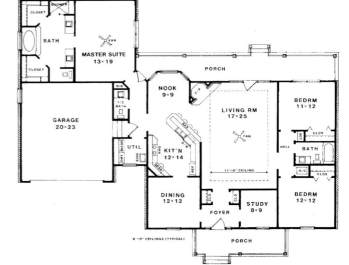

MASTER SUITE
13 x 19

GARAGE
20 x 23

NOOK
9 x 9

PORCH

LIVING RM
17 x 25

BEDRM
11 x 12

KIT'N
12 x 14

UTIL

DINING
12 x 12

STUDY
8 x 9

FOYER

BEDRM
12 x 12

PORCH

Copyright by designer/architect.

Images provided by
designer/architect.

Plan #171013

Dimensions: 74' W x 72' D

Levels: 1

Square Footage: 3,084

Bedrooms: 4

Bathrooms: 3½

Foundation: Crawl space or slab

Materials List Available: Yes

Price Category: G

Bonus Room
Copyright by designer/architect.

Future Rm

Copyright by designer/architect.

Plan #291002

Dimensions: 63' W x 37' D

Levels: 1

Square Footage: 1,550

Bedrooms: 3

Bathrooms: 2

Foundation: Basement

Materials List Available: Yes

Price Category: C

Images provided by
designer/architect.

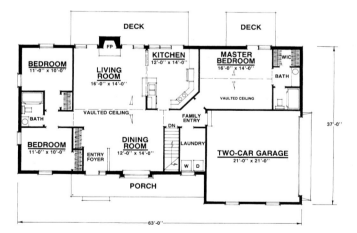

Copyright by designer/architect.

Rear View

Plan #181151

Dimensions: 50' W x 46' D
Levels: 2
Square Footage: 2,283
Main Level Sq. Ft.: 1,274
Second Level Sq. Ft.: 1,009
Bedrooms: 3
Bathrooms: 2½
Foundation: Basement
Materials List Available: Yes
Price Category: F

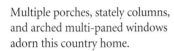

Multiple porches, stately columns, and arched multi-paned windows adorn this country home.

Features:

• Ceiling Height: 8 ft. unless otherwise noted.

• Great Room: The second-floor mezzanine overlooks this great room. With its soaring ceiling, this dramatic room is the centerpiece of a spacious and flowing design that is just as suited to entertaining as it is to family life.

• Dining Area: Guests will naturally flow into this dining area when it is time to eat. After dinner they can step directly out onto the porch to enjoy coffee and dessert when the weather is fair.

• Kitchen: This efficient and well-designed kitchen has double sinks and offers a separate eating area for those impromptu family meals.

• Master Suite: This master retreat has a walk-in closet and its own sumptuous bath.

• Home Office: Whether you work at home or just need a place for the family computer and keeping track of family finances, this home office fills the bill.

Front View

Main Level Floor Plan

21'-0" X 20'-8"
6,30 X 6,20

46'-0"
13,8 m

17'-0" X 11'-8"
5,10 X 3,50

9'-8" X 8'-8"
2,90 X 2,60

9'-8" X 10'-0"
2,70 X 3,00

10'-0" X 12'-0"
3,00 X 3,60

9'-8" X 9'-4"
2,90 X 2,80

12'-0" X 20'-8"
3,60 X 6,20

50'-0"
15,0 m

Upper Level Floor Plan

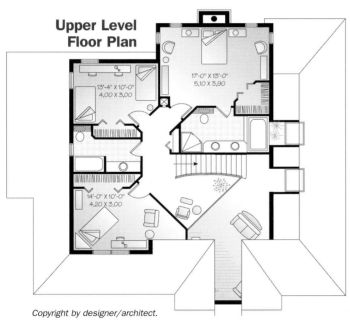

13'-4" X 10'-0"
4,00 X 3,00

17'-0" X 13'-0"
5,10 X 3,90

14'-0" X 10'-0"
4,20 X 3,00

Copyright by designer/architect.

SMARTtip

Coping Chair Rails

If the teeth of your rasp tend to break out thin edges of the cope, try wrapping the rasp with sandpaper to make fine adjustments.

Dining Room

Living Room

Master Bath

Plan #181085

Dimensions: 56'4" W x 44' D
Levels: 2
Square Footage: 2,183
Main Level Sq. Ft.: 1,232
Second Level Sq. Ft.: 951
Bedrooms: 3
Bathrooms: 2½
Foundation: Basement
Materials List Available: Yes
Price Category: G

This country home features an inviting front porch and a layout designed for modern living.

Images provided by designer/architect.

Features:

- Ceiling Height: 8 ft.
- Solarium: Sunlight streams through the windows of this solarium at the front of the house.
- Living Room: Walk through French doors, and you will enter this inviting living room. Family and friends will be drawn to the corner fireplace.
- Formal Dining Room: Usher your guests directly from the living room into this formal dining room. The kitchen is located on the

other side of the dining room for convenient service.

- Kitchen: This generously sized kitchen is a delight, it offers a center island, separate eat-in area, and access to the back deck.
- Bonus Room: This room just off the entry hall can become a family room, a bedroom, or an office.
- Master Suite: Curl up by the corner fireplace in this master retreat, with its walk-in closet and lavish bath with separate shower and tub.

Main Level Floor Plan

Upper Level Floor Plan

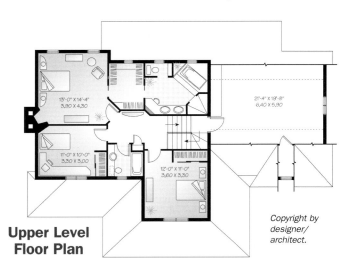

Copyright by designer/architect.

Plan #161024

Dimensions: 54'4" W x 26'8" D
Levels: 2
Square Footage: 1,698
Main Level Sq. Ft.: 868
Upper Level Sq. Ft.: 830
Bonus Space Sq. Ft.: 269
Bedrooms: 3
Bathrooms: 2½
Foundation: Basement
Materials List Available: Yes
Price Category: C

This home, as shown in the photograph, may differ from the actual blueprints. Images provided by designer/architect. For more detailed information, please check the floor plans carefully.

The covered porch, dormers, and center gable that grace the exterior let you know how comfortable your family will be in this home.

Features:

- Great Room: Walk from windows overlooking the front porch to a door into the rear yard in this spacious room, which runs the width of the house.

- Dining Room: Adjacent to the great room, the dining area gives your family space to spread out and makes it easy to entertain a large group.

- Kitchen: Designed for efficiency, the kitchen area includes a large pantry.

- Master Suite: Tucked away on the second floor, the master suite features a walk-in closet in the bedroom and a luxurious attached bathroom.

- Bonus Room: Finish the 269-sq.-ft. area over the 2-bay garage as a guest room, study, or getaway for the kids.

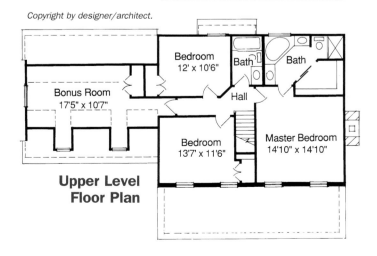

Copyright by designer/architect.

Main Level Floor Plan

Two-car Garage 20' x 20'
Kitchen 8'4" x 11'4"
Breakfast 9'6" x 14'6"
Great Room 14'6" x 25'4"
Laun.
Foyer
Porch

Upper Level Floor Plan

Bonus Room 17'5" x 10'7"
Bedroom 12' x 10'6"
Bath
Bath
Hall
Bedroom 13'7" x 11'6"
Master Bedroom 14'10" x 14'10"

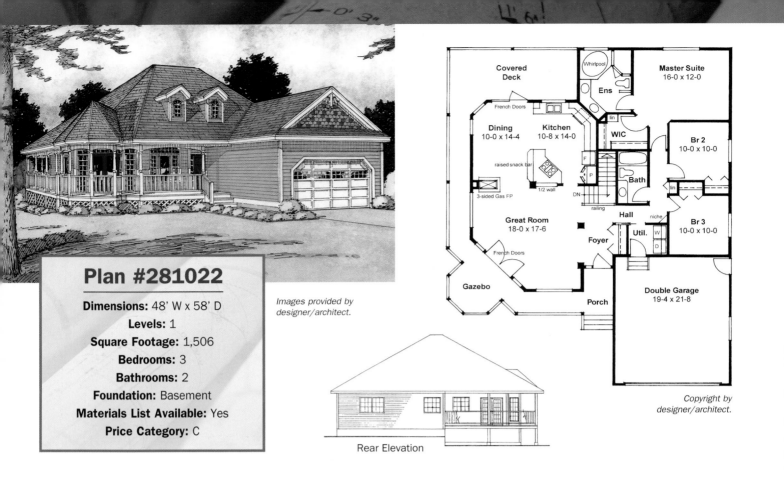

Plan #281022

Dimensions: 48' W x 58' D

Levels: 1

Square Footage: 1,506

Bedrooms: 3

Bathrooms: 2

Foundation: Basement

Materials List Available: Yes

Price Category: C

Images provided by designer/architect.

Rear Elevation

Copyright by designer/architect.

Plan #111043

Dimensions: 42' W x 49' D

Levels: 2

Square Footage: 1,737

Main Level Sq. Ft.: 1,238

Upper Level Sq. Ft.: 499

Bedrooms: 3

Bathrooms: 2½

Foundation: Crawl space

Materials List Available: Yes

Price Category: C

Images provided by designer/architect.

Main Level Floor Plan

Upper Level Floor Plan

Copyright by designer/architect.

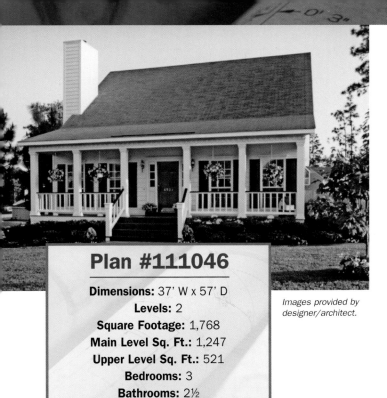

Main Level Floor Plan

Wood Deck 12'6"x 8'

Covered Porch 12'2"x 10'

Ext. Storage

Master Bath

WIC

Breakfast 11'10" x 9'6"

Utility

Master Bedroom 12'6"x 15'6"

1/2 Ba.

Kitchen 10'x 11'6"

Dining 13'x 12'

Living 14'4"x 17'6"

Porch 32'x 5'

Images provided by designer/architect.

Upper Level Floor Plan

Bedroom 12'6"x 14'

Bedroom 10'6"x 13'2"

Balcony

Ba.

Copyright by designer/architect.

Plan #111046

Dimensions: 37' W x 57' D

Levels: 2

Square Footage: 1,768

Main Level Sq. Ft.: 1,247

Upper Level Sq. Ft.: 521

Bedrooms: 3

Bathrooms: 2½

Foundation: Crawl space

Materials List Available: Yes

Price Category: D

MBR. 13'4" X 14'8"

LIV. VAULTED CEILING 13'8" X 18'0"

'DIRECT VENT GAS FIREPLACE

DIN. 12'0" X 10'8"

SCREEN PORCH 14'0" X 16'0"

KIT. 12'0" X 12'6"

STORAGE 14'0" X 7'8"

E. VAULTED CEILING

BR. #2 11'6" X 11'8"

BR. #3 11'0" X 11'8"

2 CAR GAR. 22'0" X 22'0"

46'-0"

60'-4"

Copyright by designer/architect.

Images provided by designer/architect.

CAD FILE AVAILABLE

Plan #221008

Dimensions: 60'4" W x 46' D

Levels: 1

Square Footage: 1,540

Bedrooms: 3

Bathrooms: 2

Foundation: Basement

Materials List Available: Yes

Price Category: C

Rear Elevation

Plan #121010

Dimensions: 50' W x 62' D
Levels: 1
Square Footage: 1,902
Bedrooms: 2
Bathrooms: 2
Foundation: Basement
Materials List Available: Yes
Price Category: D

CAD FILE AVAILABLE · CAD ·

Images provided by designer/architect.

This home is replete with architectural details that provide a convenient and gracious lifestyle.

Features:

- Ceiling Height: 8 ft.

- Great Room: The entry enjoys a long view into this room. Family and friends will be drawn to the warmth of its handsome fireplace flanked by windows.

- Breakfast Area: You'll pass through cased openings from the great room into the cozy breakfast area that

will lure the whole family to linger over informal meals.

- Kitchen: Another cased opening leads from the breakfast area into the well-designed kitchen with its convenient island.

- Master Bedroom: To the right of the great room special ceiling details highlight the master bedroom where a cased opening and columns lead to a private sitting area.

- Den/Library: Whether you are listening to music or relaxing with a book, this special room will always enhance your lifestyle.

Copyright by designer/architect.

SMARTtip

Accentuating Your Fireplace with Faux Effects

Experiment with faux effects to add an aged look or a specific style to a fireplace mantel and surround. Craft stores sell inexpensive kits with directions for adding the appearance of antiqued or paneled wood or plaster, rusticated stone, marble, terra cotta, and other effects that make any style achievable.

Plan #391051

Dimensions: 63'6" W x 42'8" D
Levels: 2
Square Footage: 1,738
Main Level Sq. Ft.: 1,164
Upper Level Sq. Ft.: 574
Bedrooms: 3
Bathrooms: 2
Foundation: Crawl space, slab, or basement
Material List Available: Yes
Price Category: C

This home, as shown in the photograph, may differ from the actual blueprints. For more detailed information, please check the floor plans carefully.

Images provided by designer/architect.

Simple can be stupendous. The classic lines of this farmhouse-style design make it an instant favorite.

Features:

- **Living Room:** As you arrive home, you enter this spacious living room, which is full of natural light from the two front windows. In the evening, the light from the fireplace fills this room.

- **Solar Room:** An optional solar greenhouse and large triple-glazed windows make the most of the sun's warmth.

- **Master Suite:** Access to a rear private patio is just one amenity of this retreat. It also boasts

his and her closets and a sumptuous master bath complete with a large tub.

- **Upper Level:** The upstairs has two ample bedrooms and a full bathroom.

Rear View

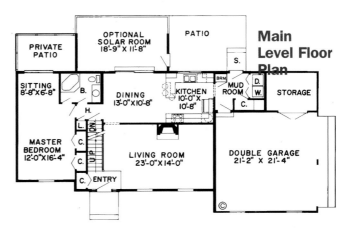

Main Level Floor Plan

OPTIONAL SOLAR ROOM 18'-9" X 11'-8"
PATIO
PRIVATE PATIO
SITTING 8'-8" X 6'-8"
DINING 13'-0" X 10'-8"
KITCHEN 10'-0" X 10'-8"
MUD ROOM
STORAGE
MASTER BEDROOM 12'-0" X 16'-4"
LIVING ROOM 23'-0" X 14'-0"
DOUBLE GARAGE 21'-2" X 21'-4"
ENTRY

Upper Level Floor Plan

BEDROOM 16'-6" X 10'-8"
BEDROOM 12'-0" X 17'-4"
OPEN TO LIVING ROOM

Copyright by designer/architect.

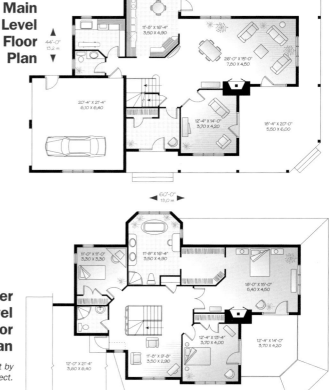

Main Level Floor Plan

44'-0"
13,2 m

11'-8" X 16'-4"
3,50 X 4,90

26'-0" X 15'-0"
7,80 X 4,50

20'-4" X 21'-4"
6,10 X 6,40

12'-4" X 14'-0"
3,70 X 4,20

18'-4" X 20'-0"
5,50 X 6,00

60'-0"
18,0 m

Upper Level Floor Plan

11'-0" X 11'-0"
3,30 X 3,30

11'-8" X 16'-4"
3,50 X 4,90

18'-0" X 15'-0"
5,40 X 4,50

12'-4" X 13'-4"
3,70 X 4,00

12'-4" X 14'-0"
3,70 X 4,20

11'-8" X 9'-8"
3,50 X 2,90

12'-0" X 21'-4"
3,60 X 6,40

Plan #181034

Dimensions: 60' W x 44' D
Levels: 2
Square Footage: 2,687
Main Level Sq. Ft.: 1,297
Upper Level Sq. Ft.: 1,390
Bedrooms: 3
Bathrooms: 2½
Foundation: Full basement
Materials List Available: Yes
Price Category: H

Main Level Floor Plan

61'-6"

DECK

MUD ROOM

KITCHEN

BREAKFAST AREA

FAMILY ROOM

PWDR

PAN.

3 CAR GARAGE

DINING ROOM

FOYER

LIVING ROOM

Plan #641001

Dimensions: 61'6" W x 56' D
Levels: 2
Square Footage: 3,034
Main Level Sq. Ft.: 1,323
Upper Level Sq. Ft.: 1,711
Bedrooms: 4
Bathrooms: 2½
Foundation: Basement
Materials List Available: Yes
Price Category: G

Upper Level Floor Plan

MASTER BATH

WIC

BATH

LAUNDRY

BEDROOM 2

MASTER BEDROOM

BEDROOM 1

BEDROOM 3

LOFT

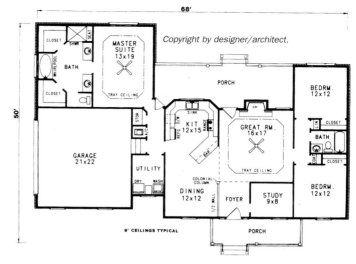

Plan #171009

Dimensions: 68' W x 50' D
Levels: 1
Square Footage: 1,771
Bedrooms: 3
Bathrooms: 2
Foundation: Crawl space, slab
Materials List Available: Yes
Price Category: C

*Images provided by
designer/architect.*

SMARTtip

Deck Awnings

Awnings come in bright colors. As light filters through, it will cast a hue to anything under the deck. Warm colors, such as red or pink, will create a rosy glow; cool colors, such blues or greens, will enhance the shade.

Plan #191003

Dimensions: 56' W x 42' D
Levels: 1
Square Footage: 1,785
Bedrooms: 3
Bathrooms: 3
Foundation: Crawl space, slab, or basement
Materials List Available: Yes
Price Category: C

*Images provided by
designer/architect.*

56'-0" Width

Plan #181081

Dimensions: 58' W x 33' D

Levels: 2

Square Footage: 2,350

Main Level Sq. Ft.: 1,107

Second Level Sq. Ft.: 1,243

Bedrooms: 3

Bathrooms: 2½

Foundation: Basement

Materials List Available: Yes

Price Category: G

Images provided by designer/architect.

This traditional country home features a wrap-around porch and a second-floor balcony.

Features:

- Ceiling Height: 8 ft. unless otherwise noted.

- Family Room: Double French doors and a fireplace in this inviting front room enhance the beauty and warmth of the home's open floor plan.

- Kitchen: You'll love working in this bright and convenient kitchen. The breakfast bar is the perfect place to gather for informal meals.

- Master Suite: You'll look forward to retiring to this elegant upstairs suite at the end of a busy day. The suite features a private bath with separate shower and tub, as well as dual vanities.

- Secondary Bedrooms: Two family bedrooms share a full bath with a third room that opens onto the balcony.

- Basement: An unfinished full basement provides plenty of storage and the potential to add additional finished living space.

Main Level Floor Plan

Copyright by designer/architect.

Upper Level Floor Plan

Plan #191009

Dimensions: 62' W x 76' D

Levels: 1

Square Footage: 2,172

Bedrooms: 4

Bathrooms: 2

Foundation: Crawl space, slab

Materials List Available: Yes

Price Category: D

Images provided by designer/architect.

This charming home is equally attractive in a rural or a settled area, thanks to its classic lines.

Features:

- Porches: Covered front and back porches emphasize the comfort you'll find in this home.

- Great Room: A tray ceiling gives elegance to this spacious room, where everyone is sure to gather. A fireplace makes a nice focal point, and French doors open onto the rear covered porch.

- Dining Room: Arched openings give distinction to this room, where it's easy to serve meals for the family or host a large group.

- Kitchen: You'll love the cooktop island, walk-in pantry, wall oven, snack bar, and view out of the windows in the adjoining breakfast area.

- Master Suite: The large bedroom here gives you space to spread out and relax, and the bath includes a corner whirlpool tub, shower, and dual sinks. An 8-ft. x 10-ft. walk-in closet is off the bath.

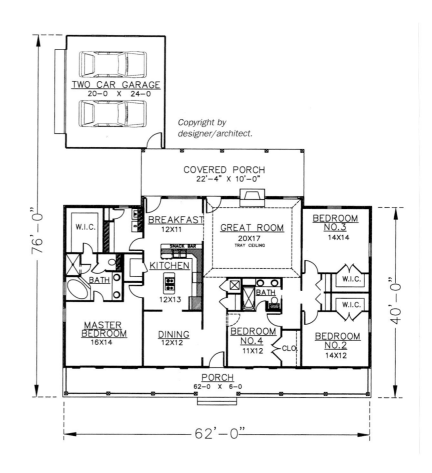

Copyright by designer/architect.

Plan #321054

Dimensions: 70'6" W x 55'6" D
Levels: 2
Square Footage: 2,828
Main Level Sq. Ft.: 2,006
Upper Level Sq. Ft.: 822
Bedrooms: 5
Bathrooms: 3½
Foundation: Basement
Materials List Available: Yes
Price Category: F

Images provided by designer/architect.

The wraparound porch welcomes visitors to this spacious home built for a large family.

Features:

- Foyer: Flanked by the study on one side and the dining room on the other, the foyer leads to the staircase, breakfast room, and family room.

- Family Room: You'll feel comfortable in this room, with its vaulted ceiling, wet bar, ample window area, and door to the patio.

- Kitchen: A center island adds work space to this well-planned room with large corner windows and a convenient door to the outside patio.

- Master Suite: Doors to the covered porch flank the fireplace here, and the luxurious bath includes a corner tub, two vanities, and separate shower. A huge walk-in closet is in the hall.

- Upper Floor: You'll find four bedrooms, each with a large closet, and two full baths here. Bay windows grace the two front bedrooms.

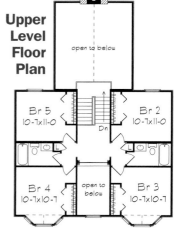

Copyright by designer/architect.

Plan #321041

Dimensions: 64' W x 34' D
Levels: 2
Square Footage: 2,286
Main Level Sq. Ft.: 1,283
Upper Level Sq. Ft.: 1,003
Bedrooms: 4
Bathrooms: 2½
Foundation: Crawl space, slab, or basement
Materials List Available: Yes
Price Category: E

Images provided by designer/architect.

If you love the way these gorgeous windows look from the outside, you'll be thrilled with the equally gracious interior of this home.

Features:

- Entryway: This two-story entryway shows off the fine woodworking on the railing and balustrades.

- Living Room: The large front windows form a glamorous background in this spacious room.

- Family Room: A handsome fireplace and a sliding glass door to the backyard enhance the open design of this room.

- Breakfast Room: Large enough for a crowd, this room makes a perfect dining area.

- Kitchen: The angled bar and separate pantry are highlights in this step-saving design.

- Master Suite: Enjoy this suite's huge walk-in closet, vaulted ceiling, and private bath, which features a double vanity, tub, and shower stall.

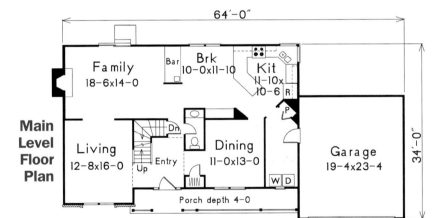

Main Level Floor Plan

Upper Level Floor Plan

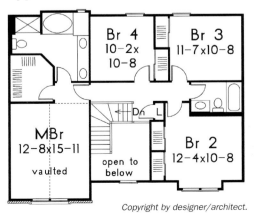

Front View

Copyright by designer/architect.

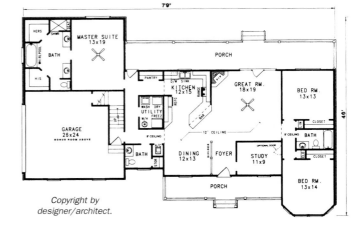

Images provided by designer/architect.

Copyright by designer/architect.

Plan #171015

Dimensions: 79' W x 52' D

Levels: 1

Square Footage: 2,089

Bedrooms: 3

Bathrooms: 2½

Foundation: Crawl space, slab

Materials List Available: Yes

Price Category: D

Bonus Area

Plan #561006

Dimensions: 61'4" W x 72'8" D

Levels: 1

Square Footage: 2,408

Bedrooms: 3

Bathrooms: 2½

Foundation: Basement

Material List Available: Yes

Price Category: D

Images provided by designer/architect.

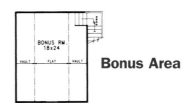

Copyright by designer/architect.

Rear Elevation

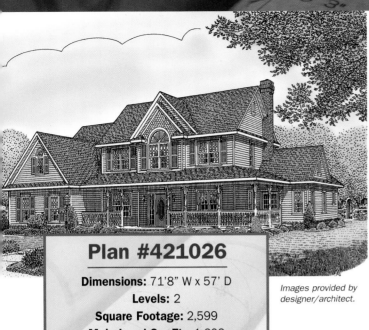

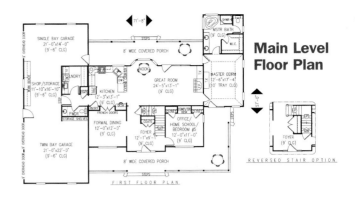

Main Level Floor Plan

Plan #421026

Dimensions: 71'8" W x 57' D

Levels: 2

Square Footage: 2,599

Main Level Sq. Ft.: 1,602

Upper Level Sq. Ft.: 997

Bedrooms: 5

Bathrooms: 2½

Foundation: Basement, crawl space, slab

Materials List Available: Yes

Price Category: E

Images provided by designer/architect.

Copyright by designer/architect.

Upper Level Floor Plan

Plan #131043

Dimensions: 65'8" W x 43'10" D

Levels: 1.5

Square Footage: 1,945

Main Level Sq. Ft.: 1,375

Upper Level Sq. Ft.: 570

Bedrooms: 3

Bathrooms: 2½

Foundation: Crawl space or slab; basement for fee

Materials List Available: Yes

Price Category: E

Images provided by designer/ architect.

Main Level Floor Plan

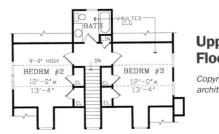

Upper Level Floor Plan

Copyright by designer/ architect.

Plan #111013

Dimensions: 33' W x 59' D

Levels: 1

Square Footage: 1,606

Bedrooms: 3

Bathrooms: 2

Foundation: Slab

Materials List Available: No

Price Category: D

Images provided by designer/architect.

This is the home you have been looking for to fit on that narrow building lot.

Features:

• Living Room: Entering this home from the front porch, you arrive in this gathering area. The corner fireplace adds warmth and charm to the area.

• Kitchen: This island kitchen features two built-in pantries and is open to the breakfast room. The oversize laundry room is close by and has room for the large items the kitchen needs to store.

• Master Suite: Located toward the rear of the home to give some extra privacy, this suite boasts a large sleeping area. The master bath has amenities such as his and her walk-in closets, dual vanities, and a whirlpool tub.

• Rear Porch: Just off the breakfast room is this covered rear porch with storage area. On nice days you can sit outside in the shaded area and watch the kids play outside.

Copyright by designer/architect.

Plan #401039

Dimensions: 69'8" W x 46' D

Levels: 2

Square Footage: 2,462

Main Level Sq. Ft.: 1,333

Upper Level Sq. Ft.: 1,129

Bedrooms: 4

Bathrooms: 2½

Foundation: Basement

Materials List Available: Yes

Price Category: E

Images provided by designer/architect.

A large wraparound porch graces the exterior of this home and gives it great outdoor livability.

Features:

- Foyer: This raised foyer spills into a hearth-warmed living room and the bay-windowed dining room beyond; French doors open from the breakfast and dining rooms to the spacious porch.

- Family Room: Built-ins surround a second hearth in this cozy gathering room.

- Study: Located in the front, this room is adorned by a beamed ceiling and, like the family room, features built-ins.

- Bedrooms: You'll find three family bedrooms on the second floor.

- Master Suite: This restful area, located on the second floor, features a walk-in closet and private bath.

- Garage: Don't miss the workshop area in this garage.

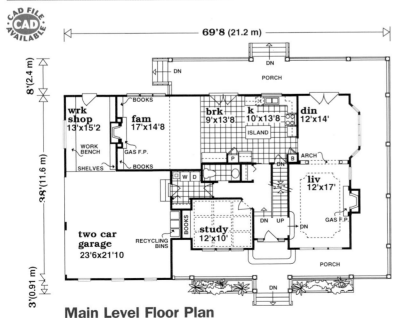

Main Level Floor Plan

Upper Level Floor Plan

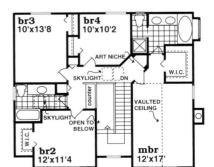

Copyright by designer/architect.

Plan #161061

Dimensions: 90' W x 69'10" D
Levels: 2
Square Footage: 3,816
Main Level Sq. Ft.: 2,725
Upper Level Sq. Ft.: 1,091
Bedrooms: 4
Bathrooms: 3½
Foundation: Basement, walkout basement
Materials List Available: Yes
Price Category: H

Luxurious amenities make living in this spacious home a true pleasure for the whole family.

Features:

- **Great Room:** A fireplace, flanking built-in shelves, a balcony above, and three lovely windows create a luxurious room that's always comfortable.

- **Hearth Room:** Another fireplace with surrounding built-ins and double doors to the outside deck (with its own fireplace) highlight this room.

- **Kitchen:** A butler's pantry, laundry room, and mudroom with a window seat and two walk-in closets complement this large kitchen.

- **Library:** Situated for privacy and quiet, this spacious room with a large window area may be reached from the master bedroom as well as the foyer.

- **Master Suite:** A sloped ceiling and windows on three walls create a lovely bedroom, and the huge walk-in closet, dressing room, and luxurious bath add up to total comfort.

Main Level Floor Plan

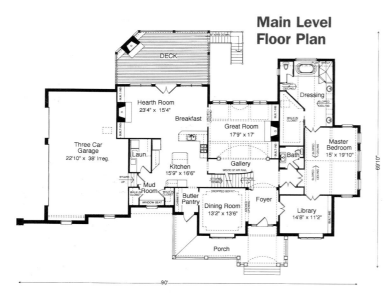

Upper Level Floor Plan

Copyright by designer/architect.

Rear Elevation

Right Side Elevation

Left Side Elevation

Great Room

Hearth Room

Kitchen

Dining Room

Library

Plan #181074

Dimensions: 42' W x 40' D

Levels: 2

Square Footage: 1,760

Main Level Sq. Ft.: 880

Upper Level Sq. Ft.: 880

Bedrooms: 3

Full Baths: 2½

Foundation: Basement; Crawl space, slab; walkout for fee

Materials List Available: Yes

Price Category: F

-A front porch and a standing-seam metal roof add to the country charm of this home.

CAD FILE AVAILABLE

Images provided by designer/architect.

Features:

- **Great Room:** Imagine coming home from a hard day of working or chauffeuring the kids and being welcomed by comfy couch and warm fire. This is the perfect room to help you unwind.

- **Kitchen:** From culinary expert to family cook, everyone will find this kitchen's workspaces and storage just what they need to create special meals. A sun-drenched family area shares the space and opens onto the future patio.

- **Second Floor:** For a restful atmosphere, the bedrooms are separated from the hum of daily life. The spacious master bedroom receives light from the bay windows. The area features a walk-in closet and a private bathroom. The two additional bedrooms share access to a Jack-and-Jill bathroom.

- **Garage:** A single-car garage adds convenience to this plan. It can be used as additional storage space.

Main Level Floor Plan

Copyright by designer/architect.

Upper Level Floor Plan

Plan #281018

Dimensions: 50' W x 52'6" D
Levels: 1
Square Footage: 1,565
Bedrooms: 3
Bathrooms: 2
Foundation: Basement
Materials List Available: Yes
Price Category: C

Images provided by designer/architect.

You'll love the arched window that announces the grace of this home to the rest of the world.

Features:

- Living Room: Scissor trusses on the ceiling and a superb window design make this room elegant.

- Dining Room: Open to the living room, this dining room features an expansive window area and contains a convenient, inset china closet.

- Family Room: A gas fireplace in the corner and a doorway to the patio make this room the heart of the house.

- Breakfast Room: The bay window here makes it a lovely spot at any time of day.

- Kitchen: A raised snack bar shared with both the family and breakfast rooms adds a nice touch to this well-planned, attractive kitchen.

- Master Suite: A bay window, walk-in closet, and private bath add up to luxurious comfort in this suite.

Rear Elevation

Left Side Elevation

Right Side Elevation

Copyright by designer/architect.

Plan #121123

Dimensions: 54' W x 52' D
Levels: 1.5
Square Footage: 2,277
Main Level Sq. Ft.: 1,570
Upper Level Sq. Ft.: 707
Bedrooms: 4
Bathrooms: 2½
Foundation: Basement;
crawl space for fee
Material List Available: Yes
Price Category: E

Images provided by designer/architect.

This country-style home, with its classic wraparound porch, is just the plan you have been searching for.

Features:

- Entry: This two-story entry gives an open and airy feeling when you enter the home. A view into the dining room and great room adds to the open feeling.

- Great Room: This grand gathering area with cathedral ceiling is ready for your friends and family to come and visit. The fireplace, flanked by large windows, adds a cozy feeling to the space.

- Kitchen: The chef in the family will love how efficiently this island kitchen was designed. An abundance of cabinets and counter space is always a plus.

- Master Suite: This main level oasis will help you relieve all the stresses from the day. The master bath boasts dual vanities and a large walk-in closet.

- Secondary Bedrooms: Three generously sized bedrooms occupy the upper level. The full bathroom is located for easy access to all three bedrooms.

Main Level Floor Plan

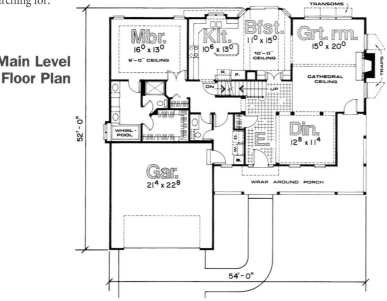

Upper Level Floor Plan

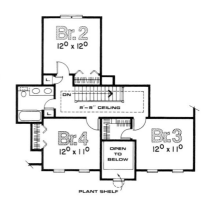

Copyright by designer/architect.

Plan #121167

Dimensions: 84'10" W x 102'3" D

Levels: 1.5

Square Footage: 4,629

Main Level Sq. Ft.: 3,337

Upper Level Sq. Ft.: 1,292

Bedrooms: 4

Bathrooms: 4½

Foundation: Slab; basement for fee

Material List Available: Yes

Price Category: I

The exquisite exterior of this stunning design offers hints of the stylish features waiting inside.

Images provided by designer/architect.

Features:

- Family Room: This large entertaining area features a coffered ceiling and a beautiful fireplace. French doors allow access to the rear yard.

- Kitchen: This island workspace has everything the chef in the family could want. The breakfast room merges with the main kitchen, allowing conversation during cleanup.

- Master Suite: This ground-level suite features a cathedral ceiling and access to the rear yard. The master bath has a marvelous whirlpool tub, dual vanities, and a separate toilet room.

- Upper Level: A large game room, with an overhead view of the family room, and bedrooms 3 and 4 occupy this level. Each bedroom has a private bathroom.

Upper Level Floor Plan

Copyright by designer/architect.

Main Level Floor Plan

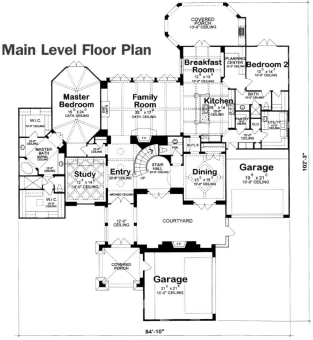

Plan #461092

Dimensions: 81' W x 54' D
Levels: 2
Square Footage: 2,844
Main Level Sq. Ft.: 2,128
Upper Level Sq. Ft.: 716
Bedrooms: 4
Bathrooms: 4
Foundation: Slab or basement; crawl space for fee
Material List Available: Yes
Price Category: F

Images provided by designer/architect.

Enjoy country living at its best in this well-designed home.

Features:

- Dining Room: Located at the entry, this formal dining room features a nook for your hutch. Pocket doors lead into the foyer, adding the ability for the space to work as a home office.

- Guest Suite: This main-level suite offers your guests privacy while staying connected to what is happening in other parts of the house. The accessible full bathroom is a bonus for the area.

- Master Suite: Located on the main level, this retreat boasts two large walk-in closets. The master bath features a whirlpool tub and a stall shower.

- Upper Level: This level is home to the two secondary bedrooms, each with a walk-in closet. Each bedroom has a private bathroom.

Rear View

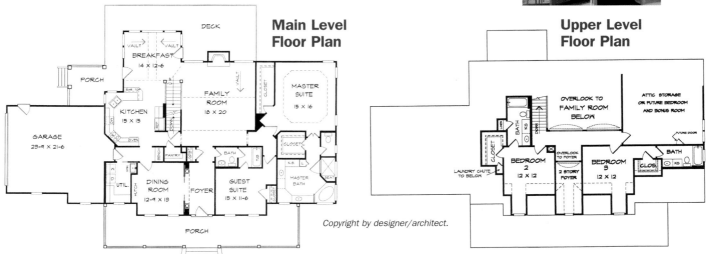

Main Level Floor Plan

Upper Level Floor Plan

Copyright by designer/architect.

Plan #281032

Dimensions: 66' W x 49' D
Levels: 2
Square Footage: 2,904
Main Level Sq. Ft.: 1,494
Upper Level Sq. Ft.: 1,410
Bedrooms: 4
Bathrooms: 2½
Foundation: Basement
Material List Available: Yes
Price Category: F

Images provided by designer/architect.

Country style is alive and well in this attractive home.

Features:

- Front Porch: This front porch welcomes guests to your home. It's the perfect spot to sit and sip lemonade while visiting with friends or family.

- Family Room: Opening onto the rear porch, which comes in handy for enjoying the outdoors, this family room also features a fireplace for the times you would rather stay inside.

- Kitchen: This efficiently designed space features an L-shaped work area, pantry, and island with a raised eating bar. The room opens to the breakfast nook, giving meal times plenty of possibilities.

- Master Suite: Imagine a relaxing breakfast in bed in this luxurious master suite. It contains two large walk-in closets and a full master bath.

Rear Elevation

Main Level Floor Plan

Copyright by designer/architect.

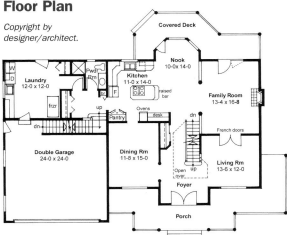

Upper Level Floor Plan

Plan #391056

Dimensions: 73'10" W x 53'4" D
Levels: 2
Square Footage: 2,607
Main Level Sq. Ft.: 1,429
Upper Level Sq. Ft.: 1,178
Bedrooms: 3
Bathrooms: 2½
Foundation: Basement
Materials List Available: Yes
Price Category: F

Images provided by designer/architect.

The spectacular pavilion front with Palladian window creates a dramatic picture indoors and out.

Features:

- Walk up the steps, onto the porch, and then through the front door with sidelights, this entry opens into a two-story space and feels light and airy. The nearby coat closet is a convenient asset.
- Living Room: This "sunken" room features a cozy fireplace flanked by two doors, allowing access to the wraparound deck. The dining room is open to the area, creating a nice flow between the two spaces.
- Family Room: This casual relaxing area is one step down from the kitchen; it boasts another fireplace and access to the large wraparound deck.
- Kitchen: This island kitchen features plenty of cabinet and counter space and is waiting for the chef in the family to take control. The breakfast area with bay window is the perfect place to start the day.
- Upper Level: This area is dedicated to the master suite with full master bath and two family bedrooms. Enjoy the dramatic view as you look down into the entry.

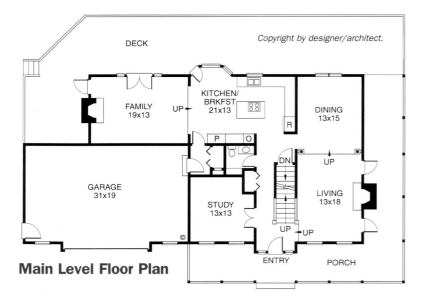

Main Level Floor Plan

Upper Level Floor Plan

Rear View

Kitchen

Living Room

Master Bath

Master Bedroom

Bedroom

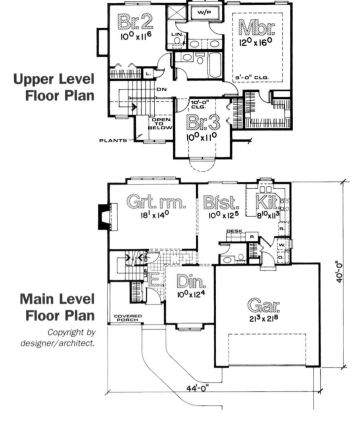

Upper Level Floor Plan

Br. 2
10⁰ x 11⁶

Mbr.
12⁰ x 16⁰

W/P

LIN.

9'-0" CLG.

DN

10'-0" CLG.

OPEN TO BELOW

Br. 3
10⁰ x 11⁰

PLANTS

Main Level Floor Plan

Copyright by designer/architect.

Grt. rm.
18¹ x 14⁰

Bfst.
10⁰ x 12⁵

Kit
8¹⁰ x 11³

DESK

Din.
10⁰ x 12⁴

Gar.
21³ x 21⁸

COVERED PORCH

40'-0"

44'-0"

Plan #121112

Dimensions: 44' W x 40' D

Levels: 2

Square Footage: 1,650

Main Level Sq. Ft.: 891

Upper Level Sq. Ft.: 759

Bedrooms: 3

Bathrooms: 2½

Foundation: Basement; crawl space for fee

Material List Available: Yes

Price Category: C

Images provided by designer/architect.

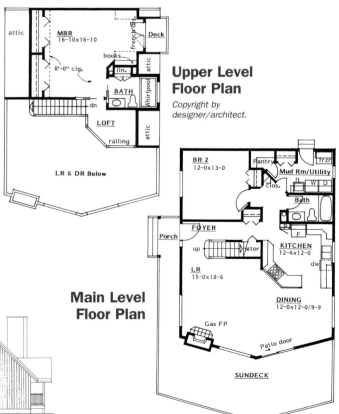

Upper Level Floor Plan

Copyright by designer/architect.

attic

MBR
16-10x16-10

Deck

8'-0" clg.

books

lin.

BATH

Whirlpool

dn

LOFT

railing

attic

LR & DR Below

Main Level Floor Plan

BR 2
12-0x13-0

pantry

frzr

Mud Rm/Utility

clos.

Bath

W D

Porch

FOYER

stor

KITCHEN
12-4x12-0

up

dw

LR
15-0x18-6

DINING
12-0x12-0/9-9

Gas FP

Patio door

SUNDECK

Plan #281014

Dimensions: 66' W x 49' D

Levels: 2

Square Footage: 2,904

Main Level Sq. Ft.: 1,494

Upper Level Sq. Ft.: 1,410

Bedrooms: 2

Bathrooms: 2

Foundation: Crawl space; slab, basement or walkout for fee

Materials List Available: Yes

Price Category: F

Images provided by designer/architect.

CAD FILE AVAILABLE

Rear Elevation

Plan #401008

Dimensions: 87' W x 44' D

Levels: 1

Square Footage: 1,541

Bedrooms: 3

Bathrooms: 2

Foundation: Basement

Materials List Available: Yes

Price Category: C

Images provided by designer/architect.

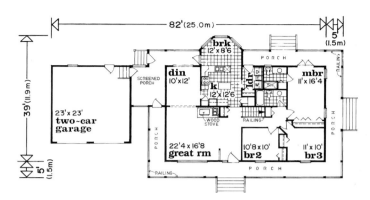

Copyright by designer/architect.

Plan #521006

Dimensions: 99'2" W x 47'5" D

Levels: 1.5

Square Footage: 2,818

Main Level Sq. Ft.: 1,787

Upper Level Sq. Ft.: 1,031

Bedrooms: 4

Bathrooms: 3½

Foundation: Crawl space

Material List Available: Yes

Price Category: F

Images provided by designer/architect.

CAD FILE AVAILABLE

Main Level Floor Plan

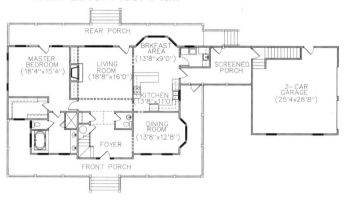

Upper Level Floor Plan

Copyright by designer/architect.

Plan #391211

Dimensions: 58' W x 40' D

Levels: 1

Square Footage: 1,461

Bedrooms: 3

Bathrooms: 2

Foundation: Basement

Material List Available: Yes

Price Category: B

Images provided by designer/architect.

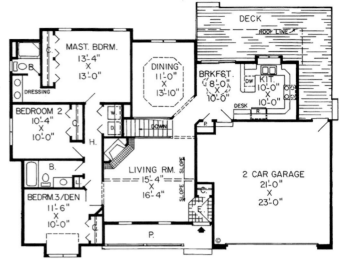

Copyright by designer/architect.

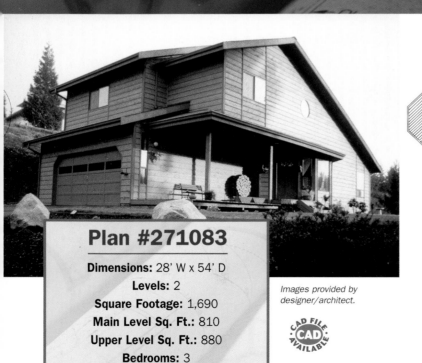

Plan #271083

Dimensions: 28' W x 54' D

Levels: 2

Square Footage: 1,690

Main Level Sq. Ft.: 810

Upper Level Sq. Ft.: 880

Bedrooms: 3

Bathrooms: 2½

Foundation: Crawl space

Materials List Available: Yes

Price Category: C

Images provided by designer/architect.

CAD FILE AVAILABLE

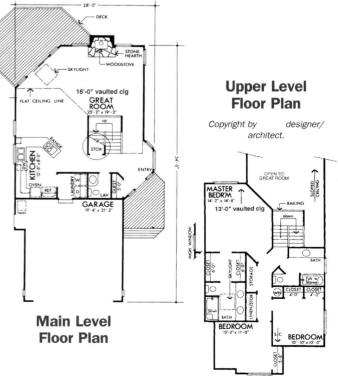

Upper Level Floor Plan

Copyright by designer/architect.

Main Level Floor Plan

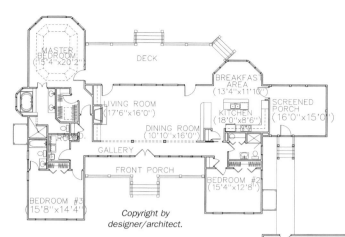

Plan #521017

Dimensions: 94'11" W x 94'10" D
Levels: 1
Square Footage: 2,359
Bedrooms: 3
Bathrooms: 3
Foundation: Slab
Material List Available: Yes
Price Category: E

Images provided by designer/architect.

Copyright by designer/architect.

Rear View

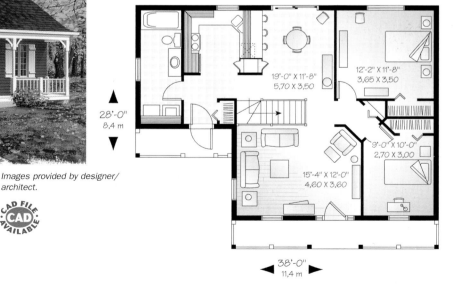

Copyright by designer/architect.

Plan #181001

Dimensions: 38' W x 28' D
Levels: 1
Square Footage: 920
Bedrooms: 2
Bathrooms: 1
Foundation: Basement
Materials List Available: Yes
Price Category: A

Images provided by designer/architect.

Plan #151490

Dimensions: 52' W x 69'6" D

Levels: 1

Square Footage: 1,869

Bedrooms: 3

Bathrooms: 2

Foundation: Crawl space or slab

CompleteCost List Available: Yes

Price Category: D

Images provided by designer/architect.

Beautiful brick and wood siding impart warmth to this French Country design.

Features:

- Open Plan: Elegance is achieved in this home by using boxed columns and 10-ft.-high ceilings. The foyer and dining room are lined with columns and adjoin the great room, all with high ceilings.

- Kitchen: This combined kitchen and breakfast room is great for entertaining and has access to the grilling porch.

- Master Suite: The split-bedroom plan features this suite, with its large walk-in closet, whirlpool tub, shower, and private area.

- Bedrooms: The two bedrooms and a large bathroom are located on the other side of the great room, giving privacy to the entire family.

Bonus Area Floor Plan

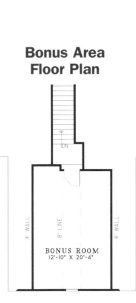

Copyright by designer/architect.

Plan #121147

Dimensions: 40' W x 51' D
Levels: 1.5
Square Footage: 2,051
Main Level Sq. Ft.: 1,497
Upper Level Sq. Ft.: 554
Bedrooms: 3
Bathrooms: 2½
Foundation: Basement;
crawl space for fee
Material List Available: Yes
Price Category: D

Images provided by designer/architect.

This home, as shown in the photograph, may differ from the actual blueprints. For more detailed information, please check the floor plans carefully.

CAD FILE AVAILABLE

Multiple rooflines add to the charm of this home.

Features:

• Family Room: This room is sure to be your family's headquarters, thanks to the sloped ceiling, central location, and cozy fireplace.

• Kitchen: This island kitchen with double sink includes a snack bar open to the family room. The walk-in pantry provides ample storage

space, and the nearby computer niche comes in handy when planning meals.

• Master Suite: For the sake of privacy, this retreat is located on the main floor away from the secondary bedrooms. The large walk-in closet and luxurious private bath are welcome amenities.

• Garage: This front-loading two-car garage can keep your cars warm and dry.

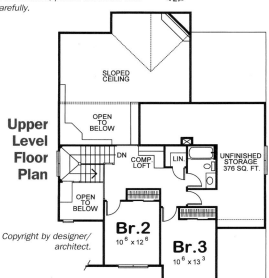

Copyright by designer/architect.

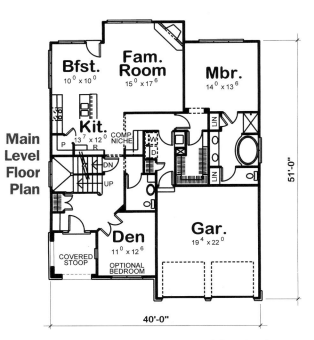

Plan #181630

Dimensions: 38' W x 31'4" D
Levels: 2
Square Footage: 2,098
Main Level Sq. Ft.: 1,092
Upper Level Sq. Ft.: 1,006
Bedrooms: 3
Bathrooms: 1½
Foundation: Basement
Material List Available: Yes
Price Category: F

This country-style home would look great in any neighborhood.

Images provided by designer/architect.

Features:

- Entry: This two-story space welcomes you to this home. The center staircase, with a balcony above, gives a spacious feeling to the home.

- Family Room: The glow of natural light from the windows and the fireplace envelops this room. Whether you are relaxing with your family or entertaining guests, this room is ideal for bringing people together.

- Dining Room: This large space has plenty of room to serve formal meals. The room's closeness to the kitchen makes serving a snap.

- Upper Level: Three bedrooms make this level their home; they share a common bathroom. The master bedroom boasts a sitting area.

Main Level Floor Plan

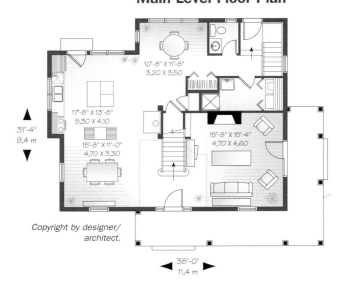

31'-4"
9,4 m

10'-8" X 11'-8"
3,20 X 3,50

17'-8" X 13'-8"
5,30 X 4,10

15'-8" X 11'-0"
4,70 X 3,30

15'-8" X 15'-4"
4,70 X 4,60

Copyright by designer/architect.

38'-0"
11,4 m

Upper Level Floor Plan

13'-8"/11'-8" X 21'-8"
4,10/3,50 X 6,50

11'-8" X 10'-0"
3,50 X 3,00

11'-8" X 12'-0"
3,50 X 3,60

Plan #321002

Dimensions: 72' W x 28' D
Levels: 1
Square Footage: 1,400
Bedrooms: 3
Bathrooms: 2
Foundation: Crawl space, basement
Materials List Available: Yes
Price Category: D

If you're looking for a well-designed compact home with contemporary amenities, this could be the home of your dreams.

Features:

- Porch: Just the right size for some rockers and a swing, this porch could become your outdoor living area when the weather is fine.

- Living Room: A vaulted ceiling adds to the spacious feeling in this room, where friends and family are sure to gather.

- Kitchen: This space-saving design, in combination with the ample counter and cabinet space, makes cooking a pleasure.

- Utility Room: This large room is fitted with cabinets for extra storage space. You'll find storage space in the large garage, too.

- Master Bedroom: This room is somewhat secluded for privacy, making it an ideal place for some quiet time at the end of the day.

Images provided by designer/architect.

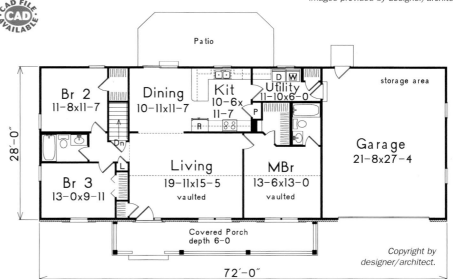

CAD FILE AVAILABLE

Copyright by designer/architect.

SMARTtip

Fabric Draping Ability

Test a fabric's draping ability by looking at a large piece in a fabric store. Gather at least two to three yards of material, holding one end in your hand. Check how it drapes. Does it fall into folds easily? Also look at the pattern when it is gathered. Does the design become lost in the folds? Ask a sales-clerk or a friend to hold the fabric, and look at it from a few feet away.

Plan #151035

Dimensions: 37'8" W x 38'4" D

Levels: 1.5

Square Footage: 1,451

Main Level Sq. Ft.: 868

Upper Level Sq. Ft: 583

Bedrooms: 3

Bathrooms: 2

Foundation: Crawl space or slab; basement or walkout for fee

CompleteCost List Available: Yes

Price Category: B

Country living meets the modern day family in this well designed home.

CAD FILE AVAILABLE

Images provided by designer/architect.

Features:

- Den: The large stone fireplace is the focal point in this gathering area. Located just off the entry porch, the area welcomes you home.

- Kitchen: This efficiently designed kitchen has an abundance of cabinets and counter space. The eat-at counter, open to the den, adds extra space for family and friends.

- Grilling Porch: On nice days, overflow your dinner guests onto this rear covered grilling porch. From the relaxing area you can watch the kids play in the backyard.

- Upper Level: Two bedrooms, with large closets, and a full bathroom occupy this level. The dormers in each of the bedrooms add more space to these rooms.

Kitchen/Den

Porch

Kitchen

Master Bedroom

Main Level Floor Plan

Upper Level Floor Plan

Images provided by designer/architect.

Den

Dining Room

Plan #391070

Dimensions: 52' W x 31' D

Levels: 2

Square Footage: 1,960

Main Level Sq. Ft.: 1,005

Upper Level Sq. Ft.: 955

Bedrooms: 4

Bathrooms: 2½

Foundation: Crawl space, slab, or basement

Material List Available: Yes

Price Category: D

Main Level Floor Plan

KITCHEN 14'-4" x 9'-6"

FAMILY ROOM 14'-4" x 15'-4"

GARAGE 21'-8" x 21'-4"

UTIL

DINING ROOM 10'-10" x 13'-4"

LIVING ROOM 10'-10" x 13'-4"

FOYER

PORCH

OPT. PATIO

STEP

52'-0"

31'-0"

Images provided by designer/architect.

Crawl Space/Slab Option

BATH

BEDROOM 4 9'-10" x 13'-0"

BEDROOM 3 10'-10" x 13'-0"

DRESSING AREA

C.

LINEN

HALL

MASTER BEDROOM 14'-4" x 13'-4"

BEDROOM 2 10'-10 x 10'-0"

SLOPED CEILING

VAULTED CEILING

Upper Level Floor Plan

Copyright by designer/architect.

Plan #521043

Dimensions: 36' W x 43'8" D

Levels: 2

Square Footage: 1,536

Main Level Sq. Ft.: 1,038

Upper Level Sq. Ft.: 498

Bedrooms: 3

Bathrooms: 2½

Foundation: Crawl space

Material List Available: Yes

Price Category: C

Main Level Floor Plan

Copyright by designer/architect.

MASTER BEDROOM (16'4"x11'10")

SCREENED PORCH (10'2"x10'4")

DINING AREA (9'10"x9'8")

LAUNDRY 8'2"x6'0"

KITCHEN (12'8"x8'0")

LIVING ROOM (17'8"x14'2")

ENTRY 8'6"x4'10"

8' FRONT WRAP AROUND PORCH

CAD FILE AVAILABLE

Images provided by designer/architect.

Side View

BEDROOM #2 (11'4"x9'10")

BATH

BEDROOM #3 (11'4"x9'10")

Upper Level Floor Plan

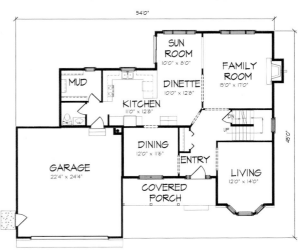

Main Level Floor Plan

Upper Level Floor Plan

Copyright by designer/architect.

Plan #271062

Dimensions: 54' W x 45' D

Levels: 2

Square Footage: 2,356

Main Level Sq. Ft.: 1,222

Upper Level Sq. Ft.: 1,134

Bedrooms: 4

Bathrooms: 2½

Foundation: Daylight basement

Materials List Available: Yes

Price Category: E

Images provided by designer/architect.

Upper Level Floor Plan

Main Level Floor Plan

Copyright by designer/architect.

Plan #521030

Dimensions: 41'8" W x 41' D

Levels: 2

Square Footage: 1,660

Main Level Sq. Ft.: 1,034

Upper Level Sq. Ft.: 626

Bedrooms: 4

Bathrooms: 2½

Foundation: Crawl space

Material List Available: Yes

Price Category: C

Images provided by designer/architect.

CAD FILE AVAILABLE

Plan #121118

Dimensions: 42' W x 59'8" D

Levels: 1

Square Footage: 1,636

Bedrooms: 3

Bathrooms: 2

Foundation: Basement; crawl space for fee

Material List Available: Yes

Price Category: C

Images provided by designer/architect.

Copyright by designer/architect.

Plan #391060

Dimensions: 58' W x 34'4" D

Levels: 1

Square Footage: 1,359

Bedrooms: 3

Bathrooms: 2

Foundation: Crawl space, slab or basement

Materials List Available: Yes

Price Category: B

Images provided by designer/architect.

Rear View

Plan #521040

Dimensions: 42'2" W x 57' D
Levels: 1
Square Footage: 1,555
Bedrooms: 3
Bathrooms: 2½
Foundation: Slab
Material List Available: Yes
Price Category: C

Copyright by designer/architect.

Images provided by designer/architect.

This home, as shown in the photographs, may differ from the actual blueprints. For more detailed information, please check the floor plans carefully.

Front View

Rear View

Plan #321030

Dimensions: 61' W x 51' D
Levels: 1
Square Footage: 2,029
Bedrooms: 4
Bathrooms: 2
Foundation: Crawl space, slab, basement, or walkout
Materials List Available: Yes
Price Category: F

Images provided by designer/architect.

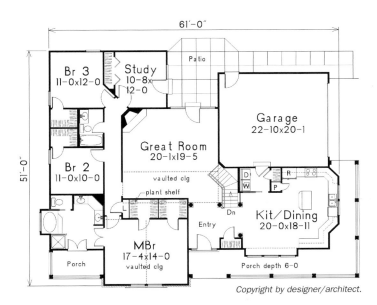

Copyright by designer/architect.

SMARTtip

Measuring Angles

A sure-fire way to accurately measure the wall-frame acute angle is to cut a piece of scrap lumber to emulate the angle, and then measure it.

Plan #181126

Dimensions: 35' W x 30' D
Levels: 2
Square Footage: 1,468
Main Level Sq. Ft.: 958
Upper Level Sq. Ft.: 510
Bedrooms: 3
Bathrooms: 2
Foundation: Basement
Materials List Available: Yes
Price Category: B

Images provided by designer/architect.
This home, as shown in the photograph, may differ from the actual blueprints. For more detailed information, please check the floor plans carefully.

A multiple-gabled roof and a covered entry give this home a charming appearance.

Features:

- Entry: You'll keep heating and cooling costs down with this air-lock entry. There is also a large closet here.

- Kitchen: This efficient L-shaped eat-in kitchen has access to the rear deck.

- Great Room: This two-story space has a cozy fireplace and is open to the kitchen.

- Master Bedroom: Located on the main level, this area has access to the main bathroom, which has an oversized tub and a compartmentalized lavatory.

- Bedrooms: The two secondary bedrooms are located on the upper level and share a common bathroom.

Great Room

Main Level Floor Plan

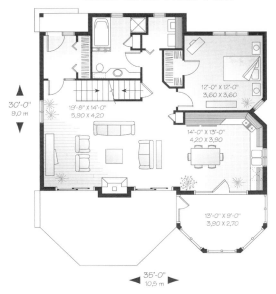

30'-0"
9,0 m

35'-0"
10,5 m

19'-8" X 14'-0"
5,90 X 4,20

12'-0" X 12'-0"
3,60 X 3,60

14'-0" X 13'-0"
4,20 X 3,90

13'-0" X 9'-0"
3,90 X 2,70

10'-0" X 11'-0"
3,00 X 3,30

15'-0" X 11'-0"
4,50 X 3,30

Upper Level Floor Plan

Copyright by designer/architect.

Rear View

Dining Room

Kitchen

Stairs

Plan #211069

Dimensions: 58' W x 42' D
Levels: 1.5
Square Footage: 1,600
Main Level Sq. Ft.: 1,136
Upper Level Sq. Ft.: 464
Bedrooms: 3
Bathrooms: 2
Foundation: Crawl space
Materials List Available: Yes
Price Category: C

Enjoy the large front porch on this traditionally styled home when it's too sunny for the bugs, and use the screened back porch at dusk and dawn.

Features:

• Living Room: Call this the family room if you wish, but no matter what you call it, expect friends and family to gather here, especially when the fireplace gives welcome warmth.

• Kitchen: You'll love the practical layout that pleases everyone from gourmet chefs to beginning cooks.

• Master Suite: Positioned on the main floor to give it privacy, this suite has two entrances for convenience. You'll find a large walk-in closet here as well as a dressing room that includes a separate vanity and mirror makeup counter.

• Storage Space: The 462-sq.-ft. garage is roomy enough to hold two cars and still have space to store tools, out-of-season clothing, or whatever else that needs a dry, protected spot.

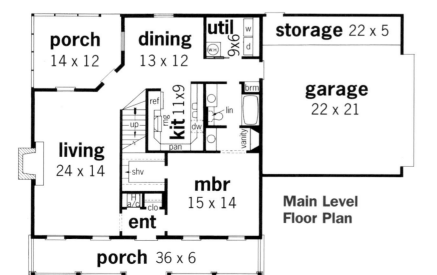

Main Level Floor Plan

Upper Level Floor Plan

Copyright by designer/architect.

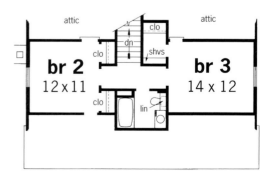

Plan #121212

Dimensions: 54' W x 44' D
Levels: 2
Square Footage: 2,219
Main Level Sq. Ft.: 1,132
Upper Level Sq. Ft.: 1,087
Bedrooms: 4
Bathrooms: 2½
Foundation: Basement;
crawl space for fee
Material List Available: Yes
Price Category: E

Images provided by designer/architect.

Country charm abounds in this lovely home.

Features:

• **Entry:** The central location of this large entry allows access to the dining room or great room. The area features a handy closet.

• **Great Room:** This gathering area features a 10-ft.-high ceiling and large windows, which allow plenty of natural light into the space.

• **Upper Level:** Three bedrooms and the master suite occupy this level. The master suite features a tray ceiling and a well-appointed bath.

• **Garage:** A front-loading two-car garage with additional storage completes the floor plan.

Rear View

Main Level Floor Plan

Copyright by designer/architect.

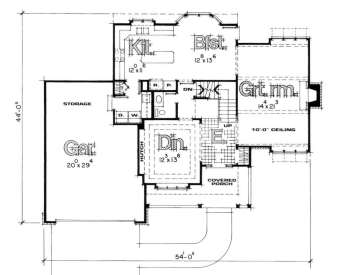

Upper Level Floor Plan

Plan #161037

Dimensions: 46' W x 59'4" D
Levels: 1
Square Footage: 2,469
Main Level Sq. Ft.: 1,462
Basement Level Sq. Ft.: 1,007
Bedrooms: 2
Bathrooms: 2½
Foundation: Walkout; basement for fee
Materials List Available: Yes
Price Category: E

Images provided by designer/architect.

A brick-and-stone facade welcomes you into this lovely home, which is designed to fit into a narrow lot.

Features:

- **Foyer:** This entrance, with vaulted ceiling, introduces the graciousness of this home.

- **Great Room:** A vaulted center ceiling creates the impression that this large great room and dining room are one space, making entertaining a natural in this area.

- **Kitchen:** Designed for efficiency with ample storage and counter space, this kitchen also allows casual dining at the counter.

- **Master Suite:** A tray ceiling sets this room off from the rest of the house, and the lavishly equipped bathroom lets you pamper yourself.

- **Lower Level:** Put extra bedrooms or a library in this finished area, and use the wet bar in a game room or recreation room.

Dining Room

Rear Elevation

Copyright by designer/architect.

Main Level Floor Plan

Optional Screened Porch 12 x 12
Deck
Dining 13' x 15'4"
Great Room 15' x 18'6"
Master Bedroom 16'4" x 14'
Kitchen 13' x 12'6"
Foyer
Dress.
Bath
Laun.
walk-in closet
Porch
Garage 22'2" x 26'5"
59'4"
46'

Basement Level Floor Plan

Library 12'7" X 12'
Bath
Hall
Rec Room 22'6" X 18'7"
Bedroom 14'5" X 14'10"
Wet Bar
Basement
Unexcavated
Unexcavated

Plan #121144

Dimensions: 40' W x 48'8" D

Levels: 1

Square Footage: 1,195

Bedrooms: 3

Bathrooms: 2

Foundation: Basement; crawl space for fee

Material List Available: Yes

Price Category: B

This is the right design if you want a home that will be easy to expand as your family grows.

Features:

- **Front Porch:** Hang baskets of plants from the roof of this porch, which is just the right size for a couple of comfortable rocking chairs and a side table.

- **Family Room:** This family room welcomes you as you enter the home. A crackling fire enhances the ambiance of the room.

- **Kitchen:** This intelligently designed kitchen has an efficient U-shape layout. A serving bar open to the dining area is a feature that makes entertaining easier.

- **Master Suite:** This is a compact space that is designed to feel large, and it includes a walk-in closet. The master bath is an added bonus.

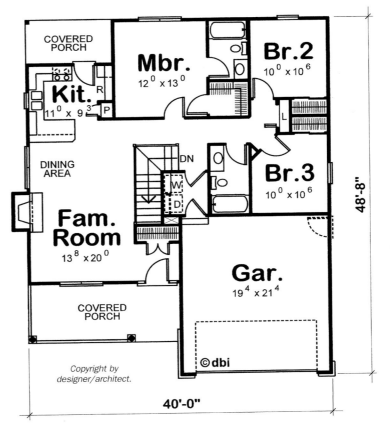

Copyright by designer/architect.

Plan #131029

Dimensions: 56'4" W x 45'10" D
Levels: 2
Square Footage: 2,718
Main Level Sq. Ft.: 1,515
Upper Level Sq. Ft.: 1,203
Bedrooms: 4
Bathrooms: 2½
Foundation: Crawl space or slab; basement for feet
Materials List Available: Yes
Price Category: G

This home, as shown in the photograph, may differ from the actual blueprints. For more detailed information, please check the floor plans carefully.

Images provided by designer/architect.

This home is ideal if you love the look of a country-style farmhouse.

Features:

- Foyer: Walk across the large wraparound porch that defines this home to enter this two-story foyer.
- Living Room: French doors from the foyer lead into this living room.

- Family Room: The whole family will love this room, with its vaulted ceiling, fireplace, and sliding glass doors that open to the wooden rear deck.
- Kitchen: A beautiful sit-down center island opens to the family room. There's also a breakfast nook with a lovely bay window.
- Master Suite: Luxury abounds with vaulted ceilings, walk-in closets, private bath with whirlpool tub, separate shower, and dual sinks.
- Loft: A special place with vaulted ceiling and view into the family room below.

Main Level Floor Plan

Copyright by designer/architect.

Upper Level Floor Plan

Rear Elevation

Dining Room

Breakfast Area

Kitchen Island

Kitchen

Master Bathroom

Plan #311009

Dimensions: 68' W x 56'6" D
Levels: 1
Square Footage: 1,894
Bedrooms: 3
Bathrooms: 2½
Foundation: Crawl space, slab, or basement
Materials List Available: Yes
Price Category: E

Images provided by designer/architect.

Perfectly at home on a tree-lined street in a quiet neighborhood, this sweet design is a contemporary version of an old-fashioned standard.

Features:

• **Great Room:** Gather by the glowing fire on cold nights, or expand your entertaining space any other time. This great room is at the center of everything and has plenty of space for friends, family, and anyone else you can think to invite.

• **Kitchen:** Plenty of workspace, ample storage, a convenient snack bar, and close proximity to both the dining room and breakfast area make this kitchen ideal for chefs and entertainers of all kinds. The kitchen layout simplifies hectic mornings, family dinners, and formal parties.

• **Master Suite:** You'll be close to your family, but in a world of your own in this master suite. The design simplifies your life with dual walk-in closets, his and her sinks, and separate tub and shower.

• **Secondary Bedrooms:** These bedrooms boast ample closet space and equal distance to a full bathroom. They're also off the beaten path, creating a calmer space for study and sleep.

Rear View

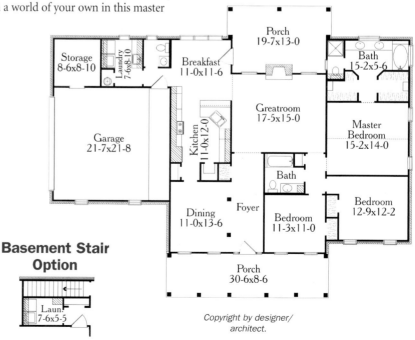

Copyright by designer/ architect.

Basement Stair Option

Laun.
7-6x5-5

Plan #161032

Dimensions: 75'8 W x 70'6" D
Levels: 2
Square Footage: 4,517
Main Level Sq. Footage: 2,562
Lower Level Sq. Footage: 1,955
Bedrooms: 3
Bathrooms: 2 full, 2 half
Foundation: Basement
Material List Available: Yes
Price Category: I

SMARTtip

Art Underfoot

Make a simple geometric pattern with your flooring materials. Create a focal point in a courtyard or a small area of a patio by fashioning an intricate mosaic with tile, stone, or colored concrete. By combining elements and colors, a simple garden room floor becomes a wonderful work of art. Whether you commission a craftsman or do it yourself, you'll have a permanent art installation right in your own backyard.

The brick-and-stone exterior, a recessed entry, and a tower containing a large library combine to convey the strength and character of this enchanting house.

Features:

• **Hearth Room:** Your family or guests will enjoy this large, comfortable hearth room, whcih has a gas fireplace and access to the rear deck, perfect for friendly gatherings.

• **Kitchen:** This spacious kitchen features a walk-in pantry and a center island.

• **Master Suite:** Designed for privacy, this master suite includes a sloped ceilng and opens to the rear deck. It also features a deluxe whirlpool bath, walk-in shower, separate his-and-her vanities, and a walk-in closet.

• **Lower Level:** This lower level includes a separate wine room, exercise room, sauna, two bedrooms, and enough space for a huge recreation room.

Rear Elevation

Rear Elevation

Images provided by designer/architect.

Main Level Floor Plan

Lower Level Floor Plan

Copyright by designer/architect.

Plan #121160

Dimensions: 66'4½" W x 49'9½" D
Levels: 1.5
Square Footage: 2,188
Main Level Sq. Ft.: 1,531
Upper Level Sq. Ft.: 657
Bedrooms: 3
Bathrooms: 2½
Foundation: Slab; basement for fee
Materials List Available: Yes
Price Category: D

The standing-seam roof on the wraparound porch gives this home a charming country look.

Images provided by designer/architect.

Features:

- **Family Room:** The open design that leads to the adjoining breakfast area makes this space airy and welcoming. The room also features a tray ceiling. The fireplace adds to the comfortable feel of the space.

- **Dining Room / Sunroom:** Featuring three exterior walls with windows, this space can either be your formal dining room or your casual sunroom.

- **Kitchen:** This peninsula kitchen boasts a raised bar open to the breakfast room. The walk-in pantry is always a welcome feature.

- **Master Suite:** Located on the main level, this retreat features a bay window with a view of the backyard. The master bath features a large walk-in closet and dual vanities.

Front View

Main Level Floor Plan

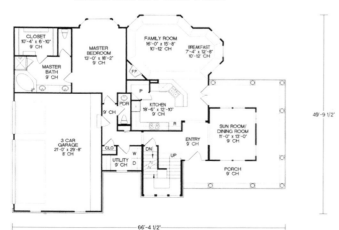

Upper Level Floor Plan

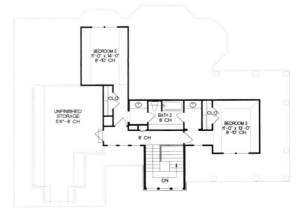

Copyright by designer/architect.

Plan #321033

Dimensions: 38' W x 46' D
Levels: 1
Square Footage: 1,268
Bedrooms: 3
Bathrooms: 2
Foundation: Basement
Materials List Available: Yes
Price Category: B

Clean lines and a layout fit for contemporary living create a graceful and efficient update to a simple cottage design that is perfect for families just starting out.

Features:

- **Great Room:** At the center of everything, this great room will be the heart of the home. Its unhampered transition into the dining areas and kitchen creates a feeling of openness that will welcome guests into your home.

- **Kitchen:** This kitchen maximizes space and efficiency with simple transitions and plenty of workspace. The laundry room is adjacent for easy cleanup; the dining room and breakfast area are just steps away; and a snack bar provides the only barrier between the kitchen and great room. Cookouts are also simplified by easy access to the back patio.

- **Master Suite:** Everyone knows that the master bath makes the master suite, and this home is no different. His and her sinks, a large tub with a view, and a separate standing shower combine to create both a retreat and a remedy for hectic mornings.

- **Secondary Bedrooms:** Bedroom 2 has plenty of closet space and would be perfect for a nursery or even a converted office. Bedroom 3 also has ample closet space and is opened up by a vaulted ceiling. Both are in a space of their own with a nearby full bathroom.

Images provided by designer/architect.

Copyright by designer/architect.

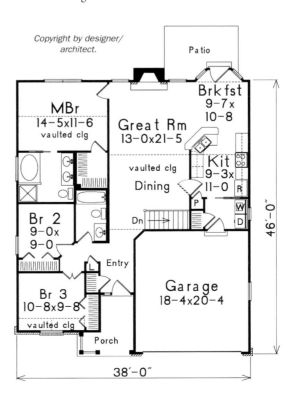

Plan #131030

Dimensions: 51' W x 41'10" D
Levels: 2
Square Footage: 2,470
Main Level Sq. Ft.: 1,290
Upper Level Sq. Ft.: 1,180
Bedrooms: 4
Bathrooms: 2½
Foundation: Crawl space or slab; basement or walkout for fee
Materials List Available: Yes
Price Category: F

This home, as shown in the photograph, may differ from the actual blueprints. For more detailed information, please check the floor plans carefully.

Master Bedroom

Master Bathroom

Entry

If high ceilings and spacious rooms make you happy, you'll love this gorgeous home.

Features:

- **Family Room:** An 18-ft. vaulted ceiling that's open to the balcony above, a corner fireplace, and a wall of windows make this room feel special.

- **Dining Room:** This formal room, which flows into the living room, also opens to the front porch and optional backyard deck.

- **Kitchen:** A bright breakfast room joins with this kitchen and opens to the backyard deck.

- **Master Suite:** You'll smile when you see the 11-ft. vaulted ceiling, stunning arched window, and two walk-in closets in the bedroom. A skylight lets natural light into the private bath, with its spa tub, separate shower, and dual-sink vanity.

- **Bedrooms:** To reach these three charming bedrooms, you'll admire the view into the family room below as you walk along the balcony hall.

Main Level Floor Plan

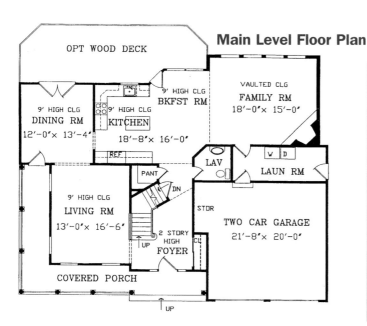

OPT WOOD DECK

9' HIGH CLG
DINING RM
12'-0"× 13'-4"

9' HIGH CLG
KITCHEN
18'-8"× 16'-0"

9' HIGH CLG
BKFST RM

VAULTED CLG
FAMILY RM
18'-0"× 15'-0"

REF

PANT

LAV

W D
LAUN RM

9' HIGH CLG
LIVING RM
13'-0"× 16'-6"

DN

UP

2 STORY
HIGH
FOYER

STOR

CL

TWO CAR GARAGE
21'-8"× 20'-0"

COVERED PORCH

UP

Upper Level Floor Plan

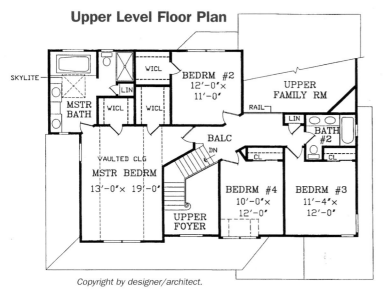

SKYLITE

MSTR
BATH

WICL

LIN

WICL WICL

BEDRM #2
12'-0"×
11'-0"

UPPER
FAMILY RM

RAIL

LIN

BATH
#2

VAULTED CLG
MSTR BEDRM
13'-0"× 19'-0"

BALC

DN

CL

CL

BEDRM #4
10'-0"×
12'-0"

BEDRM #3
11'-4"×
12'-0"

UPPER
FOYER

Copyright by designer/architect.

Kitchen/Breakfast Area

Dining Room

Living Room

Kitchen/Breakfast Area

Color

No other decorating component has more power and greater effect at such little cost than color. It can fill a space and make furnishings look fresh and new. Color can also show off fine architectural details or downplay a room's structural flaws. A particular color can make a cold room cozy, while another hue can cool down a sunny cooker. And color comes cheap, giving a tremendous impact for your decorating dollar: elbow grease, supplies, prep work, and paint will all cost pretty much the same if you choose a gorgeous hue over plain white.

But finding the color—the right color—isn't easy. Where do you begin to look? Like the economy, color has leading indicators. You have a market basket full of choices, and there are lots of signposts to direct you where to go.

The Lay of the Land

For the past 200 years, white has been the most popular choice for American home exteriors. And it still is, followed by tan, brown, and beige. You can play it safe and follow the leader. But you should also think about the architecture of your house and where you live when you're considering exterior color. For example, traditional Colonials have a color-combination range of about two that look appropriate: white with black or green shutters and gray with white trim. Mediterranean-style houses typically pick up the colors of terra-cotta and the tile that are indigenous to the regions that developed the architecture—France, Italy, and Spain. A ranch-style house shouldn't be overdone—it is, after all, usually a modest structure. On the other hand, a cottage can be fanciful. Whimsical colors also look charming on Victorian houses in San Francisco, but they would be out of place in conservative Scarsdale, New York, where you must check with the local building board even when you want to change the exterior color of your house.

How's the Weather?

Like exteriors, interiors often take their color cues from their environs and local traditions. In the rainy and often chilly Pacific Northwest, cozy blanket plaids in strong reds and black abound. In the hot-and-arid climate of the West, indigo or brown ticking-stripes and faded denim look appropriately casual and cool. Subtle grays and neutrals, reflecting steel, limestone, and concrete, look apropos for sophisticated city life. In extremely warm southern climates, the brilliant sun tends to overpower lighter colors. That explains the popularity of strong hues in tropical, sun-drenched locales.

Natural Light. That's the one you don't pay for. Its direction and intensity greatly affects color. A room with a window that faces trees will look markedly different in summer, when warm white sunlight is filtered through the leaves, than in winter, when the trees are bare and the color of natural light takes on a cool blue cast. Time of day affects color, too. Yellow walls that are pleasant and cheerful in the early morning can be stifling and blinding in the afternoon. That's because afternoon sun is stronger than morning sun.

When you're choosing a color for an interior, always view it at different times

The yellow-colored wall, above, complements the antique painted dresser.

Warm neutral-color walls, opposite, and touches of red make this bedroom cozy.

of day, but especially during the hours in which you will inhabit the room.

Artificial Light. Because artificial light affects color rendition as much as natural light, don't judge a color in the typically chilly fluorescence of a hardware store. The very same color chip will look completely different when you bring it home, which is why it's so important to test out a paint color in your own home. Most fluorescent light is bluish and distorts colors. It depresses red and exaggerates green, for example. A romantic faded rose on your dining room walls will just wash out in the kitchen if your use a fluorescent light there. Incandescent light, the type produced by the standard bulbs you probably use in your chandelier and in most of your home's light fixtures, is warm but slightly yellow. Halogen light, which comes from another newer type of incandescent bulb, is white and the closest to natural sunlight. Of all three types of bulbs, halogen is truest in rendering color.

red

RED is powerful, dramatic, motivating. Red is also hospitable, and it stimulates the appetite, which makes it a favorite choice for dining rooms. Some studies have indicated that a red room actually makes people feel warmer.

yellow

YELLOW illuminates the colors it surrounds. It warms rooms that receive north-
ern light but can be too bright in a sunny room. It's best for daytime rooms, not
bedrooms. It has a short range, which means as white is added to yellow, it disap-
pears. Yellow highlights and calls attention to features—think of bright taxicabs.

green

GREEN is tranquil, nurturing, rejuvenating. It is a psychological primary, and because it is mixed from yellow and blue, it can appear both warm and cool. Time seems to pass more quickly in green rooms. Perhaps that's why waiting rooms off-stage are called "green rooms."

 # neutrals

GRAY goes with all colors—it is a good neighbor. Various tones of gray range from dark charcoal to pale oyster.

BLACK (technically the absence of color) enhances and brightens other colors, making for livelier decorating schemes when used as an accent.

 # pink

PINK is perceived as outgoing and active. It's also a color that flatters skin tones. Hot shades are invigorating, while soft, toned-down versions can be relaxed and charming.

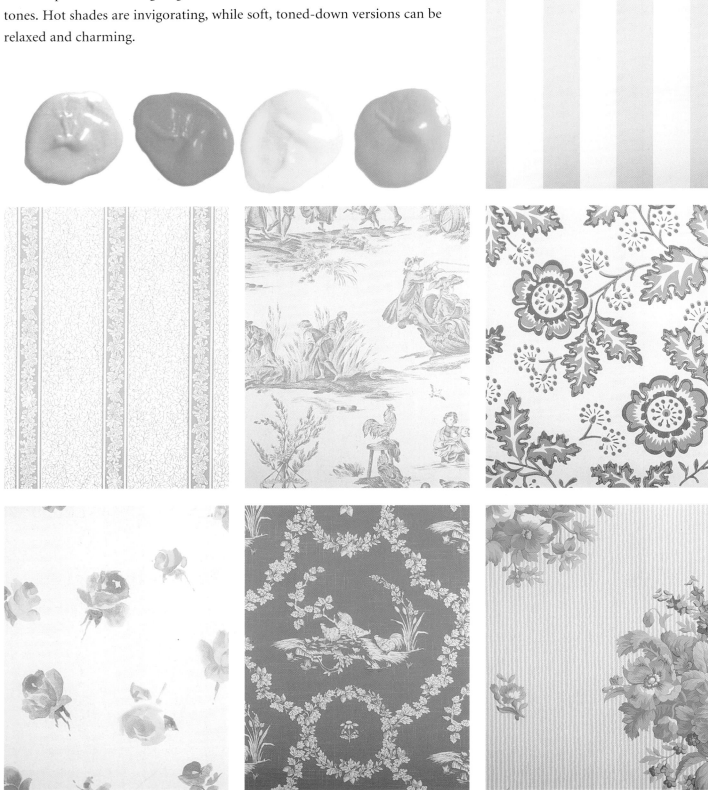

blue

BLUE, with its associations of sea and sky, offers serenity, which is why it is a favorite in bedrooms. Studies have shown that people think better in blue rooms. Perhaps that explains the popularity of the navy blue suit. Cooler blues show this color's melancholy side, however.

Plan #291015

Dimensions: 88'6" W x 58'3" D
Levels: 1.5
Square Footage: 2,901
Main Level Sq. Ft.: 2,078
Upper Level Sq. Ft.: 823
Bedrooms: 3
Bathrooms: 2½
Foundation: Basement
Materials List Available: Yes
Price Category: F

Upon entering this home, a cathedral-like timber-framed interior fills the eye.

Features:

- **Great Room:** This large gathering area's ceiling rises up two stories and is open to the kitchen. The beautiful fireplace is the focal point of this room.

- **Kitchen:** This island kitchen is open to the great room and the breakfast nook. Warm woods of all species enhance the great room and this space.

- **Master Suite:** This suite has a sloped ceiling and adjoins a luxurious master bath with twin walk-in closets that open to a sunroom with a private balcony.

- **Upper Level:** This upper level has an open lounge that leads to two bedrooms with vaulted ceilings and a generous second bath.

Images provided by designer/architect.

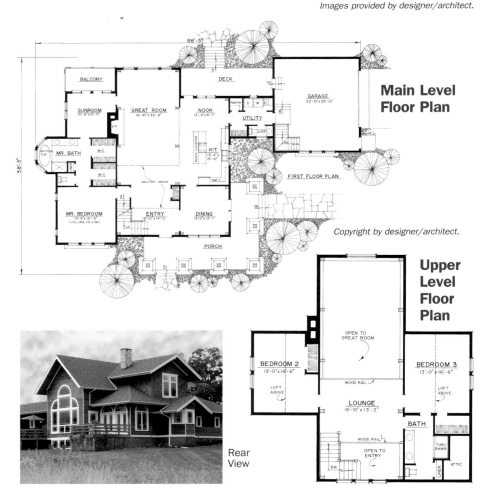

Main Level Floor Plan

Copyright by designer/architect.

Rear View

Upper Level Floor Plan

Great Room

Dining Room

Kitchen

Rear Porch

Plan #181221

Dimensions: 60' W x 44' D
Levels: 2
Square Footage: 3,411
Main Level Sq. Ft.: 1,488
Upper Level Sq. Ft.: 603
Basement Level Sq. Ft.: 1,321
Bedrooms: 3
Bathrooms: 2½
Foundation: Basement
Materials List Available: Yes
Price Category: I

Images provided by designer/architect.

This stone- and wood-sided home will be a joy to come home to.

Features:

- **Living Room:** This large entertaining area features a fireplace and large windows.

- **Kitchen:** Any cook would feel at home in this island kitchen, which has an abundance of cabinets and counter space.

- **Master Bedroom:** Located on the main level for privacy, this room features a walk-in closet and access to the main-level full bathroom.

- **Bedrooms:** One bedroom is located on the upper level and the other is located on the main level. Each has a large closet.

Study

Living Room

Main Level Floor Plan

44'-0"
13,2 m

60'-0"
18.0 m

17'-0" X 14'
5,10 X 4,30

13'-4" X 14'
4,00 X 4,25

16'-4" X 22'
4,90 X 6,80

15'-0" X 15'
4,50 X 4,60

12'-0" X 10'
3,60 X 3,00

Upper Level Floor Plan

Copyright by designer/architect.

12'-6" X 14'
3,75 X 4,20

14'-1" X 11'
4,22 X 3,40

Basement Level Floor Plan

19'-8" X 28'
4,70 X 8,50

13'-0" X 14'
3,90 X 4,20

11'-8" X 13'-4"
3,50 X 4,00

Dining Room/ Kitchen

Foyer

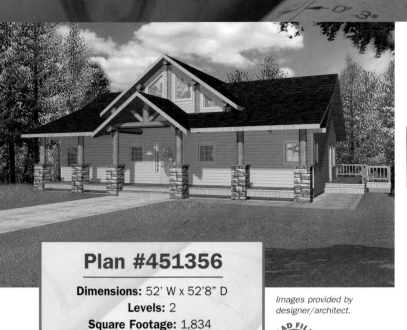

Main Level Floor Plan

COVERED ENTRY PORCH

KITCHEN
12'0" X 13'0"

FOYER

DINING ROOM
12'0" X 12'0"

GREAT ROOM
20'0" X 17'0"

MASTER SUITE
12'0" X 15'0"

DECK AREA

DECK AREA

Upper Level Floor Plan

LOFT AREA
20'0" X 17'0"

ATTIC STORAGE
12'0" X 13'0"
UNFINISHED

ATTIC STORAGE
12'0" X 13'0"
UNFINISHED

OPEN TO BELOW

Plan #451356

Dimensions: 52' W x 52'8" D

Levels: 2

Square Footage: 1,834

Main Level Sq. Ft.: 1,444

Basement Level Sq. Ft.: 390

Bedrooms: 3

Bathrooms: 2½

Foundation: Walkout -- insulated concrete form

Material List Available: Yes

Price Category: D

Images provided by designer/architect.

CAD FILE AVAILABLE

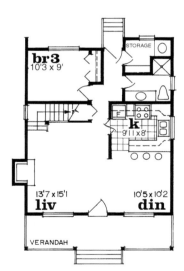

FUTURE OFFICE
11'5" X 11'4"
UNFINISHED

STORAGE
UNFINISHED

MECH
11'5" X 11'8"
UNFINISHED

BDRM. #3
11'5" X 14'0"

RECREATION ROOM
20'0" X 17'0"

BDRM. #2
11'5" X 14'0"

Basement Level Floor Plan

Copyright by designer/architect.

br3
10'3 x 9'

STORAGE

Main Level Floor Plan

Copyright by designer/architect.

k
9'11 x 8'

liv
13'7 x 15'1

din
10'5 x 10'2

VERANDAH

Plan #401007

Dimensions: 25' W x 36'6" D

Levels: 2

Square Footage: 1,286

Main Level Sq. Ft.: 725

Upper Level Sq. Ft.: 561

Bedrooms: 3

Bathrooms: 2

Foundation: Crawl space

Materials List Available: Yes

Price Category: B

Images provided by designer/architect.

CAD FILE AVAILABLE

Rear Elevation

br2
13'4 x 10'6

STORAGE

STORAGE

Upper Level Floor Plan

13'4 x 12'
mbr

BALCONY

Main Level Floor Plan

DECK

LIVING ROOM
15'-0" x 29'-6"

BEDROOM 2
14'-6" x 12'-5"

BEDROOM 1
14'-6" x 12'-5"

DINING
16'-7" x 10'-5"

KITCHEN
10'-6" x 14'-0"

BATH

BATH

PORCH

52'-0"

58'-0"

Copyright by designer/architect.

Images provided by designer/architect.

CAD FILE AVAILABLE

Upper Level Floor Plan

BEDROOM 3
10'-0" x 11'-0"

LOFT
10'-0" x 11'-5"

Rear View

Plan #641010

Dimensions: 58' W x 32' D
Levels: 1½
Square Footage: 1,833
Main Level Sq. Ft.: 1,441
Basement Level Sq. Ft.: 392
Bedrooms: 3
Bathrooms: 3
Foundation: Crawl space; slab basement or walkou for fee
Material List Available: Yes
Price Category: D

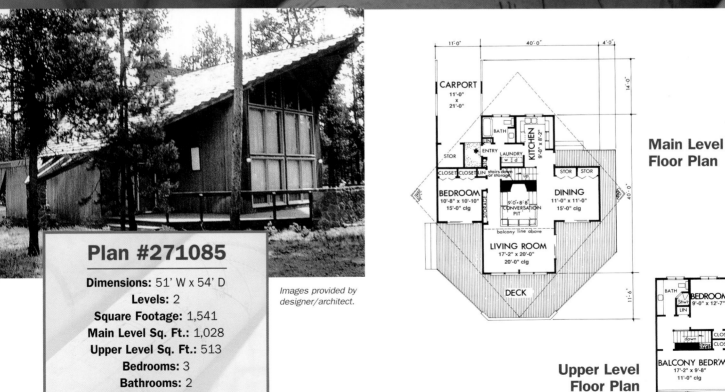

Plan #271085

Dimensions: 51' W x 54' D
Levels: 2
Square Footage: 1,541
Main Level Sq. Ft.: 1,028
Upper Level Sq. Ft.: 513
Bedrooms: 3
Bathrooms: 2
Foundation: Basement
Materials List Available: Yes
Price Category: C

Images provided by designer/architect.

Main Level Floor Plan

11'-0"   40'-0"   4'-0"

CARPORT
11'-0" x 21'-0"

14'-0"

BATH

KITCHEN
9'-0" x 8'-2"

ENTRY

STOR

LAUNDRY
w d

STOR STOR

CLOSET CLOSET LIN

stairs down or storage

up

40'-0"

BEDROOM
10'-8" x 10'-10"
15'-0" clg

STORAGE

CONVERSATION PIT
9'-0" x 8'-8"

DINING
11'-0" x 11'-0"
15'-0" clg

balcony line above

LIVING ROOM
17'-2" x 20'-0"
20'-0" clg

11'-6"

DECK

Upper Level Floor Plan

BATH

Shwr

LIN

BEDROOM
9'-0" x 12'-7"

down

CLOS

CLOS

BALCONY BEDR'M
17'-2" x 9'-8"
11'-0" clg

railing

upper part of living room

Copyright by designer/architect.

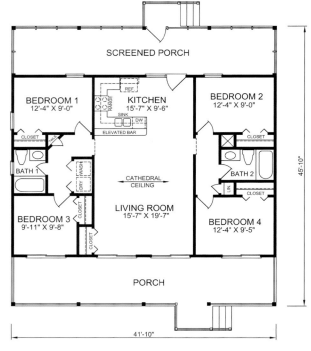

Plan #341227

Dimensions: 41'10" W x 45'10" D

Levels: 1

Square Footage: 1,248

Bedrooms: 4

Bathrooms: 2

Foundation: Crawl space, slab, basement or walkout

Material List Available: Tes

Price Category: B

Images provided by designer/architect.

Copyright by designer/architect.

Within floor plan:
SCREENED PORCH
BEDROOM 1 12'-4" X 9'-0"
KITCHEN 15'-7" X 9'-6"
BEDROOM 2 12'-4" X 9'-0"
CLOSET
ELEVATED BAR
BATH 1
CATHEDRAL CEILING
BATH 2
BEDROOM 3 9'-11" X 9'-8"
LIVING ROOM 15'-7" X 19'-7"
BEDROOM 4 12'-4" X 9'-5"
PORCH
45'-10"
41'-10"

Plan #641011

Dimensions: 62' W x 48' D

Levels: 1.5

Square Footage: 2,838

Main Level Sq. Ft.: 2,588

Upper Level Sq. Ft.: 250

Bedrooms: 3

Bathrooms: 2

Foundation: Basement; crawl space, slab or walkout for fee

Material List Available: Yes

Price Category: F

Images provided by designer/architect.

Main Level Floor Plan

DECK
DINING ROOM
GREAT ROOM
COVERED PORCH
MASTER BEDROOM
KITCHEN
SUN ROOM
BEDROOM
BATH
BEDROOM 2
ENTRY
WC
WC
MASTER BATH
62'-0

Upper Level Floor Plan

LOFT 14'-0 X 18'-0

Copyright by designer/architect.

Front Elevation

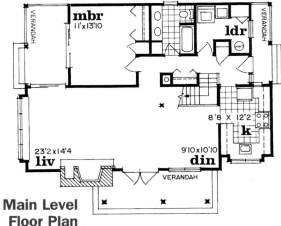

Plan #401006

Dimensions: 43' W x 35'4" D

Levels: 1½

Square Footage: 1,670

Main Level Sq.Ft.: 1,094

Upper Level Sq.Ft.: 576

Bedrooms: 3

Bathrooms: 2

Foundation: Crawl space

Materials List Available: Yes

Price Category: C

Images provided by designer/architect.

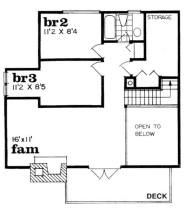

Main Level Floor Plan

Upper Level Floor Plan

Copyright by designer/architect.

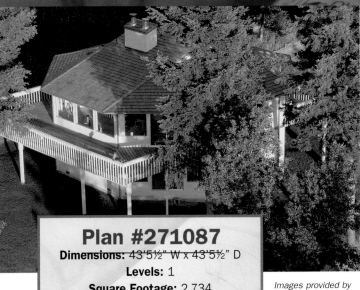

Plan #271087

Dimensions: 43'5½" W x 43'5½" D

Levels: 1

Square Footage: 2,734

Main Level Sq. Ft.: 1,564

Lower Level Sq. Ft.: 1,170

Bedrooms: 4

Bathrooms: 3

Foundation: Crawl space or walkout basement

Material List Available: Yes

Price Category: F

Images provided by designer/architect.

Main Level Floor Plan

Basement Level Floor Plan

Copyright by designer/architect.

Plan #181106

Dimensions: 32'4" W x 25'6" D

Levels: 1

Square Footage: 1,648

Main Level Sq. Ft.: 824

Upper Level Sq. Ft.: 824

Bedrooms: 3

Bathrooms: 2

Foundation: Basement or walkout

Material List Available: Yes

Price Category: E

Images provided by designer/architect.

This vacation-styled home makes a perfect year-round residence, giving the feeling of the great outdoors.

Features:

• Porch: This porch occupies the front and one side of the home, providing plenty of room to relax with family and friends.

• Family Room: The cathedral ceiling in this family room extends into the kitchen. The two-story windows allow an abundance of light into this area.

• Kitchen: This L-shaped kitchen features an eating area and a triple sliding glass door onto the front deck. The fireplace, which it shares with the family room, will warm this area on cold mornings.

• Lower Level: Two bedrooms and a den with a wood stove highlight this area. The full bathroom has room for the washer and dryer.

Lower Level Floor Plan

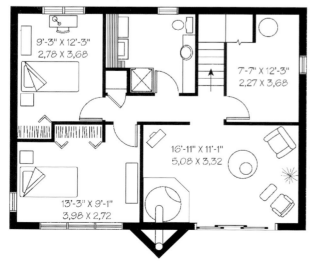

Main Level Floor Plan

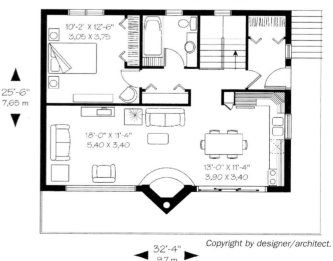

Copyright by designer/architect.

Plan #441009

Dimensions: 94' W x 53' D
Levels: 1
Square Footage: 2,650
Bedrooms: 4
Bathrooms: 2½
Foundation: Crawl space; slab or basement available for fee
Materials List Available: Yes
Price Category: G

You'll love to call this plan home. It's large enough for the whole family and has a façade that will make you the envy of the neighborhood.

Images provided by designer/architect.

Features:

• Foyer: The covered porch protects the entry, which has a transom and sidelights to brighten this space.

• Great Room: To the left of the foyer, beyond decorative columns, lies this vaulted room, with its fireplace and media center. Additional columns separate the room from the vaulted formal dining room.

• Kitchen: A casual nook and this island work center are just around the corner from the great room. The second covered porch can be reached via a door in the nook.

• Master Suite: This luxurious space boasts a vaulted salon, a private niche that could be a small study, and a view of the front yard. The master bath features a spa tub, separate shower, compartmented toilet, huge walk-in closet, and access to the laundry room.

• Bedrooms: The two additional bedrooms are located at the back of the plan and share the Jack-and-Jill bathroom.

Copyright by designer/architect.

Rear Elevation

Plan #561002

Dimensions: 61' W x 75' D
Levels: 1.5
Square Footage: 3,416
Main Level Sq. Ft.: 2,479
Upper Level Sq. Ft.: 937
Bedrooms: 4
Bathrooms: 3½
Foundation: Basement
Material List Available: Yes
Price Category: G

Images provided by designer/architect.

Traditional Cape Cod styling provides this home with incredible street appeal.

CAD FILE AVAILABLE

Features:

- Great Room: There is plenty of room for your family and friends to gather in this large room. The fireplace will add a feeling of coziness to the expansive space

- Kitchen: Open to the great room and a dining area, this island kitchen adds to the open feeling of the home. Additional seating, located at the island, enables guests to mingle with the chef of the family without getting in the way.

- Lower Level: This level (finishing is optional) adds a fourth bedroom suite, enough space for a family room or media room, and a wet bar for entertaining.

- Garage: Split garages allow the daily drivers their spaces plus a separate garage for that special vehicle or even a golf cart.

Main Level Floor Plan

Upper Level Floor Plan

Copyright by designer/architect.

Basement Level Floor Plan

Great Room

Great Room

Kitchen

Office

Master Bedroom

Master Bath

Plan #491003

Dimensions: 46' W x 28' D
Levels: 2
Square Footage: 1,235
Main Level Sq. Ft.: 893
Second Level Sq. Ft.: 342
Bedrooms: 3
Bathrooms: 2
Foundation: Walk out
Materials List Available: Yes
Price Category: B

Images provided by designer/architect.

he rear-oriented view makes this home perfect for lake-front property.

Features:

• **Living Room:** This gathering area, with its vaulted ceiling and fireplace, has skylights, which flood the space with natural light.

• **Kitchen:** An island kitchen is always a welcome feature. This one is open to the dining and living rooms and makes the home feel spacious.

• **Master Suite:** The upper level is dedicated to this private oasis with vaulted ceiling. The secluded sun deck is the perfect place to watch the sun set.

• **Secondary Bedrooms:** Located on the main level are these two equal-size bedrooms with private closets. Each room also has a view of the backyard.

Front Elevation

Front Elevation

Main Level Floor Plan

SUNDECK
GREENHOUSE WINDOW
BR3 9' x 10'
BR2 9' x 10'2"
KIT. 10' x 10'4"
SKYLIGHTS
DIN. RM. 11'6" x 8'8" 16'11" VAULTED CLG.
FOYER 16'11" VAULTED CLG.
LIV. RM. 13'6" x 12'4" 16'11" VAULTED CLG.
COVERED PORCH
28'-0"
46'-0"

Upper Level Floor Plan

Front/Side Elevation

SUNDECK
SKYLIGHTS
MBR 13'6" x11'8" 11' VAULTED CLG. PLANT LEDGE OVER
OPEN TO BELOW
DN
OPEN TO BELOW
OPEN TO BELOW

Plan #441026

Dimensions: 60' W x 52' D
Levels: 2
Square Footage: 3,623
Main Level Sq. Ft.: 1,835
Upper Level Sq. Ft.: 1,788
Bedrooms: 4
Bathrooms: 2½
Foundation: Crawl space
Materials List Available: Yes
Price Category: J

Images provided by designer/architect.

Crazy about Craftsman styling? This exquisite plan has it in abundance and doesn't skimp on the floor plan, either. Massive stone bases support the Arts and Crafts columns at the entry porch.

Features:

• Living Room: This large gathering area features a cozy fireplace.

• Dining Room: This formal room is connected to the island kitchen via a butler's pantry.

• Master Suite: Located upstairs, this suite features a walk-in closet and luxury bath.

• Bedrooms: The three family bedrooms share a centrally located compartmented bathroom.

Rear Elevation

Main Level Floor Plan

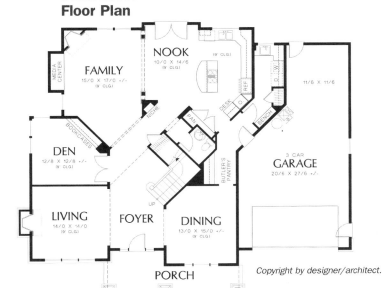

Copyright by designer/architect.

Upper Level Floor Plan

Plan #111049

Dimensions: 60' W x 50' D
Levels: 2
Square Footage: 2,205
Main Level Sq. Ft.: 1,552
Upper Level Sq. Ft.: 653
Bedrooms: 3
Bathrooms: 2
Foundation: Pier
Materials list available: Yes
Price Code: F

Images provided by designer/architect.

This stately beach home offers many waterfront views.

Features:

- Ceiling Height: 8 ft.

- Entrance: This home features raised stairs, with two wings that lead to the central staircase.

- Front Porch: This area is 110 square feet.

- Living Room: This huge room features a wood-burning fireplace and large windows, and it leads to the rear covered porch and a spacious deck. It is also open to the kitchen and dining area.

- Kitchen: This room has ample counter space and an island that is open to the dining area.

- Master Suite: This upper level room has a large balcony. This balcony is a perfect place to watch the sun set over the beach. This room also a walk-in closet.

- Master Bath: This room has all the modern amenities, with separate vanities, large corner tub and walk-in shower.

- Lower Level Bedrooms: These rooms each have a walk in closet and share a bathroom.

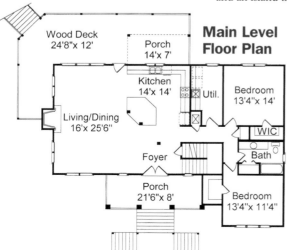

Main Level Floor Plan

Wood Deck 24'8"x 12'
Porch 14'x 7'
Kitchen 14'x 14'
Util.
Living/Dining 16'x 25'6"
Bedroom 13'4"x 14'
WIC
Bath
Foyer
Porch 21'6"x 8'
Bedroom 13'4"x 11'4"

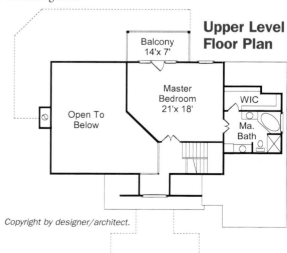

Upper Level Floor Plan

Balcony 14'x 7'
Master Bedroom 21'x 18'
WIC
Open To Below
Ma. Bath

Copyright by designer/architect.

Removing Carpet Stains in Kid's Rooms

Kids will be kids, and so accidents will happen. The cardinal rule for removing a stain from carpeting is to always clean up a spot or spill immediately, using white cloths or paper towels. Blot, never rub or scrub, a stain. Work from the outer edge in toward the center of the spot, and then follow up with clean water to remove any residue of the stain. Blot up any moisture remaining from the cleanup by layering white paper towels over the spot and weighing them down with a heavy object.

To remove a water-soluble stain, blot as much of it as possible with white paper towels that have been dampened with cold water. If necessary, mix a solution of 1¼ teaspoon of clear, mild, nonbleach laundry detergent with 32 ounces of water, and then spray it lightly onto the spot. Blot it repeatedly with white paper towels. Rinse it with a spray of clean water; then blot it dry.

To treat soils made by urine or vomit, mix equal parts of white vinegar and water, and blot it onto the spot with white paper towels; then clean with detergent solution.

To remove an oil-based stain, blot as much of it as you can; then apply a nonflammable spot remover made specifically for grease, oil, or tar to a clean, white paper towel. Don't apply the remover directly to the carpet, or you may damage the backing. Blot the stain with the treated towel. Wear rubber gloves to protect your hands. Use this method for stains caused by crayons, cosmetics, ink, paint, and shoe polish.

For spots made by cola, chocolate, or blood, apply a solution of 1 tablespoon of ammonia and 1 cup of water to the stain; then go over it with the detergent solution. Do not use ammonia on a wool carpet. Try an acid stain remover—lemon juice or white vinegar diluted with water.

To remove chewing gum or candle wax, try freezing the spot with ice cubes, and then gently scrape off the gum or wax with a blunt object. Follow this with a vacuuming. If this doesn't work, apply a commercial gum remover to the area, following the manufacturer's directions.

Rear View

Plan #271048

Dimensions: 60' W x 32'6" D
Levels: 2
Square Footage: 2,143
Main Level Sq. Ft.: 1,200
Upper Level Sq. Ft.: 943
Bedrooms: 4
Bathrooms: 3
Foundation: Crawl space, basement
Materials List Available: Yes
Price Category: D

Images provided by designer/architect.

With a nod to historical architecture, this authentic Cape Cod home boasts a traditional exterior with an updated floor plan.

Features:

- Living Room: This spacious area is warmed by an optional fireplace and merges with the dining room.

- Kitchen: Efficient and sunny, this walk-through kitchen handles almost any task with aplomb.

- Family Room: The home's second optional fireplace can be found here, along with a smart log-storage bin that can be loaded from the garage. Sliding-glass-door access to a backyard patio is a bonus.

- Guest Bedroom: Private access to a bath and plenty of room to relax make this bedroom a winner.

- Master Suite: Amenities abound in the master bedroom, including two closets, a separated dressing spot, and a dormer as a sitting area.

Copyright by designer/architect.

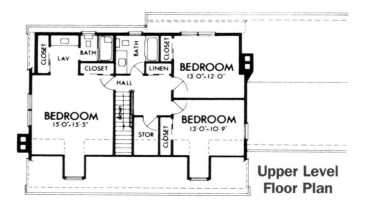

Plan #391001

Dimensions: 32' W x 40' D
Levels: 2
Square Footage: 2,015
Main Level Sq. Ft.: 1,280
Upper Level Sq. Ft.: 735
Bedrooms: 3
Bathrooms: 2½
Foundation: Crawl space
Materials List Available: Yes
Price Category: D

Images provided by designer/architect.

- **Kitchen:** This L-shaped kitchen features an expansive cooktop/lunch counter.
- **Utility Areas:** A utility room handles the laundry and storage, and a half bath with linen closet takes care of other necessities.
- **Master Suite:** This main-floor master suite is just that—sweet! The spa-style bath features

a corner tub nestled against a greenhouse window. Plus, there are double sinks and a separate shower.

- **Upstairs:** The sun-washed loft overlooks the activity below while embracing two dreamy bedrooms and a sizable bath with double sinks.

Follow your dream to this home surrounded with decking. The A-frame front showcases bold windowing (on two levels), and natural lighting fills the house.

Features:

- **Dining Room:** This dining room and the family room are completely open to each other, perfect for hanging out in the warmth of the hearth.

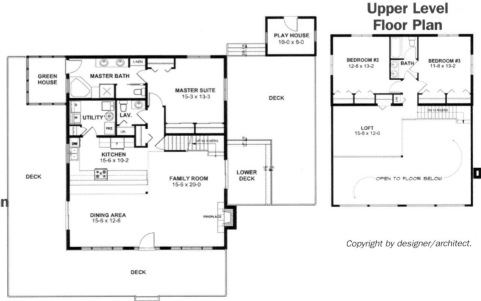

Main Level Floor Plan

Upper Level Floor Plan

Copyright by designer/architect.

Plan #111047

Dimensions: 36' W x 54' D
Levels: 2
Square Footage: 1,863
Main Level Sq. Ft.: 1,056
Upper Level Sq. Ft.: 807
Bedrooms: 4
Bathrooms: 3
Foundation: Pier
Materials List Available: Yes
Price Category: E

Designed for a coastline, this home is equally appropriate as a year-round residence or a vacation retreat.

Features:

- Orientation: The rear-facing design gives you an ocean view and places the most attractive side of the house where beach-goers can see it.

- Entryway: On the waterside, a large deck with a covered portion leads to the main entrance.

- Carport: This house is raised on piers that let you park underneath it and that protect it from water damage during storms.

- Living Room: A fireplace, French doors, and large windows grace this room, which is open to both the kitchen and the dining area.

- Master Suite: Two sets of French doors open to a balcony on the ocean side, and the suite includes two walk-in closets and a fully equipped bath.

Main Level Floor Plan

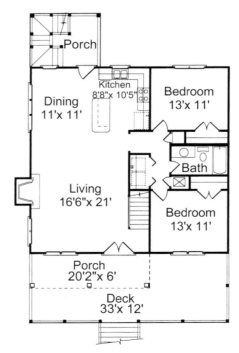

Upper Level Floor Plan

Plan #451360

Dimensions: 59' W x 69'2" D
Levels: 2
Square Footage: 2,600
Main Level Sq. Ft.: 1,523
Upper Level Sq. Ft.: 1,077
Bedrooms: 3
Bathrooms: 2½
Foundation: Walkout –
insulated concrete form
Material List Available: Yes
Price Category: F

This rustic-looking home would suit the bustle of a busy neighborhood or the quietness of a secluded lake.

Features:

- **Great Room:** This area is the interior high-light of the home. The large, exciting space features a soaring ceiling, massive fireplace, and magnificent window wall to capture the view.

- **Kitchen:** An abundance of cabinets and counter space makes this kitchen functional as well as attractive. The built-in pantry is large enough to hold supplies and extra treats.

- **Master Suite:** Pamper yourself in this lavish master suite. Enjoy the privacy and convenience of a main-level location. The master bath boasts an oversized stall shower and a whirlpool tub.

- **Secondary Bedrooms:** Located on the upper level are two bedrooms joined by an open loft.

Main Level Floor Plan

Upper Level Floor Plan

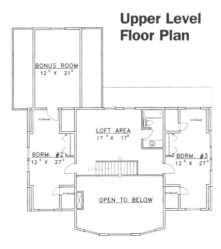

Basement Level Floor Plan

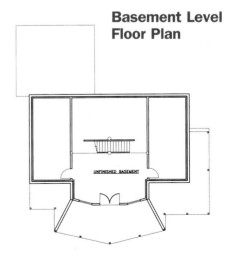

Plan #271053

Dimensions: 70' W x 33'10" D
Levels: 2
Square Footage: 2,458
Main Level Sq. Ft.: 1,067
Upper Level Sq. Ft.: 346
Bedrooms: 3
Bathrooms: 2½
Foundation: Crawl space or daylight basement
Materials List Available: Yes
Price Category: E

The octagonal shape and window-filled walls of this home create a powerful interior packed with panoramic views.

Features:

• **Great Room:** Straight back from the angled entry, this room is brightened by sunlight through windows and sliding glass doors. Beyond the doors, a huge wraparound deck offers plenty of space for tanning or relaxing. A spiral staircase adds visual interest.

• **Kitchen:** This efficient space includes a convenient pantry.

• **Master Suite:** On the upper level, this romantic master suite overlooks the great room below. Several windows provide scenic outdoor views. A walk-in closet and a private bath round out this secluded haven.

• **Basement:** The optional basement includes a recreation room, as well as an extra bedroom and bath.

Images provided by designer/architect.

Copyright by designer/architect.

Main Level Floor Plan

Upper Level Floor Plan

Optional Basement Level Floor Plan

Images provided by designer/architect.

Plan #111021

Dimensions: 34' W x 44' D
Levels: 2
Square Footage: 2,221
Main Level Sq. Ft.: 1,307
Upper Level Sq. Ft.: 914
Bedrooms: 4
Bathrooms: 3
Foundation: Pier
Materials List Available: Yes
Price Category: F

If you've got a view you want to admire, choose this well-designed home, with its comfortable front porch and spacious second-floor balcony.

Features:

• Porch: Double doors open to both the living and dining rooms for complete practicality.

• Living Room: The spacious living room anchors the open floor plan in this lovely home.

• Dining Room: Natural light pours into this room from the large front windows.

• Kitchen: An angled snack bar that's shared with the dining room doubles as a large counter.

• Master Suite: Double doors lead from the bedroom to the balcony. The bath includes a tub, separate shower, and double vanity.

• Sitting Area: This quiet area is nestled into a windowed alcove between the study and the master suite.

Main Level Floor Plan

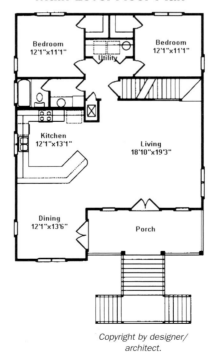

Copyright by designer/architect.

Upper Level Floor Plan

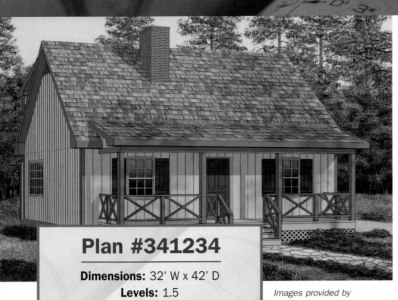

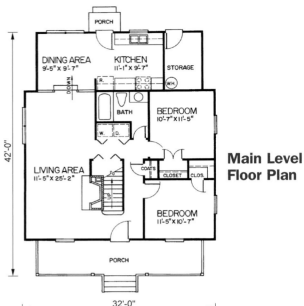

Main Level Floor Plan

PORCH
DINING AREA 9'-5" X 9'-7"
KITCHEN 11'-1" X 9'-7"
STORAGE
W.H.
BATH
BEDROOM 10'-7" X 11'-5"
W. D.
LIVING AREA 11'-5" X 25'-2"
COATS
CLOSET
CLOS.
UP
BEDROOM 11'-5" X 10'-7"
PORCH
42'-0"
32'-0"

Upper Level Floor Plan

BEDROOM 11'-5" X 11'-5"
BATH
CLOS.
BEDROOM 11'-5" X 11'-5"
LINEN
CLOSET
CLOSET
DOWN

Copyright by designer/architect.

Images provided by designer/architect.

Plan #341234

Dimensions: 32' W x 42' D

Levels: 1.5

Square Footage: 1,476

Main Level Sq. Ft.: 1,049

Upper Level Sq. Ft.: 427

Bedrooms: 4

Bathrooms: 2

Foundation: Crawl space, slab, basement or walkout

Material List Available: Yes

Price Category: B

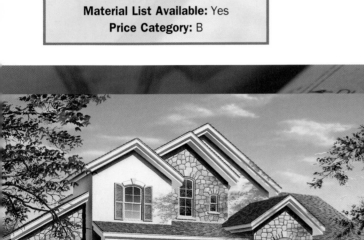

Main Level Floor Plan

53'-2" 15.95 m
56'-0" 16.8 m

Upper Level Floor Plan

OPEN TO BELOW

BONUS ROOM 20'-4" X 14'-0" 6.10 X 4.20

Copyright by designer/architect.

Images provided by designer/architect.

CAD FILE AVAILABLE

Plan #181053

Dimensions: 56' W x 53'2" D

Levels: 2

Square Footage: 2,353

Main Level Sq. Ft.: 1,606

Upper Level Sq. Ft.: 747

Bedrooms: 3

Bathrooms: 2½

Foundation: Basement, crawl space

Materials List Available: Yes

Price Category: E

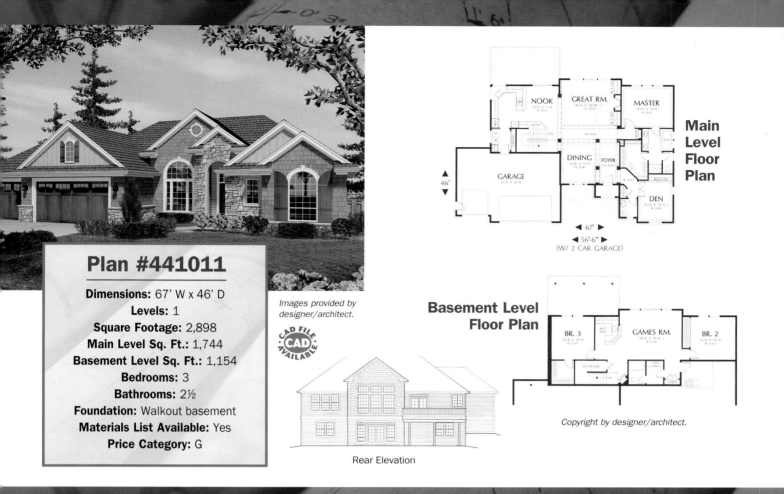

Plan #441011

Dimensions: 67' W x 46' D

Levels: 1

Square Footage: 2,898

Main Level Sq. Ft.: 1,744

Basement Level Sq. Ft.: 1,154

Bedrooms: 3

Bathrooms: 2½

Foundation: Walkout basement

Materials List Available: Yes

Price Category: G

Images provided by designer/architect.

CAD FILE AVAILABLE

Rear Elevation

Main Level Floor Plan

Basement Level Floor Plan

Copyright by designer/architect.

Plan #181120

Dimensions: 32' W x 40' D

Levels: 2

Square Footage: 1,480

Main Level Sq. Ft.: 1,024

Second Level Sq. Ft.: 456

Bedrooms: 2

Bathrooms: 2

Foundation: Basement

Materials List Available: Yes

Price Category: E

Images provided by designer/architect.

CAD FILE AVAILABLE

Front Elevation

Main Level Floor Plan

Copyright by designer/architect.

Upper Level Floor Plan

Plan #111010

Dimensions: 34' W x 38' D
Levels: 3
Square Footage: 1,804
Main Level Sq. Ft.: 731
Upper Level Sq. Ft.: 935
Third Level Sq.Ft.: 138
Bedrooms: 3
Bathrooms: 3
Foundation: Piers
Materials List Available: Yes
Price Category: E

This vacation home is designed for practicality and convenience.

Features:

- Porch: This cozy porch opens to the dining room and the living room. Relax on the porch, and invite a passing neighbor to join you for a cup of coffee.

- Living Room: French doors connect this brightly lit room to the porch. The corner fireplace adds warmth and elegance to the area.

- Kitchen: This island kitchen, with a snack bar, is open to the dining room and living room. A full bathroom and the laundry area are just a few steps away.

- Master Suite: This private retreat is located on the upper level close to the secondary bedrooms. Pass his and her closets that lead into the private bath, complete with an oversized tub.

Main Level Floor Plan

Deck 14'x 10'
Kitchen 10'6"x 13'9"
Dining 9'x 13'8"
Living 14'x 19'
Screen Porch 19'6"x 10'

Upper Level Floor Plan

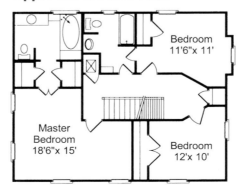

Bedroom 11'6"x 11'
Master Bedroom 18'6"x 15'
Bedroom 12'x 10'

Third Level Floor Plan

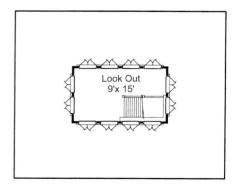

Look Out 9'x 15'

Plan #531040

Dimensions: 42' W x 81' D

Levels: 2

Square Footage: 3,325

Main Level Sq. Ft.: 1,272

Upper Level Sq. Ft.: 2,053

Bedrooms: 3

Bathrooms: 3½

Foundation: Slab

Material List Available: Yes

Price Category: G

This home is tailor-made for a site with dramatic views.

CAD FILE AVAILABLE

Features:

- **Dining Room:** This dining room is located just off the foyer and features a built-in butler's pantry. Large windows will flood this area with natural light.

- **Kitchen:** This island kitchen is open to the family room and has access to the tower above. The breakfast nook offers great views and additional seating at the bar.

- **Master Suite:** Also located on the upper level, this oasis has access to the rear lanai. The master bath features a large walk-in closet and a whirlpool tub.

- **Lower Level:** The third bedroom, with a large walk-in closet, is located on this level. The game room and office make their home here as well.

Main Level Floor Plan

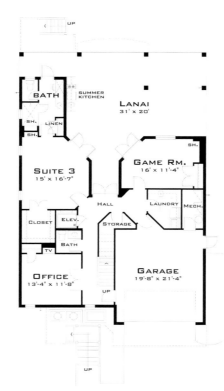

Upper Level Floor Plan

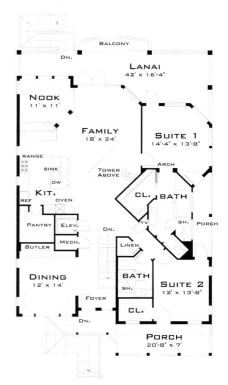

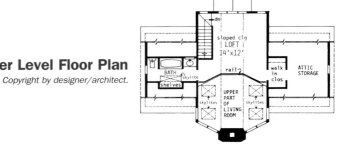

Main Level Floor Plan

Plan #431004

Dimensions: 41' W x 30' D
Levels: 2
Square Footage: 1,156
Main Level Sq. Ft.: 810
Upper Level Sq. Ft.: 346
Bedrooms: 2
Bathrooms: 2
Foundation: Crawl space
Material List Available: Yes
Price Category: B

Images provided by designer/architect.

Upper Level Floor Plan

Copyright by designer/architect.

Plan #321007

Dimensions: 76' W x 55'2" D
Levels: 1
Square Footage: 2,695
Bedrooms: 3
Bathrooms: 2½
Foundation: Basement
Materials List Available: Yes
Price Category: G

Images provided by designer/architect.

Copyright by designer/architect.

SMARTtip

Decorative Poles

Drapery poles are supported by the brackets fastened to the window frame or wall. The brackets that are provided with the poles generally coordinate and blend in with the pole finish. Brackets can be simple but also decorative. If you opt for a spectacular, attention-grabbing bracket, consider choosing less showy finials for the ends of the pole.

Main Level Floor Plan

Images provided by designer/architect.

Upper Level Floor Plan

Copyright by designer/architect.

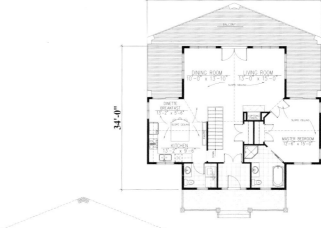

Plan #471019

Dimensions: 31' W x 36' D
Levels: 2
Square Footage: 1,024
Main Level Sq. Ft.: 710
Upper Level Sq. Ft.: 314
Bedrooms: 2
Bathrooms: 2
Foundation: Crawl space or basement
Material List Available: Yes
Price Category: C

Plan #571039

Dimensions: 40' W x 34' D
Levels: 1
Square Footage: 2,144
Main Level Sq. Ft.: 1,072
Lower Level Sq. Ft.: 1,072
Bedrooms: 3
Bathrooms: 2½
Foundation: Basement
Material List Available: Yes
Price Category: D

Images provided by designer/architect.

Basement Level Floor Plan

Copyright by designer/architect.

Plan #611069

Dimensions: 61'8" W x 75' D
Levels: 2
Square Footage: 5,445
Main Level Sq. Ft.: 2,900
Upper Level Sq. Ft.: 2,545
Bedrooms: 6
Bathrooms: 4
Foundation: Slab
Material List Available: Yes
Price Category: J

Images provided by designer/architect.

- **Family Room:** An open snack bar faces this room, which will become a favorite for the family to enjoy a movie and popcorn. On nice days or evenings you can step out the double doors and onto the rear covered porch.
- **Master Suite:** This private oasis features a large sleeping area, a sitting area, and an exercise room complete with a sauna and

steam room. The large master bath features a spa tub, dual vanities, a separate shower, and a private lavatory area.

- **Bedrooms:** Five additional bedrooms, each with a private full bathroom, complete the floor plan. Two bedrooms are located on the first level, with the remaining three on the upper level with the master suite.

Luxury abounds in this six-bedroom home for larger families. You'll find lavish comforts throughout the design.

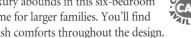

Features:

- **Living Room:** This open room hosts a bar and wine storage for entertaining family and friends. The two-story space boasts a dramatic fireplace and access to the rear covered porch.

Rear View.

Main Level Floor Plan

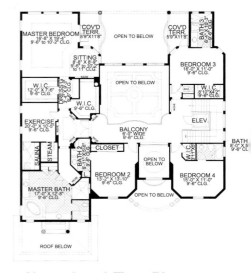

Upper Level Floor Plan

Copyright by designer/architect.

Plan #391052

Dimensions: 68' W x 34'10" D
Levels: 2
Square Footage: 1,778
Main Level Sq. Ft.: 1,306
Upper Level Sq. Ft.: 472
Bedrooms: 3
Bathrooms: 2
Foundation: Crawl space, slab, or basement
Material List Available: Yes
Price Category: C

The contemporary styling of the angled walls and center tower helps this design stand apart.

This home, as shown in the photograph, may differ from the actual blueprints. For more detailed information, please check the floor plans carefully.

Images provided by designer/architect.

Features:

• Entry: This airlock entry will help conserve energy. The two-story entry allows an overview from the master suite above.

• Kitchen: Centrally located, this kitchen has an efficiently designed work area. The raised bar divides the dining room from the kitchen, while maintaining the open floor plan.

• Master Suite: The entire upper level is dedicated to this retreat, which features a sitting area and a view down into the living room and entry. The master bath boasts dual vanities.

• Garage: Although capable of holding two cars, this garage would also make a great workshop.

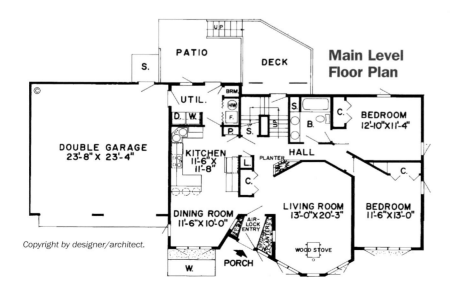

Main Level Floor Plan

PATIO

DECK

DOUBLE GARAGE 23'-8" X 23'-4"

UTIL.

KITCHEN 11'-6" X 11'-8"

DINING ROOM 11'-6" X 10'-0"

HALL

PLANTER

AIR-LOCK ENTRY

PORCH

WOOD STOVE

LIVING ROOM 13'-0" X 20'-3"

BEDROOM 12'-10" X 11'-4"

BEDROOM 11'-6" X 13'-0"

Copyright by designer/architect.

Upper Level Floor Plan

DRESSING AREA

SITTING AREA

MASTER BEDROOM SUITE 19'-2" X 15'-7"

OPEN TO ENTRY

OPEN TO LIVING ROOM

Plan #131056

Dimensions: 40' W x 54' D
Levels: 1.5
Square Footage: 1,396
Main Level Sq. Ft.: 964
Upper Level Sq. Ft.: 432
Bedrooms: 3
Bathrooms: 2
Foundation: Slab; basement for fee
Materials List Available: Yes
Price Category: C

This ruggedly handsome home is a true A-frame. The elegance of the roof virtually meeting the ground and the use of rugged stone veneer and log-cabin siding make it stand out.

Features:

- Living Room: This area is the interior highlight of the home. The large, exciting space features a soaring ceiling, a massive fireplace, and a magnificent window wall to capture a view.

- Side Porch: The secondary entry from this side porch leads to a center hall that provides direct access to the first floor's two bedrooms, bathroom, kitchen, and living room.

- Kitchen: This kitchen is extremely efficient and includes a snack bar and access to the screened porch.

- Loft Area: A spiral stairway leads from the living room to this second-floor loft, which overlooks the living room. The area can also double as an extra sleeping room.

Images provided by designer/architect.

Great Room

Main Level Floor Plan

Copyright by designer/architect

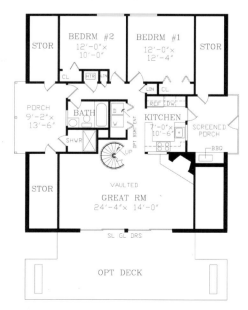

Upper Level Floor Plan

Right Side View

Rear View

Kitchen

Dining Room/Great Room

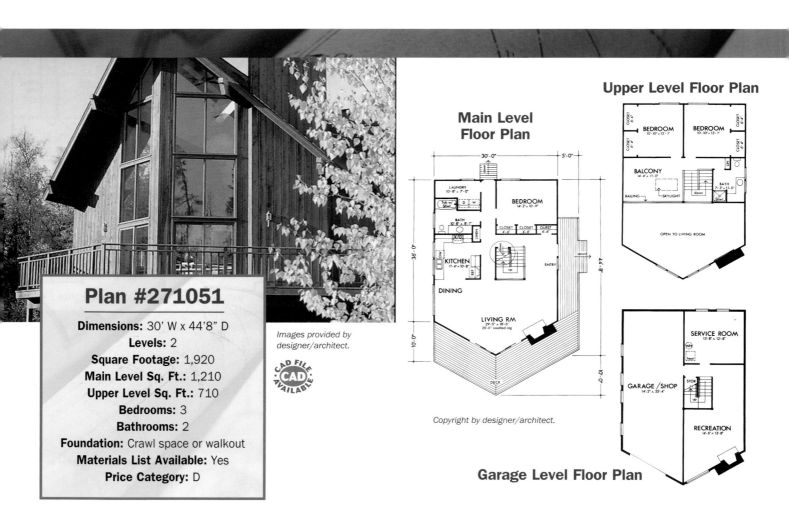

Plan #321008

Dimensions: 57' W x 52'2" D

Levels: 1

Square Footage: 1,761

Bedrooms: 4

Bathrooms: 2

Foundation: Basement

Materials List Available: Yes

Price Category: C

Images provided by designer/architect.

Copyright by designer/architect.

MBr 14-6x13-0 vaulted clg

Br 2 11-0x10-0

Br 3 11-0x10-0

Br 4 12-0x10-0 vaulted clg

Great Rm 16-0x17-10 vaulted clg

Brkfst 11-8x10-8

Kit 11-5x 12-9

Dining 12-4x10-0

Patio

Dn

Covered Porch

Garage 20-4x20-10

52'-2"

57'-0"

SMARTtip

Hanging Wallpaper

Use liner paper to smooth out a damaged wall and to provide uniform support for expensive paper.

Plan #271051

Dimensions: 30' W x 44'8" D

Levels: 2

Square Footage: 1,920

Main Level Sq. Ft.: 1,210

Upper Level Sq. Ft.: 710

Bedrooms: 3

Bathrooms: 2

Foundation: Crawl space or walkout

Materials List Available: Yes

Price Category: D

Images provided by designer/architect.

Upper Level Floor Plan

Main Level Floor Plan

LAUNDRY 10'-8" x 7'-0"

BATH 10'-8" x 6'-7"

BEDROOM 14'-3" x 10'-9"

KITCHEN 17'-4" x 9'-7"

DINING

LIVING RM 29'-0" x 18'-6" 26'-0" vaulted clg

ENTRY

DECK

30'-0"

5'-0"

36'-0"

10'-0"

44'-8"

10'-0"

BEDROOM 10'-10" x 13'-1"

BEDROOM 10'-10" x 13'-1"

BALCONY 14'-4" x 11'-0"

BATH 7'-3" x 11'-0"

RAILING

SKYLIGHT

OPEN TO LIVING ROOM

Garage Level Floor Plan

SERVICE ROOM 13'-8" x 12'-8"

GARAGE/SHOP 14'-2" x 35'-4"

RECREATION 14'-6" x 13'-6"

Copyright by designer/architect.

Main Level Floor Plan

SUNDECK

DINING
14' x 12'
16'11" VAULTED CLG.

BR.
11' x 12'4"
10' VAULTED CLG.

LIVING
16' x 15'
16'11" VAULTED CLG.

SEAT

FOYER

SITTING

UP

COVERED PORCH

LDR

10'-0"

29'-6"

53'-0"

4'-0"

Plan #491006

Dimensions: 53' W x 29'6" D
Levels: 2
Square Footage: 1,470
Main Level Sq. Ft.: 1,130
Upper Level Sq. Ft.: 340
Bedrooms: 2
Bathrooms: 2
Foundation: Crawl space
Material List Available: Yes
Price Category: B

Images provided by designer/architect.

Front View

BALCONY

BR.
12'2" x 10'
10' VAULTED CLG.

LOFT
VAULTED

OPEN TO BELOW

RAILING

PLANT LEDGE

OPEN

DN

Upper Level Floor Plan

Copyright by designer/architect.

Deck
20'4" x 8'

Deck
14'10" x 8'

Porch
20'4" x 8'

Deck
14'10" x 8'

Bedroom
13' 15'6"

Living
18'8" x 18'

Master Bedroom
14'8" x 20'

Main Level Floor Plan

Copyright by designer/architect.

Breakfast
18'8" x 11'2"

Bedroom
11'10" x 12'6"

Kitchen
18'8" x 10'

Deck
13' x 4'

Plan #111032

Dimensions: 50' W x 56' D
Levels: 3
Square Footage: 2,904
Ground Level Sq. Ft.: 449
Main Level Sq. Ft.: 2,000
Upper Level Sq. Ft.: 455
Bedrooms: 4
Bathrooms: 3
Foundation: Pier
Materials List Available: Yes
Price Category: G

Images provided by designer/architect.

Upper Level Floor Plan

Storage
12'7" x 10'4"

Bedroom
11'10" x 16'4"

Foyer
24'9" x 4'6"

Ground Level Floor Plan

Open to Below

Loft
19'8" x 21'

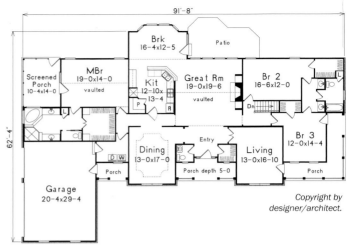

91'-8"

Brk
16-4x12-5

Patio

Screened
Porch
10-4x14-0

MBr
19-0x14-0
vaulted

Kit
12-10x
13-4

Great Rm
19-0x19-6
vaulted

Br 2
16-6x12-0

Br 3
12-0x14-4

62'-4"

Dining
13-0x17-0

Entry

Living
13-0x16-10

Porch

Porch depth 5-0

Porch

Garage
20-4x29-4

Copyright by designer/architect.

Plan #321004

Dimensions: 91'8" W x 62'4" D
Levels: 1
Square Footage: 2,808
Bedrooms: 3
Bathrooms: 2½
Foundation: Basement
Materials List Available: Yes
Price Category: H

Images provided by designer/architect.

CAD FILE AVAILABLE — CAD

SMARTtip

Ornaments in a Garden

Placement is everything with ornaments in a garden. Some elements are best sitting by themselves. Others are better when they are part of a cohesive whole, perhaps placed in the greenery at a corner or flanking a structure.

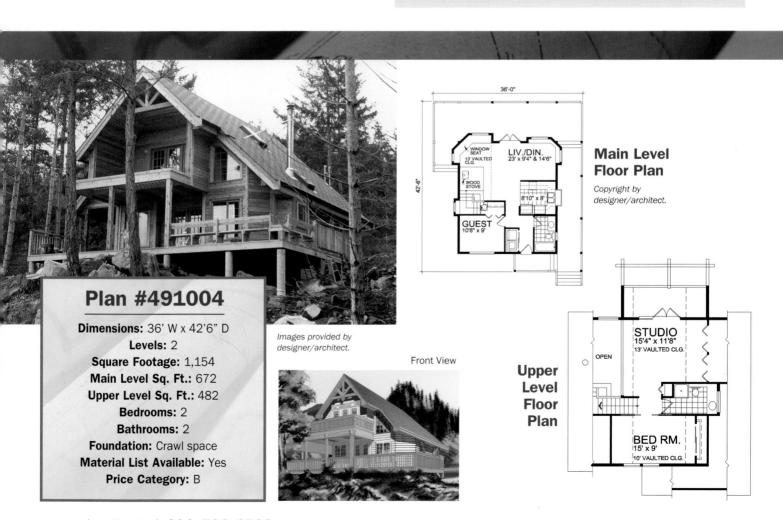

36'-0"

WINDOW SEAT
13' VAULTED CLG.

LIV./DIN.
23' x 9'4" & 14'6"

WOOD STOVE

8'10" x 8'

42'-6"

GUEST
10'8" x 9'

Main Level Floor Plan

Copyright by designer/architect.

STUDIO
15'4" x 11'8"
13' VAULTED CLG.

OPEN

Upper Level Floor Plan

BED RM.
15' x 9'
10' VAULTED CLG.

Plan #491004

Dimensions: 36' W x 42'6" D
Levels: 2
Square Footage: 1,154
Main Level Sq. Ft.: 672
Upper Level Sq. Ft.: 482
Bedrooms: 2
Bathrooms: 2
Foundation: Crawl space
Material List Available: Yes
Price Category: B

Images provided by designer/architect.

Front View

Plan #111027

Dimensions: 48' W x 57' D
Levels: 2
Square Footage: 2,601
Main Level Sq. Ft.: 1,623
Upper Level Sq. Ft.: 978
Bedrooms: 3
Bathrooms: 2
Foundation: Pier
Materials List Available: Yes
Price Category: F

Images provided by designer/architect.

Main Level Floor Plan

Dining 12'8"x 12'
Bedroom 13'x 12'
Living 18'6"x 22'
Bedroom 13'x 11'9"
Porch
Deck

Upper Level Floor Plan

Copyright by designer/architect.

Master Bedroom 18'6"x 20'
Study 13'x 15'6"
Balcony

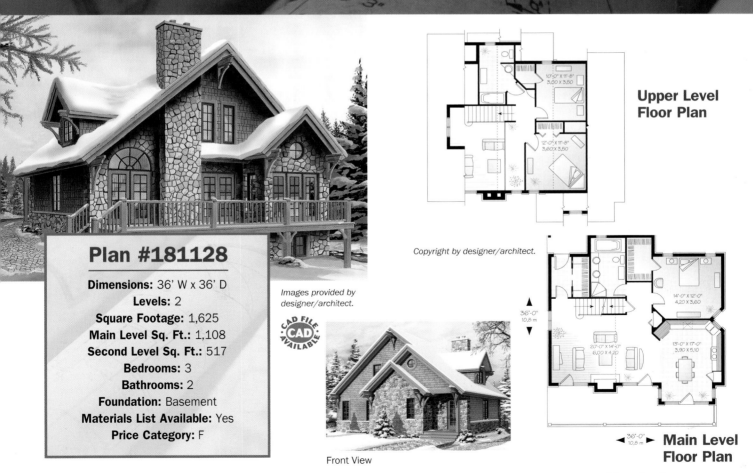

Plan #181128

Dimensions: 36' W x 36' D
Levels: 2
Square Footage: 1,625
Main Level Sq. Ft.: 1,108
Second Level Sq. Ft.: 517
Bedrooms: 3
Bathrooms: 2
Foundation: Basement
Materials List Available: Yes
Price Category: F

Upper Level Floor Plan

10'-0" X 11'-8"
3,00 X 3,50
12'-0" X 11'-8"
3,60 X 3,50

Copyright by designer/architect.

Images provided by designer/architect.

CAD FILE AVAILABLE

Front View

14'-0" X 12'-0"
4,20 X 3,60
20'-0" X 14'-0"
6,00 X 4,20
13'-0" X 17'-0"
3,90 X 5,10

36'-0"
10,8 m

Main Level Floor Plan

Plan #531020

Dimensions: 74' W x 97' D
Levels: 1
Square Footage: 3,371
Bedrooms: 4
Bathrooms: 3½
Foundation: Slab; basement or pier/pole for fee
Material List Available: Yes
Price Category: G

Beauty meets practicality in this charming home. Lovely architectural details and an interior designed with daily living in mind create an ideal environment for the growing family.

Features:

• Living Room: Open to the foyer and dining room, this gathering area boasts a fireplace flanked by built-in shelves. On nice days, expand living space by opening the doors to the rear lanai.

• Dining Room: This oversize dining room greets your guests, setting the mood for fun. A pair of large windows floods this space with natural light.

• Master Suite: Located on the opposite side of the home from the secondary bedrooms, this private oasis features an oversize sleeping area. His and her walk-in closets open to the private bath, which boasts a separate toilet area.

• Secondary Bedrooms: Three additional bedrooms and two full bathrooms are located toward the rear of the home.

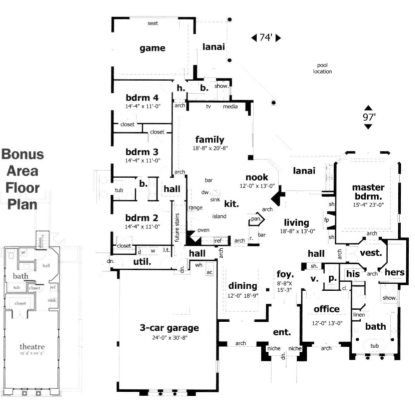

Copyright by designer/architect.

Plan #161026

Dimensions: 67'6" W x 63'6" D
Levels: 1
Square Footage: 2,041
Bedrooms: 3
Bathrooms: 2
Foundation: Basement
Materials List Available: Yes
Price Category: D

Images provided by designer/architect.

You'll love the special features of this home, which has been designed for efficiency and comfort.

CAD FILE AVAILABLE

Features:

• Foyer: This raised foyer offers a view through the great room and beyond it to the covered deck.

• Great Room: Elegant windows allow versatility — decorate casually or more formally.

• Kitchen: You'll find ample counter space and cabinets in this spacious room, which adjoins the dining room and opens onto the rear yard.

• Library: Curl up on the window seat that wraps around the tower in this quiet spot.

• Laundry Room: A tub makes this large room practical for crafts as well as laundry.

• Master Suite: A vaulted ceiling gives grace to the sitting area, and the garden bath with a walk-in closet and whirlpool tub adds luxury.

Rear Elevation

Main Level Floor Plan

Basement Level Floor Plan

Copyright by designer/architect.

Plan #321009

Dimensions: 55'8" W x 46'4" D

Levels: 1

Square Footage: 2,295

Bedrooms: 3

Bathrooms: 2

Foundation: Basement

Materials List Available: Yes

Price Category: E

Images provided by designer/architect.

CAD FILE AVAILABLE

Rear View

Copyright by designer/architect.

Optional Basement Level Floor Plan

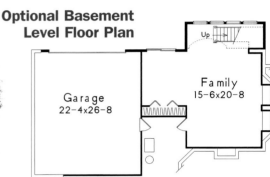

Plan #181133

Dimensions: 38' W x 40' D

Levels: 2

Square Footage: 1,832

Main Level Sq. Ft.: 1,212

Second Level Sq. Ft. 620

Bedrooms: 3

Bathrooms: 2

Foundation: Walkout; crawl space, slab, or basement for fee

Materials List Available: Yes

Price Category: G

Images provided by designer/architect.

CAD FILE AVAILABLE

Main Level Floor Plan

Upper Level Floor Plan

Copyright by designer/architect.

Plan #491005

Dimensions: 36' W x 44'6" D

Levels: 2

Square Footage: 1,333

Main Level Sq. Ft.: 768

Upper Level Sq. Ft.: 565

Bedrooms: 2

Bathrooms: 2

Foundation: Crawl space

Material List Available: Yes

Price Category: B

Images provided by designer/architect.

Main Level Floor Plan

GREAT ROOM
23' x 10'2" x& 16'6"

16' VAULTED CLG.

WOOD STOVE

KIT
8'6" x 8'

GUEST
10'8" x 11'

W
D

Upper Level Floor Plan

Copyright by designer/architect.

RAILING

OPEN

STUDIO
15'4" x13'4"
13' VAULTED CLG.

DN

BED RM.
15' x 11'
10' VAULTED CLG.

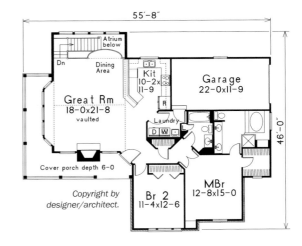

Rear View

Plan #321035

Dimensions: 55'8" W x 46' D

Levels: 1

Square Footage: 1,384

Bedrooms: 2

Bathrooms: 2

Foundation: Walkout

Materials List Available: Yes

Price Category: D

Images provided by designer/architect.

CAD FILE AVAILABLE

55'-8"

46'-0"

Atrium below

Dn

Dining Area

Kit
10-2x 11-9

Garage
22-0x11-9

Great Rm
18-0x21-8
vaulted

Laundry

D W

R

Cover porch depth 6-0

Br 2
11-4x12-6

MBr
12-8x15-0

Copyright by designer/architect.

Rear View

Optional Basement Level Floor Plan

Up

Patio

Family Rm
25-0x21-4

Unexcavated

Unfinished Basement

DESIGN IDEAS for CREATIVE HOMEOWNER®

Kitchens

NEW UPDATED EDITION includes GREEN TIPS

products | inspiration | materials   Susan Hillstrom

This article was reprinted from *Design Ideas for Kitchens* (Creative Homeowner 2009).

Choosing Your Sink

Today's kitchen sinks and faucets are making a bold design statement. While stainless steel endures as the most popular sink finish, there are more options to consider—bigger sizes, deeper bowls, new configurations, and colors and materials galore. There are also great new faucets with multiple spray features and accessories ranging from soap dispensers to water purification systems. Despite their glamour, sinks and faucets are still the workhorses of the kitchen, so make sure your choices look good and work hard.

Here's a helpful rule of thumb for choosing a kitchen sink—identify your practical needs first; then go for good looks. With so many choices you won't have to sacrifice one for the other. Another pointer comes from the National Kitchen & Bath Association (NKBA), an industry trade group: a standard 22 x 24-inch single-bowl sink is sufficient for kitchens that measure 150 square feet or less; for kitchens that are over that size, a larger single-bowl design or a double- or triple-bowl model are better choices.

If you haven't bought a kitchen sink for a while you'll be dazzled by your choices. You may also be surprised that many kitchens, even relatively modest ones, sport two or even three sinks. There's the primary one, located at the heart of the work area near the dishwasher and devoted to cleanup. There may also be a small prep sink, often located away from the busiest area and intended for a second cook or for a helpful dinner guest who may be washing or chopping vegetables or fruit. This secondary sink, a nice amenity for any household, is practically a necessity for a two-cook kitchen. If you have a large family or entertain often, you may want to install a bar sink that allows people to help themselves to beverages without getting in the cooks' way. If this auxiliary sink is accompanied by an undercounter refrigerator and enough counter space for a coffeemaker, you've got a beverage center.

Unless you select unusual shapes, super sizes, or deluxe materials such as natural stone, concrete, copper, brass, fire clay, or handmade ceramics, kitchen sinks are not especially big-ticket items. An investment of a couple of hundred dollars will get you a high-quality single- or double-bowl model in porcelain, stainless steel, or a composite material. The price could go up several hundred more for color, multiple bowls, or solid surfacing. You'll also pay a premium for an apron-front farmhouse sink of any material.

In this unusual melding of form with function, an antique pot of hammered copper works beautifully as a kitchen sink, opposite.

This integrated stainless-steel double sink, top, contrasts with the butcher-block counter material.

This shallow prep sink, above, with a self-draining bottom grid is ideal for rinsing fruits and vegetables.

Popular Materials

When it's time to choose a kitchen sink, you can go for the glamour, selecting a material such as stone, hand-painted china, or even glass. But if you want to make a more conventional choice, there are some solid options for your consideration.

The familiar look of glossy white porcelain over cast iron has great appeal for many people, and this durable material is also available in myriad colors. Stains that may develop over time are generally easy to remove. A perfect match for trendy pro-style appliances, **stainless steel** is affordable, easy-care, and long lasting; 18- or 20-gauge steel promises durability and strength, and a satin finish disguises most water spots and scratches. Other metals, such as **copper** and **brass**, look great but require lots of care and polishing. Used alone or molded into a countertop, **solid surfacing** comes in many colors and stone-looks. It's pricey but requires little maintenance; the occasional scratch, dent, or stain can be successfully repaired. Often used for trendy farmhouse sinks, **concrete** and **soapstone** are costly but practically indestructible. Soapstone comes in several earthy colors, and concrete can be tinted any shade you like.

This brushed stainless-steel sink, top, features a sculptural shape, elegant corners, and generous dimensions.

A polyester-acrylic double sink, above, in bright blue provides a bold pop of color at a reasonable price.

Three Main Composite Materials

Ever since plastic laminate was cooked up in a laboratory early in the last century, product engineers have been working to create materials that supply the look and durability of stone but cost less. One case in point: composites, which are available in three basic types.

- **Polyester/acrylic** is the least expensive and least durable of the big three. It's somewhat soft, so it scratches and stains easily. Still, if your budget is tight, you'll like its price, glossy surface, and bright colors.

- **Quartz composite**, a mixture of crushed quartz and resin fillers, is durable and resistant to most stains and scratches. Its moderate price and earthy or bright colors—including a brilliant blue and zippy yellow—make it appealing.

- **Granite composite**, a mixture of crushed granite and resin fillers, is the most expensive—and most durable—of the composites, offering high resistance to chips, stains, scratches, and burns. It's available in a number of colors and in several neutrals.

In this traditional-style kitchen, above, the exposed-apron sink matches the warm metallic of the faucet.

A 90-deg.—or "zero radius"—sink looks especially cutting edge mounted under a bright solid-surface countertop, below left.

Because the color goes all the way through, this retro-pattern composite countertop, below right, is unlikely to fade over time.

Installation Styles

- **Self-rimming (drop-in) sinks** are the least costly and most common. Available in any material, they are set into the counter with the edges overlapping. The downside: crumbs, water splashes, other debris, and germs can collect along the seam of the rim.

- **Undermounted sinks** attach below the countertop. With no visible edges, they make a smooth transition between sink and counter. To avoid warping or buckling, choose a water-resistant counter material.

- **Integral sinks**, made of the same material as the counter, look seamless and sleek and provide no crevices where food can lodge. They can be fabricated of any moldable material, such as stainless steel, solid surfacing, composites, and concrete.

- **Exposed-apron sinks** are undermounted but reveal the sink's front panel. They can be made from most types of sink materials.

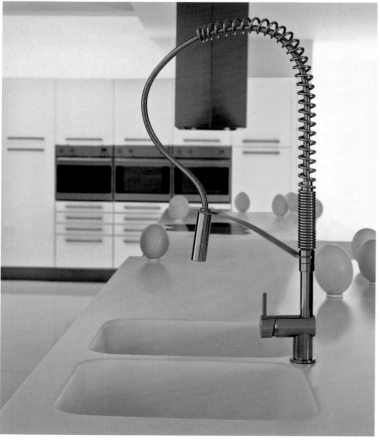

This under-mounted single-bowl kitchen sink, top, is deep enough to accommodate whatever can fit in the oven.

The clean look of this contemporary kitchen, left, is enhanced by the integral double sinks made of pure white solid-surfacing material.

This humble farmhouse-style sink, above, gets a sophisticated makeover in sleek black.

This tiny marble vessel was cleverly installed in an antique dry sink, left.

Bar sinks are so small that you can afford to splurge a little with a fancy faucet set or a gleaming hammered-copper finish, below.

Prep and Bar Sinks

In addition to the primary sink, prep and bar sinks are becoming standard equipment.

You'll welcome a prep sink if your kitchen is large, if two cooks often work together in it, or if you entertain frequently. Especially useful when two cooks are working simultaneously or when a dinner guest is pressed into service to scrub some vegetables or make a salad, prep sinks are placed away from the work zone. Typically drop-in or undermount models, they are small, ranging in size from 9-inch. rounds to 18-inch. squares, although some are smaller. Because such a diminutive sink doesn't represent a major investment or get hard use, you can splurge a little bit on sexy materials that wouldn't hold up well in the primary work area—gleaming copper or brass, or a hand-painted ceramic or glass bowl, for example.

The popularity of bar sinks is a direct result of the kitchen's current status as a living center. With one cook busy at the main sink and a helper using the prep sink, a third sink where hot or cold drinks can be served is useful.

A swan-neck spout is both graceful and practical—it allows plenty of clearance for tall pots, right.

This integral, zero-radius sink, below, is a kitchen star thanks to its unusual size, shape, color, and material.

Standard Sizes

Sink Type	Width	Front to Rear	Basin Depth
Single-bowl	25	21–22	8–9
Double-bowl	33, 36	21–22	8–9
Side-disposal	33	21–22	8–9, 7
Triple-bowl	43	21–22	8, 6, 10
Corner (each way)	17–18	21–11	8–9
Bar	15–25	15	5½–6

Note: Sink dimensions (in inches)

How To Choose a Kitchen Sink

It's tempting to put looks first, but give some thought to your day-to-day practical needs, too. If you have a dishwasher, a large single-bowl sink may be sufficient; add a prep sink if yours is a two-cook household—but only if you have space for it. No dishwasher? You'll need a double-bowl design with equal-size basins. Other double-bowl options include one large and one medium or one small bowl.
A triple-bowl sink with two deep basins for washing and rinsing and a small basin is a good choice for a kitchen with no dishwasher and no space for a separate prep sink. If you entertain, a bar sink is a bonus.

Match the sink with the decor, too. Stainless steel, for example, looks good in a contemporary room, but it's also at home in any style kitchen, as are solid-surface and composite-stone designs. Copper sinks, or porcelain sinks in white or a pretty color, blend beautifully with traditional or country decors. Concrete or soapstone designs have a handsome, sturdy quality. Depending on the other elements in the kitchen, they can look rustic or refined.

A single-hole faucet with a swivel spout can easily service a two-bowl sink.

Plan #121066

Dimensions: 46' W x 41'5" D

Levels: 2

Square Footage: 2,078

Main Level Sq. Ft.: 1,113

Upper Level Sq. Ft.: 965

Bedrooms: 4

Bathrooms: 2½

Foundation: Basement

Materials List Available: Yes

Price Category: D

Images provided by designer/architect.

This lovely home has an unusual dignity, perhaps because its rooms are so well-proportioned and thoughtfully laid out.

Features:

- Gathering Room: This room is sunken, giving it an unusually cozy, comfortable feeling. Its abundance of windows let natural light stream in during the day, and the fireplace warms it when the weather's chilly.

- Dining Room: This dining room links to the parlor beyond through a cased opening.

- Parlor: A tall, angled ceiling highlights a large, arched window that's the focal point of this room.

- Breakfast Area: A wooden rail visually links this bayed breakfast area to the family room.

- Master Suite: A roomy walk-in closet adds a practical touch to this luxurious suite. The bath features a skylight, whirlpool tub, and separate shower.

Main Level Floor Plan

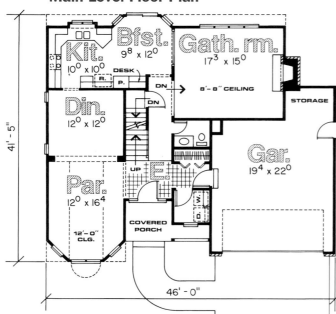

Upper Level Floor Plan

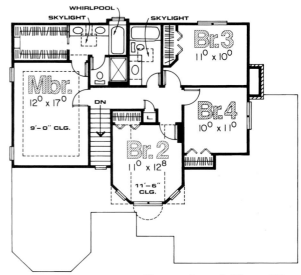

Copyright by designer/architect.

Plan #441031

Dimensions: 78'2" W x 68' D
Levels: 2
Square Footage: 4,150
Main Level Sq. Ft.: 2,572
Upper Level Sq. Ft.: 1,578
Bedrooms: 4
Bathrooms: 4½
Foundation: Crawl space;
slab or basement available for fee
Materials List Available: Yes
Price Category: J

Images provided by designer/architect.

Features:

- **Great Room:** The main level offers this commodious room, with its beamed ceiling, alcove, fireplace, and built-ins.
- **Kitchen:** Go up a few steps to the dining nook and this kitchen, and you'll find a baking center, walk-in pantry, and access to a covered side porch.

- **Formal Dining Room:** This formal room lies a few steps up from the foyer and sports a bay window and hutch space.
- **Guest Suite:** This suite, which is located at the end of the hall, features a private bathroom and walk-in closet.
- **Master Suite:** A fireplace flanked by built-ins warms this suite. Its bath contains a spa tub, compartmented toilet, and huge shower.

Graceful and gracious, this superb shingle design delights with handsome exterior elements. A whimsical turret, covered entry, upper-level balcony, and bay window all bring their charm to the facade.

CAD FILE AVAILABLE

Main Level Floor Plan

Upper Level Floor Plan

Copyright by designer/architect.

Plan #161102

Dimensions: 99'6" W x 84'2" D
Levels: 1
Square Footage: 6,659
Main Level Sq. Ft.: 3,990
Lower Level Sq. Ft: 2,669
Bedrooms: 4
Bathrooms: 4 full, 2 half
Foundation: Walkout; basement for fee
Material List Available: Yes
Price Category: K

Images provided by designer/architect.

A brick-and-stone exterior with lime-stone trim and arches decorates the exterior, while the interior explodes with design elements and large spaces to dazzle all who enter.

Features:

- Great Room: The 14-ft. ceiling height in this room is defined with columns and a fireplace wall. Triple French doors with an arched transom create the rear wall, and built-in shelving adds the perfect spot to house your big-screen TV.

- Kitchen: This spacious gourmet kitchen opens generously to the great room and allows everyone to enjoy the daily activities. A two-level island with cooktop provides casual seating and additional storage.

- Breakfast Room: This room is surrounded by windows, creating a bright and cheery place to start your day. Sliding glass doors to the covered porch in the rear add a rich look for outdoor entertaining, and the built-in fire place provides a cozy, warm atmosphere.

- Master Suite: This master bedroom suite is fit for royalty, with its stepped ceiling treatment, spacious dressing room, and private exercise room.

- Lower Level: This lower level is dedicated to fun and entertaining. A large media area, billiards room, and wet bar are central to sharing this spectacular home with your friends.

Front View

Rear Elevation

Right Side Elevation

Left Side Elevation

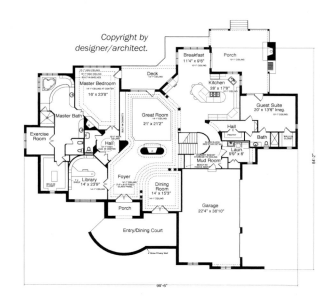

Master Bedroom
16' x 23'8"

Master Bath

Deck

Breakfast
11'4" x 9'6"

Porch

Kitchen
28' x 17'8"

Great Room
21' x 21'2"

Guest Suite
20' x 13'6" Irreg.

Exercise Room

Hall

Bath

Library
14' x 23'9"

Laun.
9'9" x 8'

Mud Room

Foyer

Dining Room
14' x 15'3"

Porch

Garage
22'4" x 36'10"

Entry/Dining Court

99'-6"

84'-2"

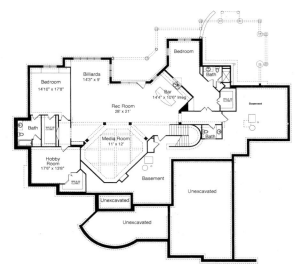

Bedroom

Billiards
14'3" x 9'

Bedroom
14'10" x 17'8"

Bar
14'4" x 10'6" Irreg.

Bath

Rec Room
28' x 21'

Basement

Bath

Bath

Media Room
11' x 12'

Hobby Room
17'6" x 13'8"

Basement

Unexcavated

Unexcavated

Unexcavated

Basement Level Floor Plan

Foyer/Dining Room

Kitchen

Great Room

Porch

Plan #151032

Dimensions: 84'8" W x 48'4" D
Levels: 2
Square Footage: 2,824
Main Level Sq. Ft.: 2,279
Upper Level Sq. Ft.: 545
Bedrooms: 4
Bathrooms: 3
Foundation: Crawl space, slab;
basement option for fee
CompleteCost List Available: Yes
Price Category: F

This luxurious two-story home combines a stately exterior with a large, functional floor plan.

Features:

- Great Room: The spacious foyer leads directly into this room, which opens to the rear yard, providing natural light and views of the outdoors.

- Kitchen: This fully equipped kitchen is located to provide the utmost convenience in serving both the formal dining room and the informal breakfast area. The combination of breakfast room, hearth room, and kitchen creatively forms a comfortable family gathering place.

- Master Suite: Located on the main level for privacy, this private retreat has a boxed ceiling in the sleeping area. The master bath boasts a large tub, dual vanities, and a walk-in closet.

- Upper Level: This level is where you'll find the two secondary bedrooms. Each has ample space, and they share the full bathroom.

Upper Level Floor Plan

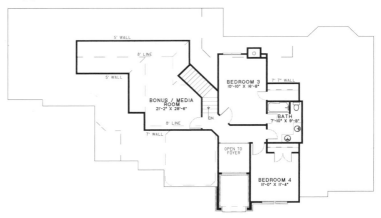

Plan #271093

Dimensions: 74' W x 52' D
Levels: 2
Square Footage: 2,813
Main Level Sq. Ft.: 1,828
Upper Level Sq. Ft.: 985
Bedrooms: 3
Bathrooms: 3
Foundation: Basement
Materials List Available: Yes
Price Category: F

This Craftsman-style home will be the envy of your neighbors.

Images provided by designer/architect.

Features:

- **Entry:** Enter the home through the covered porch and into this entry with a view into the great room.

- **Great Room:** This large gathering area, with two-sided fireplace, has window looking out to the backyard.

- **Kitchen:** This peninsula kitchen has plenty of cabinets and counter space. The garage is just a few steps away though the laundry room.

- **Hearth Room:** Just off the kitchen this hearth room shares the fireplace with the great room and is open into the dining room.

- **Master Suite:** Located upstairs, with a secondary bedroom, this suite has a sitting area, large closet, and master bath.

Great Room

Kitchen

Main Level Floor Plan

Copyright by designer/architect.

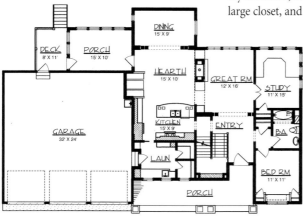

Upper Level Floor Plan

Plan #161033

Dimensions: 78'2" W x 74'6" D
Levels: 2
Square Footage: 3,809
Main Level Sq. Ft.: 2,782
Upper Level Sq. Ft.: 1,027
Optional Lower Level Sq. Ft.: 1,316
Bedrooms: 4
Bathrooms: 3½
Foundation: Basement
Materials List Available: Yes
Price Category: H

Images provided by designer/architect.

The dramatic design of this home, combined with its comfort and luxuries, suit those with discriminating tastes.

Features:

• Great Room: Let the fireplace and 14-ft. ceilings in this room set the stage for all sorts of gatherings, from casual to formal.

• Dining Room: Adjacent to the great room and kitchen fit for a gourmet, the dining room allows you to entertain with ease.

• Music Rom: Give your music the space it desreves in this specially-designed room.

• Library: Use this room as an office, or reserve it for quiet reading and studying.

• Master Suite: You'll love the separate dressing area and walk-in closet in the bedroom.

• Lower Level: A bar and recreational area give even more space for entertaining.

Rear view

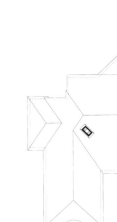

**Main Level
Floor Plan**

**Upper Level
Floor Plan**

*Copyright by
designer/architect.*

**Optional Lo
Level Floor F

Plan #271069

Dimensions: 63'5" W x 51'8" D
Levels: 2
Square Footage: 2,376
Main Level Sq. Ft.: 1,248
Upper Level Sq. Ft.: 1,128
Bedrooms: 4
Bathrooms: 2½
Foundation: Crawl space, basement
Materials List Available: Yes
Price Category: E

Images provided by designer/architect.

This home's Federal-style facade has a simple elegance that is still popular among today's homeowners.

Features:

- **Living Room:** This formal space is perfect for serious conversation or thoughtful reflection. Optional double doors would open directly into the family room beyond.

- **Dining Room:** You won't find a more elegant room than this for hosting holiday feasts.

- **Kitchen:** This room has everything the cook could hope for—a central island, a handy pantry, and a menu desk. Sliding glass doors in the dinette let you step outside for some fresh air with your cup of coffee.

- **Family Room:** Here's the spot to spend a cold winter evening. Have hot chocolate in front of a crackling fire!

- **Master Suite:** With an optional vaulted ceiling, the sleeping chamber is bright and spacious. The private bath showcases a splashy whirlpool tub.

Main Level Floor Plan

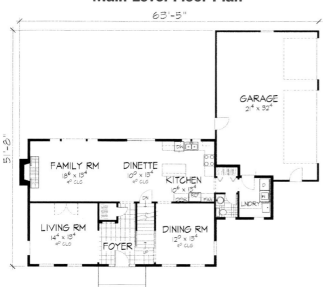

Upper Level Floor Plan

Copyright by designer/architect.

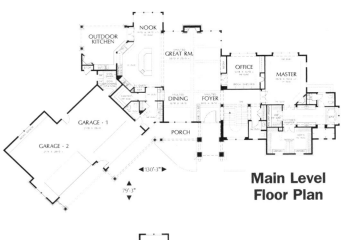

Main Level
Floor Plan

Images provided by designer/architect.

Basement Level
Floor Plan

Copyright by designer/architect.

Plan #441015

Dimensions: 130'3" W x 79'3" D

Levels: 1

Square Footage: 4,732

Main Level Sq. Ft.: 2,902

Lower Level Sq. Ft.: 1,830

Bedrooms: 4

Bathrooms: 3 full, 2 half

Foundation: Walkout basement

Materials List Available: Yes

Price Category: J

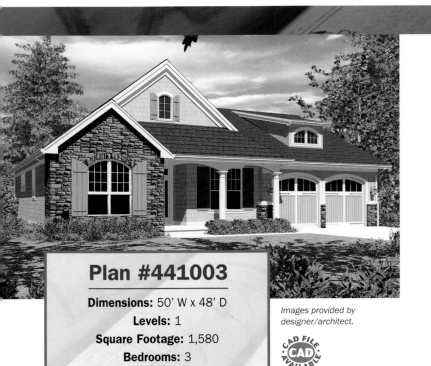

Images provided by designer/architect.

Copyright by designer/architect.

Plan #441003

Dimensions: 50' W x 48' D

Levels: 1

Square Footage: 1,580

Bedrooms: 3

Bathrooms: 2½

Foundation: Crawl space;
slab or basement available for fee

Materials List Available: Yes

Price Category: E

Rear Elevation

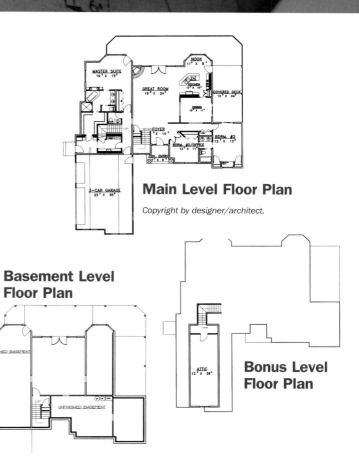

Main Level Floor Plan

Copyright by designer/architect.

Plan #451359

Dimensions: 70' W x 86'8" D
Levels: 2
Square Footage: 3,039
Main Level Sq. Ft.: 2,558
Upper Level Sq. Ft.: 481
Bedrooms: 3
Bathrooms: 2½
Foundation: Basement – insulated concrete form
Material List Available: Yes
Price Category: G

Images provided by designer/architect.

Basement Level Floor Plan

Bonus Level Floor Plan

Main Level Floor Plan

Plan #151731

Dimensions: 55' W x 58'6" D
Levels: 1.5
Square Footage: 2,099
Bedrooms: 3
Bathrooms: 2
Foundation: Crawl space, slab
CompleteCost List Available: Yes
Price Category: D

Images provided by designer/architect.

Upper Level Floor Plan

Copyright by designer/ architect

Plan #271021

Dimensions: 38'4" W x 58' D
Levels: 2
Square Footage: 1,551
Main Level Sq. Ft.: 1,099
Upper Level Sq. Ft.: 452
Bedrooms: 3
Bathrooms: 2½
Foundation: Basement
Materials List Available: Yes
Price Category: C

Images provided by designer/architect.

The exterior of this cozy country-style home boasts a charming combination of woodwork and stone that lends an air of England to the facade.

Features:

• Living Room: An arched entryway leads into the living room, with its vaulted ceiling, tall windows, and fireplace.

• Dining Room: This space also features a vaulted ceiling, plus a view of the patio.

• Master Suite: Find a vaulted ceiling here, too, as well as a walk-in closet, and private bath.

Living Room

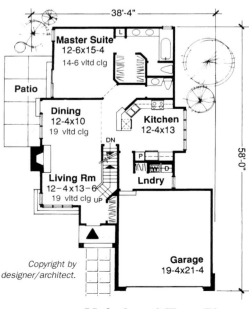

Copyright by designer/architect.

Main Level Floor Plan

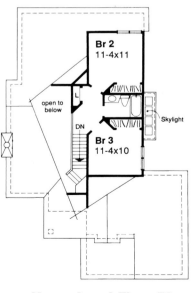

Upper Level Floor Plan

Plan #441025

Dimensions: 70' W x 100'6" D
Levels: 2
Square Footage: 3,457
Main Level Sq. Ft.: 2,222
Upper Level Sq. Ft.: 1,235
Bedrooms: 4
Bathrooms: 3 full, 2 half
Foundation: Crawl space; slab or basement for fee
Materials List Available: Yes
Price Category: I

Images provided by designer/architect.

Classic Craftsman tradition shines through in this spectacular two-story home.

Features:

- **Great Room:** This open room features two sets of double doors to the rear yard, a fireplace, and a built-in media center.

- **Kitchen:** Casual dining takes place in the breakfast nook, which is open to this island kitchen and leads to a vaulted porch.

- **Master Suites:** One master suite is found on the first floor. It glows with appointments, from double-door access to the rear yard to a fine bath with spa tub, separate shower, and double sinks. The second master suite, on the second floor, holds a window seat and a private bath with spa tub.

- **Bedrooms:** Two additional bedrooms (or a bedroom and a study) share a full bathroom with private vanities for each room.

- **Garage:** This four-car garage connects to the main house at a laundry/mud room with a half-bath, coat closet, built-in bench, and washer/dryer space. Extra room in the garage can be used as a workshop or for storage space.

Main Level Floor Plan

Upper Level Floor Plan

Copyright by designer/architect.

Plan #441014

Dimensions: 119'6" W x 87'6" D
Levels: 1
Square Footage: 3,940
Bedrooms: 3
Bathrooms: 3 full, 2 half
Foundation: Crawl space;
slab or basement available for fee
Materials List Available: Yes
Price Category: J

CAD FILE AVAILABLE

Though this is but a single-story home, it satisfies and delights on many levels. The exterior has visual appeal, with varied rooflines, a mixture of materials, and graceful traditional lines.

Features:

- **Great Room:** This huge room boasts a sloped, vaulted ceiling, a fireplace, and built-ins. There is also a media room with double-door access.

- **Kitchen:** This kitchen has an island, two sink prep areas, a butler's pantry connecting it to the formal dining room, and a walk-in pantry.

- **Bedrooms:** Family bedrooms sit at the front of the plan and are joined by a Jack-and-Jill bathroom.

- **Master Suite:** This master suite is on the far right side. Its grand salon has an 11-ft.-high ceiling, a fireplace, built-ins, a walk-in closet, and a superb bathroom.

- **Garage:** If you need extra space, there's a bonus room on an upper level above the three-car garage.

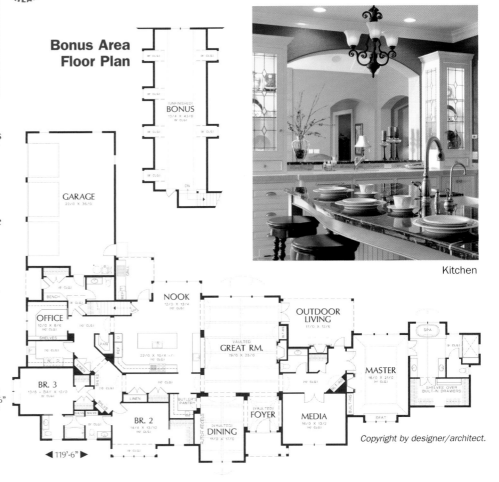

Bonus Area Floor Plan

Kitchen

Copyright by designer/architect.

Plan #151536

Dimensions: 37' W x 74'4" D

Levels: 1

Square Footage: 1,933

Bedrooms: 3

Bathrooms: 2

Foundation: Crawl space or slab

CompleteCost List Available: Yes

Price Category: D

The design of this home reflects the attention to detail of the Craftsman style.

Features:

- Foyer: The covered porch leads to this foyer, which separates the secondary bedrooms from the rest of the home.

- Great Room: This gathering room has eight-inch-diameter columns that add to the drama of the design. Additional amenities include a media center, a cozy fireplace, and a hidden computer center for study time or to serve as a small office.

- Kitchen: This spacious kitchen, with snack bar seating, has a wall of windows for plenty of natural light. Conveniently located just off the kitchen is a kids' play nook that helps keep the work area clutter free.

- Master Suite: A 10-ft.-high boxed ceiling, a large walk-in closet, whirlpool tub, and a separate shower, with built-in seat, make this master suite the ultimate in privacy and relaxation.

Images provided by designer/architect.

Copyright by designer/architect.

Plan #211008

Dimensions: 56' W x 93' D

Levels: 1

Square Footage: 2,259

Bedrooms: 3

Bathrooms: 2½

Foundation: Slab

Materials List Available: Yes

Price Category: E

If you're looking for a design that suits a narrow building lot, you'll love this home, with its exterior that resembles an old European cottage.

Features:

- Ceiling Height: 10-ft. except as noted.

- Courtyards: Use formal gardens full of easy-care plants to make the most of the lovely courtyards.

- Living Room: The massive glass wall in this room with 16-ft. ceilings looks out to the entry courtyard. In cool weather you'll love the fireplace, which is flanked by lovely built-ins that can hold everything from books to collectables.

- Kitchen: With a contemporary layout and up-to-date conveniences, this kitchen is as convenient as it is attractive.

- Master Suite: Relax beside the bedroom fireplace, or luxuriate in the bath, with its two walk-in closets, soaking tub, shower, two vanities, linen closet, and private room for toilet and bidet.

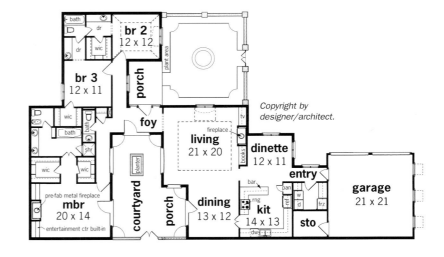

Plan #151529

Dimensions: 43' W x 66'6" D
Levels: 1
Square Footage: 1,474
Bedrooms: 2
Bathrooms: 2
Foundation: Crawl space or slab
CompleteCost List Available: Yes
Price Category: B

This elegant design is reflective of the Arts and Crafts era. Copper roofing and carriage style garage doors warmly welcome guests into this split-bedroom plan.

Features:

- Great Room: With access to the grilling porch as a bonus, this large gathering area features a 10-ft.-high ceiling and a beautiful fireplace.

- Kitchen: This fully equipped island kitchen has a raised bar and a built-in pantry. The area is open to the great room and dining room, giving an open and airy feeling to the home.

- Master Suite: Located on the opposite side of the home from the secondary bedroom, this retreat offers a large sleeping area and two large closets. The master bath features a spa tub, a separate shower, and dual vanities.

- Bedroom: This secondary bedroom has a large closet and access to the full bathroom in the hallway.

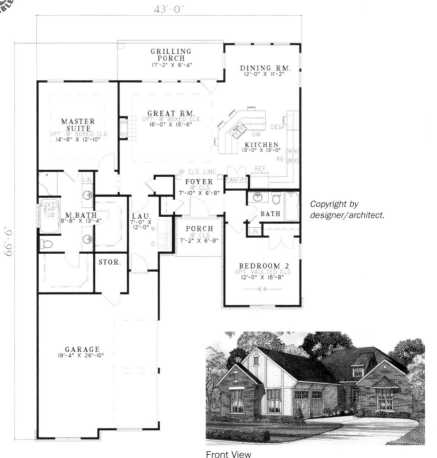

Front View

Plan #441002

Dimensions: 70' W x 51' D

Levels: 1

Square Footage: 1,873

Bedrooms: 3

Bathrooms: 2

Foundation: Crawl space

Materials List Available: Yes

Price Category: E

Images provided by designer/architect.

CAD FILE AVAILABLE · CAD

Rear Elevation

Plan #551066

Dimensions: 42' W x 58' D

Levels: 2

Square Footage: 2,415

Main Level Sq. Ft.: 1,200

Upper Level Sq. Ft.: 1,215

Bedrooms: 4

Bathrooms: 2½

Foundation: Crawl Space

Materials List Available: Yes

Price Category: E

Images provided by designer/architect.

Main Level Floor Plan

Upper Level Floor Plan

Copyright by designer/architect.

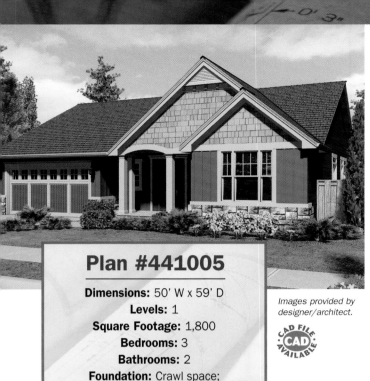

Copyright by designer/architect.

Images provided by designer/architect.

Rear Elevation

Plan #441005

Dimensions: 50' W x 59' D
Levels: 1
Square Footage: 1,800
Bedrooms: 3
Bathrooms: 2
Foundation: Crawl space; slab or basement for fee
Materials List Available: Yes
Price Category: E

CAD FILE AVAILABLE

Main Level Floor Plan

Images provided by designer/architect.

Bonus Area Floor Plan

Upper Level Floor Plan

Copyright by designer/architect.

Plan #121203

Dimensions: 67' W x 56' D
Levels: 1.5
Square Footage: 2,690
Main Level Sq. Ft.: 1,792
Upper Level Sq. Ft.: 898
Bedrooms: 4
Bathrooms: 2½
Foundation: Basement; crawl space or slab for fee
Materials List Available: Yes
Price Category: F

Main Level Floor Plan

VAULTED MASTER
11/8 X 15/0

VAULTED GREAT RM.
15/8 X 16/8

UP

DINING
11/0 X 10/0 +/-

GARAGE
19/0 X 21/6

PORCH

40'

47'

Plan #441246

Dimensions: 40' W x 47' D

Levels: 2

Square Footage: 1,866

Main Level Sq. Ft.: 1,198

Upper Level Sq. Ft.: 668

Bedrooms: 4

Bathrooms: 2½

Foundation: Crawl space

Material List Available: Yes

Price Category: E

Images provided by designer/architect.

 CAD FILE AVAILABLE

Rear Elevation

Upper Level Floor Plan

GREAT RM. BELOW

LINEN

DN

BR. 2
10/10 X 10/8

BR. 4
10/10 X 11/10

BR. 3
12/0 X 11/4

Main Level Floor Plan

50'-0"

36'-0"

DINING ROOM

GREAT ROOM
OPEN TO ABOVE

3 CAR GARAGE
20'-6 x 34

KITCHEN

OFFICE

COFFERED CEILING

ENTRY

ENTRY PORCH

Plan #641005

Dimensions: 50' W x 38' D

Levels: 2

Square Footage: 2,669

Main Level Sq. Ft.: 1,017

Upper Level Sq. Ft.: 1,652

Bedrooms: 3

Bathrooms: 2½

Foundation: Crawl space; Slab, basement or walkout for fee

Materials List Available: Yes

Price Category: F

Images provided by designer/architect.

 CAD FILE AVAILABLE

Upper Level Floor Plan

Copyright by designer/architect.

50'-0"

35'-0"

DECK

ROOF BELOW

SITTING AREA

DECK

MASTER BATH

OPEN TO BELOW

RAILING

BEDROOM 2
20'-6 x 3-9

WIC

LAUNDRY

BATH

DECK

MASTER SUITE

OPEN TO BELOW

BEDROOM 3
20'-6 x 3-9

UPPER DECK

Images provided by designer/architect.

Plan #161224

Dimensions: 87'4" W x 57'4" D

Levels: 1

Square Footage: 2,796

Bedrooms: 2

Bathrooms: 2 1/2

Foundation: Walkout

Materials List Available: Yes

Price Category: F

Plan #441006

Dimensions: 48' W x 64' D

Levels: 1

Square Footage: 1,891

Bedrooms: 3

Bathrooms: 2

Foundation: Crawl space; slab or basement for fee

Materials List Available: Yes

Price Category: E

Images provided by designer/architect.

CAD FILE AVAILABLE

Rear Elevation

Copyright by designer/architect.

Plan #121125

Dimensions: 54' W x 58'8" D
Levels: 1
Square Footage: 1,978
Bedrooms: 3
Bathrooms: 2½
Foundation: Basement; crawl space or slab for fee
Material List Available: Yes
Price Category: D

Images provided by designer/architect.

You'll love this plan if you are looking for a home with fantastic curb appeal outside and comfortable amenities inside.

Features:

- **Living Room:** Family and friends will love to gather in this large area, which features a 10-ft.-high ceiling.

- **Dining Room:** This formal dining area is open to the entry foyer and features a stepped ceiling. The triple-window unit, with the transom above, floods the space with natural light.

- **Kitchen:** Convenience marks this well-laid-out kitchen, where you'll love to cook for family and friends. Open to both the family room and the breakfast room, the space has an airy feeling.

- **Master Suite:** The 10-ft.-high boxed ceiling in the sleeping area makes this space feel airy. The master bath features dual vanities and a whirlpool tub.

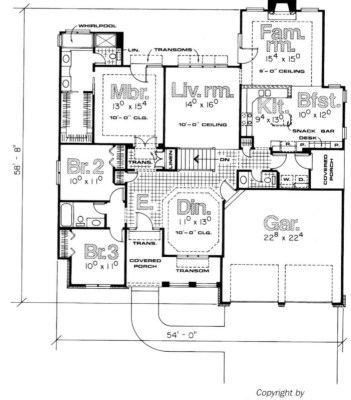

Copyright by designer/architect.

Plan #441016

Dimensions: 50' W x 45' D
Levels: 2
Square Footage: 1,893
Main Level Sq. Ft.: 1,087
Upper Level Sq. Ft.: 806
Bedrooms: 3
Bathrooms: 2½
Foundation: Crawl space; slab or basement for fee
Material List Available: Yes
Price Category: E

It's a classic. This two-story home delivers comfort and beauty that will serve your family for years to come.

CAD FILE AVAILABLE

Images provided by designer/architect.

Features:

• Den: Just off the foyer and through double doors is this cozy space, which features a view of the front yard.

• Kitchen: Equipped with an island, this L-shape kitchen hosts workstations for multiple cooks. The panrty stretches the storage space.

• Master Suite: This master suite includes a bedroom with ample wall space for positioning of furniture, a walk-in closet, and a private master bath with twin sinks, a tub, and a shower.

• Bedrooms: The two additional bedrooms boast large closets and share the other full-size bath.

Copyright by designer/architect.

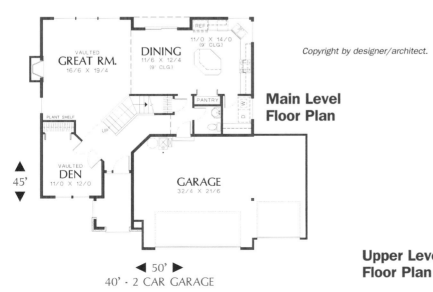

Main Level Floor Plan

Upper Level Floor Plan

Plan #121121

Dimensions: 47'4" W x 45'8" D
Levels: 1
Square Footage: 1,341
Bedrooms: 3
Bathrooms: 2
Foundation: Basement;
crawl space for fee
Material List Available: Yes
Price Category: C

Images provided by designer/architect.

This traditional home is charming and bound to make your life simpler with all its amenities.

Features:

- Great Room: Already equipped with an entertainment center, bookcase and a fireplace by which you can enjoy those books, this room has endless possibilities. This is a room that will bring the whole family together.

- Kitchen: This design includes everything you need and everything you want: a pantry waiting to be filled with your favorite foods, plenty of workspace, and a snack bar that acts as a useful transition between kitchen and breakfast room.

- Breakfast Room: An extension of the kitchen, this room will fill with the aroma of coffee and a simmering breakfast, so you'll be immersed in your relaxing morning. With peaceful daylight streaming in through a window-lined wall, this will easily become the best part of your day.

- Master Suite: Plenty of breathing room for both of you, there will be no fighting for sink or closet space in this bedroom. The full master bath includes dual sinks, and the walk-in closet will hold everything you both need. Another perk of this bathroom is the whirlpool bathtub.

- Garage: This two-car garage opens directly into the home, so there is no reason to get out of your warm, dry car and into unpleasant weather.

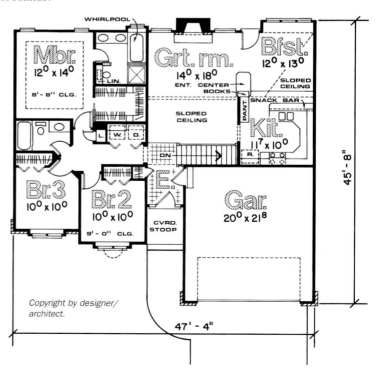

Plan #441008

Dimensions: 60' W x 50' D
Levels: 1
Square Footage: 2,001
Bedrooms: 3
Bathrooms: 2
Foundation: Crawl space;
slab or basement available for fee
Materials List Available: Yes
Price Category: F

Images provided by designer/architect.

A fine design for a country setting, this one-story plan offers a quaint covered porch at the entry, cedar shingles in the gables, and stonework at the foundation line.

Features:

• Entry: The pretty package on the outside is prelude to the fine floor plan on the inside. It begins at this entry foyer, which opens on the right to a den with a 9-ft.-high ceiling and space for a desk or closet.

• Great Room: This entertaining area is vaulted and contains a fireplace and optional media center. The rear windows allow a view onto the rear deck.

• Kitchen: Open to the dining room and great room to form one large space, this kitchen boasts a raised bar and a built-in desk.

• Master Suite: The vaulted ceiling in this master suite adds an elegant touch. The master bath features a dual vanities and a spa tub.

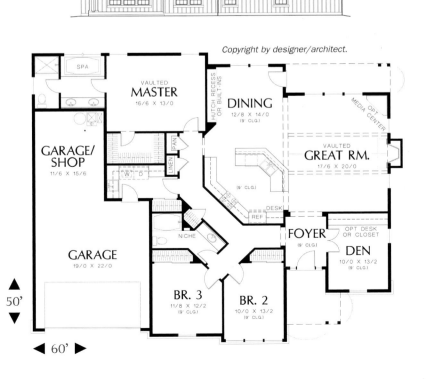

Copyright by designer/architect.

Plan #121032

Dimensions: 54' W x 45'4" D

Levels: 2

Square Footage: 2,339

Main Level Sq. Ft.: 1,665

Upper Level Sq. Ft.: 674

Bedrooms: 4

Bathrooms: 2½

Foundation: Basement

Materials List Available: Yes

Price Category: E

Images provided by designer/architect.

This home is designed for gracious living and is distinguished by many architectural details.

Features:

- Ceiling Height: 8 ft. unless otherwise noted.
- Foyer: This is truly a grand foyer with a dramatic ceiling that soars to 18 ft.
- Great Room: The foyer's 18-ft. ceiling extends into the great room where an open staircase adds architectural windows. Warm yourself by the fireplace that is framed by windows.

- Kitchen: An island is the centerpiece of this handsome and efficient kitchen that features a breakfast area for informal family meals. The room also includes a handy desk.
- Private Wing: The master suite and study are in a private wing of the house.
- Room to Expand: In addition to the three bedrooms, the second level has an unfinished storage space that can become another bedroom or office.

CAD FILE AVAILABLE

Main Level Floor Plan

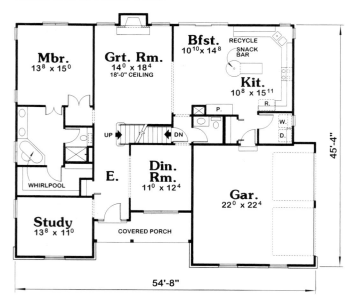

Upper Level Floor Plan

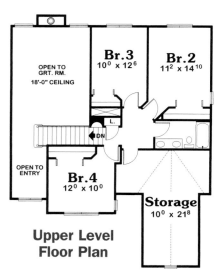

Copyright by designer/architect.

Plan #441049

Dimensions: 50' W x 47'6" D
Levels: 2
Square Footage: 2,124
Main Level Sq. Ft.: 1,157
Upper Level Sq. Ft.: 967
Bedrooms: 3
Bathrooms: 2½
Foundation: Crawl space; slab or basement for fee
Materials List Available: Yes
Price Category: F

Take a quaint cottage design, and expand naturally with a second-floor addition over the garage-the result is a comfortable home with all the charm of bungalow style.

Features:

• Foyer: Enter the home through the covered entry porch, with Arts and Crafts columns, into this foyer brightened by sidelights and a transom at the front door. The half-bathroom and coat closet make the entry area convenient.

• Great Room: This gathering area features a vaulted ceiling and a fireplace. Tall windows allow the room to be flooded with natural light, giving a warm and airy feeling.

• Kitchen: This island kitchen boasts long counters lined with cabinetry, making it a gourmet's delight to prepare meals in the area. The raised bar is open to the great room and dining room.

• Upper Level: This upper level is devoted to sleeping space. There is the vaulted master salon with private master bath and walk-in closet, plus the two family bedrooms, which that share the other full bathroom. Note the large linen closet in the upper-level hall.

Images provided by designer/architect.

Rear Elevation

Main Level Floor Plan

Upper Level Floor Plan

Copyright by designer/architect.

Plan #351206

Dimensions: 71' W x 77' D
Levels: 1
Square Footage: 2,140
Bedrooms: 4
Bathrooms: 2 1/2
Foundation: Crawl space, slab or basement
Materials List Available: Yes
Price Category: D

Images provided by designer/architect.

CAD FILE AVAILABLE

Bonus Level Floor Plan

Bonus Room 14-0 x 33-4

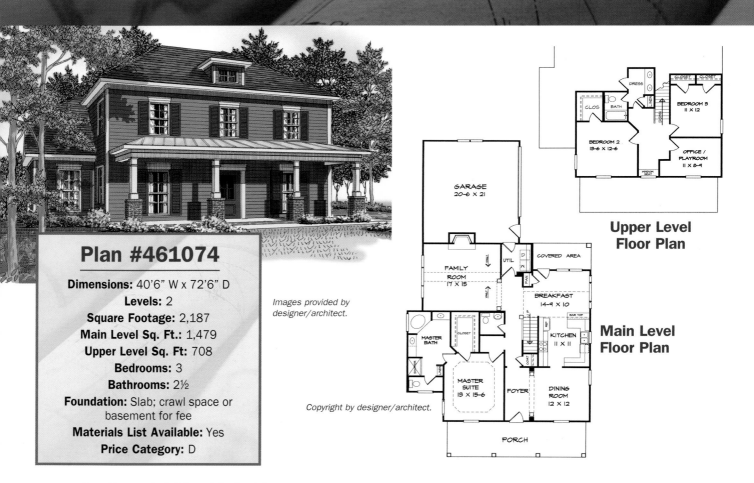

Plan #461074

Dimensions: 40'6" W x 72'6" D
Levels: 2
Square Footage: 2,187
Main Level Sq. Ft.: 1,479
Upper Level Sq. Ft.: 708
Bedrooms: 3
Bathrooms: 2½
Foundation: Slab; crawl space or basement for fee
Materials List Available: Yes
Price Category: D

Images provided by designer/architect.

Upper Level Floor Plan

Main Level Floor Plan

Copyright by designer/architect.

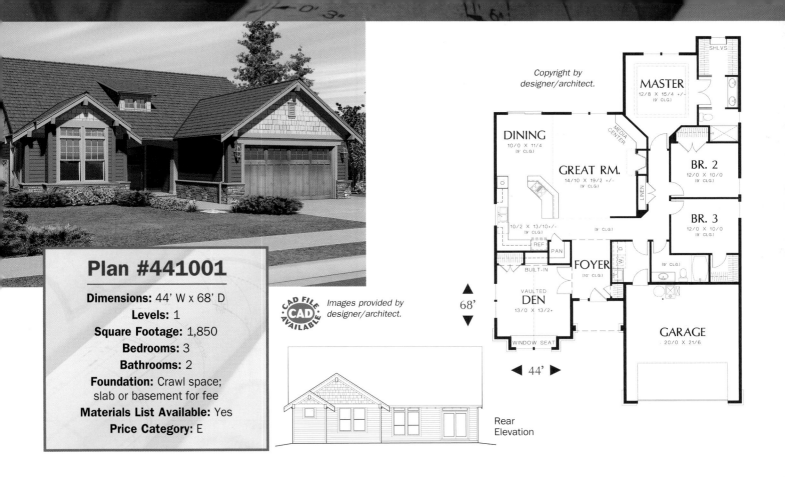

Plan #441001

Dimensions: 44' W x 68' D

Levels: 1

Square Footage: 1,850

Bedrooms: 3

Bathrooms: 2

Foundation: Crawl space;
slab or basement for fee

Materials List Available: Yes

Price Category: E

*Images provided by
designer/architect.*

Rear
Elevation

Plan #151530

Dimensions: 38'10" W x 70'4" D

Levels: 2

Square Footage: 2,146

Main Level Sq. Ft.: 1,654

Upper Level Sq. Ft.: 492

Bedrooms: 3

Bathrooms: 2½

Foundation: Crawl space or slab

CompleteCost List Available: Yes

Price Category: D

*Images provided by
designer/architect.*

**Upper Level
Floor Plan**

*Copyright by
designer/architect.*

Main Level Floor Plan

Front View

Trimwork Basics

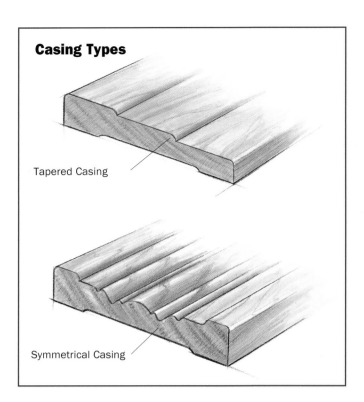

Tapered Casing

Symmetrical Casing

There are two basic types of window casings: tapered and symmetrical. Tapered casing is thinner on the edge closest to the window or door and thicker on the outside edge. Stock Colonial and clamshell casings are tapered casings. When you form corners with tapered casings, you must miter the joints.

Symmetrical casing is the same thickness on both edges and has a uniform pattern across its face. This type of casing rests on top of a plinth block or window stool and joins corner blocks or headers with square-cut butt joints. These casings often look more decorative than stock Colonial-style casings, and they are easier for most do-it-yourselfers to install because you don't have to miter symmetrical casings.

Casing Reveals

The edge of a doorjamb is flush with the surface of the adjoining wall, and there is usually a narrow gap between the jamb and the nearby drywall. Casing has to bridge that gap. Typically, the door side of the casing covers most but not all of the jamb, leaving a narrow edge called a reveal. This helps to add definition to the molding and avoids an unsightly seam where the edge of one board lines up directly over another.

When you're working on a new jamb, you have to establish the reveal and stick with it to maintain a uniform appearance. If you're replacing existing trim, you may need to clean up the edge of an old jamb with a sharp scraper and a sander even if you duplicate the old reveal. Although there are several varieties of casing treatments, they all share this detail—a slight setback of at least ⅛ inch from the edge of the jamb. If you install plinths or corner blocks, which are slightly wider than the casing, you may need to experiment with their exact placement to maintain the reveal.

A typical reveal between a doorjamb and casing creates a handsome transition at cased openings.

Door casings can be built up with molding, including an outer strip of backband molding, showing multiple reveals.

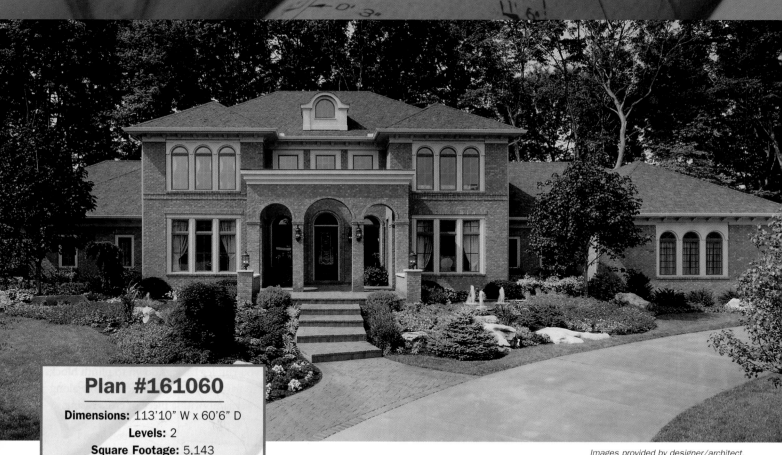

Plan #161060

Dimensions: 113'10" W x 60'6" D
Levels: 2
Square Footage: 5,143
Main Level Sq. Ft.: 3,323
Upper Level Sq. Ft.: 1,820
Bedrooms: 4
Bathrooms: 3½
Foundation: Basement, walkout basement
Materials List Available: Yes
Price Category: J

Images provided by designer/architect.

Luxury, comfort, beauty, spaciousness—this home has everything you've been wanting, including space for every possible activity.

Features:

- Courtyard: Enjoy the privacy here before entering this spacious home.

- Great Room: Open to the foyer, dining area, and kitchen, this great room has a fireplace flanked by windows and leads to the open rear deck.

- Dining Room: Situated between the foyer and the kitchen, this room is ideal for formal dining.

- Library: Located just off the foyer, this library offers a calm retreat from activities in the great room.

- Utility Area: The mudroom, pantry, half-bath and laundry room add up to household convenience.

- Master Suite: You'll love the huge walk-in closet, extensive window feature, and bath with a dressing room and two vanities.

Left Side Elevation

Stairs

Rear Elevation

Right Side Elevation

Dining Room

Media Room

**Main Level
Floor Plan**

*Copyright by designer/
architect.*

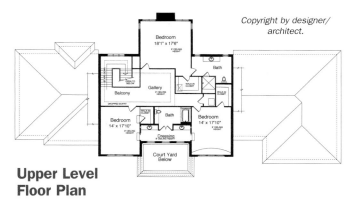

**Upper Level
Floor Plan**

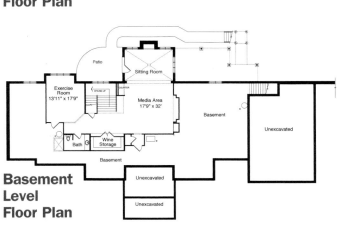

**Basement
Level
Floor Plan**

Great Room

Kitchen

Plan #121064

Dimensions: 44' W x 40' D

Levels: 2

Square Footage: 1,846

Main Level Sq. Ft.: 919

Upper Level Sq. Ft.: 927

Bedrooms: 4

Bathrooms: 2½

Foundation: Basement

Materials List Available: Yes

Price Category: D

Images provided by designer/architect.

You'll love the features and design in this compact but amenity-filled home.

Features:

- **Entry:** A balcony overlooks this two-story entry, where a plant shelf tops the coat closet.
- **Great Room:** A trio of tall windows points up the large dimensions of this room, which is sure to be the hub of your home. Arrange the

furniture to create a cozy space around the fireplace, or leave it open to the room.

- **Kitchen:** You'll love to work in this well-designed kitchen area.
- **Master Suite:** On the second floor, this master suite features a tiered ceiling and two walk-in closets. In the bath, you'll find a double vanity, whirlpool tub, and separate shower.

Main Level Floor Plan

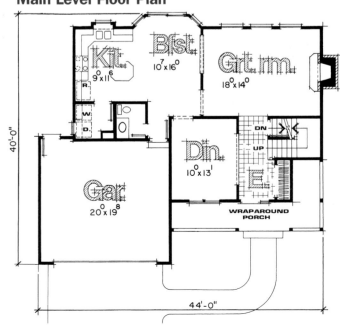

Upper Level Floor Plan

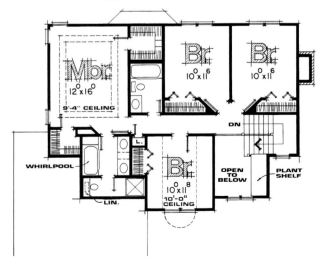

Copyright by designer/architect.

Plan #351002

Dimensions: 64' W x 45'10" D
Levels: 1
Square Footage: 1,751
Bedrooms: 3
Bathrooms: 2
Foundation: Crawl space, slab, or basement
Materials List Available: Yes
Price Category: D

This is a beautiful classic traditional home with a European touch.

Features:

- **Great Room:** This gathering area has a gas log fireplace that is flanked by two built-in cabinets. The area has a 10-ft.-tall tray ceiling.

- **Kitchen:** This L-shaped island kitchen has a raised bar and is open to the eating area and great room. The three open spaces work together as one large room.

- **Master Suite:** Located on the opposite side of the home from the secondary bedrooms, this suite has a vaulted ceiling. The master bath has dual vanities and a garden tub.

- **Bedrooms:** The two secondary bedrooms share a hall bathroom and have ample closet space.

Images provided by designer/architect.

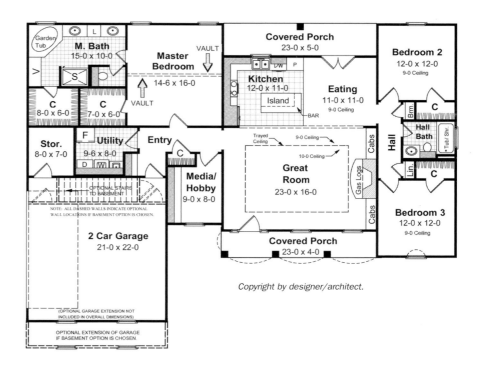

Copyright by designer/architect.

Plan #131003

Dimensions: 60' W x 39'10" D
Levels: 1
Square Footage: 1,466
Bedrooms: 3
Bathrooms: 2
Foundation: Crawl space or slab; basement for fee
Materials List Available: Yes
Price Category: C

Victorian styling adds elegance to this compact and easy-to-maintain ranch design.

This home, as shown in the photograph, may differ from the actual blueprints. For more detailed information, please check the floor plans carefully.

Images provided by designer/ar

Features:

- **Ceiling Height:** 8 ft.
- **Foyer:** Bridging between the front door and the great room, this foyer is a surprise feature.
- **Great Room:** A 10-ft. ceiling adds to the spacious feeling of this room, while the corner fireplace gives it an intimate feeling. Sliding glass doors at the rear of the room open to the backyard.

- **Dining Room:** This formal room adjoins the great room, allowing guests and family to flow between the rooms.
- **Breakfast Room:** Turrets add a Victorian feeling to this room that's just off the kitchen and overlooks the front porch.
- **Master Suite:** Privacy is assured in this suite, which is separated from the main part of the house. A separate toilet room and large walk-in closet add convenience to its beauty.

Copyright by designer/architect.

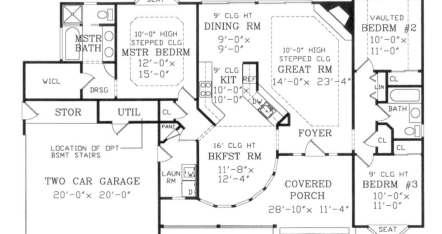

Plan #111006

Dimensions: 56' W x 67' D
Levels: 1
Square Footage: 2,241
Bedrooms: 4
Bathrooms: 2½
Foundation: Slab
Materials List Available: Yes
Price Category: F

Images provided by designer/architect.

You'll love this plan if you're looking for a home with fantastic curb appeal on the outside and comfortable amenities on the inside.

Features:

• **Foyer:** This lovely foyer opens to both the living and dining rooms.

• **Dining Room:** Three columns in this room accentuate both its large dimensions and its slightly formal air.

• **Living Room:** This room gives an airy feeling, and the fireplace here makes it especially inviting when the weather's cool.

• **Kitchen:** This G-shaped kitchen is designed to save steps while you're working, and the ample counter area adds even more to its convenience. The breakfast bar is a great gathering area.

• **Master Suite:** Two walk-in closets provide storage space, and the bath includes separate vanities, a standing shower, and a deluxe corner bathtub.

Front Elevation

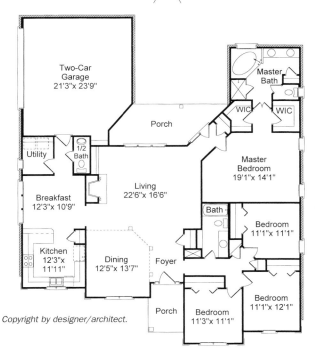

Copyright by designer/architect.

Plan #161041

Dimensions: 63'4" W x 48' D
Levels: 2
Square Footage: 2,738
Main Level Sq. Ft.: 1,915
Upper Level Sq. Ft.: 823
Bedrooms: 4
Bathrooms: 3½
Foundation: Basement
Materials List Available: Yes
Price Category: F

Images provided by designer/architect.

This two-level European country home is perfect for a large family, and makes entertaining a pleasure.

Features:

• Great Room: From the foyer, view the dramatic great room with its high windows and fireplace. Open stairs with rich wood trim lead to the second floor. The balcony on the second floor draws the eye up to the vaulted ceiling and also gives an exciting bird's eye view for those looking down. You can enter the formal dining room from either the great room or the kitchen.

• Breakfast Room/Hearth Room: Appreciate these rooms as two cozy nooks or as one large space for entertaining.

• Master Bedroom: The master bedroom encourages pampering in its private sitting room with an 11-ft. ceiling and garden bath.

• Additional bedrooms: You'll find a bedroom with a private bath, and two others that share a bath on the second floor.

• Basement and Garage: A full basement and two-car garage add extra storage capabilities to this family-friendly home.

Rear Elevation

Main Level Floor Plan

Upper Level Floor Plan

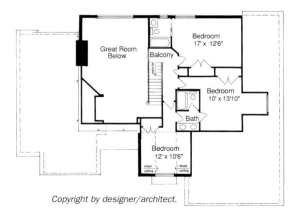

Copyright by designer/architect.

Plan #121018

Dimensions: 95'9" W x 70'2" D
Levels: 2
Square Footage: 3,950
Main Level Sq. Ft: 2,839
Upper Level Sq. Ft. : 1,111
Bedrooms: 4
Bathrooms: 2 full, 2 half
Foundation: Basement
Material List Available: Yes
Price Category: H

Images provided by designer/architect.

A spectacular two-story entry with a floating curved staircase welcomes you home.

Features:

• Ceiling Height: 8 ft. except as noted.

• Den: To the left of the entry, French doors lead to a spacious and stylish den featuring a spider-beamed ceiling.

• Living Room: The volume ceiling, transom windows, and large fireplace evoke a gracious traditional style.

• Gathering Rooms: There is plenty of space for large-group entertaining in the gathering rooms that also feature fireplaces and transom windows.

• Master Suite: Here is the height of luxurious living. The suite features an oversized walk-in closet, tiered ceilings, and a sitting room with fiireplace. THe pampering bath has a corner whirlpool and shower.

Garage: An angle minimizes the appearance of the four-car garage.

Main Level Floor Plan

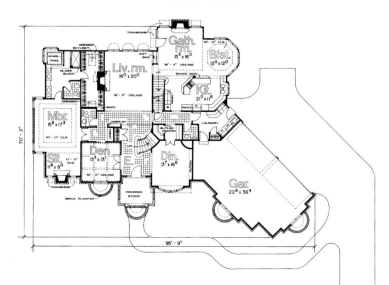

Upper Level Floor Plan

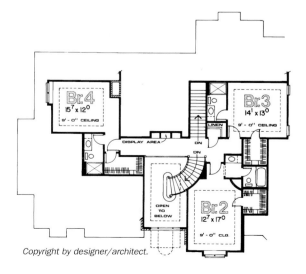

Copyright by designer/architect.

Images provided by designer/architect.

Plan #291014

Dimensions: 102' W x 54' D
Levels: 2
Square Footage: 4,372
Main Level Sq. Ft.: 3,182
Upper Level Sq. Ft.: 1,190
Bedrooms: 3
Bathrooms: 3 full, 2 half
Foundation: Basement
Materials List Available: Yes
Price Category: I

Cottage-like architectural details and an abundance of windows add warmth and personality to this generously designed home.

Features:

- **Entry:** Welcome family and friends from a shaded porch into this grand foyer. A curving stairway ahead and a vaulted library to the left make an elegant impression.

- **Kitchen:** The heart of any home, this kitchen will be the center of all your entertaining. Plenty of workspace, a nearby pantry, and an island complete with cooktop will appease chefs of any skill level. The kitchen's proximity to the dining room, the living room, and the sunlit morning room, as well as to a small back porch, creates a simple transition for any kind of dining.

- **Master Suite:** This area is a sybaritic retreat where you can shut out the frenzied world and simply relax. The attached master bath includes dual walk-in closets, his and her sinks, a standing shower, and a separate tub-perfect for busy mornings and romantic evenings.

- **Second Floor:** Great for guests or growing siblings, both secondary bedrooms have ample closet space and private bathrooms. A bonus room over the three-car garage and laundry area can fulfill whatever need you have. Create a quiet study environment or a fully featured entertainment area.

Main Level Floor Plan

Copyright by designer/architect.

Upper Level Floor Plan

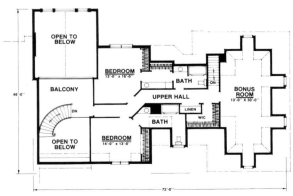

Plan #221054

Dimensions: 63'8" W x 75'4" D
Levels: 2
Square Footage: 3,206
Main Level Sq. Ft.: 2,064
Upper Level Sq. Ft.: 1,142
Bedrooms: 4
Bathrooms: 3½
Foundation: Basement
Materials List Available: Yes
Price Category: G

The large turret of this European beauty is sure to capture your attention as you enter the two-story home.

Features:

- **Great Room:** This room features a two-story ceiling, a wall of windows, and a see-through fireplace to the master suite.

- **Kitchen:** This kitchen, with its eat-in island overlooking the dining room and hearth room, works together with those two rooms to create a comfortable living area.

- **Master Suite:** You'll be impressed by the large walk-in closet of this suite, which opens directly to a main floor laundry room, as well as the spacious master bath.

- **Bedrooms:** Upstairs you can look over the railing into the great room below as you proceed to one of the three additional bedrooms. Bedroom 4 has its own full bathroom, while the remaining two share a Jack and Jill bathroom.

Images provided by designer/architect.

Upper Level Floor Plan
Copyright by designer/architect.

Rear Elevation

Main Level Floor Plan

Plan #161029

Dimensions: 87' W x 82' D
Levels: 2
Square Footage: 4,470
Main Level Sq. Ft.: 3,300
Upper Level Sq. Ft.: 1,170
Bedrooms: 4
Bathrooms: 3 full, 2 half
Foundation: Basement
Materials List Available: Yes
Price Category: I

Images provided by designer/architect.

This gracious home is so impressive — inside and out — that it suits the most discriminating tastes.

Features:

- Foyer: A balcony overlooks this gracious area decorated by tall columns.

- Hearth Room: Visually open to the kitchen and the breakfast area, this room is ideal for any sort of gathering.

- Great Room: Colonial columns also form the entry here, and a magnificent window treatment that includes French doors leads to the terrace.

- Library: Built-in shelving adds practicality to this quiet retreat.

- Kitchen: Spread out on the oversized island with a cooktop and seating.

- Additional Bedrooms: Walk-in closets and private access to a bath define each bedroom.

Main Level Floor Plan

Upper Level Floor Plan

Copyright by designer/architect.

Rear View

Living Room

Living Room/Kitchen

Ideas for Entertaining

Whether an everyday family meal or a big party for 50, make it memorable and fun. With a world of options, it's easier than you think. Be imaginative with food and decoration. Although it is true that great hamburgers and hot dogs will taste good even if served on plain white paper plates, make the meal more fun by following a theme of some sort—color, occasion, or seasonal activity, for example. Be inventive with the basic elements as well as the extraneous touches, such as flowers and lighting. Here are some examples to get you started.

- For an all-American barbecue, set a picnic table with a patchwork quilt having red, white, and blue in it. Use similar colors for the napkins, and perhaps even bandannas. Include a star-studded centerpiece.

- Make a children-size dining set using an old door propped up on crates, and surround it with appropriate-size benches or chairs. Cover the table with brightly colored, easy-to-clean waxed or vinyl-covered fabric.

- If you're planning an elegant dinner party, move your dining room table outside and set it with your best linens, china, silver, and crystal. Add romantic lighting with candles in fabulous candelabras, and set a beautiful but small floral arrangement at each place setting.

- Design a centerpiece showcasing the flowers from your garden. Begin the arrangement with a base of purchased flowers, and fill in with some of your homegrown blooms. That way your flower beds will still be full of blossoms when the guests arrive.

- Base your party theme on the vegetables growing in your yard, and let them be the inspiration for the menu. When your zucchini plants are flowering, wow your family or guests by serving steamed squash blossoms. Or if the vegetables are starting to develop, lightly grill them with other young veggies—they have a much more delicate flavor than mature vegetables do.

- During berry season, host an elegant berry brunch. Serve mixed-berry crepes on your prettiest plates.

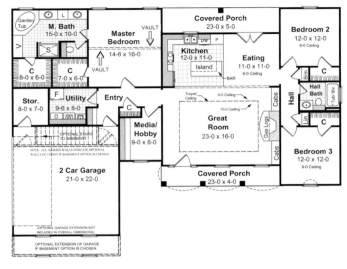

Images provided by designer/architect.

CAD FILE AVAILABLE

Plan #351003

Dimensions: 64' W x 45'10" D

Levels: 1

Square Footage: 1,751

Bedrooms: 3

Bathrooms: 2

Foundation: Crawl space, slab, or basement

Materials List Available: Yes

Price Category: D

Copyright by designer/architect.

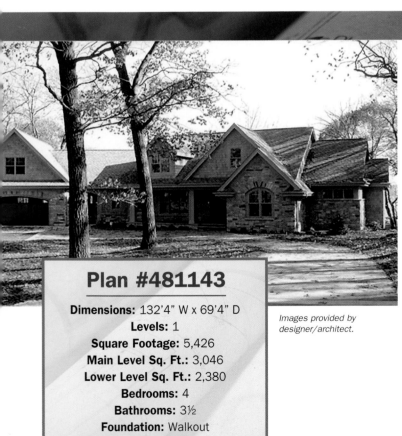

Main Level Floor Plan

Basement Level Floor Plan

Images provided by designer/architect.

Plan #481143

Dimensions: 132'4" W x 69'4" D

Levels: 1

Square Footage: 5,426

Main Level Sq. Ft.: 3,046

Lower Level Sq. Ft.: 2,380

Bedrooms: 4

Bathrooms: 3½

Foundation: Walkout

Material List Available: Yes

Price Category: J

Copyright by designer/architect.

Main Level Floor Plan

Images provided by designer/architect.

CAD FILE AVAILABLE

Plan #181079

Dimensions: 60' W x 47'8" D

Levels: 2

Square Footage: 3,016

Main Level Sq. Ft.: 1,716

Upper Level Sq. Ft.: 1,300

Bedrooms: 6

Bathrooms: 4½

Foundation: Crawl space

Material List Available: Yes

Price Category: G

Upper Level Floor Plan

Copyright by designer/architect.

Upper Level Floor Plan

Plan #121081

Dimensions: 76'8" W x 68' D

Levels: 1.5

Square Footage: 3,623

Main Level Sq. Ft.: 2,603

Upper Level Sq. Ft.: 1,020

Bedrooms: 4

Bathrooms: 4 full, 1 half

Foundation: Basement

Material List Available: Yes

Price Category: G

Images provided by designer/architect.

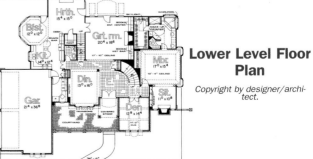

Lower Level Floor Plan

Copyright by designer/architect.

Plan #181224

Dimensions: 36' W x 39'8" D

Levels: 2

Square Footage: 1,727

Main Level Sq. Ft.: 837

Upper Level Sq. Ft.: 890

Bedrooms: 3

Bathrooms: 2

Foundation: Basement

Material List Available: Yes

Price Category: E

Images provided by designer/architect.

CAD FILE AVAILABLE

This elegant home occupies a small footprint.

Features:

- **Living Room:** This two-story gathering place features a cozy fireplace and tall windows, which flood the room with natural light.

- **Kitchen:** This island kitchen has plenty of cabinet and counter space. It is open to the breakfast room.

- **Upper Level:** On this level you will find a balcony that overlooks the living room. Also, there are three bedrooms and a large bathroom.

- **Garage:** This one-car garage has room for a car plus some storage area.

Kitchen

Main Level Floor Plan

Copyright by designer/architect.

Upper Level Floor Plan

Plan #351086

Dimensions: 82'6" W x 65' D
Levels: 1
Square Footage: 2,201
Bedrooms: 3
Bathrooms: 2½
Foundation: Crawl space or slab
Material List Available: Yes
Price Category: E

This stunning European country home is designed with the contemporary family in mind.

CAD FILE AVAILABLE

Features:

- **Porches:** Beautiful brick arches welcome guests into your covered front porch, indicating the warmth and hospitality within the home. A screened back porch, accessible from the dining area, is ideal for enjoying meals in the fresh air.

- **Great Room:** Three entrances from the covered porch, elegant archways into the kitchen and dining area, raised ceilings, a fireplace, and built-in cabinets combine to make this an ideal space for entertaining.

- **Kitchen:** The efficient L-shaped design of this work area includes an island with a vegetable sink and raised bar. The kitchen is open to the dining area and great room to provide a feeling of openness and informality.

- **Master Suite:** This suite features vaulted ceilings and a walk-in closet. But the compartmentalized master bath, with its second walk-in closet, his and her sinks and linen cabinets, standing shower, vanity, and jetted tub, really makes the suite special.

- **Secondary Bedrooms:** The secondary bedrooms have a wing of their own, and both include computer desks, large closets, and shared access to a bathtub through their individual half-baths.

- **Garages:** Two separate garages house up to three cars, or use the one-car bay for storage or hobby needs.

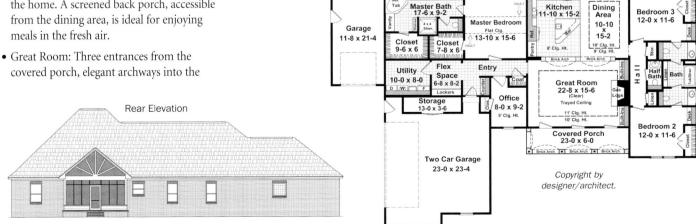

Rear Elevation

Copyright by designer/architect.

Plan #211049

Dimensions: 73' W x 66' D
Levels: 1
Square Footage: 2,023
Bedrooms: 3
Bathrooms: 2
Foundation: Slab
Materials List Available: Yes
Price Category: D

This European-style home features an open floor plan that maximizes use and flexibility of space.

Features:

• Ceiling Height: 8 ft. unless otherwise noted.

• Living/Dining Area: This combined living-and-dining area features high ceilings, which make the large area seem even more spacious. Corner windows will fill the room with light. The wet bar and cozy fireplace make this the perfect place for entertaining.

• Backyard Porch: This huge covered backyard porch is accessible from the living/dining

area, so the entire party can step outdoors on a warm summer night.

• Kitchen: More than just efficient, this modern kitchen is actually an exciting place to cook. It features a dramatic high ceiling and plenty of work space.

• Utility Area: Located off the kitchen, this area has extra freezer space, a walk-in pantry, and access to the garage.

• Eating Nook: Informal family meals will be a true delight in this nook that adjoins the kitchen and faces a lovely private courtyard.

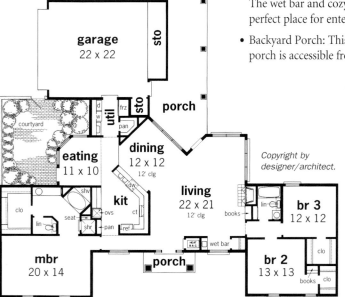

Copyright by designer/architect.

SMARTtip

Outdoor Lighting Safety

Lighting is necessary for walkways, paths, stairways, and transition areas (from the deck to the yard, hot tub, or pool) to prevent accidents. Choose from low-voltage rail, path, and post lighting for these areas. The corners of planters or built-in seating should also be delineated with lighting. Consider installing floodlights near doorways or large open spaces for security reasons.

Plan #161105

Dimensions: 90'2" W x 104'5" D
Levels: 2
Square Footage: 6,806
Main Level Sq. Ft.: 4,511
Upper Level Sq. Ft.: 2,295
Bedrooms: 4
Bathrooms: 4 full, 2 half
Foundation: Walkout basement
Material List Available: Yes
Price Category: K

The opulence and drama of this European-inspired home features a solid brick exterior with limestone detail, arched dormers, and a parapet.

Images provided by designer/architect.

Features:

- Foyer: A large octagonal skylight tops a water fountain feature displayed in this exquisite entryway. The formal dining room and library flank the entry and enjoy a 10-ft. ceiling height.

- Family Living Area: The gourmet kitchen, breakfast area, and cozy hearth room comprise this family activity center of the home. Wonderful amenities such as a magnificent counter with seating, a celestial ceiling over the dining table, an alcove for an entertainment center, a stone-faced wood-burning fireplace, and access to the rear porch enhance the informal area.

- Master Suite: This luxurious suite enjoys a raised ceiling, a seating area with bay window, and access to the terrace. The dressing room pampers the homeowner with a whirlpool tub, a ceramic tile shower enclosure, two vanities, and a spacious walk-in closet.

- Upper Level: Elegant stairs lead to the second-floor study loft and two additional bedrooms, each with a private bathroom and large walk-in closet. On the same level, and located for privacy, the third bedroom serves as a guest suite, showcasing a cozy sitting area and private bathroom.

Optional Basement Level Floor Plan

Copyright by designer/architect.

Upper Level Floor Plan

Main Level Floor Plan

Plan #401050

Dimensions: 81' W x 61' D
Levels: 2
Square Footage: 6,841
Main Level Sq. Ft.: 2,596
Upper Level Sq. Ft.: 2,233
Finished Basement Sq. Ft.: 2,012
Bedrooms: 4
Bathrooms: 3 full, 2 half
Foundation: Basement
Materials List Available: Yes
Price Category: I

Images provided by designer/architect.

This grand two-story European home is adorned with a facade of stucco and brick, meticulously appointed with details for gracious living.

Features:

- Foyer: Guests enter through a portico to find this stately two-story foyer.

- Living Room: This formal area features a tray ceiling and a fireplace and is joined by a charming dining room with a large bay window.

- Kitchen: A butler's pantry joins the dining room to this gourmet kitchen, which holds a separate wok kitchen, an island work center, and a breakfast room with double doors that lead to the rear patio.

- Family Room: Located near the kitchen, this room enjoys a built-in aquarium, media center, and fireplace.

- Den: This room with a tray ceiling, window seat, and built-in computer center is tucked in a corner for privacy.

- Master Suite: The second floor features this spectacular space, which has a separate sitting room, an oversized closet, and a bath with a spa tub.

Right Side Elevation

Kitchen

Rear Elevation

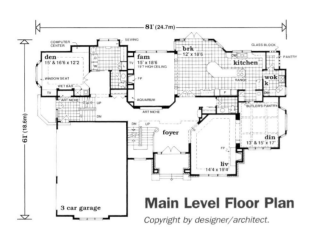

Main Level Floor Plan

Copyright by designer/architect.

81' (24.7m)

61' (18.6m)

COMPUTER CENTER
SEWING
GLASS BLOCK

den
15' & 16'6 x 12'2

fam
15' x 18'6
19'7 HIGH CEILING

brk
12' x 18'6

kitchen

PANTRY

WINDOW SEAT

WET BAR

TV

ART NICHE

UP

DN

AQUARIUM

ART NICHE

wok
k

RANGE

F

DW

BUTLER'S PANTRY

ART NICHE

foyer

DN
UP

din
13' & 15' x 17'

FP

liv
14'4 x 19'4

3 car garage

Upper Level Floor Plan

VAULTED CEILING

br4
11'2 x 12'2

br3
11' x 14'10

SEAT

SHOWER/STEAM RM

SEAT

SKYLIGHT

OPEN TO BELOW

br2
12' x 14'6

SOAKER TUB

WINDOW SEAT

PLANT LEDGE

W.I.C.

W.I.C.

ensuite

SKYLIGHT

SKYLIGHT

GALLERY

W.I.C.

MAKE UP

DN

RAILING

ART NICHE

ARCH

OPEN OVER

OPEN TO BELOW

F.P.

sitting
13' x 10'

T.V.

VAULTED CEILING

mbr
15' x 19'6

VAULTED CEILING

games rm

media rm

card rm

hobby rm/
br5

BUILT-IN MEDIA CENTER

WET BAR

HRV
VACUUM
HRV

mech

STORAGE

ARCH

FURNACE

HWT

UP

UP

wine

exercise rm

storage

Basement Level Floor Plan

Master Bedroom

Great Room

Master Bathroom

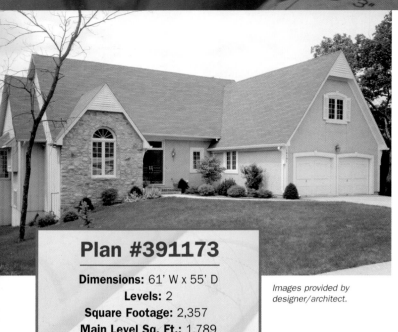

Main Level Floor Plan

Plan #391173

Dimensions: 61' W x 55' D

Levels: 2

Square Footage: 2,357

Main Level Sq. Ft.: 1,789

Upper Level Sq. Ft.: 568

Bedrooms: 3

Bathrooms: 2½

Foundation: Basement

Material List Available: Yes

Price Category: E

Upper Level Floor F

Copyright by designer/arc.

Plan #561003

Dimensions: 58'8" W x 67'4" D

Levels: 1.5

Square Footage: 3,164

Main Level Sq. Ft.: 2,085

Upper Level Sq. Ft.: 1,079

Bedrooms: 4

Bathrooms: 3½

Foundation: Basement

Material List Available: Yes

Price Category: G

*Copyright by
designer/architect.*

Main Level Floor Plan

Upper Level Floor Plan

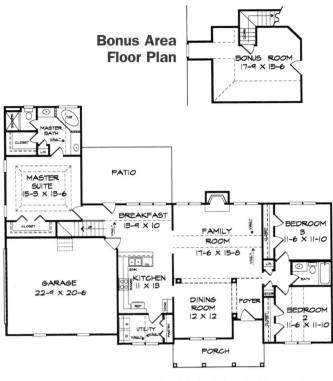

Bonus Area Floor Plan

BONUS ROOM 17-9 X 15-6

Plan #461033

Dimensions: 67'6" W x 50'9"D

Levels: 1

Square Footage: 1,802

Bedrooms: 3

Bathrooms: 2

Foundation: Slab; crawl space, or basement for fee

Material List Available: Yes

Price Category: D

Images provided by designer/architect.

MASTER BATH

MASTER SUITE 15-3 X 13-6

PATIO

BREAKFAST 13-9 X 10

FAMILY ROOM 17-6 X 15-8

BEDROOM 3 11-6 X 11-10

GARAGE 22-9 X 20-6

KITCHEN 11 X 13

DINING ROOM 12 X 12

FOYER

BATH

BEDROOM 2 11-6 X 11-10

UTILITY

PORCH

Copyright by designer/architect.

Main Level Floor Plan

TERRACE

Nook 10x5

Great Room 19x16

Kitchen

PANTRY

TERRACE

BAR POWDER

UP DN.

Den 13x13

Foyer

Dining 13x12

Util.

Portico 20x16

Garage 38x24

UP

Porch

Copyright by designer/architect.

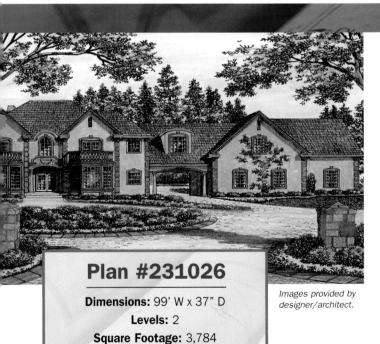

Plan #231026

Dimensions: 99' W x 37" D

Levels: 2

Square Footage: 3,784

Main Level Sq. Ft: 1,668

Upper Level Sq. Ft: 2,116

Bedrooms: 4

Bathrooms: 3 full, 2 half

Foundation: Basement

Material List Available: Yes

Price Category: H

Images provided by designer/architect.

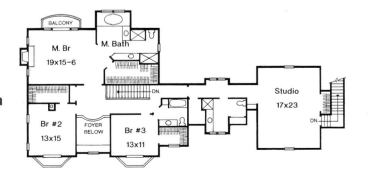

Upper Level Floor Plan

BALCONY

M. Br 19x15-6

M. Bath

DN.

Studio 17x23

Br #2 13x15

FOYER BELOW

Br #3 13x11

DN.

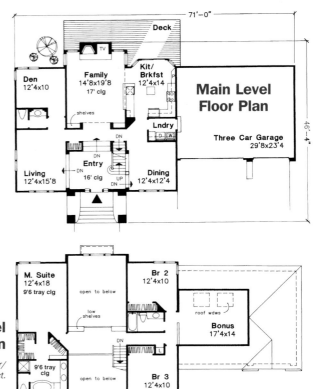

Plan #271041

Dimensions: 71' W x 47' D

Levels: 2

Square Footage: 2,416

Main Level Sq. Ft.: 1,416

Upper Level Sq. Ft.: 1,000

Bedrooms: 4

Bathrooms: 2½

Foundation: Basement

Materials List Available: Yes

Price Category: E

Images provided by designer/architect.

Main Level Floor Plan

Upper Level Floor Plan

Copyright by designer/architect.

Plan #161104

Dimensions: 130' W x 84'6" D

Levels: 2

Square Footage: 8,088

Main Level Sq. Ft.: 5,418

Upper Level Sq. Ft.: 2,670

Bedrooms: 4

Bathrooms: 4 full, 2 half

Foundation: Basement

Material List Available: Yes

Price Category: L

Images provided by designer/architect.

Main Level Floor Plan

Upper Level Floor Plan

Basement Level Floor Plan

Copyright by designer/architect.

Main Level Floor Plan

Images provided by designer/architect.

CAD FILE AVAILABLE

Plan #151025

Dimensions: 71' W x 55' D

Levels: 2

Square Footage: 3,914

Main Level Sq. Ft.: 2,291

Upper Level Sq. Ft.: 1,623

Bedrooms: 3

Bathrooms: 3

Foundation: Crawl space, slab; full basement or walkout for fee

CompleteCost List Available: Yes

Price Category: H

Upper Level Floor Plan

Copyright by designer/architect

Main Level Floor Plan

Copyright by designer/architect.

Plan #221077

Dimensions: 57'8" W x 44' D

Levels: 2

Square Footage: 2,440

Main Level Sq. Ft.: 1,206

Upper Level Sq. Ft.: 1,234

Bedrooms: 4

Bathrooms: 2½

Foundation: Basement; crawl space or slab for fee

Material List Available: Yes

Price Category: E

Images provided by designer/architect.

CAD FILE AVAILABLE

Rear Elevation

Upper Level Floor Plan

Main Level Floor Plan

Upper Level Floor Plan

Optional Basement Level Floor Plan

Copyright by designer/architect.

Images provided by designer/architect.

Plan #161103

Dimensions: 89'10" W x 89'4" D
Levels: 2
Square Footage: 5,633
Main Level Sq. Ft.: 3,850
Upper Level Sq. Ft.: 1,783
Bedrooms: 4
Bathrooms: 3½
Foundation: Walkout; basement for fee
Material List Available: Yes
Price Category: J

Main Level Floor Plan

Upper Level Floor Plan

Copyright by designer/architect.

Images provided by designer/architect.

Plan #181710

Dimensions: 32'4" W x 40'4" D
Levels: 2
Square Footage: 1,767
Main Level Sq. Ft.: 857
Upper Level Sq. Ft.: 910
Bedrooms: 3
Bathrooms: 2½
Foundation: Basement
Materials List Available: Yes
Price Category: E

Main Level Floor Plan

Copyright by designer/architect.

35'-0"
10,5 m

33'-0"
9,9 m

Upper Level Floor Plan

Rear Elevation

Plan #181617

Dimensions: 33' W x 35' D

Levels: 2

Square Footage: 1,745

Main Level Sq. Ft.: 805

Upper Level Sq. Ft.: 940

Bedrooms: 3

Bathrooms: 2½

Foundation: Basement

Materials List Available: Yes

Price Category: E

Images provided by designer/architect.

CAD FILE AVAILABLE

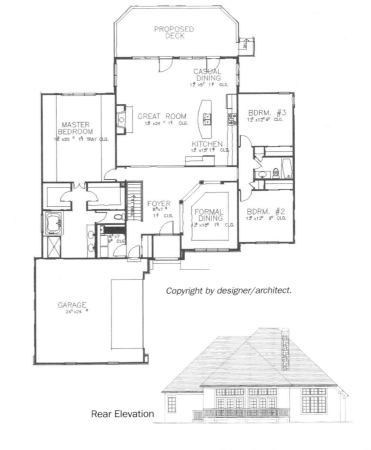

PROPOSED DECK

CASUAL DINING

GREAT ROOM

MASTER BEDROOM

KITCHEN

BDRM. #3

FOYER

FORMAL DINING

BDRM. #2

GARAGE

Copyright by designer/architect.

Rear Elevation

Plan #561005

Dimensions: 58'4" W x 71' D

Levels: 1

Square Footage: 2,358

Bedrooms: 3

Bathrooms: 2

Foundation: Basement

Material List Available: Yes

Price Category: E

Images provided by designer/architect.

CAD FILE AVAILABLE

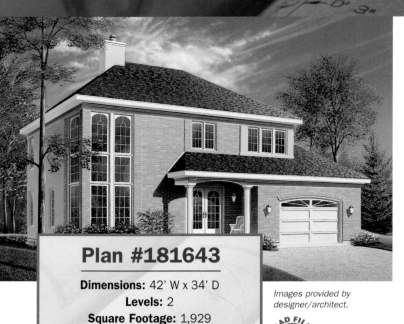

Main Level Floor Plan

Plan #181643

Dimensions: 42' W x 34' D

Levels: 2

Square Footage: 1,929

Main Level Sq. Ft.: 938

Upper Level Sq. Ft.: 991

Bedrooms: 4

Bathrooms: 2½

Foundation: Basement

Materials List Available: Yes

Price Category: F

Images provided by designer/architect.

CAD FILE AVAILABLE

Upper Level Floor Plan

Copyright by designer/architect.

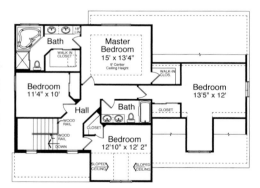

Upper Level Floor Plan

Main Level Floor Plan

Plan #161114

Dimensions: 50' W x 36'8" D

Levels: 2

Square Footage: 2,246

Main Level Sq. Ft.: 1,072

Upper Level Sq. Ft.: 1,174

Bedrooms: 4

Bathrooms: 2½

Foundation: Basement; crawl space for fee

Material List Available: Yes

Price Category: E

Images provided by designer/architect.

Rear Elevation

Copyright by designer/architect.

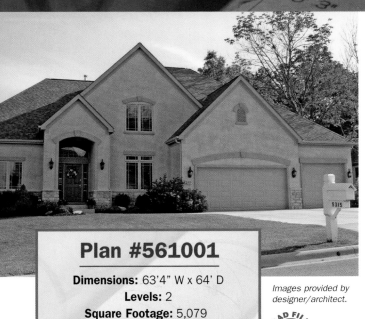

Main Level Floor Plan

Upper Level Floor Plan

Copyright by designer/architect.

Images provided by designer/architect.

CAD FILE AVAILABLE CAD

Plan #561001

Dimensions: 63'4" W x 64' D
Levels: 2
Square Footage: 5,079
Main Level Sq. Ft.: 3,301
Upper Level Sq. Ft.: 1,778
Bedrooms: 3
Bathrooms: 2½
Foundation: Basement
Material List Available: Yes
Price Category: J

Main Level Floor Plan

Upper Level Floor Plan

Images provided by designer/architect.

CAD FILE AVAILABLE CAD

Copyright by designer/architect.

Plan #151851

Dimensions: 73'4" W x 86'8" D
Levels: 1.5
Square Footage: 2,846
Main Level Sq. Ft.: 2,560
Upper Level Sq. Ft.: 286
Bedrooms: 4
Bathrooms: 3½
Foundation: Crawl space or slab; basement or walkout for fee
CompleteCost List Available: Yes
Price Category: F

Plan #181615

Dimensions: 36' W x 40' D
Levels: 2
Square Footage: 1,613
Main Level Sq. Ft.: 845
Upper Level Sq. Ft.: 768
Bedrooms: 3
Bathrooms: 1½
Foundation: Basement
Materials List Available: Yes
Price Category: E

Images provided by designer/architect.

Copyright by designer/architect.

Main Level Floor Plan

Upper Level Floor Plan

Rear Elevation

Plan #151849

Dimensions: 54'6" W x 59' D
Levels: 2
Square Footage: 2,095
Main Level Sq. Ft.: 1,839
Upper Level Sq. Ft.: 256
Bedrooms: 3
Bathrooms: 2
Foundation: Crawl space or slab; basement or walkout for fee
CompleteCost List Available: Yes
Price Category: D

Images provided by designer/architect.

Main Level Floor Plan

Upper Level Floor Plan

Copyright by designer/architect.

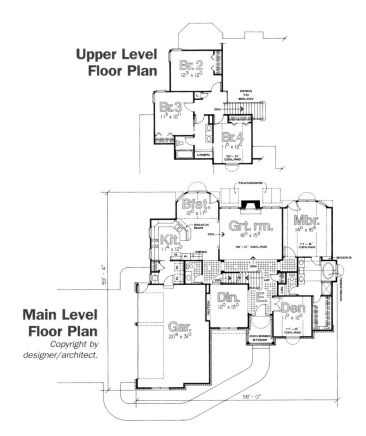

Upper Level Floor Plan

Main Level Floor Plan
Copyright by designer/architect.

Plan #121127

Dimensions: 58' W x 59'4" D

Levels: 1.5

Square Footage: 2,496

Main Level Sq. Ft.: 1,777

Upper Level Sq. Ft.: 719

Bedrooms: 4

Bathrooms: 2½

Foundation: Basement; crawl space for fee

Material List Available: Yes

Price Category: E

Images provided by designer/architect.

CAD FILE AVAILABLE

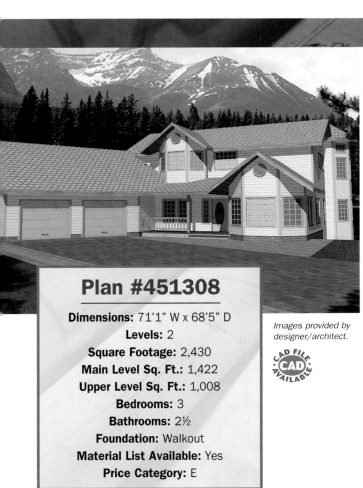

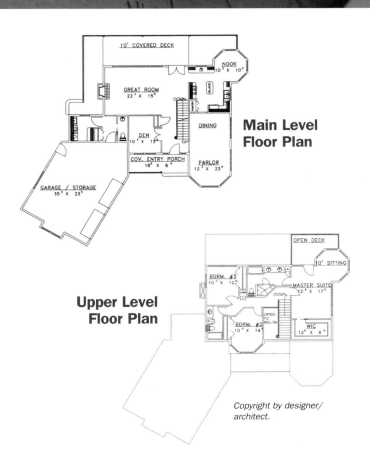

Main Level Floor Plan

Upper Level Floor Plan

Copyright by designer/architect.

Plan #451308

Dimensions: 71'1" W x 68'5" D

Levels: 2

Square Footage: 2,430

Main Level Sq. Ft.: 1,422

Upper Level Sq. Ft.: 1,008

Bedrooms: 3

Bathrooms: 2½

Foundation: Walkout

Material List Available: Yes

Price Category: E

Images provided by designer/architect.

CAD FILE AVAILABLE

Plan #181253

Dimensions: 68' W x 50' D

Levels: 2

Square Footage: 3,614

Main Level Sq. Ft.: 1,909

Upper Level Sq. Ft.: 1,705

Bedrooms: 3

Bathrooms: 3½

Foundation: Basement

Material List Available: Yes

Price Category: J

Images provided by designer/architect.

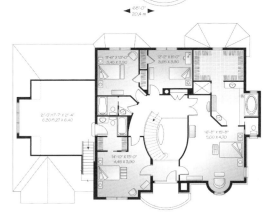

Main Level Floor Plan

Upper Level Floor Plan

Plan #121094

Dimensions: 40'8" W x 46' D

Levels: 2

Square Footage: 1,768

Main Level Sq. Ft.: 905

Upper Level Sq. Ft.: 863

Bedrooms: 3

Bathrooms: 2½

Foundation: Basement

Materials List Available: Yes

Price Category: C

Images provided by designer/architect.

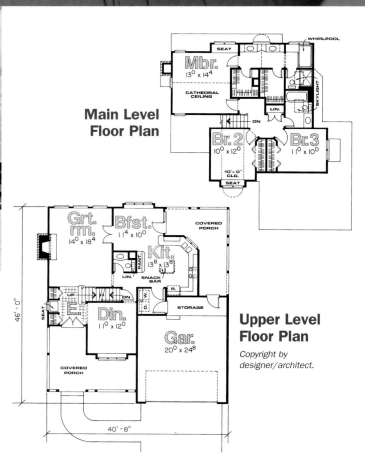

Main Level Floor Plan

Upper Level Floor Plan

Copyright by designer/architect.

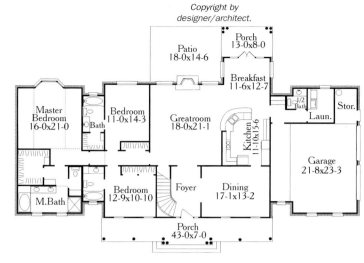

Patio
18-0x14-6

Porch
13-0x8-0

Breakfast
11-6x12-7

Master
Bedroom
16-0x21-0

Bath

Bedroom
11-0x14-3

Greatroom
18-0x21-1

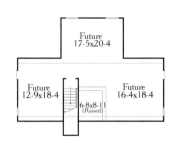

Kitchen
11-10x15-6

1/2
Bath

Laun.

Stor.

Garage
21-8x23-3

M.Bath

Bedroom
12-9x10-10

Foyer

Dining
17-1x13-2

Porch
43-0x7-0

Images provided by
designer/architect.

**Bonus Area
Floor Plan**

Future
17-5x20-4

Future
12-9x18-4

6-8x8-11
(Raised)

Future
16-4x18-4

Plan #311005

Dimensions: 87' W x 57'3" D

Levels: 1

Square Footage: 2,497

Bedrooms: 3

Bathrooms: 3½

Foundation: Crawl space, slab,
or basement

Materials List Available: Yes

Price Category: F

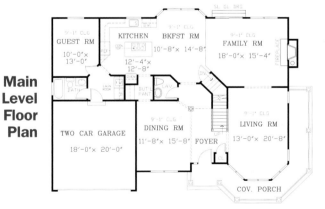

**Main
Level
Floor
Plan**

9'-1" CLG
GUEST RM
10'-0"x
13'-0"

KITCHEN
12'-4"x
12'-8"

9'-1" CLG
BKFST RM
10'-8"x 14'-8"

SL GL DRS

9'-1" CLG
FAMILY RM
18'-0"x 15'-4"

FIREPLACE

BATH

LAUN
ROOM

BUT.
PAN.

LAV.

TWO CAR GARAGE
18'-0"x 20'-0"

9'-1" CLG
DINING RM
11'-8"x 15'-8"

FOYER

9'-1" CLG
LIVING RM
13'-0"x 20'-8"

COV. PORCH

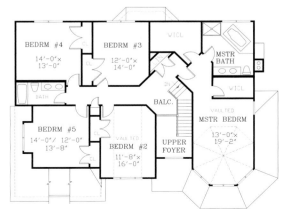

Upper Level Floor Plan

BEDRM #4
14'-0"x
13'-0"

BEDRM #3
12'-0"x
14'-0"

WICL

MSTR
BATH

BATH

WICL

BEDRM #5
14'-0"/ 12'-0"
13'-8"

VAULTED

BEDRM #2
11'-8"x
16'-0"

BALC.

DN

UPPER
FOYER

VAULTED
MSTR BEDRM
13'-0"x
19'-2"

Plan #131069

Dimensions: 52' W x 38' D

Levels: 2

Square Footage: 3,169

Main Level Sq. Ft.: 1,535

Upper Level Sq. Ft.: 1,634

Bedrooms: 5

Bathrooms: 3½

Foundation: Crawl space;
basement for fee

Material List Available: Yes

Price Category: H

Images provided by
designer/architect.

Plan #161036

Dimensions: 74'10" W x 65' D
Levels: 2
Square Footage: 3,664
Main Level Sq. Ft.: 2,497
Upper Level Sq. Ft.: 1,167
Bedrooms: 4
Bathrooms: 2½
Foundation: Basement
Materials List Available: Yes
Price Category: H

Images provided by designer/architect.

The traditional European brick-and-stone facade on the exterior of this comfortable home will thrill you and make your guests feel welcome.

Features:

• **Pub:** The beamed ceiling lends a casual feeling to this pub and informal dining area between the kitchen and the great room.

• **Dining Room:** Columns set off this formal dining room, from which you can see the fireplace in the expansive great room.

• **Library:** Close to the master suite, this room lends itself to quiet reading or work.

• **Master Suite:** The ceiling treatment makes the bedroom luxurious, while the tub, double-bowl vanity, and large walk-in closet make the bath a pleasure.

• **Upper Level:** Each of the three bedrooms features a large closet and easy access to a convenient bathroom.

Main Level Floor Plan

Upper Level Floor Plan

Copyright by designer/architect.

Rear Elevation

Left Elevation

Right Elevation

Kitchen

Dining Room

Living Room

Living Room

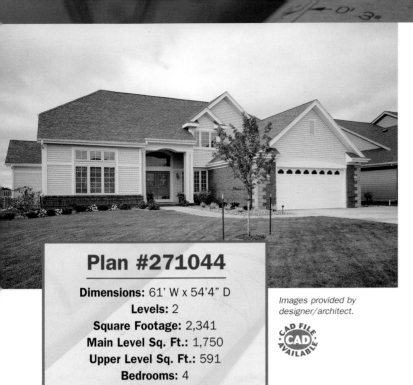

Plan #271044

Dimensions: 61' W x 54'4" D
Levels: 2
Square Footage: 2,341
Main Level Sq. Ft.: 1,750
Upper Level Sq. Ft.: 591
Bedrooms: 4
Bathrooms: 2½
Foundation: Basement
Materials List Available: Yes
Price Category: E

Images provided by designer/architect.

CAD FILE AVAILABLE

Main Level Floor Plan

M Br 14x17–8 15 vaulted clg
Patio
Deck
Family Rm 14x17–8 17 vaulted clg
Brkfst 8x10–8
Kit
Living Rm 14x14 15 vaulted clg
Dining 11–8x12
Lndry
Garage 21x21–8

Upper Level Floor Plan

Br 2 10–6x11
open to below
Br 4 12x11–4
Br 3 11x13

Copyright by designer/architect.

Plan #391003

Dimensions: 47' W x 39' D
Levels: 2
Square Footage: 1,907
Main Street Sq. Ft.: 1,269
Upper Street Sq. Ft.: 638
Bedrooms: 3
Bathrooms: 2½
Foundation: Crawl space, slab, or basement
Materials List Available: Yes
Price Category: D

Images provided by designer/architect.

Slab/Crawl Space Option

Upper Level Floor Plan

slope
skylight
open to below
Balcony
Br 2 10-4 x 14
Br 3 11 x 14
plant ledge

Main Level Floor Plan

Optional Deck
Living Rm 13 x 19-6
Ldry
wood stove
Kitchen 11 x 12
MBr 1 13-6 x 14
Dining Rm 12-10 x 13-6
Foyer

Copyright by designer/architect.

Main Level Floor Plan

Plan #441012

Dimensions: 65' W x 55' D
Levels: 1
Square Footage: 3,682
Main Level Sq. Ft.: 2,192
Basement Level Sq. Ft.: 1,490
Bedrooms: 4
Bathrooms: 4
Foundation: Walk out
Materials List Available: Yes
Price Category: J

Images provided by designer/architect.

CAD FILE AVAILABLE

Basement Level Floor Plan

Rear Elevation

Copyright by designer/architect.

Plan #151029

Dimensions: 59'4" W x 74'2" D
Levels: 1½
Square Footage: 2,777
Main Level Sq. Ft.: 2,082
Upper Level Sq. Ft.: 695
Bedrooms: 4
Bathrooms: 2½
Foundation: Crawl space, slab; basement for fee
CompleteCost List Available: Yes
Price Category: F

Images provided by designer/architect.

CAD FILE AVAILABLE

Main Level Floor Plan

Upper Level Floor Plan

Copyright by designer/architect.

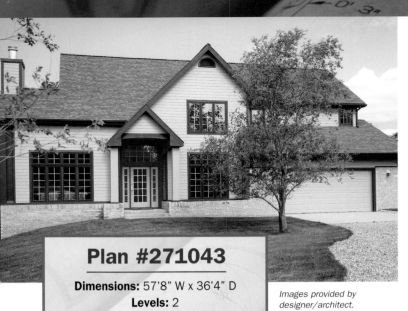

Plan #271043

Dimensions: 57'8" W x 36'4" D
Levels: 2
Square Footage: 2,396
Main Level Sq. Ft.: 1,238
Upper Level Sq. Ft.: 1,158
Bedrooms: 4
Bathrooms: 2½
Foundation: Basement
Materials List Available: Yes
Price Category: E

Images provided by designer/architect.

CAD FILE AVAILABLE

Main Level Floor Plan

Upper Level Floor Plan

Copyright by designer/architect.

Plan #351085

Dimensions: 70'6" W x 65' D
Levels: 1
Square Footage: 2,200
Bedrooms: 3
Bathrooms: 2½
Foundation: Crawl space or slab
Material List Available: Yes
Price Category: E

Images provided by designer/architect.

CAD FILE AVAILABLE

Copyright by designer/architect.

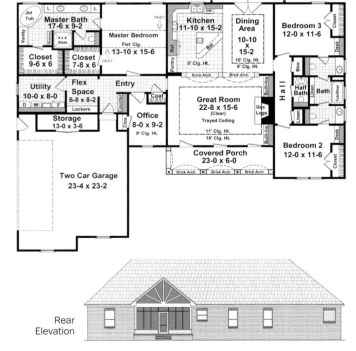

Rear Elevation

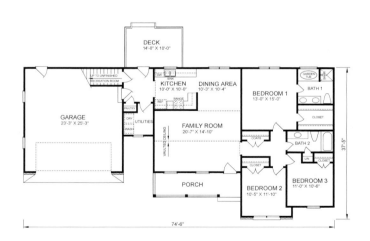

Main Level Floor Plan

Images provided by designer/architect.

CAD FILE AVAILABLE

Upper Level Floor Plan

Copyright by designer/architect.

Plan #151024

Dimensions: 60' W x 73'8" D
Levels: 2
Square Footage: 3,623
Main Level Sq. Ft.: 2,391
Upper Level Sq. Ft.: 1,232
Bedrooms: 3
Bathrooms: 3½
Foundation: Crawl space, slab; full basement for fee
CompleteCost List Available: Yes
Price Category: H

Images provided by designer/architect.

CAD FILE AVAILABLE

Plan #341285

Dimensions: 74'6" W x 37'5" D
Levels: 1
Square Footage: 1,481
Bedrooms: 3
Bathrooms: 2
Foundation: Crawl space, slab, basement, or walkout
Material List Available: Yes
Price Category: B

Copyright by designer/architect.

Main Level Floor Plan

Upper Level Floor Plan

Images provided by designer/architect.

CAD FILE AVAILABLE

Copyright by designer/architect.

Plan #181252

Dimensions: 92' W x 50' D
Levels: 2
Square Footage: 3,631
Main Level Sq. Ft.: 2,153
Upper Level Sq. Ft.: 1,478
Bedrooms: 3
Bathrooms: 3½
Foundation: Basement
Materials List Available: Yes
Price Category: J

Main Level Floor Plan

SHOP 10/6 X 11/6 | OFFICE 12/4 X 11/0 (9' CLG.) | MEDIA CENTER | GREAT RM. 15/0 X 17/6 +/- (2 STORY OR OPT. 9' CLG.)

GARAGE 19/6 X 22/6 | STOR | UP | DINING 11/6 X 14/0 (9' CLG.)

14/0 X 13/0 (9' CLG.)

42'
50'

Upper Level Floor Plan

Copyright by designer/architect.

VAULTED MASTER 17/6 X 12/6 | OPTIONAL GAMES RM. 15/0 X 15/0 (9' CLG.)

BENCH OR DRAWERS | LINEN | VAULTED | DN | LINEN | FOYER BELOW | BR. 2 10/6 X 16/0 +/- (9' CLG.)

SPA | VAULTED BR. 3 14/0 X 11/0

Plan #441047

Dimensions: 50' W x 42' D
Levels: 2
Square Footage: 2,605
Main Level Sq. Ft.: 1,142
Upper Level Sq. Ft.: 1,463
Bedrooms: 3
Bathrooms: 2½
Foundation: Crawl space;
slab or basement available for fee
Material List Available: Yes
Price Category: G

Images provided by designer/architect.

CAD FILE AVAILABLE

Rear Elevation

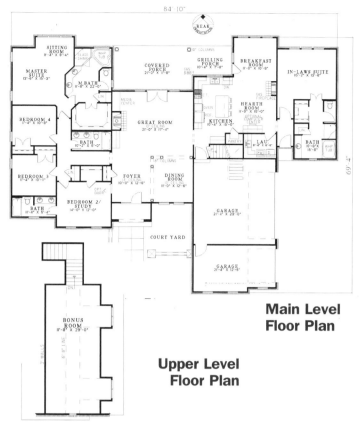

Plan #151845

Dimensions: 84'10" W x 69'4" D
Levels: 1
Square Footage: 3,003
Bedrooms: 5
Bathrooms: 4
Foundation: Crawl space, slab
CompleteCost List Available: Yes
Price Category: G

Images provided by designer/architect.

CAD FILE AVAILABLE

Main Level Floor Plan

Upper Level Floor Plan

BONUS ROOM 11'-8" X 29'-0"

Plan #161034

Dimensions: 56' W x 53' D
Levels: 2
Square Footage: 2,156
Main Level Sq. Ft.: 1,605
Upper Level Sq. Ft.: 551
Bedrooms: 3
Bathrooms: 2½
Foundation: Basement
Materials List Available: Yes
Price Category: D

Main Level Floor Plan

Copyright by designer/architect.

Images provided by designer/architect.

Upper Level Floor Plan

Rear View

Plan #481024

Dimensions: 87'2" W x 59'8" D

Levels: 1

Square Footage: 3,458

Main Level Sq. Ft.: 2,016

Lower Level Sq. Ft.: 1,442

Bedrooms: 4

Bathrooms: 3

Foundation: Walkout basement

Material List Available: Yes

Price Category: G

Images provided by designer/architect.

Basement Level Floor Plan

Copyright by designer/architect.

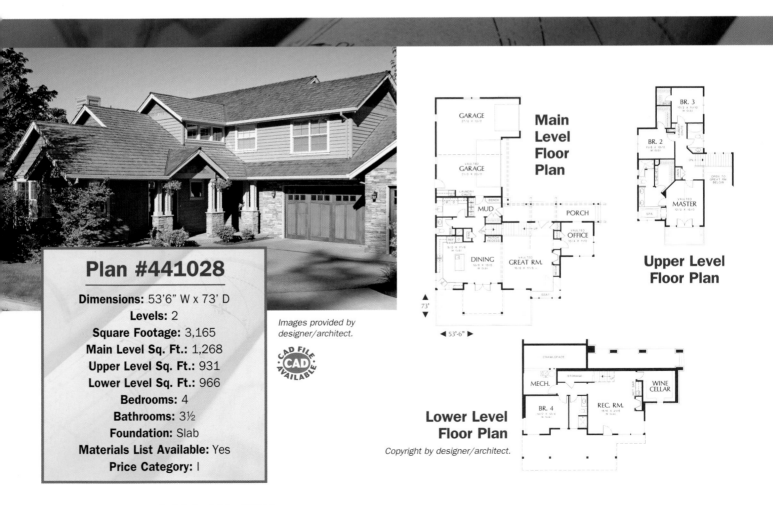

Plan #441028

Dimensions: 53'6" W x 73' D

Levels: 2

Square Footage: 3,165

Main Level Sq. Ft.: 1,268

Upper Level Sq. Ft.: 931

Lower Level Sq. Ft.: 966

Bedrooms: 4

Bathrooms: 3½

Foundation: Slab

Materials List Available: Yes

Price Category: I

Images provided by designer/architect.

Main Level Floor Plan

Upper Level Floor Plan

Lower Level Floor Plan

Copyright by designer/architect.

Plan #161093

Dimensions: 70'8" W x 64' D
Levels: 1
Square Footage: 4,328
Main Level Sq. Ft.: 2,582
Lower Level Sq. Ft.: 1,746
Bedrooms: 3
Bathrooms: 3½
Foundation: Walkout
Materials List Available: Yes
Price Category: I

Main Level Floor Plan

Images provided by designer/architect.

Lower Level Floor Plan

Copyright by designer/architect.

Plan #441004

Dimensions: 55' W x 48' D
Levels: 1
Square Footage: 1,728
Bedrooms: 2
Bathrooms: 2
Foundation: Crawl space; slab or basement available for fee
Materials List Available: Yes
Price Category: E

CAD FILE AVAILABLE

Images provided by designer/architect.

Copyright by designer/architect.

Rear Elevation

Plan #151524

Dimensions: 79'10" W x 60'6" D

Levels: 2

Square Footage: 4,461

Main Level Sq. Ft.: 2,861

Upper Level Sq. Ft.: 1,600

Bedrooms: 5

Bathrooms: 4½

Foundation: Crawl space or slab; basement or walkout available for fee

CompleteCost List Available: Yes

Price Category: H

This home is the culmination of classic French design and ambiance.

CAD FILE AVAILABLE

Images provided by designer/architect.

Features:

- Great Room: This gathering area features a vaulted ceiling and a built-in media center. Step through the French doors to the rear porch.

- Kitchen: An island kitchen is the most desirable layout in today's home. The raised bar in this kitchen is open to the breakfast room.

- Master Suite: The tray ceiling in this room adds a unique look to the sleeping area. The master bath features a large walk-in closet, vaulted ceiling, and whirlpool tub.

- Secondary Bedrooms: Four bedrooms and three bathrooms are located on the upper level.

Upper Level Floor Plan

Copyright by designer/architect.

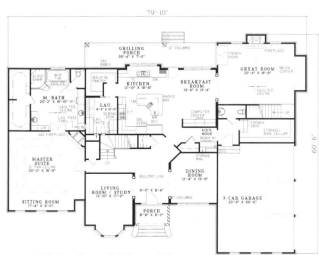

Main Level Floor Plan

Plan #221025

Dimensions: 69'8" W x 72' D

Levels: 2

Square Footage: 3,009

Main Level Sq. Ft.: 2,039

Upper Level Sq. Ft.: 970

Bedrooms: 4

Bathrooms: 2½

Foundation: Basement; crawl space for fee

Materials List Available: Yes

Price Category: G

Images provided by designer/architect.

Designed to resemble a country home in France, this two-story beauty will delight you with its good looks and luxurious amenities.

CAD FILE AVAILABLE CAD

Features:

- **Great Room:** You'll look into this great room as soon as you enter the two-story foyer. A fireplace flanked by built-in bookcases and large windows looking out to the deck highlight this room.

- **Dining Room:** This formal room is located just off the entry for the convenience of your guests.

- **Kitchen:** A huge central island and large pantry make this kitchen a delight for any cook. The large nook looks onto the deck and opens to the lovely three-season porch.

- **Master Suite:** You'll love this suite, with its charming bay shape, great windows, walk-in closet, luxurious bath, and door to the deck.

- **Upper Level:** Everyone will love the two bedrooms, large bath, and huge game.

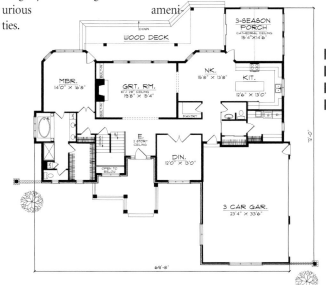

Main Level Floor Plan

Upper Level Floor Plan

Copyright by designer/architect.

Plan #451180

Dimensions: 74' W x 60' D
Levels: 2
Square Footage: 4,272
Main Level Sq. Ft.: 2,213
Upper Level Sq. Ft.: 1,822
Lower Lever Sq. Ft.: 237
Bedrooms: 3
Bathrooms: 3½
Foundation: Walkout
Material List Available: Yes
Price Category: I

CAD FILE AVAILABLE

Images provided by designer/architect.

Classic style shines through in this spectacular two-story home.

Features:

- Foyer: This large, open foyer welcomes you home and features a convenient coat closet. The angled stairs add drama to the space.

- Mud Room: This family entrance is perfect for coats, hats, book bags, sporting equipment, and the like. There is even a handy sink.

- Great Room: This large gathering area features a cozy fireplace and French doors that lead to the rear deck. The two-story ceiling imparts an open and airy feeling to the space.

- Lower Level: In addition to a four-car garage, there is a utility room, which holds the washer and dryer.

Copyright by designer/architect.

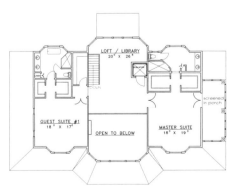

Main Level Floor Plan

Upper Level Floor Plan

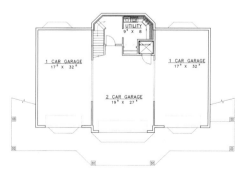

Basement Level Floor Plan

Plan #441038

Dimensions: 59' W x 51'6" D
Levels: 2
Square Footage: 2,518
Main Level Sq. Ft.: 1,464
Upper Level Sq. Ft.: 1,054
Bedrooms: 4
Bathrooms: 3
Foundation: Crawl space;
slab or basement available for fee
Materials List Available: Yes
Price Category: G

Features:

- Kitchen: This kitchen contains gourmet appointments with an island countertop, a large pantry, and a work desk built in.
- Dining Room: This formal room connects directly to the kitchen for convenience.
- Master Suite: This suite features a fine bath with a spa tub and separate shower.

- Bedrooms: A bedroom (or make it a home office) is tucked away behind the two-car garage and has the use of a full bathroom across the hall. Three additional bedrooms are found on the upper level, along with a large bonus space that could be developed later into bedroom 5.

Victorians are such a cherished style; it's impossible not to admire them. This one begins with all the classic details and adds a most up-to-date floor plan.

CAD FILE AVAILABLE

Main Level Floor Plan

Upper Level Floor Plan

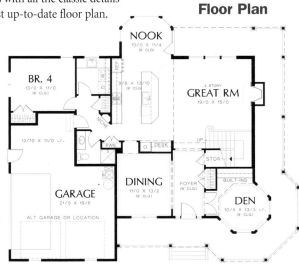

Copyright by designer/architect.

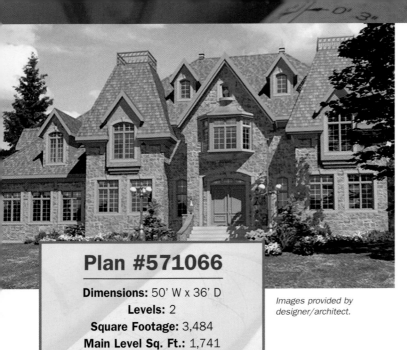

Main Level Floor Plan

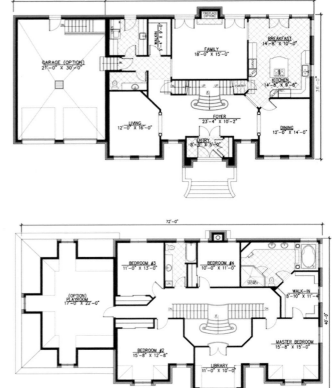

Plan #571066

Dimensions: 50' W x 36' D

Levels: 2

Square Footage: 3,484

Main Level Sq. Ft.: 1,741

Upper Level Sq. Ft.: 1,743

Bedrooms: 3

Bathrooms: 2½

Foundation: Basement

Material List Available: Yes

Price Category: D

Images provided by designer/architect.

Upper Level Floor Plan

Copyright by designer/architect.

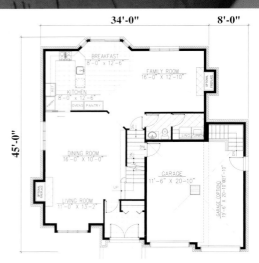

Main Level Floor Plan

Plan #571103

Dimensions: 34' W x 45' D

Levels: 2

Square Footage: 2,459

Main Level Sq. Ft.: 1,127

Garage Level Sq. Ft.: 1,332

Bedrooms: 4

Bathrooms: 2½

Foundation: Basement

Material List Available: Yes

Price Category: E

Images provided by designer/architect.

Garage Level Floor Plan

Copyright by designer/architect.

Bonus Area Floor Plan

Copyright by designer/architect.

Bonus Room
14-10 x 19-10

Future Bath

Plan #351106

Dimensions: 65'2" W x 61' D

Levels: 1

Square Footage: 2,202

Bedrooms: 4

Bathrooms: 2½

Foundation: Crawl space or slab

Material List Available: Yes

Price Category: E

Images provided by designer/architect.

CAD FILE AVAILABLE

His Clo.
9-4 x 5-6

Master Bedroom
14-2 x 15-8

M. Bath
9-4 x 17-0

Her Clo.
13-6 x 6-2

Covered Porch
17-4 x 7-2

Breakfast
11-0 x 9-10

Utility
9-10 x 7-8

Half Bath

Storage
8-2 x 8-0

Bedroom 3
11-8 x 11-2

Great Room
17-0 x 19-0

Kitchen
11-0 x 12-10

Hall Bath

Dining
11-0 x 11-6

Two-Car Garage
23-10 x 22-8

Bedroom 2
11-8 x 11-2

Bedroom 4/ Study
11-8 x 11-2

Foyer
6-4 x 8-0

Covered Porch
7-8 x 6-6

Main Level Floor Plan

Master Suite
14'-10" X 12'-0"

Covered Porch
26'-6" X 8'-4"

M. Bath

Great Room

Breakfast Room

Bedroom 3
10'-0" X 10'-0"

Bath

Dining
10'-0" X 10'-0"

Kitchen

Bedroom 2
10'-0" X 10'-0"

Foyer

Covered Entry

Garage
20'-0" X 22'-6"

Court Yard

Plan #151840

Dimensions: 44'3" W x 72' D

Levels: 2

Square Footage: 1,875

Main Level Sq. Ft.: 1,588

Upper Level Sq. Ft.: 287

Bedrooms: 4

Bathrooms: 3

Foundation: Crawl space or slab; basement or walkout for fee

CompleteCost List Available: Yes

Price Category: D

Images provided by designer/architect.

CAD FILE AVAILABLE

Bath

Computer Center

Open to Below

Optional Bridge

Bonus Room/ Home Theater
10'-0" X 15'-6"

Bedroom 4
11'-0" X 10'-0"

Open to Below

Plant Ledge

Attic Storage

Upper Level Floor Plan

Copyright by designer/architect.

Plan #481034

Dimensions: 84'8" W x 77'8" D
Levels: 2
Square Footage: 2,830
Main Level Sq. Ft.: 1,673
Upper Level Sq. Ft.: 1,157
Bedrooms: 3
Bathrooms: 2½
Foundation: Walkout
Materials List Available: Yes
Price Category: F

This European-influenced two-story home has stone accents and wide board siding.

Images provided by designer/architect.

Features:

- Great Room: The fireplace, flanked by built-in cabinets, is the focal point of this gathering area. Because the area is located just off the foyer, your guests can easily enter this area.

- Dining Room: This formal dining area features a built-in cabinet and a 9-ft,-high ceiling. The triple window has a view of the front yard.

- Kitchen: This large island kitchen is a bonus in any home. Open to the dinette and the great room, the area has a light and open feeling. The built-in pantry is ready to store all of your supplies.

- Master Suite: Occupying most of the upper level, this retreat boasts a vaulted ceiling in the sleeping area and a large walk-in closet. The master bath features his and her vanities and a large stall shower.

Rear View

Main Level Floor Plan

Upper Level Floor Plan

Copyright by designer/architect.

Plan #401017

Dimensions: 79' W x 44' D
Levels: 2
Square Footage: 2,632
Main Level Sq. Ft.: 1,362
Upper Level Sq. Ft.: 1,270
Bedrooms: 4
Bathrooms: 2½
Foundation: Crawl space or basement
Material List Available: Yes
Price Category: F

Rich in Victorian details-scalloped shingles, wraparound porch, and turrets-this beautiful facade conceals a modern floor plan.

Images provided by designer/architect.

Features:

- **Living Room:** Archways announce this distinctive living room, which features a lovely tray ceiling.

- **Den:** This octagonal den, located across the foyer from the living room, is the perfect private spot for reading or studying.

- **Kitchen:** This U-shaped island kitchen holds an octagonal breakfast bay and a pass-through breakfast bar that connects to the family room.

- **Master Suite:** This master suite is complete with a sitting room and a bay window. A well-appointed master bath is located in one of the turrets.

- **Secondary Bedrooms:** Three family bedrooms share a bathroom. One of the bedrooms is located within a turret.

Rear Elevation

Main Level Floor Plan

Copyright by designer/architect.

Upper Level Floor Plan

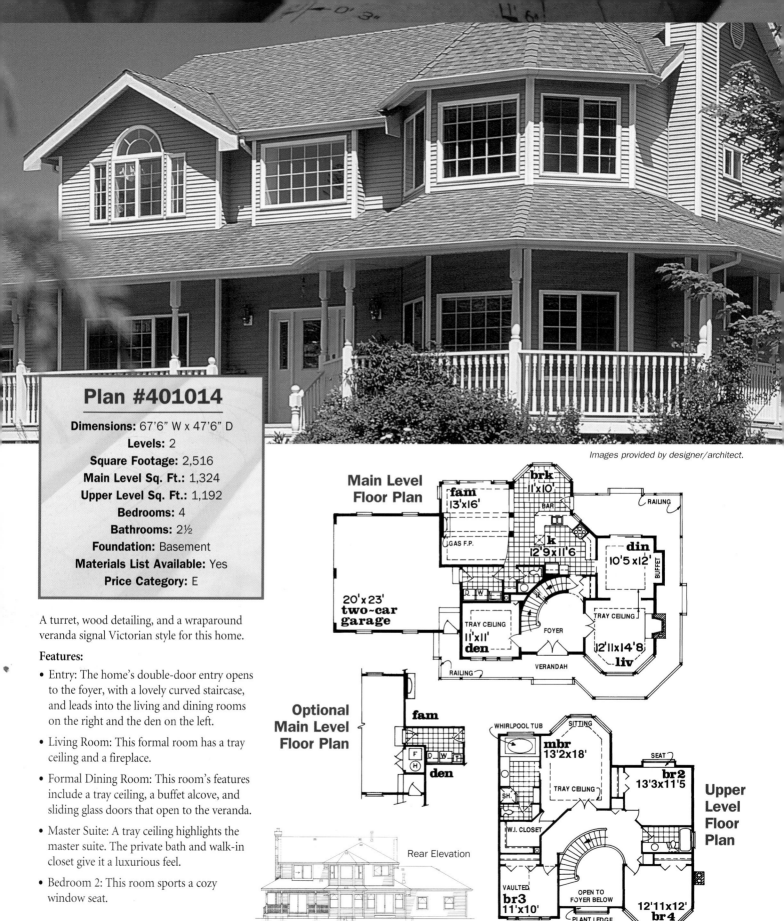

Plan #401014

Dimensions: 67'6" W x 47'6" D
Levels: 2
Square Footage: 2,516
Main Level Sq. Ft.: 1,324
Upper Level Sq. Ft.: 1,192
Bedrooms: 4
Bathrooms: 2½
Foundation: Basement
Materials List Available: Yes
Price Category: E

A turret, wood detailing, and a wraparound veranda signal Victorian style for this home.

Features:

• **Entry:** The home's double-door entry opens to the foyer, with a lovely curved staircase, and leads into the living and dining rooms on the right and the den on the left.

• **Living Room:** This formal room has a tray ceiling and a fireplace.

• **Formal Dining Room:** This room's features include a tray ceiling, a buffet alcove, and sliding glass doors that open to the veranda.

• **Master Suite:** A tray ceiling highlights the master suite. The private bath and walk-in closet give it a luxurious feel.

• **Bedroom 2:** This room sports a cozy window seat.

Images provided by designer/architect.

Main Level Floor Plan

fam 13'x16'
GAS F.P.
brk 11'x10'
BAR
RAILING
k 12'9"x11'6"
din 10'5"x12'
BUFFET
20'x23' two-car garage
TRAY CEILING 11'x11' den
FOYER
TRAY CEILING
D W
RAILING
VERANDAH
12'11"x14'8" liv

Optional Main Level Floor Plan

fam
F D W T
H
den

Upper Level Floor Plan

WHIRLPOOL TUB
SITTING
mbr 13'2x18'
SEAT
br2 13'3x11'5
TRAY CEILING
SH.
W.I. CLOSET
VAULTED br3 11'x10'
OPEN TO FOYER BELOW
PLANT LEDGE
12'11x12' br4

Rear Elevation

Copyright by designer/architect.

Images provided by designer/architect.

Plan #391002

Dimensions: 76'4" W x 45'10" D
Levels: 2
Square Footage: 2,281
Main Level Sq. Ft.: 1,260
Upper Level Sq. Ft.: 1,021
Bedrooms: 3
Bathrooms: 2½
Foundation: Crawl space, slab, or basement
Materials List Available: Yes
Price Category: E

The luxurious amenities in this compact, well designed home are sure to delight everyone in the family.

Features:

• Ceiling Height: 9-ft. ceilings add to the spacious feeling created by the open design.

• Family Room: A vaulted ceiling and large window area add elegance to this comfortable room, which will be the heart of this home.

• Dining Area: Adjoining the kitchen, this room features a large bayed area as well as French doors that open onto the back deck.

• Kitchen: This step-saving design will make cooking a joy for everyone in the family.

• Utility Room: Near the kitchen, this room includes cabinets and shelves for extra storage space.

• Master Suite: A triple window, tray ceiling, walk-in closet, and luxurious bath make this area a treat.

Main Level Floor Plan

Copyright by designer/architect.

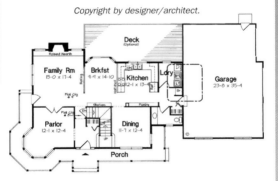

Alternate Crawl Space/Slab

Upper Level Floor Plan

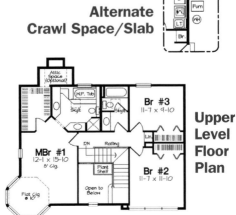

Plan #121102

Dimensions: 128'5" W x 77' D
Levels: 1½
Square Footage: 3,689
Main Level Sq. Ft.: 2,617
Upper Level Sq. Ft.: 1,072
Bedrooms: 4
Bathrooms: 4½
Foundation: Basement;
crawl space or slab for fee
Material List Available: Yes
Price Category: H

Gorgeous details make this home unique and luxurious.

Images provided by designer/architect.

Features:

• Living Room: You and your guests will love to spend time in this living room, with its 10 ft. ceiling, wet bar, and transom windows for beautiful views.

• Kitchen: This beautiful kitchen is great for cooking meals, in addition to grabbing quick snacks or hanging out at the snack bar. The adjoining breakfast nook is a wonderful place to relax in the mornings before a busy day.

• Master Suite: An 11 ft. ceiling, whirlpool tub, his-and-her sinks, compartmentalized toilet, and spacious walk-in closet make this suite a place you will never want to leave.

Front Elevation

Copyright by designer/architect.

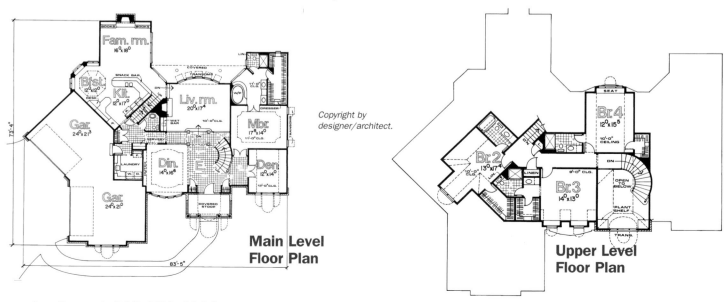

Main Level Floor Plan

Upper Level Floor Plan

Plan #481035

Dimensions: 99' W x 64' D
Levels: 2
Square Footage: 3,204
Main Level Sq. Ft.: 1,701
Upper Level Sq. Ft.: 1,503
Bedrooms: 3
Bathrooms: 2½
Foundation: Walkout
Material List Available: Yes
Price Category: G

Images provided by designer/architect.

Distinctive design details set this home apart from others in the neighborhood.

Features:

• Foyer: This large foyer welcomes you home and provides a view through the home and into the family room. The adjoining study can double as a home office.

• Family Room: This two-story gathering space features a fireplace flanked by built-in cabinets. The full-height windows on the rear wall allow natural light to flood the space.

• Kitchen: This island kitchen flows into the nearby family room, allowing mingling between both spaces when friends or family are visiting. The adjacent dinette is available for daily meals.

• Master Suite: This private retreat waits for you to arrive home. The tray ceiling in the sleeping area adds elegant style to the area.

Rear Elevation

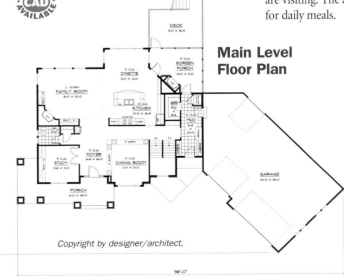

**Main Level
Floor Plan**

Copyright by designer/architect.

**Upper Level
Floor Plan**

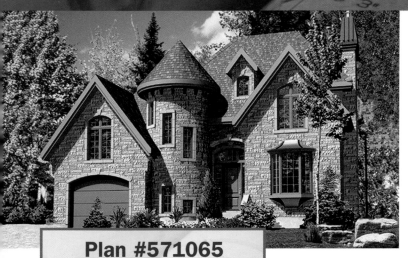

Plan #571065

Dimensions: 42' W x 34' D

Levels: 2

Square Footage: 1,610

Main Level Sq. Ft.: 798

Upper Level Sq. Ft.: 812

Bedrooms: 3

Bathrooms: 1½

Foundation: Basement

Materials List Available: Yes

Price Category: C

Images provided by designer/architect.

Main Level Floor Plan

Upper Level Floor Plan

Copyright by designer/architect.

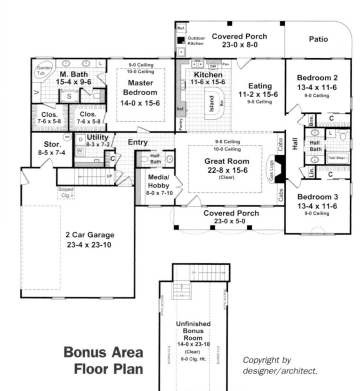

Plan #351105

Dimensions: 69' W x 59'10" D

Levels: 1

Square Footage: 2,000

Bedrooms: 3

Bathrooms: 2½

Foundation: Crawl space or slab

Material List Available: Yes

Price Category: E

Images provided by designer/architect.

CAD FILE AVAILABLE

Bonus Area Floor Plan

Copyright by designer/architect.

Plan #351107

Dimensions: 69'6" W x 80'6" D

Levels: 1

Square Footage: 2,400

Bedrooms: 4

Bathrooms: 3

Foundation: Crawl space or slab

Material List Available: Yes

Price Category: F

Images provided by designer/architect.

CAD FILE AVAILABLE

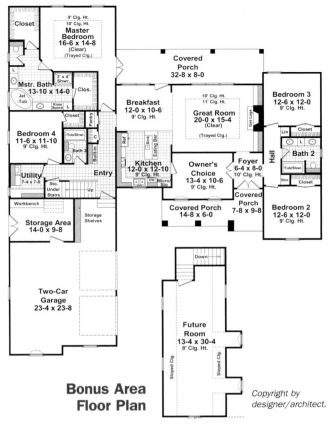

Bonus Area Floor Plan

Copyright by designer/architect.

Plan #221055

Dimensions: 69' W x 88'8" D

Levels: 2

Square Footage: 3,551

Main Level Sq. Ft.: 1,882

Upper Level Sq. Ft.: 1,669

Bedrooms: 4

Bathrooms: 3½

Foundation: Basement

Material List Available: Yes

Price Category: H

Images provided by designer/architect.

CAD FILE AVAILABLE

Main Level Floor Plan

Copyright by designer/architect.

Rear Elevation

Upper Level Floor Plan

Plan #161100

Dimensions: 89' W x 59'2" D

Levels: 1

Square Footage: 5,377

Main Level Sq. Ft.: 2,961

Basement Level Sq. Ft.: 2,416

Bedrooms: 3

Bathrooms: 2 full, 2 half

Foundation: Walkout; basement for fee

Material List Available: Yes

Price Category: J

This luxury home is perfect for you and your family.

Images provided by designer/architect.

Features:

- **Foyer:** This beautiful foyer showcases the two-sided fireplace, which warms its space, as well as that of the great room.

- **Gathering Areas:** The kitchen, breakfast area, and hearth room will quickly become a favorite gathering area, what with the warmth of the fireplace and easy access to a covered porch. Expansive windows with transoms create a light and airy atmosphere.

- **Master Suite:** This suite makes the most of its circular sitting area and deluxe dressing room with platform whirlpool tub, dual vanities, commode room with closet, and two-person shower.

- **Lower Level:** This lower level is finished with additional bedrooms and areas dedicated to entertaining, such as the wet bar, billiards area, media room, and exercise room

Rear View

Copyright by designer/architect.

Plan #281015

Dimensions: 32' W x 48' D
Levels: 2
Square Footage: 1,660
Main Level Sq. Ft.: 964
Upper Level Sq. Ft.: 696
Bedrooms: 4
Bathrooms: 2½
Foundation: Basement
Materials List Available: Yes
Price Category: C

Images provided by designer/architect.

You'll love the gracious features and amenities in this charming home, which is meant for a narrow lot.

Features:

- **Foyer:** This two-story foyer opens into the spacious living room.

- **Living Room:** The large bay window in this room makes a perfect setting for quiet times alone or entertaining guests.

- **Dining Room:** The open flow between this room and the living room adds to the airy feeling.

- **Family Room:** With a handsome fireplace and a door to the rear patio, this room will be the heart of your home.

- **Kitchen:** The U-shaped layout, pantry, and greenhouse window make this room a joy.

- **Master Suite:** The bay window, large walk-in closet, and private bath make this second-floor room a true retreat.

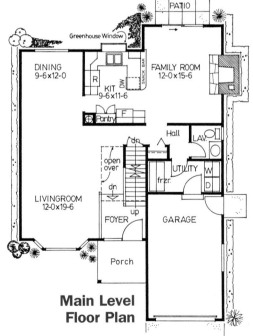

Main Level Floor Plan

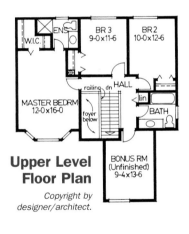

Upper Level Floor Plan

Copyright by designer/architect.

Rear Elevation

Left Side Elevation

Right Side Elevation

Plan #481036

Dimensions: 84'8" W x 82'4" D
Levels: 1
Square Footage: 4,258
Main Level Sq. Ft.: 2,440
Basement Level Sq. Ft.: 1,818
Bedrooms: 4
Bathrooms: 3½
Foundation: Walkout
Material List Available: Yes
Price Category: I

Old-world style with a modern floor plan makes this home perfect for you.

Rear Elevation

Features:

- Great Room: With a 12-ft.-high ceiling and a glowing fireplace, this room welcomes you home. Relax with your family, or entertain your friends.

- Study: Located off the foyer, this room would make a perfect home office; clients can come and go without disturbing the family.

- Master Suite: Unwind in this private space, and enjoy its many conveniences. The full master bath includes a standing shower, his and her sinks, a large tub, and a spacious walk-in closet.

- Garage: This large storage space has room for three full-size cars and includes a convenient sink. The stairs to the storage area in the basement will help keep things organized.

Front View

Main Level
Floor Plan

Basement Level
Floor Plan

Copyright by designer/architect.

Breakfast Room/Kitchen

Master Bath

Study

Great Room

Plan #441024

Dimensions: 90'6" W x 84' D
Levels: 2
Square Footage: 3,517
Main Level Sq. Ft.: 2,698
Upper Level Sq. Ft.: 819
Bedrooms: 3
Bathrooms: 3½
Foundation: Crawl space; slab or basement available for fee
Materials List Available: Yes
Price Category: J

You'll feel like royalty every time you pull into the driveway of this European-styled manor house.

Images provided by designer/architect.

Features:

- Kitchen: This gourmet chef's center hosts an island with a vegetable sink. The arched opening above the primary sink provides a view of the fireplace and entertainment center in the great room. A walk-in food pantry and a butler's pantry are situated between this space and the dining room.

- Master Suite: Located on the main level, this private retreat boasts a large sleeping area and a sitting area. The grand master bath features a large walk-in closet, dual vanities, a large tub, and a shower.

- Bedrooms: Two secondary bedrooms are located on the upper level, and each has its own bathroom.

- Laundry Room: This utility room houses cabinets, a folding counter, and an ironing board.

- Garage: This large three-car garage has room for storage. Family members entering the home from this area will find a coat closet and a place to stash briefcases and backpacks.

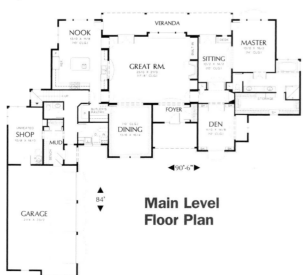

Main Level Floor Plan

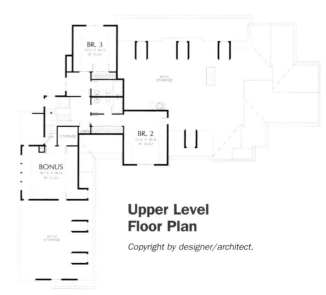

Upper Level Floor Plan

Copyright by designer/architect.

Plan #391050

Dimensions: 67' W x 51' D
Levels: 2
Square Footage: 2,674
Main Level Sq. Ft.: 1,511
Upper Level Sq. Ft.: 1,163
Bedrooms: 3
Bathrooms: 2½
Foundation: Crawl space, slab, or basement
Materials List Available: Yes
Price Category: F

This home, as shown in the photograph, may differ from the actual blueprints. For more detailed information, please check the floor plans carefully.

Images provided by designer/architect.

This home truly transforms tutor styling for today. Charming Old World half-timbering dramatizes exterior dormers and the deeply recessed pillared porch, while New World surprises fill the interior.

Features:

• Kitchen: Beyond the living room and study and past the double-entry stairway, this elaborately open-ended kitchen feeds into other important spaces, including the breakfast room, which is bathed in natural light on three sides as it looks out on the patio and three-season porch.

• Family Room: This open family room is also a big draw, with its fireplace, two-story cathedral ceilings, and porch access.

• Master Suite: The second level, enjoying the spacious aura of the vaulted ceiling, high lights this master suite, with its generous windowing, spectacular closeting, and bathroom with tub situated in a wide windowed corner.

• Bedrooms: Two additional bedrooms feature plentiful closeting and pretty front-view windows (one with window seat) and share a second full bath.

Main Level Floor Plan

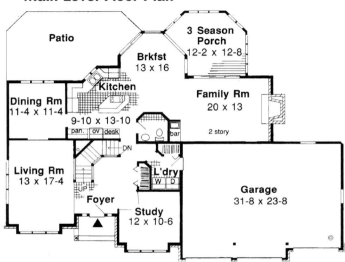

Upper Level Floor Plan

Copyright by designer/architect.

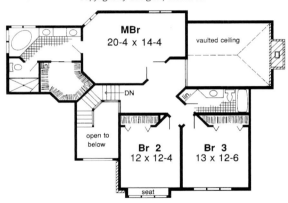

Plan #401012

Dimensions: 48' W x 52'6" D
Levels: 2
Square Footage: 2,301
Main Level Sq. Ft.: 1,180
Upper Level Sq. Ft.: 1,121
Bedrooms: 3-4
Bathrooms: 2½
Foundation: Basement
Materials List Available: Yes
Price Category: E

A turret roof, prominent bay window, and wraparound veranda designate this four bedroom design as classic Victorian. The plans include two second-level layouts – one with four bedrooms or one with three bedrooms and a vaulted ceiling over the family room.

Features:

- **Living Room:** This formal room has windows that overlook the veranda.

- **Family Room:** This gathering space includes a fireplace for atmosphere.

- **Kitchen:** This U-shaped kitchen has a sunny breakfast bay; you'll find a half-bath and a laundry room in the service area that leads to the two-car garage.

- **Master Suite:** This lavish area has an octagonal tray ceiling in the sitting room, a walk-in closet, and a private bath with a colonnaded whirlpool spa and separate shower.

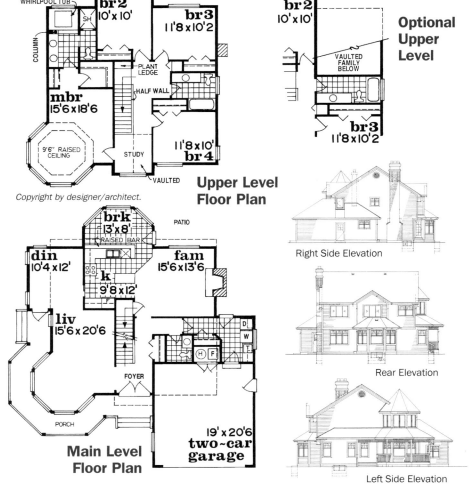

Images provided by designer/architect.

Copyright by designer/architect.

Upper Level Floor Plan

Optional Upper Level

Main Level Floor Plan

Right Side Elevation

Rear Elevation

Left Side Elevation

Plan #281016

Dimensions: 46' W x 44' D
Levels: 2
Square Footage: 1,945
Main Level Sq. Ft.: 1,211
Upper Level Sq. Ft.: 734
Bedrooms: 3
Bathrooms: 3
Foundation: Combination basement/slab
Materials List Available: Yes
Price Category: D

Images provided by designer/architect.

The fabulous window shapes on this Tudor-style home give just a hint of the beautiful interior design.

Features:

- Living Room: A vaulted ceiling in this raised room adds to its spectacular good looks.

- Dining Room: Between the lovely bay window and the convenient door to the covered sundeck, this room is an entertainer's delight.

- Family Room: A sunken floor, cozy fireplace, and door to the patio make this room special.

- Study: Just off the family room, this quiet spot can be a true retreat away from the crowd.

- Kitchen: The family cooks will be delighted by the ample counter and storage space here.

- Master Suite: A large walk-in closet, huge picture window, and private bath add luxurious touches to this second-floor retreat.

Main Level Floor Plan

Upper Level Floor Plan

Copyright by designer/architect.

Rear Elevation

Left Side Elevation

Right Side Elevation

Copyright by designer/architect.

Plan #151349

Dimensions: 47' W x 50' D
Levels: 1.5
Square Footage: 1,684
Main Level Sq. Ft.: 1,155
Upper Level Sq. Ft.: 529
Bedrooms: 3
Bathrooms: 2½
Foundation: Crawl space or slab; basement or walkout for fee
CompleteCost List Available: Yes
Price Category: C

Images provided by designer/architect.

Bonus Area Floor Plan

Main Level Floor Plan

Copyright by designer/architect.

Upper Level Floor Plan

Plan #161228

Dimensions: 64'4" W x 66'8" D
Levels: 2
Square Footage: 2,873
Main Level Sq. Ft.: 2,050
Upper Level Sq. Ft.: 823
Bedrooms: 4
Bathrooms: 2½
Foundation: Walkout
Material List Available: Yes
Price Category: F

Images provided by designer/architect.

Rear Elevation

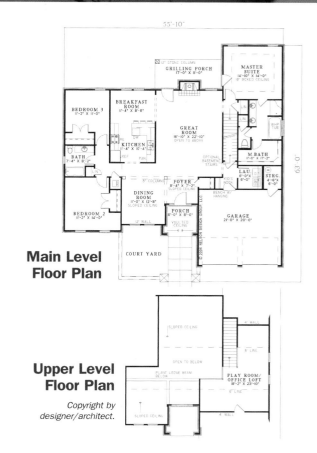

Plan #151837

Dimensions: 55'10" W x 63' D
Levels: 2
Square Footage: 2,256
Main Level Sq. Ft.: 1,935
Upper Level Sq. Ft.: 321
Bedrooms: 3
Bathrooms: 2
Foundation: Crawl space or slab; basement or walkout for fee
CompleteCost List Available: Yes
Price Category: E

Images provided by designer/architect.

CAD FILE AVAILABLE

Main Level Floor Plan

Upper Level Floor Plan

Copyright by designer/architect.

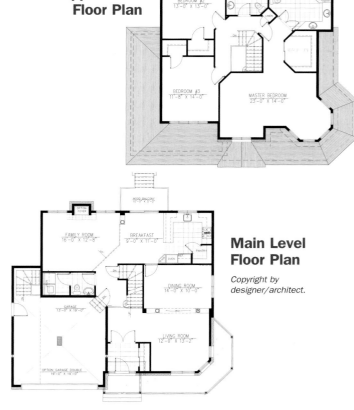

Plan #571014

Dimensions: 36' W x 39' D
Levels: 2
Square Footage: 2,134
Main Level Sq. Ft.: 1,065
Upper Level Sq. Ft.: 1,069
Bedrooms: 3
Bathrooms: 2½
Foundation: Basement
Material List Available: Yes
Price Category: D

Images provided by designer/architect.

Upper Level Floor Plan

Main Level Floor Plan

Copyright by designer/architect.

Plan #391017

Dimensions: 77' W x 41'6" D
Levels: 2
Square Footage: 2,176
Main Level Sq. Ft.: 1,671
Upper Level Sq. Ft.: 505
Bedrooms: 3
Bathrooms: 2½
Foundation: Crawl space, slab, or basement
Materials List Available: Yes
Price Category: D

Quaint, complex pitched rooflines and long, light-filled windows make this house a proper Tudor-style home befitting today's lifestyles.

Features:

- Entry: This formal entry, with its double doors, opens on a sophisticated library on one side and a formal dining room on the other.

- Living Room: This living room is central to the layout, inviting folks to gather at the fireplace, hang out on the screened porch, join the hustle bustle in the kitchen, or take meals to the outdoor patio.

- Master Suite: This master suite, with its special ceiling and dreamy full bath (tub tucked beneath a corner of windows, plus a separate shower) enjoys main-floor access to the library and a front yard view.

- Bedrooms: Upstairs, a lavishly long hallway delivers two dramatic-looking bedrooms, built around a spacious bathroom. One bedroom with picture window also features an expansive closet (cedar treatment optional). Another bedroom with wall-length closet enjoys a backyard view.

Main Level Floor Plan

Upper Level Floor Plan

Copyright by designer/architect.

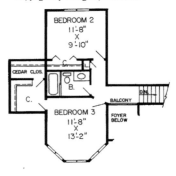

Plan #121090

Dimensions: 60' W x 58' D
Levels: 1.5
Square Footage: 2,645
Main Level Sq. Ft.: 1,972
Upper Level Sq. Ft.: 673
Bedrooms: 4
Bathrooms: 2½
Foundation: Basement
Materials List Available: Yes
Price Category: F

Images provided by designer/architect.

You'll be amazed at the amenities that have been designed into this lovely home.

Features:

• Den: French doors just off the entry lead to this lovely home, with its bowed window and spider-beamed ceiling.

• Great Room: A trio of graceful arched windows highlights the vlume ceiling in this room. You might want to curl up to read next to the see-through fireplace into the hearth room.

• Kitchen: Enjoy the good design in this room.

• Hearth Room: The shared fireplace with the great room makes this a cozy spot in cool weather.

• Master Suite: French doors lead to this well-lit area, with its roomy walk-in closet, sunlit whirlpool tubs, separate shower, and two vanities.

Main Level Floor Plan

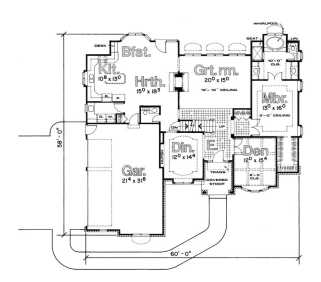

Upper Level Floor Plan

Copyright by designer/architect.

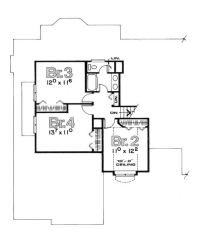

Plan #151846

Dimensions: 69'8" W x 79'6" D
Levels: 2
Square Footage: 2,609
Main Level Sq. Ft.: 2,280
Upper Level Sq. Ft.: 329
Bedrooms: 4
Bathrooms: 3
Foundation: Crawl space or slab; basement, or walkout for fee
CompleteCost List Available: Yes
Price Category: F

Images provided by designer/architect.

With all the tantalizing elements of a cottage and the comfortable space of a family-sized home, this European-style two-story design is the best of both worlds.

Features:

- Foyer: The vaulted ceiling soars up to the second level giving this foyer a dramatic feel. A view into the atrium brings the outdoors inside.

- Great Room: This large gathering area features a beautiful fireplace and a sloped ceiling. On nice days, exit through the glass door and relax on the porch.

- Kitchen: The raised snack bar in this efficient kitchen provides additional seating for informal meals. The family will enjoy lazy weekend mornings in the adjoining breakfast nook, which affords a view into the atrium.

- Master Suite: You'll spend many luxurious hours in this beautiful suite, which contains a 10-ft.-high boxed ceiling. The master bath boasts a large walk-in closet, glass shower, whirlpool tub, and double vanity.

Main Level Floor Plan

Copyright by designer/architect.

Upper Level Floor Plan

Plan #371046

Dimensions: 50'2" W x 70' D
Levels: 2
Square Footage: 2,440
Main Level Sq. Ft.: 1,809
Upper Level Sq. Ft.: 631
Bedrooms: 4
Bathrooms: 2½
Foundation: Slab
Materials List Available: Yes
Price Category: E

Ornate windows accent the exterior of this two-story home. Beautiful brick cast stone give it added charm.

Features:

• **Living Room:** This spacious formal room has a cathedral ceiling.

• **Family Room:** Large windows flood this open and airy room with natural light; the cozy fireplace makes it comfortable.

• **Dining Room:** This formal room opens into the large entry.

• **Kitchen:** This kitchen has a pantry, raised bar, and breakfast nook that opens to the family room and is great for entertaining.

• **Master Suite:** This secluded area, located downstairs, has a luxurious master bathroom with two walk-in closets.

• **Bedrooms:** Upstairs are three additional bedrooms with walk-in closets that share a convenient hall bathroom with a dressing room.

Images provided by designer/architect.

Upper Level Floor Plan

Copyright by designer/architect.

Main Level Floor Plan

Plan #351176

Dimensions: 69' W x 59' D

Levels: 1

Heated Square Footage: 2,100

Bedrooms: 4

Bathrooms: 2½

Foundation: Crawl space, slab

Material List Available: Yes

Price Category: D

Images provided by designer/architect.

The many available features and flexibility of this home make it the perfect choice for you and your family.

Features:

- **Great Room:** This great room features vaulted ceilings, built-in cabinets, a fireplace, and direct access to the rear covered porch.

- **Kitchen:** Mornings are made easy in this kitchen, which features a raised eating bar, a breakfast area, and ample counter space.

- **Master Suite:** You'll never want to leave this beautiful master suite with its coffered ceiling, two walk-in closets, whirlpool tub, and separate vanity areas.

- **Secondary Bedrooms:** Three additional bedrooms share a separate area of the home, each with its own walk-in closet.

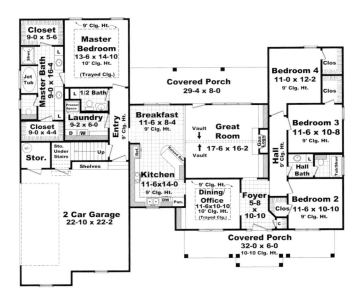

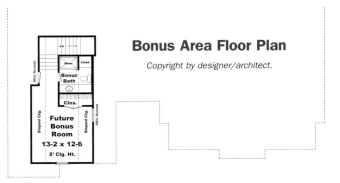

Bonus Area Floor Plan

Copyright by designer/architect.

Plan #131032

Dimensions: 69'2" W x 46' D
Levels: 2
Square Footage: 2,455
Main Level Sq. Ft.: 1,499
Upper Level Sq. Ft.: 956
Bedrooms: 4
Bathrooms: 3
Foundation: Crawl space or slab; basement for fee
Materials List Available: Yes
Price Category: F

If you love Victorian styling, you'll be charmed by the ornate, rounded front porch and the two-story bay that distinguish this home.

Images provided by designer/architect.

Features:

- Living Room: You'll love the 13-ft. ceiling in this room, as well as the panoramic view it gives of the front porch and yard.

- Kitchen: Sunlight streams into this room, where an angled island with a cooktop eases both prepping and cooking.

- Breakfast Room: This room shares an eating bar with the kitchen, making it easy for the family to congregate while the family chef is cooking.

- Guest Room: Use this lovely room on the first level as a home office or study if you wish.

- Master Suite: The dramatic bayed sitting area with a high ceiling has an octagonal shape that you'll adore, and the amenities in the private bath will soothe you at the end of a busy day.

Rear View

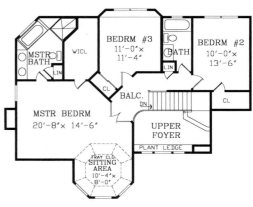

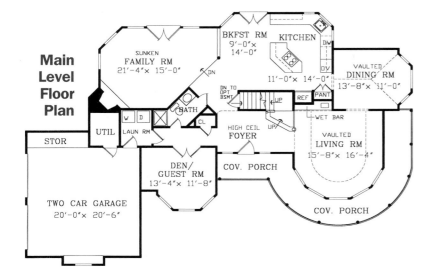

Main Level Floor Plan

Upper Level Floor Plan

Copyright by designer/architect.

Plan #121108

Dimensions: 67'4" W x 66' D
Levels: 2
Square Footage: 3,806
Main Level Sq. Ft.: 2,126
Upper Level Sq. Ft.: 1,680
Bedrooms: 4
Bathrooms: 4½
Foundation: Basement; Crawl space for fee
Material List Available: Yes
Price Category: H

Elegant architecture and stylish details define this home.

Images provided by designer/architect.

Features:

• Master Suite: This room will become your oasis with its large bedroom area, beautiful ceiling details, spacious walk-in closet, his-and-hers sinks, and a large whirlpool bath surrounded by windows for a truly relaxing experience.

• Hearth Room: This roomy hearth room features an entertainment center, open access to the kitchen, and a two-way fireplace shared with the great room.

• Kitchen: You'll love the elegant details in this kitchen, with its walk-in pantry and snack bar.

The brightly-lit connecting breakfast area is a perfect place for yourmorningcup of coffee.

Front View

Main Level Floor Plan

Copyright by designer/architect.

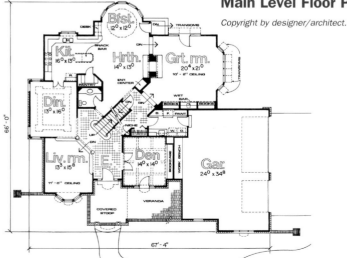

Upper Level Floor Plan

Plan #241058

Dimensions: 93' W x 57'2" D

Levels: 2

Square Footage: 4,216

Main Level Sq. Ft.: 2,384

Upper Level Sq. Ft.: 1,832

Bedrooms: 4

Bathrooms: 3½

Foundation: Slab

Material List Available: Yes

Price Category: I

Images provided by designer/architect.

A brick-and-stone exterior provides a rich solid look to this beautiful two-story home.

Features:

- Entry: This covered entry opens into the two-story foyer. The dining room is located to the right through an entry of floor-to-ceiling columns.

- Great Room: This sunken gathering area boast a fireplace flanked by windows.

- Master Suite: Located on the main level, this retreat boasts a sitting area. The master bath features a large walk-in closet and whirlpool tub.

- Bedrooms: Three secondary bedrooms are located on the upper level. A nearby play-room could serve as a spare bedroom. Two bedrooms share a Jack-and-Jill bathroom.

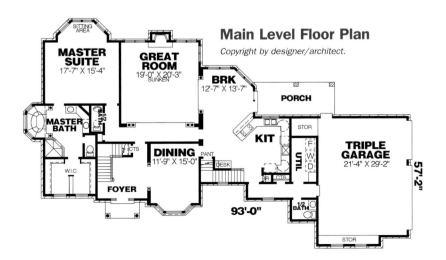

Main Level Floor Plan

Copyright by designer/architect.

Upper Level Floor Plan

Plan #151842

Dimensions: 60'4" W x 64'4" D
Levels: 1
Square Footage: 2,135
Bedrooms: 4
Bathrooms: 2
Foundation: Crawl space or slab; basement or walkout for fee
CompleteCost List Available: Yes
Price Category: D

Images provided by designer/architect.

CAD FILE AVAILABLE

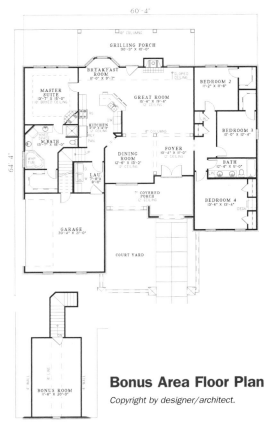

Bonus Area Floor Plan
Copyright by designer/architect.

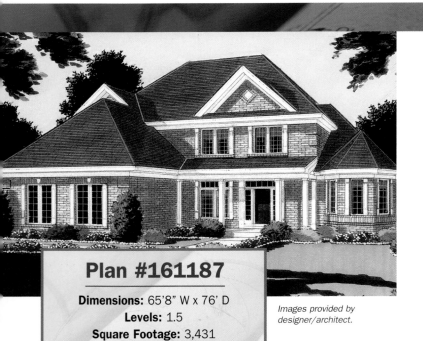

Plan #161187

Dimensions: 65'8" W x 76' D
Levels: 1.5
Square Footage: 3,431
Main Level Sq. Ft.: 2,341
Upper Level Sq. Ft.: 1,090
Bedrooms: 4
Bathrooms: 3½
Foundation: Basement
Materials List Available: Yes
Price Category: G

Images provided by designer/architect.

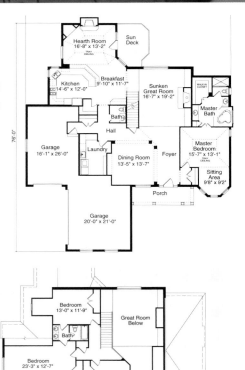

Main Level Floor Plan

Upper Level Floor Plan
Copyright by designer/architect.

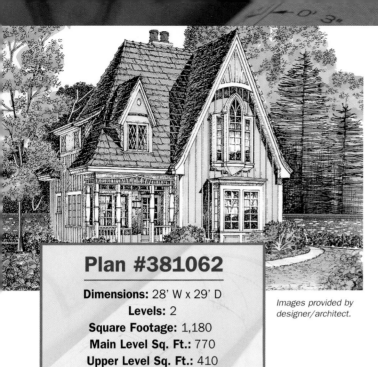

Plan #381062

Dimensions: 28' W x 29' D
Levels: 2
Square Footage: 1,180
Main Level Sq. Ft.: 770
Upper Level Sq. Ft.: 410
Bedrooms: 2
Bathrooms: 2
Foundation: Crawl space
Material List Available: Yes
Price Category: B

Images provided by designer/architect.

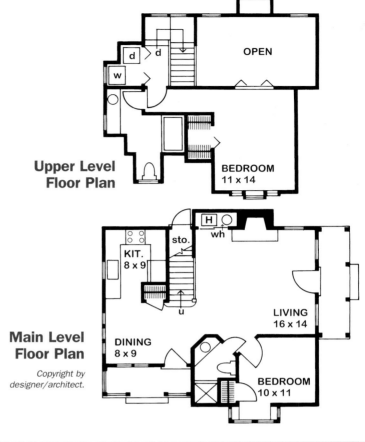

Upper Level Floor Plan

OPEN

BEDROOM
11 x 14

d | d
w

Main Level Floor Plan

Copyright by designer/architect.

KIT.
8 x 9

sto.

H

wh

u

DINING
8 x 9

LIVING
16 x 14

BEDROOM
10 x 11

Plan #381058

Dimensions: 68'5" W x 33' D
Levels: 2
Square Footage: 1,895
Main Level Sq. Ft.: 1,180
Upper Level Sq. Ft.: 715
Bedrooms: 4
Bathrooms: 2½
Foundation: Basement
Material List Available: Yes
Price Category: D

Images provided by designer/architect.

Upper Level Floor Plan

Copyright by designer/architect.

stor.

BEDROOM
12 x 10

BEDROOM
13 x 14

d | attic | L

stor.

BEDROOM
13 x 13

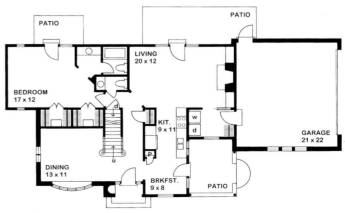

PATIO

PATIO

LIVING
20 x 12

BEDROOM
17 x 12

d

KIT.
9 x 11

w
d

GARAGE
21 x 22

DINING
13 x 11

u

P

BRKFST.
9 x 8

PATIO

Main Level Floor Plan

Today's Fireplace Technology

Handsome and romantic, but drafty. Thirty years ago, you might have described a traditional fireplace in this way. But that was before technological advancements finally made fireplaces more efficient. Now, not only can you expect your fireplace to provide ambiance and warmth, you can relax knowing that your energy dollars aren't going up in smoke. Over the centuries, people had tried to improve the efficiency of the fireplace so that it would generate the maximum heat possible from the wood consumed. But real strides didn't come until the energy crisis of the early 1970s. That's when designers of fireplaces and stoves introduced some significant innovations. Today, fireplaces are not only more efficient, but cleaner and easier to use.

The traditional fireplace is an all-masonry construction, consisting of only bricks and mortar. However, new constructions and reconstructions of masonry fireplaces often include either a metal or a ceramic firebox. This type of firebox has double walls. The space between these walls is where cool air heats up after being drawn in through openings near the floor of the room. The warm air exits through openings near the top of the firebox. Although a metal firebox is more efficient than an all-masonry firebox, it doesn't radiate heat very effectively, and the heat from the fireplace is distributed by convection—that is, the circulation of warmed air. This improvement in heating capacity comes from the warm air emitted by the upper openings. But that doesn't keep your feet toasty on a cold winter's night—remember, warm air rises.

A more recent development is the ceramic firebox, which is engineered from modern materials such as the type used in kilns. Fires in ceramic fireboxes burn hotter, cleaner, and more efficiently than in all-masonry or metal fireboxes. The main reason is that the back and the walls of a ceramic firebox absorb, retain, and reflect heat effectively. This means that during the time the fire is blazing, more heat radiates into the room than with the other fireboxes. Heat radiation is boosted by the fact that most ceramic units are made with

The warm glow of a realistic-looking modern zero-clearance gas fire, below, can make the hearth the heart of any room in the house.

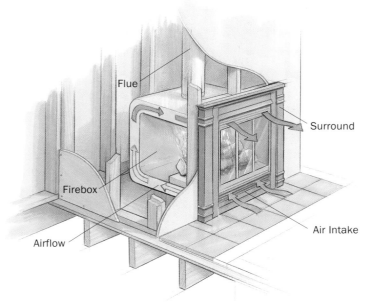

Flue

Surround

Firebox

Air Intake

Airflow

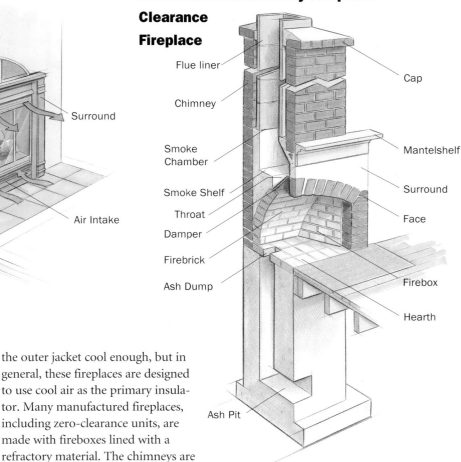

Traditional Masonry Fireplace

Flue liner

Chimney

Smoke Chamber

Smoke Shelf

Throat

Damper

Firebrick

Ash Dump

Ash Pit

Cap

Mantelshelf

Surround

Face

Firebox

Hearth

New-technology and traditional fireplaces are shown above. Woodstove-like inserts, below and opposite, make fireplaces more efficient.

thick walls, and so the fire itself is not set as deeply into the hearth as it is with all-masonry or metal fireboxes. As a bonus, because heat is absorbed and retained by the material, the firebox actually radiates a significant amount of heat many hours after the fire has died down. By contrast, a metal firebox cools quickly once the heat source goes out.

In this type of efficient fireplace construction, a metal firebox is usually less expensive than a ceramic one, but the metal does break down over time, in a process professionals refer to as burnout. In addition, an air-circulating metal firebox can only be installed in masonry constructions that are built with ports for the intake of cool air and the discharge of warmed air, or in masonry fireplaces in which such ports can be added. On the other hand, ceramic fireboxes can be installed in any type of masonry fireplace and are not subject to burnout.

Manufactured Fireplaces

The metal fireplaces that are made today can be zero-clearance or freestanding. The zero-clearance units are so named because they can be installed safely against combustible surfaces such as wood. Any of a number of methods are used to keep

the outer jacket cool enough, but in general, these fireplaces are designed to use cool air as the primary insulator. Many manufactured fireplaces, including zero-clearance units, are made with fireboxes lined with a refractory material. The chimneys are also made of metal, and a variety of designs use noncombustible material or air as insulation to keep the outer surface at a safe temperature.

The Advantages of a Manufactured Unit

There are some important pluses to choosing a zero-clearance manufactured fireplace. First is the price, which is relatively low, and second is the easy and quick installation. Also, these units are lightweight and can be installed over almost any type of flooring, including wood. This means they do not need elaborate foundations, which is another cost-saver. Manufactured fireplaces are also extremely efficient, and many are designed to provide both radiated heat from the firebox and convection heat from ducting.

Manufactured freestanding fireplaces are, in effect, stoves. They are available in an array of colors, finishes, shapes, and sizes. Like zero-clearance factory-built fireplaces, freestanding models are lightweight, offering the same advantages: no need for heavy masonry or additional reinforcement of flooring. And you have a choice of either a wood-burning or gas-powered unit. Heat efficiency is maximized because, in addition to the firebox, the chimney and all

sides of the unit radiate heat into the room. Freestanding units may be the least expensive option because installation requires only a chimney hole and, depending on the type of flooring, a noncombustible pad. A major disadvantage is the space required for placement, because you cannot install most of these units near a combustible wall. Also, a freestanding fireplace is probably not the best choice for families with young children because so much heat is radiated from the exposed surfaces.

Hybrids

If you're looking for a way to get improved efficiency from a masonry fireplace, consider a gas insert (actually a prefabricated firebox equipped with gas logs). You can purchase either a venting insert or one that's nonventing. But be prepared to pay $1,500 to several thousand dollars for the unit in addition to the cost of installation. For a fraction of that amount you can simply replace real wood logs with ceramic logs powered by gas. Like inserts, these logs may or may not require venting. Consult

an experienced plumber or heating contractor, and remember that once you convert to gas you cannot burn wood.

Improving a masonry fireplace on the inside by installing a metal firebox might also be an inspiration to think of the fireplace and mantel in a new design way. Pairing two or more finishing materials, such as metal and masonry, can make your fireplace a hybrid in more than one way. For example, combine a stone base with a metal hood and chimney to create a custom-designed fireplace that works as a room divider in a large space. The design options in terms of materials and technology are seemingly endless.

If you have plans for building an innovative custom design, carefully review them with an expert in fireplace construction and maintenance to make sure you're not doing something hazardous. Also, don't forget to check with your local building inspector so that you don't waste time and money on a project that may not comply with codes and regulations set forth where you live.

Enhancing the Basics

You can improve the efficiency of any manufactured fireplace, and of masonry and hybrid constructions as well, with a few extras. In a masonry fireplace, a device commonly referred to as a fresh-air intake accessory or an outside air kit may improve performance. A fresh-air accessory makes use of outside air instead of heated room air for combustion, thus improving the fireplace's efficiency. There is another way to make your fireplace more efficient that isn't high tech at all, however. Simply replace the traditional grate or firebasket with a superior design—one that provides greater air circulation and allows a better placement of logs. Another type, a heat-exchanger grate, works with a fan. The device draws in the room's air, reheats it quickly, and then forces it back into the room.

Capitalizing on Technology

Wood is the traditional fuel for a fireplace, and today's manufactured fireplaces offer designs that make the most of your cord of hardwood. However, wood is not the only fuel option. In fact, in some places, it's not an option at all. There are manufactured units that offer a choice of natural gas or propane as a fuel source, which heats ceramic logs designed to realistically simulate wood. The fire, complete with glowing embers, is often difficult to distinguish from one burning real wood.

In some areas of the country, fireplace emission regulations have become strict—in places such as much of Colorado and parts of Nevada and California so strict that new construction of wood-burning fireplaces has been outlawed. In these areas, manufactured units using alternative fuels allow homeowners all the benefits of a wood-burning fireplace without the adverse impact on air quality.

Most of the units available today also offer a variety of amenities, including built-in thermostatic control and remote-control devices for turning the fire on and off and regulating heat output.

The Importance of a Clean Sweep

Finally, one of the most important factors in the use of a fireplace or stove is the regular inspection and cleaning of the stovepipe, flue, and chimney. To understand why, remember that the burning of wood results in the combustion of solids as well as combustible gases. However, not everything that goes into the firebox is burned, no matter how efficient the appliance. One of the by-products of wood burning is the dark brown or black tar called creosote, a flammable substance that sticks to the linings of chimney flues.

Although the burning temperature of creosote is high, it can ignite and cause a chimney fire. It may be brief and without apparent damage, but a chimney fire may also be prolonged or intense and result in significant fire and smoke damage or, at worst, the loss of your home if the creosote buildup is great enough. Creosote causes other problems, too. It decreases the inside diameter of stovepipes and flues, causing slower burning. This makes burning less efficient and contributes to further deposits of creosote. In addition, because creosote is acidic, it corrodes mortar, metal, and eventually even stainless-steel and ceramic chimney liners.

To prevent costly and dangerous creosote buildup, have your chimney professionally cleaned by a qualified chimney sweep. How often depends on the amount of creosote deposited during the burning season, and this, in turn, depends largely on how and what kind of wood you burn. Professional sweeps usually recommend at least annual cleaning. Depending on where you live, you'll spend about $150, perhaps less, for a cleaning.

You'll enjoy a warm glow at the highest efficiency if you use a glass-front wood-burning or gas-fueled, right, fireplace insert.

Fireside Arrangements

Creating an attractive, comfortable setting around a fireplace should be easy. Who doesn't like the cozy ambiance of relaxing in front of a fire? But there are times when the presence of a fireplace in a room poses problems with the layout. A fireplace can take up considerable floor and wall space, and like any other permanent feature or built-in piece of furniture, its size or position can limit the design possibilities.

The Fireplace and the Space

What is the room's size and shape—large, small, square, long and narrow, L-shaped?

Where is the fireplace located—in the center of a wall, to the side, or in a corner? What other permanent features, such as windows, doors, bookcases, or media units, will you have to work with in your arrangement? How much clearance can you allow around the furniture for easy passage? How close do you want to be to the fire? Think of these questions as you consider the design basics presented below.

Scale and Proportion. Remember the importance of spatial relationships. For example, a fireplace may seem large in a room with a low ceiling; conversely, it may appear small in a room with a vaulted ceil-

ing. Size is relative. Applied to objects on the mantel or the wall above the fireplace, correct scale and proportion happen when the objects are the appropriate size for the wall or the fireplace.

Balance. Sometimes the architectural features of a mantel or surround are so strong, you'll have to match them with furnishings of equal visual weight. Or they may be so ornate or plain that you'll have to play them up or tone them down to make them work with the rest of the decor. That's balance. But balance also refers to arrangements: symmetrical, asymmetrical, and radial.

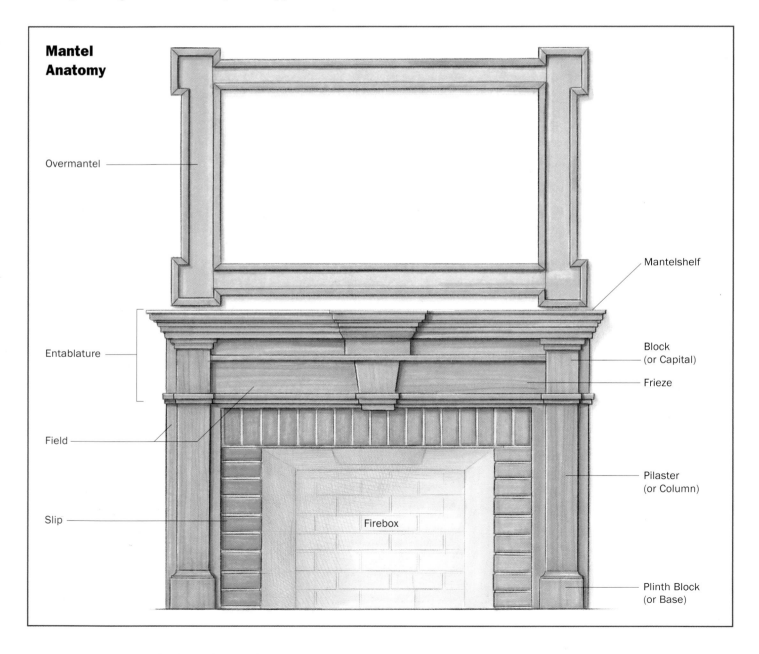

Mantel Anatomy

Overmantel

Entablature

Field

Slip

Mantelshelf

Block (or Capital)

Frieze

Pilaster (or Column)

Firebox

Plinth Block (or Base)

Line. Shape depends on line. Different types of lines suggest various qualities. Pay attention to the lines when you're creating arrangements and relationships among objects. Some lines are inherent in a room or an architectural feature, but you can modify them. For example: vertical lines are stately and dignified, which is just the look you want for your fireplace, but unfortunately, it's rather wide and squat instead. Solution? Create an arrangement above the fireplace that extends high on the wall, or hang a tall mirror or frame over than mantel.

What if the fireplace is too tall? Does it overwhelm the rest of the furniture? Add horizontal lines by moving seating pieces farther apart to the right and left of the hearth. Install wall art on the sides of the fireplace.

If the room is boxy, avoid grouping pieces at right angles to the fireplace and each other. Instead, de-emphasize the boxy shape by placing them on the diagonal to open the square. Use upholstered pieces with rounded arms or curvaceous cushions, legs, or frames. Create a radial arrangement. With the hearth as the central point, create a semicircular hub of furnishings that include seating and a small table or two.

Rhythm. Keep the eye moving at a measured pace by repeating motifs, colors, or shapes. For example, you might pick up the color from a tiled surround to use as an accent color in fabrics on upholstered pieces, curtains, pillows, throws, or other decorative accessories. Or repeat architectural features of the fireplace with other similar elements in the room, such as molding or other woodwork details.

Variety. Don't go overboard trying to match everything exactly. The most interesting rooms and arrangements mix objects of different sizes, shapes, lines, and sometimes even styles (as long as they are compatible).

Harmony. Create harmony among all of the parts of your design by connecting all of the elements either by color or motif. For example, in a display of family photos the frames may all be different shapes, styles, and heights, but because each one is made of brass, the overall appearance looks harmonious. Or you could assemble a wall vignette of frames over the fireplace, all different in finish but tied together by the subject matter of each one—all landscapes, for example, or all pink cabbage roses. Unifying diverse items in this way creates a finished-looking scheme.

How to Make a Hinged Fireboard

You'll need a hinged three-panel wooden fireplace screen, which you can buy or make. If you buy one, you'll have to sand and prime it thoroughly before applying the new finish over the existing one. Ideally, it's best to work on unfinished wood.

The screen used for this project features two 9 x 36-inch side panels and one 26 x 36-inch center panel that were cut from a ¾-inch-thick sheet of plywood. If you aren't handy with a circular saw or table saw, ask your local lumber supplier to cut the panels to your desired dimensions. Attach the side and center panels with two-way (piano) hinges, which are easy to install. Simply mark their location along the inside edges of the panel pieces, drill pilot holes, and then screw the hinges into place. To finish, prime the boards; then paint or stencil a design onto each panel. For Victorian authenticity, decoupage the panels with a motif cut out of a piece of fabric, wallpaper, old greeting cards, or postcards.

Symmetrical versus Asymmetrical Arrangements

If you like the symmetry of classic design, balance your arranged pieces accordingly. For example, position two sofas or love seats of the same size perpendicular to the fireplace and exactly opposite each other. Or place a single sofa parallel with the fireplace, with two chairs opposite one another and equidistant from both the sofa and the hearth. Try out a low coffee table or an oversize ottoman in the center of the arrangement. Leave the peripheral areas outside the main grouping for creating small impromptu conversation areas during parties and gatherings or to accommodate a modest dining area or home-office station.

If your design sense is less formal or contemporary, try an asymmetrical grouping in front of the fire. Turn seating pieces at a 45-degree angle from the hearth.

In a large open space, locate seating not directly in front of the hearth but slightly off to the side. Counterbalance the arrangement with a large table and chairs, a hutch, bookcases, or any element of relatively equal weight. This layout works especially well when the ceiling is vaulted (as most great rooms are) or when the hearth is massive. In many contemporary homes, especially where there is a zero-clearance unit, the fireplace is not on an outside wall, nor is it necessarily in a central location. This means you can put the fireplace almost anywhere.

Comfortable Arrangements

You may want an intimate environment in front of the fire, but the room is so large that it feels and looks impersonal. Large rooms afford lots of leeway for arranging, but people often make the mistake of pushing all of the furniture against the walls. If that's what you're doing, pull the major seating pieces closer together and near the fire, keeping a distance of only 4 to 10 feet between sofas and chairs. For the most comfortable result, create one or more small groupings that can accommodate up to four to six people in different areas of the room.

Modular Seating. Instead of a standard sofa and chairs, consider the convenience of modular seating, too, which comes in any number of armless and single-arm end pieces. The advantage of these separate upholstered units is that you can easily add, take away, or rearrange the modules to suit any of your layout or seating needs. Create an L or a U arrangement in front of the fire; subtract pieces, moving one or two outside of the area for an intimate

A raised hearth, above, reinforces the idea of a fireplace as a focal point, and it provides seating near the fire. Place other furniture to the sides of the hearth.

grouping. Use an area rug to further define the space. Or put the pieces together to make one large arrangement in any configuration. Versatile furnishings such as an ottoman with a hinged top or an antique trunk can double as seating, a low table, or storage.

A Quick Guide to Buying Firewood

How much wood you need to buy in a season depends on a number of factors, but there are three major variables: how often and how long you burn fires; the efficiency of your fireplace or stove; and the type of wood you burn. In general, hard, dense woods are ideal for fuel. As a rule of thumb, the wood from deciduous trees is best. (Deciduous trees are those that shed their leaves annually.) These include oak, maple, walnut, birch, beech, ash, and the wood from fruit trees such as cherry and apple.

Avoid burning wood from evergreens—those cone-bearing (coniferous) trees with needles instead of leaves. The wood of coniferous trees is soft and it will burn faster, so a greater volume of wood will be consumed per hour compared with hardwood. A greater problem with softwoods, however, is the resin content. Resin is the gummy substance that's used in the manufacture of some wood

stains and shellacs, and when resin is burned it gives off a byproduct called creosote. Creosote, which is flammable, accumulates in flues and chimneys, and this buildup represents a potential fire hazard.

The wood you purchase should also be seasoned, which means that the tree should have been cut down at least six months or, preferably, a year prior to the burning of the wood. Ideally, the wood should be cut and split soon after the tree is felled, allowing for more effective drying. The moisture in unseasoned (or green) wood tends to have a cooling effect, preventing complete combustion and making it harder to keep a fire blazing. A low-burning fire also increases creosote. (It's okay to burn green wood occasionally, but make sure to use small logs or split sticks and add them to an already hot fire.)

A simple brick wall, left, serves as a backdrop for a gleaming fireplace insert.

Mantel Vignettes

A grouping of objects on your mantel can be as simple or complex as you like. To make your display lively, choose a variety of shapes and sizes. For dramatic impact, group related objects that you can link in theme or color.

Remember that a symmetrical arrangement has classical overtones and will reinforce the formality of traditional designs. Stick with similar objects: a pair of Chinese ginger jars or antique silver candlesticks arranged in mirror fashion on either side of the mantel equidistant from the center, for example. Or keep the look simple by placing a single but important object in the center; it could be a mantel clock, a floral arrangement, or some other objet d'art.

Asymmetry, on the other hand, brings a different dynamic to a mantel vignette with mismatched pieces. Try placing a large object to one side of the mantel, and then balance that piece by massing several small objects or a different type of object of similar scale on the opposite side. An example might be an arrangement of books of varying heights and sizes at one end of the mantel and a simple large vase at the other end. Or you might oppose tall thin candlesticks with one fat candle.

Plan #161002

Dimensions: 64'2" W x 44'2" D
Levels: 1
Square Footage: 1,860
Bedrooms: 3
Bathrooms: 2
Foundation: Basement
Materials List Available: Yes
Price Category: D

CAD FILE **CAD** AVAILABLE

Images provided by designer/architect.

The brick, stone, and cedar shake facade provides color and texture to the exterior, while the unique nooks and angles inside this delightful one-level home give it character.

Features:

• **Great Room/Dining Room:** This spacious great room is furnished with a wood-burning fireplace, a high ceiling, and French doors. Wide entrances to the breakfast room and dining room expand its space to comfortably hold large gatherings.

• **Kitchen:** The breakfast bar offers additional seating. The covered porch lets you enjoy a view of the landscape and is conveniently located for outdoor meals off this kitchen and breakfast area.

• **Master Suite:** The master suite is a private retreat. An alcove creates a comfortable sitting area, and an angled entry leads to the bath with whirlpool and a double-bowl vanity.

Great Room/Foyer

Rear Elevation

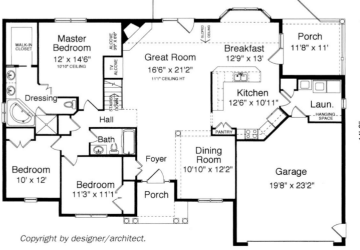

Copyright by designer/architect.

Plan #311024

Dimensions: 56' W x 45' D
Levels: 1
Square Footage: 1,492
Bedrooms: 3
Bathrooms: 2
Foundation: Crawl space, slab, or basement
Materials List Available: Yes
Price Category: C

Images provided by designer/architect.

With its uncomplicated layout, this charming, traditional house is a perfect starter or retirement home.

Features:

- **Porches:** Front and back covered porches allow you to enjoy the outdoors without leaving home. Sit out on warm summer evenings, enjoying the breeze and greeting passersby.

- **Kitchen:** This efficient layout includes a snack bar, which can act as a transition or buffet for the adjacent formal dining room.

- **Master Suite:** Enjoy a private entry to the porch, a walk-in closet, and a large master bath with his and her vanities, a large whirlpool tub, and a separate shower.

- **Secondary Bedrooms:** Two additional bedrooms have ample closet space and access to a shared bathroom, all tucked away from the main area of the home.

Rear View

Bonus Area Floor Plan

Copyright by designer/architect.

Plan #131021

Dimensions: 60' W x 52'4" D
Levels: 2
Square Footage: 3,110
Main Level Sq. Ft.: 1,818
Upper Level Sq. Ft.: 1,292
Bedrooms: 5
Bathrooms: 2½
Foundation: Crawl space or slab; basement for fee
Materials List Available: Yes
Price Category: H

This home, as shown in the photograph, may differ from the actual blueprints. For more detailed information, please check the floor plans carefully.

Amenities abound in this luxurious two-story beauty with a cozy gazebo on one corner of the spectacular wraparound front porch. Comfort, functionality, and spaciousness characterize this home.

Features:

- Ceiling Height: 8 ft.

- Foyer: This two-story high foyer is breathtaking.

- Family Room: Roomy with open views of the kitchen, the family room has a vaulted ceiling and boasts a functional fireplace and a built-in entertainment center.

- Dining Room: Formal yet comfortable, this spacious dining room is perfect for entertaining family and friends.

- Kitchen: Perfectly located with access to a breakfast room and the family room, this U-shaped kitchen with large center island is charming as well as efficient.

- Master Suite: Enjoy this sizable room with a vaulted ceiling, two large walk-in closets, and a lovely compartmented bath.

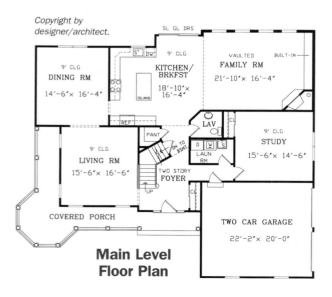

Main Level Floor Plan

Upper Level Floor Plan

Plan #101018

Dimensions: 56' W x 67' D

Levels: 2

Square Footage: 2,546

Main Level Sq. Ft.: 1,818

Upper Level Sq. Ft.: 728

Bedrooms: 4

Bathrooms: 3½

Foundation: Basement

Materials List Available: Yes

Price Category: E

CAD FILE AVAILABLE

The brick exterior of this home is accented with multilevel stucco trim and copper roof details.

Features:

• Ceiling Height: 9 ft. unless otherwise noted.

• Foyer: From the front porch you'll enter this dramatic two-story foyer highlighted by a corner niche.

• Dining Room: To one side of the foyer you will find this elegant dining room.

At 13 ft. x 12 ft., there's plenty of room for large dinner parties.

• Family Room: This dramatic room seems enormous, due to its two-story glass bay. It's open to the kitchen and the breakfast room.

• Master Suite: Just off the breakfast room is this luxurious master retreat. An enormous walk-in closet, a bath highlighted by a 5-ft. x 6-ft. whirlpool tub framed by decorative columns, and a vaulted ceiling with fixed glass above make this the most impressive area of the house.

• Secondary Bedrooms: Two of the upstairs bedrooms have direct access to their bath. All of the upper-level rooms have 8-ft. ceilings.

Main Level Floor Plan

MASTER BR 15x16

DECK

BRKFST 12x10

KITCHEN 15x13

FAMILY ROOM 21x18

3 CAR GARAGE 20x32

DINING 13x12

LIVING 13x12

OPTIONAL LAUNDRY CHUTE

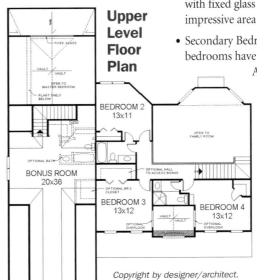

Upper Level Floor Plan

FIXED GLASS

VAULT VAULT

OPEN TO MASTER BEDROOM

PLANT SHELF BELOW

BEDROOM 2 13x11

OPEN TO FAMILY ROOM

OPTIONAL BATH

BONUS ROOM 20x36

OPTIONAL HALL TO ACCESS BONUS

BEDROOM 3 13x12

BEDROOM 4 13x12

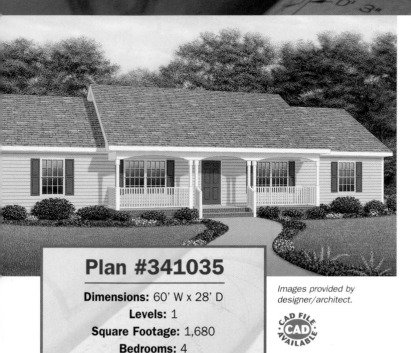

DECK
12'-0" X 10'-0"

GARDEN TUB

CLOSET

BATH 1

LIN

SHWR

KITCHEN
13'-1" X 13'-5"

REF

RANGE

SINK

DW

ISLAND

DRY

WASH

BEDROOM 2
10'-6" X 13'-5"

PANTRY

CLOSET

BATH 2

BEDROOM 3
10'-6" X 10'-11"

CLOSET

LINENS

CLOSET

28'-0"

BEDROOM 1
13'-11" X 13'-5"

DINING ROOM
12'-4" X 13'-5"

LIVING ROOM
18'-10" X 13'-5"

PREFAB VENTLESS GAS LOG FIREPLACE

COAT

SHELVES

BEDROOM 4
10'-6" X 10'-11"

PORCH

60'-0"

Images provided by designer/architect.

Copyright by designer/architect.

Plan #341035

Dimensions: 60' W x 28' D

Levels: 1

Square Footage: 1,680

Bedrooms: 4

Bathrooms: 2

Foundation: Crawl space, slab; basement option for fee

Materials List Available: Yes

Price Category: C

CAD FILE AVAILABLE

Copyright by designer/architect.

Great Rm
22-8x16-10
vaulted clg

MBr
15-8x13-9
vaulted clg

Covered Patio

Dining
12-0x12-0

Br 2
10-0x
9-0

Stor
8-0x
7-7

D

W

Laundry

Kit
Brkfst
17-4x14-2

R

Foyer

Dn

Study
Br 4
11-4x12-7
vaulted clg

Br 3
10-0x
10-0

Garage
19-4x21-0

Porch depth
5-10

48'-0"

67'-4"

Plan #321003

Dimensions: 67'4" W x 48' D

Levels: 1

Square Footage: 1,791

Bedrooms: 4

Bathrooms: 2

Foundation: Basement

Materials List Available: Yes

Price Category: E

Images provided by designer/architect.

CAD FILE AVAILABLE

Plan #131028

Dimensions: 69'2" W x 50'2" D
Levels: 2
Square Footage: 2,696
Main Level Sq. Ft.: 1,960
Upper Level Sq. Ft.: 736
Bedrooms: 4
Bathrooms: 3
Foundation: Crawl space or slab; basement for fee
Materials List Available: Yes
Price Category: F

Images provided by designer/architect.

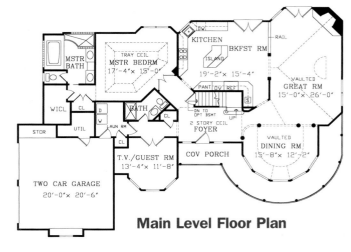

Main Level Floor Plan

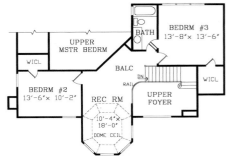

Upper Level Floor Plan

Copyright by designer/architect.

Plan #261001

Dimensions: 77'8" W x 49' D
Levels: 2
Square Footage: 3,746
Main Level Sq. Ft.: 1,965
Upper Level Sq. Ft.: 1,781
Bedrooms: 4
Bathrooms: 3½
Foundation: Basement
Materials List Available: Yes
Price Category: H

Images provided by designer/architect.

Main Level Floor Plan

Upper Level Floor Plan

Copyright by designer/architect.

Main Level Floor Plan

Images provided by designer/architect.

Plan #211077

Dimensions: 94' W x 68' D
Levels: 2
Square Footage: 5,560
Main Level Sq. Ft.: 4,208
Upper Level Sq. Ft.: 1,352
Bedrooms: 4
Bathrooms: 4 full, 2 half
Foundation: Slab; crawl space for fee
Materials List Available: Yes
Price Category: J

Upper Level Floor Plan

Copyright by designer/architect.

Plan #101012

Images provided by designer/architect.

Dimensions: 69'4" W x 62'9" D
Levels: 1
Square Footage: 2,288
Bedrooms: 3
Bathrooms: 2½
Foundation: Crawl space, slab, basement, or walkout
Materials List Available: yes
Price Category: E

Copyright by designer/architect.

Living Room

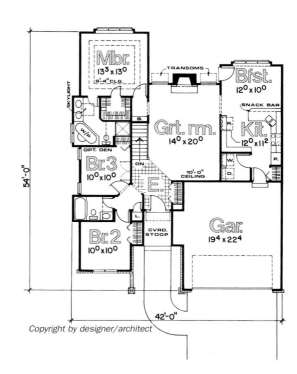

Plan #121002

Dimensions: 42' W x 54' D
Levels: 1
Square Footage: 1,347
Bedrooms: 3
Bathrooms: 2
Foundation: Basement
Materials List Available: Yes
Price Category: B

Images provided by designer/architect.

CAD FILE AVAILABLE

Copyright by designer/architect

Main Level Floor Plan

Plan #181541

Dimensions: 42' W x 50' D
Levels: 2
Square Footage: 2,017
Main Level Sq. Ft.: 1,026
Upper Level Sq. Ft.: 991
Bedrooms: 3
Bathrooms: 1½
Foundation: Basement
Material List Available: Yes
Price Category: F

Images provided by designer/architect.

CAD FILE AVAILABLE

Upper Level Floor Plan

Copyright by designer/architect.

Plan #181080

Dimensions: 44'8" W x 36' D
Levels: 2
Square Footage: 2,042
Main Level Sq. Ft.: 934
Upper Level Sq. Ft.: 1,108
Bedrooms: 3
Bathrooms: 2½
Foundation: Full basement
Materials List Available: Yes
Price Category: G

The second-floor balcony and angled tower are only two of the many design elements you'll love in this beautiful home.

Features:

• Family Room: Corner windows and sliding glass doors to the backyard let natural light pour into this spacious, open area.

• Living Room: Decorate around the deep bay to separate it from the adjacent dining area.

• Dining Room: Large windows and French doors to the kitchen are highlights here.

• Kitchen: The U-shaped counter aids efficiency, as does the handy lunch counter.

• Master Suite: From the sitting area in the bay to the walk-in closet and bath with tub and shower, this suite will pamper you.

• Balcony: Set a row of potted plants and a table and chairs on this perch above the street.

Main Level Floor Plan

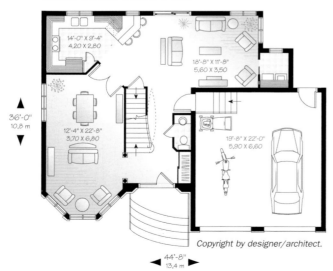

14'-0" X 9'-4"
4,20 X 2,80

18'-8" X 11'-8"
5,60 X 3,50

36'-0"
10,8 m

12'-4" X 22'-8"
3,70 X 6,80

19'-8" X 22'-0"
5,90 X 6,60

Copyright by designer/architect.

44'-8"
13,4 m

Upper Level Floor Plan

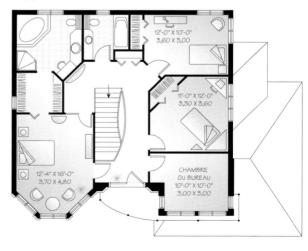

12'-0" X 10'-0"
3,60 X 3,00

11'-0" X 12'-0"
3,30 X 3,60

12'-4" X 16'-0"
3,70 X 4,80

CHAMBRE
OU BUREAU
10'-0" X 10'-0"
3,00 X 3,00

Plan #161095

Dimensions: 59' W x 49'8" D
Levels: 1
Square Footage: 3,620
Main Level Sq. Ft.: 2,068
Basement Level Sq. Ft.: 1,552
Bedrooms: 3
Bathrooms: 3
Foundation: Walkout basement
Material List Available: Yes
Price Category: H

CAD FILE AVAILABLE

Images provided by designer/architect.

This home, as shown in the photograph, may differ from the actual blueprints. For more detailed information, please check the floor plans carefully.

This elegant ranch design has everything your family could want in a home.

Features:

• Dining Room: This column-accented formal area has a sloped ceiling and is open to the great room.

• Great Room: Featuring a cozy fireplace, this large gathering area offers a view of the backyard.

• Kitchen: This fully equipped island kitchen has everything the chef in the family could want.

• Master Suite: Located on the main level for privacy, this suite has a sloped ceiling in the sleeping area. The master bath boasts a whirlpool tub, a walk-in closet, and dual vanities.

Main Level Floor Plan

Rear View

Lower Level Floor Plan

Copyright by designer/architect.

Plan #131026

Dimensions: 55'10" W x 41' D
Levels: 2
Square Footage: 2,796
Main Level Sq. Ft.: 1,481
Upper level Sq. Ft.: 1,315
Bedrooms: 4
Bathrooms: 2½
Foundation: Crawl space or slab; basement for fee
Materials List Available: Yes
Price Category: G

Images provided by designer/architect.

Handsome half rounds add to curb appeal.

Features:

- Ceiling Height: 8 ft.

- Library: This room features a 10-ft. ceiling with a bright bay window.

- Family Room: A 10-ft. ceiling adds to the spacious feeling of this room, while the fireplace gives it an intimate feeling. Sliding glass doors at the rear of the room open to the backyard.

- Dining Room: This formal room adjoins the living room, allowing guests and family to flow between the rooms, and it opens to the backyard through sliding glass doors.

- Breakfast Room: Turrets add a Victorian feeling to this room, which is just off the kitchen and overlooks the front porch.

- Master Suite: Privacy is assured in this suite, which is separated from the main part of the house. A separate toilet room and large walk-in closet add convenience to its beauty.

Master Bathroom

Family Room

Rear
Elevation

Upper Level Floor Plan

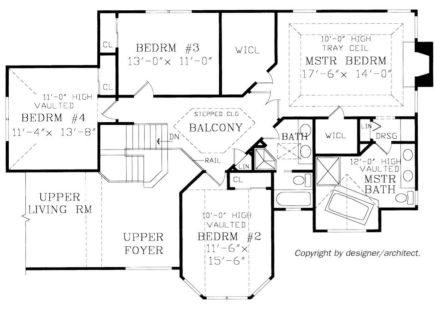

BEDRM #3
13'-0"× 11'-0"

CL

CL

WICL

10'-0" HIGH
TRAY CEIL
MSTR BEDRM
17'-6"× 14'-0"

11'-0" HIGH
VAULTED
BEDRM #4
11'-4"× 13'-8"

STEPPED CLG
BALCONY

DN

RAIL

BATH

WICL

LIN

DRSG

LIN

CL

12'-0" HIGH
VAULTED
MSTR
BATH

UPPER
LIVING RM

UPPER
FOYER

10'-0" HIGH
VAULTED
BEDRM #2
11'-6"×
15'-6"

Copyright by designer/architect.

Main Level Floor Plan

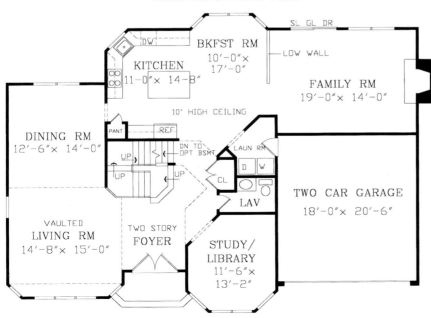

SL GL DR

BKFST RM
10'-0"×
17'-0"

LOW WALL

DW

KITCHEN
11'-0"× 14'-8"

FAMILY RM
19'-0"× 14'-0"

10' HIGH CEILING

DINING RM
12'-6"× 14'-0"

PANT

REF

DN TO
OPT BSMT

LAUN RM

UP

UP

UP

D W

CL

LAV

TWO CAR GARAGE
18'-0"× 20'-6"

VAULTED
LIVING RM
14'-8"× 15'-0"

TWO STORY
FOYER

STUDY/
LIBRARY
11'-6"×
13'-2"

Plan #121024

Dimensions: 60' W x 58' D
Levels: 2
Square Footage: 3,057
Main Level Sq. Ft.: 1,631
Second Level Sq. Ft.: 1,426
Bedrooms: 4
Bathrooms: 2½
Foundation: Basement
Materials List Available: Yes
Price Category: G

Images provided by designer/architect.

This distinctive home offers plenty of space and is designed for gracious and convenient living.

Features:

• Ceiling Height: 8 ft. unless otherwise noted.

• Foyer: A curved staricase in this elegant entry will greet your guests.

• Living Room: This room invites you with a volume ceiling flanked by transom-topped windows that flood the room with sunlight.

• Screened Veranda: On warm summer nights, throw open the French doors in the living room and enjoy a breeze on the huge screened veranda.

• Dining Room: This distinctive room is overlooked by the veranda.

• Family Room: At the back of the home is this comfortable family retreat with its soaring cathedral ceiling and handsome fireplace flanked by bookcases.

• Master Suite: This bayed bedroom features a 10-ft. vaullted ceiling.

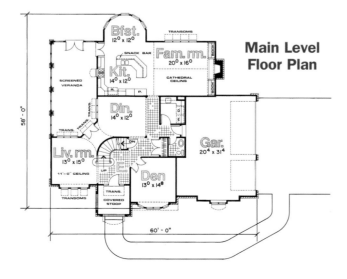

Main Level Floor Plan

Upper Level Floor Plan

Copyright by designer/architect.

Plan #401015

Dimensions: 56' W x 50'4" D

Levels: 2

Square Footage: 2,618

Main Level Sq. Ft.: 1,464

Upper Level Sq. Ft.: 1,154

Bedrooms: 3

Bathrooms: 3

Foundation: Basement

Materials List Available: Yes

Price Category: F

Images provided by designer/architect.

High vaulted ceilings and floor-to-ceiling windows enhance the spaciousness of this home. Decorative columns separate the living room from the tray-ceiling dining room.

Features:

- Kitchen: This gourmet kitchen offers a center food-preparation island, a pantry, and a pass-through to the family room and breakfast bay.

- Family Room: This spacious room boasts a fireplace and vaulted ceiling open to the second-level hallway.

- Den: This room has a wall closet and private access to a full bath. It can be used as extra guest space if needed.

- Master Suite: Located on the second floor, this area holds a bay-windowed sitting area, a walk-in closet, and a bath with a whirlpool tub and separate shower.

- Bedrooms: Family bedrooms are at the other end of the hall upstairs and share a full bath.

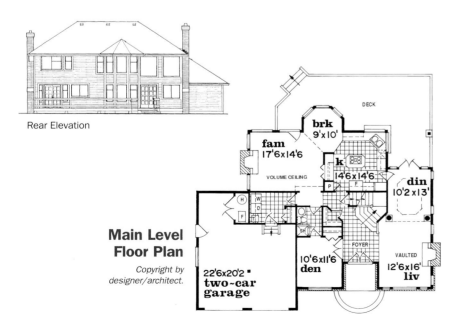

Rear Elevation

Main Level Floor Plan

Copyright by designer/architect.

Upper Level Floor Plan

Plan #161018

Dimensions: 74'4" W x 69'11" D
Levels: 2
Square Footage: 2,816
+ 325 Sq. Ft. bonus room
Main Level Sq. Ft.: 2,231
Upper Level Sq. Ft.: 624
Bedrooms: 3
Bathrooms: 2 full, 2 half
Foundation: Basement
Materials List Available: yes
Price Category: F

If you love classic European designs, look closely at this home with its multiple gables and countless conveniences and luxuries.

Features:

• Foyer: Open to the great room, the 2-story foyer offers a view all the way to the rear windows.

• Great Room: A fireplace makes this room cozy in any kind of weather.

• Kitchen: This large room features an island with a sink, and an angled wall with French doors to the back yard.

• Dining Room: The furniture alcove and raised ceiling make this room both formal and practical.

• Master Suite: You'll love the quiet in the bedroom and the luxuries—a tub, separate shower, and double vanities—in the bath.

• Basement: The door from the basement to the side yard adds convenience to outdoor work.

Main Level Floor Plan

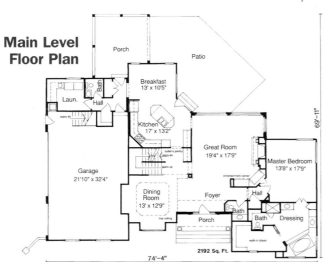

Upper Level Floor Plan

Copyright by designer/architect.

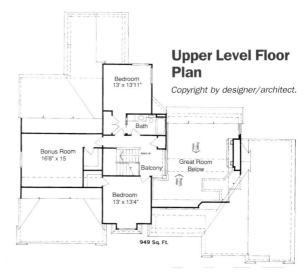

Rear View

Rear Elevation

Foyer/Dining Room

Living Room

Plan #121093

Dimensions: 62' W x 60'8" D
Levels: 2
Square Footage: 2,603
Main Level Sq. Ft.: 1,800
Upper Level Sq. Ft.: 803
Bedrooms: 4
Bathrooms: 3½
Foundation: Basement
Materials List Available: Yes
Price Category: F

Images provided by designer/architect.

If you love family life but also treasure your privacy, you'll appreciate the layout of this home.

Features:

• Entry: This two-story, open area features plant shelves to display a group of lovely specimens.

• Dining Room: Open to the entry, this room features 12-ft. ceilings and corner hutches.

• Den: French doors lead to this quiet room, with its bowed window and spider-beamed ceiling.

• Gathering Room: A three-sided fireplace, shared with both the kitchen and the breakfast area, is the highlight of this room.

• Master Suite: Secluded for privacy, this suite also has a private covered deck where you can sit and recharge at any time of day. A walk-in closet is practical, and a whirlpool tub is pure comfort.

CAD FILE AVAILABLE

Main Level Floor Plan

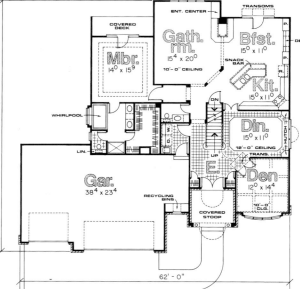

Upper Level Floor Plan

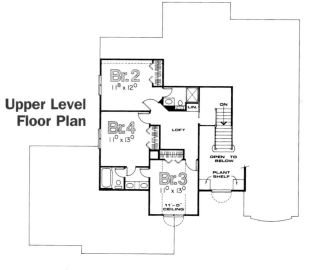

Copyright by designer/architect.

Plan #161094

Dimensions: 68'8" W x 56'8" D
Levels: 2
Square Footage: 3,366
Main Level Sq. Ft.: 1,759
Upper Level Sq. Ft.: 1,607
Bedrooms: 5
Bathrooms: 4
Foundation: Walkout basement
Material List Available: Yes
Price Category: G

This home, as shown in the photograph, may differ from the actual blueprints. For more detailed information, please check the floor plans carefully.

Images provided by designer/architect.

This luxurious two-story home combines a stately exterior style with a large, functional floor plan.

Features:

- **Great Room:** The volume ceiling in this room is decorated with wood beams and reaches a two-story height, while 9-ft. ceiling heights prevail throughout the rest of the first floor.

- **Bright and Open:** Split stairs lead to the second-floor balcony, which offers a dramatic view of the great room. Light radiates through the multiple rear windows

to flood the great room, breakfast area, and kitchen with natural daylight.

- **Master Suite:** Built-in bookshelves flank the entrance to this lavish retreat, with its large sitting area, which is surrounded by windows, and deluxe master bath, which sports spacious closets, dual vanities, and an oversized whirlpool tub.

- **Bedrooms:** Three more bedrooms, each with large closets and private access to the bathroom, complete this family-friendly home.

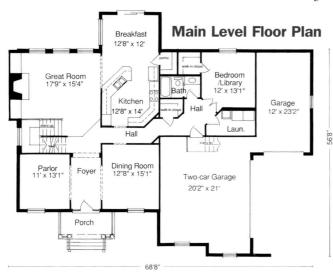

Main Level Floor Plan

Upper Level Floor Plan

Copyright by designer/architect.

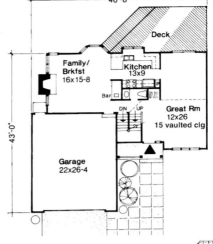

Main Level Floor Plan

Family/Brkfst 16x15-8

Kitchen 13x9

Deck

Bar

Great Rm 12x26 15 vaulted clg

DN UP

Garage 22x26-4

46'-8"

43'-0"

Images provided by designer/architect.

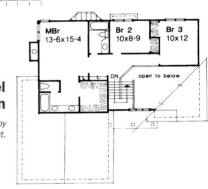

MBr 13-6x15-4

Br 2 10x8-9

Br 3 10x12

DN

open to below

Upper Level Floor Plan

Copyright by designer/architect.

Plan #271010

Dimensions: 46'8" W x 43' D

Levels: 2

Square Footage: 1,724

Main Level Sq. Ft.: 922

Upper Level Sq. Ft.: 802

Bedrooms: 3

Bathrooms: 2½

Foundation: Basement

Materials List Available: Yes

Price Category: C

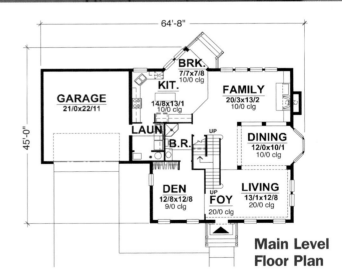

64'-8"

45'-0"

GARAGE 21/0x22/11

KIT. 14/8x13/1 10/0 clg

BRK. 7/7x7/8 10/0 clg

FAMILY 20/3x13/2 10/0 clg

LAUN

B.R.

UP

DINING 12/0x10/1 10/0 clg

DEN 12/8x12/8 9/0 clg

UP FOY 20/0 clg

LIVING 13/1x12/8 20/0 clg

Main Level Floor Plan

Images provided by designer/architect.

BR. 2 11/0x11/10

M. BA.

M. BR. 13/2x16/4

B.R.

DN

W.I.C.

BR. 3 13/0x13/10

OPEN TO BELOW

Upper Level Floor Plan

Copyright by designer/architect.

Plan #271305

Dimensions: 64'8" W x 45' D

Levels: 2

Square Footage: 2,526

Main Level Sq. Ft.: 1,555

Upper Level Sq. Ft.: 971

Bedrooms: 3

Bathrooms: 3

Foundation: Slab

Material List Available: Yes

Price Category: E

Upper Level Floor Plan

Main Level Floor Plan

Copyright by designer/architect.

Plan #181101

Dimensions: 58' W x 43' D

Levels: 2

Square Footage: 1,936

Main Level Sq. Ft.: 1,044

Second Level Sq. Ft.: 892

Bedrooms: 3

Bathrooms: 2½

Foundation: Basement

Materials List Available: Yes

Price Category: F

Images provided by designer/architect.

CAD FILE AVAILABLE · CAD

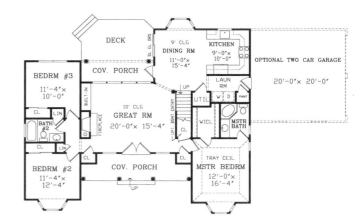

Copyright by designer/architect.

Plan #131014

Dimensions: 48' W x 43'4" D

Levels: 1

Square Footage: 1,380

Bedrooms: 3

Bathrooms: 2

Foundation: Crawl space or slab; basement or walkout for fee

Materials List Available: Yes

Price Category: C

Images provided by designer/architect.

CAD FILE AVAILABLE · CAD

Rear Elevation

Bonus Room

FUTURE EXPANSION
20'-0" x 15'-4"

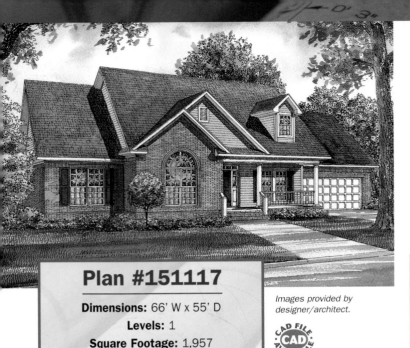

Copyright by designer/architect.

Images provided by designer/architect.

CAD FILE AVAILABLE

Plan #151117

Dimensions: 66' W x 55' D

Levels: 1

Square Footage: 1,957

Bedrooms: 3

Bathrooms: 3

Foundation: Crawl space or slab; basement for fee

CompleteCost List Available: Yes

Price Category: D

Bonus Area

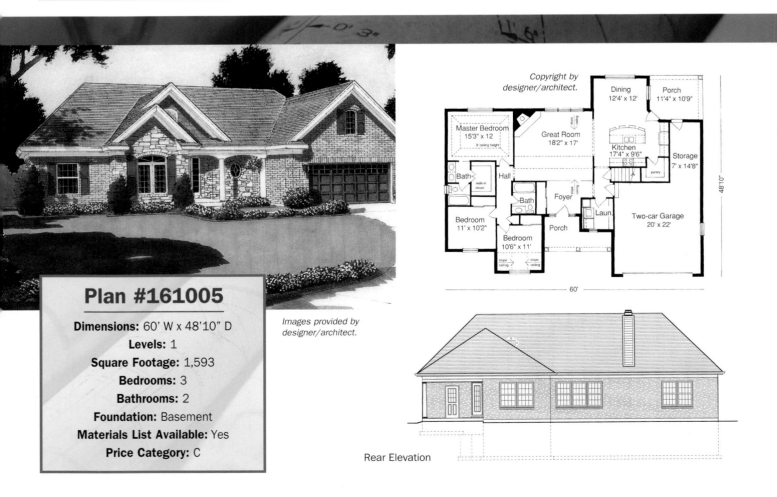

Copyright by designer/architect.

Images provided by designer/architect.

Plan #161005

Dimensions: 60' W x 48'10" D

Levels: 1

Square Footage: 1,593

Bedrooms: 3

Bathrooms: 2

Foundation: Basement

Materials List Available: Yes

Price Category: C

Rear Elevation

Plan #151168

Dimensions: 66' W x 65'2" D

Levels: 1

Square Footage: 2,261

Bedrooms: 4

Bathrooms: 2½

Foundation: Crawl space, slab, basement, or daylight basement

CompleteCost List Available: Yes

Price Category: E

Images provided by designer/architect.

Copyright by designer/architect.

Bonus Room

Plan #151853

Dimensions: 73'2" W x 86'8" D

Levels: 1.5

Square Footage: 2,885

Main Level Sq. Ft.: 2,599

Upper Level Sq. Ft.: 286

Bedrooms: 4

Bathrooms: 3½

Foundation: Crawl space, slab

CompleteCost List Available: Yes

Price Category: F

Images provided by designer/architect.

Main Level Floor Plan

Upper Level Floor Plan

Copyright by designer/architect.

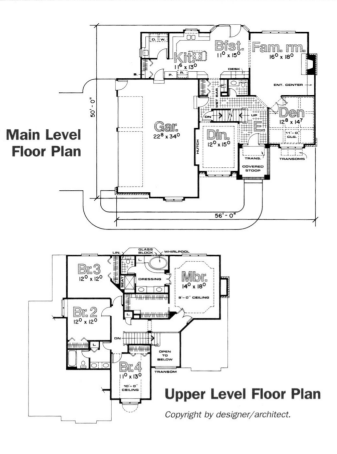

Main Level Floor Plan

Images provided by designer/architect.

This home, as shown in the photograph, may differ from the actual blueprints. For more detailed information, please check the floor plans carefully.

Upper Level Floor Plan

Copyright by designer/architect.

Plan #121091

Dimensions: 56' W x 50' D
Levels: 2
Square Footage: 2,689
Main Level Sq. Ft.: 1,415
Upper Level Sq. Ft.: 1,274
Bedrooms: 4
Bathrooms: 2½
Foundation: Basement
Materials List Available: Yes
Price Category: F

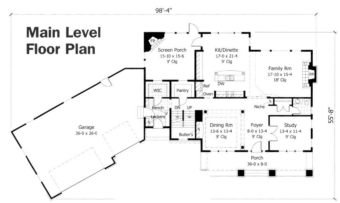

Main Level Floor Plan

Images provided by designer/architect.

Upper Level Floor Plan

Plan #481021

Dimensions: 98'4" W x 55'8" D
Levels: 2
Square Footage: 3,289
Main Level Sq. Ft.: 1,680
Upper Level Sq. Ft.: 1,609
Bedrooms: 3
Bathrooms: 2½
Foundation: Walkout
Material List Available: Yes
Price Category: G

Copyright by designer/architect.

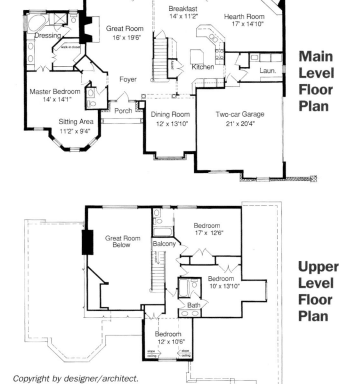

Main Level Floor Plan

Great Room 16' x 19'6"
Breakfast 14' x 11'2"
Hearth Room 17' x 14'10"
Dressing
walk-in closet
Foyer
Kitchen
Laun.
Master Bedroom 14' x 14'1"
Sitting Area 11'2" x 9'4"
Porch
Dining Room 12' x 13'10"
Two-car Garage 21' x 20'4"

Upper Level Floor Plan

Great Room Below
Balcony
Bedroom 17' x 12'6"
Bedroom 10' x 13'10"
Bath
Bedroom 12' x 10'6"
slope ceiling   slope ceiling

Images provided by designer/architect.

This home, as shown in the photograph, may differ from the actual blueprints. For more detailed information, please check the floor plans carefully.

CAD FILE AVAILABLE

Copyright by designer/architect.

Plan #161025

Dimensions: 63'4" W x 48' D
Levels: 2
Square Footage: 2,738
Main Level Sq. Ft.: 1,915
Upper Level Sq. Ft.: 823
Bedrooms: 4
Bathrooms: 3½
Foundation: Basement
Materials List Available: Yes
Price Category: F

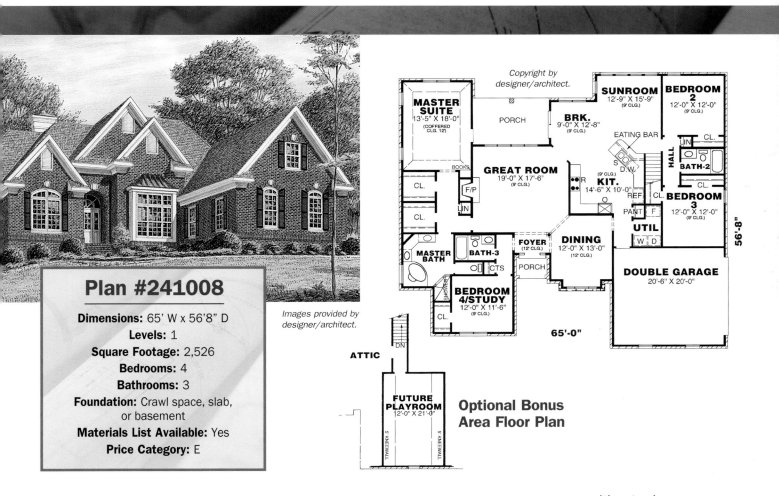

Copyright by designer/architect.

MASTER SUITE 13'-5" X 18'-0" (COFFERED CLG. 12)
PORCH
BRK. 9'-0" X 12'-8" (9' CLG.)
SUNROOM 12'-9" X 15'-9" (9' CLG.)
BEDROOM 2 12'-0" X 12'-0" (9' CLG.)
BOOKS
EATING BAR
GREAT ROOM 19'-0" X 17'-6" (9' CLG.)
F/P
KIT. 14'-6" X 10'-0" (9' CLG.)
HALL
LIN   CL.
BATH-2
CL.
LIN
REF   CL.
PANT   F
BEDROOM 3 12'-0" X 12'-0" (9' CLG.)
MASTER BATH
BATH-3
CTS
FOYER (12' CLG.)
DINING 12'-0" X 13'-0" (12' CLG.)
UTIL
W   D
PORCH
BEDROOM 4/STUDY 12'-0" X 11'-6" (9' CLG.)
CL.
DOUBLE GARAGE 20'-6" X 20'-0"
56'-8"
65'-0"

Images provided by designer/architect.

Plan #241008

Dimensions: 65' W x 56'8" D
Levels: 1
Square Footage: 2,526
Bedrooms: 4
Bathrooms: 3
Foundation: Crawl space, slab, or basement
Materials List Available: Yes
Price Category: E

ATTIC
DN
FUTURE PLAYROOM 12'-0" X 21'-0"
5 KNEEWALL   5 KNEEWALL

Optional Bonus Area Floor Plan

Plan #121114

Dimensions: 64' W x 52' D
Levels: 1.5
Square Footage: 2,115
Main Level Sq. Ft.: 1,505
Upper Level Sq. Ft.: 610
Bedrooms: 4
Bathrooms: 2½
Foundation: Basement; crawl space for fee
Materials List Available: Yes
Price Category: D

This contemporary home is not only beautifully designed on the outside; it has everything you need on the inside. It will be the envy of the neighborhood.

CAD FILE AVAILABLE

Features:

- **Great Room:** The cathedral ceiling and cozy fireplace strike a balance that creates the perfect gathering place for family and friends. An abundance of space allows you to tailor this room to your needs.

- **Kitchen/Breakfast Room:** This combined area features a flood of natural light, workspace to spare, an island with a snack bar, and a door that opens to the backyard, creating an ideal space for outdoor meals and gatherings.

- **Dining Room:** A triplet of windows projecting onto the covered front porch creates a warm atmosphere for formal dining.

- **Master Bedroom:** Away from the busy areas of the home, this master suite is ideal for shedding your daily cares and relaxing in a romantic atmosphere. It includes a full master bath with skylight, his and her sinks, a stall shower, a whirlpool tub, and a walk-in closet.

- **Second Floor:** Three more bedrooms and the second full bathroom upstairs give you plenty of room for a large family. Or if you only need two extra rooms, use the fourth bedroom as a study or entertainment area for the kids.

Upper Level Floor Plan

Copyright by designer/architect.

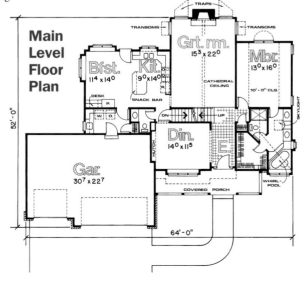

Main Level Floor Plan

Plan #121086

Dimensions: 55'4" W x 37'8" D

Levels: 2

Square Footage: 1,998

Main Level Sq. Ft.: 1,093

Upper Level Sq. Ft.: 905

Bedrooms: 3

Bathrooms: 2½

Foundation: Basement

Materials List Available: Yes

Price Category: D

Images provided by designer/architect.

You'll love the open design of this comfortable home if sunny, bright rooms make you happy.

Features:

• Entry: Walk into this two-story entry, and you're sure to admire the open staircase and balcony from the upper level.

• Dining Room: To the left of the entry, you'll see this dining room, with its special ceiling detail and built-in display cabinet.

• Living Room: Located immediately to the right, this living room features a charming bay window.

• Family Room: French doors from the living room open into this sunny space, where a handsome fireplace takes center stage.

• Kitchen: Combined with the breakfast area, this kitchen features an island cooktop, a large pantry, and a built-in desk.

Upper Level Floor Plan

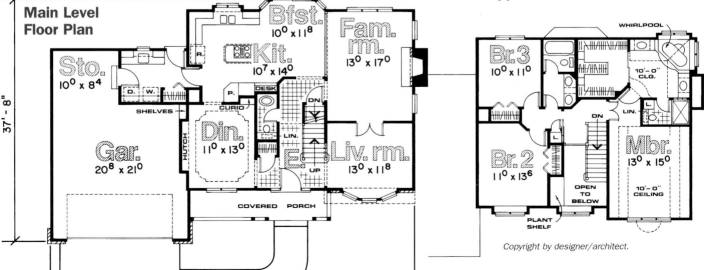

Copyright by designer/architect.

Plan #131007

Dimensions: 59'10" W x 47'8" D
Levels: 1
Square Footage: 1,595
Bedrooms: 3
Bathrooms: 2
Foundation: Crawl space or slab; basement or walkout for fee
Materials List Available: Yes
Price Category: D

Images provided by designer/architect.

Imagine living in this home, with its traditional country comfort and individual brand of charm.

Features:

- Exterior elements: The mixture of a front porch with a cameo front door, decorative posts, bay windows, and dormers will delight you.

- Great Room: A tray ceiling gives distinction to this large room, and a wet bar eases entertaining.

- Screened Porch: At dusk and dawn, this porch is sure to be your favorite outdoor spot.

- Kitchen: Eat any meal in this large kitchen for a touch of homey charm.

- Dining Room: Perfect for hosting a formal dinner, this bayed dining room can increase your enjoyment of simple family meals.

- Master Bedroom: For the sake of privacy, this room is somewhat secluded. Decorate to emphasize the elegant tray ceiling.

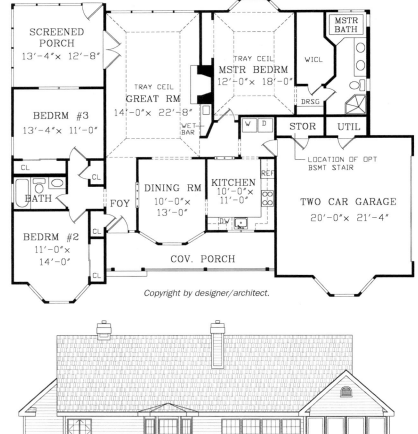

Copyright by designer/architect.

Rear Elevation

Alternate Front View

Foyer / Dining Room

Great Room

SMARTtip

Add the Extras

Simple or plain, it's the little conveniences and miscellaneous touches that push the dining experience to perfection. Here are some extra things to think about.

- You can never have too many serving trays when you entertain outside. For carrying food or drinks from the kitchen or the grill, trays are indispensable.

- A serving cart on wheels makes a perfect movable outdoor bar and provides an additional serving surface. Look for one at yard sales or buy one new.

- Chances are you won't have a sideboard, but a few small tables to hold excess items are great substitutes for one. They're also easier to position in the different places where you need them.

- For cooler weather or even a summer's evening with a bit of nip in the air, nothing beats an outdoor fireplace for comfort. You could build one into the house, but various types of stand-alone units are sold in home centers. To add a Southwest ambiance, consider a chiminea, a clay fireplace. Try burning some piñon pine, and you'll feel as if you're in Santa Fe. Be sure to follow manufacturers' instructions when using these fireplaces. You might also have to store them during the winter.

- Pots of fragrant plants—lavender, scented geraniums, flowering tobacco, or jasmine—provide a sensual aroma. Flowers such as roses climbing up an arbor or trellis are beautiful, evoke a romantic feeling, and lend a delicate scent to the atmosphere as well.

Nothing adds romance and intrigue to an evening soiree as candlelight does. Include just a few candles for an intimate dinner. Use more for a larger gathering, placing one or more on each table. Scatter luminaries around the yard. As the beautiful evening dusk begins, light candles, a few at a time, so your eyes can adjust to the dimming light. Not only do the candles illuminate the night in a magical way but they can also keep bugs at bay.

Plan #151118

Dimensions: 54'2" W x 73'6" D
Levels: 2
Square Footage: 2,784
Main Level Sq. Ft.: 1,895
Upper Level Sq. Ft.: 889
Bedrooms: 4
Bathrooms: 2½
Foundation: Crawl space, slab, or basement
CompleteCost List Available: Yes
Price Category: F

Images provided by designer/architect.

Upper Level Floor Plan

Main Level Floor Plan

Copyright by designer/architect.

Plan #311002

Dimensions: 56'6" W x 82' D
Levels: 1
Square Footage: 2,402
Bedrooms: 4
Bathrooms: 2½
Foundation: Crawl space, slab
Materials List Available: Yes
Price Category: F

Images provided by designer/architect.

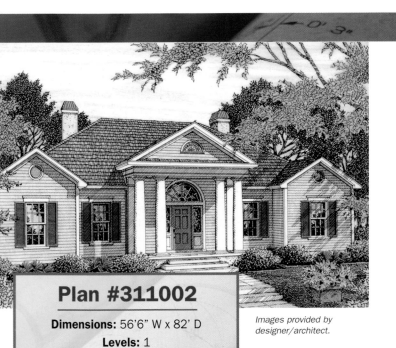

Bonus Area

Main Level Floor Plan

Copyright by designer/architect.

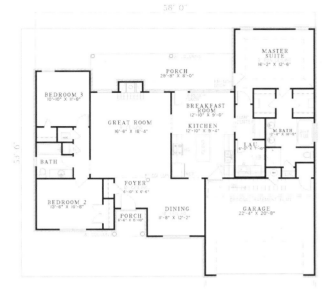

Copyright by designer/architect.

Plan #151173

Dimensions: 58' W x 53'6" D
Levels: 1
Square Footage: 1,739
Bedrooms: 3
Bathrooms: 2
Foundation: Crawl space, slab, basement, or walkout
CompleteCost List Available: Yes
Price Category: C

Images provided by designer/architect.

CAD FILE AVAILABLE

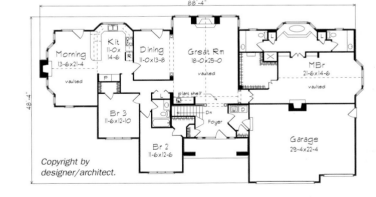

Copyright by designer/architect.

Plan #321018

Dimensions: 88'4" W x 48'4" D
Levels: 1
Square Footage: 2,523
Bedrooms: 3
Bathrooms: 2
Foundation: Basement
Materials List Available: Yes
Price Category: E

Images provided by designer/architect.

CAD FILE AVAILABLE

SMARTtip

Tiebacks

You don't have to limit yourself to tiebacks made from matching or contrasting fabric. Achieve creative custom looks by making tiebacks from unexpected items. Some materials to consider are old cotton bandannas or silk scarves, strings of beads, lengths of leather, or old belts and chains.

Plan #131023

Dimensions: 78'8" W x 36'2" D
Levels: 2
Square Footage: 2,460
Main Level Sq. Ft.: 1,377
Upper Level Sq. Ft.: 1,083
Bedrooms: 4
Bathrooms: 3½
Foundation: Crawl space or slab; basement for fee
Materials List Available: Yes
Price Category: F

Images provided by designer/architect.

You'll love the modern floor plan inside this traditional two-story home, with its attractive facade.

Features:

- Ceiling Height: 8 ft.

- Living Room: The windows on three sides of this room make it bright and sunny. Choose the optional fireplace for cozy winter days and the wet bar for elegant entertaining.

- Family Room: Overlooking the rear deck, this spacious family room features a fireplace and a skylight.

- Dining Room: The convenient placement of this large room lets guests flow into it from the living room and allows easy to access from the kitchen.

- Kitchen: The island cooktop and built-in desk make this space both modern and practical.

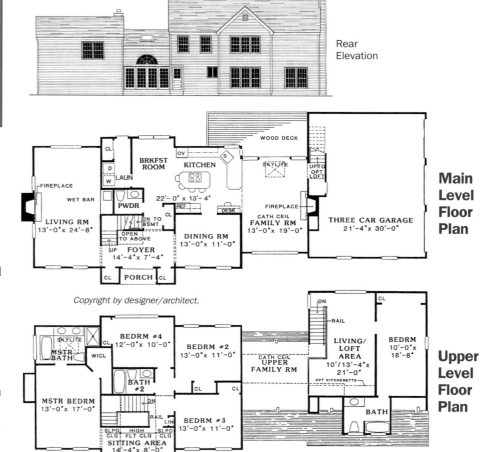

Rear Elevation

Main Level Floor Plan

Copyright by designer/architect.

Upper Level Floor Plan

Plan #271001

Dimensions: 52'8" W x 35'4" D
Levels: 1
Square Footage: 1,400
Bedrooms: 3
Bathrooms: 2
Foundation: Basement
Materials List Available: Yes
Price Category: B

Images provided by designer/architect.

This contemporary design builds on the basics, creating a comfortable home that offers possibilities for entertaining or quiet downtime.

Features:

• Great room: The heart of the home, this massive gathering room features a handsome fireplace and a handy wet bar, and flows into the dining space. Sliding glass doors between the two spaces lead to a deck.

• Kitchen/Breakfast: This combination space uses available space efficiently and comfortably.

• Master Suite: The inviting master bedroom includes a private bath.

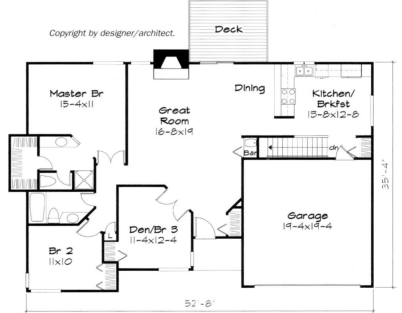

Copyright by designer/architect.

SMARTtip

Candid Camera for Your Landscaping

To see your home and yard as others see them, take some camera shots. Seeing your house and landscaping on film will create an opportunity for objectivity. Problems will become more obvious, and you will then be better able to prioritize your home improvements, as well as your landscaping plan.

Plan #321001

Dimensions: 83' W x 42' D

Levels: 1

Square Footage: 1,721

Bedrooms: 3

Bathrooms: 2

Foundation: Crawl space, slab, or basement

Materials List Available: Yes

Price Category: E

You'll love the atrium which creates a warm, naturally lit space inside this gracious home, as well as the roof dormers that give the house wonderful curb appeal from the outside.

Features:

- Great Room: Bathed in light from the atrium window wall, this room, with its vaulted ceiling, will be the hub of your family life.

- Dining Room: This room also has a vaulted ceiling and is lit by the atrium, but you can draw drapes at night to create a cozy, warm feeling.

- Kitchen: Designed for functionality, this step-saving kitchen is easy to organize and makes cooking a pleasure.

- Breakfast Room: For convenience, this room is located between the kitchen and the rear covered porch.

- Master Suite: Retire with pleasure to this lovely retreat, with its luxurious bath.

Rear View

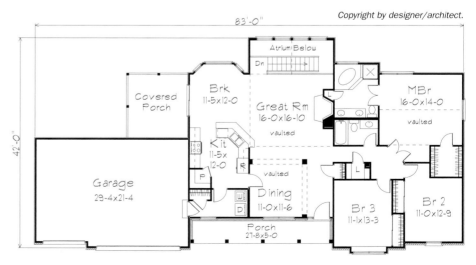

Plan #121072

Dimensions: 64' W x 53'4"D

Levels: 2

Square Footage: 3,031

Main Level Sq. Ft.: 1,640

Upper Level Sq. Ft.: 1,391

Bedrooms: 4

Bathrooms: 2½

Foundation: Basement; slab for fee

Materials List Available: Yes

Price Category: G

If you're looking for a home with well-designed rooms and interesting architectural innovations, this could be your heart's desire.

Features:

- **Foyer:** This foyer has an impressive two-story ceiling and is lit by the arched transom and sidelights at the entryway.

- **Living Room:** Just off the foyer, this room has a 12-ft. angled ceiling. Decorate to emphasize the arched window here.

- **Den:** French doors open to the den, where a spider-beamed ceiling sets an elegant tone.

- **Kitchen:** This well-designed kitchen is sure to be the delight of every cook in the family.

- **Master Suite:** French doors open into this suite, with built-in dressers tucked into a huge closet and a bath with a whirlpool tub and two vanities.

Images provided by designer/architect.

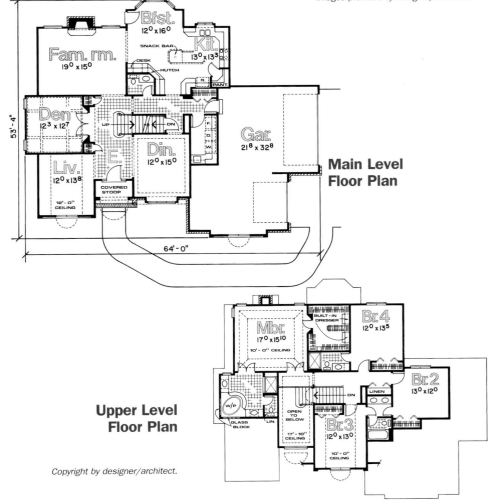

Main Level Floor Plan

Upper Level Floor Plan

Copyright by designer/architect.

57'-6" OVERALL
(77'-10" W/ OPT. GARAGE)

OPTIONAL
TWO CAR GARAGE
20'-0" x 20'-0"

42'-4" OVERALL
(54'-0" W/ OPT. GARAGE)

Plan #131044

Dimensions: 65'4" W x 45'10" D

Levels: 1

Square Footage: 1,892

Bedrooms: 3

Bathrooms: 2½

Foundation: Crawl space or slab; basement for fee

Materials List Available: Yes

Price Category: E

Images provided by designer/ architect.

Rear Elevation

Bonus Area

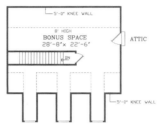

BONUS SPACE
28'-8" x 22'-6"

ATTIC

Copyright by designer/ architect.

51'-6"

49'-10"

GRILLING PORCH
10'-8" X 8'-2"

DINING ROOM
11'-0" X 9'-6"

COVERED PORCH
13'-2" X 9'-2"

M. BATH
15'-8" X 10'-8"

BRKFAST ROOM
10'-0" X 8'-0"

KITCHEN
15'-2" X 11'-0"

GREAT ROOM
13'-6" X 19'-8"

MASTER SUITE
15'-8" X 12'-0"

BEDROOM 2
10'-2" X 10'-8"

BEDROOM 3 / STUDY
10'-0" X 10'-8"

FOYER

GARAGE
20'-10" X 20'-0"

COVERED PORCH
16'-6" X 5'-0"

Plan #151169

Dimensions: 51'6" W x 49'10" D

Levels: 1

Square Footage: 1,525

Bedrooms: 3

Bathrooms: 2

Foundation: Crawl space of slab; basement or walkout for fee

CompleteCost List Available: Yes

Price Category: C

Images provided by designer/architect.

Copyright by designer/architect.

Rear Elevation

Plan #151528

Dimensions: 41'4" W x 84'2" D
Levels: 1
Square Footage: 1,747
Bedrooms: 2
Bathrooms: 2
Foundation: Crawl space or slab
CompleteCost List Available: Yes
Price Category: C

Images provided by designer/architect.

Copyright by designer/architect.

Front View

Plan #461168

Dimensions: 58' W x 35'6" D
Levels: 2
Square Footage: 1,756
Main Level Sq. Ft.: 874
Upper Level Sq. Ft.: 882
Bedrooms: 3
Bathrooms: 2½
Foundation: Crawl space, slab
Material List Available: Yes
Price Category: C

Images provided by designer/architect.

Main Level Floor Plan

Upper Level Floor Plan

Copyright by designer/architect.

Plan #121163

Dimensions: 65'10" W x 75'6" D
Levels: 1
Square Footage: 2,679
Bedrooms: 4
Bathrooms: 3
Foundation: Slab; basement for fee
Material List Available: Yes
Price Category: F

Large rooms give this home a spacious feel in a modest footprint.

Features:

• Family Room: This area is the central gathering place in the home. The windows to the rear fill the area with natural light. The fireplace take the chill off on cool winter nights.

• Kitchen: This peninsula kitchen with raised bar is open into the family room and the breakfast area. The built-in pantry is a welcomed storage area for today's family.

• Master Suite: This secluded area features large windows with a view of the backyard. The master bath boasts a large walk-in closet, his and her vanities and a compartmentalized lavatory area.

• Secondary Bedrooms: Bedroom 2 has its own access to the main bathroom, while bedrooms 3 and 4 share a Jack-and-Jill bathroom. All bedrooms feature walk-in closets.

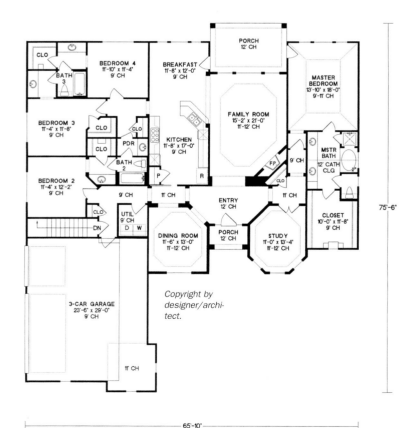

Copyright by designer/architect.

Plan #321005

Dimensions: 69' W x 53'8" D
Levels: 1
Square Footage: 2,483
Bedrooms: 3
Bathrooms: 2
Foundation: Basement
Materials List Available: Yes
Price Category: F

You'll love the grand feeling of this home, which combines with the very practical features that make living in it a pleasure.

Features:

- **Porch:** The open brick arches and Palladian door set the tone for this magnificent home.

- **Great Room:** An alcove for the entertainment center and vaulted ceiling show the care that went into designing this room.

- **Dining Room:** A tray ceiling sets off the formality of this large room.

- **Kitchen:** The layout in this room is designed to make your work patterns more efficient and to save you steps and time.

- **Study:** This quiet room can be a wonderful refuge, or you can use it for a fourth bedroom if you wish.

- **Master Suite:** Made for relaxing at the end of the day, this suite will pamper you with luxuries.

Copyright by designer/architect.

SMARTtip

Art in Pools

The tiled walls and floor of a pool make great canvases for art, so incorporate a serious or whimsical design. Also, make the stairs wide and shallow to form a wading area for kids.

Plan #151232

Dimensions: 79'6" W x 71'4" D
Levels: 1.5
Square Footage: 3,901
Main Level Sq. Ft.: 3,185
Upper Level Sq. Ft.: 716
Bedrooms: 3
Bathrooms: 4
Foundation: Crawl space or slab
CompleteCost List Available: Yes
Price Category: H

This elegant brick home has something for everyone

Features:

- **Great Room:** This large gathering area has a fireplace and access to the rear grilling porch.

- **Hearth Room:** Relaxing and casual, this cozy area has a fireplace and is open to the kitchen.

- **Kitchen:** This large island kitchen has a built-in pantry and is open to the breakfast nook.

- **Master Suite:** A private bathroom with a corner whirlpool tub and a large walk-in closet turn this area into a spacious retreat.

- **Bonus Room:** This large space located upstairs near the two secondary bedrooms can be turned into a media room.

Images provided by designer/architect.

Main Level Floor Plan

Copyright by designer/architect.

Upper Level Floor Plan

Foyer

Great Room

Living Room

Great Room

Kitchen

Kitchen

Master Bedroom

Master Bath

Plan #151170

Dimensions: 57' W x 64'4" D

Levels: 1

Square Footage: 1,965

Bedrooms: 4

Bathrooms: 2

Foundation: Crawl space, slab; basement or daylight basement for fee

CompleteCost List Available: Yes

Price Category: E

Images provided by designer/architect.

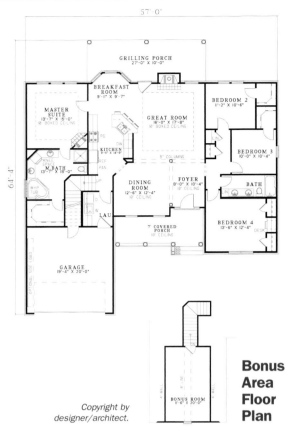

Copyright by designer/architect.

Bonus Area Floor Plan

Plan #311001

Dimensions: 65'11" W x 67'9" D

Levels: 1

Square Footage: 2,085

Bedrooms: 3

Bathrooms: 2½

Foundation: Crawl space, slab, or basement

Materials List Available: Yes

Price Category: E

Images provided by designer/architect.

Rear View

designer/

Optional Bonus Area

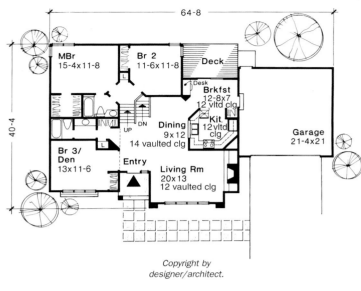

64-8

40-4

MBr
15-4x11-8

Br 2
11-6x11-8

Deck

Desk

Brkfst
12-8x7
12 vltd clg

Kit
12 vltd
clg

Dining
9x12
14 vaulted clg

DN

UP

Br 3/
Den
13x11-6

Entry

Living Rm
20x13
12 vaulted clg

Garage
21-4x21

Images provided by designer/architect.

Copyright by designer/architect.

Plan #271003

Dimensions: 64'8" W x 40'4" D

Levels: 1

Square footage: 1,452

Bedrooms: 3

Bathrooms: 2

Foundation: Full basement

Materials List Available: Yes

Price Category: B

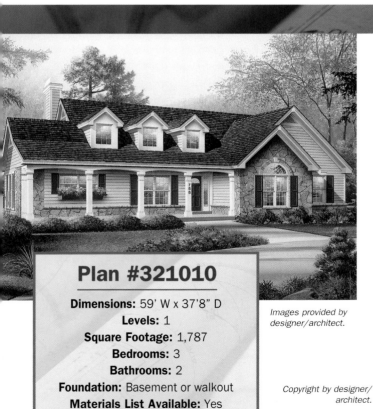

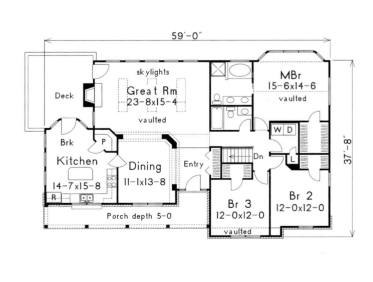

59'-0"

Deck

skylights

Great Rm
23-8x15-4
vaulted

MBr
15-6x14-6
vaulted

37'-8"

Brk

P

Kitchen
14-7x15-8

Dining
11-1x13-8

Entry

Dn

W D

L

R

Br 3
12-0x12-0

Br 2
12-0x12-0

Porch depth 5-0

vaulted

Images provided by designer/architect.

Copyright by designer/architect.

Plan #321010

Dimensions: 59' W x 37'8" D

Levels: 1

Square Footage: 1,787

Bedrooms: 3

Bathrooms: 2

Foundation: Basement or walkout

Materials List Available: Yes

Price Category: C

Plan #391049

Dimensions: 78' W x 52'4" D
Levels: 1
Square Footage: 4,064
Main Level Sq. Ft.: 2,466
Lower Level Sq. Ft.: 1,598
Bedrooms: 4
Bathrooms: 3
Foundation: Basement
Materials List Available: Yes
Price Category: I

Images provided by designer/architect.

This home proves that elegance can be comfortable. No need to sacrifice one for the other. Here, a peaked roofline creates a well-mannered covered front porch and classical columns announce the beauty of the dining room.

Features:

• Living Areas: High windows and a fireplace light up the living room, while an open hearth room shares the glow of a three-sided fireplace with the breakfast area and kitchen.

• Kitchen: To please the cook there's a built-in

kitchen desk, cooking island, food-preparation island, double sinks, and pantries.

• Master Suite: To soothe the busy executive, th[e] first-floor master suite includes a lavish bath and nearby study.

• Recreation: The lower level entertains some b[ig] plans for entertaining--a home theater, wet bar, and large recreation room with a double-sided f[ire]place.

• Bedrooms: Two additional bedrooms with ex[cel]lent closet spaace and a shared full bath keep fa[mily] or guests in stylish comfort.

Living Room

Main Level Floor Plan

Main Level

Lower Level Floor Plan

Copyright by designer/architect.

Plan #221018

Dimensions: 67' W x 53' D
Levels: 1
Square Footage: 2,007
Bedrooms: 3
Bathrooms: 2
Foundation: Basement
Materials List Available: Yes
Price Category: D

Images provided by designer/architect.

You'll love this ranch design, with its traditional stucco facade and interesting roofline.

Features:

- Ceiling Height: 9 ft.

- Great Room: A cathedral ceiling points up the large dimensions of this room, and the handsome fireplace with tall flanking windows lets you decorate for a formal or a casual feeling.

- Dining Room: A tray ceiling imparts elegance to this room, and a butler's pantry just across from the kitchen area lets you serve in style.

- Kitchen: You'll love the extensive counter space in this well-designed kitchen. The adjoining nook is large enough for a full-size dining set and features a door to the outside deck, where you can set up a third dining area.

- Master Suite: Located away from the other bedrooms for privacy, this suite includes a huge walk-in closet, windows overlooking the backyard, and a large bath with a whirlpool tub, standing shower, and dual-sink vanity.

Rear Elevation

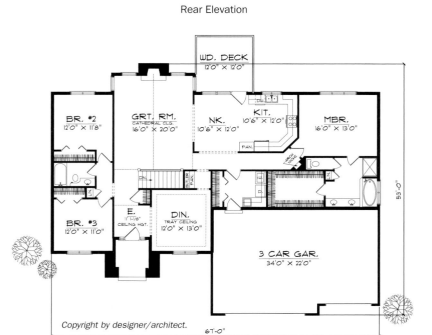

Copyright by designer/architect.

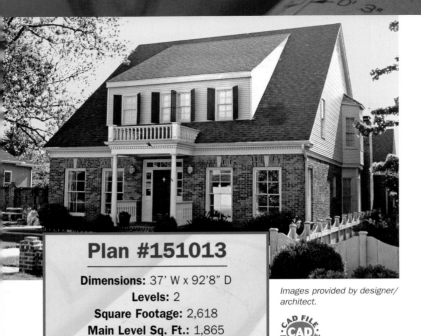

Upper Level Floor Plan

Copyright by designer/architect.

Plan #151013

Dimensions: 37' W x 92'8" D

Levels: 2

Square Footage: 2,618

Main Level Sq. Ft.: 1,865

Upper Level Sq. Ft.: 753

Bedrooms: 3

Bathrooms: 2½

Foundation: Crawl space or slab; basement available for fee

CompleteCost List Available: Yes

Price Category: F

Images provided by designer/architect.

CAD FILE AVAILABLE

Main Level Floor Plan

Upper Level Floor Plan

Copyright by designer/architect.

Plan #271009

Dimensions: 54' W x 36' D

Levels: 2

Square Footage: 1,909

Main Level Sq. Ft.: 994

Upper Level Sq. Ft.: 915

Bedrooms: 4

Bathrooms: 2½

Foundation: Basement

Materials List Available: Yes

Price Category: D

Images provided by designer/architect.

Rear Elevation

Images provided by designer/architect.

Copyright by designer/architect.

Plan #221015

Dimensions: 69'8" W x 46' D

Levels: 1

Square Footage: 1,926

Bedrooms: 3

Bathrooms: 2½

Foundation: Basement; walkout basement for fee

Materials List Available: Yes

Price Category: D

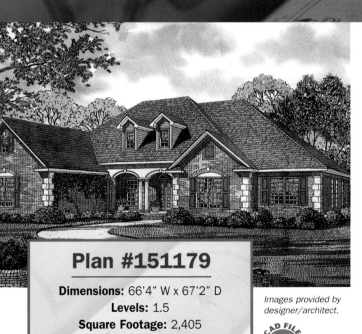

Images provided by designer/architect.

CAD FILE AVAILABLE

Plan #151179

Dimensions: 66'4" W x 67'2" D

Levels: 1.5

Square Footage: 2,405

Opt. Bonus Level Sq. Ft.: 358

Bedrooms: 4

Bathrooms: 3

Foundation: Crawl space, slab; basement or walkout for fee

CompleteCost List Available: Yes

Price Category: E

Copyright by designer/architect.

Bonus Area Floor Plan

Plan #161017

Dimensions: 61' W x 37'6" D
Levels: 2
Square Footage: 2,653
Main Level Sq. Ft.: 1,365
Upper Level Sq. Ft.: 1,288
Bedrooms: 4
Bathrooms: 2½
Foundation: Basement
Materials List Available: Yes
Price Category: F

CAD FILE AVAILABLE • CAD

If a traditional look makes you feel comfortable, you'll love this spacious, family-friendly home.

Features:

• **Family Room:** Accessorize with cozy cushions to make the most of this sunken room. Windows flank the fireplace, adding warm, natural light. Doors leading to the rear deck make this room a family "headquarters."

• **Living and Dining Rooms:** These formal rooms open to each other, so you'll love hosting gatherings in this home.

• **Kitchen:** A handy pantry fits well with the traditional feeling of this home, and an island adds contemporary convenience.

• **Master Suite:** Relax in the whirlpool tub in your bath and enjoy the storage space in the two walk-in closets in the bedroom.

Main Level Floor Plan

Deck

Sunken Family Room 18 x 15-4

Breakfast 9-10 x 13-3

Kitchen 8-10 x 11-11

stairs up

stairs dn

Laun.

Bath

Hall

Two-car Garage 22-4 x 22

Living Room 14-8 x 12-7

Foyer

Dining Room 14-8 x 12-7

Porch

Copyright by designer/ architect.

Upper Level Floor Plan

Bath

Bedroom 12-5 x 10-11

Bedroom 10-10 x 10-11

walk-in closet

walk-in closet

shelves

stairs dn

Bath

sky-light

laun. chute

Balcony

Master Bedroom 14-8 x 16-2

Foyer Below

Bedroom 12-3 x 12-7

plant shelf

Plan #121028

Dimensions: 54'8" W x 42' D
Levels: 2
Square Footage: 2,644
Main Level Sq. Ft.: 1,366
Upper Level Sq. Ft.: 1,278
Bedrooms: 4
Bathrooms: 2½
Foundation: Basement
Materials List Available: Yes
Price Category: F

This home is filled with special touches and amenities that add up to gracious living.

Features:

• Ceiling Height: 8 ft.

• Formal Living Room: This large, inviting room is the perfect place to entertain guests.

• Family Room: This cozy, comfortable room is accessed through elegant French doors in the living room. It is sure to be the favorite family gathering place with its bay window, see-through fireplace, and bay window.

• Breakfast Area: This area is large enough for the whole family to enjoy a casual meal as they are warmed by the other side of the see-through fireplace. The area features a bay window and built-in bookcase.

• Master Bedroom: Upstairs, enjoy the gracious and practical master bedroom with its boxed ceiling and two walk-in closets.

• Master Bath: Luxuriate in the whirlpool bath as you gaze through the skylight framed by ceiling accents.

Main Level Floor Plan

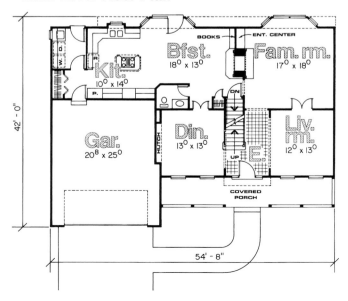

Upper Level Floor Plan

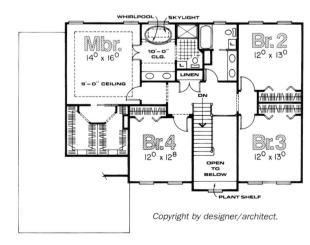

Copyright by designer/architect.

Plan #131019

Dimensions: 83'6" W x 53'4" D
Levels: 1
Square Footage: 2,243
Bedrooms: 3
Bathrooms: 2½
Foundation: Crawl space or slab; basement or walkout for fee
Materials List Available: Yes
Price Category: F

Images provided by designer/architect.

Rear Elevation

Copyright by designer/architect.

Plan #151037

Dimensions: 50' W x 56' D
Levels: 1
Square Footage: 1,538
Bedrooms: 3
Bathrooms: 2
Foundation: Crawl space, slab, or basement
CompleteCost List Available: Yes
Price Category: C

Images provided by designer/architect.

CAD FILE AVAILABLE

Copyright by designer/architect.

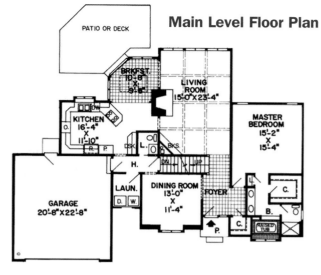

Main Level Floor Plan

PATIO OR DECK

BRKFST 10'-8" X 9'-6"

LIVING ROOM 15'-0"X 23'-4"

KITCHEN 16'-4" X 11'-10"

MASTER BEDROOM 15'-2" X 15'-4"

LAUN.

DINING ROOM 13'-0" X 11'-4"

FOYER

GARAGE 20'-8"X22'-8"

RAISED TUB

Images provided by designer/architect.

BEDROOM 2 11'-10" X 13'-0"

BEDROOM 3 12'-8" X 11'-4"

Upper Level Floor Plan

Copyright by designer/architect.

Plan #391131

Dimensions: 63'4" W x 47'10" D
Levels: 2
Square Footage: 2,183
Main Level Sq. Ft.: 1,584
Upper Level Sq. Ft.: 599
Bedrooms: 3
Bathrooms: 2
Foundation: Basement
Material List Available: Yes
Price Category: D

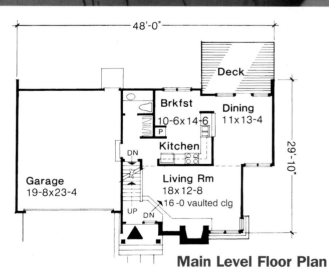

48'-0"

Deck

Brkfst 10-6x14-6

Dining 11x13-4

Kitchen

Garage 19-8x23-4

Living Rm 18x12-8
16-0 vaulted clg

29'-10"

DN

UP DN

Main Level Floor Plan

MBr 11-8x13

Loft/ Br 3 9x11

Br 2 10x9-8

DN

skylight

open to below

Upper Level Floor Plan

Copyright by designer/architect.

Plan #271012

Dimensions: 48' W x 29'10" D
Levels: 2
Square Footage: 1,359
Main Level Sq. Ft.: 668
Upper Level Sq. Ft.: 691
Bedrooms: 3
Bathrooms: 2½
Foundation: Basement
Materials List Available: Yes
Price Category: B

Images provided by designer/architect.

This home, as shown in the photograph, may differ from the actual blueprints. For more detailed information, please check the floor plans carefully.

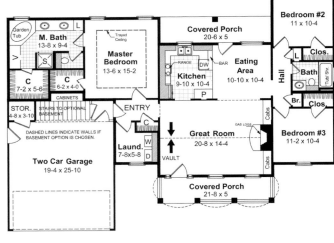

Plan #351005

Dimensions: 61' W x 47'4" D

Levels: 1

Square Footage: 1,501

Bedrooms: 3

Bathrooms: 2

Foundation: Crawl space, slab, or basement

Materials List Available: Yes

Price Category: C

Images provided by designer/architect.

CAD FILE AVAILABLE

Copyright by designer/architect.

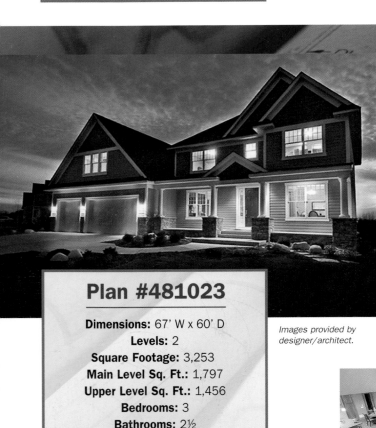

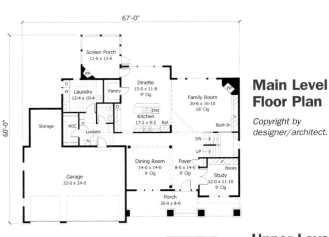

Plan #481023

Dimensions: 67' W x 60' D

Levels: 2

Square Footage: 3,253

Main Level Sq. Ft.: 1,797

Upper Level Sq. Ft.: 1,456

Bedrooms: 3

Bathrooms: 2½

Foundation: Walkout

Material List Available: Yes

Price Category: G

Images provided by designer/architect.

Main Level Floor Plan

Copyright by designer/architect.

Upper Level Floor Plan

Great Room

Plan #151050

Dimensions: 69'2" W x 74'10" D

Levels: 1

Square Footage: 2,096

Bedrooms: 3

Bathrooms: 2½

Foundation: Crawl space, slab, or basement

CompleteCost List Available: Yes

Price Category: F

Images provided by designer/architect.

CAD FILE AVAILABLE

Optional Front View

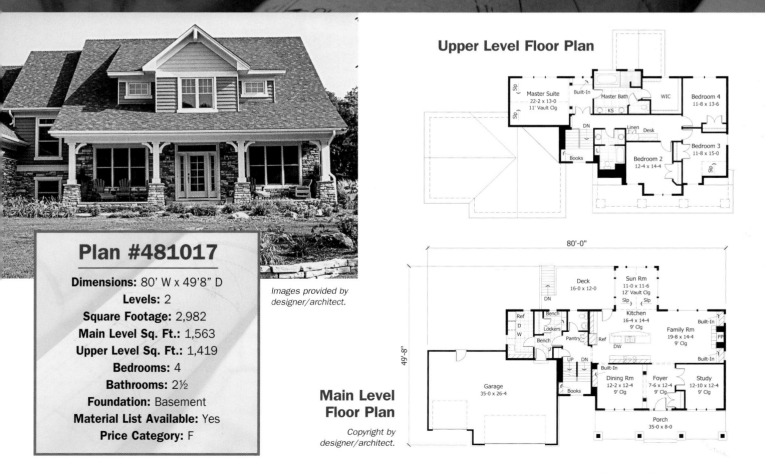

Plan #481017

Dimensions: 80' W x 49'8" D

Levels: 2

Square Footage: 2,982

Main Level Sq. Ft.: 1,563

Upper Level Sq. Ft.: 1,419

Bedrooms: 4

Bathrooms: 2½

Foundation: Basement

Material List Available: Yes

Price Category: F

Images provided by designer/architect.

Upper Level Floor Plan

Main Level Floor Plan

Copyright by designer/architect.

Plan #161009

Dimensions: 60'9" W x 49' D
Levels: 1
Square Footage: 1,651
Bedrooms: 3
Bathrooms: 2
Foundation: Basement
Materials List Available: Yes
Price Category: C

The warm, textured exterior combines with the elegance of double-entry doors to preview both the casual lifestyle and formal entertaining capabilities of this versatile home.

Features:

- **Great Room:** Experience the openness provided by the sloped ceiling topping both this great room and the formal dining area. Enjoy the warmth and light supplied by the gas fireplace and dual sliding doors.

- **Kitchen:** This kitchen, convenient to the living space, is designed for easy work patterns and features an open bar that separates the work area from the more richly decorated gathering rooms.

- **Master Bedroom:** Separated for privacy, this master bedroom includes a tray ceiling and lavishly equipped bath.

- **Basement:** This full basement allows you to expand your living space to meet your needs.

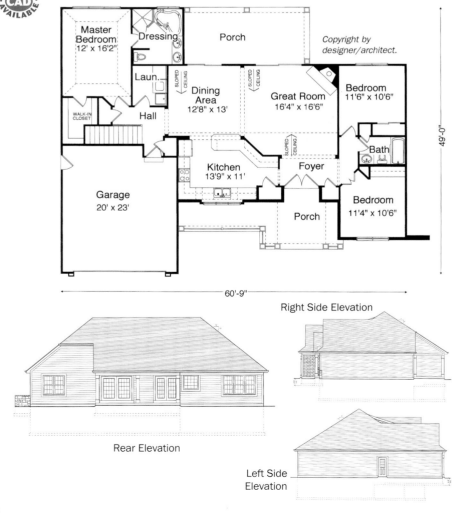

Images provided by designer/architect.

Copyright by designer/architect.

Rear Elevation

Right Side Elevation

Left Side Elevation

Plan #351007

Dimensions: 73'8"W x 53'2" D

Levels: 1

Square Footage: 2,251

Bedrooms: 3

Bathrooms: 2½

Foundation: Crawl space, slab, or basement

Materials List Available: Yes

Price Category: E

Images provided by designer/architect.

This three-bedroom brick home with arched window offers traditional styling that features an open floor plan.

Features:

- **Great Room:** This room has a 12-ft.-high ceiling and a corner fireplace.

- **Kitchen:** This kitchen boasts a built-in pantry and a raised bar open to the breakfast area.

- **Dining Room:** This area features a vaulted ceiling and a view of the front yard.

- **Master Bedroom:** This private room has an office and access to the rear porch.

- **Master Bath:** This bathroom has a double vanity, large walk-in closet, and soaking tub.

Bonus Room

Copyright by designer/architect.

58'-6"

64'-6"

ATRIUM DOOR

HEARTH ROOM
10' BOX CEILING
19'-4" X 17'-2"

MASTER SUITE
10' BOX CEILING
14'-8" X 15'-4"

KITCHEN
12'-4" X 11'-10"

GREAT ROOM
10' BOX CEILING
17'-8" X 18'-0"

BEDROOM 3
12'-2" X 14'-6"

BATH

GLASS BLOCKS

WHP TUB

M.BATH
15'-6" X 12'-4"

LAU.

8" COLUMN

FOYER
11' CEILING

BEDROOM 2
12'-2" X 12'-2"

DINING ROOM
11' CEILING
12'-8" X 13'-0"

PORCH
9'-8" X 4'-4"

GARAGE
22'-4" X 21'-8"

Plan #151034

Dimensions: 58'6" W x 64'6" D

Levels: 1

Square Footage: 2,133

Bedrooms: 3

Bathrooms: 2

Foundation: Crawl space or slab; basement or walkout for fee

CompleteCost List Available: Yes

Price Category: D

Images provided by designer/architect.

This home, as shown in the photograph, may differ from the actual blueprints. For more detailed information, please check the floor plans carefully.

CAD FILE AVAILABLE

Copyright by designer/architect.

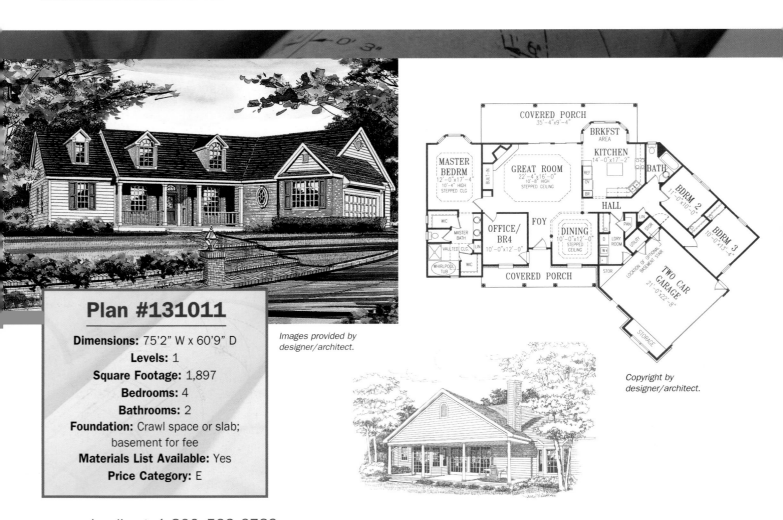

COVERED PORCH
35'-4"x9'-4"

BRKFST AREA

KITCHEN
14'-0"x17'-2"

MASTER BEDRM
12'-0"x17'-4"
10'-4" HIGH STEPPED CLG

GREAT ROOM
22'-4"x15'-0"
10'-8" HIGH STEPPED CEILING

BATH

BDRM 2
11'-0"x10'-0"

BDRM 3
10'-0"x13'-4"

WIC

MASTER BATH
VAULTED CLG

OFFICE/
BR4
10'-0"x12'-0"

FOY

DINING
10'-0"x12'-0"
STEPPED CEILING

HALL

LDRY ROOM

UTILITY

LOCATION OF OPTIONAL BASEMENT STAIR

WHIRLPOOL TUB

WIC

STOR

TWO CAR GARAGE
21'-0"x22'-8"

COVERED PORCH

STORAGE

Plan #131011

Dimensions: 75'2" W x 60'9" D

Levels: 1

Square Footage: 1,897

Bedrooms: 4

Bathrooms: 2

Foundation: Crawl space or slab; basement for fee

Materials List Available: Yes

Price Category: E

Images provided by designer/architect.

Copyright by designer/architect.

CAD FILE AVAILABLE

Plan #121001

Dimensions: 56' W x 58' D

Levels: 1

Square Footage: 1,911

Bedrooms: 3

Bathrooms: 2

Foundation: Basement

Materials List Available: Yes

Price Category: D

Plan #161008

Dimensions: 64'2" W x 46'6" D

Levels: 1

Square Footage: 1,860

Bedrooms: 3

Bathrooms: 2

Foundation: Slab

Materials List Available: Yes

Price Category: D

CAD FILE AVAILABLE

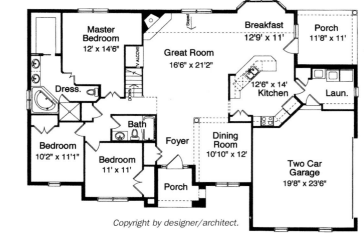

SMARTtip

Espaliered Fruit Trees

Try a technique used by the royal gardeners at Versailles—espalier. They trained the fruit trees to grow flat against the walls, creating patterns. It's not difficult, especially if you go to a reputable nursery and purchase an apple or pear tree that has already been espaliered. Plant it against a flat surface that's in a sunny spot.

Copyright by designer/architect.

Plan #221020

Dimensions: 69'8" W x 43' D

Levels: 1

Square Footage: 1,859

Bedrooms: 3

Bathrooms: 2½

Foundation: Basement

Materials List Available: Yes

Price Category: D

Images provided by designer/architect.

CAD FILE AVAILABLE · CAD

Rear Elevation

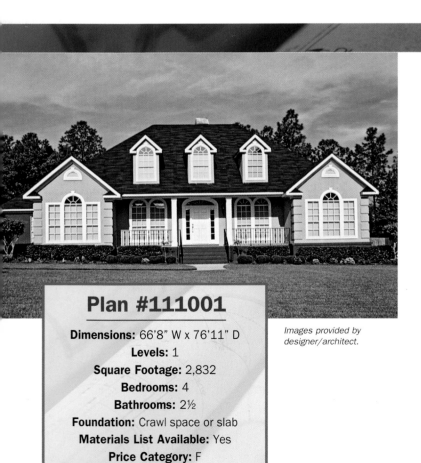

Plan #111001

Dimensions: 66'8" W x 76'11" D

Levels: 1

Square Footage: 2,832

Bedrooms: 4

Bathrooms: 2½

Foundation: Crawl space or slab

Materials List Available: Yes

Price Category: F

Images provided by designer/architect.

Copyright by designer/architect.

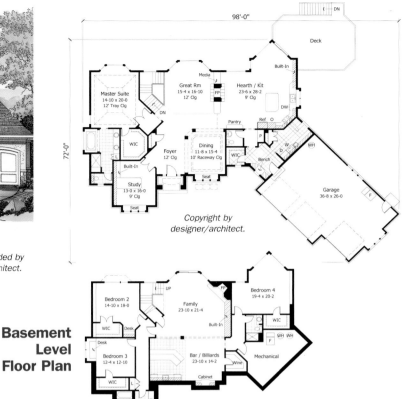

Copyright by
designer/architect.

*Images provided by
designer/architect.*

Plan #481031

Dimensions: 98' W x 72' D

Levels: 1

Square Footage: 4,707

Main Level Sq. Ft.: 2,518

Basement Level Sq. Ft.: 2,189

Bedrooms: 4

Bathrooms: 3½

Foundation: Walkout basement

Material List Available: Yes

Price Category: I

Basement Level Floor Plan

Main Level Floor Plan

LOWER LEVEL

3 CAR GARAGE OPTION

Plan #101017

Dimensions: 57' W x 51' D

Levels: 2

Square Footage: 2,253

Main Level Sq. Ft.: 1,719

Upper Level Sq. Ft.: 534

Opt. Upper Level Bonus Sq. Ft.: 247

Bedrooms: 4

Bathrooms: 3

Foundation: Basement

Materials List Available: Yes

Price Category: E

*Images provided by
designer/architect.*

CAD FILE AVAILABLE

Upper Level Floor Plan

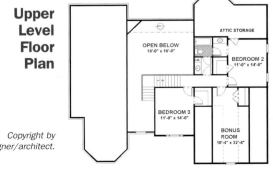

Copyright by
designer/architect.

Plan #161045

Dimensions: 57' W x 49'8" D

Levels: 2

Square Footage: 2,077

Main Level Sq. Ft.: 1,532

Upper Level Sq. Ft.: 545

Bedrooms: 3

Bathrooms: 2½

Foundation: Basement; crawl space or slab for fee

Materials List Available: Yes

Price Category: D

Images provided by designer/architect.

Multiple gables, arched windows, and the stone accents that adorn the exterior of this lovely two-story home create a dramatic first impression.

Features:

• Great Room: With multiple windows to light your way, grand openings, varied ceiling treatments, and angled walls let you flow from room to room. Enjoy the warmth of the gas fireplace in both this great room and the dining area.

• Master Suite: Experience the luxurious atmosphere of this master suite, with its coffered ceiling and deluxe bath.

• Additional Bedrooms: Angled stairs lead to a balcony with writing desk and to two additional bedrooms.

• Porch: Exit two sets of French doors to the rear yard and a covered porch, perfect for relaxing in comfortable weather.

Main Level Floor Plan

Copyright by designer/architect.

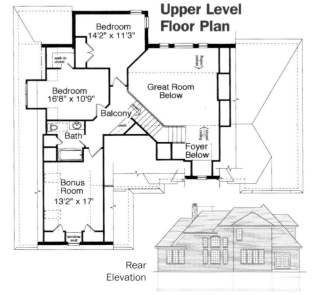

Upper Level Floor Plan

Rear Elevation

Plan #481028

Dimensions: 86'8" W x 53' D
Levels: 1
Square Footage: 3,980
Main Level Sq. Ft.: 2,290
Lower Level Sq. Ft.: 1,690
Bedrooms: 3
Bathrooms: 2½
Foundation: Walkout basement
Material List Available: Yes
Price Category: H

Images provided by designer/architect.

• Lower Level: For fun times, this lower level is finished to provide a wet bar and a recreation room. Two bedrooms, which share a full bathroom, are also on this level. Future expansion can include an additional bedroom.

Rear View

This home, with its Southwestern flair, invites friends and family in for some down-home hospitality.

Features:

• Foyer: A 12-ft-high ceiling extends an open welcome to all. With a view through the great room, the open floor plan makes the home feel large and open.

• Kitchen: This spacious gourmet kitchen opens generously to the hearth room, which features an angled fireplace. A two-level island, which contains a two-bowl sink, provides casual seating and additional storage.

• Master Suite: This romantic space features a 10-ft.-high stepped ceiling and a compartmentalized full bath that includes his and her sinks and a whirlpool tub.

Copyright by designer/architect.

Main Level Floor Plan

THREE CAR CARRIAGE HOUSE

WRAP AROUND PORCH

FAMILY ENTRY

FAMILY ROOM
22'-0" x 14'-2"

OPT BOOKCASE

OPT BOOKCASE

KITCHEN
13'-0" x 13'-0"

MORNING ROOM
14'-0" x 13'-0"

DINING ROOM

LAV.

FP

CABINET

OPT BOOKCASE

OPT LIBRARY CABINETS

STUDY LIBRARY
14'-0" x 12'-0"

LIVING ROOM
14'-0" x 18'-0"

ENTRY FOYER

72'-0"

75'-0"

Images provided by designer/architect.

Copyright by designer/architect.

Upper Level Floor Plan

FUTURE LIVING AREA
16'-0" x 31'-0"

Adds 516 square feet

REAR HALL

75'-0"

MASTER BATH

HER WIC

WHIRL POOL TUB

HIS WIC

MASTER BEDROOM
26'-5" x 13'-0"

SLOPED CEILING

FP

PETIT DEJEUNER

BOOKCASE

BEDROOM
12'-0" x 14'-2"

DRESSING   BATH

BEDROOM
12'-0" x 12'-0"

UPPER HALL

BEDROOM
12'-0" x 12'-0"

65'-0"

Plan #291013

Dimensions: 72' W x 75' D
Levels: 2
Square Footage: 3,553
Main Level Sq. Ft.: 1,830
Upper Level Sq. Ft.: 1,723
Bedrooms: 4
Bathrooms: 2½
Foundation: Basement
Materials List Available: Yes
Price Category: H

Dining
13' x 11'6"

Screened Porch
19' x 12'

Great Room
16' x 17'2"

Master Bedroom
11'9" x 15'

walk-in closet

10' corner ceiling height

Kitchen
11' x 15'6"

Two-Car Garage
20'8" x 21'

Dressing

Laun.

Foyer

10' ceiling height

Bath

Bedroom
10'8" x 11'6"

Porch

Bedroom
10'6" x 10'6"

66'-4"

43'-10"

Copyright by designer/architect.

Images provided by designer/architect.

CAD FILE AVAILABLE

Rear Elevation

Plan #161007

Dimensions: 66'4" W x 43'10" D
Levels: 1
Square Footage: 1,611
Bedrooms: 3
Bathrooms: 2
Foundation: Basement; crawl space option for fee
Materials List Available: Yes
Price Category: C

Main Level Floor Plan

Plan #131050

Dimensions: 72'8" W x 47' D

Levels: 2

Square Footage: 2,874

Main Level Sq. Ft.: 2,146

Upper Level Sq. Ft.: 728

Bedrooms: 4

Bathrooms: 3

Foundation: Crawl space or slab; basement for fee

Materials List Available: Yes

Price Category: G

Images provided by designer/architect.

This home, as shown in the photograph, may differ from the actual blueprints. For more detailed information, please check the floor plans carefully.

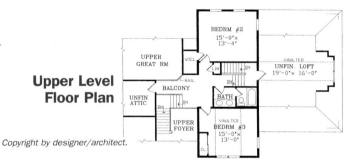

Upper Level Floor Plan

Copyright by designer/architect.

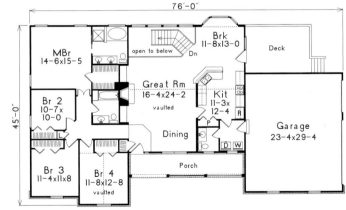

Plan #321006

Dimensions: 76' W x 45' D

Levels: 1, optional lower

Square Footage: 1,977

Optional Basement Level Sq. Ft.: 1,416

Bedrooms: 4

Bathrooms: 2½

Foundation: Basement

Materials List Available: Yes

Price Category: E

Images provided by designer/architect.

Optional Basement Level Floor Plan

Copyright by designer/architect.

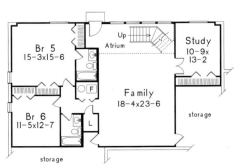

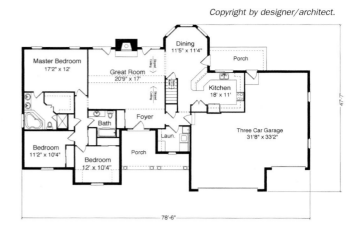

Images provided by designer/architect.

Rear Elevation

Plan #161006

Dimensions: 78'6" W x 47'7" D

Levels: 1

Square Footage: 1,755

Bedrooms: 3

Bathrooms: 2

Foundation: Basement

Materials List Available: Yes

Price Category: C

Plan #151009

Dimensions: 44' W x 86'2" D

Levels: 1

Square Footage: 1,601

Bedrooms: 3

Bathrooms: 2

Foundation: Crawl space or slab

CompleteCost List Available: Yes

Price Category: C

Images provided by designer/architect.

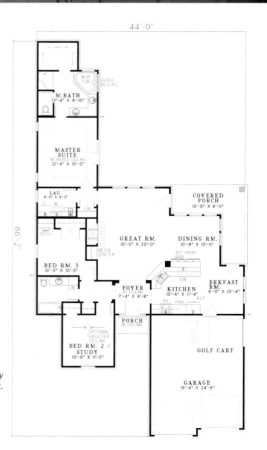

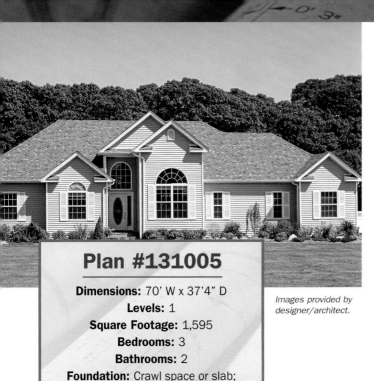

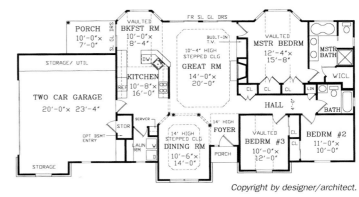

Copyright by designer/architect.

Plan #131005

Dimensions: 70' W x 37'4" D
Levels: 1
Square Footage: 1,595
Bedrooms: 3
Bathrooms: 2
Foundation: Crawl space or slab; basement for fee
Materials List Available: Yes
Price Category: C

Images provided by designer/architect.

Copyright by designer/architect.

Plan #221001

Dimensions: 87' W x 60' D
Levels: 1
Square Footage: 2,600
Bedrooms: 3
Bathrooms: 2½
Foundation: Basement
Materials List Available: Yes
Price Category: F

Images provided by designer/architect.

CAD FILE AVAILABLE

Rear Elevation

Kitchen

Main Level
Floor Plan

Images provided by designer/architect.

Plan #661124

Dimensions: 45' W x 68'10 D
Levels: 1
Square Footage: 2,392
Bedrooms: 3
Bathrooms: 2 full, 1 half
Foundation: Slab
Materials List Available: Yes
Price Category: E

Upper Level
Floor Plan

Copyright by designer/architect.

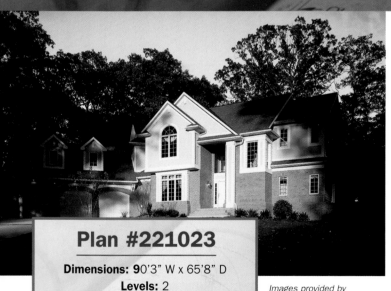

Plan #221023

Dimensions: 90'3" W x 65'8" D
Levels: 2
Square Footage: 3,511
Main Level Sq. Ft.: 1,931
Upper Level Sq. Ft.: 1,580
Bedrooms: 4
Bathrooms: 3
Foundation: Basement
Materials List Available: Yes
Price Category: H

Images provided by designer/architect.

Main Level
Floor Plan

Upper Le
Floor F

Copyright by designer/archite

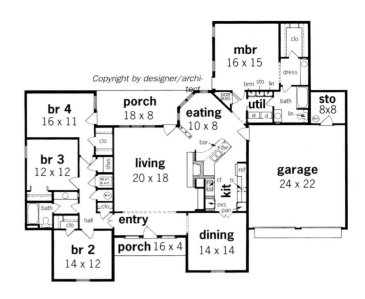

Copyright by designer/architect

Floor plan labels:
- br 4 — 16 x 11
- br 3 — 12 x 12
- br 2 — 14 x 12
- porch — 18 x 8
- eating — 10 x 8
- living — 20 x 18
- kit
- dining — 14 x 14
- porch 16 x 4
- entry
- hall
- bath
- mbr — 16 x 15
- util
- sto — 8x8
- garage — 24 x 22
- clo, dress, bath, lin, pan, ref, ct, tc, ovs, bar, dw

Images provided by designer/architect.

Plan #211007

Dimensions: 72' W x 60' D
Levels: 1
Square Footage: 2,252
Bedrooms: 4
Bathrooms: 2
Foundation: Slab
Materials List Available: Yes
Price Category: E

Front View

Plan #271024

Dimensions: 75' W x 44' D
Levels: 2
Square Footage: 3,107
Main Level Sq. Ft.: 1,639
Upper Level Sq. Ft.: 1,468
Bedrooms: 4
Bathrooms: 2½
Foundation: Basement
Materials List Available: Yes
Price Category: G

Images provided by designer/architect.

Main Level Floor Plan

Floor plan labels:
- DECK
- BRKFST — 11'-0"x12'-0"
- FAMILY — 24'-0"x16'-0"
- MUD LNDRY
- KITCHEN
- GARAGE — 24'-0"x36'-0"
- DINING — 14'-6"x12'-0"
- LIVING — 14'-0"x16'-0"

Upper Level Floor Plan

Copyright by designer/architect.

Floor plan labels:
- M BATH
- MASTER BEDROOM — 16'-0"x15'-6" 12'-0" VAULTED CEILING
- BDRM 2 — 11'-0"x12'-6"
- BDRM 3 — 12'-0"x12'-0"
- BDRM 4 — 14'-3"x13'-6"
- OPEN TO BELOW

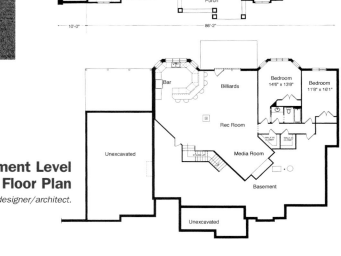

Main Level Floor Plan

Plan #161056

Dimensions: 86'2" W x 63'8" D

Levels: 1

Square Footage: 3,171

Bedrooms: 3

Bathrooms: 2½

Foundation: Basement or walkout, crawl space for fee

Material List Available: Yes

Price Category: G

Images provided by designer/architect.

CAD FILE AVAILABLE

Basement Level Floor Plan

Copyright by designer/architect.

Plan #151534

Dimensions: 37'8" W x 71'6" D

Levels: 2

Square Footage: 2,237

Main Level Sq. Ft.: 1,708

Upper Level Sq. Ft.: 529

Bedrooms: 3

Bathrooms: 2½

Foundation: Crawl space or slab

CompleteCost List Available: Yes

Price Category: E

Images provided by designer/architect.

CAD FILE AVAILABLE

Upper Level Floor Plan

Copyright by designer/architect.

Main Level Floor Plan

Front View

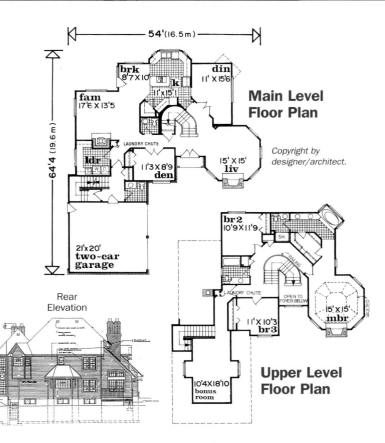

Main Level Floor Plan

Copyright by designer/architect.

Upper Level Floor Plan

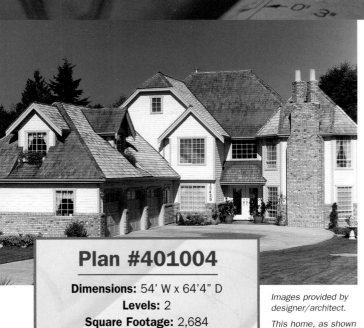

Plan #401004

Dimensions: 54' W x 64'4" D

Levels: 2

Square Footage: 2,684

Main Level Sq. Ft.: 1,620

Upper Level Sq. Ft.: 1,064

Bedrooms: 3

Bathrooms: 2 full, 2 half

Foundation: Basement

Materials List Available: Yes

Price Category: F

Images provided by designer/architect.

This home, as shown in the photograph, may differ from the actual blueprints. For more detailed information, please check the floor plans carefully.

Rear Elevation

Main Level Floor Plan

Copyright by designer/architect.

Upper Level Floor Plan

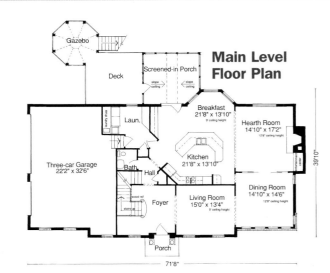

Plan #161023

Dimensions: 71'8" W x 39'10" D

Levels: 2

Square Footage: 3,445

Main Level Sq. Ft.: 1,666

Mid Level Sq. Ft.: 743

Upper Level Sq. Ft.: 1,036

Bedrooms: 4

Bathrooms: 3½

Foundation: Basement

Materials List Available: Yes

Price Category: G

Images provided by designer/architect.

Plan #151484

Dimensions: 53'6" W x 76'10" D
Levels: 1.5
Square Footage: 2,211
Bedrooms: 3
Bathrooms: 2
Foundation: Crawl space or slab
CompleteCost List Available: Yes
Price Category: E

Images provided by designer/architect.

This traditional design, perfect for narrow lot, incorporates 10-ft.-tall boxed ceilings and 8-in. round columns.

Features:

- Dining Room: This room is centrally located and looks through to the great room, which allows access to the rear grilling porch.

- Master Suite: The split-bedroom plan gives the ultimate in privacy to this suite, complete with a large walk-in closet and a bath with amenities galore.

- Kitchen: At the other end of the house from the master suite is this kitchen and breakfast room combo with island seating, a built-in bench seat, and a walk-in pantry.

- Den: Down the hall from the kitchen is this den or extra bedroom. Private access to the full bathroom makes it great for guests.

Front View

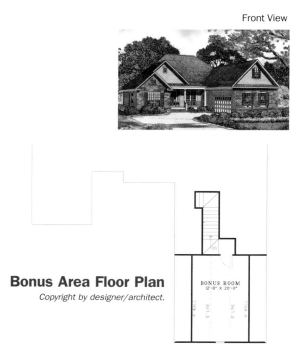

Bonus Area Floor Plan
Copyright by designer/architect.

Plan #121011

Dimensions: 50' W x 50' D
Levels: 1
Square Footage: 1,724
Bedrooms: 3
Bathrooms: 2
Foundation: Slab, basement
Materials List Available: Yes
Price Category: C

This home, as shown in the photograph, may differ from the actual blueprints. For more detailed information, please check the floor plans carefully.

This one-level home is perfect for retirement or for convenient living for the growing family.

Features:

• Ceiling Height: 8 ft.

• Master Suite: For privacy and quiet, the master suite is segregated from the other bedrooms.

• Family Room: Sit by the fire and read as light streams through the windows flanking the fireplace. Or enjoy the built-in entertainment center.

• Breakfast Area: Located just off the family room, the sunny breakfast areaa will lure you to linger over impromptu family meals. Here you will find a built-in desk for compiling shopping lists and menus.

• Private Porch: Step out of the breakfast area to enjoy a breeze on this porch.

• Kitchen: Efficient and attractive, this kitchen offers an angled pantry and an island that doubles as a snack bar.

SMARTtip

Measuring for Kitchen Countertops

Custom cabinetmakers will sometimes come to your house to measure for a countertop, but home centers and kitchen stores may require that you come to them with the dimensions already in hand. Be sure to double-check measurements carefully. Being off by only ½ in. can be quite upsetting.

To ensure accuracy, sketch out the countertop on a sheet of graph paper. Include all the essential dimensions. To be on the safe side, have some one else double-check your numbers.

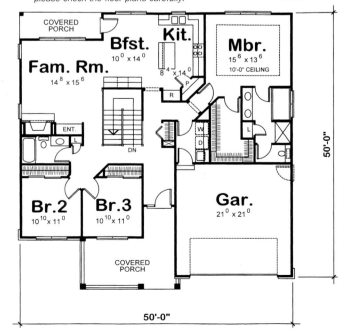

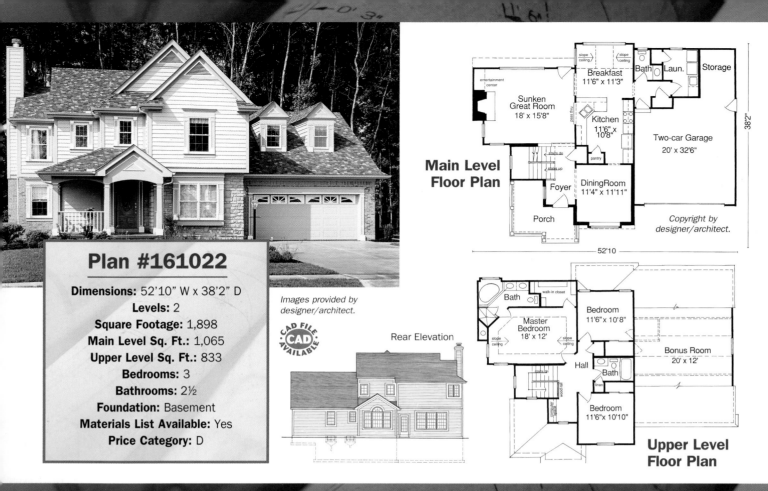

Main Level Floor Plan

entertainment center

Breakfast 11'6" x 11'3"

Bath Laun. Storage

slope ceiling slope ceiling

Sunken Great Room 18' x 15'8"

Kitchen 11'6" x 10'8"

Two-car Garage 20' x 32'6"

38'2"

pass thru

stairs do
stairs up

pantry

DiningRoom 11'4" x 11'11"

Foyer

Porch

Copyright by designer/architect.

52'10

Images provided by designer/architect.

CAD FILE AVAILABLE

Rear Elevation

Bath

walk-in closet

Master Bedroom 18' x 12'

slope ceiling slope ceiling

Bedroom 11'6" x 10'8"

Bonus Room 20' x 12'

Hall

Bath
linen

computer

wood rail

Bedroom 11'6"x 10'10"

Upper Level Floor Plan

Plan #161022

Dimensions: 52'10" W x 38'2" D
Levels: 2
Square Footage: 1,898
Main Level Sq. Ft.: 1,065
Upper Level Sq. Ft.: 833
Bedrooms: 3
Bathrooms: 2½
Foundation: Basement
Materials List Available: Yes
Price Category: D

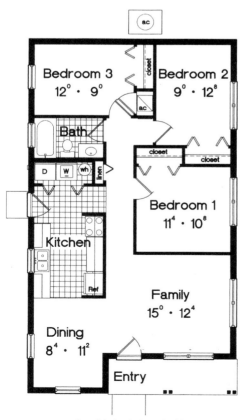

a.c.

Bedroom 3 12⁰ · 9⁰

Bedroom 2 9⁰ · 12⁸

closet

a.c.

Bath

closet closet

D W wh

linen

Bedroom 1 11⁴ · 10⁸

Kitchen

Ref

Family 15⁰ · 12⁴

Dining 8⁴ · 11²

Entry

Plan #661021

Dimensions: 24'4" W x 43'8" D
Levels: 1
Square Footage: 966
Bedrooms: 3
Bathrooms: 1
Foundation: Slab
Materials List Available: Yes
Price Category: A

Images provided by designer/architect.

CAD FILE AVAILABLE

Copyright by designer/architect.

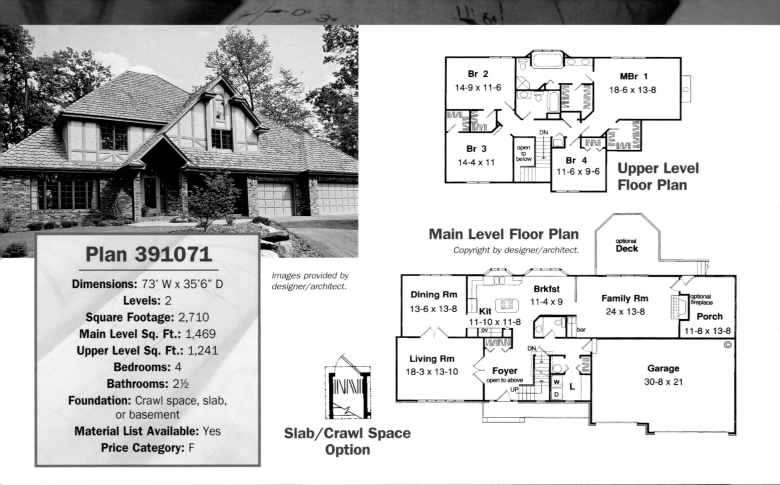

Plan 391071

Dimensions: 73' W x 35'6" D
Levels: 2
Square Footage: 2,710
Main Level Sq. Ft.: 1,469
Upper Level Sq. Ft.: 1,241
Bedrooms: 4
Bathrooms: 2½
Foundation: Crawl space, slab, or basement
Material List Available: Yes
Price Category: F

Images provided by designer/architect.

Upper Level Floor Plan

Br 2
14-9 x 11-6

MBr 1
18-6 x 13-8

Br 3
14-4 x 11

open to below

DN

Br 4
11-6 x 9-6

Main Level Floor Plan
Copyright by designer/architect.

optional **Deck**

Dining Rm
13-6 x 13-8

Kit
11-10 x 11-8

Brkfst
11-4 x 9

Family Rm
24 x 13-8

optional fireplace

Porch
11-8 x 13-8

Living Rm
18-3 x 13-10

Foyer
open to above

DN

UP

Garage
30-8 x 21

Slab/Crawl Space Option

Plan #271097

Dimensions: 60' W x 42' D
Levels: 2
Square Footage: 1,645
Main Level Sq. Ft.: 1,136
Upper Level Sq. Ft.: 509
Bedrooms: 3
Bathrooms: 2
Foundation: Basement
Materials List Available: Yes
Price Category: C

Images provided by designer/architect.

60'-0"

PORCH

DINING
10'-0"x10'-4"

KITCH
11'-0"x12'-8"

GARAGE
21'-8"x25'-4"

42'-0"

LIVING
13'-4"x23'-0"
8'-6" CLG

BATH

BEDROOM 1
14'-4"x13'-4"

FOYER

Main Level Floor Plan

PORCH

UP

BEDRM 3
9'-4"x11'-10"

HALL

BEDRM 2
10'-10"x14'-6"

OPEN TO BELOW

Upper Level Floor Plan

Copyright by designer/architect.

Plan #481005

Dimensions: 67'4" W x 53' D
Levels: 2
Square Footage: 2,825
Main Level Sq. Ft.: 1,412
Upper Level Sq. Ft.: 1,413
Bedrooms: 4
Bathrooms: 2½
Foundation: Walkout basement
Material List Available: Yes
Price Category: F

Images provided by designer/architect.

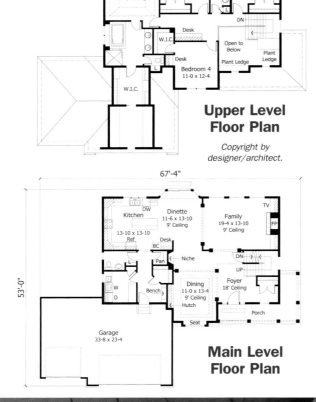

Upper Level Floor Plan

Copyright by designer/architect.

Main Level Floor Plan

Plan #461174

Dimensions: 70'4" W x 67' D
Levels: 2
Square Footage: 3,753
Main Level Sq. Ft.: 2,519
Upper Level Sq. Ft.: 1,234
Bedrooms: 4
Bathrooms: 3½
Foundation: Basement, crawl space, slab
Material List Available: Yes
Price Category: H

Images provided by designer/architect.

Main Level Floor Plan

Copyright by architect.

Upper Level Floor Plan

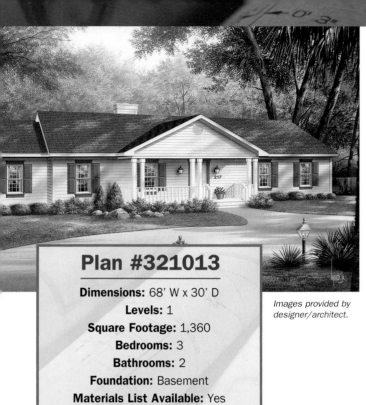

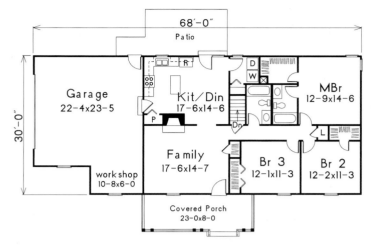

Plan #321013

Dimensions: 68' W x 30' D

Levels: 1

Square Footage: 1,360

Bedrooms: 3

Bathrooms: 2

Foundation: Basement

Materials List Available: Yes

Price Category: B

Images provided by designer/architect.

Copyright by designer/architect.

Plan #151684

Dimensions: 65'2" W x 63' D

Levels: 1

Square Footage: 1,994

Bedrooms: 3

Bathrooms: 2

Foundation: Crawl space, slab, basement, or walkout

CompleteCost List Available: Yes

Price Category: D

Images provided by designer/architect.

CAD FILE AVAILABLE

Copyright by designer/architect.

Plan #391069

Dimensions: 56' W x 48' D

Levels: 1

Square Footage: 1,492

Bedrooms: 3

Bathrooms: 2

Foundation: Crawl space, slab, or basement

Materials List Available: Yes

Price Category: B

Images provided by designer/architect.

This design opens wide from the living room to the kitchen and dining room. All on one level, even the bedrooms are easy to reach.

Features:

- **Living Room:** This special room features a fireplace and entry to the deck.

- **Dining Room:** This formal room shows off special ceiling effects.

- **Bedrooms:** Bedroom 3 is inspired by a decorative ceiling, and bedroom 2 has double closet doors. There's a nearby bath for convenience.

- **Master Suite:** This private area features a roomy walk-in closet and private bath.

Copyright by designer/architect.

Optional Floor Plan

Plan #271027

Dimensions: 61' W x 44' D
Levels: 2
Square Footage: 2,463
Main Level Sq. Ft.: 1,380
Upper Level Sq. Ft.: 1,083
Bedrooms: 4
Bathrooms: 2½
Foundation: Basement
Materials List Available: Yes
Price Category: D

Images provided by designer/architect.

This post-modern design uses half-round transom windows and a barrel-vaulted porch to lend elegance to its facade.

Features:

• Living Room: A vaulted ceiling and a striking fireplace enhance this formal gathering space.

• Dining Room: Introduced from the living room by square columns, this formal dining room is just steps from the kitchen.

• Kitchen: Thoroughly modern in its design, this walk-through kitchen includes an island cooktop and a large pantry. Nearby, a sunny, bayed breakfast area offers sliding-glass-door access to an angled backyard deck.

• Family Room: Columns provide an elegant preface to this fun gathering spot, which sports a vaulted ceiling and easy access to the deck.

• Master suite: A vaulted ceiling crowns this luxurious space, which includes a private bath and bright windows.

Main Level Floor Plan

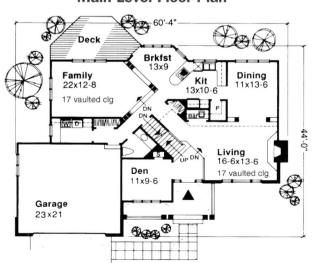

Upper Level Floor Plan

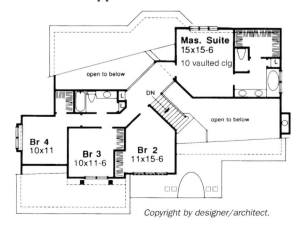

Copyright by designer/architect.

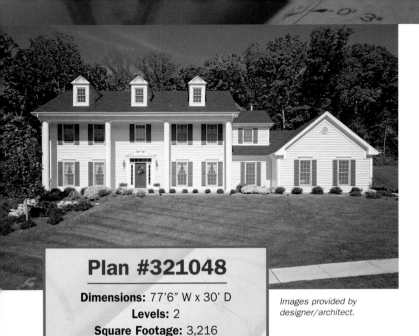

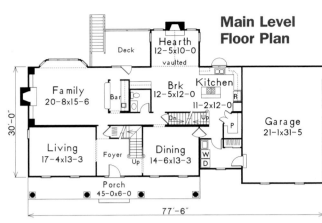

Main Level Floor Plan

Deck

Hearth 12-5x10-0 vaulted

Family 20-8x15-6

Bar

Brk 12-5x12-0

Kitchen

Garage 21-1x31-5

Living 17-4x13-3

Foyer

Up

Dining 14-6x13-3

Porch 45-0x6-0

30'-0"

77'-6"

Images provided by designer/architect.

Plan #321048

Dimensions: 77'6" W x 30' D

Levels: 2

Square Footage: 3,216

Main Level Sq. Ft.: 1,834

Upper Level Sq. Ft.: 1,382

Bedrooms: 4

Bathrooms: 4½

Foundation: Basement

Materials List Available: Yes

Price Category: G

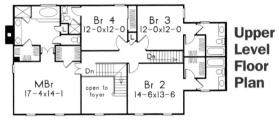

Upper Level Floor Plan

Br 4 12-0x12-0

Br 3 12-0x12-0

MBr 17-4x14-1

Dn

open to foyer

Br 2 14-6x13-6

Copyright by designer/architect.

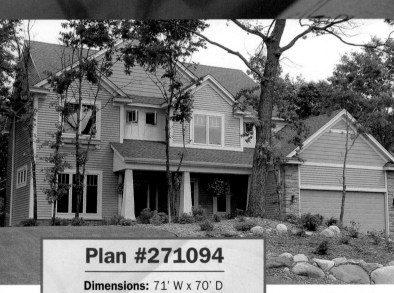

Plan #271094

Dimensions: 71' W x 70' D

Levels: 2

Square Footage: 3,242

Main Level Sq. Ft.: 1,552

Upper Level Sq. Ft.: 1,690

Bedrooms: 5

Bathrooms: 2½

Foundation: Full basement

Materials List Available: Yes

Price Category: G

Images provided by designer/architect.

CAD FILE AVAILABLE

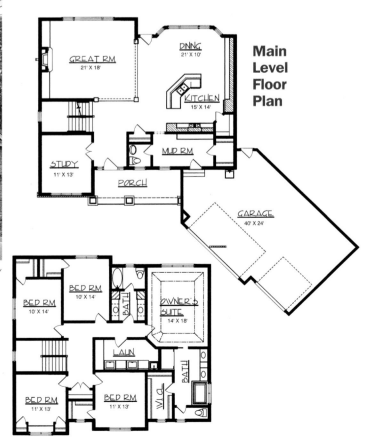

Main Level Floor Plan

GREAT RM 21' X 18'

DINING 21' X 10'

KITCHEN 15' X 14'

STUDY 11' X 13'

MUD RM

PORCH

GARAGE 40' X 24'

Upper Level Floor Plan

Copyright by designer/architect.

BED RM 10' X 14'

BED RM 10' X 14'

BATH

OWNER'S SUITE 14' X 18'

LAUN

BATH

BED RM 11' X 13'

BED RM 11' X 13'

W.I.C.

BATH

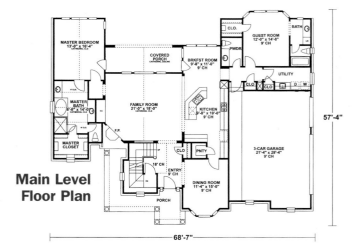

**Main Level
Floor Plan**

*Images provided by
designer/architect.*

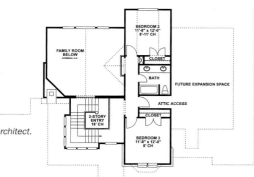

**Upper Level
Floor Plan**

Copyright by designer/architect.

Plan #121150

Dimensions: 68'7" W x 57'4" D

Levels: 1.5

Square Footage: 2,639

Main Level Sq. Ft.: 2,087

Upper Level Sq. Ft.: 552

Bedrooms: 4

Bathrooms: 3½

Foundation: Slab; crawl space
or basement for fee

Material List Available: Yes

Price Category: F

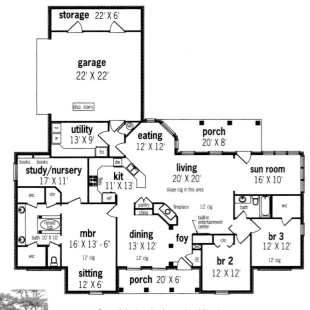

Plan #211130

Dimensions: 68' W x 70' D

Levels: 1

Square Footage: 2,280

Bedrooms: 3

Bathrooms: 2

Foundation: Slab

Materials List Available: Yes

Price Category: E

*Images provided by
designer/architect.*

Front View

Copyright by designer/architect.

Plan #281033

Dimensions: 40' W x 40' D
Levels: 2
Square Footage: 2,391
Main Level Sq. Ft.: 1,358
Garage Level Sq. Ft.: 1,033
Bedrooms: 4
Bathrooms: 3
Foundation: Basement
Material List Available: Yes
Price Category: E

This home, as shown in the photograph, may differ from the actual blueprints. For more detailed information, please check the floor plans carefully.

The interesting floor plan and gorgeous exterior are sure to make this home a hit with your family.

Features:

• Living Room: The bay window brings natural light into this gathering area, while the fireplace adds a glow of its own. Because it is open to the dining room, guests flow easily between the two areas.

• Kitchen: This U-shaped kitchen, with its breakfast nook, is located next to the dining room to make serving guests easy.

• Bedrooms: A master and two secondary bedrooms are located on the upper level. The master bedroom boasts a private bathroom.

• Garage: A two-car front-loading garage has room for cars or for storage.

Main Level Floor Plan

Garage Level Floor Plan

Plan #151242

Dimensions: 74'4" W x 77' D
Levels: 2
Square Footage: 2,710
Main Level Sq. Ft.: 1,819
Upper Level Sq. Ft.: 891
Bedrooms: 4
Bathrooms: 2½
Foundation: Crawl space or slab; basement or walkout for fee
CompleteCost List Available: Yes
Price Category: F

Images provided by designer/architect.

Multiple rooflines give this home an elegant and unique look.

Features:

- Great Room: This large entertaining area features a gas fireplace flanked by built-in cabinets. The atrium doors, which lead to the rear covered porch, will allow plenty of natural light to fill this room.

- Dining Room: The 8-inch-diameter round columns at the entry add elegance to this formal eating area. The kitchen is close by, making serving guests convenient.

- Kitchen: This efficient kitchen features a raised bar to handle the overflow from the breakfast room. The pantry cabinet is always a welcome bonus.

- Master Suite: Located on the lower level for privacy, this retreat boasts a large sleeping area allowing for many different furniture layouts. Pamper yourself in the elegant master bath, complete with glass shower, whirlpool tub, and dual vanities.

Upper Level Floor Plan
Copyright by designer/architect.

Main Floor

Plan #191055

Dimensions: 60' W x 76' D

Levels: 1

Square Footage: 2,123

Bedrooms: 3

Bathrooms: 2½

Foundation: Crawl space or slab

Material List Available: Yes

Price Category: D

Images provided by designer/architect.

Copyright by designer/ architect.

60'-0" WIDE
76'-0" DEEP

M. BATH

CLOSET
8'-5" X 10'-0"

MASTER BEDROOM
19'-0" X 18'-0"

PORCH 2
7' DEEP

BEDROOM 3
12'-0" X 11'-8"

PORCH 2
11' DEEP

LAUNDRY
7'-0" X 10'-2"

PANTRY
8'-0" X 7'-2"

GREAT ROOM
22'-4" X 16'-0"

KITCHEN
13'-10" X 11'-10"

BEDROOM 2
11'-10" X 12'-10"

SITTING
7'-8" X 8'-0"

FOYER

1/2 B.

DINING AREA
13'-10" X 12'-0"

PORCH 1
6' DEEP

Plan #151005

Dimensions: 58' W x 54'10" D

Levels: 1

Square Footage: 1,940

Bedrooms: 4

Bathrooms: 2

Foundation: Crawl space, slab, or basement

CompleteCost List Available: Yes

Price Category: D

Images provided by designer/architect.

58'-0"

BREAKFAST ROOM
9'-4" X 10'-11"

COVERED PORCH
18'-5" X 4'-0"

BEDROOM 4
13'-6" X 14'-6"

MASTER SUITE
15'-0" X 15'-0"
9' PAN CEILING

GREAT ROOM
15'-0" X 19'-6"
9' BOX CEILING

BATH

KITCHEN

BUILT-INS

M. BATH
15'-0" X 11'-8"

DINING ROOM
11'-6" X 9'-8"

FOYER
7'-0" X 7'-0"

BEDROOM 3
10'-0" X 10'-4"

STORAGE

4' PORCH

BEDROOM 2
12'-4" X 10'-6"

GARAGE
20'-10" X 20'-0"

Copyright by designer/ architect.

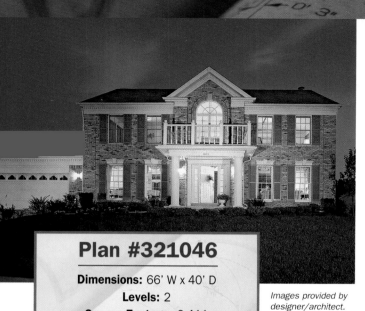

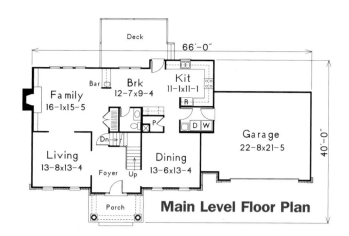

Main Level Floor Plan

66'-0"

40'-0"

Deck

Family 16-1x15-5

Bar

Brk 12-7x9-4

Kit 11-1x11-1

R

Garage 22-8x21-5

Living 13-8x13-4

Dn

P

Dining 13-6x13-4

D W

Foyer

Up

Porch

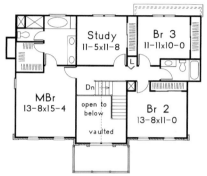

Upper Level Floor Plan

Copyright by designer/ architect.

Study 11-5x11-8

Br 3 11-11x10-0

L

MBr 13-8x15-4

Dn

open to below

vaulted

Br 2 13-8x11-0

Plan #321046

Dimensions: 66' W x 40' D

Levels: 2

Square Footage: 2,411

Main Level Sq. Ft.: 1,293

Upper Level Sq. Ft.: 1,118

Bedrooms: 3

Bathrooms: 2½

Foundation: Basement

Materials List Available: Yes

Price Category: E

Images provided by designer/architect.

This home, as shown in the photograph, may differ from the actual blueprints. For more detailed information, please check the floor plans carefully.

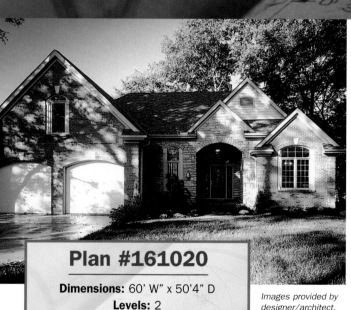

Bedroom 11'1" x 13'3"

Bedroom 11'5" x 12'0"

linen

Bath

bookshelves

computer desk

Balcony

Foyer Below

wood rail

Bonus Room 11'0" x 22'0"

wood rail

Upper Level Floor Plan

Master Bedroom 13'6" x 15'1"

Triple French Doors w/ arched window above

Great Room 17'4" x 21'2"

12' high ceiling

Dining Room 10'10" x 14'0"

Bath

Bath

hanging space

Laun.

walk-in closet

Foyer

pass thru

Kitchen 12'4" x 11'6"

50'4"

Two-car Garage 22'9" x 22'0"

wood rail

pantry

Breakfast 11' x 9'4"

Main Level Floor Plan

Copyright by designer/ architect.

60'

Plan #161020

Dimensions: 60' W" x 50'4" D

Levels: 2

Square Footage: 2,082; 2,349 with bonus space

Main Level Sq. Ft.: 1,524

Upper Level Sq. Ft.: 558

Bedrooms: 3

Bathrooms: 2½

Foundation: Basement

Materials List Available: Yes

Price Category: D

Images provided by designer/architect.

Plan #391019

Dimensions: 56' W x 32' D

Levels: 1

Square Footage: 1,792

Bedrooms: 3

Bathrooms: 2

Foundation: Basement

Materials List Available: Yes

Price Category: C

Images provided by designer/architect.

Copyright by designer/architect.

MAIN AREA

Plan #641004

Dimensions: 56' W x 52' D

Levels: 2

Square Footage: 3,030

Main Level Sq. Ft.: 1,778

Upper Level Sq. Ft.: 1,252

Bedrooms: 3

Bathrooms: 3½

Foundation: Crawl space, slab, or basement

Material List Available: Yes

Price Category: G

Images provided by designer/architect.

Main Level Floor Plan

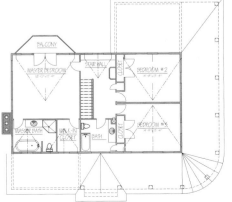

Upper Level Floor Plan

Copyright by designer/architect.

Main Level Floor Plan

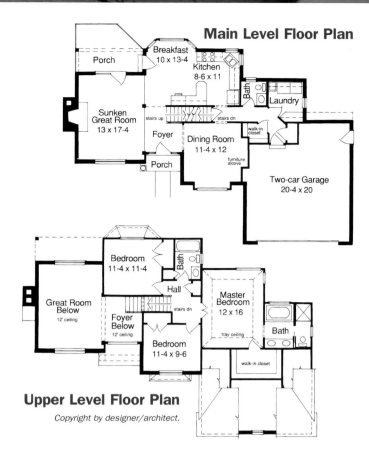

Porch

Breakfast
10 x 13-4

Kitchen
8-6 x 11

Bath

Laundry

Sunken
Great Room
13 x 17-4

stairs up

stairs dn

walk-in closet

Foyer

Dining Room
11-4 x 12

furniture alcove

Two-car Garage
20-4 x 20

Porch

Bedroom
11-4 x 11-4

Bath

Great Room Below
12' ceiling

Hall

Master Bedroom
12 x 16

stairs dn

Foyer Below
12' ceiling

tray ceiling

Bath

Bedroom
11-4 x 9-6

walk-in closet

Upper Level Floor Plan

Copyright by designer/architect.

Plan #161015

Dimensions: 55'4" W x 40'4" D

Levels: 2

Square Footage: 1,768

Main Level Sq. Ft.: 960

Upper Level Sq. Ft.: 808

Bedrooms: 3

Bathrooms: 2½

Foundation: Walkout

Materials List Available: Yes

Price Category: C

Images provided by designer/architect.

Upper Level Floor Plan

Copyright by designer/architect.

Master Suite
15-8 x 18-6
pan vault

whirlpool

Br 2
12-0 x 11-4

Br 4
12-8 x 13-0

open to foyer

Br 3
11-0 x 13-0

Main Level Floor Plan

Deck

Brkfst
15-8 x 10-0

Kitchen
15-8 x 14-10

Family Rm
17-0 x 22-0

built-ins

pantry

desk

Study
12-8 x 13-1

Ldry

Dining Rm
11-0 x 17-0

Foyer

Living Rm
13-0 x 19-7

Garage
31-8 x 23-8

Plan #391066

Dimensions: 78' W x 60' D

Levels: 2

Square Footage: 3,526

Main Level Sq. Ft.: 2,054

Upper Level Sq. Ft.: 1,472

Bedrooms: 4

Bathrooms: 3½

Foundation: Crawl space, slab, or basement

Material List Available: Yes

Price Category: H

Images provided by designer/architect.

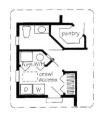

pantry

furn.W/H

crawl access

Alternate Foundation Option

Plan #351033

Dimensions: 64' W x 39' D

Levels: 1

Heated Square Footage: 1,654

Bedrooms: 3

Bathrooms: 2

Foundation: Crawl space, slab, or basement

Materials List Available: Yes

Price Category: C

This gorgeous three-bedroom brick home would be the perfect place to raise your family.

Features:

- **Great Room:** This terrific room has a gas fireplace with built-in cabinets on either side.

- **Kitchen:** This island kitchen with breakfast area is open to the great room.

- **Master Suite:** This private room features a vaulted ceiling and a large walk-in closet. The bath area has a walk-in closet, jetted tub, and double vanities.

- **Bedrooms:** The two additional bedrooms share a bathroom located in the hall.

Copyright by designer/architect.

Plan #131025

Dimensions: 62'4" W x 65'10" D
Levels: 1½
Square Footage: 3,204
Main Level Sq. Ft.: 2,196
Upper Level Sq. Ft.: 1,008
Bedrooms: 4
Bathrooms: 4
Foundation: Crawl space or slab; basement for fee
Materials List Available: Yes
Price Category: H

Images provided by designer/architect.

You'll appreciate the flowing layout that's designed for entertaining but also suits an active family.

Features:

• Ceiling Height: 8 ft.

• Great Room: Decorative columns serve as the entryway to the great room that's made for entertaining. A fireplace makes it warm in winter; built-in shelves give a classic appearance; and the serving counter it shares with the kitchen is both practical and attractive.

• Kitchen: A door into the backyard makes outdoor entertaining easy, and the full bathroom near the door adds convenience.

• Master Suite: Enjoy the sunny sitting area that's a feature of this suite. A tray ceiling adds character to the room, and a huge walk-in closet is easy to organize. The bathroom features a corner spa tub.

• Bedrooms: Each of the additional 3 bedrooms is bright and cheery.

Main Level Floor Plan

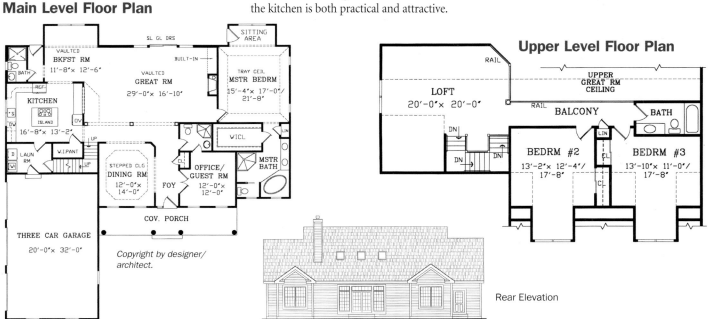

Copyright by designer/architect.

Rear Elevation

Optional Basement Level Floor Plan

Copyright by designer/architect.

Images provided by designer/architect.

Plan #391064

Dimensions: 54' W x 28' D

Levels: 1

Square Footage: 988

Bedrooms: 3

Bathrooms: 2

Foundation: Crawl space, basement

Materials List Available: Yes

Price Category: A

Kitchen 8-6 x 8-3

Mstr. Br. 13-7 x 11-6

Kitchen 8-6 x 8-3

Dining 8-10 x 11-6

Covered Patio

Br 2 9-8 x 11-8

Br 3 11-0 x 10-2

Living Rm 15-8 x 11-7

Garage 13-9 x 19-5

Optional 2-Car Garage

Crawl Access

Plant Box

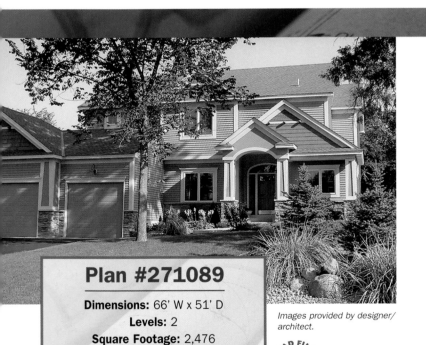

Plan #271089

Dimensions: 66' W x 51' D

Levels: 2

Square Footage: 2,476

Main Level Sq. Ft.: 1,266

Upper Level Sq. Ft.: 1,210

Bedrooms: 3

Bathrooms: 2½

Foundation: Daylight basement

Materials List Available: Yes

Price Category: E

Images provided by designer/architect.

CAD FILE AVAILABLE

Main Level Floor Plan

DINING RM 12' X 14'

GREAT RM 17' X 14'

KITCHEN 20' X 14'

STUDY 11' X 11'

ENTRY

MUD RM

GARAGE 32' X 24'

Upper Level Floor Plan

Copyright by designer/architect.

OWNER'S SUITE 15' X 14'

BED RM 11' X 13'

HALL

BATH

BED RM 11' X 13'

Main Level Floor Plan

Images provided by designer/architect.

CAD FILE AVAILABLE

Plan #181084

Dimensions: 69'8" W x 73'8" D
Levels: 2
Square Footage: 4,084
Main Level Sq. Ft.: 2,579
Upper Level Sq. Ft.: 1,469
Bedrooms: 4
Bathrooms: 3½
Foundation: Basement
Material List Available: Yes
Price Category: K

Upper Level Floor Plan

Copyright by designer/architect.

Plan #211108

Dimensions: 66' W x 66' D
Levels: 2
Square Footage: 2,954
Main Level Sq. Ft.: 1,984
Upper Level Sq. Ft.: 970
Bedrooms: 4
Bathrooms: 3½
Foundation: Crawl space, slab, or basement
Materials List Available: Yes
Price Category: F

Images provided by designer/architect.

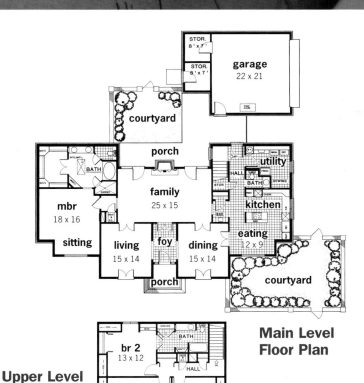

Main Level Floor Plan

Upper Level Floor Plan

Copyright by designer/architect.

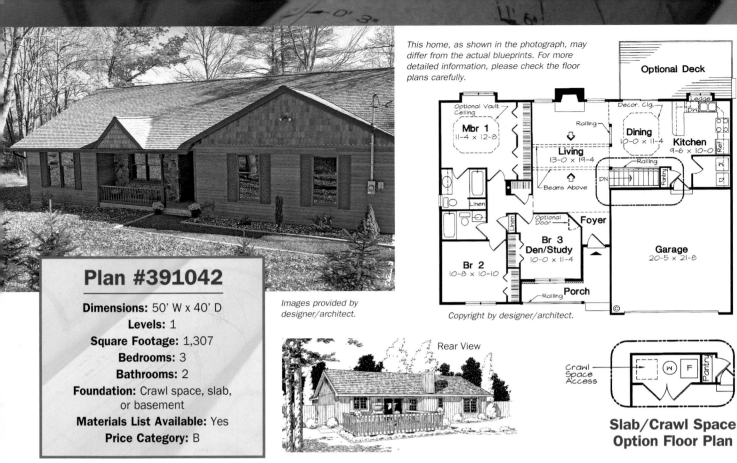

Optional Deck

Optional Vault Ceiling

Mbr 1
11-4 x 12-8

Railing

Dining
10-0 x 11-4

Decor. Clg.

Kitchen
9-6 x 10-0

DW

Ref

Living
13-0 x 19-4

Railing

Beams Above

DN

Pantry

Linen

DN

Optional Door

Foyer

Linen

Br 3
Den/Study
10-0 x 11-4

Garage
20-5 x 21-8

Br 2
10-8 x 10-10

Railing

Porch

©

Images provided by designer/architect.

Copyright by designer/architect.

Rear View

Crawl Space Access

M | F

Pantry

Slab/Crawl Space Option Floor Plan

Plan #391042

Dimensions: 50' W x 40' D
Levels: 1
Square Footage: 1,307
Bedrooms: 3
Bathrooms: 2
Foundation: Crawl space, slab, or basement
Materials List Available: Yes
Price Category: B

Plan #151171

Dimensions: 63'10" W x 72'2" D
Levels: 1
Square Footage: 2,131
Bedrooms: 3
Bathrooms: 2½
Foundation: Crawl space or slab; basement or walkout for fee
CompleteCost List Available: Yes
Price Category: D

Images provided by designer/architect.

63'-10"

GRILLING PATIO
13'-4" X 12'-0"

SCREENED PORCH
29'-8" X 12'-0"

MASTER SUITE
13'-0" X 17'-2"

GREAT RM.
18'-0" X 22'-0"

DINING
13'-8" X 13'-8"

M. BATH
15'-0" X 17'-4"

SKYLIGHTS

VAULTED CEILING

KITCHEN
12'-10" X 10'-6"

BATH

COMPUTER CENTER

FOYER
7'-7" X 11'-0"

STORM SHELTER

LAU.
8'-7" X 7'-8"

BEDROOM 2
14'-8" X 12'-6"

BEDROOM 3 / DEN
13'-6" X 14'-2"

72'-2"

COVERED PORCH
36'-8" X 8'-0"

OPTIONAL BASEMENT PLAN

GARAGE
21'-0" X 27'-4"

Copyright by designer/architect.

Main Level Floor Plan

Images provided by designer/architect.

Plan #271090

Dimensions: 78' W x 49' D

Levels: 2

Square Footage: 2,708

Main Level Sq. Ft.: 1,430

Upper Level Sq. Ft.: 1,278

Bedrooms: 3

Bathrooms: 2½

Foundation: Daylight basement

Materials List Available: Yes

Price Category: F

Upper Level Floor Plan

Copyright by designer/architect.

Plan #271007

Dimensions: 52' W x 41' D

Levels: 1

Square Footage: 1,283

Bedrooms: 3

Bathrooms: 2

Foundation: Basement

Materials List Available: Yes

Price Category: B

Images provided by designer/architect.

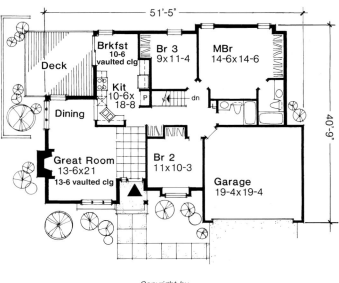

Copyright by designer/architect.

Plan #121216

Dimensions: 40' W x 47'8" D
Levels: 1
Square Footage: 1,205
Bedrooms: 2
Bathrooms: 2
Foundation: Basement; crawl space or slab for fee
Material List Available: Yes
Price Category: B

This home boasts a beautiful arched entry.

Features:

- Great Room: Enter this large gathering area from the foyer; the warmth of the fireplace welcomes you home. The 10-ft.-high ceiling gives the area an open feeling.

- Kitchen: Family and friends will enjoy gathering in this cozy kitchen, with its attached breakfast room. The area provides access to a future rear patio. The garage and laundry area are just a few steps away.

- Master Suite: This private area features a stepped ceiling in the sleeping area and a large window for backyard views. The master bath boasts a whirlpool bathtub, a separate shower, and dual vanities.

- Secondary Bedroom: A large front window brings light into this comfortable bedroom. A full bathroom is located nearby.

Images provided by designer/architect.

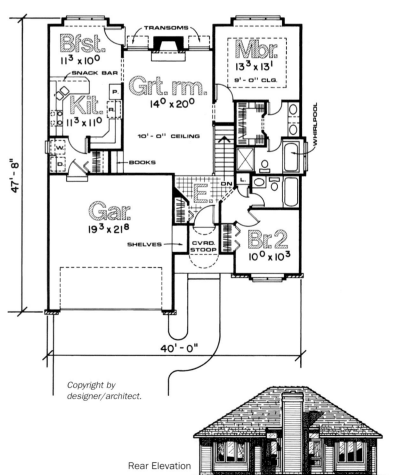

Copyright by designer/architect.

Rear Elevation

Plan #151026

Dimensions: 34' W x 66'8" D
Levels: 2
Square Footage: 1,574
Main Level Sq. Ft.: 1,131
Upper Level Sq. Ft.: 443
Bedrooms: 3
Bathrooms: 2½
Foundation: Crawl space, slab, full basement for fee
Complete Cost Available: Yes
Price Category: C

Images provided by designer/architect.

This French Country home gives space for entertaining and offers privacy.

Features:

• Great Room: Move through the gracious foyer framed by wooden columns into the great room with its lofty 10-ft. ceilings and gas fireplace.

• Dining Room: Set off by 8-in. columns, the dining room opens to the kitchen, both with 9-ft. ceilings.

• Master Suite: Enjoy relaxing in the bedroom with its 10-ft. boxed ceiling and well-placed windows. Atrium doors open to the backyard, where you can mmake a secluded garden. A glass-bricked corner whirlpool tub, corner shower, and double vanity make the master bath luxurious.

• Bedrooms: Upstairs, two large bedrooms with a walk-throuugh bath provide plenty of room as well as privacy for kids and guests.

Main Level Floor Plan

Copyright by designer/architect.

Upper Level Floor Plan

Plan #131006

Dimensions: 61' W x 53'6" D
Levels: 1
Square Footage: 2,193
Bedrooms: 3
Bathrooms: 2
Foundation: Crawl space or slab;
basement for fee
Materials List Available: Yes
Price Category: E

Images provided by designer/architect.

Copyright by designer/architect.

Alternate Floor Plan

Plan #251012

Dimensions: 57'9" W x 62'10" D
Levels: 2
Square Footage: 2,009
Main Level Sq. Ft.: 1,520
Upper Level Sq. Ft.: 489
Bedrooms: 3
Bathrooms: 2½
Foundation: Basement
Material List Available: Yes
Price Category: G

Images provided by designer/architect.

T

Upper Level Floor Plan

Main Level Floor Plan

Copyright by designer/architect.

Main Level Floor Plan

12'-0" X 15'-0"
3,60 X 4,50

17'-0" X 15'-0"
5,10 X 4,50

12'-4" X 24'-4"
3,70 X 7,30

29'-0"
8,70 m

14'-0" X 12'-4"
4,20 X 3,70

45'-6"
13,65 m

Plan #181157

Dimensions: 45' 6" W x 29' D

Levels: 2

Square Footage: 1,795

Main Level Sq. Ft.: 890

Upper Level Sq. Ft.: 905

Bedrooms: 3

Bathrooms: 2½

Foundation: Full basement

Materials List Available: Yes

Price Category: E

Images provided by designer/architect.

CAD FILE AVAILABLE

Upper Level Floor Plan

Copyright by designer/architect.

10'-8" X 12'-0"
3,20 X 3,60

10'-8" X 12'-0"
3,20 X 3,60

12'-4" X 24'-0"
3,70 X 7,20

15'-0" X 15'-0"
4,50 X 4,50

Main Level Floor Plan

KITCHEN

FAMILY ROOM

STORAGE

LAUNDRY

PANTRY

2 CAR GARAGE

DINING

ENTRY

LIVING

61'-0"

Plan #641009

Dimensions: 61' W x 37'6" D

Levels: 2

Square Footage: 2,648

Main Level Sq. Ft.: 1,373

Upper Level Sq. Ft.: 1,275

Bedrooms: 4

Bathrooms: 2½

Foundation: Basement; crawl space, slab or walkout for fee

Materials List Available: Yes

Price Category: F

Images provided by designer/architect.

CAD FILE AVAILABLE

Upper Level Floor Plan

BEDROOM 3

BEDROOM 4

MASTER BEDROOM

UNFINISHED BONUS ROOM

HALL

BATH

WC

WC

BEDROOM 2

MASTER BATH

Copyright by designer/architect.

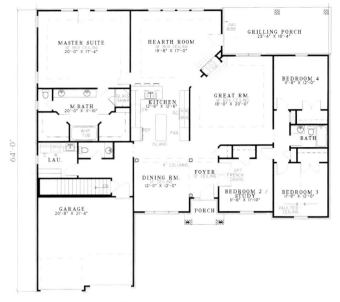

Plan #151063

Dimensions: 64' W x 60'2" D

Levels: 1

Square Footage: 2,554

Bedrooms: 4

Bathrooms: 2½

Foundation: Crawl space or slab; basement or walkout for fee

CompleteCost List Available: Yes

Price Category: D

Images provided by designer/architect.

Copyright by designer/architect.

Plan #331002

Dimensions: 62'2" W x 66'8" D

Levels: 2

Square Footage: 2,299

Main Level Sq. Ft.: 1,517

Upper Level Sq. Ft.: 782

Bedrooms: 3

Bathrooms: 2½

Foundation: Crawl space, slab, or basement

Materials List Available: Yes

Price Category: E

Images provided by designer/architect.

Main Level Floor Plan

Upper Level Floor Plan

Copyright by designer/architect.

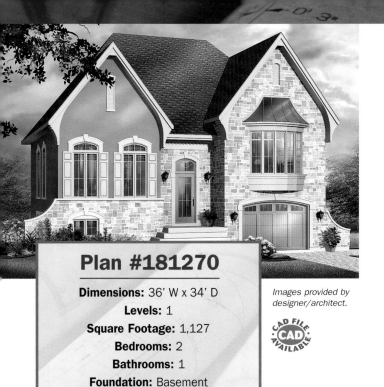

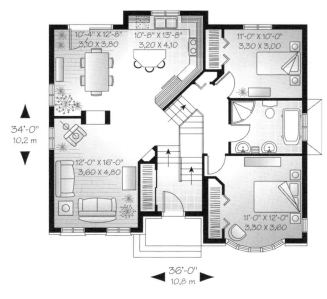

Plan #181270

Dimensions: 36' W x 34' D

Levels: 1

Square Footage: 1,127

Bedrooms: 2

Bathrooms: 1

Foundation: Basement

Materials List Available: Yes

Price Category: D

Images provided by designer/architect.

CAD FILE AVAILABLE

34'-0"
10,2 m

36'-0"
10,8 m

10'-4" X 12'-8"
3,10 X 3,80

10'-8" X 13'-8"
3,20 X 4,10

11'-0" X 10'-0"
3,30 X 3,00

12'-0" X 16'-0"
3,60 X 4,80

11'-0" X 12'-0"
3,30 X 3,60

Copyright by designer/architect.

Plan #181506

Dimensions: 26' W x 26'4" D

Levels: 2

Square Footage: 1,365

Main Level Sq. Ft.: 689

Upper Level Sq. Ft.: 676

Bedrooms: 3

Bathrooms: 2

Foundation: Basement

Material List Available: Yes

Price Category: B

Images provided by designer/architect.

CAD FILE AVAILABLE

Main Level Floor Plan

Copyright by designer/architect.

26'-4"
7,9 m

26'-0"
7,8 m

14'-0" X 12'-2"
4,20 X 3,65

10'-8" X 10'-0"
3,20 X 3,00

8'-0" X 14'-4"
2,40 X 4,30

Upper Level Floor Plan

12'-0" X 11'-10"
3,60 X 3,55

10'-0" X 9'-8"
3,00 X 2,90

10'-0" X 10'-0"
3,00 X 3,00

Rear Elevation

Main Level Floor Plan

Deck

Hearth Rm
13-4 x 14-8

Kit
11-4 x 12

Living Rm
13-8 x 22
17'-0" ceiling height

Ldry

Garage
21-8 x 21-4

UP

DN

Balcony above

Foyer

Dining Rm
13 x 13-6

plant shelf

MBr 1
14-4 x 15-4
ceiling vaulted

Images provided by designer/architect.

Upper Level Floor Plan

Copyright by designer/architect.

slope
plant shelf

Guest Br 4
11-4 x 11-8

Br 3
12-2 x 13-4

open to below

DN

Balcony

open to below

Br 2
13 x 11-2

plant shelf

Plan #391041

Dimensions: 61' W x 52' D
Levels: 2
Square Footage: 2,563
Main Level Sq. Ft.: 1,737
Upper Level Sq. Ft.: 826
Bedrooms: 4
Bathrooms: 3½
Foundation: Basement
Materials List Available: Yes
Price Category: E

Upper Level Floor Plan

Copyright by designer/architect.

MASTER BEDROOM

OPEN BELOW

BEDROOM #2

BATH

BONUS ROOM

BALCONY

MASTER BATH

OPEN BELOW

BEDROOM #3

Plan #641002

Dimensions: 75'6" W x 52' D
Levels: 2
Square Footage: 2,655
Main Level Sq. Ft.: 1,512
Upper Level Sq. Ft.: 1,143
Bedrooms: 3
Bathrooms: 3
Foundation: Basement; crawl space, slab or walkout for fee
Material List Available: Yes
Price Category: F

Images provided by designer/architect.

CAD FILE AVAILABLE

Main Level Floor Plan

WOOD DECK

LIVING

BREAKFAST

OPEN ABOVE

KITCHEN

LAUNDRY

BATH

3-CAR GARAGE

PANTRY

CLOSET

DEN

ENTRY

DINING

PORCH

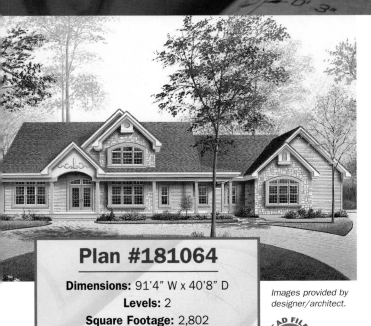

Plan #181064

Dimensions: 91'4" W x 40'8" D

Levels: 2

Square Footage: 2,802

Main Level Sq. Ft.: 2,219

Upper Level Sq. Ft.: 583

Bedrooms: 4

Bathrooms: 2½

Foundation: Crawl space; slab or basement for fee

Materials List Available: Yes

Price Category: F

Images provided by designer/architect.

CAD FILE AVAILABLE

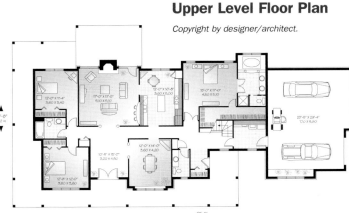

Upper Level Floor Plan

Copyright by designer/architect.

Main Level Floor Plan

Plan #651011

Dimensions: 67' W x 76 D

Levels: 2

Square Footage: 4,169

Main Level Sq. Ft.: 2,939

Upper Level Sq. Ft.: 1,230

Bedrooms: 4

Bathrooms: 3 full, 2 half

Foundation: Slab

Materials List Available: Yes

Price Category: I

Images provided by designer/architect.

CAD FILE AVAILABLE

Main Level Floor Plan

Upper Level Floor Plan

Copyright by designer/architect.

Plan #121170

Dimensions: 68'4" W x 68' D
Levels: 1.5
Square Footage: 3,459
Main Level Sq. Ft.: 2,348
Upper Level Sq. Ft.: 1,111
Bedrooms: 4
Bathrooms: 3½
Foundation: Basement; crawl space for fee
Material List Available: Yes
Price Category: G

This home, as shown in the photograph, may differ from the actual blueprints. For more detailed information, please check the floor plans carefully.

CAD FILE AVAILABLE

Large rooms make this home very attractive.

Features:

- **Dining Room:** When you enter this home, your eyes are drawn to this elegant formal eating area. The stepped ceiling adds to the feeling of grandeur.

- **Den:** Featuring French door access to the front porch, this den could function as a home office. The fireplace adds a focal point to the room.

- **Master Suite:** This main-level master suite boasts a 10-ft.-high ceiling. The master bath features a stall shower and dual vanities.

- **Upper Level:** Three secondary bedrooms are located on this level. Bedroom 2 boasts a private bathroom.

Front View

Main Level Floor Plan

Upper Level Floor Plan

Copyright by designer/architect.

Plan #321042

Dimensions: 71' W x 54'7" D
Levels: 2
Square Footage: 3,368
Main Level Sq. Ft.: 2,150
Upper Level Sq. Ft.: 1,218
Bedrooms: 4
Bathrooms: 3 full, 2 half
Foundation: Basement
Materials List Available: Yes
Price Category: G

Inside this traditional exterior lies a home filled with contemporary amenities and design features that are sure to charm the whole family.

Features:

• Great Room: Relax in this sunken room with a cathedral ceiling, wooden beams, skylights, and a masonry fireplace.

• Breakfast Room: Octagon-shaped with a domed ceiling, this room leads to the outdoor patio.

• Library: Situated for privacy and quiet, this room opens up from the master bedroom and the foyer.

• Kitchen: The central island here adds to the ample work and storage space.

• Dining Room: Just off the foyer, this room is ideal for formal dinners and quiet times.

• Master Suite: Enjoy the large bedroom and bath with a luxurious corner tub, separate shower, two vanities, walk-in closet, and dressing area.

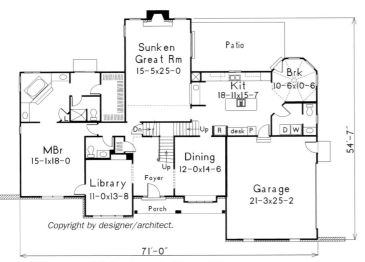

Main Level Floor Plan

Upper Level Floor Plan

Main Level Floor Plan

GRILLING PORCH
31'-6" X 10'-0"

GREAT RM.
18'-2" X 14'-0"

BREAKFAST ROOM
11'-6" X 14'-0"

DINING RM.
11'-6" X 13'-0"

KITCHEN
12'-6" X 14'-0"

COMPUTER DESK

BATH

FORMAL LIVING
11'-6" X 16'-10"

GARAGE
22'-4" X 26'-0"

GUEST RM.
11'-0" X 11'-2"

FOYER
8'-10" X 18'-8"
OPEN ABOVE

PORCH

Upper Level Floor Plan

MASTER SUITE

M. BATH

BEDROOM 4

BONUS RM.

LAU.

BEDROOM 3

BATH

BEDROOM 2

OPEN TO BELOW

Images provided by designer/architect.

Copyright by designer/architect.

Plan #151087

Dimensions: 55'4" W x 53'10" D
Levels: 2
Square Footage: 2,942
Main Level Sq. Ft.: 1,547
Upper Level Sq. Ft.: 1,395
Bedrooms: 5
Bathrooms: 4
Foundation: Crawl space or slab; basement or walkout for fee
CompleteCost List Available: Yes
Price Category: F

CAD FILE AVAILABLE

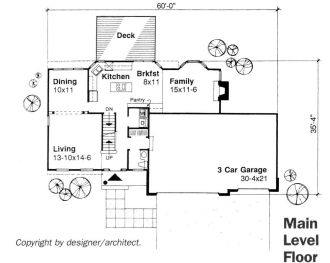

Main Level Floor Plan

Deck

Dining
10x11

Kitchen

Brkfst
8x11

Family
15x11-6

Living
13-10x14-6

Pantry

3 Car Garage
30-4x21

60'-0"

35'-4"

Copyright by designer/architect.

Upper Level Floor Plan

Br 4
10-4x10

Br 3
11x10

Mas. Suite
14x15-6
11-6 vaulted clg

Br 2
12-8x10

open to below

High Glass above

Plan #271038

Dimensions: 60' W x 35'4" D
Levels: 2
Square Footage: 1,820
Main Level Sq. Ft.: 987
Upper Level Sq. Ft.: 833
Bedrooms: 4
Bathrooms: 2½
Foundation: Basement
Materials List Available: Yes
Price Category: D

Images provided by designer/architect.

Extra Storage
19'4"x 3'4"

Two-Car
Carport
20'0"x 24'0"

Patio
20'0"x 8'0"

Utility

Great Room
22'8"x 14'0"

Breakfast
10'0"x 10'0"

Master
Bath

WIC

Kitchen
11'4"x
10'10"

Master
Bedroom
13'6"x 13'0"

Dining
Room
11'4"x 12'0"

Porch
11'0"x 5'0"

Main Level Floor Plan

Open to
Below

Bedroom
11'4"x 15'0"

Bedroom
10'4"x 10'6"

Study
11'10"x 9'2"

Upper Level Floor Plan

Images provided by designer/architect.

Copyright by designer/architect.

Plan #111008

Dimensions: 43' W x 69' D
Levels: 2
Square Footage: 2,011
Main Level Sq. Ft.: 1,331
Upper Level Sq. Ft.: 680
Bedrooms: 3
Bathrooms: 2½
Foundation: Slab or basement
Materials List Available: Yes
Price Category: E

Main Level Floor Plan

61'-0"

skylts

Deck

Great Rm
22-1x18-2
vaulted

Brk
10-8x15-1
vaulted

Kit
9-10x12-2

Bar

Dn

Dining
12-3x12-5

MBr
17-0x16-0

Up

Entry

Garage
20-8x20-1

Porch depth 4-0

49'-4"

open to
below

Br 4
14-8x11-1

Dn

Upper Level Floor Plan

Br 3
17-0x11-0

skylt

Br 2
12-3x12-8

Images provided by designer/architect.

CAD FILE AVAILABLE
CAD

Copyright by designer/architect.

Plan #321044

Dimensions: 61' W x 49'4" D
Levels: 2
Square Footage: 2,618
Main Level Sq. Ft.: 1,804
Upper Level Sq. Ft.: 814
Bedrooms: 4
Bathrooms: 2½
Foundation: Basement
Materials List Available: Yes
Price Category: F

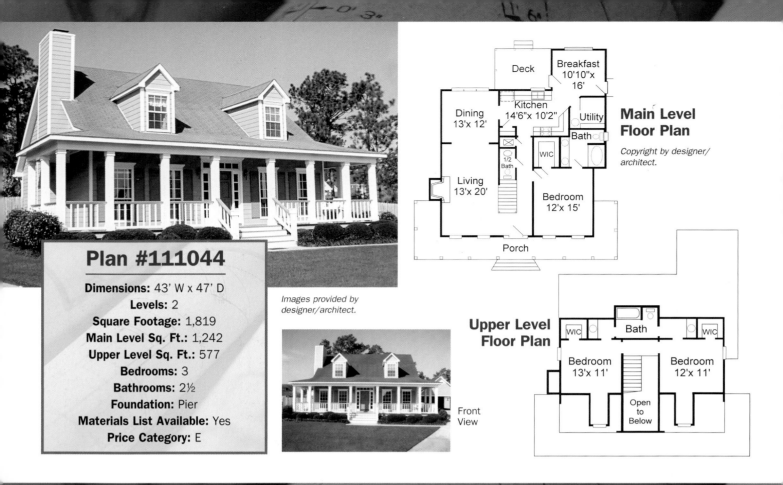

Plan #111044

Dimensions: 43' W x 47' D

Levels: 2

Square Footage: 1,819

Main Level Sq. Ft.: 1,242

Upper Level Sq. Ft.: 577

Bedrooms: 3

Bathrooms: 2½

Foundation: Pier

Materials List Available: Yes

Price Category: E

Images provided by designer/architect.

Main Level Floor Plan

Copyright by designer/architect.

Deck

Breakfast 10'10"x 16'

Dining 13' x 12'

Kitchen 14'6"x 10'2"

Utility

Bath

1/2 Bath

WIC

Living 13' x 20'

Bedroom 12' x 15'

Porch

Upper Level Floor Plan

WIC

Bath

WIC

Bedroom 13' x 11'

Bedroom 12' x 11'

Open to Below

Front View

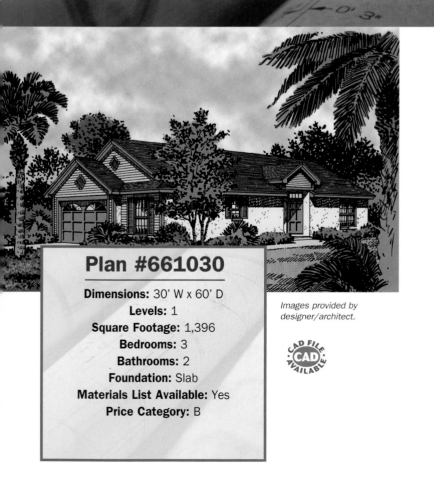

Plan #661030

Dimensions: 30' W x 60' D

Levels: 1

Square Footage: 1,396

Bedrooms: 3

Bathrooms: 2

Foundation: Slab

Materials List Available: Yes

Price Category: B

Images provided by designer/architect.

CAD FILE AVAILABLE

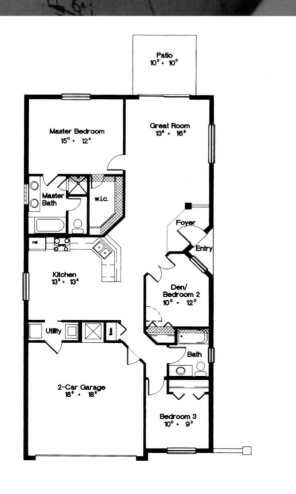

Patio 10° · 10°

Master Bedroom 15° · 12⁴

Great Room 13⁴ · 16°

Master Bath

w.l.c.

Foyer

Entry

Kitchen 13° · 13°

Den/ Bedroom 2 10° · 12°

Utility

Bath

2-Car Garage 18° · 18°

Bedroom 3 10° · 9°

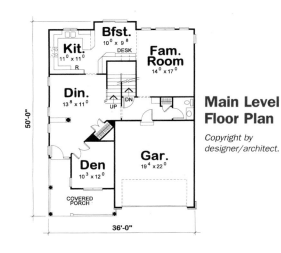

**Main Level
Floor Plan**

*Copyright by
designer/architect.*

36'-0"

50'-0"

Bfst.
10⁰ x 9⁰

Kit.
11⁰ x 11⁰

Fam.
Room
14⁰ x 17⁰

Din.
13⁸ x 11⁰

Den
10³ x 12⁰

Gar.
19⁴ x 22⁰

COVERED
PORCH

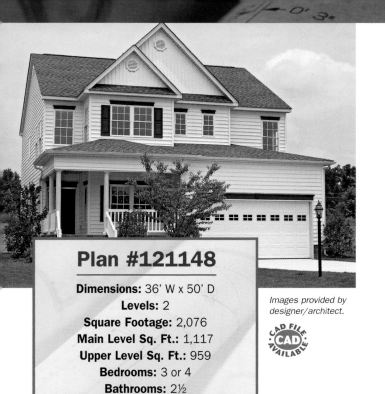

Plan #121148

Dimensions: 36' W x 50' D
Levels: 2
Square Footage: 2,076
Main Level Sq. Ft.: 1,117
Upper Level Sq. Ft.: 959
Bedrooms: 3 or 4
Bathrooms: 2½
Foundation: Basement;
crawl space or slab for fee
Material List Available: Yes
Price Category: D

*Images provided by
designer/architect.*

CAD FILE AVAILABLE

**Upper Level
Floor Plan**

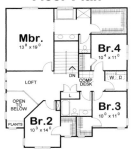

Mbr.
13⁸ x 19⁰

Br.4
10⁴ x 11⁰

LOFT

OPEN TO BELOW

Br.3
10⁰ x 11⁰

Br.2
10³ x 14⁰

PLANTS

**Optional Upper
Level Floor Plan**

Mbr.
13⁸ x 11⁰

OPEN TO BELOW

OPEN TO BELOW

Br.3
10⁰ x 11⁰

Br.2
10³ x 14⁰

PLANTS

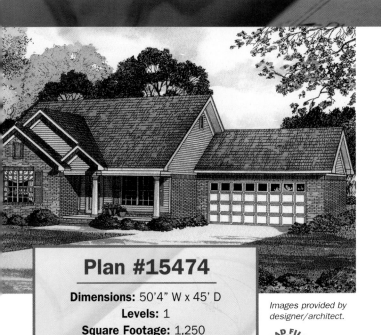

Plan #15474

Dimensions: 50'4" W x 45' D
Levels: 1
Square Footage: 1,250
Bedrooms: 3
Bathrooms: 2
Foundation: Crawl space or slab;
basement or walkout for fee
Complete Cost Available: Yes
Price Category: B

*Images provided by
designer/architect.*

CAD FILE AVAILABLE

50'-4"

45'-0"

STORAGE
15'-7" X 3'-0"

MASTER
SUITE
OPT. 9' BOXED
CEILING
12'-0" X 14'-7"

W.I.C.

M.
BATH

KITCHEN
11'-4" X 14'-7"

GARAGE
20'-0" X 20'-7"

BEDROOM 2
14'-0" X 10'-3"

BREAKFAST
NOOK

BATH

GREAT ROOM
15'-0" X 18'-7"

BEDROOM 3
14'-0" X 11'-0"

COVERED
PORCH
15'-6" X 6'-0"

*Copyright by
designer/architect.*

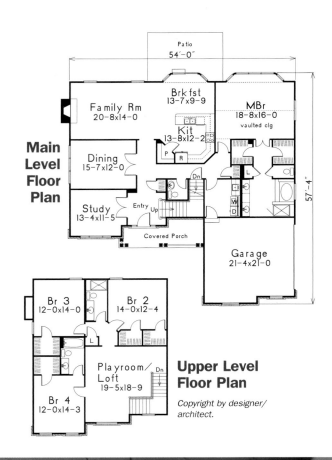

Plan #321062

Dimensions: 54' W x 57'4" D
Levels: 2
Square Footage: 3,138
Main Level Sq. Ft.: 1,958
Upper Level Sq. Ft.: 1,180
Bedrooms: 4
Bathrooms: 3½
Foundation: Basement
Materials List Available: Yes
Price Category: G

Images provided by designer/architect.

This home, as shown in the photograph, may differ from the actual blueprints. For more detailed information, please check the floor plans carefully.

Main Level Floor Plan

Upper Level Floor Plan

Copyright by designer/ architect.

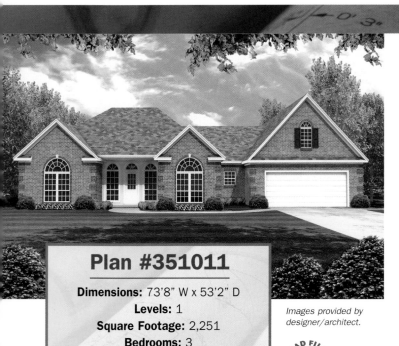

Plan #351011

Dimensions: 73'8" W x 53'2" D
Levels: 1
Square Footage: 2,251
Bedrooms: 3
Bathrooms: 2½
Foundation: Crawl space, slab, or basement
Materials List Available: Yes
Price Category: F

Images provided by designer/architect.

Main Level Floor Plan

Upper Level Floor Plan

Copyright by designer/ architect.

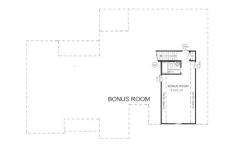

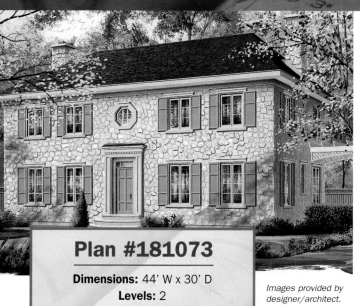

Main Level Floor Plan

44'-0"
13,2 m

30'-0"
9,0 m

Images provided by designer/architect.

Upper Level Floor Plan

Copyright by designer/architect.

Plan #181073

Dimensions: 44' W x 30' D

Levels: 2

Square Footage: 2,663

Main Level Sq. Ft.: 1,343

Upper Level Sq. Ft.: 1,320

Bedrooms: 3

Bathrooms: 2½

Foundation: Basement

Material List Available: Yes

Price Category: H

CAD FILE AVAILABLE

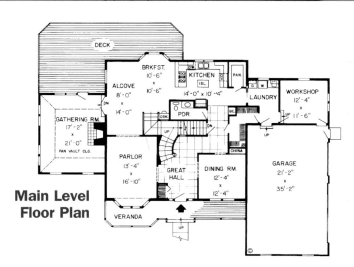

Main Level Floor Plan

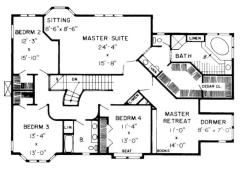

Upper Level Floor Plan

Copyright by designer/architect.

Plan #391055

Dimensions: 76'6" W x 55' D

Levels: 2

Square Footage: 4,217

Main Level Sq. Ft.: 2,108

Upper Level Sq. Ft.: 2,109

Bedrooms: 4

Bathrooms: 2½

Foundation: Basement

Material List Available: Yes

Price Category: I

Images provided by designer/architect.

This home, as shown in the photograph, may differ from the actual blueprints. For more detailed information, please check the floor plans carefully.

Plan #121155

Dimensions: 65'6" W x 56'10" D
Levels: 1.5
Square Footage: 2,638
Main Level Sq. Ft.: 1,844
Upper Level Sq. Ft.: 794
Bedrooms: 4
Bathrooms: 3½
Foundation: Slab; basement for fee
Material List Available: Yes
Price Category: F

This home, as shown in the photograph, may differ from the actual blueprints. For more detailed information, please check the floor plans carefully.

Images provided by designer/architect.

This traditional home is so attractive that passersby will want to stop and visit.

Features:

• Study: Situated in close proximity to the entry, this study would function well as a home office. The triple-window unit adds light to the area.

• Kitchen: This gourmet peninsula kitchen offers a handy pantry. The attached breakfast room offers easy access to the veranda.

• Master Suite: This master suite boasts a vaulted ceiling and two walk-in closets. The private bath shows off a whirlpool tub and dual vanities.

• Secondary Bedrooms: Residing on the upper level are three family bedrooms. Bedroom 4 boasts its own private bath, while bedrooms 2 and 3 share a Jack-and-Jill bathroom.

Upper Level Floor Plan

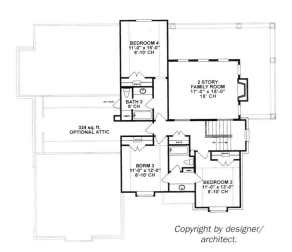

Copyright by designer/architect.

Main Level Floor Plan

Plan #121020

Dimensions: 64' W x 46' D
Levels: 2
Square Footage: 2,480
Main Level Sq. Ft.: 1,369
Upper Level Sq. Ft.: 1,111
Bedrooms: 4
Bathrooms: 2½
Foundation: Basement
Materials List Available: Yes
Price Category: E

Images provided by designer/architect.

Tapered columns and an angled stairway give this home a classical style.

Features:

• Ceiling Height 8 ft.

• Living Room: Just off the dramatic two-story entry is this distinctive living room, with its apered columns, transom-topped windows, and boxed ceiling.

• Formal Dining Room: The tapered columns, transom-topped windows, and boxed ceiling

found in the living room continue into this gracious dining space.

• Family Room: Located on the opposite side of the house from the living room and dining room, the family room features a beamed ceiling and fireplace framed by windows.

• Kitchen: An island is the centerpiece of this convenient kitchen.

• Master Suite: Upstairs, a tiered ceiling and corner windows enhance the master bedroom, which is served by a pampering bath.

Main Level Floor Plan

Upper Level Floor Plan

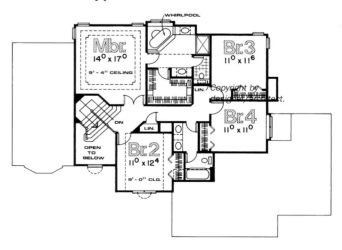

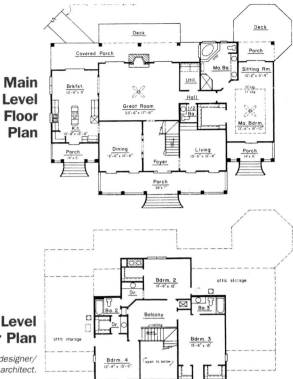

Main Level Floor Plan

Plan #111036

Dimensions: 66' W x 47' D

Levels: 2

Square Footage: 3,149

Main Level Sq. Ft.: 2,033

Upper Level Sq. Ft.: 1,116

Bedrooms: 4

Bathrooms: 3½

Foundation: Slab

Materials List Available: Yes

Price Category: H

Photo provided by designer/architect.

Upper Level Floor Plan

Copyright by designer/architect.

Plan #181505

Dimensions: 30' W x 28' D

Levels: 2

Square Footage: 1,650

Main Level Sq. Ft.: 825

Upper Level Sq. Ft.: 825

Bedrooms: 3

Bathrooms: 2

Foundation: Basement

Material List Available: Yes

Price Category: E

Images provided by designer/architect.

Main Level Floor Plan

Copyright by designer/architect.

28'-0"
8,4 m

30'-0"
9,0 m

Rear Elevation

Upper Level Floor Plan

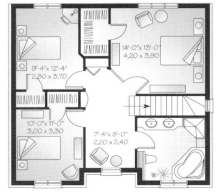

Main Level Floor Plan

Images provided by designer/architect.

Plan #121149

Dimensions: 75'1 1/2" W x 38' D
Levels: 2
Square Footage: 2,715
Main Level Sq. Ft.: 1,400
Upper Level Sq. Ft.: 1,315
Bedrooms: 4
Bathrooms: 3½
Foundation: Slab; basement for fee
Material List Available: Yes
Price Category: F

Upper Level Floor Plan

Copyright by designer/architect.

Main Level Floor Plan

Images provided by designer/architect.

Plan #281001

Dimensions: 54' W x 47' D
Levels: 2
Square Footage: 2,423
Main Level Sq. Ft.: 1,388
Second Level Sq. Ft.: 1,035
Bedrooms: 3
Bathrooms: 2½
Foundation: Basement
Materials List Available: Yes
Price Category: E

Upper Level Floor Plan

Copyright by designer/architect.

Main Level Floor Plan

- Laun. 11'8" x 8'8"
- Bath
- Breakfast 11'4" x 10'4"
- Family Room 17'5" x 15'4"
- Kitchen 15'6" x 10'6"
- Two-car Garage 19'8" x 23' 0"
- Living Room 13'6" x 14'2"
- Dining Room 11'6" x 13'6" to 15'6"
- Foyer
- Porch
- 41'10"
- 54'6"

Copyright by designer/architect.

Upper Level Floor Plan

- Bedroom 11'6" x 12'0"
- Master Bedroom 15'0" x 14'5"
- walk-in closet
- Bedroom 11'8" x 11'0"
- Bath
- Bath
- Balcony
- stairs dn
- Foyer Below
- Bedroom 11'4" x 13'6"
- plant shelf

Plan #161019

Dimensions: 54'6" D x 41'10" W
Levels: 2
Square Footage: 2,428
Main Level Sq. Ft.: 1,309
Upper Level Sq. Ft.: 1,119
Bedrooms: 4
Bathrooms: 2½
Foundation: Basement
Materials List Available: Yes
Price Category: E

Images provided by designer/architect.

Main Level Floor Plan

- GARAGE 28'-0" X 21'-0"
- UTILITY
- BREAKFAST 14'-0" X 11'-10"
- KITCHEN 15'-2" X 13'-4"
- FAMILY ROOM 19'-0" X 23'-0"
- PATIO
- MASTER BEDROOM 18'-0" X 21'-10"
- M BATH
- BEDROOM 2 / STUDY 12'-10" X 12'-0"
- DINING 13'-8" X 16'-8"
- ENTRY
- LIVING ROOM 19'-8" X 25'-0"

Upper Level Floor Plan

- BEDROOM 5 13'-8" X 13'-8"
- DECK
- BEDROOM 4 13'-10" X 15'-8"
- SKY LIGHTS
- DOWN
- OPEN TO ENTRY
- STORAGE
- ATTIC
- BEDROOM 3 13'-8" X 15'-2"

Copyright by designer/architect.

Plan #391054

Dimensions: 111' W x 72'6" D
Levels: 2
Square Footage: 5,254
Main Level Sq. Ft.: 4,075
Upper Level Sq. Ft.: 1,179
Bedrooms: 5
Bathrooms: 5
Foundation: Slab
Material List Available: Yes
Price Category: J

Images provided by designer/architect.

Rear View

Plan #151140

Dimensions: 67'2" W x 55'10" D

Levels: 1

Square Footage: 2,525

Bedrooms: 4

Bathrooms: 3

Foundation: Crawl space, slab

Materials List Available: Yes

Price Category: E

Images provided by designer/architect.

Copyright by designer/architect.

Plan #211070

Dimensions: 46' W x 68' D

Levels: 2

Square Footage: 1,700

Main Level Sq. Ft.: 1,160

Upper Level Sq. Ft.: 540

Bedrooms: 3

Bathrooms: 2½

Foundation: Crawl space or slab; basement option for fee

Materials List Available: Yes

Price Category: C

Images provided by designer/architect.

Upper Level Floor Plan

Main Level Floor Plan

Copyright by designer/architect.

Main Level Floor Plan

Copyright by designer/architect.

GARAGE 21'-0"X20'-10"

63'-0"

KITCHEN 14'-0" X 13'-0"

NOOK 9'-10" X 11'-4"

PATIO

FAMILY ROOM 13'-10"X18'-2"

BAR

M.BEDROOM 15'-0" X 17'-0"

DINING 13'-0" X 13'-0"

FOYER

LIVING ROOM 18'-0"X19'-6"

76'-0"

Images provided by designer/architect.

BEDROOM 12'-10"X11'-0"

BEDROOM 12'-10"X11'-0"

Upper Level Floor Plan

BEDROOM 13'-0"X11'-10"

LIBRARY

Plan #391053

Dimensions: 76' W x 63' D

Levels: 2

Square Footage: 3,128

Main Level Sq. Ft.: 2,277

Upper Level Sq. Ft.: 851

Bedrooms: 4

Bathrooms: 3½

Foundation: Crawl space, slab, or basement

Material List Available: Yes

Price Category: G

WOOD BALCONY

WICL

MSTR BATH

BEDRM #3 11'-0"x 15'-6"

Upper Level Floor Plan

VAULTED MSTR BEDRM 13'-0"x 18'-6"

WICL

BATH

BALCONY

BEDRM #4 12'-6"x 15'-4"

UPPER LIVING ROOM

UPPER FOYER

VAULTED BEDRM #2 10'-0"x 12'-0"

43'-6" OVERALL

SL GL DR

KITCHEN 12'-0"x 13'-0"

BKFST RM 10'-0"x 15'-0"

LAUN RM

48'-6" OVERALL

FAMILY RM 13'-0"x 18'-6"

PANT

DINING RM 17'-0"x 12'-6"

Main Level Floor Plan

VAULTED LIVING RM 15'-0"x 21'-0"

TWO STORY FOYER

DN TO BSMT

UP

TWO CAR GARAGE 17'-4"x 19'-8"

Plan #131066

Dimensions: 43'6" W x 48'6" D

Levels: 2

Square Footage: 2,760

Main Level Sq. Ft.: 1,483

Upper Level Sq. Ft.: 1,277

Bedrooms: 4

Bathrooms: 2½

Foundation: Crawl space or basement

Material List Available: Yes

Price Category: G

Images provided by designer/architect.

Copyright by designer/architect.

Main Level Floor Plan

Plan #131074

Dimensions: 56' W x 41' D
Levels: 2
Square Footage: 2,085
Main Level Sq. Ft.: 1,240
Upper Level Sq. Ft.: 845
Bedrooms: 4
Bathrooms: 2½
Foundation: Slab or basement
Material List Available: Yes
Price Category: E

This home, as shown in the photograph, may differ from the actual blueprints. For more detailed information, please check the floor plans carefully.

Optional Bonus Area Floor Plan

Upper Level Floor Plan

Copyright by designer/architect.

Plan #161021

Dimensions: 48' W x 38' D
Levels: 2
Square Footage: 1,897
Main Level Sq. Ft.: 1,036
Upper Level Sq. Ft.: 861
Bedrooms: 3
Bathrooms: 2½
Foundation: Basement
Materials List Available: Yes
Price Category: D

Images provided by designer/architect.

Rear Elevation

Main Level Floor Plan

Upper Level Floor Plan

Copyright by designer/architect.

Main Level Floor Plan

Images provided by designer/architect.

This home, as shown in the photograph, may differ from the actual blueprints. For more detailed information, please check the floor plans carefully.

Upper Level Floor Plan

Copyright by designer/architect.

Plan #331004

Dimensions: 81' W x 49'10" D
Levels: 2
Square Footage: 3,146
Main Level Sq. Ft.: 2,150
Upper Level Sq. Ft.: 996
Bedrooms: 4
Bathrooms: 3½
Foundation: Crawl space, slab, or basement
Materials List Available: Yes
Price Category: G

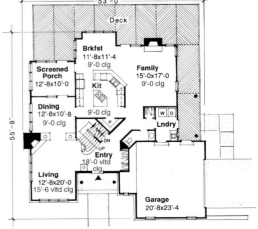

Upper Level Floor Plan

Images provided by designer/architect.

Main Level Floor Plan

Copyright by designer/architect.

Plan #271029

Dimensions: 53' W x 55'8" D
Levels: 2
Square Footage: 3,039
Main Level Sq. Ft.: 1,612
Upper Level Sq. Ft.: 1,427
Bedrooms: 4
Bathrooms: 2½
Foundation: Basement
Materials List Available: Yes
Price Category: G

Main Level Floor Plan

Copyright by designer/architect.

SCREENED PORCH VAULTED CEILING

FAMILY ROOM 18'-0" x 22'-0"

KITCHEN 12'-6" x14'-6"

DINETTE 10'-6"x13'-0"

DINING RM. 14'-8"x14'-0"

PANT. PANT.

DESK

BR.

SKYLT.

HIP VAULT CEILING

FOYER OPEN TO ABOVE

LAUNDRY/ SEWING 11'-2"x11'-2"

BENCH

CABINETS

GARAGE 23'-8" x 25'-7"

LIVING RM. 14'-6"x16'-0"

DEN/STUDY 11'-0"x12'-4"

DRIVEWAY

Images provided by designer/architect.

Plan #391040

Dimensions: 69' W x 55'6" D
Levels: 2
Square Footage: 3,276
Main Level Sq. Ft.: 1,786
Upper Level Sq. Ft.: 1,490
Bedrooms: 4
Bathrooms: 2½
Foundation: Basement
Materials List Available: Yes
Price Category: G

JACUZZI

SHWR.

CAB. ABV.

LIN.

BOOKS

M. BEDROOM 18'-0" x 17'-8" VAULTED CEILING

Upper Level Floor Plan

OPEN TO FOYER

BOOKS

BOOKS

BEDROOM 4 11'-4" x15'-4"

BEDROOM 2 11'-0"x14'-4"

BEDROOM 3 11'-4"x12'-4"

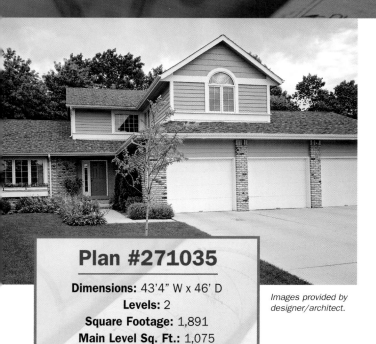

Plan #271035

Dimensions: 43'4" W x 46' D
Levels: 2
Square Footage: 1,891
Main Level Sq. Ft.: 1,075
Upper Level Sq. Ft.: 816
Bedrooms: 3
Bathrooms: 2½
Foundation: Basement
Materials List Available: Yes
Price Category: D

Images provided by designer/architect.

43'-4"

Deck

Main Level Floor Plan

Dining

Kit 10x13

Family 17-4x16-8

Great Room 13x25-4 13-6 vltd clg

46'-0"

Garage 19-8x19-8

Br 2 10-9x12-4

Br 3 10-9x12-4

open to below

MBr 14x16 11 vaulted clg

Upper Level Floor Plan

Copyright by designer/architect.

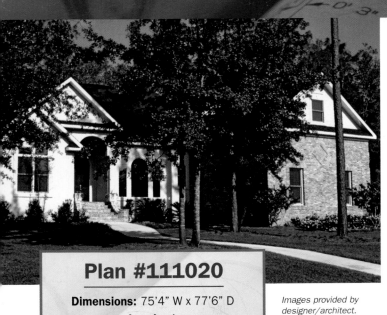

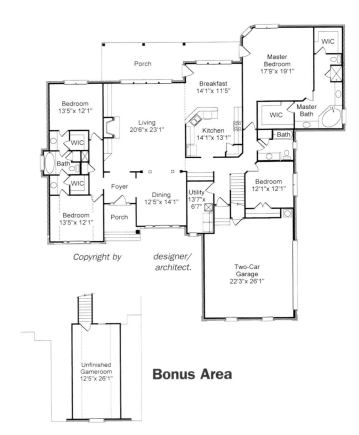

Copyright by designer/architect.

Images provided by designer/architect.

Bonus Area

Plan #111020

Dimensions: 75'4" W x 77'6" D

Levels: 1

Square Footage: 2,987

Bedrooms: 4

Bathrooms: 3

Foundation: Slab

Materials List Available: Yes

Price Category: G

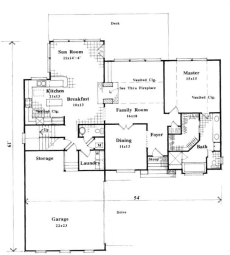

Main Level Floor Plan

Copyright by designer/architect

Images provided by designer/architect.

Plan #251014

Dimensions: 53'8" W x 61' D

Levels: 2

Square Footage: 2,210

Main Level Sq. Ft.: 1,670

Upper Level Sq. Ft.: 540

Bedrooms: 3

Bathrooms: 2 1/2

Foundation: Crawl space or basement

Materials List Available: Yes

Price Category: E

Upper Level Floor Pla

Main Level Floor Plan

Images provided by designer/architect.

Copyright by designer/architect.

Upper Level Floor Plan

Plan #461028

Dimensions: 69' W x 65' D

Levels: 2

Square Footage: 3,663

Main Level Sq. Ft.: 2,516

Upper Level Sq. Ft.: 1,147

Bedrooms: 4

Bathrooms: 4½

Foundation: Basement, slab

Material List Available: Yes

Price Category: H

Rear Elevation

Images provided by designer/architect.

CAD FILE AVAILABLE

Plan #111018

Dimensions: 67' W x 79' D

Levels: 1

Square Footage: 2,745

Bedrooms: 4

Bathrooms: 3½

Foundation: Slab or walkout

Materials List Available: Yes

Price Category: G

Copyright by designer/architect.

**Main Level
Floor Plan**

*Images provided by
designer/architect.*

CAD FILE AVAILABLE

**Upper Level
Floor Plan**

*Copyright by designer/
architect.*

Plan #151019

Dimensions: 63'4" W x 53'10" D

Levels: 2

Square Footage: 2,653

Main Level Sq. Ft.: 1,407

Upper Level Sq. Ft.: 1,246

Bedrooms: 3

Bathrooms: 2½

Foundation: Crawl space, slab;
optional full basement plan available
for extra fee

CompleteCost List Available: Yes

Price Category: F

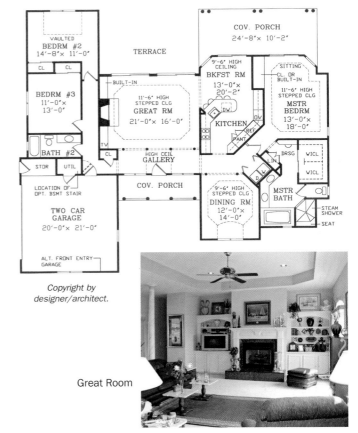

*Images provided by
designer/architect.*

*Copyright by
designer/architect.*

Great Room

Plan #131009

Dimensions: 64'10" W x 57'8" D

Levels: 1

Square Footage: 2,018

Bedrooms: 3

Bathrooms: 2

Foundation: Crawl space or slab;
basement or walkout for fee

Materials List Available: Yes

Price Category: E

Main Level Floor Plan

Images provided by designer/architect.

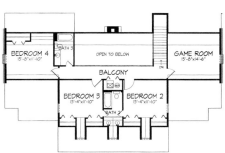

Upper Level Floor Plan

Copyright by designer/architect.

Plan #271098

Dimensions: 68'10" W x 81'5" D

Levels: 2

Square Footage: 3,382

Main Level Sq. Ft.: 2,136

Upper Level Sq. Ft.: 1,246

Bedrooms: 4

Bathrooms: 3½

Foundation: Slab

Materials List Available: Yes

Price Category: G

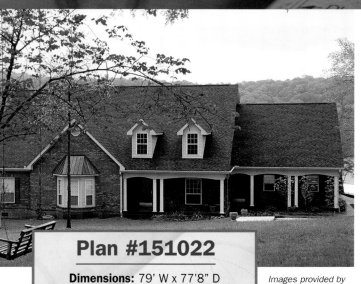

Main Level Floor Plan

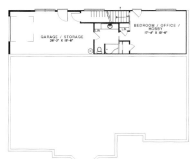

Upper Level Floor Plan

Copyright by designer/architect.

Plan #151022

Dimensions: 79' W x 77'8" D

Levels: 2

Square Footage: 3,059

Main Level Sq. Ft.: 2,650

Upper Level Sq. Ft.: 409

Bedrooms: 4

Bathrooms: 4

Foundation: Crawl space, slab, or basement

CompleteCost List Available: Yes

Price Category: G

Images provided by designer/architect.

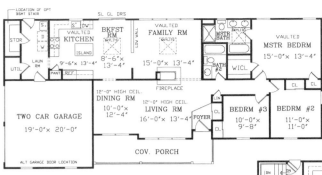

Plan #131010

Dimensions: 70' W x 34'4" D
Levels: 1
Square Footage: 1,667
Bedrooms: 3
Bathrooms: 2
Foundation: Crawl space or slab; basement for fee
Materials List Available: Yes
Price Category: D

Images provided by designer/architect.

Family Room /
Kitchen
Living Room

Optional Laundry Room with Basement Floor Plan

Plan #121165

Dimensions: 46' W x 55' D
Levels: 1
Square Footage: 1,678
Bedrooms: 3
Bathrooms: 2
Foundation: Basement; crawl space for fee
Material List Available: Yes
Price Category: C

Images provided by designer/architect.

This home, as shown in the photograph, may differ from the actual blueprints. For more detailed information, please check the floor plans carefully.

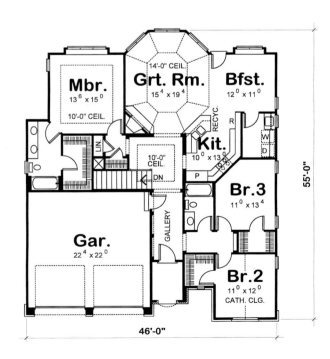

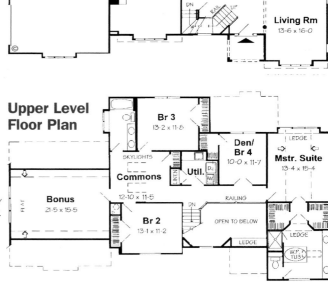

Main Level Floor Plan

Porch

Brkfst. 10-0 x 9-6

Kitchen 10-11 13-8

Dining Rm 11-0 15-5

Family Rm 13-5 x 19-5

Garage 21-5 x 27-4

OPEN TO ABOVE

Living Rm 13-6 x 16-0

Images provided by designer/architect.

Upper Level Floor Plan

Br 3 13-2 x 11-8

Den/Br 4 10-0 x 11-7

Mstr. Suite 13-4 x 15-4

LEDGE

SKYLIGHTS

Commons 12-10 x 11-5

Util.

LINEN

Copyright by designer/architect.

Bonus 21-5 15-5

Br 2 13-1 11-2

OPEN TO BELOW

LEDGE

W.P. TUB

Plan #391067

Dimensions: 69'8" W x 42' D

Levels: 2

Square Footage: 2,897

Main Level Sq. Ft.: 1,435

Upper Level Sq. Ft.: 1,462

Bedrooms: 4

Bathrooms: 2½

Foundation: Crawl space, slab, or basement

Material List Available: Yes

Price Category: F

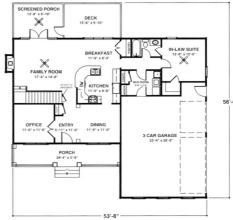

SCREENED PORCH 13-8 x 9-10

DECK 15-6 x 9-10

BREAKFAST 11-9 x 8-3

IN-LAW SUITE 12-6 x 12-0

Main Level Floor Plan

FAMILY ROOM 17-3 x 14-8

KITCHEN 11-9 x 9-8

MUD ROOM

56'-0"

OFFICE 11-0 x 11-6

ENTRY 5-11 x 11-0

DINING 11-9 x 11-0

3 CAR GARAGE 23-4 x 28-9

PORCH 29-4 x 5-9

53'-8"

UPPER DECK 11-10 x 9-10

SITTING

MASTER SUITE 21-4 x 14-9

2'6 SPA TUB

3'x6' SHOWER

SEAT

OPEN BELOW 17-3 x 18-3

TRAY CEILING

CLOSET 13-6 x 5-11

OPTIONAL MASTER CLOSET EXPANSION OR STORAGE 7-10 x 30-0

BEDROOM 2 12-0 x 11-0

BEDROOM 3 12-0 x 11-0

5' HIGH KNEE WALLS

Upper Level Floor Plan

Copyright by designer/architect.

Plan #101138

Dimensions: 53'8" W x 56' D

Levels: 2

Square Footage: 2,234

Main Level Sq. Ft.: 1,274

Upper Level Sq. Ft.: 960

Bedrooms: 4

Bathrooms: 3

Foundation: Basement

Materials List Available: Yes

Price Category: E

Images provided by designer/architect.

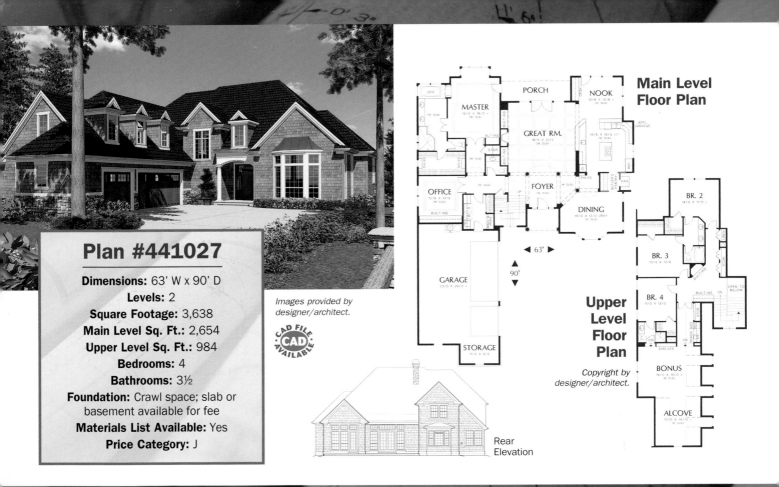

Plan #441027

Dimensions: 63' W x 90' D

Levels: 2

Square Footage: 3,638

Main Level Sq. Ft.: 2,654

Upper Level Sq. Ft.: 984

Bedrooms: 4

Bathrooms: 3½

Foundation: Crawl space; slab or basement available for fee

Materials List Available: Yes

Price Category: J

Images provided by designer/architect.

CAD FILE AVAILABLE

Main Level Floor Plan

MASTER · PORCH · NOOK · GREAT RM. · OFFICE · FOYER · DINING · GARAGE · STORAGE

Upper Level Floor Plan

BR. 2 · BR. 3 · BR. 4 · BONUS · ALCOVE

Copyright by designer/architect.

Rear Elevation

Plan #111014

Dimensions: 78' W x 47' D

Levels: 1

Square Footage: 1,865

Bedrooms: 4

Bathrooms: 2

Foundation: Slab

Materials List Available: Yes

Price Category: E

Images provided by designer/architect.

Master Bedroom 14'8"x 14' · Porch · Breakfast · Bedroom 11'x 10' · Living 19'4"x 15'6" · Bedroom 10'6"x 11'6" · Dining 10'6"x 11'6" · Bedroom 11'x 10'6" · Porch · Two Car Garage 19'6"x 22'8"

Copyright by designer/architect.

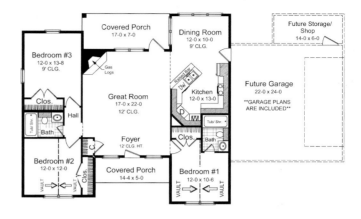

Images provided by designer/architect.

CAD FILE AVAILABLE

Plan #351018

Dimensions: 40'8" W x 38'6" D

Levels: 1

Square Footage: 1,251

Bedrooms: 3

Bathrooms: 2

Foundation: Crawl space or slab

Materials List Available: Yes

Price Category: B

Copyright by designer/architect.

Images provided by designer/architect.

CAD FILE AVAILABLE

Plan #341024

Dimensions: 49'6" W x 39'8" D

Levels: 1

Square Footage: 1,310

Bedrooms: 3

Bathroom: 2

Foundation: Crawl space

Materials List Available: Yes

Price Category: B

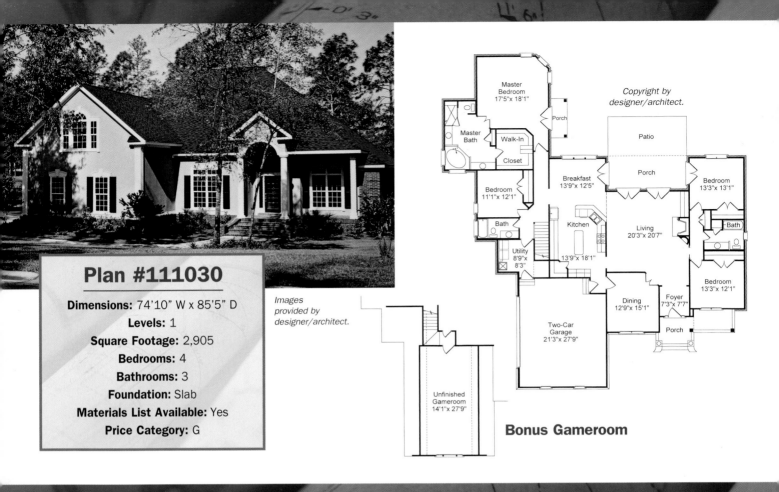

Plan #111030

Dimensions: 74'10" W x 85'5" D

Levels: 1

Square Footage: 2,905

Bedrooms: 4

Bathrooms: 3

Foundation: Slab

Materials List Available: Yes

Price Category: G

Images provided by designer/architect.

Copyright by designer/architect.

Bonus Gameroom

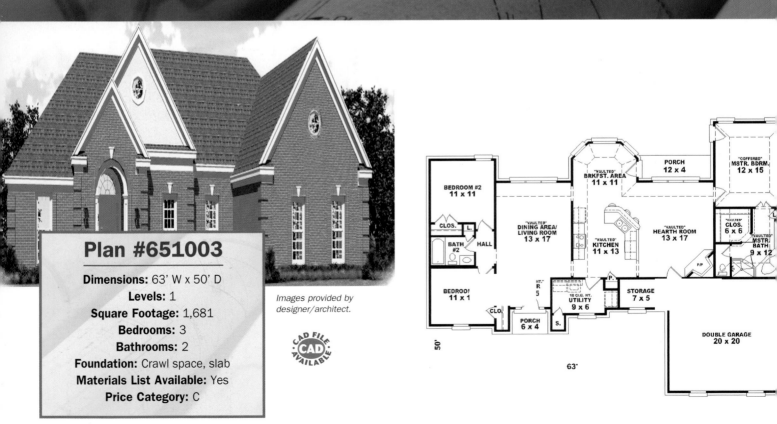

Plan #651003

Dimensions: 63' W x 50' D

Levels: 1

Square Footage: 1,681

Bedrooms: 3

Bathrooms: 2

Foundation: Crawl space, slab

Materials List Available: Yes

Price Category: C

Images provided by designer/architect.

CAD FILE AVAILABLE

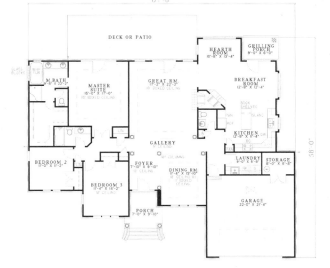

Main Floor

Plan #151277

Dimensions: 67'8" W x 58' D

Levels: 1

Square Footage: 2,216

Bedrooms: 3

Bathrooms: 2 1/2

Foundation: Crawl space or slab

CompleteCost List Available: Yes

Price Category: E

Images provided by designer/architect.

CAD FILE AVAILABLE CAD

Main Level Floor Plan

Plan #181087

Dimensions: 32'8" W x 38' D

Levels: 2

Square Footage: 1,909

Main Level Sq. Ft.: 880

Upper Level Sq. Ft.: 1,029

Bedrooms: 4

Bathrooms: 2½

Foundation: Basement

Material List Available: Yes

Price Category: F

Images provided by designer/architect.

CAD FILE AVAILABLE CAD

Upper Level Floor Plan

Copyright by designer/architect.

Plan #161135

Dimensions: 42' W x 75' D
Levels: 2
Square Footage: 2,495
Main Level Sq. Ft.: 1,847
Upper Level Sq. Ft.: 648
Bedrooms: 3
Bathrooms: 3
Foundation: Slab or basement; crawl space for fee
Material List Available: Yes
Price Category: E

Images provided by designer/architect.

This charming cottage-style home is both practical and beautiful-the perfect place to raise a family and welcome friends.

Features:

- **Foyer:** Enter the home through the covered porch into this foyer. The sidelights around the front door brighten the area. The bathroom and walk-in closet add to the convenience of the entry area.

- **Great Room:** The main gathering area of this home is this two-story great room. A corner fireplace adds a focal point to the room.

- **Master Suite:** This retreat features a large sleeping area and access to the patio. The master bath boasts dual vanities, a separate shower, a spa tub, and a very large walk-in closet.

- **Upper Level:** This optional area can be finished to include a loft with a view down into the great room. There is also room for a guest suite.

Main Level Floor Plan

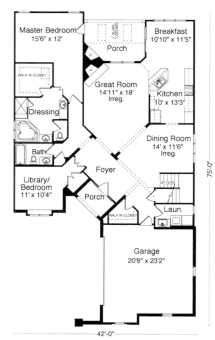

Upper Level Floor Plan

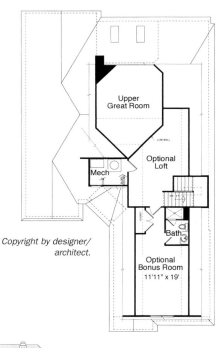

Copyright by designer/architect.

Rear Elevation

Plan #271091

Dimensions: 68' W x 43' D
Levels: 2
Square Footage: 2,854
Main Level Sq. Ft.: 1,219
Upper Level Sq. Ft.: 1,635
Bedrooms: 3
Bathrooms: 2½
Foundation: Daylight basement
Materials List Available: Yes
Price Category: F

This Craftsman-style home has a unique design to accommodate the needs of a growing family.

Features:

- **Porch:** A long covered porch shelters guests from the elements or gives you outdoor living space where you can sit and greet the neighbors.

- **Great Room:** This large gathering room, with a two-sided fireplace it shares with the study, draws you in to share good times. Open to the dining room and kitchen, it allows friends and family to flow among all three spaces.

- **Master Suite:** Located on the upper level with the secondary bedrooms, this retreat offers privacy. The master bath boasts a double-bowl vanity and whirlpool tub to offer luxury and comfort.

- **Garage:** A large front-load three-car garage can hold cars or other items you need to store.

Images provided by designer/architect.

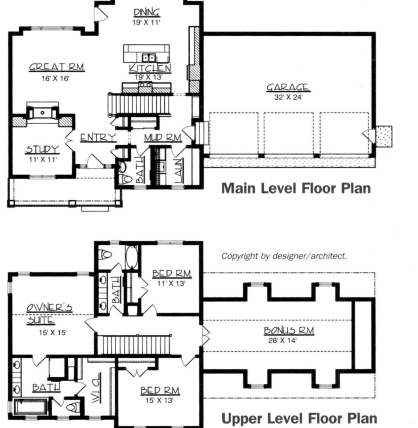

Main Level Floor Plan

Copyright by designer/architect.

Upper Level Floor Plan

Plan #161133

Dimensions: 42' W x 70'8" D
Levels: 2
Square Footage: 2,412
Main Level Sq. Ft.: 1,820
Upper Level Sq. Ft.: 552
Bedrooms: 3
Bathrooms: 3
Foundation: Slab or basement; crawl space or walkout for fee
Material List Available: Yes
Price Category: F

Dramatic design coupled with elegant architectural detailing contributes to the lovely façade of this home.

Features:

- **Great Room:** With its cathedral ceiling and glowing fireplace, this room welcomes you home. Relax with your family or entertain your friends.

- **Kitchen:** Release the chef inside of you with this gourmet kitchen, complete with seating at the peninsula and access to the breakfast area. Step through the glass door to enjoy the fresh air on the rear porch.

- **Master Suite:** Located on the main level for convenience and privacy, this retreat offers a large sleeping area. The master bath boasts dual vanities and a stall shower.

- **Upper Level:** A loft, with a view down to the great room, is located on this level. A bonus room with a full bathroom can be finished as a guest suite.

Main Level Floor Plan

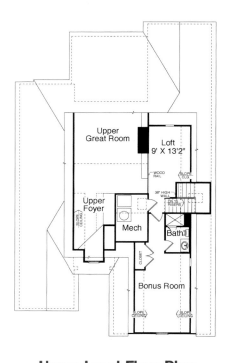

Upper Level Floor Plan

Rear Elevation

Plan #161134

Dimensions: 50' W x 75' D
Levels: 2
Square Footage: 2,605
Main Level Sq. Ft.: 1,953
Upper Level Sq. Ft.: 652
Bedrooms: 3
Bathrooms: 3
Foundation: Slab or basement; crawl space or walkout for fee
Material List Available: Yes
Price Category: F

This home would be great for a new family or an empty nester couple.

Images provided by designer/architect.

Features:

- Great Room: Angled walls and a sloped ceiling add drama to this gathering area. The fireplace will add cozy warmth when your friends visit.
- Library: A bay window adds style to this library located just off the foyer. A large walk-in closet creates the option to make this room an additional bedroom.
- Dining Room: The unique shape of this area adds elegance to this formal eating area. The kitchen is close by, making serving guests convenient.
- Kitchen: This peninsula kitchen boasts long counters lined with cabinetry, making it a gourmet's delight to prepare meals in the area. The raised snack bar is open to the great room and breakfast room.

Main Level Floor Plan

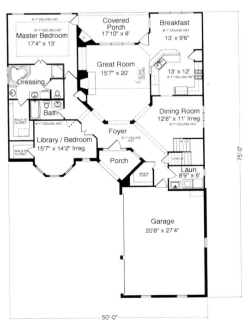

Upper Level Floor Plan

Copyright by designer/architect.

Rear Elevation

Plan #151106

Dimensions: 70' W x 81' D
Levels: 1.5
Square Footage: 3,568
Main Level Sq. Ft.: 3,051
Upper Level Sq. Ft.: 517
Bedrooms: 3
Bathrooms: 3 full, 2 half
Foundation: Crawl space or slab; basement or walkout for fee
CompleteCost List Available: Yes
Price Category: F

Images provided by designer/architect.

Satisfy your personal needs with this home.

Features:

- **Great Room:** This large gathering space has a cozy fireplace and built-ins for casual get-togethers. French doors lead to a future rear patio.

- **Kitchen:** This efficient U-shaped kitchen has a raised snack bar that looks into the adjoining breakfast room. The laundry room is located just off this space.

- **Master Suite:** This suite, with its sitting area, is the perfect place for an escape after a busy day. The master bath has two walk-in closets, dual vanities, a shower, and a large tub.

- **Secondary Bedrooms:** Bedroom 2 and 3 share a Jack-and-Jill bathroom and are located near the master suite.

Main Level Floor Plan

Upper Level Floor Plan

Copyright by designer/architect.

Plan #131078

Dimensions: 72'8" W x 47' D
Levels: 2
Square Footage: 3,278
Main Level Sq. Ft.: 2,146
Upper Level Sq. Ft.: 1,132
Bedrooms: 3
Bathrooms: 3
Foundation: Foundation: Crawl space or slab; basement for fee
Material List Available: Yes
Price Category: H

This attractive home is a delight when viewed from the outside and features a great floor plan inside.

Images provided by designer/architect.

Features:

• Great Room: This spacious room, with a vaulted ceiling and skylights, is the place to curl up by the fireplace on a cold winter night. Sliding glass doors lead out to the backyard.

• Kitchen: A center island adds convenience to this well-planned kitchen. The bayed breakfast area adds extra room for a table.

• Master Suite: The 10-ft.-high stepped ceiling sets the tone for this secluded area, which features a large walk-in closet. The master bath boasts a whirlpool tub and dual vanities.

• Bonus Room: Located above the garage, this space can be finished as a fourth bedroom or home office.

Rear View

Main Level Floor Plan

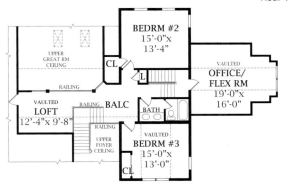

Upper Level Floor Plan

Copyright by designer/architect.

Plan #161138

Dimensions: 42' W x 70'8" D
Levels: 2
Square Footage: 2,112
Main Level Sq. Ft.: 1,616
Upper Level Sq. Ft.: 496
Bedrooms: 3
Bathrooms: 3
Foundation: Slab or basement; crawl space for fee
Material List Available: Yes
Price Category: D

Indoor and outdoor enjoyment is featured in this narrow-lot patio home.

Features:

- Great Room: This elegant area, with a gas fireplace and high ceiling, enjoys a view of the backyard. The open floor plan allows the kitchen and dining area to become an extension of the great room, creating a roomy gathering space.

- Kitchen: Located off the great room, your family will enjoy meals together in this expansive kitchen. It features a raised eating bar and is open into the dining room.

- Master Suite: Luxury enhances your lifestyle in this romantic master suite. A spacious bedroom leads into a full bath, which contains his and her sinks, a separate shower, and a whirlpool tub.

- Bonus Room: A bonus space is available on the second floor. A loft overlooks the great room, and an optional bedroom and bath offer privacy to overnight visitors.

Images provided by designer/architect.

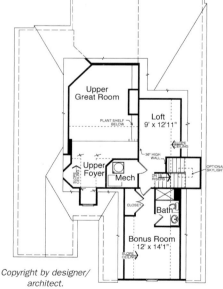

Main Level Floor Plan

Copyright by designer/architect.

Upper Level Floor Plan

Rear Elevation

Let Us Help You
Plan Your Dream Home

Whether you've always dreamed of building your own home or you can't find the right house from among the dozens you've toured, our collection of ultimate plans can help you achieve the home of your dreams. You could have an architect create a one-of-a-kind home for you, but the design services alone could end up costing up to 15 percent of the cost of construction---a hefty premium for any building project. Isn't it a better idea to select from among the hundreds of unique designs shown in our collection for a fraction of the cost?

What Does Creative Homeowner Offer?

In this book, Creative Homeowner provides hundreds of home plans from North America's best architects and designers. Our designs are among the most popular available. By using this book or visiting our Web site, **ultimateplans.com,** you will be sure to find the house design best suited to you and your family. Our plan packages include detailed drawings to help you or your builder construct your dream house. **(See page 598.)**

Can I Make Changes to the Plans?

Creative Homeowner offers three ways to help you achieve a truly unique home design. Our customizing service allows for extensive changes to our designs—a custom home for thousands of dollars less. **(See page 599.)** We also provide reverse images of our plans, or we can give you and your builder the tools for making minor changes on your own. **(See page 602.)**

Can You Help Me Manage My Costs?

To help you stay within your budget, Creative Homeowner has teamed up with North America's leading estimating company to provide one of the most accurate, complete, and reliable building material take-offs in the industry, which will help you price out construction costs. **(See page 600.)** If that is too much detail for you, we can provide you with general construction costs based on your zip code. **(See page 602.)** If you don't want a take-off, you have the option of buying a materials list with many of our plans.

How Do I Begin the Building Process?

To get started building your dream home, fill out the order form on page 603, call our order department at **1-800-523-6789,** or visit our Web site, **ultimateplans.com**. If you plan on doing all or part of the work yourself, or want to keep tabs on your builder, we offer best-selling building and design books at **creativehomeowner.com.**

Our Plans Packages Offer:

"Square footage" refers to the total "heated square feet" of this plan. This number does not include the garage, porches, or unfinished areas. All of our home plans are the result of many hours of work by leading architects and professional designers. Most of our home plans include each of the following:

Frontal Sheet

This artist's rendering of the front of the house gives you an idea of how the house will look once it is completed and the property landscaped.

Detailed Floor Plans

These plans show the size and layout of the rooms. They also provide the locations of doors, windows, fireplaces, closets, stairs, and electrical outlets and switches.

Foundation Plan

A foundation plan gives the dimensions of basements, walk-out basements, crawl spaces, pier foundations, and slab construction. Each house design lists the type of foundation included. If the plan you choose does not have the foundation type you require, our customer service department can help you customize the plan to meet your needs.

Roof Plan

In addition to providing the pitch of the roof, these plans also show the locations of dormers, skylights, and other elements.

Exterior Elevations

These drawings show the front, rear, and sides of the house as if you were looking at it head on. Elevations also provide information about architectural features and finish materials.

Interior Elevations and Details

Interior elevations show specific details of such elements as fireplaces, kitchen and bathroom cabinets, built-ins, and other unique features of the design.

Cross Sections

This shows the structure as if it were sliced to reveal construction requirements, such as insulation, flooring, and roofing details.

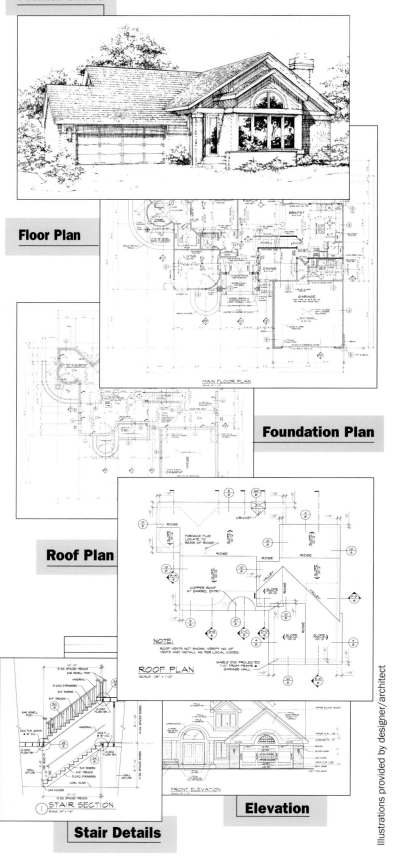

Frontal Sheet

Floor Plan

Foundation Plan

Roof Plan

Elevation

Stair Details

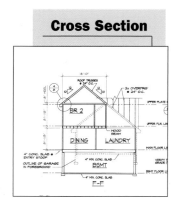

Cross Section

Illustrations provided by designer/architect

Customize Your Plans in 4 Easy Steps

1 **Select the home plan** that most closely meets your needs. Purchase of a reproducible master, PDF files or CAD files is necessary in order to make changes to a plan.

2 **Call 1-800-523-6789 to place your order.** Tell our sales representative you are interested in customizing your plan, and provide your contact information. Within a day or two you will be contacted (via phone or email) to provide a list or sketch of the changes requested to one of our plans. There is no consultation fee for this service.

3 **Within three business days** of receipt of your request, a detailed cost estimate will be provided to you.

4 **Once you approve the estimate,** you will purchase either the reproducible master, PDF files, or CAD files, and customization work will begin. During all phases of the project, you will receive progress prints by fax or email. On average, the project will be completed in two or three weeks. After completion of the work, modified plans will be shipped. You will receive one set of blueprints in addition to a reproducible master or CAD files, depending on which package you purchased.

Modification Pricing Guide

Categories	Average Cost For Modification
Add or remove living space	Quote required
Bathroom layout redesign	Starting at $150
Kitchen layout redesign	Starting at $120
Garage: add or remove	Starting at $600
Garage: front entry to side load or vice versa	Starting at $300
Foundation changes	Starting at $220
Exterior building materials change	Starting at $200
Exterior openings: add, move, or remove	$75 per opening
Roof line changes	Starting at $600
Ceiling height adjustments	Starting at $280
Fireplace: add or remove	Starting at $90
Screened porch: add	Starting at $300
Wall framing change from 2x4 to 2x6	Starting at $250
Bearing and/or exterior walls changes	Quote required
Non-bearing wall or room changes	$65 per room
Metric conversion of home plan	Starting at $495
Adjust plan for handicapped accessibility	Quote required
Adapt plans for local building code requirements	Quote required
Engineering stamping only	Quote required
Any other engineering services	Quote required
Interactive illustrations (choices of exterior materials)	Quote required

Note: *Any home plan can be customized to accommodate your desired changes. The average prices above are provided only as examples of the most commonly requested changes, and are subject to change without notice. Prices for changes will vary according to the number of modifications requested, plan size, style, and method of design used by the original designer. To obtain a detailed cost estimate, please contact us.*

Terms & Copyright

These home plans are protected under the terms of United States Copyright Law and may not be copied or reproduced in any way, by any means, unless you have purchased reproducible masters, which clearly indicate your right to copy or reproduce. We authorize the use of your chosen home plan as an aid in the construction of one single-family home only. You may not use this home plan to build a second or multiple dwellings without purchasing another blueprint or blueprints, or paying additional home plan fees.

Architectural Seals

Because of differences in building codes, some cities and states now require an architect or engineer licensed in that state to review and "seal" a blueprint, or officially approve it, prior to construction. Delaware, Nevada, New Jersey, New York, and some other states require that all plans for houses built in those states be redrawn by an architect licensed in the state in which the home will be built. We strongly advise you to consult with your local building official for information regarding architectural seals.

Before Customization

After

Turn your dream home into reality with

a **Material Take-off** and **ProServices**

LOWE'S®

When purchasing a home plan with Creative Homeowner, we recommend you order one of the most complete materials lists in the industry.

Quote

- Basis of the entire estimate.

- Detailed list of all the framing materials needed to build your project, listed from the bottom up, in the order that each one will actually be used.

Comments

- Details pertinent information beyond the cost of materials.

- Includes any notes from our estimator.

Express List

- A version of the Quote with space for SKU numbers listed for purchasing the items at your local lumberyard.

- Your local lumberyard can then price out the materials list.

Construction-Ready Framing Diagrams

- Your "map" to exact roof and floor framing.

Millwork Report

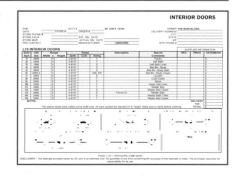

- A complete count of the windows, doors, molding, and trim.

Man-Hour Report

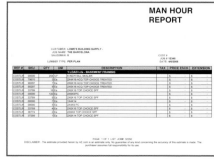

- Calculates labor on a line-by-line basis for all items quoted and presented in man-hours.

Accurate. Professional estimators break down each individual item from the blueprints using advanced software, techniques, and equipment.

Timely. You will be able to start your home-building project quickly — knowing the exact framing materials you need and how to get them with Lowe's.

Detailed. Work with your Lowe's associate to select the remaining products needed for your new home and get a final, accurate quote.

3

Pricing is determined by the total square feet of the home plan — including living area, garages, decks, porches, finished basements, and finished attics.

Square Feet Range	MT Tier*	Price
Up to 5,000 total square feet	XB	$345.00
5,001 to 10,000 total square feet	XC	$545.00

*Please see the Plan Index to determine your plan's Material Take-off Tier (MT Tier).
Note: All prices subject to change.

Call our toll-free number (800-523-6789), or visit ultimateplans.com to order your Material Take-off (also called Ultimate Estimate online).

4

When you purchase your products from Lowe's you may receive a gift card for the amount of your **Material Take-off.** Please go to **UltimatePlans.com** and select **Ultimate Estimate** located under "Quick Links" for complete details of the program.

The Lowe's Advantage:

What's more is you can save an **additional 10%** (up to $500.00) on your first building material purchase.* You will receive details on this program with your order.

Turn your dream home into reality.

*Good for a single purchase of any in-stock or Special Order merchandise only up to $5,000 (maximum discount $500). Not valid on previous sales, service or installation fees, the purchase of gift cards, or any products by Fisher & Paykel, Electrolux, John Deere, or Weber.

Decide What Type of Plan Package You Need

How many Plans Should You Order?

Standard 8-Set Package. We've found that our 8-set package is the best value for someone who is ready to start building. The 8-set package provides plans for you, your builder, the subcontractors, mortgage lender, and the building department.

Minimum 5-Set Package. If you are in the bidding process, you may want to order only five sets for the bidding round and reorder additional sets as needed.

1-Set Study Package. The 1-set package allows you to review your home plan in detail. The plan set is not a complete construction package and will be marked as a study print. It is illegal to build a house from a study print alone. It is a violation of copyright law to reproduce a blueprint without permission. This plan cannot be exchanged or returned, it can only be upgraded to a full build set of the same plan.

Buying Additional Sets. If you require additional copies of blueprints for your home construction, you can order additional sets within 60 days of the original order date at a reduced price. The cost is $50.00 for each additional set. For more information, contact customer service.

Reproducible Masters

If you plan to make minor changes to one of our home plans, you can purchase reproducible masters. These plans are printed on bond or vellum paper that is easy to alter. They clearly indicate your right to modify, copy, or reproduce the plans. Reproducible masters allow an architect, designer, or builder to alter our plans to give you a customized home design. This package allows you to print as many copies of the modified plans as you need for the construction of one home.

PDF Files

PDF files are a complete set of home plans in electronic file format sent to you via email. These files cannot be altered electronically, once printed changes can be hand drawn. A PDF file gives you the license to modify the plans to fit your needs and build one home. Not available for all plans. Please contact our order department or visit our Web site to check the availability of PDF files for your plan.

CAD (Computer-Aided Design) Files

CAD files are the complete set of home plans in an electronic file format. Choose this option if there are multiple changes you wish made to the home plans and you have a local design professional able to make the changes. Not available for all plans. Please contact our order department or visit our Web site to check the availability of CAD files for your plan.

Mirror-Reverse Sets/Right-Reading Reverse

Plans can be printed in mirror-reverse—we can "flip" plans to create a mirror image of the design. This is useful when the house would fit your site or personal preferences if all the rooms were on the opposite side than shown. As the image is reversed, the lettering and dimensions will also be reversed, meaning they will read backwards. Therefore, when ordering mirror-reverse drawings, you must order at least one set of the original plan unreversed. A $50.00 fee per plan order will be charged for mirror-reverse (regardless of the number of mirror-reverse sets ordered). Some plans are available in right-reading reverse; this feature will show the plan in reverse, but the writing on the plan will be readable. A $150.00 fee per plan order will be charged for right-reading reverse (regardless of the number of right-reading reverse sets ordered). Please contact our order department or visit our Web site to check the availibility of this feature for your chosen plan.

EZ Quote® : Home Cost Estimator

EZ Quote® is our response to a frequently asked question we hear from customers: "How much will the house cost me to build?" EZ Quote®: Home Cost Estimator will enable you to obtain a calculated building cost to construct your home, based on labor rates and building material costs within your zip code area. This summary is useful for those who want to get an idea of the total construction costs before purchasing sets of home plans. It will also provide a level of comfort when you begin soliciting bids. The cost is $29.95 for the first EZ Quote and $19.95 for each additional one in the same order. Available only in the U.S. and Canada.

Materials List

Available for most of our plans, the Materials List provides you an invaluable resource in planning and estimating the cost of your home. Each Materials List outlines the quantity, dimensions, and type of materials needed to build your home (with the exception of mechanical systems). You will get faster, more-accurate bids from your contractors and building suppliers. A Materials List may only be ordered with the purchase of at least five sets of home plans.

CompleteCost Estimator

CompleteCost Estimator is a valuable tool for use in planning and constructing your new home. It provides more detail than a materials list and will act as a checklist for all items you will need to select or coordinate during your building process. CompleteCost Estimator is only available for certain plans (please see Plan Index) and may only be ordered with the purchase of at least five sets of home plans. The cost is $125.00 for CompleteCost Estimator

Lowe's Material Take-off (See page 600.)

Material Take-off may take 2 to 3 weeks for delivery.

Order Toll Free by Phone	Order Online	Canadian Customers
1-800-523-6789	**www.ultimateplans.com**	**Order Toll Free 1-800-393-1883**
By Fax: 201-760-2431	**Mail Your Order**	**Mail Your Order (Canada)**
	Creative Homeowner	Creative Homeowner Canada
Orders received 3PM ET, will be processed and shipped within two business days.	Attn: Home Plans	Attn: Home Plans
	24 Park Way	113-437 Martin St., Ste. 215
	Upper Saddle River, NJ 07458	Penticton, BC V2A 5L1

Before You Order

Our Exchange Policy

Blueprints are nonrefundable. However, should you find that the plan you have purchased does not fit your needs, you may exchange that plan for another plan in our collection within 60 days from the date of your original order. The entire content of your original order must be returned before an exchange will be processed. You will be charged a processing fee of 20% of the amount of the original order, the cost difference between the new plan set and the original plan set (if applicable), and all related shipping costs for the new plans. Contact our order department for more information. Please note: reproducible masters may only be exchanged if the package is unopened. PDF files and CAD files cannot be exchanged and are nonrefundable.

Building Codes and Requirements

All plans offered for sale in this book and on our Web site (www.ultimateplans.com) are continually updated to meet the latest International Residential Code (IRC). Because building codes vary from area to area, some drawing modifications and/or the assistance of a professional designer or architect may be necessary to comply with your local codes or to accommodate specific building site conditions. We strongly advise you to consult with your local building official for information regarding codes governing your area.

Multiple Plan Discount

Purchase **3** different home plans in the **same order** and receive **5% off** the plan price.

Purchase **5** or more different home plans in the **same order** and receive **10% off** the plan price. (Please Note: Study sets do not apply.)

Blueprint Price Schedule

Price Code	1 Set	5 Sets	8 Sets	Reproducible Masters or PDF Files	CAD	Materials List
A	$431	$494	$572	$693	$1,181	$89
B	$488	$567	$646	$777	$1,376	$89
C	$551	$651	$730	$861	$1,549	$89
D	$604	$704	$782	$914	$1,654	$100
E	$656	$767	$845	$971	$1,759	$100
F	$725	$830	$908	$1,040	$1,890	$100
G	$756	$861	$940	$1,071	$1,937	$100
H	$767	$872	$950	$1,097	$1,995	$100
I	$1,045	$1,150	$1,229	$1,355	$2,216	$110
J	$1,250	$1,355	$1,433	$1,565	$2,415	$110
K	$1,255	$1,360	$1,439	$1,570	$2,415	$110
L	$1,302	$1,402	$1,481	$1,612	$2,520	$110

Note: All prices subject to change

Lowe's Material Take-off (MT Tier)

MT Tier*	Price
XB	$345
XC	$545

* Please see the Plan Index to determine your plan's Lowe's Material Take-off (MT Tier).

Shipping & Handling

	1–4 Sets	5–7 Sets	8+ Sets or Reproducibles	CAD
US Regular (7–10 business days)	$18	$20	$25	$25
US Priority (3–5 business days)	$35	$40	$45	$45
US Express (1–2 business days)	$45	$60	$80	$50
Canada Express (3–4 business days)	$100	$100	$100	$100
Worldwide Express (3–5 business days)	** Quote Required **			

Note: All delivery times are from date the blueprint package is shipped (typically within 1-2 days of placing order).

Order Form
Please send me the following:

Plan Number: _____ **Price Code:** _____ (See Plan Index.)

Indicate Foundation Type: (Select ONE. See plan page for availability.)
- ❏ Slab ❏ Crawl space ❏ Basement ❏ Walk-out basement
- ❏ Optional Foundation for Fee _____ $_____
  (Please enter foundation here)

*Please call all our order department or visit our website for optional foundation fee

Basic Blueprint Package — Cost
- ❏ CAD Files — $_____
- ❏ PDF Files — $_____
- ❏ Reproducible Masters — $_____
- ❏ 8-Set Plan Package — $_____
- ❏ 5-Set Plan Package — $_____
- ❏ 1-Set Study Package — $_____
- ❏ Additional plan sets:
  __ sets at $50.00 per set — $_____
- ❏ Print in mirror-reverse: $50.00 per order — $_____
  Please call all our order department or visit our website for availibility
- ❏ Print in right-reading reverse: $150.00 per order — $_____
  Please call all our order department or visit our website for availibility

Important Extras
- ❏ Lowe's Material Take-off (See Price Tier above.) — $_____
- ❏ Materials List — $_____
- ❏ CompleteCost Materials Report at $125.00 — $_____
  Zip Code of Home/Building Site _____
- ❏ EZ Quote® for Plan #_____ at $29.95 — $_____
- ❏ Additional EZ Quotes for Plan #s_____ at $19.95 each — $_____
- **Shipping** (see chart above) — $_____
- **SUBTOTAL** — $_____
- **Sales Tax** (NJ residents only, add 7%) — $_____
- **TOTAL** — $_____

Order Toll Free: **1-800-523-6789** By Fax: 201-760-2431
Creative Homeowner (Home Plans Order Dept.)
24 Park Way
Upper Saddle River, NJ 07458

Name _____
(Please print or type)

Street _____
(Please do not use a P.O. Box)

City _____ State _____

Country _____ Zip _____

Daytime telephone ( ) _____

Fax ( ) _____
(Required for reproducible orders)

E-Mail _____

Payment ❏ Bank check/money order. No personal checks.
Make checks payable to Creative Homeowner

❏ ❏ ❏ ❏

Credit card number _____

Expiration date (mm/yy) _____

Signature _____

Please check the appropriate box:
❏ Building home for myself ❏ Building home for someone else

SOURCE CODE **LA302**

Copyright Notice

All home plans sold through this publication are protected by copyright. Reproduction of these home plans, either in whole or in part, including any form and/or preparation of derivative works thereof, for any reason without prior written permission is strictly prohibited. The purchase of a set of home plans in no way transfers any copyright or other ownership interest in it to the buyer except for a limited license to use that set of home plans for the construction of one, and only one, dwelling unit. The purchase of additional sets of the home plans at a reduced price from the original set or as a part of a multiple-set package does not convey to the buyer a license to construct more than one dwelling.

Similarly, the purchase of reproducible home plans (sepias, mylars) carries the same copyright protection as mentioned above. It is generally allowed to make up to a maximum of 10 copies for the construction of a single dwelling only. To use any plans more than once, and to avoid any copyright license infringement, it is necessary to contact the plan designer to receive a release and license for any extended use. Whereas a purchaser of reproducible plans is granted a license to make copies, it should be noted that because blueprints are copyrighted, making photocopies from them is illegal.

Copyright and licensing of home plans for construction exist to protect all parties. Copyright respects and supports the intellectual property of the original architect or designer. Copyright law has been reinforced over the past few years. Willful infringement could cause settlements for statutory damages to $150,000.00 plus attorney fees, damages, and loss of profits.

Index

For pricing, see page 603.

...ter direct: 1-800-523-6789